Reforming Rural Russia

Studies of the Harriman Institute
COLUMBIA UNIVERSITY

Founded as the Russian Institute in 1946, the W. Averell Harriman Institute for Advanced Study of the Soviet Union is the oldest research institution of its kind in the United States. The book series *Studies of the Harriman Institute*, begun in 1953, helps bring to a wider audience some of the work conducted under its auspices by professors, degree candidates, and visiting fellows. The faculty of the Institute, without necessarily agreeing with the conclusions reached in these books, believes their publication will contribute to both scholarship and a greater public understanding of the Soviet Union. A list of the *Studies* appears at the back of the book.

Reforming Rural Russia

STATE, LOCAL SOCIETY, AND
NATIONAL POLITICS, 1855–1914

Francis William Wcislo

PRINCETON UNIVERSITY PRESS

PRINCETON, NEW JERSEY

Copyright © 1990 by Princeton University Press
Published by Princeton University Press, 41 William Street,
Princeton, New Jersey 08540
In the United Kingdom: Princeton University Press, Oxford

Library of Congress Cataloging-in-Publication Data

Wcislo, Francis William, 1951–
Reforming rural Russia : state, local society, and national politics,
1855–1914 / Francis William Wcislo.
p.   cm. — (Studies of the Harriman Institute)
Includes bibliographical references.
1. Soviet Union—Politics and government—1855–1881. 2. Soviet
Union—Politics and government—1881–1894. 3. Soviet Union—
Politics and government—1894–1917. 4. Soviet Union—Economic
conditions—1861–1917. 5. Soviet Union—Rural conditions.
I. Title. II. Series.
DK221.W25   1990   947.08'09734—dc20   89-70242

ISBN 0-691-05574-2 (alk. paper)

This book has been composed in Linotron Sabon

Printed in the United States of America by Princeton University Press,
Princeton, New Jersey
10 9 8 7 6 5 4 3 2 1

For Jane Schulte

Contents

Bibliography

Index

Introduction

CONSIDER, at the outset, what a Russian born in 1839 might have experienced during a single lifetime. In 1855, at age sixteen, amid the debacle of the Crimean War, he or she confronted what was still very much an agrarian order whose economy, society, politics, and culture all revealed the particularistic distinctions that so fundamentally shaped Russian life. Fueled by the labor of serfs and the manorial operations of the hereditary nobility, the empire's economy rested upon the regional networks of agriculture, handicrafts, trades, and manufacturing that distinguished a country only just entering the industrial age. Russian public life, given the structure of disparate legal orders (*sostoianiia*) or estates (*sosloviia*) through which it was organized—and even more the kaleidoscopic localism of a rural population that these constructs but partially rationalized—bore slight resemblance to the more urbanized and homogenous civil existence of western Europe. The ideals of popular sovereignty and national independence, however ambivalently the West defined them at midcentury, were difficult to advocate in Russian official discourse so long as autocracy purportedly guaranteed impartial justice and commonweal. As important as the monopoly of power and authority that belonged to the tsar, however, was the centralized, but underdeveloped hierarchy of ministries through which the sovereign ruled. Here, the very effort to administer more often than not reinforced societal particularism. Lacking sufficient resources and personnel to impose its will in local affairs, the central government instead subordinated groups of the population to estate institutions, and supervisory officials, and delegated to them the obligation to self-administer (*samoupravlenie*) those matters that the state deemed necessary to the common good. The tsar was indeed, as folklore had it, far away. Subordination and obligation were the reality through which most imperial subjects experienced mid-nineteenth-century autocracy.

If this same individual was still alive in 1914, the septuagenerian regarded a country that although in many ways still familiar, had undergone profound alterations as well. The abolition of serfdom and the industrialization of the later nineteenth century had created a national industrial economy, which, despite its continued dependence upon peasant agriculture, provided the supports for a more populous and urbanized society. Estate categories were still to be found in both law and culture, but the growing complexity of all social structures left little doubt that the phenomenon of civil society was a much more tangible reality than had been the case in 1855. Politically, such sweeping economic and social change challenged, and partially altered, the patterns of authority and power that defined autocratic rule. Such, at least, seemed to be the lessons of the revolution of 1905 and the subsequent fragile coexistence of autocracy and national representative institutions that it created. By the early twentieth century, a heritage of subordination and obligation was being transformed, and from it was emerging a new historical experience of civil freedom, popular sovereignty, and mass politics.

Although historians must beware of a chronology that becomes teleology, they by now acknowledge that the roots of Russia's twentieth-century revolutions are to be found in these decades of sweeping yet transitional and contradictory change. Historians of central Europe especially will appreciate that few other continental countries experienced a modernization more compressed in time, a transformation of its socioeconomic and political structures more unresolved, and a resulting systemic crisis more resoundingly evident than ancien régime Russia. Increasingly in recent years, however, scholars have also appreciated that the interpretive framework within which the revolutionary phenomenon must be understood extends beyond these objective processes to encompass the problem of *mentalité* or social identity. In particular, there is burgeoning interest in examining how the consciousness of societal change—the divergent ways in which the constituent groups of Russian society received and interpreted their historical milieu—in turn influenced the character of that social reality. Examining how workers, hereditary nobles, or entrepreneurs experienced the dictates of industrial modernity, even as they escaped a heritage of serfdom, service, and subordination to a superordinate state power, has opened new avenues for understanding the causes of Russia's twentieth-century revolutionary crisis.[1]

This work aims to extend such analytical concerns into what is too often considered the domain of political history. It studies the repeated attempts of imperial bureaucratic elites to reform the civil administration of local rural society, perhaps the most critical mediating link between the autocratic state and the developing society that it ruled. A rich literature already illuminates the problem of nineteenth- and twentieth-century rural administrative reform—and this for good reason. Given the frequency with which the issue was addressed, primary sources are copious.

---

[1] Moshe Lewin, "Social Crises and Political Structures in the USSR," in idem, *The Making of the Soviet System: Essays in the Social History of Interwar Russia* (Pantheon, 1985), pp. 3–45; Leopold Haimson, "The Problem of Social Identities in Early Twentieth Century Russia" *Slavic Review* 47, no. 1 (Spring 1988): 1–29; Alfred J. Rieber, *Merchants and Entrepreneurs in Late Imperial Russia* (University of North Carolina Press, 1982); and Diane Koenker, *Moscow Workers and the 1917 Revolution* (Princeton University Press, 1981).

Moreover, because issues of national import formally remained, at least until the 1905 Revolution, the prerogative of the autocratic sovereign and his ministers, discussions of "local" administration and self-administration were often nothing more than an Aesopian context in which to debate questions of central importance to both state and society. Mining this vein has allowed Soviet and Western historians to rework some basic assumptions of their respective literatures. In the case of the former, where a rigidly structuralist class analysis nearly predetermined the anachronistic, semifeudal character of tsarist policy, consideration of local reform has renewed interest in the perplexing interpretive problem of an autocratic bureaucracy displaying "bourgeois," reformist tendencies and frequently sacrificing the interests of its dominant landowning class.[2] For Western scholars, this research has considerably expanded our understanding of autocratic state-building and, more broadly, of the capacity of the system in the late imperial period to reform itself from above. It has also emphasized that a central part of the methodology of political history must be the attempt to understand autocratic state power within the historical context of the society and culture from which it evolved.[3]

Monographic bounty, of course, is preferable to famine, especially when it allows the historian to place the problem of local reform within a chronological context spanning the entire post-emancipation era: a frame of reference essential to an analysis of bureaucratic identity. Students of late imperial history will recognize how frequently contemporaries of that era, albeit from quite different perspectives, found their circum-

[2] V. S. Diakin, "Stolypin i dvorianstvo (proval mestnoi reformy)," in *Problemy krest'ianskogo zemlevladeniia i vnutrennoi politiki Rossii, dooktiabr'skoi period* (Leningrad, 1972), pp. 238–82; idem, *Samoderzhavie, burzhuaziia i dvorianstvo v 1907–1911 gg.* (Leningrad, 1978), and L. G. Zakharova, *Samoderzhavie i otmena krepostnogo prava v Rossii, 1856–1861* (Moscow, 1984). See also P. N. Zyrianov, "Sotsial'naia struktura mestnogo upravleniia kapitalisticheskoi Rossii (1861–1914)," *Istoricheskie zapiski* 107 (Moscow, 1982); S. M. Troitskii, *Russkii absoliutizm i dvorianstvo v XVIII v. Formirovanie biurokratii* (Moscow, 1974); A. Ia. Avrekh, "Russkii absoliutizm i ego rol' v utverzhdenii kapitalizma v Rossii," *Istoriia SSSR*, no. 2 (1968); and B. V. Ananych, V. S. Diakin et al., eds., *Krizis samoderzhaviia v Rossii, 1895–1917 gg.* (Leningrad, 1984).

[3] David A. J. Macey, *Government and Peasant in Russia, 1861–1906: The Prehistory of the Stolypin Reforms* (Northern Illinois University Press, 1987); James I. Mandel, "Paternalistic Authority in the Russian Countryside, 1856–1906" (Ph.D. diss., Columbia University, 1978); Daniel T. Orlovsky, *The Limits of Reform: The Ministry of Internal Affairs in Imperial Russia, 1802–1881* (Harvard University Press, 1981); Thomas S. Pearson, "Ministerial Conflict and Local Self-Government in Russia, 1877–1890" (University of North Carolina Ph.D. diss., 1977); S. Frederick Starr, *Decentralization and Self-Government in Russia, 1830–1870* (Princeton University Press, 1972); Neil B. Weissman, *Reform in Tsarist Russia: The State Bureaucracy and Local Government, 1900–1914* (Rutgers University Press, 1981); Richard S. Wortman, *The Development of a Russian Legal Consciousness* (University of Chicago Press, 1976); and George L. Yaney, *The Urge to Mobilize: Agrarian Reform in Russia, 1861–1930* (University of Illinois Press, 1982).

stances still dominated by the objective results and symbolic importance of those mid-nineteenth-century events that we label the Great Reforms. This was especially true of bureaucratic officials, who, because they were agents of the reformed order that had been created in the 1860s, were frequently confronted with the heritage of serfdom that those great compromises had but partially overcome. In few other areas was this duality more graphically apparent than in the recurrent debates regarding local rural administration and the agrarian society it was intended to supervise.

Indeed, from the time of emancipation until the First World War, the record of institutional reform reveals officials acutely aware of and struggling to understand Russia's slow, ill-defined transformation from one sociopolitical order, the superordinate autocratic state that in 1861 ruled a particularistic society of estates (*sosloviia*), toward another, the national state governing a civil society (*grazhdanskoe obshchestvo*), which some deemed it to have become by 1914.[4] Of course, rather than an object clarified by post-facto analytical insight, contemporaries instead confronted, as the work of George Yaney has suggested, an amorphous reality that accommodated quite divergent conceptions of autocratic power and authority, the nature of the society in which both were utilized, and, based on these views, the role the bureaucratic state was obliged to assume in overseeing Russia's development.[5] The debates that arose over these issues were both divisive and fundamental. What was the nature of Russian social development, and how should the state organize its institutions in response? Were legality and the rule of law necessary for, and were they compatible with, the exercise of autocratic state power? Ought the personalized and often arbitrary authority of autocracy be constrained by rational norms that regularized administration—even if such action curtailed the power of individuals, whether in the center or distant countryside, to address the needs (*nuzhdy*) of the populace? And perhaps most critical: Would the system of centralized ministerial bureaucracy and legal estates through which, under serfdom, the autocracy had imposed obligations upon its population be able to uphold the authority of a modern bureaucratic state, as ever-broader strata of society began to

---

[4] Leopold H. Haimson, "The Parties and the State: The Evolution of Political Attitudes," in Michael Cherniavsky, ed., *The Structure of Russian History* (Random House, 1970), pp. 309–40; Gregory L. Freeze, "The Soslovie (Estate) Paradigm and Russian Social History," *American Historical Review* 91, no. 1 (Feb. 1986): 11–36; Seymour Becker, *Nobility and Privilege in Late Imperial Russia* (Northern Illinois University Press, 1985); and Rieber, *Merchants and Entrepreneurs.*

[5] George L. Yaney, *The Systematization of Russian Government: Social Evolution in the Domestic Administration of Imperial Russia, 1711–1905* (University of Illinois Press, 1973). See also Orlovsky, *Ministerial Power*, and Macey, *Government and Peasant.*

experience a more autonomous civic life and feel the aspirations of political nationhood?

Beginning with the administrative reforms proposed by "enlightened bureaucrats" in the late 1850s, a succession of reformist statesmen assumed the inevitability of a "Western" future for Russia, and therefore urged the incorporation of greater legal rationality, civil equality, and public initiative into the autocratic administrative system. This study, drawing from existing investigations of bureaucratic behavior, emphasizes how two different bureaucratic traditions motivated such reformist thinking. The generalist or statist (*étatist*) official, heir in the nineteenth century to the cameralist theory of the European police state (*Polizeistaat*), was perhaps the most prominent "persona" in late imperial administration. Educated in the law and entrusted with the power to define and articulate general state interests, these executive agents of an "impartial" autocracy deemed themselves qualified to govern because they alone possessed the universalistic perspective and means necessary to mediate the interests of a populace unaccustomed to the responsibilities of civil life.[6] Yet, by the end of Alexander II's reign and the so-called first crisis of autocracy, Russian educated opinion with growing assertiveness was refusing to acknowledge the authority of administrators whose enlightened supervision it regarded as uninvited tutelage (*opeka*). That challenge not only undermined exclusive claims to rule, but also, combined as it was with the nagging social instability and violent radicalism of those years, often reinforced officials' convictions that their analysis of civil evolution was correct and necessitated reforms to strengthen the authority of the autocracy in this emerging civil society.

As moderate dissidence and radicalism became the national and mass politics of the early twentieth century, however, an ethos of bureaucratic innovation and social engineering, which had its roots in the statist transformation of the Petrine era, introduced an important new component into the reformist perspective. Statesmen represented most notably by Sergei Witte and, following him, P. A. Stolypin, shared the generalist's propensity to define overarching state interests and wield the instrumentalities of state power in achieving them. Yet they also utilized law, administration, and power as means to foster and even accelerate the coun-

---

[6] Marc Raeff, *The Well-Ordered Police State: Social and Institutional Change Through Law in the Germanies and Russia, 1600–1800* (Yale University Press, 1983) and idem, *Michael Speransky: Statesman of Imperial Russia (1772–1839)* (Mouton, 1957); Wortman, *Russian Legal Consciousness*; Walter M. Pintner and Don Karl Rowney, eds., *Russian Officialdom: The Bureaucratization of Russian Society from the Seventeenth to the Twentieth Century* (University of North Carolina Press, 1980); and Mack Walker, *German Home Towns: Community, State, and General Estate, 1648–1871* (Cornell University Press, 1971).

try's civil and political transformation. The integrity of the state's power—and, by the time of the 1905 Revolution, the legitimacy of its authority—required state intervention in society not merely in order to supervise it more effectively, but also in order to transform it: economically, socially, and, as we shall see in the last decades of the old regime, politically as well.[7]

As Weberian analyses of autocratic government suggest, however, even reformers remained subject to the peculiarities of Russian administrative history; paradoxically, the societal particularism whose transformation they considered inevitable weighed heavily against the possibility that autocratic officialdom might ever become a modern bureaucracy coexisting with an autonomous civil society.[8] Historically, Russian society possessed little tradition of autonomous public activity sanctioned by custom, natural law, or civil code. Its capacity to articulate the general interest of the body politic, to evolve a conception of social contract defining the relations of state and citizen, had been limited or repressed. Thus, officials drawn from this same milieu lacked articulate abstractions of community and political rights in whose context they could define themselves as members of a civil service, an independent corporate entity subject only to established, legal definitions of the commonweal. Instead, they were state servants, subordinate to the dictates of hierarchical power and to the potentially unconstrained definitions of state interest that were implicit in the ministerial government of the empire. Although the civil and political development of Russian society after emancipation mitigated these tendencies, even reformers—historians need only recall Witte's ardent pursuit of industrialization or Stolypin's "bonapartism"—remained subject to this heritage of autocratic rule.

What was true to a degree for reformers was a much more pronounced tendency among their bureaucratic opponents, who can be labeled police officials. As Daniel Orlovsky has argued in his study of the Ministry of Internal Affairs (Ministerstvo Vnutrennykh Del—MVD), for many such individuals in the post-emancipation era statist regulation of societal change became an end in itself, an instrument of repression and a looming

---

[7] Macey, *Government and Peasant in Russia*, chap. 1; Orlovsky, *Ministerial Power*, chaps. 3 and 5; Yaney, *Urge To Mobilize*; and Raeff, *Well-Ordered Police State*.

[8] Hans J. Torke, "Continuity and Change in the Relations between Bureaucracy and Society in Russia, 1613–1861," *Canadian Slavic Studies* 5, no. 4 (Winter 1971): 457–76; Marc Raeff, "The Well-Ordered Police State and the Development of Modernity in Seventeenth- and Eighteenth-Century Europe: An Attempt at a Comparative Approach," *American Historical Review* 80, no. 5 (December 1975): 1221–43; and John P. LeDonne, *Ruling Russia: Politics and Administration in the Age of Absolutism, 1762–1796* (Princeton University Press, 1984).

impediment to reform.[9] Consistently reinforcing this hegemonic imperative was an interpretation of agrarian social development that differed starkly from that embraced by reformers. In this view, rural society was dominated by a peasantry ill-prepared to assimilate the responsibilities of civil freedom; this society was not so much a sociological phenomenon as it was an administrative objective that had been established at the time of emancipation. Segregated within an estate (*soslovie*) system of laws, institutions, and landholding, the peasant populace after 1861 began to display all the alarming symptoms characteristic of the unstable mass populations threatening civil order and property in industrial Europe. In this milieu, social change offered few prospects of future civil stability; instead, it increased the necessity of preserving uncontested ministerial power over a subordinate population to protect against the political disorder and social conflict endemic in modern life. Such arguments would work against the reformists' advocacy of rural civil and political reform.

Indeed, however "progressive" they might seem to an outside observer, these reformist initiatives conveyed anomalous, even alien values to an old-regime society in which patterns of personalized authority, superordinate power, and ascriptive status still bore great significance. This was certainly true at its apex, where the persona of the sovereign tsar incarnated a dynamic tension between conflicting political and social values.[10] As emperor, the sovereign upheld civic order; in the person of the tsar, he guaranteed the justice and moral well-being that a "premodern" rural populace required. The emperor governed through an institutionalized ministerial system; the tsar provided reward and punishment through networks of personalized relationships that tied individuals and families to his service. The emperor issued and executed the laws needed to regulate public life; the tsar mediated, in a supra-legal fashion, the disparate interests of the legal estates subordinated to his rule. The sovereign presided over an increasingly complex institutional system that exercised autocratic power and authority; the tsar, through the unrestricted autocratic authority that was the birthright of the Romanov house, remained the ultimate source of power in the state and the sole guarantee of its legitimacy.

In the final analysis, a study of the reformist initiatives that aimed to implant the values of civic culture in rural public life brings into sharp focus the particularism of the Russian sociopolitical order, a particular-

[9] Orlovsky, *Limits of Reform*; and Richard Pipes, *Russia Under the Old Regime* (Scribner's, 1974), chap. 11.

[10] Michael Cherniavsky, *Tsar and People: Studies in Russian Myths* (Yale University Press, 1961); David L. Ransel, *The Politics of Catherinian Russia: The Panin Party* (Yale University Press, 1975); and Andrew M. Verner, *The Crisis of Russian Autocracy: Nicholas II and the 1905 Revolution* (Princeton University Press, 1990).

ism that had existed in Russia before the abolition of serfdom and that retained its resilience not only at the apex, but also in the rural regions of old-regime society. Such a study can also demonstrate the challenge and threat that bureaucratic reformism generally posed to the traditional political culture of autocracy. Throughout the late imperial era, its traditions and values resonated within the imperial court, the ministerial bureaucracy, educated society, and, particularly, the provincial nobility (*pomestnoe dvorianstvo*)—a landowning elite whose social identity remained fundamentally influenced by its heritage as the "first service estate of the realm."[11] From these bastions of the ancien régime powerful rationales could (and did) issue, decrying the contention that Russia was destined to assimilate the social and political structures of the West. In the last analysis, sociopolitical change shaped not only the attempts of the autocratic state to reform itself, but also the staunch traditionalist opposition, in both state and society, upon which these efforts were to founder.

[11] Roberta Thompson Manning, *The Crisis of the Old Order In Russia: Gentry and Government* (Princeton University Press, 1982); Leopold H. Haimson, ed., *The Politics of Rural Russia, 1905–1914* (Indiana University Press, 1979).

Acknowledgments

I WOULD LIKE to thank those institutions and individuals who have helped in the writing of this book. The International Research and Exchanges Board and the USSR Ministry of Higher Education funded archival research in the Soviet Union during the 1978–79 academic year. I am grateful especially to my *rukovoditel'*, Professor Boris Vasil'evich Ananych, and to Serafima Grigorevna Sakharova of the Central State Historical Archive in Leningrad. The Kennan Institute of the Woodrow Wilson Center, the Vanderbilt University Research Council, and the Harriman (née Russian) Institute of Columbia University have all, at various stages, supported this work. Special thanks are due both to the Harriman Institute, for funding a postdoctoral fellowship that allowed me to complete revisions during the 1987–88 academic year, and to its faculty and graduate students, for providing a challenging and stimulating environment. Finally, as promised, my thanks to the many undergraduates at Vanderbilt who helped me articulate my understanding of Russia's history.

The author would like to thank the editors of *Russian History* for permission to reprint materials in chapter 3 and the editors of *Russian Review* for permission to reprint materials in chapters 6 and 7.

Many people have read drafts and discussed versions of this manuscript, and it has benefited greatly from their insightful criticism. My gratitude to Boris Ananych, Valentina Chernukha, Valentin Diakin, William Duggan, Thomas Fallows, Heather Hogan, Ronald Petrusha, Norman Pereira, Jonathan Sanders, Timothy Mixter, Dwight Van Horn, and Mark Von Hagen. Special thanks are due Robert Moellar, David McDonald, Daniel Orlovsky, Andrew Verner, and Richard Wortman. I would like to note as well the skillful work of Princeton University Press, especially that of my copyeditor, Adrienne Shirley. I would also like to thank my teachers: William Rosenberg, for instilling an ideal; Andrzej Kaminski; Sheila Fitzpatrick; Moshe Lewin; and Marc Raeff, who generously shared his knowledge of the autocracy and its bureaucracy. I learned much from them about Russian history as a discipline and a profession. Finally, I thank Leopold Haimson, a teacher, mentor, critic, and friend. As do so many others, I acknowledge his intellect, which is exceeded only by his heart.

To conclude with a personal note. My daughter Katherine has spent most of her first seven years with this manuscript, only recently discovering, with some bemusement, that her father actually "wrote books."

My son Daniel, a two-year-old during the final revisions, frequently did without his absentee father, settling instead for the kaleidoscope of New York, which he may have thought was a better than fair trade. Both of them should know how much joy and pleasure they give by assuring that life extends beyond history. Finally, my wife, Jane Schulte Wcislo, has contributed more than she imagines. She is a humanitarian who has found room in her own life and career to encourage the independence of others. For that I am grateful, and I dedicate this book to her.

Harriman Institute
New York City
June 1988

Abbreviations

AO	Administrativnoe otdelenie redaktsionnykh komissii
BE	*Bol'shaia entsiklopediia*
ES	*Entsiklopedicheskii slovar'*
GUMKh	Glavnoe upravlenie po delam mestnogo khoziastva
GUZiZ	Glavnoe upravlenie zemleustroistva i zemledeliia
KA	*Krasnyi arkhiv*
MF	Ministerstvo finansov
MRK	Materialy redaktsionnykh komissii
MVD	Ministerstvo vnutrennykh del
OP	Obshchee prisutstvie
PSZ	Polnoe sobranie zakonov
SOGD	Stenograficheskii otchet Gosudarstvennoi Dumy
SOGS	Stenograficheskii otchet Gosudarstvennogo Soveta
TsGIA	Tsentral'nyi Gosudarstvennyi Istoricheskii Arkhiv
TsGAOR	Tsentral'nyi Gosudarstvennyi Arkhiv Oktiabr'skoi Revo-liutsii
Trudy o.k.	Trudy osoboi komissii (Kakhanov Commission)

TRANSLITERATION AND CALENDAR

Transliteration of the Russian language generally follows the Library of Congress system. All dates are old style and accord with the Julian calendar, which lagged thirteen days behind the Gregorian calendar used in the West.

Reforming Rural Russia

Prologue

ON THE EVE of the abolition of serfdom, the Russian Empire was the most agrarian society on the European continent. Imprecise estimates indicate a total population of some sixty-six million people, the vast majority of which was rural, agricultural, and peasant.[1] Less than one of every ten Russians lived in cities or, as was more likely, in smaller towns. In 1863 only the two capitals of St. Petersburg and Moscow approached the size of one-half million residents.[2] Outside these centers lived a population whose provincial existence in large measure remained unaffected by the unifying bonds of a national market economy or the ideological forces of the age. Russia was a particularistic society, riven by myriad distinctions of geography, ethnicity, religion, privilege, and law.

Most evident was the vast inequality of legal privilege dividing the country's westernized elite, (often called "educated society"—*obrazovannoe obshchestvo*—in the later nineteenth century) from its majority, peasant populace (*narod*). More so than in other European countries at mid-century, social status in Russia reflected the long-term efforts of the autocratic state to create hierarchies of service-rendering and tax-bearing ranks and thereby extract from the population needed personnel and revenues. The institution of the head tax in the early eighteenth century, which generalized taxed and untaxed legal standing (*podatnye i nepodatnye sostoianiia*), clarified a social cleavage between the privileged minority and the subordinate majority, a cleavage that remained a characteristic feature of rural society to the end of the old regime. Bearing the head tax, a condition that in 1858 described some 90 percent of the population, required that an individual be registered in a local tax list (*podushnyi oklad*)—thus fixed to a place of residence (*mesto*)—and subject to the military recruitment and corvée labor obligations through which these lists provided personnel. To be exempt from it, as was the remaining 10 percent of the empire's subjects, was one distinguishing mark of privilege.[3]

[1] A. Troinitskii, *Krepostnoe naselenie v Rossii, po 10-i narodnoi perepisi* (St. Petersburg, 1861), pp. 82–83. The figure excludes the populations of Russian Poland, Finland, and the Caucasus. See also M. Kabuzan, *Izmeneniia v razmeshchenii naseleniia Rossii v XVIII-pervoi polovine XIX v. (Po materialam revizii).* (Moscow, 1971), pp. 167–78; and A. G. Rashin, *Naselenie Rossii za 100 let, 1811–1913 gg.* (Moscow, 1956), pp. 28–29.

[2] P. I. Liashchenko, *History of the National Economy of Russia* (Macmillan, 1949), p. 273 and pp. 91, 95.

[3] Kabuzan, *Izmeneniia*, pp. 175–78. See also P. N. Miliukov, *Gosudarstvennoe kho-*

Students of Russian cultural history, however, will recognize that social status did not derive solely from law. The attempt of the eighteenth-century state to regulate obligation accentuated, but did not create, social disparities; these were rooted in a much older past. A similar symbiosis of law and sociocultural history was evident in the structure of ascriptive service estates (*soslovie*) that even in the modern era separated the Russian population into distinct social groups. Although its antecedents can be found in the seventeenth century, if not earlier, the estate system was first codified in the ninth volume of the *Digest of Laws*, which was published in 1832 and reedited in 1857.[4] Categorizing the "various types of legal standing [*raznye rody sostoianii*]" occupied by the empire's subjects, the code extended legal standing (*sostoianie*) to three ethnic groups ("native" ethnic Slavs, non-Russian national minorities [*inorodtsy*], and foreign-born nationals [*inostrantsy*]), as well as to four "primary kinds of people [*rod liudei*]: the nobility; the clergy; town residents; and rural residents." These four it labeled "estates," and it declared that all ethnic Russians belonged to one of them, thereby legitimating a social structure of legal orders almost a half-century after the French Revolution had initiated the demise of similar hierarchies in Western Europe.[5]

The imperial scholar Vasilii Kliuchevskii believed the estate structure to have been a legal artifice through which the autocracy regulated the privileges and obligations of service.[6] To be sure, each estate was an institutional structure constituted from distinguishable laws, administrative structures, and legal obligations that the population subordinate to it owed the state.[7] Moreover, from the seventeenth century on, the autocracy exhibited the characteristic drive of the absolutist state to rationalize the particularistic society over which it ruled—an effort not only essential to the project of aggrandizing power but also necessary in order to create the civil structures that would subordinate imperial subjects to state law

---

ziastvo vo pervoi chetverti XVIII stoletiia i reforma Petra Velikogo, 2d ed. (St. Petersburg, 1905), chap. 1.

[4] *Svod zakonov Rossiiskoi imperii poveleniem gosudaria imperatora Nikolaia Pavlovicha sostavlennyi*, vol. 9, *Zakony o sostoianiiakh* (St. Petersburg, 1832), and *Svod zakonov Rossiiskoi imperii izdannyi 1857 goda*, vol. 9, *Zakony o sostoianiiakh* (St. Petersburg, 1857). See also historical antecedents in *Ulozhenie gosudaria, tsaria i velikogo kniazia Alekseia Mikhailovicha: Perepechatano iz Polnogo sobraniia zakonov.* (St. Petersburg, 1913), especially chap. 7 ("O sluzhbe vsiakikh ratnykh liudei Moskovskogo Gosudarstva"), chap. 11 ("Sud' o krest'ianakh"), chap. 19 ("O posadskikh liudiakh"), and chap. 20 ("Sud' o kholopakh").

[5] *Svod zakonov* (1857), articles 1–3.

[6] V. O. Kliuchevskii, *Istoriia soslovii v Rossii* (St. Petersburg, 1886).

[7] *Svod zakonov* (1857), book 1, "O raznykh rodakh sostoianii, i razlichii prav im prisvoennykh," sections 1–6 (dvorianstvo, dukhovenstvo, gorodskie obyvateli, sel'skie obyvateli, sostoianie inorodtsev, sostoianie inostrantsev).

and state definitions of commonweal. Yet, as historians have recently emphasized, this attempt at rationalization could only take place through existing legal-administrative hierarchies, which themselves had been constructed in earlier times to define the services and obligations that distinct "kinds of people" were to render to the crown. The efforts of the state thereby reinforced existing cultural distinctions that possessed normative power for social structure, group mentalities, and autocratic government.[8]

Indeed, to read the history of the estate system only as a halting process of institutionalization is to ignore the dynamic tension that drove the state to impose generalized categories on a particularistic social reality. What some historians labeled the consequences of an underdeveloped civil society were not simply distortions visited upon society by the statist traditions of autocracy. Rather, because Russian society was particularistic—because region, privilege, ethnicity, historical culture, and estate exerted a profound influence on social structure—the state was impelled to secure its values and norms through institutions that incorporated estate groups of the population and not civil society as a whole. The act, moreover, exacerbated rather than diminished the particularism of estate society, offering an inviting target for further statist regulation. Such a pattern is especially evident for the two estates that concern this study of rural Russia, the nobility and the peasantry.

Of the empire's four legal estates, the noble service estate (*dvorianstvo*)—in 1858 a small elite numbering some 890,000 individuals—seemed least to display the particularism of the rural milieu from which, in large measure, it had been constituted.[9] Hoping to accentuate if not create a civil function for the service nobility, the eighteenth-century state had granted it both personal and corporative rights as part of a campaign to relocate noble service from the center to the provinces, where it might be used to administer and provide enlightened civic leadership.[10] These privileges, enacted by the 1785 Charter to the Nobility, had been reaffirmed in the early nineteenth century by the *Digest of Laws*. To the noble's person attached the right of exclusive ownership of serfs and the

---

[8] See, in particular, Freeze, "The Soslovie (Estate) Paradigm," and Haimson, "The Problem of Social Identities in Early Twentieth Century Russia." Also the more dated, but still provocative, A. E. Presniakov, *Moskovskoe tsarstvo* (Petrograd, 1918).

[9] A. P. Korelin, *Dvorianstvo v poreformennoi Rossii, 1861–1904 gg.* (Moscow, 1979), p. 302; V. M. Kabuzan, S. M. Troitskii, "Izmeneniia v chislennosti, udel'nom vese i razmeshchenii dvorianstva v Rossii v 1782–1858 gg.," *Istoriia SSSR* no. 4 (1971): 164–65; and Rashin, *Naselenie*, p. 259. See also Marc Raeff, *The Origins of the Russian Intelligentsia: The Eighteenth-Century Nobility* (Harcourt, Brace and World, 1966), chap. 2.

[10] Robert Jones, *The Emancipation of the Russian Nobility, 1762–1785* (Princeton University Press, 1973); S. A. Korf, *Dvorianstvo i ego soslovnoe upravlenie za stoletie 1762–1855* (St. Petersburg, 1906); and LeDonne, *Ruling Russia*.

standing of an "untaxed" individual, which meant exemption not only from the head tax, but also from military recruitment, corporal punishment, and corvée. As a corporative body, the nobility of each province was empowered to self-administer its own estate affairs. It was allowed the right to convene periodically, to elect officers (the marshals of the nobility), and to petition the sovereign. Each provincial nobility also delegated a number of local administrative officials, especially the primary executive authority in the rural county (*uezd*), the police sheriff (*ispravnik*).[11]

Yet, for all this institutional coherence, the first estate of the realm was more noteworthy for having subsumed within itself quite divergent historical experiences of nobility. The nineteenth and twentieth centuries would often illustrate how differing self-perceptions of noble identity, and attempts to act upon them, could all be justified by the one legal construct that defined the noble estate. For example, the extension of corporate structures and rights to the nobility of each province reinforced an ingrained localism rooted in sixteenth-century service lands (*pomest'e*) and furthered by late-eighteenth-century provincial reform. The conferral of a tacit legitimacy on the divergent origins of a family's nobility—the law had established six different categories to differentiate such status—preserved in statute a much older dichotomy between status ascribed by birth and that earned through service. This contradiction appeared as well in the legal distinction drawn between hereditary and personal nobility. The latter category implicitly denigrated officialdom by denying hereditary standing to a growing pool of individuals who had obtained noble status through state service.[12] Finally, the legal title of hereditary nobleman concealed profound differences of socioeconomic status. While many nobles owned substantial estates or romped in the capitals, imprecise estimates suggest that the hard lot of the poor, rural smallholder fell to as much as 40 percent of the empire's "first estate."[13]

The definition of the peasant legal estate, however, was even less capable of transcending the societal particularism that its legal codification and administrative hierarchies were intended to level. "Rural residents [*sel'skie obyvateli*]" constituted some 83 precent of the empire's population in 1857–58.[14] Table P-1, which utilizes the contemporary la-

---

[11] *Svod zakonov* (1857), vol. 9, book 1, section 1 ("O dvorianstve"), chaps. 2–3.

[12] *Svod zakonov* (1857), vol. 9, articles 15, 17, and generally chap. 1 ("O priobretenii prav dvorianskogo sostoianiia i dokazatel'stvakh onogo"). In 1858, thirty percent of all nobles, via successful promotion in state service, had obtained personal noble status, which was not inheritable. The law denied them voting rights in noble assemblies and prohibited their ownership of serfs. Korelin, *Dvorianstvo*, pp. 35–37 and 302.

[13] Troinitskii, *Krepostnoe naselenie*, p. 65, and Korelin, *Dvorianstvo*, pp. 61–63.

[14] Kabuzan, *Izmeneniia*, p. 175, and Rashin, *Naselenie*, p. 259.

bels of appanage, state, and seigneurial peasantries, details the distribution of population among them in 1857. That section of the *Digest of Laws* codifying the peasant estate was a much more complex mélange of descriptive statutes than these appellations imply. Developing categories to describe the diversity of peasant existence was itself a task to test the skill of the legislator. Drawing on a tradition of bondage to land, the *Digest* in its first article delineated "different kinds" of peasants according to "the land on which they [were] settled."[15] By 1857 these kinds of land included the private holdings of hereditary noble serfowners, the personal property allowed to some peasants, and three different categories of state lands.[16] As the second article illustrated, however, these categories themselves entailed cumbersome descriptions—twenty-nine separate subsections were required to define "rural residents settled on crown lands" alone.[17]

If the mere task of describing a rational organization of peasant life necessitated such generalization, the actual administration of these populations—organizing their resources, assuring their orderly life, creating conditions for their public well-being—was an overwhelming task. In the

TABLE P.1
Peasant Population of the Russian Empire, 1857

Category of Peasantry	Population	% of Total Peasants
appanage (*udel'nye*)	1,885,668	4.1
state (*gosudarstvennye*)	23,469,550	48.7
seigneurial (*krepostnye*)	22,676,084	47.2
Total	48,031,302	100.0

Source: Kabuzan, *Izmeneniia*, pp. 167–75.

[15] *Svod zakonov* (1857), vol. 9, book 1, section 4 ("O sel'skikh obyvateliakh"), articles 613–1207.

[16] *Svod zakonov* (1857), vol. 9, book 1, section 4, article 613 (*kazennoe, udel'noe, dvortsovoe, vladel'cheskoe, sobstvennoe*).

[17] *Svod zakonov* (1857), article 614. This statutory language summarized the history of state tenure over lands belonging to neither church nor secular landowners: lands in the sixteenth century supporting the tsar's court (*dvortsovoe*); state (*gosudarstvennye*) lands created by Peter the Great; northern Russian "free peasants" (*chernososhnye krest'iane*); nationalities such as the Tatars, assimilated before the eighteenth century; the populations of the Polish partitions; petty state servitors (*odnodvortsy*) in the southern steppe; monastic peasants from church holdings secularized in the eighteenth century; and seigneurial serfs freed since 1801 who retained peasant status. See also N. M. Druzhinin, *Gosudarstvennye krest'iane i reforma P. D. Kiseleva* (Moscow, 1946), vol. 1, pp. 25–45, and A. P. Zablotskii-Desiatovskii, *Graf P. D. Kiselev i ego vremia* (St. Petersburg, 1882), vol. 2, pp. 24–30.

first half of the nineteenth century, the autocratic state did undertake a significant expansion of parallel administrative hierarchies charged with overseeing scattered rural territories and the diverse populace settled upon them. By so doing, however, it greatly exacerbated the particularism it was attempting to combat.

The case of the appanage peasants—*udel'nye krest'iane*—is illustrative. Appanage peasant territories, created by Paul I in 1797 to provide "lands and incomes" for collateral members of the Romanov family, were to be found scattered throughout European Russia.[18] This disparate collection of local territories and populations existed as a legal category solely by virtue of the underdeveloped administrative structure surrounding it. A centralized Department of Appanage Lands (*Departament udelov*), responsible directly to the emperor, utilized provincial officials of the Ministry of Finance to manage networks of crown-appointed officials whose name, the appanage expedition (*udel'naia ekspeditsiia*), conveyed some sense of the plenipotentiary character of the structure that the state flung into the provinces. These, in turn, supervised peasant-elected officials in large township territories (*volost'*) and appanage villages. In excruciating and futile detail, the administrative network was charged to extract revenues and prevent the moral and economic ruin of the population that was obliged to provide them—a delicate balancing act that it notoriously failed to accomplish.[19]

Like that of "appanage peasant," the legal category "state peasant" connoted an inchoate administrative structure that had evolved haphazardly through the eighteenth century. Yet during the reign of Nicholas I this apparatus became the primary focus of the autocracy's efforts to effect a basic transformation of peasant life. The so-called Kiselev reforms of 1837–38, which resulted from both traditional fiscal concerns and a desire to establish precedents for the eventual eradication of serfdom, attempted to create a coherent administrative system capable of rationalizing state peasant rights and obligations. Through this generalized legal

---

[18] This category of settled land was amalgamated from lands belonging to the imperial court and private estates purchased from hereditary nobles. By 1857, appanage peasants were concentrated in provinces surrounding Moscow, the Petersburg-Novgorod region, the northern Urals, and Simbirsk province, where fully one-third of all appanage peasants resided. Kabuzan, *Izmeneniia*, p. 167. Also *Polnoe sobranie zakonov rossisskoi imperii* (hereafter *PSZ*), series 1 (1649–1825) (St. Petersburg, 1830), "Uchrezhdenie ob imperatorskoi familii" (5 April 1797), no. 17906, otdelenie 1, and V. A. Bogoliubov, "Udel' nye krest'iane," in A. K. Dzhivelegov et al., eds., *Velikaia reforma: Russkoe obshchestvo i krest'ianskii vopros v proshlom i nastoiashchem* (Moscow, 1911), vol. 2, pp. 242–44 and 250–54.

[19] *PSZ*, "Uchrezhdenie," sections 6, 8; Bogoliubov, "Udel' nye krest'iane," pp. 242–44, 250–54, and M. V. Klochkov, *Ocherki pravitel'stvennoi deiatel'nosti vremeni Pavla I*, in *Zapiski istoriko-filologicheskogo fakul'teta Imperatorskogo Petrogradskogo Universiteta* (Petrograd, 1916), pp. 527 ff.

and administrative structure the state hoped to create a civil environment where it could, in Kiselev's own words, assure "the public welfare [*bla-gosostoianie*] of state peasants" by assuming "the most immediate stewardship [*pokrovitel'stvo*]" over them.[20] To achieve the goals it had set for itself, however, the state utilized institutions that operated to isolate (*obosobit'*) a diverse local population within distinct administrative structures. The drive to effect rural civil transformation thus strengthened particularism in rural society.

While state peasants subject to government authority possessed the "standing of free rural residents [*sostoianie svobodnykh sel'skikh oby-vateliakh*]," the *Digest of Laws* classified seigneurial serfs simply as "people of enserfed status [*liudi krepostnogo sostoianiia*]."[21] The rubric tacitly acknowledged that despite the pretense of the law, this large population remained outside the purview of the state and subject only to the arbitrary power that the noble lord wielded over the seigneurial estate and the peasant community that was bound to it.[22] In the code were the trappings of legalistic uniformity: the paternal and maternal hereditary lines which created a serf; the extent of the landowner's authority over serfs; the limitations placed upon trade in serfs; the responsibilities of the *pomeshchik* (landowner) for the well-being of serfs; and the means to terminate the status of a serf. But these ineffective regulations of the particularistic reality that in fact so dominated Russian life bespoke little more than futility. The state had recognized this reality and had delegated uncontested police, judicial, and moral power to the administrative apparatus of the seigneurial manor. More than one article in the code echoed the mandate that all serfs would "peacefully remain at their vocation [*zvanie*], be obedient to their landowners, and fulfill exactly all . . . obligations imposed upon them by the laws."[23]

[20] Zablotskii-Desiatovskii, *Graf P. D. Kiselev*, 1:53 and generally 53–73; also Druzhinin, *Gosudarstvennye krest'iane*, 1:346–53; and Henry H. Hirschbiel III, "The District Captains of the Ministry of State Properties in the Reign of Nicholas I: A Case Study of Russian Provincial Officialdom, 1838–1856," New York University Ph.D. diss., 1978, pp. 68–71.

[21] *Svod zakonov* (1832), vol. 9, article 389, and *Svod zakonov* (1857), vol. 9, chaps. 2, 7.

[22] *Svod zakonov* (1857), book 1, section 4, chap. 7, "O liudiakh krepostnogo sosto-ianiia."

[23] Ibid., article 1027. See also I. I. Ignatovich, *Pomeshchich'e krest'iane nakanune osvo-bozhdeniia* (St. Petersburg, 1902), pp. 1–36; and Jerome Blum, *Lord and Peasant in Russia from the Ninth to the Nineteenth Century* (Princeton University Press, 1961), chaps. 21–22. Contemporaries labeled seigneurial power "votchina authority (*votchinnaia vlast'*)." In the 1857 *Svod zakonov*, the lord, or, as was more likely, the estate steward, was allowed the use of "domestic corrective measures," generally corporal punishment or confinement, against "disobedience [*nepovinovenie*]" and "all kinds of vice, quarrels, brawls, and similar disorders." These uncontested police powers were supported by the lord's informal adjudication of "disputes and suits" among estate serfs. *Svod zakonov* (1857), book 1, section 4, articles 1034–36, and Ignatovich, *Pomeshchich'e krest'iane*, pp. 1–21.

The historical literature amply details how intolerable this situation had become, both morally and administratively, for the generation of Russian statesmen that exercised power under Nicholas I. It also details their inability to alter it. Throughout the Nicholaevan years, a succession of secret committees made various, ultimately ineffective efforts to regulate an institution whose influence permeated every facet of Russian life and extended far beyond the confines of legal categories or administrative structures. Indeed, no more eloquent testimony to the symbiotic relationship of pre-reform autocratic government and its society of estates need be found than this legacy of failure. Nicholas I and his advisers dwelt in the realm of legal and civil abstraction—seeking to codify serfdom as a first step toward its elimination, or creating precedents for this act in state peasant reforms and statutes encouraging nobles to renounce their rights of ownership voluntarily, as enlightened men should. Yet the futile work of secret committees did nothing to alter the autocracy's reliance on the personalized power of individual seigneurs to administer some forty-eight million people, whose "civil" life the state remained powerless to influence.[24]

In 1855 all these efforts bespoke an autocracy whose institutions and attitudes were enmeshed in, and themselves exacerbated, the cultural and legal particularism of Russian society. Only a crisis as jolting as military defeat at the hands of other Western powers, an event profound enough to stir the first manifestations of civil consciousness in society, would convince autocratic statesmen that Russian national survival dictated a transformation of the social and political foundations of the old regime. A new era in Russian history was beginning.

---

[24] V. P. Alekseev, "Sekretnye komitety pri Nikolae I," in Dzhivelegov, ed., *Velikaia reforma*, vol. 1, and V. I. Semevskii, *Krest'ianskii vopros v Rossii v XVIII i pervoi polovine XIX veka*, vol. 2 (St. Petersburg, 1888).

CHAPTER I

The Abolition of Serfdom

No OTHER event so dominated the late imperial era as that which marked its beginnings: the abolition of serfdom. Analysts with divergent perspectives have long disputed its meaning for Russian history.[1] Most do agree, however, that emancipation belongs among those episodes of state reform that periodically characterized Russian history. Patronized by Tsar Alexander II, a handful of ministerial officials were able to direct state power and law to effect the civil transformation of a rural society that had seemed immutable. Their work reinforced an ethos of state-sponsored change that would continue to influence, and be influenced by, the historical development of Russian autocracy in the post-emancipation era. Yet because both officials and the instrumentalities of state they utilized were themselves shaped by the historical experience of serfdom, their efforts to transform the institution exacerbated the social and political peculiarities of the old regime, thereby intensifying the dilemmas of reform that the autocracy confronted. Like the emancipation's legacy of reform, these dilemmas would also become a constituent element of autocracy's history over the subsequent seven decades.

THE GORDIAN KNOT: SERFDOM VIEWED BEFORE THE GREAT REFORMS

Given the obscurantism of Russian public life in 1851, few could have expected that the autocratic government a decade later would declare serfdom to be abolished. Despite persistent attempts by officials in the reign of Nicholas I to untie what contemporaries called the Gordian knot of serfdom, it remained, frustratingly snarled within the mid-nineteenth-century ancien régime. Any attempt to abolish the legal category had to encompass so many other fundamental issues of rural socioeconomic and political relations that the daunting task reinforced a hesitancy to undertake significant change of any kind. Russian serfdom on the eve of the Great Reforms continued to exist because both government and nobility lacked the will or the vision to alter it.

[1] See especially Daniel Field, *The End of Serfdom: Nobility and Bureaucracy in Russia, 1855–1861* (Harvard University Press, 1976); Terrence Emmons, *The Russian Landed Gentry and the Peasant Emancipation of 1861* (Cambridge University Press, 1968); P. A. Zaionchkovskii, *Otmena krepostnogo prava* (Moscow, 1968); and L. G. Zakharova, *Samoderzhavie i otmena.*

The hesitancy of the Nicolaevan autocracy is often attributed to the increasing incidence of "peasant disorders" and fear that the substantive reform of serfdom might encourage social instability.[2] Indeed, in a 1842 speech before the Imperial State Council, Nicholas I himself—as always, convinced that serfdom was "an obvious evil keenly felt by everyone"— nevertheless repudiated the "premature and impossible" extension of freedom to seigneurial serfs. "In the present era," the tsar maintained, such an act would constitute a "criminal encroachment upon public tranquility and the welfare of the state," and he summoned forth the memory of the eighteenth-century insurrection led by the peasant Pugachev to prove "how far the explosiveness of the dark masses [*buistvo cherni*]" could go."[3] Yet because Nicholas dispensed these cautionary missives to support legislation creating the so-called obligated peasants—legislation that sought to ameliorate serfdom through voluntary contractual agreements between individual noble landowners and their serfs—his actions suggest that a fear of peasant disorder did not so much constrain reform as it fueled the regulation, through legal and administrative channels, that characterized state relations with all categories of the rural population during the Nicolaevan era.[4] An awareness of the fragility of the pre-reform social order, in turn, arose not from the threat of peasant retribution, but from the recognition that the state had failed to extend its own civil values into rural life.

That was the judgment tendered by the Smolensk provincial marshal of the nobility, M. V. Drutskoi-Sokolinskii, when he objected in 1842 to the law regarding obligated peasants. It was impossible, Sokolinskii explained, to engage in contractual relations with serfs who did not recognize the legal rights and "mutual dependency of members of civil societies [*grazhdanskie obshchestva*]." They neither comprehended that such "consciousness was necessary," he wrote, nor understood "freedom in a civil sense—freedom embedded in the forms of civil life and protected by legal statute." "In a word," he concluded, "their [capacity to] reason is still in a childlike state; and with such people the pomeshchik simply will not begin to negotiate."[5] Minister of Internal Affairs L. D. Perovskii voiced similar trepidation when he stated that his own cultural standards were virtually irrelevant among the masses of the population. In a report of 1845 that advocated the use of inventories to regulate relations between noble lords or noble landowners and peasants, he was forced to recognize that the false expectations of peasants who still lacked the civil

[2] Ignatovich, *Pomeshch'iche krestiane*, pp. 168–74 and idem, "Krest'ianskie volneniia" in Dzhivelegov, ed., *Velikaia reforma*, 3:41–65. Also Zaionckovskii, *Otmena*, pp. 9–52.

[3] Semevskii, *Krest'ianskii vopros*, 2:60–62.

[4] Field, *End of Serfdom*, pp. 35–50.

[5] *Russkaia starina* 8 (1873): 915–16.

values of the educated Russian made more sweeping initiatives impossible. "In the popular understanding, freedom [*vol'nost'*] means essentially, total anarchy and insubordination," Perovskii wrote, noting as proof that state peasants called themselves "crown peasants" or "sovereign's peasants" in recognition that "the estate of state peasants, in their understanding, is *not* free [*svobodnoe*]" as the law had decreed it to be.[6]

Given the perceived fragility of a civil structure dominated by the institution of serfdom, the instruments that preserved what order and culture existed in the countryside, in particular noble property and the administrative mechanism provided by the manorial estate, assumed all that much more significance in the eyes of government officials. For example, P. D. Kiselev, the most prominent rural reformer of the Nicolaevan state, recognized as early as 1840 that any future emancipation must assure adequate peasant landholding in order to avoid the social instability of industrializing England or Russia's own Baltic provinces. Yet he found the prospect of the expropriation of noble landholding, which was necessary to assure such an outcome, equally unpalatable. Not only would the act violate the "right of property of the hereditary nobility," but it would also "weaken the economic viability [*samostoiatel'nost'*] of the highest estate" and thereby undermine "the most important moral force through which the supreme authority influences the people."[7] Given this quandary, it was not surprising that a government secret committee in 1846 rationalized the status quo with the argument that all "legal orders [*sostoianiia*]"—a rubric that here included seigneurial peasants—enjoyed "freedom" under autocracy. "Each [estate] individually" was secure "from the impositions of another," and "all were subordinate to laws that issue from one supreme source." Yet equal security for all estates could not then mean legal equality, particularly when the noble servitor was regarded as the sole purveyor of civic values in the countryside. The state could protect serfs from individual nobles who abused their power, but it could not abandon the single foundation on which public order rested: "The authority of the pomeshchik . . . is an instrument and a support of autocratic authority; it is the closest guardian over a population of 24 million people [*sic*] and upon it rests the responsibility, before autocratic authority, for the tranquility and well-being of this vast portion of its subjects."[8]

From the perspective of the government, then, the very fragility of civil culture, and the social and political complexities embedded in any attempt to stabilize it, created intricate obstacles that obstructed any initi-

---

[6] Semevskii, *Krest'ianskii vopros*, 2:136–37.

[7] Ibid., pp. 34–42.

[8] Ibid., pp. 144–45. Twenty million was actually the number of adult males; the serf population of Russia was substantially larger.

ation of reform. Moreover, because the government prohibited most public debate of the system, frustration and pessimism within chancellery walls could find little articulated contradiction outside them. Indeed, the views of the serf-owning hereditary nobility, which alone could have served as a major source of nongovernmental opinion in the pre-reform period, acted only to perpetuate the seeming immutability of the system.

Historians generally agree that Russian serf-owners lacked a coherent ideological defense of their way of life, one that might be comparable to that described, for example, among slaveowners in the antebellum American South. The Russian nobility, unchallenged by any "abolitionist" sentiment and favored by the state, felt little need to question or defend the social order that assured their income and thereby their identity as the first service estate of the realm.[9] Moreover, specialists have long disputed whether the pre-reform nobility, subject as it was to the obligation or allure of state service, even possessed any established economic and cultural ties to rural regions. Many scholars maintain that service simply fostered noble absenteeism from the seigneurial landed estate, despite unsuccessful state efforts to combat this phenomenon.[10] Yet to the extent that nobiliar views were discernible in the first half of the century, they did not indicate indifference to serfdom. Indeed, in important ways, nobles repeated the rhetoric of the autocratic government as a justification of their role as serf-owners.

Since at least the mid-eighteenth century, some could be heard to argue that the cultural peculiarities of the Russian peasantry rendered them at worst semi-human and at best simply unable to share the burdens of civic enlightenment that the serf-owning nobility shouldered unselfishly—and of necessity.[11] One of the most recognizable advocates of this view was the historian M. N. Karamzin. His *Memoir on Ancient and Modern Russia*, which displayed the romantic emphasis upon historical organicity that Karamzin grafted onto the Russian lexicon, warned that noble serf-owners occupied a key mediating position between the autocracy and the seigneurial peasantry. Through rural administration and their landed estates, Karamzin insisted, an enlightened nobility preserved order and a modicum of good morals in the provinces. Injudicious or legalistic tampering with serf-owning acted to undermine not only this form of noble

[9] Field, *End of Serfdom*, pp. 8–21, and Peter Kolchin, *Unfree Labor: American Slavery and Russian Serfdom* (Harvard University Press, 1987), chaps. 2–3.

[10] Raeff, *Origins*, pp. 111–47; Jones, *Emancipation*, especially chap. 7; Anatole Leroy-Beaulieu, *The Empire of the Tsars and the Russians* (Putnam's, 1893), vol. 1, pp. 346–403; and A. V. Romanovich-Slavatinskii, *Dvorianstvo v Rossii ot nachala XVIII veka do otmeny krepostnogo prava* (St. Petersburg, 1870), chap. 5.

[11] Romanovich-Slavatinskii, *Dvorianstvo v Rossii*, pp. 375–79, and Kolchin, *Unfree Labor*, pp. 170–74.

service but also the public order it maintained—and, he added (perhaps only for effect), even the autocracy:

> Freed from the surveillance of the masters . . . the peasants will take to drinking and villainy—what a gold mine for taverns and corrupt police officials, but what a blow to morals and to the security of the state. In short, at the present time, the hereditary nobility, dispersed throughout the state, assists the sovereign in preserving peace and order; divesting them of this supervisory authority, he would, like Atlas, take all of Russia upon his shoulders. Could he bear it? The collapse would be frightful.[12]

Others echoed Karamzin's emphasis on the critical service that nobles fulfilled by inculcating, or at least defending, what contemporaries considered to be civil culture in the countryside. A Kharkov serfowner in 1811 explained his role in the countryside as that of "the hereditary official [*nasledstvennyi chinovnik*]" to whom the supreme power had given land and "the care of people" that lived upon it, even as he called "Russian noble landowners . . . nothing less than the plenipotentiaries [*namestniki*] of their grand princes, each in the local region entrusted to him."[13] In 1847, a Smolensk county marshal justified the nobility's unwillingness to convert their serfs to the status of obligated peasants by arguing that "the ignorance of the peasants, their superstitions, incorrigibility, and irreversible attachment to the old ways make them incapable of accepting legal statutes and assimilating the consciousness of civil dependency." Who but "the noble landowner, possessing direct supervision over the entire existence of the simple people," could "prevent all the departures from order and good morals" that occurred in this milieu?[14]

In the aftermath of the 1848 revolutions in Europe, a distant crisis that produced severe political reaction in Russia, such views of the nobility's role and significance in the countryside became perhaps even more pronounced. In February 1849 M. V. Drutskoi-Sokolinskii, writing an addendum to his earlier critique of the imperial decree on obligated peasants, reiterated his fears of social instability by drawing sweeping and groundless historical parallels to the customary right of peasant movement revoked in the late sixteenth century with the declaration of the forbidden years. Rhetorically, he noted the dangers of allowing peasants free rein over their own existence:

> Millions of people left their places to seek something better, not because need dictated it but because they had a right [to do so]. . . . [I]ndustry suffered, there

---

[12] Richard Pipes, ed. and trans., *Karamzin's Memoir on Ancient and Modern Russia* (Atheneum, 1966), pp. 165–66.

[13] Romanovich-Slavatinskii, *Dvorianstvo v Rossii*, pp. 379, 386.

[14] Ibid., p. 394.

was disorder without end, the collection of state taxes and the military drafts were conducted irregularly; in famine years thousands of unsettled peasant families, seeking sustenance for themselves, roamed the roads, died from hunger and cold, unable to find a haven [*pristanishcha*].[15]

Sokolinskii's references to the administrative, economic, and civil disorder caused in the past indicated the dangers of altering existing rural order now, at a time when "noble landowners face the state and are responsible to it for the safety [*tselost'*] of millions of people."[16]

More strident in asserting the primacy of nobiliar authority and the necessity of its preservation during the uncertain times of 1848 was an anonymous note of that October, a protest against a government directive allowing wealthy serfs to purchase their freedom at auctions of bankrupt noble estates. To the author, such policy was tantamount to teaching "the people the lessons of communism: about the advantages of destroying authorities and dividing up their riches." Soon, he continued,

> noble properties, and with them landowner authority, this link [*zveno*] which binds the people and the sovereign, will disappear entirely. Who does not know that the strength and tranquility of the state is based upon the people seeing in the pomeshchiki the expression of tsarist authority and in the tsar the earthly God? How the enemies of Russia hate this simple and firm state structure. They understand that only by eliminating this general bond can they undermine the throne and the empire.[17]

Although exceptional for its time, the bold assertion of autocratic dependence upon the service of the hereditary noble estate was a line that would run throughout the post-emancipation years. For the moment, however, it was yet another thread binding serfdom, rural society, and autocratic state power into a seemingly unloosable Gordian knot.

Hence, before 1855 the views of autocratic officials and hereditary nobles complemented each other in constraining any attempt to alter the status quo of serfdom. Nicholas's advisers, despite persistent efforts to ameliorate serfdom in the short term, simply found the task of its wholesale transformation too complex and daunting. It required addressing not only the economic and social consequences of change, but also the very real problem of undermining the noble estate, the primary instrument of state power and cultural order in the countryside. Nobles, correctly seeing their identity as an estate threatened by significant changes in serfdom, agreed that societal and political instability was the most likely consequence of any assault on their status and incomes. Taken to-

---

[15] *Russkaia starina* 8 (1873): 928–30.
[16] Ibid., p. 936.
[17] Semevskii, *Krest'ianskii vopros*, vol. 2, pp. 193–94.

gether, both perspectives—that of the nobility and that of officialdom—reinforced the conceptual muddle that when placed within the hierarchical and restorationist milieu of the Nicolaevan era, had constrained reformist initiatives for a generation.[18]

AUTOCRATIC WILL AND AUTOCRATIC POLITICS: ENDS AND MEANS

From London in summer 1856, Alexander Herzen began publishing a new journal, *Voices from Russia*. Its inaugural essay, authored by the liberal activists B. N. Chicherin and K. D. Kavelin, expressed wonder that Russia now seemed to rouse itself from the long somnolence of the Nicolaevan years:

> The unusual political events of recent times have summoned forth extraordinary, unprecedented phenomena in the intellectual and moral life of Russia. From the tsar to the lowest day-worker, she has awakened from a deathlike trance in which, until now, she has been entrapped, with amazement has taken the measure of her impoverished condition, and, as if by magic, has given birth to a vast manuscript literature, which is attempting to answer the thousands of questions of contemporary Russian life.[19]

Indeed, the magnitude of the events that had occurred in Russia by the time these words appeared abroad had shattered the imposing facade of the previous three decades. Amid the travails of the Crimean War, Russia learned that its iron-willed emperor Nicholas I had died. With the succession of Alexander II, who soon was forced to accept the humiliating surrender of Sevastopol and a peace dictated by the Western allies, a new reign replaced that of Nicholas, who had bequeathed to Russia military defeat, financial bankruptcy, intellectual suffocation, and political crisis. Although Alexander was very much his father's son and felt obliged to preserve inviolate the power and authority he had inherited, he also took from Nicholas an uncompromising sense of duty to Russia's welfare—a duty that impelled him to initiate and guide fundamental reforms of the autocratic order.[20] The fact that he made his desire to abolish serfdom

[18] On the Nicolaevan state, see especially Marc Raeff, *Understanding Imperial Russia: State and Society in the Old Regime* (Columbia University Press, 1984). Also I. M. Kataev, *Doreformennaia biurokratiia po zapiskam, memuaram i literature* (St. Petersburg, 1911); A. E. Presniakov, *Emperor Nicholas I: The Apogee of Autocracy* (Academic International Press, 1974); and Nicholas Riasanovsky, *Nicholas I and Official Nationality in Russia, 1825–1855* (University of California Press, 1969).

[19] Akademiia nauk SSSR, Institut istorii, M. V. Nechkina, ed., *Golosa iz Rossii: Sborniki A. I. Gertsena i N. P. Ogareva* (Moscow, 1974), vol. 1, pt. 1, p. 9; dates and authorship from editor's commentary, vol. 4, pp. 9, 44.

[20] On Alexander's personal role, see Alfred J. Rieber, *The Politics of Autocracy* (Mouton, 1966); N.G.O. Pereira, "Alexander II and the Decision to Emancipate the Russian Serfs,

clear as early as March 1856 contributed to the milieu of heightened expectations and deep uncertainty that now dominated educated circles in both government and society.[21]

The tsar had revealed for the first time a tenacious personal commitment to abolishing serfdom without undermining the autocracy. Yet ahead of him loomed the arduous task of mediating what was to be a protracted struggle to determine the structure of a reformed rural order and the means of constructing it. Western and Soviet authors have portrayed this process in rich detail. Of interest here is one aspect of the mosaic: the conjuncture of events and actors within the autocratic government that allowed a handful of central government officials to orient the state toward a fundamental restructuring of servile society.

Although still a secondary factor in the closed world of autocratic high politics, public opinion in the late 1850s was beginning to influence the thinking of those who proposed new laws. The idea of emancipation—not only that of serfs from their lords but also of Russia from serfdom—fed a mood of expectation in both the salons and press of St. Petersburg and Moscow, and the provinces as well, where the government in 1858 orchestrated the participation of noble committees in discussions of emancipation. Diverse and increasingly outspoken public opinion not only reinforced the seeming inevitability of reform, but also raised the potential for disillusionment should change not be forthcoming.[22] Yet, against this backdrop, the primary drama was occurring within the government apparatus, among actors and factions competing for influence over the tsar.

Perhaps the most powerful voice there belonged to the so-called *sanovniki*, the high ministerial advisors and aristocratic councillors whose personal relations with the emperor assured their influence over the legislative process.[23] Their presence was evident in the Secret Committee (after February 1858 the Main Committee on Peasant Affairs), which was a small plenipotentiary body established by Alexander in January 1857 to oversee the development of the statute. Two such individuals, General Ia. I. Rostovtsev and Count V. N. Panin, played critical roles as chairmen of

---

1855–1861," *Canadian Slavonic Papers* 22, no. 1 (March 1980): 99–115; W. Bruce Lincoln, *Nicholas I: Emperor and Autocrat of All the Russias* (Indiana University Press, 1978), pp. 352–56.

[21] A. A. Kornilov, *Krest'ianskaia reforma* (St. Petersburg, 1905), pp. 31–35 and "Tsirkuliar ministra vnutrennykh del" in Nechkina, ed., *Golosa iz Rossii*, vol. 1, pt. 1, pp. 31–45.

[22] In general see A. A. Kornilov, *Obshchestvennoe dvizhenie pri Aleksandre II* (Moscow, 1909); Emmons, *Russian Landed Gentry*, chaps. 1–5; Zakharova, *Samoderzhavie*, pp. 54–107, which includes a judicious assessment of the influence of peasant unrest; and Field's use of "the engineering of assent" in *End of Serfdom*, pp. 57–114.

[23] Field, *End of Serfdom*, especially chaps. 2, 3, and 8. Also, the discussion of clan networks in autocratic politics, Ransel, *Politics in Catherinian Russia*.

the interministerial Editing Commissions, the institution that, from its creation in February 1858, was most responsible for hammering out the principles and language of the emancipation legislation. And because their familial pedigree or history of loyal service imparted high status in St. Petersburg politics, men such as Minister of State Properties M. N. Muraviev, Count V. F. Adlerberg, or Prince V. A. Dolgorukov were influential figures, particularly in the final stages of deliberations that occurred in the Imperial State Council in early 1861.[24]

Two characteristics distinguished all these men. Theirs was a voice of caution. Exemplars of the Nicolaevan era, they honored the sovereign's desire to eliminate serfdom, but also supported his insistence on averting, at all costs, any threats to public order or noble property interests. The influential Rostovtsev, writing in early 1857, saw reform as a process with an end still distant in time, which required scrupulous state "guardianship [popechitel'stvo]" given the low "moral level" of the serfs. It was quite impossible, he noted, to "suddenly transfer half-educated people from full slavery to full freedom"; similarly, in July 1857 P. D. Kiselev warned Alexander that "this huge mass [was] not prepared for total legal freedom."[25] Throughout 1857, such weighty rationales constrained the discussion of reform in the Secret Committee, where members were resolved that the actual work of emancipation required long preparatory and transitional periods before it could even be initiated.[26] After Alexander decided in late 1857 that such preliminaries would consume at most twelve years, Rostovtsev swayed the tsar to consider appointing plenipotentiary governors-general and county administrators to exercise scrupulous oversight of the entire process.[27]

The sanovnik, however, was above all else a loyal servitor of the tsar, an individual who could be counted on to harness the government apparatus to autocratic will. This certainly was true of Rostovtsev, the person most responsible, after the tsar, for the achievement of emancipation. Rostovtsev rose to prominence in the summer of 1858, when for personal reasons that remain unexplained he began to advocate a much more thorough and far-reaching abrogation of serfdom than he had earlier contemplated. His views, set forth in letters written to Alexander II, provided a general set of guidelines by which the tsar could both achieve emancipation and create a new rural economic and civil life after serfdom was abolished.[28]

[24] Zaionchkovskii, Otmena, p. 68; P. A. Valuev, Dnevnik P. A. Valueva, ministra vnutrennykh del, edited by P. A. Zaionchkovskii (Moscow, 1961), vol. 1, pp. 363–65.

[25] Zaionchkovskii, Otmena, pp. 69–71, 76–77.

[26] Zakharova, Samoderzhavie, pp. 92–103, and Field, End of Serfdom, pp. 143–49.

[27] Starr, Decentralization and Self-Government, pp. 136–50.

[28] On Rostovtsev, see Field, End of Serfdom, pp. 165–72. Generally, see "Deiateli reformy," in Dzhivelegov, ed., Velikaia reforma, 5:1–163.

To be successful, Rostovtsev noted in his correspondence, reform legislation had to assure an expectant peasant "that his life had improved," a suspicious pomeshchik that his interests were not damaged irreparably, and the tsar himself that "powerful authority was not weakened for a moment on the local level" or "public order" undermined. Those goals necessitated enlightened state intervention in both the administrative and the economic structures that had been built around serfdom. The nobility's authority over seigneurial peasants, which Rostovslev now deemed "impossible within the new order of things," had become expendable. Moreover, Rostovtsev outlined his belief that emancipated serfs required sufficient manorial arable land to guarantee their independence and prosperity; given the ruined state of the empire's finances, the peasants would supply necessary compensation to their former lords for lost land and labor. The final statute, he was convinced, could "strengthen the possibility that peasants would [one day] become landed proprietors [*pozemel'nye sobstvenniki*]" and, at the same time, summon "Russia to a new life without burdening the state [financially] . . . and without destroying the rights of noble landowners [*dvoriane-pomeshchiki*]." Ever the loyal adherent of the "impartial" autocracy, Rostovtsev implicitly believed, as did his sovereign, that the autocratic state was capable of mediating "the interests of two estates [*sosloviia*], which up until now have been organically connected—without confrontations."[29] He was also prepared to guarantee that it could oversee the country's transformation to a new era of civil relations.

The pivotal influence of Rostovtsev, and the alliance that he established with his sovereign, testified to the continuing weight of personal relations and influence within the autocratic system. Until he died in January 1860, Rostovtsev worked to assure Alexander that the tsar controlled the state apparatus and could indeed mediate the conflicts that statist intervention inevitably would produce. Yet Rostovtsev's own alliances, and the patronage that he himself extended to a small cadre of "enlightened" officials, were of equal importance in the development of the emancipation legislation. Rostovtsev relied on ministerial officials who provided him not only with a reservoir of legislative expertise but also with assurances that the state could indeed effect an orderly and rational transformation of rural society. These so-called men of state (*gosudarstvenniki*) played a role in government policy that far exceeded their minority status in the bureaucratic hierarchy.[30] As K. F. Golovnin recalled, "the best people

[29] A. I. Skrebitskii, ed., *Krestianskoe delo v tsarstvovanii Imperatora Aleksandra II: Materialy dlia istorii osvobozhdeniia krest'ian. Gubernskie komitety, ikh deputaty i Redaktsionnye kommissii v krest'ianskom dele* (Bonn am Rhein, 1862–68), vol. 1, pp. 908–10.

[30] W. Bruce Lincoln, "The Genesis of an 'Enlightened' Bureaucracy in Russia, 1825–1856," *Jahrbücher für Geschichte Osteuropas* 20, no. 3 (September 1972): 321–30; and

from the ranks of officialdom . . . saw more clearly and further than the majority of landowners, even though the latter sat upon the land and the former only behind a green blotter." They were "bureaucrats of the purest sort, but bureaucrats who were very enlightened [and] strongly shaped by the general standard of society at that time." Their dream, he concluded, was "the renewal of Russia from above"—a dream that could not be realized without "a dose of general-ism [*generalina* (*sic*)]."[31]

Officials such as N. A. Miliutin, Ia. A. Solov'ev, N. K. Giers, A. P. Zablotskii-Desiatovskii, and P. P. and N. P. Semenov had been young subalterns in Kiselev's Ministry of State Properties and L. D. Perovskii's MVD during the reform-minded early 1840s. They were generalists schooled in the primacy of state interests and the hegemonic imperative that both ministries had displayed in their administration of the countryside.[32] As landless, career civil servitors they were divorced from the interests of noble landowning and more easily derived their identity and livelihood from the higher calling of life-service to the state. They were distinguished, moreover, by education at university juridical faculties or specialized institutes like the Alexander Lyceum or the Imperial School of Jurisprudence.[33] Here, to be sure, they encountered a curriculum that often favored rote learning of statutes over the analysis of law, and the accumulation of encyclopedic knowledge over comprehension of theory— and they often discovered only outside the classroom that "a student could study science [*nauka*] rather than learning lectures by heart."[34]

Yet they imbibed an elitism and corporate spirit from these institutions that—particularly at the university juridical faculties in Moscow and St. Petersburg—reinforced the universalist philosophical perspective of German idealism and Hegelianism dominating Russian intellectual life since the 1830s. The experience had convinced a generation that history was an inevitable and rational process, revealed above all in state law and the

W. Bruce Lincoln, *Nikolai Miliutin: An Enlightened Russian Bureaucrat* (Oriental Research Partners, 1977). Orlovsky shows their minority status through a statistical analysis of MVD career patterns and generational cohorts. Daniel T. Orlovsky, "High Officials in the Ministry of Internal Affairs, 1855–1881," in Pintner and Rowney, eds., *Russian Officialdom*, pp. 250–82.

[31] Golovnin, *Moi vospominaniia* (St. Petersburg, 1908), vol. 1, pp. 3–5.

[32] See especially Orlovsky's discussion of the MVD. Orlovsky, *Limits of Reform*, especially pp. 123–32, emphasizes that the marriage of a statist, interventionist ministerial tradition to the goal of emancipation declared by Alexander II motivated this powerful administrative apparatus to reform the economic and administrative structures of serfdom.

[33] Walter M. Pintner, "The Evolution of Civil Officialdom, 1755–1855," in Pintner and Rowney, eds., *Russian Officialdom*, pp. 190–226; Wortman, *Russian Legal Consciousness*, chap. 3; and P. A. Zaionchkovskii, *Pravitel'stvennyi apparat samoderzhavnoi Rossii v XIX v.* (Moscow, 1978), chap. 2.

[34] V. V. Bervi-Flerovskii, *Zapiski revoliutsionera-mechtatelia* (Moscow-Leningrad, 1929), pp. 13–16.

actions of men who were its agents.[35] Again to quote K. F. Golovnin, for university students in the 1840s and 1850s "development [*razvitie*] . . . was a favored word." The phenomenon sometimes encouraged "idle talk," he continued, but it undoubtedly instilled in the individual a sense of personal creative power when "working independently and thinking in ways other than by the book."[36] Through personal bonds and a shared intellectual universe, education also allowed officials to partake of the intelligentsia culture spreading throughout the enlivened public milieu of the 1850s. It assured them an intensifying cross-pollination of ideas and exposure to the ethic of obligation and progress that informed the mentality of the intelligentsia to such a great extent.[37] Even a future Finance Ministry official as plodding as F. G. Terner, who disdained the widespread "romanticized feeling" for "alma mater," wrote of invigorating salon discussions that "touched upon various public questions" or the discovery, born of the statistical discourses in Chernyshevskii's *Sovremennik*, that "one could study economic questions with interest."[38]

In their own self-perception, these officials were the elite of their era. Skilled generalists with long experience in the state apparatus, they were in a position to be the legitimate agents of orderly societal transformation. They believed themselves to be able to understand the irresistible, universalizing power of law over society and to possess, in the state, the vehicle to assure its realization. Like the impartial autocracy they served, they too could mediate the conflicting private interests loosed by changes in the old order and thereby prepare Russia for a new social and economic era. By late 1858, with Rostovtsev's rise to preeminence, they were provided with the opportunity to do so.

Although much of the groundwork had been accomplished within the Ministry of Internal Affairs during the preceding twelve months, the outlines of the emancipation statute as it would emerge in February 1861 first became apparent in October and December 1858, when Rostovtsev assumed the chairmanship of the Main Committee on Peasant Affairs, and when, through him, enlightened officials assumed their extraordinary

[35] Isaiah Berlin, "A Remarkable Decade," in idem, *Russian Thinkers* (Penguin, 1979), pp. 114–209, and Martin Malia, *Alexander Herzen and the Birth of Russian Socialism* (Harvard University Press, 1961), especially chaps. 10–13.

[36] Golovin, *Moi vospominaniia*, 1:13.

[37] W. Bruce Lincoln, "The Circle of the Grand Duchess Yelena Pavlovna, 1847–1861," *Slavic and East European Review* 48, no. 112 (July 1970): 373–87; and, more broadly, Haimson, "The Parties and the State," pp. 309–13.

[38] F. G. Terner, *Vospominaniia zhizni F. G. Ternera* (St. Petersburg, 1910), pp. 51, 33–51; also D. D. Obolenskii, "Nabroski iz vospominanii D. D. Obolenskogo," *Russkii arkhiv*, no. 3, pt. 1 (1894), 256–69; A. E. Egorov, *Stranitsy iz proshlogo* (Odessa, 1913), vol. 1, pp. 38–44; and the comprehensive treatment in Wortman, *Russian Legal Consciousness*, pp. 204–34.

influence upon the legislative process.[39] The journal of the Main Committee on Peasant Affairs for 26 October sanctioned Rostovtsev's letters of the summer as guidelines for reform and decreed that emancipation would be accomplished by means of "a single statute-general for all of Russia." The following February the Editing Commissions were formally invested with this work. These were chaired by Rostovtsev and staffed by the "enlightened bureaucrats" and appointed provincial noble experts who shared their reformist proclivities, although often not their statist perspective.[40]

The legislative principles approved by the Main Committee in the so-called journal of 4 December were sweeping. State institutions and the law would be used to sever both economic and institutional relations binding serfs to their lords. First, by granting the seigneurial peasantry such personal and property rights as the Code of Laws extended to other categories of peasants, the committee intended to incorporate it into the "general structure of free rural estates in the state." Second, the pomeshchik was to be removed from his position of immediate administrative authority over the village. All "authority over the person of the peasant, for [his] fulfillment or breach of obligations," the committee stated, would be invested in self-administering "village communities [*sel'skoe obshchestvo*]" (a still undefined territorial unit based loosely on the peasant commune [*obshchina, mir*] and the seigneurial estate), their elected peasant officials, and, implicitly, a local apparatus of bureaucratic officialdom.[41] This second legislative principle also represented a profound intervention in local affairs, for as recently as the previous April the Ministry of Internal Affairs had promised to preserve some form of pomeshchik authority, which it labelled "manorial police powers [*votchinnaia politsiia*]," in the village.[42] Third, the journal of 4 December clarified for the first time that the government would assist "peasants in the redemption of their [allotment] lands" and assure that they "would gradually become land proprietors [*pozemel'nye sobstvenniki*]." Although the process still required definition, the emphasis on redemption revealed an intention to redefine rural property relations altogether.[43]

That Rostovtsev and the officials of the Editing Commissions intended

[39] On the MVD, see Skrebitskii, *Krest'ianskoe delo*, 1:v–viii and xxiv–xxxi; Field, *End of Serfdom*, p. 84; and Zakharova, *Samoderzhavie*, p. 77.

[40] Skrebitskii, *Krest'ianskoe delo*, 1:lvi–lix and lxi–lxvi.

[41] The MVD had announced the previous spring its intention to create county (*uezd*) boards "for mediation of misunderstandings arising between pomeshchiki and peasants," Skrebitskii, *Krest'ianskoe delo*, 1:vii, and had begun discussions that February of county administrative-police reform, MVD, *Trudy komissii o gubernskikh i uezdnykh uchrezhdeniiakh* (St. Petersburg, 1860–63), vol. 1, pts. 1–2, pp. 5–6.

[42] Skrebitskii, *Krest'ianskoe delo*, 1:xxx and viii.

[43] Ibid., pp. lix–lxi and general discussion in Field, *End of Serfdom*, pp. 159–65.

the state to supervise the beginnings of a new era as it was terminating the old one became unmistakable over the next five months. Rostovtsev first detailed the principles of the land redemption operation, brokered through state credit but funded with "annual payments by the peasants," in a meeting of the Editing Commissions on 5 March. His remarks had been written by P. P. Semenov and reviewed by Nikolai Miliutin.[44] Insisting again on "strict fairness and impartiality," Rostovtsev explained that redemption would provide the nobles with "fair, fully adequate compensation for their lands" and allow peasants "the opportunity to obtain as property from noble landowners" land sufficient enough to preserve their sedentary "way of life [*byt*]." Concerned that "the redemption of landed property by the peasants be consummated or at least initiated" as quickly as possible, Rostovtsev committed state administrative and financial resources to "hastening" the process.[45]

To be sure, the Editing Commissions did not support the calls for obligatory and immediate redemption proffered by some provincial noble committees outside the black-earth, agricultural region. The financial particulars of the redemption operation, which when announced on 20 May also included the state peasantry, made clear that redemption was to be "voluntary [*poliubovnyi*; literally, 'amicable']." This position satisfied Alexander II's desire to respect noble property rights and assuaged legitimate government uncertainty as to whether the state's economy or credit could weather immediate change on such a grand scale.[46] Yet, a policy tying state interests to peasant tenure of arable land, which, moreover, foresaw the market sale of redeemed land to individuals of any estate,[47] already assumed both the inevitability of the operation and government responsibility for the new social and economic relations obtaining on the land.

Opponents were quick to recognize the change. A notable protest by St. Petersburg provincial marshal of the nobility Count P. P. Shuvalov and Prince F. I. Paskevich in May charged that the Editing Commissions were "joining together two [different] goals . . . the abolition of serfdom and voluntary redemption of land by the peasants."[48] The chairman and the officials behind him were, however, quite aware of this fact. Rostovtsev was quoted in the official summary of proceedings for 6, 9, and 13 May as saying that "the logical course of the Editing Commissions' labors demands that the statutes primarily focus not on the provisional-obligatory

---

[44] Zakharova, *Samoderzhavie*, p. 150.

[45] Skrebitskii, *Krest'ianskoe delo*, 1:lxvii–lxix.

[46] Ibid., 1:lxxxii–lxxxiv, and 4:295–96.

[47] Ibid., 4:461.

[48] Ibid., 1:lxxxviii; Field, *End of Serfdom*, pp. 253–58; and Zakharova, *Samoderzhavie*, 151–55.

period, but the final period, i.e., when peasants constitute a free rural estate [and] have no obligatory relations with the pomeshchiki." To encourage pomeshchiki to move to this goal, the government in good bureaucratic style would declare its intentions to "undertake measures" after twelve years "for bringing the provisional-obligatory period to a conclusion." With redemption, peasant "rights of property were to be restricted only by their debt obligations to the government." This "conditional relationship," Rostovtsev believed, was not onerous; it represented nothing more than the contractual obligations obtaining between "a debtor and a creditor."[49]

By spring 1859, then, a basic framework for emancipation had been established. Its codification was to occupy the Editing Commissions for most of two stormy years. The task required the detailed elaboration of draft legislation. Heated confrontations with elected delegates of provincial noble committees were also in the offing. Added to this turmoil was the death, on 6 February 1860, of Rostovtsev, and his replacement by Panin, a known opponent of redemption.[50] And yet the first principles of reform established after December 1858 to guide the work of the Editing Commissions remained intact, for the same understanding of state interests continued to inform the "enlightened" officials and noble experts who constituted its membership.

In the autumn of 1858 Rostovtsev, responding to the first wave of provincial criticism against the Editing Commissions, had written the tsar that "the commissions have state necessity and state law [*gosudarstvennoe pravo*]; [provincial nobles] have civil law [*grazhdanskoe pravo*] and private interests [*chastnye interesy*]." The numerous compromises that the commissions eventually incorporated into their work to accommodate the economic concerns of noble landowners demonstrated that neither Rostovtsev nor his subordinates, as the chairman then noted, aimed "to rob the nobles" or abandon "the interests of noble landowners," who constituted the country's "honored and most enlightened class."[51] Nevertheless, one overriding precedent brooking no compromise now shaped the work of the Editing Commissions: given "state imperative [*neobkhodimost'*] and on the basis of state law," Rostovtsev said, in language

[49] Skrebitskii, *Krest'ianskoe delo*, 1:lxxxv–lxxxvi.

[50] This appointment so alarmed the Editing Commissions that nineteen members despatched a report to Panin explaining why emancipation was unrealizable without the land settlement as currently established. "Osobaia zapiska 19-ti chlenov Redaktsionnoi komisii po krest'ianskomu delu, o bezsrochnom polzovanii krest'ian zemleiu, predstavlennaia grafu Paninu," in N. P. Semenov, *Osvobozhdenie krest'ian v tsarstvovanii imperatora Aleksandra II: Khronika deiatel'nosti komisii po krest'ianskomu delu* (St. Petersburg, 1889–93), vol. 3, pt. 1, pp. 475–79.

[51] Semenov, *Osvobozhdenie krest'ian*, 2:928–29, and Field, *End of Serfdom*, chap. 7.

neatly capturing his conception of the autocracy's prerogatives, "this reform is legal, sacred, and necessary."[52]

RESTRUCTURING RURAL SOCIETY: LAW AND ADMINISTRATION IN THE EDITING COMMISSIONS, 1859–1860

Through the summer of 1860, the Editing Commissions worked at the task of codification. Theory and vision had to be squared with administrative practice and societal reality, a difficult task indeed. Prince V. A. Cherkasskii, one of the most prominent noble experts on the commissions, remarked at a February 1860 banquet that "the more highly we regard science [*nauka*] . . . the more prepared we must be to make rational concessions, even if only to allow her to penetrate gradually into the real world and subordinate it to herself." Such, at least, was the task of "a statesman who seriously desired the triumph of truth and the good of humanity [*blago chelovechestva*]." However unpalatable the concession, Cherkasskii continued, the statesman was still obliged "religiously to preserve in his soul a consciousness of the bits of evil he had allowed . . . and be able to maintain, amidst all the unfavorable conditions of external reality, clarity of reason, freedom of conscience, and moral independence of spirit."[53] Although the timing might have been coincidental, Cherkasskii's remarks vividly portrayed the ideational conflict seen time and again in the deliberations of the Editing Commissions.

Commission officials indeed confronted intractable "external realities." Complex enough was the task of framing economic legislation that would assure peasant prosperity in the future. Much more problematic was the creation of laws and administrative institutions that would foster rural civil evolution, because, to paraphrase Cherkasskii, some "evil" was inevitable if traditional statist concerns for police and fiscal order were to be allayed. The task of codification thus was herculean, but officials shouldered it with startling ease and theoretical conviction. Their unlimited faith in the power of law and their own generalist perspective, fraught with future disillusionment as it was, provided certainty that the particularistic complexities of the servile order would yield to an orderly, progressive national life.

The conclusions of the commissions' Economic Division, which was chaired by N. A. Miliutin, were illustrative. Long an advocate of landed emancipation, Miliutin deemed allotments of arable land the means both to abolish serfdom and to foster a more developed peasant agriculture.[54] The formal report of his division outlined in panoramic scale the new era

---

[52] Semenov, *Osvobozhdenie krest'ian*, 2:929.
[53] Ibid., 2:916 (speech of 10 February 1860 in honor of French economist de Molinari).
[54] Zakharova, *Samoderzhavie*, pp. 47–50; Lincoln, *Nikolai Miliutin*, pp. 39–43.

in Russian life that state legislation would begin to establish within a decade's time. The following passage deserves full quotation, for it illustrates the perception that state law represented—indeed, created—the long-term interests of the country as a whole:

[Hereditary noble] landowning, which for two and a-half centuries positivist law has upheld through the obligatory relations of the peasant to the soil, would undoubtedly experience significant and inevitable disruption if this same law . . . immediately replaced serfdom with unconditional freedom. . . . In most instances, pomeshchik economies would not withstand the sudden elimination of all the obligations that had hitherto assured them of inexpensive labor or reliable renters. The burden of economic transformation [*ekonomicheskoe preobrazovanie*], intended only as the gradual re-creation of the mutual relations of two classes, thus inevitably, instantly, and exclusively would fall on [just] one of these estates. On the other hand, it is also not possible to sacrifice indefinitely the best interests of the peasant estate to the demands of the pomeshchik economy. . . . [Recognizing] that not only the welfare of the large peasant estate but also the general interest of the entire country [*obshchii interes vsei strany*] demands the quickest possible establishment of a more correct economic existence [*bolee pravil'nyi ekonomicheskii byt*] and more independent estate relations, the Editing Commissions consider it possible to restrict [the transitional] period to nine years.[55]

In order to assure this transformation, yet preserve state revenues, military recruitment, and patterns of rural settlement, required voluminous codification.[56] Regulation of land, income, and peasant mobility, though it contradicted the very essence of evolutionary change, was nevertheless deemed to be justified: without a rationalized public order, a future civil society could not evolve. "In general," Miliutin said at one of the Editing Commissions' sessions in the summer, "given the evolution of consciousness and the construction of a new way of life, all of this, as it was hitherto done amidst the primitive coarseness and ignorance of the simple people, cannot continue. . . . All of this ought to have proper forms [*pravil'nye formy*]."[57]

Two examples suffice. The Economic Division took pains to protect "the right of each individual peasant" to refuse a land allotment and depart [*vykhodit'*] from the commune, which was a significant principle of laissez-faire economics. Yet concerns for the tax-paying capacities of village communities or the patterns of fixed residence necessary to maintain tax and army draft lists underlay an array of regulations that greatly re-

---

[55] Skrebitskii, *Krest'ianskoe delo*, vol. 2, pt. 1, pp. 483–85.

[56] *Materialy redaktsionnykh komissii* (hereinafter, *MRK*); *Pervoe izdanie materialov* (St. Petersburg, 1859), vol. 8 ("Svod zakliuchenii po dokladam khoziastvennogo otdeleniia").

[57] Semenov, *Osvobozhdenie krest'ian*, 1:495.

stricted its application. Nevertheless, the Economic Division was convinced that even in this limited manner a sufficient first step toward peasant smallholding had been taken. Life and law would take care of the rest: "to jump farther ahead in resolving such questions prematurely is not only fruitless, but positively harmful and almost impossible."[58]

Similar reasoned compromises of principle were to be found in the treatment of communal land tenure, which was to be in subsequent decades one of the most debated legacies of the emancipation era. Slavophile opinion, eloquently represented on the Editing Commissions by Iurii Samarin, held that the communal land relations of the peasantry were the only viable foundation of independent public life in autocratic Russia.[59] This ideological commitment, however, was not widespread among commission members. According to V. A. Cherkasskii, he and most others considered "the future collapse of the structure of the commune to be inevitable," and Rostovtsev in March 1858 had instructed that the entire issue be left "to the natural course of events."[60] The Economic Division, in turn, was willing to allow majorities in each village community to limit communal land repartition or convert to hereditary family holdings. Yet, "for the present," the division was willing to accept, for its own utilitarian purposes, the Slavophile claim that the organizational foundation of communal land tenure provided "a powerful instrument for assuring [fiscal] obligations and stabilizing peasant independence" vis-à-vis their former lords.[61] No one objected that present legal obligation might impede future public independence—primarily, it would seem, because communal institutions were deemed to provide peasants with that modicum of organization necessary to fulfill their public responsibilities and begin the transition to more developed forms of civil life.

This assumption certainly underlay the system of self-administration that the Editing Commissions projected to supervise emancipated peas-

[58] Skrebitskii, *Krest'ianskoe delo*, vol. 2, pt. 1, pp. 505, 497–505, and *MRK*, 8:41–46 (articles 15–23).

[59] Semenov, *Osvobozhdenie krest'ian*, 1:215 (OP no. 19, 3 June 1859). See also Skrebitskii, *Krest'ianskoe delo*, 2:394–424. Samarin's views were noticeable among a small minority of provincial noble committees: Nizhnii-Novgorod minority report; Pskov; Samara majority; Vilno; Kursk majority report, *MRK*, vol. 1, pt. 2, "Doklad administrativnogo otdeleniia (hereinafter, AO) No. 4," pp. 6–8, and *MRK*, vol. 2, pt. 4, "Dopol'nitelnyi doklad AO No. 4," pp. 6–12.

[60] Semenov, *Osvobozhdenie krest'ian*, 1:215 (OP no. 19, 3 June 1859), and Skrebitskii, *Krest'ianskoe delo*, 1:lxviii–lxix.

[61] Skrebitskii, *Krest'ianskoe delo*, vol. 2, pt. 1, pp. 516, 516–29; *MRK*, 8:50–51 (articles 35–40). This view also had its antecedents in earlier government discussions, e.g., P. D. Kiselev's argument in 1841 that communal allotments guaranteed both pomeshchik income and the peasantry's "means of existence." Semevskii, *Krest'ianskii vopros*, 2:45–46, 51–54.

ants. As it was explained in the reports of the Administrative Division, the foundation of this structure—the village community (*sel'skoe obshchestvo*)—if possible would encompass the household plots and arable land allotted by a single noble landowner.[62] The Administrative Division quite deliberately cast an institutional shield about the commune, hoping in this way to prevent "the damage to the material and moral interests of the peasants" that, implicitly, interfering seigneurs could inflict.[63] Thus there would be created "an order of administration" to prepare peasants "for the acquisition, after a certain number of years, of full freedom [*polnaia svoboda*] to work the land and dispose of their labor."[64] The creation of the village community, however, resolved only one of the objectives confronting the Editing Commissions. Indeed, this initial separation of lords and peasants immediately raised three other issues: how to eliminate seigneurial power over the new institution; how to order, if not create altogether, the civil relations of the newly emancipated peasants; and how to secure government supervisory authority in the reformed locale. Each step drew the Commissions more deeply into the thicket of rural reality, where principles of law and rational administration could be applied only with increasing difficulty—or with more demanding leaps of faith.

The Editing Commissions were resolved to abrogate seigneurial authority over the former serfs, one of the primary underpinnings, in their eyes, of the entire servile order. In characteristically rationalistic language, the Administrative Division of the commissions explained that the pomeshchik's "former unaccountable [*bezotchetnaia*] police power and . . . judicial role" were to be replaced by "a correct police and judicial-administrative structure for the peasants."[65] Judging from private correspondence between Rostovtsev and the tsar, however, a second factor buttressed this principled commitment to rationalizing rural authority: the perception that peasants expected such action from the government. In a letter of September 1859 Rostovtsev rebutted the charge of Orel provincial marshal V. V. Apraksin that a "radical elimination" of pomeshchik authority would produce "pernicious consequences" for rural public order. Quieting such objections by retaining "landowner influence over the person of the peasant," Rostovtsev warned, "would signify the retention of servile dependency and artificially [*sic*] ensure an unend-

---

[62] The village community thus was not a territorial jurisdiction for an entire local area, and, for reasons of administrative convenience, the structure did not always correspond to the pattern of seigneurial land allotments. Large villages might be divided into smaller units, and smaller ones combined into a single *sel'skoe obshchestvo* (village community), *MRK*, vol. 1, pt. 1, "Doklad AO No. 2," pp. 11–17.

[63] Ibid., pp. 7–8.

[64] Ibid., p. 2.

[65] Ibid., "Doklad AO No. 1," p. 5.

ing struggle between landowners and peasant farmers."[66] A decade later, Iurii Samarin was still reiterating that "the expectations of the peasants had reached very far" on the eve of emancipation. Thus he defended the elimination of seigneurial authority by referring to the Editing Commissions' fear that any hint of preserving noble power might have produced peasant "disillusionment" of potentially "dangerous" proportions.[67]

Relieving the pomeshchik of his position of power left a void in rural civil administration that the Editing Commissions intended to fill. Given the disorganized state of existing rural institutions, the question was: With what? That serfs were unprepared for independent civil life was, with the notable exception of Iurii Samarin, a virtually unquestioned maxim for most members, who assumed that peasants, if left to themselves, would tend to their private agriculture and shirk public responsibilities.[68] Equally evident was the inadvisability of subordinating new peasant institutions to the existing rural police, as had happened during the state peasant reform. Indeed, at this time two of the commissions' most influential members, Miliutin and Ia. A. Solov'ev, were also serving on the MVD's Commission on Provincial and County Institutions (the so-called Police Commission), which, in a report of April 1860 written by Solov'ev, decried an administrative status quo where, "in one local area, and not infrequently in one settlement, various public and estate [soslovie] authorities" together constituted "a strip system [cherezpolositsa] of rural departments and administrations."[69] Extensive repairs, Solov'ev concluded, were required to transform an arbitrary and disorganized local officialdom into "an organ of government authority [pravitel'-stvennaia vlast'], equally just and equally solicitous of [the welfare of] all estates and interests".[70] The necessity of such reform, however, kept the Editing Commissions from subjecting peasant institutions directly to police authorities, in effect replacing one arbitrary power, the nobility, with another, that of the local police.

Instead, the Editing Commissions proposed the creation of a second peasant institution distinct from the village community. Township (volost') self-administration would become the locus for "all relations between [seigneurial] peasants and the government," as well as all "affairs

---

[66] Semenov, *Osvobozhdenie krest'ian*, 2:912–13; Apraksin note in Skrebitskii, *Krest'ianskoe delo*, 1:636–37.

[67] Iu. Samarin, *Revoliutsionnyi konservatizm* (Berlin, 1875), pp. 30–31.

[68] *MRK*, vol. 1, pt. 2, "Doklad AO No. 1," pp. 7–8.

[69] "Obshchiaia ob"iasnitel'naia zapiska k proektam ob uezdnykh uchrezhdeniiakh," in *Trudy komissii o gubernskikh i uezdnykh uchrezhdeniiakh*, vol. 1, pt. 2, p. 105. On the Police Commission, see Orlovsky, *Limits of Reform*, pp. 145–50; 58–61 and Starr, *Decentralization*, chap. 3.

[70] *Trudy Komissii o gubernskikh i uezdnykh uchrezdeniiakh*, vol. 1, pt. 2, p. 114.

affecting [their] civil life [*grazhdanskaia zhizn'*] as members of the [village] community."[71] All village communities in each such jurisdiction would be obliged to fund an elder (*starshina*), an advisory council (*skhod*), and a township court (*volostnoi sud*)—the last viewed as a concession to reality that would relieve overburdened local officials and imperial courts of adjudicating civil and criminal misdemeanors.[72] The elder, of course, was the primary focus of the township project: he would be the chief executive of peasant self-administration responsible for "future public welfare [*blagoustroistvo*]" and "general order and peace" in the area.[73] The draft statute described these arenas of administrative obligation with excruciating detail, using some twenty-four different categories to cover the responsibilities that the Editing Commissions were investing in this former serf: he would oversee crime; public order, morality, and health; tax assessment and collection; famine relief; passports; military recruitment; the implementation of "legal demands" by higher officials; and the power to levy fines and to imprison people.[74]

Even though this statutory detail reflected, above all else, the underdevelopment prevailing in mid-nineteenth-century Russian society generally, there was more than a hint of ambiguity in an institution charged to foster peasant civil life while simultaneously overseeing the most traditional fiscal and police concerns of the state. Plainly, the elder, despite his status as an executive of peasant self-administration, was to be an agent of the state; his police authority would extend to "all individuals of taxed status" who resided in the village communities, whether they participated in its land affairs or not.[75] Similarly, the Editing Commissions supported the contention of both Miliutin and Nikolai Semenov that although "police power" belonged primarily to the township elder, officials of the village community would of necessity have to bear some responsibility for these matters of state as well.[76] Finally, this same ambiguity between the interests of peasant public life and the demands of state was reflected in the objectives of the arbiters of the peace (*mirovye posredniki*). In the original projections of the Police Commission, where the particulars of

[71] *MRK*, vol. 1, pt. 2, "Doklad AO No. 1," p. 11.

[72] Semenov, *Osvobozhdenie krest'ian*, vol. 3, pt. 1, pp. 338–39; and *MRK*, vol. 8, "Svod zakliuchenii po dokladam administrativnogo otdeleniia," pp. 34–38.

[73] *MRK*, vol. 1, pt. 2, "Doklad AO No. 1," pp. 2, 5; and Semenov, *Osvobozhdenie krest'ian*, 1:193.

[74] *MRK*, vol. 2, pt. 4, "Dopolnitel'nyi doklad AO No. 6," pp. 44–45. The proceedings of the Editing Commissions in December 1859 demonstrate that the MVD Police Commission was decisive in assuring police influence over peasant administration. Semenov *Osvobozhdenie krest'ian*, 2:325–32, 343–46.

[75] Semenov, *Osvobozhdenie krest'ian*, 1:529–30; and *MRK* vol. 1, pt. 2, "Doklad AO No. 1," p. 10.

[76] Semenov, *Osvobozhdenie krest'ian*, 1:195–197.

this legislation were initially formulated, these "temporary" officials were to implement the emancipation statute and initiate land redemption. Eventually a territorial structure of local law courts and county police administration, which would supervise the entire local population, would replace them. Yet from the outset the Police Commission also intended the peace arbiter to execute initially some general administrative responsibilities, at least by resolving complaints against illegal actions taken by peasant officials. In this regard, the peace arbiter would provide "leadership and supervision" to the new peasant institutions, a function particularly necessary when a "portion of the administrative power that had formerly been concentrated in the hands of the landowner" was devolving on them. Although the commission repudiated any desire to establish "a distinct [osobyi] administration" for private peasants alone, it recognized the utility, "in certain situations, of a local authority that could serve as control and protection for rural public administration"—a step toward the estate segregation (soslovnaia obosoblennost') that would later dominate peasant life.[77]

To the extent that motivation and perception are at issue in this discussion, however, emphasis must be placed on the goals that peasant institutions were intended to achieve, not merely on the statist context in which they were defined or the fate that we now know to have fallen to them. As all rural administration was the subject of intense reformist speculation, it was that much easier for officials of the Editing Commissions to compromise their principles—or assume that the legalization and rationalization of administrative practice would limit the impact of those "rational concessions" that Cherkasskii had admitted all statesmen had to allow. In one session Nikolai Miliutin admitted as much when he defended township self-administration against excessive administrative or judicial interference. Such "subordination," he said, was wrong:

> Elected individuals are only strong when they are independent of police and judicial institutions. We, of course, must recognize that our institutions are far from complete. Yet the posts of provincial and county marshals of the nobility are honorable most of all because they are independent. . . . The more independent the marshals, the more they have significance [znachenie, i.e., authority], whereas other individuals delegated by the nobility alone become petty officials. There is more order and success . . . where there is less dependency.[78]

[77] Skrebitskii, Krest'ianskoe delo, 1:701–14; and Semenov, Osvobozhdenie krest'ian, vol. 3, pt. 1, pp. 327–41. On the peace arbiter, see M. M. Kataev, Mestnye krest'ianskie uchrezhdeniia, 1861, 1874 i 1889: Istoricheskii ocherk ikh obrazovaniia i norm deiatel'nosti (St. Petersburg, 1911–12), vol. 1, pp. 41–48, 99–109; V. G. Chernukha, Krest'ianskii vopros v pravitel'stvennoi politike Rossii (Leningrad, 1972), chap. 1; and Zaionchkovskii, Otmena, pp. 142–49.

[78] Semenov, Osvobozhdenie krest'ian, 1:497 (OP no. 34, 29 July 1859).

Of course, as Miliutin also knew, law guaranteed the marshals their independence and character as public officials. So too would it influence elected peasant officials, making them conduits for the civil development of the countryside that the state, in the guise of the Editing Commissions, desired as much as fiscal and social order.

Even among some members of the Editing Commissions, however, such faith in the transformative power of rationalistic law was not always professed so readily. In June 1860, for example, N. P. Semenov persuaded the Editing Commissions that the arbiter of the peace, as defined by the Police Commission, bore an excessively bureaucratic character. Despite Miliutin's protests that the absence of a rural "public structure [*obshchestvennoe ustroistvo*]" made this unreasonable, a majority voted to allow noble nomination and peasant election of peace arbiters one year after the first round of gubernatorial appointments.[79] This measure, and the broadened jurisdiction over peasant civil and criminal misdemeanors that the commissions also approved, were together taken to counter bureaucratic influence, in hopes of establishing a "historical path" to more fully developed justices of the peace and the rule of law that they could establish.[80]

The most heated protests, and revealing debates, were sparked by the Slavophile Iurii Samarin. Suspicious of the statist tendencies dominating legislative discussions, Samarin insisted that theoretical distinctions between police obligations and peasant self-administration were fictitious and in fact threatened all forms of peasant development, economic and civil. In proceedings of both June and December 1859, he demanded the removal of all police responsibilities from peasant officials of the village community, charging that such obligations would "corrupt" them and turn them "into petty officials [*chinovniki*]." He challenged his colleagues to recognize that the imposition of police responsibilities guaranteed the atrophy of communal life: "In Russia the people are not yet prepared for this, not educated; consequently, without the complete separation of the village community and the police, [its elected official] will be totally consumed by the [role of] official [*chinovnik*], and this, in my conviction, is the greatest evil."[81] Moreover, Samarin saw no value in a township administration that instead of protecting the economic independence of the village community, provided police officials with access to it.

His colleagues reacted with predictable disbelief, wondering with some

---

[79] Ibid., vol. 3, pt. 1, pp. 316 and 346–49. Eventually the State Council mandated that the peace arbiter be subordinate only to the Governing Senate.

[80] Ibid., vol. 3. pt. 1, pp. 327–29, 358, 361; and Skrebitskii, *Krest'ianskoe delo*, 1:729–33.

[81] Semenov, *Osvobozhdenie krest'ian*, 1:327 and June commentary in ibid., 1:214–16 and 198–99.

justification who was playing the ideologue. "Where," the chair of the Administrative Division P. A. Bulgakov queried, "will administration be when we jettison everything having to do with the police?" Ia. A. Solov'ev reminded the Editing Commissions that police functions were "a category of authority recognized by the entire world." Yet it fell to V. A. Cherkasskii, another Slavophile expert from the nobility whose own convictions more readily accommodated the statist concerns of his bureaucratic co-workers, to defend the administrative principles adopted by the Editing Commissions:

> "Well, this is what you are telling us: you have constructed the township for nothing, there is no rational basis for it, and hence I propose to you . . . do not give it any authority, and do not give it any responsibility. This is a special theory that one might defend brilliantly; but how are you going to cope with administration?[82]

Cherkasskii, it will be recalled, was a believer in "science." Here he maintained his allegiance. Stipulating in law the police obligations of the township elder, he said, would assure self-administration of its own authority in these matters and prevent "turning him and the [village] community over into the hands of the police."[83] Like many members, he preferred to place his trust in law and a rational legal structure, rather than in a Slavophilic commitment to the commune, as a guarantee of future rural development. When Samarin retorted that all this subjugation to "the police or the government [*pravitel'stvo*]" resembled the relationship of a noble lord and his house serf, Cherkasskii responded with outrage. The "relationship of a free individual to the government," he said, was "completely different than that of a serf to his lord."

> Iurii Fedorovich is convinced that the village is the fundamental component of the state, an antediluvian fact that no administration can destroy; indeed, Iurii Fedorovich thinks that the commune will never fall apart. From his point of view this certainty is unshakable, but we, at least the majority of members who are known to me, think that with freedom the commune will fall apart—so what kind of support can a voiceless official [without administrative authority] give to his village institution?

Samarin's protests were soundly rejected.[84]

By the summer of 1860, the Editing Commissions had produced the economic and administrative components of an emancipation statute. The village community, township self-administration, township court,

[82] Ibid., 1:328.
[83] Ibid., 1:327 and 343–46.
[84] Ibid., 1:329.

arbiter of the peace, and, inseparable from the overall direction of reform thinking, the restructuring of county administration would together establish the rationalized, legal administrative structure that would assure both the abolition of serfdom and the future development of rural society. Yet even in their internal debates, no member had been able to resolve entirely the evident contradictions between the lofty goals of their plans and the institutional means available to effect them. Most, like Miliutin or Cherkasskii, could compromise their principles in the name of realpolitik; others, like Samarin, could not. Before an audience generally less sympathetic to officialdom, however, the inconsistencies loomed quite large indeed.

AND THE NOBILITY?

That audience appeared in St. Petersburg only in August through October 1859 and again in the winter of 1860, when the first and then second convocations of noble deputies produced an outburst of criticism against the Editing Commissions. That which reformers insisted to be the dictates of legal principle and reasoned interests of state, critics from quite different perspectives condemned as the continuing consolidation of arbitrary bureaucratic hegemony. Leveled against the Editing Commissions' definitions of state interest, these attacks also reflected the mosaic of alternatives that the nobility detailed in its efforts to override official opinion. However, few of them were able to rise above the particularism of the social milieu in which the deputies and their identity as a service estate were trapped—a fact, ironically enough, that provided a final foundation stone for the statist conviction that law and administrative power were the only instruments available to transform it.

Certainly the most frequently cited source of noble criticism was the "address of the five," a petition to the tsar signed in October 1859 by five deputies of the first convocation. Written by D. A. Khrushchov of Kharkov and signed by the Tver provincial marshal A. M. Unkovskii, the address is often regarded as an early charter of Russian liberalism. The economic interests of both the peasantry and the nobility, the address maintained, were not served by the extended process of land redemption envisioned in the Editing Commissions' plans. Understating their economic self-interest as much as the officials had understated their statist concerns, the five deputies insisted that only immediate land redemption provided peasants unrestricted control of property in the long term. With the aid of the state treasury, of course, it also assured nobles of quick financial compensation for losses of land and peasant labor, which would be inevitable, albeit much less predictable, under the government plan. Moreover, they continued, the rule of law and rural well-being required reducing—if not eliminating altogether—government administrative supervision in the reformed countryside. That was only possible under public and independent courts, greater press freedom (*glasnost'*), and public institutions for self-administration elected from all estates, particularly an enlightened nobility itself freed from the coils of serfdom. Limited to the seigneurial peasants alone, self-administration would inevitably be "suppressed and destroyed by the influence of petty officials."[85]

A. M. Unkovskii, the most prominent signer of the "address of the five," had detailed his stance in a much longer essay submitted earlier to the Editing Commissions. Like other enlightened officials, Unkovskii possessed enough breadth of vision to understand that emancipation would define the future direction of rural development. As a provincial *rentier* who desired to make a profitable termination of his investment in a small, soil-poor estate, he recognized as well that the statute would transform the function and identity of the Russian nobility. And, with a perspective that challenged "enlightened" officials with the dull reality of their stultifying local officialdom, Unkovskii questioned how an administrative apparatus that itself was a product of servile society could achieve the goals of emancipation more effectively than men such as himself, who had imbibed the service tradition of the nobility and recognized the altered conditions redefining it.

Serfdom, Unkovskii maintained, had created a situation of "wholesale arbitrariness" not merely within the seigneurial manor.[86] Corruption and servility dominated a "system of administering or, better, of abusing authority," that covered "all Russia, leaving not a single place for a rational, free life." To those who imagined that the estates of the realm could "root out this evil" with legal petitions to higher authorities, Unkovskii responded that the rights of the nobility, the clergy, townsmen, and state peasants "existed only on paper." In reality, each was subject to the superordinate power of a bureaucratic chancellery and the ubiquitous response: "inappropriate interference . . . in affairs." Local petty officials, not the tsar and his ministers, were the ones who administered, and they did so "despotically, preventing the truth from reaching the government, plugging all apertures through which might be heard the cries of an oppressed people."[87] Defining emancipation quite broadly indeed, Unkovskii thus insisted that the final outcome of reform could not rely for its success "on the personal qualities of [high] officials . . . on an off chance [*na avos*]"—however laudable their intentions might be. It required the rule of law and a new structure of "general administration [*obshchee*

[85] Ibid., 2:933–39; and Field, *End of Serfdom*, pp. 306–8.
[86] Skrebitskii, *Krest'ianskoe delo*, 1:785.
[87] Ibid., 1:789–92.

upravlenie]" encompassing all estates. Yet even this system was fated to fail without the enlightened leadership of those nobles who, like Unkovskii, were prepared to transcend the "alienation of estates, one from another," and assume a new role in local life that was theirs "by moral influence alone, itself indivisible from education and some experience in public affairs [*obshchestvennye dela*]."[88] To retain "the separate administration of departments and legal estates," he warned, was to preserve a "bureaucratic administration" that would become even "more arbitrary" and formalistic after it assumed supervision of the peasantry. It was better, Unkovskii concluded—and here he assumed that individuals were the critical difference—to create "one general administration [that would] unite the interests of the people and create trustworthy organs for the undeviating execution of the supreme will."[89]

Yet despite such reasoned challenges not merely to the Editing Commissions but to the very utility of bureaucratic government, these deputies, much like the officials whom they criticized, were an enlightened minority of their own rank-and-file, better able than most to envision the transformation of the nobility's service identity in the altered circumstances of post-emancipation society. How unrepresentative such opinions were of the landowning nobility as a whole was indicated by how few other noble deputies were able to make the leap of imagination such vision required.

Some tried, particularly during the first convocation, to define the nobility's place in the post-emancipation order in terms other than the status that serfowning and service had ascribed to them.[90] Yet, even among these supposedly more liberal noble delegates, most displayed little enthusiasm for land redemption and the revocation of their property rights that it signified. Most protested as well against the intervention of officialdom into their rural areas and the elimination of seigneurial authority that went along with it. Noteworthy for the extremism of his views, Prince I. V. Gagarin of Voronezh rejected land redemption out of hand. The entire process, he testified, represented "the principle of communism by an ad-

---

[88] Ibid., 1:796.

[89] Ibid., 1:797. See also the comments of Kosagovskii (Nizhnii-Novgorod), Skrebitskii, *Krest'ianskoe delo*, 1:774 and Semenov, *Osvobozhdenie krest'ian*, 2:131; as well as those of Kn. S. V. Volkonskii and F. S. Ofrosimov (Riazan), E. A. Kardo-Sysoev (Tver), D. A. Khrushchov and A. G. Shreter (Kharkov), and D. V. Vasiliev and P. N. Dubrovin (Iaroslavl')—Skrebitskii, *Krest'ianskoe delo*, 1:776–80 and 799–804; and A. I. Koshelev (Riazan), Semenov, *Osvobozhdenie krest'ian*, 2:133; and Skrebitskii, *Krest'ianskoe delo*, 1:780–83.

[90] See, for example, S. S. Volkov (Moscow), Semenov, *Osvobozhdenie krest'ian*, 2:56, and Skrebitskii, *Krest'ianskoe delo*, 1:761–762 and 770; N. A. Nikiforov and G. F. Petrovo-Solovovo (Tambov), Semenov, *Osvobozhdenie krest'ian*, 2:62, 74; and Skrebitskii, *Krest'ianskoe delo*, 1:783–85.

ministrative path." Proclaiming that a subject of a monarchical state could not even consider such ideas unless the sovereign explicitly permitted it, he refused to discuss plans for peasant self-administration and supported the preservation of the noble landowner's manorial police powers as long as peasants owed obligations.[91] Less strident opposition to landed emancipation, containing, perhaps, more confused reflections on the need to retain some form of seigneurial authority during the uncertain years of the transitional period, were evident in the commentaries of the Chernigov, Kostroma, Pskov, Poltava, St. Petersburg, and Saratov deputies.[92]

Dmitrii Shidlovskii of Simbirsk province had no such qualms. He insisted that each serf-owner become the administrative and supervisory "chief [*nachal'nik*] of the village community," a proposal advocated in 1857–58 and then abandoned by the government. His "rights," Shidlovskii maintained, "ought to belong to him, given the natural order of things, because the property owner is the lord of his property."[93] Shidlovskii, however, stood out among his colleagues because, like Unkovskii, he drew the connection between these local concerns and the affairs of state with which they were inextricably intertwined. He petitioned Alexander II to convene elected noble representatives who, replacing the Editing Commissions, would complete the compilation of an emancipation statute. Shidlovskii fell back upon the the service traditions of the noble estate—"the unity of the autocracy with the nobility, the first and most natural protector of the throne and the fatherland"—to remind the tsar that his true interests were better guaranteed by the nobility than by officials obsessed with the "flood of Western ideas threatening to undermine order in the state." "Now, as previously," Shidlovskii declaimed, the estate of the nobility did "not fear subordinating its personal interests to the good of the people, the preservation of fundamental state laws, and the holy will of its beloved Monarch."[94]

The plea fell on deaf ears. As Alexander commented in a note to his Minister of Internal Affairs Lanskoi: "Look at what thoughts are wandering around in the heads of these gentlemen"—an indication of the un-

[91] Skrebitskii, *Krest'ianskoe delo*, 1:804–6; and Semenov, *Osvobozhdenie krest'ian*, 2:120–21.

[92] Skrebitskii, *Krest'ianskoe delo*, 1:803, 498, 654–55, 806–7, 808–10, 810–11; and Semenov, *Osvobozhdenie krest'ian*, 2:108–12, 124, 98, and 154–61.

[93] Semenov, *Osvobozhdenie krest'ian*, 2:135.

[94] Ibid., 2:939. Shidlovskii's was one of several such proposals circulating in the fall of 1859. Alexander II labeled that of M. A. Bezobrazov an attempt "to establish oligarchic rule in our country." "Zapiska kamergera Mikhaila Aleksandrovicha Bezobrazova o znachenii Russkogo dvorianstva i polozhenii, kakoe ono dolzhno zanimat' na poprishche gosudarstvennoi deiatel'nosti," Semenov, *Osvobozhdenie krest'ian*, 2:940–52. See also "Proekt polozheniia o prekrashchenii krepostnoi zavisimosti—fligel' ad"iutantskii, October 1859," ibid., 2:954–59.

compromising patronage with which the tsar was protecting his officials.[95] Yet the Editing Commissions were still subjected to a final, more vociferous round of provincial protests, this time from the second convocation of deputies, who arrived in St. Petersburg during the winter months of 1860. As Daniel Field has noted, these representatives of the nobility, drawn primarily from the black-earth, agricultural region of central European Russia, presented a collective image of "rich, hard-driving, resident squires." They came to town buoyed by the recent appointment of Count V. N. Panin to replace the deceased and suspect Rostovtsev, with high hopes that this measure signaled a more favorable reception for noble views. And they displayed remarkable unanimity by submitting seven essays critiquing the entire emancipation project.[96]

Their heated repudiation of bureaucratic interference at this critical moment in rural life, however, revealed an array of motivations as contradictory, if not more so, as those displayed by officials of the Editing Commissions. Field rightly indicates that their counterproposals to land redemption would have pleased the most Manchestrian economic liberal.[97] Less wealthy nobles were to be provided with the opportunity to liquidate their investments through immediate land redemption. Elsewhere, peasants would farm lands allotted to them from the seigneurial manor for a three-year period. Thereafter all land and labor relations would be governed by free contractual agreement between landowners and their former serfs.[98] An essential and startling precept of this laissez-faire perspective was its excoriation of the Editing Commissions' reliance upon the peasant commune, which the deputies labeled an attempt to replace servile dependency with "an even more burdensome dependency on the [village] community" and the bureacratic institutions looming above it. With more than minimal self-interest in this continuing source of labor and rental income, they rhetorically asked what improvement could be expected in the "home life" of the individual peasant householder once he was subjected to "the exclusive arbitrariness of [peasant officials] from whose capriciousness in former times he could find protection and defense in the noble landowner."[99] Plainly, the answer was "none," unless this same householder could freely leave the community and enjoy the "irrevocable right to dispose of his own labor."[100]

Yet, this quite novel insistence on economic individualism coexisted with administrative reform proposals to preserve nobiliary mediation of

---

[95] Ibid., 2:939.
[96] Field, *End of Serfdom*, pp. 333–39.
[97] Ibid., pp. 339–43.
[98] Skrebitskii, *Krest'ianskoe delo*, 1:811–16.
[99] Ibid., 1:812.
[100] Ibid., 1:816.

civil relations between state and peasantry, an essential attribute of the most traditional components of the noble service identity under serfdom. In place of the proposed peasant township self-administration, the thirty-nine deputies signing this report instead advocated a "township chief [*na-chal'nik*]." A noble landowner elected for "an indeterminate period" by the county assembly of the nobility, this chief would possess a veto over all decisions of subordinate peasant institutions and the right to exercise over them, "on his own responsibility," unlimited judicial and police authority.[101]

However much it contradicted their defense of individual economic freedom, the deputies advocated this measure because they regarded personal nobiliary authority as a fundamental guarantee, firmer than law or government supervision, against the general instability and economic uncertainty that would be inevitable once servile relations became contractual. "Until now," the deputies maintained, "internal order in the greater part of Russia was preserved by the authority of the noble landowner," and although the nobility had parted willingly with its "right to the person and labor of the servile population," it did not intend to abandon the obligation of the noble to "support decorum and order [*blagochinie i poriadok*] among people settled on his land."[102]

Indeed, it required little perspicacity to discern that only the nobility, given its historical place as the first service estate of the land, was capable of executing these responsibilities for the state. Certainly the peasants were not: the prospect of "the present servile population of Russia, divided up amongst ten thousand near republics, with an officialdom elected from the plow, assuming its responsibilities by the will of the people . . . and incapable of answering for the preservation of public order" dumbfounded the deputies. Neither were petty bureaucrats capable of doing so, these same officials who had crafted proposals so "incompatible with a powerful government authority" and, the deputies noted with some justification, so defined by "an abstract system that failed to account for either historical experience [*istoricheskii byt*] or local conditions."[103]

As had been the case during the first convocation of provincial deputies, however, the protests of these loyal noble servitors were filtered through the perspective of equally loyal ministerial officials and went largely unheeded. Indeed, even before the first calling, MVD chief Lan-

[101] Skrebitskii, *Krest'ianskoe delo*, 1:814 and 670–72.

[102] Ibid., 1:814.

[103] Ibid., 1:811–13. The final defeat of this proposal, which Minister of State Properties Muraviev had shepherded to the State Council, is described in Kataev, *Mestnye krest'ianskie uchrezhdeniia*, pp. 116–19; P. A. Valuev, "Dnevnik," *Russkaia starina* 72 (1891): 404–6; and Valuev, *Dnevnik P. A. Valueva*, 1:64 and 363–64.

skoi had predisposed Alexander against the deputies altogether. In a report of August 1859, Lanskoi emphasized the confusing array of opinion present among provincial noble committees, implicitly questioning why such diversity should delay the articulation of policy affecting the most fundamental general interests of the state.[104] Allowing that little else could be expected of individuals "born and raised" under serfdom, the minister claimed that most provincial committees exhibited "little enthusiasm for the emancipation of the peasants" and secretly sought by every means possible "the retention of their rights" and the preservation of their "personal material interest." Others, who attached "primacy" to "the estate interests of the nobility" and wanted "to create in our country a landed noble aristocracy like the English," strove to introduce "feudal principles" and create a landless emancipation with all the dangers this implied. Although in fact he had encouraged their support of redemption,[105] Lanskoi here largely avoided mention of liberal minorities in committees such as Tver, except to note their general willingness to effect "the complete elimination of serfdom" and the MVD's ongoing consideration of their proposals for local self-administration.[106]

There was an element of truth in each of these characterizations. Yet the recalcitrant serfowner and the landed aristocrat seeking a feudal order as well as nobles seeking a tidbit of local reform, were gross generalizations and accounted neither for the nuances of the noble perspective nor for the efforts from below, which resembled those of these officials, to grapple with the dilemmas of emancipation. Framing their opinion as particularistic and oppositional did serve its purpose; Lanskoi could argue convincingly and probably with conviction that in this environment only the Editing Commissions' program could achieve the goal of abolition pursued by the tsar. And he could also conclude that any effort to exert pressure on the legislative process, whether through unbridled provincial criticism of the projects or through consideration of broader "legislative questions" and "changes in the state structure," was an impermissible political act. "One cannot give way," Lanskoi warned the tsar with a phrase that would recur in later years, "to daydreams."[107]

Lanskoi's defense of generalist rationality against petty provincialism was reflected as well in the official reply to noble protests issued by the Editing Commissions' Administrative Division in mid-1860. On the one hand, officials could readily applaud the goal of general administrative reform advanced by deputies of the first convocation, a task already underway in the MVD's Police Commission. Yet they could just as easily

[104] Semenov, *Osvobozhdenie krest'ian*, 2:826–34.
[105] Field, *End of Serfdom*, pp. 213–15.
[106] Semenov, *Osvobozhdenie krest'ian*, 2:831–32, 834.
[107] Ibid., 2:834.

rebut the stinging criticism that had accompanied these proposals, since the "extreme complexity" of the work might delay "resolution of the peasant question, one of the most urgent requirements of state."[108]

On the other hand, provincial proponents of nobiliary authority, by asserting their self-interest against the self-proclaimed impartiality and mediatory role of state officials, were, by definition, illegitimate. Continued seigneurial power did not complement but rather contradicted the Editing Commissions' drive to implant legal structure and rational administration in the countryside; it therefore threatened the future well-being of the seigneurial peasantry and the general welfare of Russia as a whole. The nobility was only one estate in a society whose further civil development was a premise of the entire emancipation statute:

> On the basis of existing law, all free estates, regardless of the differences in the rights presented to them . . . enjoy full independence from each other. All of them, from the highest to the lowest, directly gravitate . . . to the vital focal point of the state structure [gosudarstvennoe ustroistvo], which reflects in itself the unity of the Russian land and the unity of its reigning supreme authority. They are all subordinate to an officialdom either placed over them by that same authority or elected by themselves (and in several instances to collegial institutions constituted on the basis of general estate representation [i.e., the prospective zemstvo]). The only exception in this regard at the moment of reform is the enserfed estate, which stands outside general law and is separated from the government by other estates. But now, when the moment to unravel the knot of serfdom has arrived, there is no basis to refuse to seigneurial peasants that which belongs to all free legal orders [svobodnye sostoianiia], and one cannot, without violating the fundamental principles of our legal code, place one newly emancipated estate under the officialdom of another.[109]

Many, of course, were already arguing that peasants were being subordinated to habitually arbitrary government supervision. But what some castigated as numbing bureaucratic hegemony, enlightened officials, from a perspective that repudiated the irrationality of serfdom, could describe as the creation of "a new, more stable shelter [priiut], covered by the shield of officiality [offitsial'nost!] and legality." Indeed, it was no more surprising in this age of transition to witness enlightened bureaucrats wielding their ethos of legality and orderly societal change against serf-owners than it had been to see noble lords proclaiming the merits of laissez-faire economics against the disdained petty officialdom. Law and administrative power, however, resided in the hands of a handful of

[108] Skrebitskii, Krest'ianskoe delo, 1:824.
[109] Ibid., 1:832.

enlightened officials, and it was their definition of legality and rationality that held sway through 1861.

There was a final factor explaining why provincial criticism had so little effect on the emancipation statute of February 1861: the tsar unflaggingly supported his officials. Indeed, at few other points in subsequent decades would the autocrat so firmly commit himself to the cause of bureaucratic reformers as Alexander did during the development of the emancipation statute. During the final legislative debates of late 1860 and early 1861, Alexander did allow important concessions to noble property rights, but despite attempts in the State Council to dissuade him, the autocrat's support of the essential legislative principles developed by his Editing Commissions was the decisive factor in their eventual promulgation on 19 February 1861.[110]

As he lay dying in January 1860, Rostovtsev, Alexander's loyal sanovnik, had composed a note for his sovereign that he considered to be his last will and testament.[111] In it he wrote that the work of the Editing Commissions had attempted "to establish the strictest balance [*samoe strogoe ravnovesie*] between the interests of the nobility and the interests of the emancipated people." They had striven to protect the one against "unjust losses" and to guarantee the other "the possibility of attaining prosperity in the future." And, above all else, they had made possible an abolition of serfdom, a transformation of the very foundation upon which the autocratic edifice rested, that could be achieved peacefully, without violating "public order and the tranquility of the state."[112] State law and state power were the mediating instruments through which Alexander could fulfill the role of just arbiter that God and history had bestowed upon the Russian autocracy—and effect its reform without causing the collapse of the edifice.

The abolition of serfdom was a triumph of bureaucratic reform. It was also a victory fraught with consequences for the future. A decade before this event, the social and political order shaped by the institution of serfdom had seemed immutable, its alteration a possibly dangerous and apparently impossible task. Moreover, because the threads of the Gordian knot bound mentalities as well, both officials in the government and

---

[110] Field, *End of Serfdom*, 344–67, Zakharova, *Samoderzhavie i otmena*, pp. 221–29, and Zaionchkovskii, *Otmena krepostnogo prava*, chaps. 2–3, emphasize especially the decreased maximum land allotments, the so-called beggar's allotment, and a commitment to reevalute in twenty year's time peasant monetary obligations on lands where redemption had not yet been initiated.

[111] "Poslednaia zapiska Rostovtseva o krest'ianskom dele, posle ego smerti priniataia Gosudarem," Semenov, *Osvobozhdenie krest'ian*, 2:968–93.

[112] Ibid., 2:993.

members of the nobility found it easier to dabble with the servile status quo than contemplate its elimination. Ten years later, rural society had been lifted off its servile foundations and placed down again within economic and administrative structures of the state's own making: a herculean act seldom rivaled in previous or subsequent Russian history.

Much of the responsibility for this achievement belonged to a handful of enlightened officials, whose influence was magnified by the uncompromising belief in legality, rationalism, and state power that education and service had inspired in them. Ensconced in ministerial institutions and sheltered by the most traditional trappings of personalized autocratic power, the patronage of the sanovnik Rostovtsev and the commitment of the sovereign tsar Alexander II, these officials maneuvered the state toward a goal that had eluded the preceding generation. And they strengthened, if not created altogether, the example and tradition of statist reform for those who succeeded them.

Yet the emancipation also left a range of unresolved dilemmas for which these officials also bore ultimate responsibility. First, many of the administrative reforms that the Editing Commissions had assumed would accompany abolition were not realized—although here the growing reluctance of Alexander II to pursue the far-reaching changes he had patronized earlier must be acknowledged as well. General administrative reform was never achieved during the reign of Alexander II. And state and appanage peasants, the other half of Russia's peasant population, received their emancipation under separate legislative acts only later in the 1860s.[113] Local self-administration, created by the zemstvo statute of 1864 to address important administrative concerns and involve the provincial nobility in local affairs, was an appendage grafted onto the state apparatus. Its institutional relations to government authority were never defined, and its role in local government was constrained from the outset.[114]

Second, although officials of the Editing Commissions had struggled to change these patterns, the results of their work also strengthened the superordinate bureaucratic and police hegemony that had been—and after 1861 increasingly continued to be—a characteristic feature of Russian administration.[115] Assuming supervision of the land redemption opera-

[113] Zaionchkovskii, *Otmena krepostnogo prava*, chap. 7.

[114] Orlovsky, *Limits of Reform*, pp. 150–54; B. B. Veselovskii, "Detsentralizatsiia upravleniia i zadachi zemstvo," in B. B. Veselovskii et al., eds., *Iubileinyi zemskii sbornik* (St. Petersburg, 1914), pp. 41–43; and N. N. Avinov, "Glavnye cherty v istorii zakonodatel'stva o zemskikh uchrezhdeniiakh 1864–1913," in Veselovskii et al., eds., *Iubileinyi zemskii sbornik*, pp. 17–18.

[115] Orlovsky, *Limits of Reform*, chap. 5; and Macey, *Government and Peasant*, pp. 11–24.

tion greatly expanded the arena of government fiscal concerns and provided a powerful economic rationale for intensifying the supervision of the state's "debtor," the peasant commune. The commissions created a new network of peasant self-administration, which, although intended as a vehicle for civil order and progress, was burdened with police and fiscal obligations and which, in turn, saddled the state with an echelon of peasant officialdom. The emancipation legislation also solidified the estate structure of society by extending administration and law to the seigneurial peasantry. As we shall have occasion to see, this institutional and legal isolation of a peasantry that enlightened officials had hoped to incorporate eventually into rural civil society rigidified the institutional separation dividing peasants from it and created grounds for what contemporaries soon would begin to call "the estate segregation of the peasants [soslovnaia obosoblennost' krest'ian]."

Third, the emancipation statute posed a number of other intractable problems for future relations between state and educated society. A reform conducted by the state in the interests of the state largely ignored the interests of a society that itself had experienced the invigorating years of the later 1850s. While the rise of the radical intelligentsia lies outside this discussion, one certainly can point to the disillusionment of noble provincial deputies in 1859–60, the disaffection generally evident among educated strata before the Polish rebellion of 1863–64, and the spurt of oppositionist, at times overtly constitutionalist sentiment, which between 1861 and 1865 became evident among some provincial noble and zemstvo assemblies.[116] Indeed, after 1866 zemstvo self-administration itself became a festering reminder of the distance separating state and society in the emancipation's aftermath.[117]

Perhaps the final and most critical consequence of emancipation was the responsibility that the state had assumed for krest'ianskoe delo—"the peasant matter." In his final report to Alexander Rostovtsev had assured the tsar that the emancipation statute would effect an orderly and impartial resolution of serfdom, guarantee the economic interests of the nobility, and assure the future prosperity of the peasantry. In order to accomplish these sweeping goals, the government would broaden its administrative and legal presence in rural society, tying the very legitimacy of autocratic authority to the order and prosperity it had promised to secure. The stakes of this game were quite high, indeed, and the round to be played of very long duration.

[116] Emmons, Russian Landed Gentry, pp. 444–62.
[117] B. B. Veselovskii, Istoriia zemstva za sorok let (St. Petersburg, 1911), 3:99–125.

CHAPTER II

The "First Crisis of Autocracy": The Reforms of Loris-Melikov and the Kakhanov Commission

IN CONTRAST to the surging enthusiasm of 1861, a deadening malaise had engulfed Russian public life by the late 1870s. In a diary entry of April 1879, P. A. Valuev wrote that radicalism and revolutionary terrorism were creating "a domestic crisis" for the government; in June he wrote that he felt as if "the ground was trembling, the [state] edifice threatening to collapse."[1] Minister of War D. A. Miliutin that same month noted "a strange mood in Petersburg." Everyone was "bantering about the necessity of radical reforms, even mentioning the word constitution; nobody," he wrote, "believe[d] in the stability of the existing order."[2] The conservative memoirist E. M. Feoktistov recalled that "dissatisfaction reigned everywhere, often appearing in the most criminal forms."[3] In the aftermath of the victorious Russo-Turkish war, the liberal historian A. D. Gradovskii recollected, educated society had been dismayed that "the poor Russian people" had bled to give Bulgaria "a new order and constitution," while themselves remaining "condemned to . . . the atmosphere of a police precinct, of ignorance and obscurantism." Why, he wondered, was the government repeating the errors of its past?—"stagnation" had contributed to the ignominious Crimean defeat, while only "a few years of progress had secured a victory" over Turkey.[4]

Soviet historians have interpreted such discontent as one aspect of a "crisis of autocracy" that occurred at the end of the 1870s and beginning of the 1880s. Caused by the capitalist transformation of Russia's semifeudal economic and social order, the crisis manifested itself politically in two ways. On the one hand, populist radicalism and terrorism, which, it is argued, posed a systemic challenge to autocratic rule, induced a cam-

---

[1] Count P. A. Valuev, *Dnevnik, 1877–1884* (Petrograd, 1919), p. 33 (15 April 1879) and p. 38 (3 June 1879).

[2] D. A. Miliutin, *Dnevnik D. A. Miliutina*, edited by P. A. Zaionchkovskii, vol. 3 (1878–80) (Moscow, 1950), p. 148 (12 June 1879).

[3] E. M. Feoktistov, *Vospominaniia E. M. Feoktistova: Za kulisami politiki i literatury* (Leningrad, 1929; reprint Oriental Research Partners, 1975), p. 226.

[4] A. D. Gradovskii, "Rokovoe piatiletie," in Gradovskii, *Itogi (1862–1907)* (Kiev, 1907), p. 6.

paign of government repression that exacerbated the "revolutionary situation" emerging in the country. On the other hand, the threat of revolution forced the central government also to undertake reforms that given the nature of the system from which they issued, could only be half-measures. The policies of the autocratic state during and briefly after the tenure of Count M. T. Loris-Melikov intensified the fragility of the old order as a whole.[5]

Crisis, of course, is a relative and ambiguous term, often applied too indiscriminately in the writing of history. To be sure, the explosion of revolutionary radicalism was an important turning point in the late imperial era, but it never approached the revolutionary challenge that Russia would face in the early twentieth century. As startling evidence of social dysfunction, however, the image of Russian youth taking up revolvers and bombs so soon after they had gone "to the people" during that fantastic summer of 1874 did influence both educated society and high officialdom. This phenomenon focused public attention on the unrealized legacy of the great reform era. Many began to doubt the legitimacy of an administrative system that had retained much of the institutional structure and superordinate practice acquired under serfdom and thus, it was thought, had prevented the development of the domestic order and civil well-being promised by emancipation. The issue of legitimacy, which was posed against officialdom but which resonated with implications for the prerogatives of the autocratic sovereign, lay at the root of the political conjuncture of 1878–85. The old regime began to experience a crisis of political values, perhaps even of political faith.

Overstating the impact of revolution, Soviet historians also misconstrue the reforms undertaken to resolve the crisis. The efforts of Loris-Melikov in 1880–81 to reorient domestic policy and the attempts of the Kakhanov Commission, despite the trauma of the assassination of Alexander II, to pursue a reformist agenda in 1882–83 were not half-measures. They were instead significant initiatives toward altering the structure of administrative power in the state and thereby revitalizing the authority of autocratic government in society. Nor was state reform a reflexive concession to political crisis. Rather, it represented a conscious reassertion of the principles and policies of the early 1860s: a concerted drive to accommodate autocratic government to the transformation of Russian society and politics it had unleashed. Twenty years after emancipation radicalism, public dissidence, and general civil disorder in Rus-

---

[5] In general, see P. A. Zaionchkovskii, *Krizis samoderzhaviia na rubezhe 1870–1880-x godov* (Moscow, 1964), and idem, *Rossiiskoe samoderzhavie v kontse XIX stoletiia* (Moscow, 1970); Orlovsky, *Limits of Reform*, chap. 6; B. B. Glinskii, "Epokha mira i uspokoeniia (istoricheskie ocherki)," *Istoricheskii vestnik*, vols. 123–26 (St. Petersburg, 1911).

sian life rendered reform once again a matter of essential state interest. A struggle to define the character, purpose, and governing values of autocratic rule ensued.

THE LEGACY OF THE GREAT REFORMS AND LORIS-MELIKOV

It is most likely that P. A. Valuev's contemporaries would have agreed with him when, in April 1878, he lamented "the complete absence of a ruling government [*pravitel'stvuiushchee pravitel'stvo*]" in Russia.[6] Alarming reports about murdered officials supported the point, but beginning in early 1879 these paled in comparison to the repetitive but sensational efforts of a conspiratorial organization, the People's Will (*Narodnaia volia*), to assassinate the sacrosanct Tsar-Emancipator Alexander II.[7] That officials could not assure the safety of the emperor dumbfounded educated opinion; it also confirmed for a variety of observers what their experience of two post-emancipation decades had suggested: autocratic government had failed to create the social stability and civil order that had been promised by the great reforms.

The most disturbing evidence came from the countryside, where the emancipation of the peasantry had secured neither prosperity nor public well-being. Harvest failures, mounting arrears of redemption payments, and the first indications of demographic pressure on arable land were all taken to signal a deterioration in the peasant standard of living.[8] Twice during the 1870s, the government reviewed the emancipation legislation to investigate the causes of this decline, but eventually changed only one feature of the statute.[9] In 1874 it abolished the arbiters of the peace and replaced them with permanent county boards for peasant affairs. This measure, which reflected the ongoing displacement of the evolutionary

[6] Valuev, *Dnevnik, 1877–1884*, p. 26 (11 April 1878).

[7] See, in particular, Franco Venturi, *Roots of Revolution: A History of the Populist and Socialist Movements in Nineteenth-Century Russia* (Grosset & Dunlap, 1960), chaps. 20–22.

[8] Macey, *Government and Peasant*, pp. 18–24; N. M. Druzhinin, *Russkaia derevnia na perelome 1861–1880 g.* (Moscow, 1970), pp. 248–65; and M. S. Siminova, "Bor'ba techenii v pravitel'stvennom lagere po voprosam agrarnoi politiki v kontse XIX v.," *Istoriia SSSR*, no. 1 (1963): 65–82. See also the growing volume of statistical work, e.g., *Statistika pozemel'noi sobstvennosti i naselennykh mest Evropeiskoi Rossii* (St. Petersburg, 1880–85); Iu. E. Ianson, *Opyt' statisticheskogo issledovaniia o krest'ianskikh nadelakh i platezhakh* (St. Petersburg, 1881); and *Obzor upravleniia gosudarstvennymi imushchestvami s 19 fevralia 1855 goda po 19 fevralia 1880 g.* (St. Petersburg, 1880).

[9] Chernukha, *Krest'ianskii vopros*, pp. 25–70 and 124–206; "Predstavlenie kommissii dlia issledovaniia sel'skoi promyshlennosti v Rossii," in S. M. Seredonin, ed., *Istoricheskii obzor deiatel'nosti Komiteta ministrov*, vol. 3, pt. 1 (St. Petersburg, 1902), pp. 92–108; *Doklad i zhurnaly vysochaishe uchrezhdennoi kommissii dlia issledovaniia nyneishnego polozheniia sel'skogo khoziastva i sel'skoi promyshlennosti v Rossii* (St. Petersburg, 1873).

concerns that had informed the statute of 1861, was ineffective and merely complicated government supervision of village fiscal and public affairs.[10]

Emancipation had not produced civil stability. Instead, future prosperity seemed more distant, bureaucratic tutelage more pervasive, and disarray in the village more widespread. By the late 1870s, Russian revolutionaries, many of whom expected peasant anarchistic rage to explode in revolutionary upheaval, were not alone in sensing the threat that an unacculturated peasantry posed to social order. Valuev complained in December 1879 that "the people" explained assassination attempts against the tsar as the work of "gentlemen or noble landowners" seeking retribution for emancipation. "These rumors are systematically penetrating the masses," he wrote, and very well might "raise the crowd against the upper stratum and lead to butchery."[11] The claim, for Valuev, was typically exaggerated; the perception of civil instability was not.

Second, contemporaries also recognized that the state's reformist activism, the source of such great public enthusiasm before 1861, had lapsed. In its place appeared once again the numbing routine of petty officialdom—that "sang-froid," said Valuev, "with which they shuffle people, beliefs, rules like cards that you can tear to pieces and throw away at will."[12] As minister of internal affairs in the 1860s, however, Valuev himself had inadvertently contributed to the resurgence of such attitudes by broadening the powers of provincial administration—a fact partially explaining this statesman's caustic disdain for incompetent local officials unable to implement the commands of the center. Moreover, zemstvo self-administration now occupied a tenuous institutional position in rural administration. Given formal jurisdiction over matters as significant as medical care and popular education but from the outset denied the authority to enforce their decisions, these organs in the later 1860s and 1870s were increasingly subjected to restrictive official supervision.[13] When terrorist violence erupted in 1878, the administrative restraint of public institutions gave way to a repression of society as a whole. Extraordinary powers for the police, administrative infringement of judicial independence in order to prosecute "state crimes," military governors-

[10] Kataev, *Mestnye krest'ianskie uchrezhdeniia*, chaps. 9–11; Chernukha, *Krest'ianskii vopros*, pp. 60–71, 85–89, 142–50.

[11] Valuev, *Dnevnik, 1877–1884*, pp. 39–40 (14 December 1879).

[12] Valuev, *Dnevnik P. A. Valueva*, 2:81 (29 November 1865).

[13] On provincial policy, see especially Orlovsky, *Limits of Reform*, pp. 74–80, 134–39, 151–54. See also Valuev's debates with Baron M. A. Korf concerning zemstvo authority in "Predstavlenie ministra VD v GosSovet, ot 26 maia 1863" and "Spisok s otnosheniia Glavnoupravliaiushchago Vtorym Otdeleniem (EIV) Kantseliarii k MVD, ot 6-ogo maia" in *Materialy po zemskomu obshchestvennomu ustroistvu* (St. Petersburg, 1886), 2:1–27 and 411–65.

general who superceded civil authorities, suspicion of political loyalty in the schools, press, and zemstvo—such was the police mentality that had come to define the government's relations with Russian society by the end of the 1870s.[14]

Third, the growth of civil culture in educated society magnified the failings of domestic administration. To be sure, the shadow of government control had loomed over a flowering public life after Karakazov's attempted assassination of the tsar in 1866.[15] Yet it could not remove the diverse historical memories of a generation that had felt the heady novelty of independent activity. Young radicals had found in a liberating nihilism the road to revolutionary politics. Educated society, having imbibed the knowledge that a realm of public affairs (obshchestvennoe delo) existed in Russian life, acquired a consciousness of civic duty. Despite haggling with the government, those who participated in the zemstvo, the zemtsy, slowly acquired practical experience in public self-administration.[16] Conservatives, awakened by "the thundering articles" of M. N. Katkov during the Polish uprising of 1863–64, did not forget how the "chaos" of liberalism began to dissipate as they acquired "a conscious regard" for the interests of the state.[17] Moderates remembered the "uplifting of spirit . . . that had reverberated within the contemporary witnesses and activists" of the great reforms.[18] By the end of the 1870s, the conviction that such endeavor was legitimate was finding expression in gestures of public disaffection as diverse as the jury acquittal of Vera Zasulich or the scattered zemstvo petitions for a consultative national assembly—that which was "given to the Bulgarians," as the Chernigov provincial assembly noted in late 1878.[19] With increasing outspokenness, educated society ar-

[14] See especially Miliutin, Dnevnik Miliutina, 3:18–19, 41, 47–48, 128–29, 133–35, 179–80 and 211–12 (24 January 1878–5 February 1880). In general, Zaionchkovskii, Krizis samoderzhaviia, pp. 59–115; Pipes, Rural Russia, pp. 296–302; and Seredonin, Istoricheskii obzor Komiteta ministrov, vol. 3, pt. 1, pp. 145–53.

[15] Valuev, Dnevnik Valueva, 2:178–85 (January 1867), and Veselovskii, Istoriia zemstva, 3:121–25.

[16] Veselovskii, Istoriia zemstva, 3:140–264. In 1871, when zemstvo institutions operated in thirty-two provinces, zemstvo expenditures totalled 21.5 million rubles; by 1881 they had increased by 54%, to 40 million rubles. Ibid., 1:15.

[17] Feoktistov, Vospominaniia, p. 137 and generally pp. 94–107; see also Count S. Iu. Witte, Vospominaniia (Moscow-Leningrad, 1923), vol. 3, pp. 54–66, and Egorov, Stranitsy iz proshlogo, pp. 90–93.

[18] Egorov, Stranitsy, pp. 105–6; "Nabroski iz vospominanii D. D. Obolenskogo," Russkii arkhiv 3 (1894): 256–61; and generally G. A. Dzhanshiev, Iz epokhi velikikh reform: Istoricheskie spravki (Moscow, 1892).

[19] On Zasulich, see Miliutin, Dnevnik Miliutina, 3:41 (2 April 1878) and Gradovskii, "Rokovoe piatiletie," pp. 8–24. On the zemstvo see Manning, "The Zemstvo and Politics," in Terence Emmons and Wayne S. Vucinich, eds., The Zemstvo in Russia (Cambridge University Press, 1982), pp. 136–37, and Veselovskii, Istoriia zemstva, 3:231–40.

ticulated ever more loudly its conviction that civil disorder was caused by the actions of an officialdom that had wrapped the lofty goals of the great reforms in the smothering embrace of government tutelage.

An essay that some twenty prominent zemstvo and public activists signed in spring 1880 illustrates this rising challenge to the legitimacy of government administration.[20] Among the participants were S. A. Muromtsev, the prorector of Moscow University, and A. I. Chuprov, perhaps the most esteemed professional zemstvo statistician in the country. The sponsors spoke both for "educated society" and in the name of a silent "common people" whose "viewpoint" they claimed to share. Disdaining revolutionary "parties," they charged that the government itself had created the grounds for this radicalism by suppressing all opportunity for moderate public initiative:

> There are dammed-up forces in society that seek a free range of activities. There are dammed-up independent opinions that are striving for free expression. The more tightly this legitimate drive is constrained, the more rapidly it will seek out the path of illegality. . . . The contingent of educated people has expanded far beyond representatives of the bureaucratic mechanism alone. A society has formed that lives and acts next to the administration. This society cannot reject the striving that is inherent in it.

Recalling the hopes of the 1860s, the sponsors found even more disillusioning the "inner contradiction" that now existed between "the most elementary rules of civil life, implanted and nurtured in us by upbringing, literature, and constant observation of that which occurs [in the West], . . . and the reality that surrounds us." They urged a resumption of state reform but insisted, as the central guarantee of its success, that an elected assembly of zemstvo representatives be summoned "to participate in state life and activities." Government measures alone, they concluded, were "inadequate to eliminate the causes of widespread dissatisfaction; the amicable cooperation of all the vital forces of Russian society" was required if autocracy was to achieve the civil order that officialdom had proven incapable of establishing.[21]

Although the tsar refused to heed these ideas, high officials, both in April 1879 and January 1880, had nevertheless discussed the convocation of an elected representative institution. The measure might "limit," Valuev observed to his diary, "the passivity of the moderate majority."[22] The

---

[20] *V pervye dni Ministerstva Gr. M. T. Loris-Melikova: Zapiska o politicheskom sostoianii Rossii vesnoi 1880 g.* (Berlin, 1881); see also Zaionchkovskii, *Krizis samoderzhaviia*, pp. 203–7.

[21] *V pervye dni*, pp. 3–4, 10–12, 18, 25–26, and 29.

[22] Valuev, *Dnevnik, 1877–1884*, pp. 51, 31–41, and 46–51; and "Konstitutsionnye proekty nachala 80-x gg. XIX v.," *KA* 31, no. 6 (1928): 118–43. In general, see V. G.

former minister, who had favored representative schemes since he first proffered them in 1862–63, was well aware, and he had written at the time, that the preservation of state power and autocratic authority "in an epoch of public excitement" required the government "to coopt social progress and lead social movement [*sotsial'noe dvizhenie*], which creates three-quarters of history."[23] His remarks then and now were a telling indication of the way in which moderate public opinion influenced the government. To be sure, at a time when political consciousness was only beginning to emerge in educated society, the public expression of representative demands was still an infrequent and quite novel event. Yet, the government also stood at a rudimentary level in its own development. Officials confronting not only radicalism, but general disarray in society—increasing rural poverty, ineffective local administration, widespread disillusionment over failed reforms—could ill afford the spread of political alienation to moderates loyal to autocracy.

That potential scenario assumed much more threatening dimensions on 5 February 1880, when a bomb, which had been concealed in a basement chamber of the Winter Palace, exploded beneath the private dining quarters of the imperial family. A week later, on 12 February, Alexander II created the Supreme Executive Commission, an ad hoc body granted extraordinary powers for the restoration of public order. Count Mikhail Tarielovich Loris-Melikov was appointed as its chair. Government domestic policy was shifting dramatically.[24]

On 15 February, the St. Petersburg official daily, *Pravitel'stvennyi vestnik*, announced this appointment and published an appeal from the new chairman addressed "To the Residents of the Capital." Requesting "society" to oppose "the criminal elements that threaten the foundation of civil order [*grazhdanskii poriadok*]," Loris-Melikov promised "the strictest measures" against sedition, but guaranteed the government's firm efforts to "assuage and protect the legitimate interests [*zakonnye interesy*] of moderate elements." "I regard the support of society," he proclaimed, "as the chief power able to assist the authorities in restoring the correct course of state life, because when it is interrupted the interests of society itself [*interesy samogo obshchestva*] suffer most of all."[25] From the government, this was public language of an astonishing sort. The liberal jurist

---

Chernukha, *Vnutrenniaia politika tsarizma s serediny 50-kh do nachala 80-kh gg. XIX v.* (Leningrad, 1978).

[23] V. V. Garmiza, "Predlozheniia i proekty P. A. Valueva po voprosam vnutrennoi politiki (1862–1866 gg.)," *Istoricheskii arkhiv*, no. 1 (1958): 143. See especially the discussion in Orlovsky, *Limits of Reform*, pp. 67–74.

[24] "Vsepoddaneishii doklad gr. P. A. Valueva i dokumenty v Verkhovnoi rasporiaditel'noi kommissii kasatel'nye," in *Russkii arkhiv*, nos. 11–12 (1915): 216–48.

[25] *Pravitel'stvennyi vestnik*, 15 February 1880, p. 1.

A. F. Koni later recalled that educated society, having "completely lost faith" in officialdom's ability to realize "the principles invested in the reforms of the 1860s," witnessed the sudden appearance of Loris-Melikov on the Petersburg stage with giddy bewilderment. It "seemed that they had opened the transom in a closed room [filled] with stale air—and many felt a fresh breeze in their souls."[26]

Behind the language stood the good public reputation and personal talents of the man. A career army officer and a hero of the recent Russo-Turkish War, Loris had been appointed military governor-general of the Ukraine in 1879. There he earned a reputation as a powerful administrator able to secure order while adhering to law and cultivating good relations with local society. His success, which he explained in a detailed report of February 1880, probably won him the appointment to the Supreme Executive Commission. In this position, and later as minister of internal affairs (August 1880–April 1881), Loris would be after his autocratic patron the dominating power in St. Petersburg, in effect the tsar's ad hoc prime minister.[27] Other personal attributes, which in 1884 Loris related personally to A. F. Koni, served him well at this critical juncture. Born in 1825 to an Armenian family with origins in the nobility, Loris remembered his father, who was by occupation a prosperous merchant, as a "half-savage man" unable to speak Russian. A boy who lacked "a cultured upbringing [*vospitanie*]," Loris obtained an education through his own efforts, first at an Armenian clerical school in Moscow and then in the military, which provided this self-made man with "a school of life" where he "started to study, read, think." Such independence of thought, perhaps accentuated by the personal insecurities of his origins, was rare within an officialdom obsessed with careerist concerns for security and status. Even "the best state people," he remarked, displayed a characteristic "tendency not to want to recognize mistakes or ignorance." "If I didn't know, I wanted to learn." When this "man of the periphery" encountered the unfamiliar world of St. Petersburg, he "started to look and listen." Finding "the deepest dissatisfaction" in educated society, he began to act.[28]

Indeed, activism was the central tenet of Loris-Melikov's brief tenure, and it was reflected in the policy of state reform that he began to implement almost immediately. The outlines of his program first appeared in a report that Alexander II approved on 11 April 1880. With its first lines, Loris insisted that "state order and public tranquility" could only be achieved "in close union with moderate people, with their enthusiastic

---

[26] A. F. Koni, *Sobranie sochinenii*, vol. 5 (Moscow, 1968), p. 187.

[27] Orlovsky, *Limits of Reform*, pp. 170–73 and generally his provocative discussion of Loris's tenure in ibid., chap. 6.

[28] Koni, *Sobranie sochineniia*, 8:194–97.

aid." The warm response that his February declaration had elicited from "people of every profession, public position, and legal status" proved that educated society retained "confidence in the wise plans of its sovereign." Yet, he continued, the public expected the government to return to the "path of prosperity" trod in the early 1860s. If it failed "to satisfy these sentiments"—if it did not again uphold the ideals that Alexander had established at the beginning of his reign—Loris warned the tsar to expect "the poison spreading in the state organism increasingly to infect more and more of its healthy parts."[29]

As willfully as any other of his contemporaries, Loris-Melikov retained subjective historical memories of the reform decade. He remembered a period of state reform that had "occupied and in many ways satisfied the intellectual powers of the developed elements of society." Reform, and the public enthusiasm it had generated, Loris emphasized, fortified "the strength of government authority [pravitel'stvennaia vlast']" and imbued "the component parts of Russian society [sostavnye chasti russkogo obshchestva] . . . with a conscious [soznatel'naia] allegiance to the person of their monarch." What was as important, he continued, was that the legislation of that decade had planted the seeds of "a legal order [zakonnyi poriadok] accommodated to the needs of the time and to Russia's historical conditions." Yet, because the administrative system of the state was left in large measure unaltered, the seeds did not take root. Officials both high and low had been unable to adapt to "a new situation that demanded different knowledge, skills, and abilities than before." Educated society, Loris admitted, was partially to blame for the "inevitable mistakes, often extremism" of its views. From such "isolated, lamentable facts," however, elements in both "society" and "influential government circles" mistakenly concluded that the reforms were "a disadvantage" and "strove not only to regulate but to eliminate" their further development. The two subsequent decades of administrative drift had undermined the promises of civil and legal order made in 1861. "An infinite number of commissions, endless [and] fruitless correspondence irritated public opinion [obshchestvennoe mnenie] and did not satisfy anyone," Loris wrote. Legislation that addressed pressing issues—the peasant question, the courts, the position of the clergy and hereditary nobility, the zemstvo, urban self-administration, the economy—"had sunk to the [level of] the chancelleries." The government, its lethargy fostering societal instability and "more or less legitimate [public] disillusionment," had

[29] "Vsepoddaneishii doklad grafa Loris-Melikova ot 11 Aprelia 1880 g. s resoliutsiiami imp. Aleksandra II," in "Konstitutsiia grafa Loris-Melikova: Materialy dlia ee istoriia," Byloe 32–33, nos. 4–5 (April–May 1918): 154–55. An analysis of commentary by public and government figures is found in Zaionchkovskii, Krizis samoderzhaviia, pp. 151–207.

created the conditions that now "weakened the foundations of the state order."[30]

How was the state to extract itself from its predicament? Loris proposed two major avenues for government policy. The first, an underlying motif throughout his brief tenure, was the unification and coordination of ministerial government. The two recommendations of this report—for a new Department of Police within the Ministry of Internal Affairs to strengthen public order and for a reorganized civil administration in the provinces to solidify state authority—reflected the importance that the self-described satrap attached to rationalized institutional hierarchies capable of executing the domestic policy of a unified central government.[31] Second, he advocated a renewed commitment to legality and reform, a task whose achievement a more unified administration would facilitate, in order to display the "intensified government activity" that educated society was demanding. Arbitrary measures of "an exclusively police character—searches, arrests, administrative exile, military courts"—by fostering dissidence, had shown their inadequacy and were to be abandoned. Legislative "measures of a positive nature" were necessary as well to address a range of pressing issues: education, religious toleration, the peasant economy, provincial civil administration, censorship. Such initiatives would convey the allegiance of the government, and the autocrat in whose name it acted, to the principles of legality and civil progress articulated in the 1860s. It was, Loris said, imperative

> to arouse in government institutions and personnel a more attentive attitude toward the manifest essential needs of the population [*potrebnosti naseleniia*] and toward its representatives. It is impermissible not to exhibit a favorably disposed concern for the needs of the clergy, toward the activity of the zemstvo, to the necessities of the cities. [We] must clear the way for those proposals of primary importance that the supreme will of your imperial majesty indicated a long time ago and whose realization has been halted in the chancelleries and in every kind of commission.[32]

With a terse "yes" written in the margin of the report, Alexander II confirmed the principles of a campaign to revitalize his government. The tsar was also aware, and Loris emphasized this point in his April report, that public spokesmen were again putting forward, as they had in the 1860s, muted demands for limited representative institutions. The so-

[30] "Vsepoddaneishii doklad ot 11 Aprelia 1880 g.," pp. 156–57.

[31] Ibid., pp. 155, 160–61. In general see Orlovsky, *Limits of Reform*, chap. 6 and Zaionchkovskii, *Krizis samoderzhaviia*, pp. 226–48.

[32] Ibid., pp. 158 and 160. The similarities between these recommendations and the programmatic demands circulating in moderate educated society were striking. See, for example, *Poriadok*, 16 February 1881, p. 1, and 19 February 1881, pp. 1–2.

called crowning of the edifice, a representative assembly intended to assure the legal order that officialdom had been unable to create, in its own way challenged the tsar as explicitly as had revolutionary terrorism. It thus confronted Loris with a Solomonic choice between two incompatible principles: autocracy and the political aspirations of civil society. His often misinterpreted "constitutional" plan, formally proposed in January 1881 but present in broad outline as early as the April report, proffered a middle course between these two extremes. It reflected both the limitations and potential of his drive to solidify the authority of autocratic government.[33]

In April, Loris proposed only that "knowledgeable [*sveduiushchie*] and loyal" experts be appointed from the provincial assemblies of the nobility, provincial zemstvos, and some municipal assemblies to participate in ministerial discussions of legislation that affected "local needs." This policy, he argued, would heighten the government's credit among public moderates and provide a desired infusion of local "expertise and labor" to resolve those "economic, public, and financial questions" now standing on the government's agenda.[34] Reminiscent of the Editing Commissions or the consultation that took place between government and zemstvo during the 1870s, this proposal became over subsequent months part of a broader effort to engage educated society in local reform initiatives.[35] Immediately following his appointment as minister of internal affairs in August, Loris ordered extraordinary senatorial investigations of eight provinces in order to gather data for a planned reorganization of rural administration. The following January, his Ministry of Internal Affairs requested all zemstvo assemblies to discuss reforms of peasant estate administration.[36]

When Loris formally proposed it on 28 January 1881, his representa-

[33] The three versions of this plan, each a more expansive attempt to institutionalize elected representation than the one before it, were "Vsepoddaneishii doklad ot 11 Aprelia 1880 g.," *Byloe* 32–33, nos. 4–5 (April–May 1918): 154–161; "Vsepoddaneishii doklad ot 28 ianvaria 1881 g.," in ibid., pp. 162–163; and "Vsepoddaneishii doklad gr. Loris-Melikova ot 12 aprelia 1881 g.," in ibid., pp. 183–84.

[34] "Vsepoddaneishii doklad ot 11 aprelia 1880 g.," in ibid., pp. 159–60.

[35] Since 1864 the government had consulted zemstvo assemblies on some thirty different administrative issues, including zemstvo-town relations (1870), head-tax reform (1873), and the grain reserve-famine relief system, Veselovskii, *Istoriia zemstva*, 3:152–53.

[36] "Senatorskie revizii 1880 goda," *Russkii arkhiv*, no. 11 (1912): 417–29, includes "Vsepoddaneishii doklad ministra vnutrennykh del 11-ogo avgusta 1880 g." and "Osoboe nastavlenie senatoram." The zemstvo discussions of peasant administration are gathered unsystematically in *Trudy osoboi kommissii dlia sostavleniia proektov mestnogo upravleniia* (hereafter *Trudy ok*), *Materialy po preobrazovaniiu mestnogo upravleniia* (St. Petersburg, 1884), and are summarized in V. Iu. Skalon, *Zemskie vzgliady na reformu mestnogo upravleniia: obzor zemskikh otzyvov i proektov* (Moscow, 1884), and James I. Mandel, "Paternalistic Authority in the Russian Countryside, 1856–1906" (Ph.D. diss., Columbia University, 1978), pp. 126–43.

tive scheme, although by no means a constitution, did crown this jerry-built edifice of public participation in legislative decision making. The plan established an electoral mechanism for designating representatives from provincial zemstvo assemblies and large municipal councils—the nobility was no longer mentioned. After elections targeted for the regular zemstvo session of winter 1881–82, delegates would join officials in a "general commission" to examine draft legislation affecting rural administration, the redemption operation, zemstvo and municipal self-administration, famine relief, and tax and passport laws. Final approval of these bills would rest in a State Council temporarily expanded to include some fifteen public representatives.[37]

One factor influencing this bolder proposal was public opinion. In the preceding months, the capital press and some zemstvo circles had expressed a growing impatience with the pace of Loris's reforms.[38] In September, he had given a well-publicized interview to St. Petersburg editors, in which he spoke disparagingly of unwarranted speculation about constitutional plans.[39] While praising this unprecedented breach of "the impenetrable veil" that usually surrounded official activity, the journal *Otechestvennye zapiski* noted its disappointment that Loris appeared to be limiting his reforms to local initiatives alone.[40] Coincidentally, only two days before the report of 28 January, the zemstvo liberal A. A. Golovachev, writing in the Petersburg daily *Poriadok*, greeted the government's "return to those tendencies projected in the reforms of the early sixties." He worried, however, that Loris-Melikov's September comments indicated merely "a return to the initial point of departure, and not essential changes in our public structure." An article criticizing "the principles spawned by [serfdom] throughout the bureaucratic structure of our life" left little doubt about the elected representative assembly it was implicitly advocating.[41]

[37] "Vsepoddaneishii doklad ministra vnutrennykh del grafa M. T. Loris-Melikova ot 28 ianvaria 1881 g.," in "Konstitutsiia grafa Loris-Melikova," pp. 164–65. Although approving the report on 16 February 1881, a special conference chaired by the future Alexander III recommended against including elected representatives in the State Council. On 1 March, Alexander II approved only the further discussion of this revised draft by the Committee of Ministers, "Zhurnal osobogo soveshchaniia, sozvannogo dlia obsuzhdeniia dokladnoi zapiski ministra vnutrennykh del," in "Konstitutsiia grafa Loris-Melikova," pp. 167–73.

[38] On the articulate and unfettered character of press and zemstvo opinion in these months, see the reviews of the 1880–81 winter zemstvo assemblies in *Poriadok*, especially 17 January 1881, p. 1, 20 January 1881, p. 1, and 16 February 1881, p. 1. See also Valuev, *Dnevnik, 1877–1884*, pp. 92–109 passim (May–August 1880); Veselovskii, *Istoriia zemstva*, 3:248–56; Gradovskii, "Rokovoe piatiletie," pp. 71–73.

[39] *Otechestvennye zapiski*, 252 (September 1880), p. 141; also Zaionchkovskii, *Krizis samoderzhaviia*, p. 236, and Gradovskii, "Rokovoe piatiletie," pp. 65–67.

[40] *Otechestvennye zapiski* 252 (October 1880): 240–42.

[41] A. A. Golovachev, "Obshchie voprosy dnia," *Poriadok*, 26 January 1881, pp. 1–2.

In his January report Loris hinted that such criticism motivated him to support elections. Noting the continuing public enthusiasm for his policies, he urged "making use of this mood" before it dissipated. Even those who favored "representative forms," Loris maintained, were in fact articulating a "matured need to serve in public affairs [*sozrevshaia potrebnost' sluzhit' obshchestvennomu delu*]." Under present conditions, his plan was "the most practical means to give [it] legal expression." Elections could not only "relieve" this pressure, but—as important—allow the government to utilize in its legislative decisions "the experience of local activists who stand closer to popular life than the officials [*chinovniki*] of central institutions."[42] Yet, Loris reiterated, he did not intend to satisfy but rather to divert constitutional sentiments and preserve "the right of the sovereign authority to raise legislative questions."[43] He explained that the parliamentary structure favored by some was "unthinkable for Russia" at a time when the personal authority of the autocrat still held great sway in the peasant village. To create a second legislative power, an idea "alien to the Russian people," might "undermine its fundamental political views [*politicheskie vozzreniia*] and [produce] total chaos [*smuta*], whose consequences are difficult to foresee."[44] An assembly of the land [*zemskii sobor*] with its representation of estates, which others favored as a more genuinely Russian alternative, was simply "a dangerous experiment of returning to the past"; it invited aristocratic pretensions and contradicted the very character of the evolution of civil life already evident in educated society.[45]

In one respect, such reservations were tactical, as Alexander II's anti-constitutionalism was well-known in the byzantine corridors of St. Petersburg politics. In another respect, however, Loris's hesitancy derived

---

Poriadok, which began publication in January 1881, was edited by M. M. Stasiulevich and had among its contributors I. S. Turgenev, Iu. E. Ianson, P. V. Annenkov, A. A. Golovachev, K. D. Kavelin, and G. K. Gradovskii. The newspaper was considered a leading voice of moderate educated society, *ES*, 48:654.

[42] "Vsepoddaneishii doklad ot 28 ianvaria 1881," in "Konstitutsiia grafa Loris-Melikova," pp. 165–66.

[43] Ibid., pp. 162–63; also "Vsepoddaneishii doklad ot 11 aprelia 1880 g.," in ibid., pp. 159–60; and (ed.), E. A. Perets, *Dnevnik E. A. Peretsa (1880–1883)*, edited by A. A. Sergeev (Moscow-Leningrad, 1927), p. 8 (October 1880).

[44] Senators sent to investigate provincial administration during summer 1880 were instructed, among their other duties, to "elucidate the attitudes of the peasant population: have uprisings recently occurred, what caused them, and how were they halted; pay particular attention to whether expectations and rumors of a new allotment of land, the so-called 'black repartition' are discernible among the peasants . . . ; and determine what can help in stopping these false rumors and calming the minds of the peasants." "Senatorskie revizii 1880 goda," *Russkii arkhiv*, no. 11 (1912): 420.

[45] "Vsepoddaneishii doklad ot 28 ianvaria 1881," in "Konstitutsia grafa Loris-Melikova," p. 163.

from personal conviction: his perceptions of a society in flux legitimated the state's superordinate role in Russian life. The reform program of 1880–81 assumed that the transformations initiated in the 1860s had barely taken root. A legal order that legitimated state authority and power was still mocked by the reality of an arbitrary officialdom. Civil order in the countryside was still threatened by an unacculturated peasantry. Hence, at a time when these goals were becoming political issues, autocracy remained a first principle of statecraft, essential to any efforts to effect gradual societal change. In August 1880 Loris not surprisingly conveyed this message when he addressed the investigating senators whom he was despatching to the provinces. Their work, he said, would assist the task of administrative reform, which was a necessary prerequisite to the still distant day when Russia would achieve the stable civil order it now lacked: "I know that there are people who dream about parliaments, about a central zemstvo duma, but I do not belong to their number. This task will fall to our sons and grandsons, whereas we have to prepare the groundwork."[46]

While preserving the mediatory role of the state, Loris had nevertheless taken a bold step toward redefining it. By January 1881 he had established the argument that the legitimacy of government, and thus ultimately that of the autocrat for whom it acted, depended on public confidence. The latter could be obtained only if the state guaranteed legal order, addressed the urgent social and economic needs of the country, and somehow took into account the legitimate political aspirations slowly coalescing in educated society. Moreover, failing to adopt these principles of reform, an arbitrary officialdom could only repress but never defuse the public dissatisfaction and anomie that sheltered a more threatening radical challenge. Hence, without legal order, autocratic authority itself could only look to an uncertain future in an immature, largely agrarian country only twenty years removed from serfdom. In a state where authority and power were still entangled in the autocracy's mediation of the estate system, this conclusion groped far beyond the entrenched, traditional patterns of autocratic rule.

STATE REFORM, LOCAL REFORM, AND THE KAKHANOV COMMISSION

Loris-Melikov is said to have spoken of his fears that "some boy with a toy revolver could destroy all my plans."[47] Whether accurate or apocryphal, the statement conveys the shattering blow visited upon Loris and his reform program on 1 March 1881, when Alexander II was assassi-

---

[46] Zaionchkovskii, *Krizis samoderzhaviia*, pp. 217–18.

[47] "Iz dnevnika V. A. Bilbasova, mart 1881 g.," in "Konstitutsiia grafa Loris-Melikova," p. 189; and Koni, *Sobranie sochinenii*, 5:197–98.

nated by members of the radical group the People's Will. Two days after the murder of the Tsar-Emancipator, an imperial command ordered all peasants to swear allegiance to the new Tsar Alexander, an obligation of citizenship that, twenty-six years earlier, their masters had assumed for them.[48] The poignant moment recalled both the accomplishments of the reform era and the grave uncertainty with which it ended. The new reign, as one Petersburg newspaper remarked, was beginning with "convulsive tremors" that might "accelerate or alter the organic course of the country's evolution."[49]

Standing first on its agenda was the Loris-Melikov "constitution." Since January, the tsarevich had not concealed his opposition to a plan that he equated with popular representation.[50] Nevertheless, on 6 March, as Tsar Alexander III, he approved a press release announcing the measure, only to decide, at the urging of his former tutor K. P. Pobedonostsev, to discuss the project at a meeting of the Committee of Ministers instead.[51] This took place on 8 March at the closely guarded Winter Palace. Alexander III took the chair, and the meeting provoked a vitriolic debate among the ministers, advisers, and grand dukes who attended.[52]

A majority of Alexander II's advisers supported Loris. Their loyalty testified to the influence he had obtained over the government: D. A. Miliutin (War), Valuev (Committee of Ministers), A. A. Abaza (Finance), A. A. Saburov (Education), D. N. Nabokov (Justice), D. M. Sol'skii (State Comptroller), and the Grand Duke Konstantin Nikolaevich.[53] A small

[48] *Poriadok*, 4 March 1881, p. 1.

[49] Ibid., 3 March 1881, p. 1.

[50] Chernukha, *Vnutrenniaia politika*, pp. 109–33; also "Zhurnal osobogo soveshchaniia . . . (17 February 1881)," in "Konstitutsiia grafa Loris-Melikova," pp. 167–73, and Valuev, *Dnevnik, 1877–1884*, pp. 47–48 (9 Jan. 1880).

[51] "Iz dnevnika Bil'basova," in "Konstitutsiia grafa Loris-Melikova," pp. 189–90. Alexander III's approval of a government press release, "2-i proekt pravitel'stvennogo soobshcheniia," ibid., pp. 177–80, can be found in "Vsepoddanneishii doklad ministra vnutrennykh del grafa M. T. Loris-Melikova ot 6 marta 1881 g.," in "Konstitutsiia grafa Loris-Melikova," p. 177. Also see the letter of 6 March from K. P. Pobedonostsev to Alexander, which urges the replacement of Loris, an end to the "liberal direction" of domestic policy and all talk of press freedoms or representative assemblies, and a reassertion of autocratic prerogative. K. P. Pobedonostsev, *Pis'ma Pobedonostseva k Aleksandru III* (Moscow, 1925), vol. 1, pp. 315–18.

[52] Perets, *Dnevnik Peretsa*, pp. 31–46; also Miliutin, *Dnevnik Miliutina*, 4:32–37, and Zaionchkovskii, *Krizis samoderzhaviia*, pp. 325–32, who relies heavily on the detailed descriptions of Perets.

[53] Perets, pp. 35–45 passim. Abaza's comments were characteristic. The great reforms "had summoned Russia to a new life." Although acknowledging the "disturbing phenomena" of contemporary life, he said that they were "acceptable and almost necessary in a situation of transition [*perekhodnoe polozhenie*] from total stagnation to rational civil freedom [*razumnaia grazhdanskaia svoboda*]." He agreed that recent events made the times perilous, but for the government to ignore the validity and necessity of Loris-Melikov's

minority—the octogenarian Count S. G. Stroganov, the former minister of internal affairs L. A. Makov, and Ober-Prokurator of the Holy Synod Pobedonostsev—termed the plan an ignominious encroachment upon autocratic authority and the first step toward the catastrophe of constitutionalism. Indeed, Pobedonostsev's speech, D. A. Miliutin remarked, was "a direct, indiscriminate repudiation of everything accomplished in the previous reign," even of "Western civilization" itself.[54]

Although a majority favored Loris's proposal, a hesitant tsar ordered it withheld for further review. For six weeks the bureaucratic rumor mills ran rampant with speculation about the future direction of state policy and the fate of the two "parties" contesting it.[55] Given Alexander's own authoritarian predilections, however, the influence of Pobedonostsev was decisive. On 21 April, the tsar complained to him in a letter that "Loris, Miliutin, and Abaza are continuing the same policy and want somehow to lead us into a representative government." They were simply mouthing phrases, Alexander impatiently exclaimed, "read out of our lousy journalism and bureaucratic liberalism. I am more and more convinced that I cannot wait for something good from these ministers."[56] On the 27th he approved Pobedonostsev's draft of an imperial manifesto pledging to preserve "the power and justice of autocratic authority . . . from any pretensions to it." On the morning of the 29th it was proclaimed. Loris-Melikov resigned that day, and Abaza the next; for reasons of protocol Miliutin,

proposals was myopic: "one cannot forget that, besides the simple narod, educated classes of society [obrazovannye klassy obshchestva] are also [counted] in the population of the state. It is necessary to whatever degree possible to attract them to participation in administration, to hear out their opinion, and not to disregard their counsel, which is frequently very intelligent." Ibid., pp. 40–41.

[54] Miliutin, Dnevnik Miliutina, 4:35; also "Iz dnevnika V. A. Bil'basova, mart 1881 g." in Konstitutsiia, p. 90. Pobedonostsev argued that the plan to summon the "so-called representatives of the zemstvo" was the culmination of a process of westernization and liberalism, which had begun with the great reforms, that was undermining autocratic power, the source of all social cohesion in Russian life. The newly emancipated peasants were "a mass of backward and ignorant people [temnye liudi]," who lacked the "proper authority over them" and were victimized by "innkeepers, kulaks, Jews, and usurers." Public self-administration were "forums" controlled by debauched people "thinking only of personal advantage, seeking popularity, and inducing chaos everywhere." In independent courts, "a forum for lawyers," "the most horrible crimes" went unpunished. The press, "this most horrible forum . . . abused and defied authority, . . . incited the people to the most flagrant illegal acts." Perets, Dnevnik Peretsa, pp. 39–40.

[55] Perets, Dnevnik Peretsa, pp. 47–69, and Zaionchkovskii, Krizis samoderzhaviia, pp. 370–77. Loris-Melikov's reform program, presented for Alexander III's approval, is "Vsepoddaneishii doklad gr. Loris-Melikova ot 12 aprelia 1881 g.," in "Konstitutsiia grafa Loris-Melikova," pp. 183–84.

[56] K. P. Pobedonostsev, K. P. Pobedonostsev i ego korrespondenty (Moscow, 1923), vol. 1, pt. 1, p. 49. See also his letters of c. 21 March and 30 March, ibid., pp. 45–48.

the only minister still in the office he had held in 1861, waited until 12 May to leave his post.[57]

The manifesto of 29 April 1881, however, had decided only the personal fate of Loris-Melikov. As the tone of the Petersburg press reaction to events indicated, it had resolved little else. On 7 May *St. Peterburgskie vedomosti* lamented the departure of Loris-Melikov, but used the moment to emphasize that his policies had raised public "faith in a stable future"; three weeks later *Poriadok* openly attacked government "conservatives [*okhraniteli*]" for undermining "public cooperation and participation in affairs of general interest."[58] In its New Year's Eve "political review" of the year 1881, *Poriadok* even more insistently referred to representative institutions. It cited various events as evidence of the continuing "uncertainty and expectancy" present among all classes of society: the summer's wave of pogroms against Jews, the unceasing rumors of peasants seizing lands, and the eight provincial zemstvo assemblies that had discussed elected representation during their recently completed meetings. True public order, the paper insisted, was impossible under "a system at whose base lies distrust of society, . . . suspicious tutelage of all branches of public life, and evisceration of [all] public independence." It was necessary, the newspaper said, to hear "the voice of the people."[59]

The appointment of Count N. P. Ignat'ev to succeed Loris-Melikov at the Ministry of Internal Affairs added to the uncertainty that prevailed in the first year of Alexander III's reign.[60] Ignatev, a former diplomat and leading spokesman of the Pan-Slavist movement, was regarded as a proponent of conservative slavophilism, and his program, first announced on 7 May, reflected that rhetoric and perspective.[61] Absent were the references to legality, civil order, and public opinion that had characterized the statements of Loris. Instead, Ignat'ev premised all government policy upon the unquestionable legitimacy of autocratic authority, the undisputed "will of the Supreme Leader" that stood in union with "the multimillion people" and "the best sons of the native land." Rather than encouraging public participation in state life, Ignat'ev expected more cooperation in the struggle against treason and held liberal ambivalence partly to blame for the violent death of Alexander II.

[57] Ibid., vol. 1, pt. 1, pp. 50–52; Miliutin, *Dnevnik Miliutina*, 4:61–66; and Perets, *Dnevnik Peretsa*, pp. 67–71. All these resignations were announced publicly after the fact. *Poriadok*, 6 May 1881, 7 May 1881, 24 May 1881.

[58] *Poriadok*, 7 May 1881, p. 2, and 23 May 1881, p. 1.

[59] *Poriadok*, 30 January 1881, p. 1.

[60] See esp. Zaionchkovskii, *Krizis samoderzhaviia*, pp. 450–60, which cites the archival document "Vospominaniia Ignat'eva," in which the minister explained his policies as a middle path between "the expansion of police measures that could only have driven dissatisfaction deeper" and "the path of concessions" advocated by Loris-Melikov.

[61] *Poriadok*, 7 May 1881, p. 2.

Although his views reflected a very different understanding of Russian society (indicating again how easily statesmen could derive conflicting perceptions from the same phenomena), Ignat'ev asserted autocratic prerogative and the rhetoric of Slavophilism to reorient, not overturn, the reform initiatives of Loris. Indeed, within ten months Ignat'ev was urging the tsar to convene an assembly of the land.[62] In his statement of 7 May, he guaranteed the government's solicitous attention to the needs of society, but did so by affirming the historic "rights" of the service nobility, the "entire Russian zemstvo," and "urban estates." Nor did he shy away from the reform of local rural government, which he, too, regarded as an essential forum for engaging the "lively participation of local activists in implementing imperial commands" and for assuring the necessary improvements of the peasantry's "public structure and economic existence."[63]

During the summer his work began. Ignat'ev twice summoned appointed marshals of the nobility and zemtsy to government conferences to discuss ways of addressing the economic decline in peasant life.[64] On 4 September 1881, the tsar approved the creation of a special commission to reform provincial and county administration. Assistant ministers from most central government departments and the four senatorial investigators were appointed to its membership. The commission was to base its work on the extensive local data gathered by the senators, as well as the studies of peasant estate administration presently underway in the zemstvo assemblies. With ministerial approval, the commission chair, Mikhail Sergeev'ich Kakhanov, a former assistant minister of internal affairs under Loris-Melikov, was empowered to invite local "prominent" experts and other useful individuals to participate in deliberations.[65] This body—the Special Commission for the Compilation of Projects for Local Administration—understandably became known as the Kakhanov Commission.[66]

---

[62] Zaionchkovskii, *Krizis samoderzhaviia*, pp. 450–60, and Veselovskii, *Istoriia zemstva*, 3:246–47.

[63] *Poriadok*, 7 May 1881, p. 1.

[64] Veselovskii, *Istoriia zemstva*, 3:246–47 and 267–77.

[65] Zaionchkovskii, *Krizis samoderzhaviia*, pp. 430–31, and Seredonin, *Istoricheskii obzor*, vol. 4, pt. 1, pp. 80–81.

[66] On the Kakhanov Commission, see Zaionchkovskii, *Rossiiskoe samoderzhavie*, chap. 4; Thomas Pearson, "Ministerial Conflict and Local Self-Government Reform, 1877–1890" (Ph. D. diss., University of North Carolina, 1976); M. V. Islavin, *Obzor trudov vysochaishe utverzhdennoi pod predsedatel'stvom stats-sekretaria Kakhanova osoboi kommissii* (St. Petersburg, 1905); V. Iu. Skalon, *Zemskie vzgliady na reformy mestnogo upravleniia: Obzor zemskikh otzyvov i proektov* (Moscow, 1884); and I. M. Strakhovskii, "Krest'ianskii vopros v zakonodatel'stve i zakonosoveshchatel'nykh kommissiakh posle 1861 g.," in P. D.

Reports of the new commission and its mandate first appeared in the press on 1 November.[67] A reformed civil administration in the territorial jurisdictions of the empire's provinces and counties, the government announced, was intended to strengthen state authority in local life. This goal, in turn, required legal guarantees allowing organs of public self-administration to execute their statutory functions effectively. As described in the idiom peculiar to such official announcements, the organizational principles of the commission's work together were intended to create a rationalized local government from the existing incoherence of local administration:

> a local structure imbued in all its parts with a unifying organizational principle [*edinstvo rukovodiashchego nachala*]; the greatest possible reduction in the number of separate institutions and councils; the strengthening of a local executive authority in general and the curtailment of restrictive formalism; . . . a vital bond between the administration [*administratsiia*] and public administration, an exact delimitation of [the latter's] rights and obligations, and a definition of the direct responsibilities [of both].[68]

Although they approved the announcement, moderate St. Petersburg press organs worried that the commission's program and bureaucratic membership—both of which seemed to favor increased administrative power over the development of public self-administration—boded nothing good for effective civil government. *Vestnik evropy* urged more attention to zemstvo and peasant "public administration," and hoped to see a plan that "lessen[ed] . . . the distinctions among estates." Success required "a new step toward equality of rights [*ravnopravnost'*], which constitutes the essence of all the reforms of the preceding reign."[69] The newspaper *Poriadok* was much less circumspect. "The resolution of the 'provincial question,' " it wrote on 5 November 1881, could not be divorced from discussion of "general state conditions." If legal guarantees "for free private and public activities . . . , for freedom of conscience and the press, for the certainty of tomorrow" did not "constitute local requirements, if the proper structure and course of local life [did] not depend upon this," then the commission's goals were "incomprehensible." This pillar of moderate educated opinion explicitly contrasted its vision of legal and civil order to the reality of exisiting administrative structures and a "bureaucracy [*biurokratiia*]" that "has the tragic capacity to eviscerate public life . . . and, branching out into hundreds of departments and sets of bosses of every kind imaginable, to obstruct public initiative and visit fear

Dolgorukov and S. Tolstoi, eds., *Krest'ianskii stroi: Sbornik statei* (St. Petersburg, 1905), pp. 421–27.
[67] *Pravitel'stvennyi vestnik*, 1 November 1881, p. 1.
[68] Ibid.
[69] *Vestnik evropy*, no. 6 (1881): 853–58.

and trembling upon society."[70] Such comments expressed the growing disillusion of the hopes held by moderates for government reform after the fall of Loris-Melikov.

Yet the continuity between Loris and the initial reform plans of the Kakhanov Commission was more pronounced than circumspect official pronouncements indicated. Perhaps the most important bond was constituted by the commission chairman, M. S. Kakhanov.[71] A graduate of the elite Imperial School of Jurisprudence, he served during the 1860s as a vice-governor and governor in the provinces, where he had supervised the initial implementation of the great reform legislation. By 1870 he was governor of Pskov and had been convinced that institutional irrationality and the arbitrary use of official power were causing public confidence in government authority to decline.[72] He then worked under Loris-Melikov as assistant minister of internal affairs; called Loris's "adjutant" by one observer, Kakhanov had written the January 1881 plan for elected zemstvo representation.[73] In late 1881 his commission set out to establish a rural government that could mediate legal and civil evolution in Russian life.[74]

At its initial organizational meeting on 20 November 1881, the Kakhanov Commission approved a report detailing the historical causes of local administrative disarray and setting forth in broad outline the already familiar perspective of Loris-Melikov.[75] The report explained that unlike England, local institutions in Russia had not arisen from "a natural

---

[70] "Reforma mestnogo upravleniia," *Poriadok*, 5 November 1881, pp. 1–2; also "Predely i tseli mestnoi reformy," *Poriadok*, 8 November 1881, pp. 1–2, and "Nasha expertiza po vnutrennym delam," *Poriadok*, 22 November 1881, pp. 1–2.

[71] Tsentral'nyi gosudarstvennyi istoricheskii arkhiv (hereafter TsGIA), f. 1162, op. 6, d. 230, ll. 77–99 (formuliarnyi spisok).

[72] Yaney, *Urge To Mobilize*, pp. 18–20.

[73] Valuev, *Dnevnik, 1877–1884*, pp. 126–27 (6 November 1880). On Kakhanov's authorship of the January 1881 representative plan, see *Russkii arkhiv*, 54 (1916): 21 and 26.

[74] A letter written by Loris-Melikov to his private secretary A. A. Skal'kovskii in October 1881 portrayed the connection that the former minister saw between his program and local reform: "the majority of our ministers . . . tried to prove that public institutions were the nest of our nihilism. . . . These nihilists have nothing in common with the mass of the population or its representatives. . . . Nihilism will collapse when society joins all its powers and sympathies to the government. . . . In my opinion, we ought immediately to begin a review of the entire zemstvo statute, urban self-administration, and even provincial institutions; on them rests the entire matter, and our future prosperity and peace are bound to their correct structure. I will say more: the more firmly and clearly [the government] frames the issue of an all-estate zemstvo, adapted to the contemporary conditions of our life, the more quickly zemstvo institutions are extended to the other provinces of the empire, the more protected we will be from the striving of a known but insignificant part of society toward a constitution, so inappropriate for Russia." "Ispoved' grafa Loris-Melikova," *Katorga i ssylka*, no. 2 (1925): 118–25.

[75] *Pravitel'stvennyi vestnik*, 24 April 1882, p. 2; also Seredonin, *Istoricheskii obzor*, vol. 3, pt. 1, pp. 81–82.

evolution of public life" and, unlike those in France or Prussia, did not constitute "a theoretically coherent" hierarchical structure. Rather, by applying contradictory administrative theories to provincial life, government officials since the eighteenth century had failed to create any kind of institutional system. The great reforms were no exception; indeed, they were perhaps much more consequential. The "unparalleled peaceful revolution [*perevorot*]" of emancipation had required "the combined and amicable exertion of all the country's intellectual forces" in order to support order and channel "the desires awakening in all strata of society . . . toward the general welfare [*obshchee blago*]." Instead, new public, administrative, and judicial institutions had been grafted onto the police-bureaucratic apparatus created under serfdom. "The absence of the necessary bond and proper definition of authority and jurisdiction among local institutions sowed and fostered antagonism [*rozn'*] not only between government and public organs but [also] among [state] institutions themselves." What resulted was the "powerlessness [*bezsilie*]" of local administration and a "noticeable decline" in the quality of officialdom as the best "public *and* government activists" avoided service in it.[76] Not suprisingly, the commission maintained, this situation had affected "the public mood [*obshchestvennoe nastroenie*]" and fostered "the antigovernment and antisocial phenomena" of Alexander II's last years. The political consequences of a local administration that had "impeded the establishment of order and the evolution of popular welfare, [our] best shields against anarchistic tendencies," required little explanation in the aftermath of a regicide.

Thus, understanding that its institutional objectives encompassed the problems of civil instability and political dissent, the commission concluded this first statement of principle by declaring that only a unified rural government could eliminate "the idea, which had taken root in society and even in some government organs, that some institutions possess[ed] goals distinct from service in the work of the sovereign [*sluzhenie Gosudarevu delu*]." To counter this threatening divisiveness, the commission would create from above an administrative system that delineated lines of authority among state and public institutions—a legal milieu forcing local officials to recognize that they acted "both in the interests of the government and in the legitimate interests of the local population, which are becoming one with general state interests [*zakonnye mestnye interesy . . . slivaiiushchiesia v obshchikh gosudarstvennykh interesakh*]." From below, a reformed order would revitalize the authority of local official-

[76] Emphasis added. Senatorial investigations emphasized low landowner voting turnout in zemstvo elections, e.g., *Trudy o. k.*, I. I. Shamshin, *Zapiska po voprosam osobogo nastavleniia revizuiushchim senatoram, otnosiashchimsia k zemskim uchrezhdeniiam* (St. Petersburg, n.d.), pp. 1–10 and 121–22.

dom by generating an influx of local talent, "the best public forces," into both administrative and zemstvo service.[77] The commission's drive to transform local officialdom, stabilize rural civil life, and strengthen the legitimacy of government authority indeed represented an attempt to continue the state reforms contemplated by Loris.

A Plan for Rural Government

Within five months, by April 1882, the Kakhanov Commission had issued an agenda of work that encompassed all rural civil administration, beginning with the village community and ending with the governor.[78] It contained three organizational objectives. The first was unified government in the provincial capital and county seat. Collegial boards that regulated the numerous ministerial, police, and public organs at present scattered throughout their respective territories were intended to effect state supervision of local society and officialdom.[79] Second, the plan had the goal of defining the jurisdiction and authority of zemstvo self-administration, especially within village administration. This would ensure greater public confidence in the government and a resurgence of public enthusiasm for local affairs. Third, it intended to eliminate most peasant estate institutions in the village and township and to replace them with all-estate jurisdictions. This measure was essential to the commission's work. It would incorporate the entire rural populace under civil administration, allow the zemstvo greater influence upon rural affairs, and promote the peasantry's gradual acculturation into civil society.

In order to draft legislative statutes, Kakhanov designated a small conference of commission members to work under his supervision.[80] They were a remarkable group of generalist officials and public activists whose careers were rooted in the reforms of the 1860s. The four senators I. I. Shamshin, S. A. Mordvinov, A. A. Polovtsev, and M. E. Kovalevskii were

[77] *Pravitel'stvennyi vestnik*, 24 April 1882, pp. 2–3.

[78] *Pravitel'stvennyi vestnik*, 24 April 1882, pp. 2–3. The organizational plan is detailed in *Trudy o.k.. Ocherk predpolozhenii bol'shinstva chlenov soveshchaniia osoboi kommissii po sostavleniiu proektov mestnogo upravleniia* (hereinafter *Ocherk*) (St. Petersburg, n.d.).

[79] County administration was divided among some twenty-three different administrative and police offices, "Perechen' predmetov zaniatii kommissii," *Pravitel'stvennyi vestnik*, 24 April 1882, pp. 2–3. On the disorganized rural administration of the later nineteenth century, Weissman, *Reform in Tsarist Russia*, chap. 1 and P. N. Zyrianov, "Sotsial'naia struktura," pp. 226–304.

[80] *Pravitel'stvennyi vestnik*, 14 May 1882, pp. 1–2. Its proposals are in *Trudy o.k., Ocherk, Polozhenie ob ustroistve mestnogo upravleniia* (hereinafter *Polozhenie*) (St. Petersburg, n.d.), and *Ob"iasnitel'nye zapiski k proektu polozhenii ob ustroistve mestnogo upravleniia, sostavlennye Soveshchaniem vydelennym iz sostava Vysochaishe uchrezhdennoi kommissii* (hereinafter *Ob"iasnitel'nye zapiski*) (St. Petersburg, n.d.).

participants. Both Polovtsev and Kovalevskii had graduated from the Imperial School of Jurisprudence. The former had served in the Senate since 1851. Kovalevskii had been a member since 1862, winning respect for his work on the judicial reform of 1865 and peasant customary law in 1871.[81]

Also a member was P. P. Semenov, a graduate of the physics-mathematics faculty at St. Petersburg University, who had played a prominent role in the Editing Commissions. He developed this expertise in peasant affairs by directing the Central Statistical Committee of the Ministry of Internal Affairs (1864–80).[82] F. L. Barykov, who in 1882 had headed the ministry's Land Section, had also been a member of the Editing Commissions. His knowledge of peasant inheritance customs, as well as a study of the repartitional commune that he conducted for the Free Economic Society in 1880, were both highly regarded.[83] Two other men brought public experience to the conference proceedings: N. A. Vaganov was a former provincial zemstvo board chair in Pskov, where Kakhanov had been governor, and I. E. Andreevskii held professorships on the juridical faculty of St. Petersburg University and at the Imperial School of Jurisprudence. Andreevskii's two-volume work on police law was the standard reference of the period.[84] Working until the spring of 1883, these men detailed a reorganization of rural government based, to be sure, on legal theory and not on legislative practice. Their reform plan nevertheless conveyed again the striking conviction that law could alter historical reality.

Zemstvo institutions, and the jurisdictional conflict that afflicted their relations with the state, occupied a prominent place in the conference's thinking. Its members contended that the original intent of the 1864 statute, the establishment of elected "state institutions" to supervise some "affairs of local administration" had been distorted when the government failed to define the zemstvo's authority and grant it executive power. Consequently, the new institution had been subject to the caprice of local police and administrative officials. This situation fostered the erroneous but nevertheless accepted view, evident in the public theory of self-administration, that the zemstvo was an elected government supervising those local affairs that the central administration chose to neglect. Functioning "alongside existing government institutions," the zemstvo had assumed

[81] P. A. Zaionchkovskii, "A. A. Polovtsev, biograficheskii ocherk," in Polovtsev, *Dnevnik*, 1:5–11, and "M. E. Kovalevskii," *Bol'shaia entsiklopediia*, (hereinafter *BE*), 11:122.

[82] "P. P. Semenov," *BE*, 17:247.

[83] "F. L. Barykov," *BE*, 2:643; and F. L. Barykov et al., eds., *Sbornik materialov dlia izucheniia sel'skoi pozemel'noi obshchiny: Izdanie imperatorskikh Vol'no-Ekonomicheskogo i Russkogo Geograficheskogo Obshchestva*, vol. 1 (St. Petersburg, 1880).

[84] "I. E. Andreevskii," *BE*, 1:624; and I. E. Andreevskii, *Politseiskoe pravo*, 2 vols. (St. Petersburg, 1871).

"a private [*chastnyi*] character" in the eyes of both officials and society. The zemstvo, the conference noted, had been forced "to complain and seek redress" from an omnipresent officialdom like any other petitioner.[85]

Thus emerged the acrimonious jurisdictional disputes of the later 1860s and 1870s. "Antagonism toward crown institutions" provoked reflexive government "distrust . . . that naturally resulted not only in criticism of zemstvo activity but also in restrictive measures [taken] against it." As political tensions rose, the effectiveness of local administration as a whole had suffered.[86] In their senatorial investigations, both Shamshin and Kovalevskii had emphasized that education, public health, famine relief, and other important administrative affairs managed by the zemstvo had been "much less fruitful than they might have been." Considering their lack of executive authority, the zemstvos in Saratov and Samara provinces had "done more during their time than one could expect," but, Shamshin delicately noted, "leaving [them] any longer in the same situation would [create] a permanent source of various difficulties."[87] The conference concurred that zemstvo management of local public welfare, which represented a substantial improvement over the "death-like stagnation" prevailing under pre-reform bureaucratic administration, had produced "if not always a correct, at least a viable, progressive movement [*postupatel'noe dvizhenie*]."[88] Yet this conclusion only reinforced the conviction that effective local government was unattainable as long as administrative practice fostered public hostility toward state concerns. A legal institutional order that would fuse a cooperative relationship between government and zemstvo was thus imperative.

It was useless, the conference argued, to foster the illusion that one could determine "the line beyond which general state interest begins to dominate . . . and exclusively local interest ends." Close study of the actual situation in the countryside revealed that "between these two extremes lies a broad range of interests that affect both the state and local areas." If "empowered by the state [and] elected by the population," zemstvo institutions would be more capable of "supervising, within legally defined limits, those branches of local administration whose assign-

[85] *Trudy o.k., Ob"iasnitel'nye zapiski*. (Uezdnoe upravlenie), pp. 1–2. See also P. P. Gronskii, "Teorii samoupravleniia v russkom nauke," in Veselovskii and Frenkel, eds., *Iubileinyi zemskii sbornik*, pp. 76–86. See also A. I. Vasil'chikov, *O samoupravlenii* (St. Petersburg, 1869); A. I. Koshelev, *Golos iz zemstva* (Moscow, 1869); and A. A. Golovachev, *Desiat' let reform, 1861–1871* (St. Petersburg, 1872).

[86] *Trudy o.k., Ob"iasnitel'nye zapiski* (Uezdnoe upravlenie), pp. 3–6. These views were also evident in *Trudy o.k., Materialy po preobrazovaniiu mestnogo upravleniia*, 1:131–64; and Skalon, *Zemskie vzgliady*, pp. 29–57 and 62–69.

[87] *Trudy o.k.*, I. I. Shamshin, *Izvlechenie iz vsepoddaneishago doklada*, pp. 7–8; and *Trudy o.k.*, M. E. Kovalevskii, *Izvlechenie iz vsepoddaneishago doklada*, pp. 11–12.

[88] *Trudy o.k., Ob"iasnitel'nye zapiski*, (Uezdnoe upravlenie), pp. 3–6.

ment to government officials [*chinovniki*] unfamilar with local needs would serve neither local nor state interests."[89] The zemstvo was a critical component of local administration; its rights and powers needed to be fixed in law.

To achieve zemstvo-state cooperation, the conference proposed a new county supervisory board (*kollegiia*), which also was a locus of its effort to unify local government. The confluence of the two goals was not coincidental. The proposed board was empowered to investigate the activities of any peasant, public, or crown official in the county and to resolve administrative appeals raised against them as well. Cooperation and unity, however, dictated a board membership drawn from equal numbers of officials and elected zemstvo delegates, which guaranteed "an impartial examination" of all issues. Moreover, the same objectives necessitated that the county zemstvo assembly elect the board's chair, subject to landholding and educational requirements and the confirmation of the minister of internal affairs. To place the board "under the direction [*pod nachal'stvom*]" of one government official, the conference stated, threatened to exacerbate the "enmity [*vrazhda*]" between administration and zemstvo, "in no way weakening . . . the isolation" of public institutions. To favor the county marshal of the nobility, an individual "elected by only one estate" was equally unacceptable. A zemstvo-elected chair, who possessed "the trust of the local population," could assure effective and authoritative government grounded in firm public support.[90]

The conference did not intend to hand over control of local administration to the zemstvo—although the use of public resources did free state personnel and revenues for police and provincial administration.[91] It rejected proposals current in some public circles to grant the zemstvo complete control of local administrative affairs "because in reality this would turn . . . all local administration into zemstvo [administration]."[92] It also

[89] Ibid., p. 12; also *Trudy o.k.*, Shamshin, *Izvlechenie*, pp. 7–8, 16–17, and *Trudy o.k.*, Kovalevskii, *Izvlechenie*, pp. 11–14.

[90] *Trudy o.k.*, *Ob"iasnitel'nye zapiski* (Uezdnoe upravlenie), pp. 10–12, 57–65. The board's permanent members were the police *ispravnik*, the chair of the county zemstvo board, and the elected chair of the board itself, who potentially tilted the majority to the zemstvo. The county marshal of nobility, currently chair of most county administrative boards, was not a member. *Trudy o.k.*, *Polozhenie* (Uezdnoe upravlenie), pp. 41–46, 61–67.

[91] Yaney, *Systematization of Russian Government*, pp. 346–51 takes this view of the Kakhanov Commission. He sees it as an attempt to resurrect the position that the local nobility occupied in the 1830s.

[92] *Trudy o.k.*, *Ob"iasnitel'nye zapiski* (Uezdnoe upravlenie), p. 12. Some zemstvo opinion was for county government subordinated to the zemstvo assembly, its executive board, or the local marshal of the nobility. When required, bureaucratic participation was to be limited to technical expertise. Skalon, *Zemskie vzgliady*, pp. 157–83.

worked to divest the local police of its extraneous, particularly fiscal responsibilities in order to create a more professional and powerful executive agent for the MVD.[93] Moreover, its proposals attached great significance to strengthening the power of the governor over all branches of provincial administration. Acting through a new provincial board with a bureaucratic majority, the governor was charged to investigate any public or bureaucratic institution in his territory, including the new county boards, as well as to supervise the expenditure of zemstvo funds.[94]

Yet the conference did consider zemstvo personnel, resources, and expertise to be fundamental if it was to construct effective civil government, particularly in the township and village institutions that supervised the peasant populace. Senatorial and zemstvo investigations had established that estate organs had become subordinate instruments of arbitrary officialdom and an irrational foundation for rural government. In the final analysis, the incorporation of the zemstvo into a unified local administration was justified as the means to reform peasant estate administration, the third and ultimate objective of the conference's plan.

Zemstvo commentaries, which the Kakhanov Commission reviewed and published, blamed peasant estate administration for widespread illiteracy, poverty, and corruption in the villages. The use of peasant public self-administration to assure the fiscal and police concerns of the state, it was argued, had altered the character of institutions that in 1861 had been meant to help develop rural civil affairs.[95] There was far less unanimity in zemstvo opinion about an alternative. Some assemblies advocated replacing peasant townships altogether with elected, all-estate zemstvos, the so-called small zemstvo units.[96] Others would transform the township into an administrative jurisdiction for all estates, supervised by an elected executive official responsible to the county zemstvo.[97] Finally, some assemblies, wary of tampering with peasant estate institutions, preferred zemstvo elected officials to administer peasant village and township organs.[98] All responses, however, shared a common characteristic: they excluded local officialdom from any substantive role in peasant life.

[93] *Trudy o.k., Ob"iasnitel'nye zapiski* (Politsiia) and *Polozhenie* (Politsiia), pp. 31–40.

[94] *Trudy o.k., Ob"iasnitel'nye zapiski* (Gubernskoe upravlenie), and *Polozhenie* (Gubernskoe upravlenie), pp. 68–90.

[95] *Trudy o.k., Materialy po preobrazovaniiu mestnogo upravleniia*, 1:3–129; Skalon, *Zemskie vzgliady*, pp. 76–157; Veselovskii, *Istoriia zemstva*, 3:649–67; and Mandel, "Patriarchal Authority," pp. 126–43.

[96] Skalon, *Zemskie vzgliady*, pp. 145–57.

[97] Ibid., pp. 137–45.

[98] Ibid., pp. 112–37. Within this category, some opinion was for the unification of administrative and judicial authority in one official placed over peasant institutions, i.e., the land captain.

In large measure, the conclusions of senatorial investigations seconded the charge that the combination of estate institutions and local official-dom had undermined the peasantry's civil development. Most revealing in this regard was M. E. Kovalevskii's review of Kazan' and Ufa provinces. Since 1874, Kovalevskii noted, crown-appointed county boards for peasant affairs had overseen peasant townships and their officials. Ostensibly they had been established to improve peasant public administration and hasten the day when peasants would be incorporated into "administrative institutions common for all estates." This effort to foster the goals of the emancipation statute, however, had created just another county office, one in which peasants deposited written complaints, supervisors more often than not were absent, and hired clerks monitored the paperwork of township officials.[99]

Such routinization of administrative practice, Kovalevskii continued, had two irrational consequences. On the one hand, after 1861, the township and its elder had gradually become the primary executive agent of all higher administrative, fiscal, and zemstvo organs in matters affecting general state administration. Yet formally their jurisdiction and authority encompassed only the allotment land of communal and state peasants and did not extend to "nonprivileged estates" and local noble landowners.[100] On the other hand, by investing peasant officials with diverse administrative and police obligations, the state had converted their responsibilities for rural public welfare into secondary concerns:

> The list of responsibilities invested by law in the elder alone shows that his [duty] is primarily fiscal and police administration, and not that of public welfare [*obshchestvenno-khoziastvennyi*]; the elder more often acts as the local representative of administrative and police authority. [He] . . . forces the rural population to fulfill their obligations and is not the representative of public authority [*obshchestvennaia vlast'*] in the township concerned with satisfying the needs and requirements of the township population and managing its public welfare.[101]

To find the quintessential expression of how the existing rural administration was undermining peasant public life, Kovalevskii looked no further than the township elder and his clerk, the *pisar'*. Legally the elder was the elected head of the township, but, given his "illiteracy, lack of

[99] *Trudy o.k., Zapiska Chlena Gosudarstvennogo Soveta Senatora Kovalevskogo, zakliuchaiushchaia materialy kasaiushchiesia polozheniia i deiatel'nosti krest'ianskikh uchrezhdenii po dannym, obnaruzhennym pri revizii gubernii Kazanskoi i Ufimskoi* (St. Petersburg, n.d.), pp. 4–5, 10–11, 37–39.

[100] Ibid., pp. 80–84.

[101] Ibid., pp. 87–88. See also his description of the elder's role in the complex, year-long process of regulating tax collection. Ibid., pp. 93–95.

development, and lack of experience," he was usually "only the submissive instrument" of a clerk familiar with written law. This clerk, however, was not a legal agent of government authority. He was a patronage appointee of a peasant-board supervisor, county sheriff (*ispravnik*) or marshal of the nobility, and he owed them his livelihood. Held responsible "by the bosses [*nachal'stvo*]" for the formulaic propriety of township administration, the clerk became "the leader" whom the peasant elder, for obvious reasons, followed. Indifference to peasant public welfare had been bred into an irrational system devoted to police-fiscal concerns and dominated by relations of personal influence and arbitrary power.[102]

Given his observations, Kovalevskii concluded that no basis existed "for the preservation of the exclusively peasant, estate character" of the township. It did not serve the needs of public self-administration. It was an irrational foundation that confounded the creation of a unified, territorial administrative system. And it rested in the hands of arbitrary local officials, a factor that here, as elsewhere in rural government, "dissuaded more educated and developed local residents from [entering] local public service [*mestnaia obshchestvennaia sluzhba*]."[103] In its own writings, the conference agreed with Kovalevskii's analysis:

> [The township administration], in its relations with the peasant world, is irresponsible and uncontrolled and [maintains] a defenseless, unstructured [*bezsviaznyi*] relationship with all the multitudinous authorities and individuals standing over it; it is thus an institution that satisfies neither peasant needs nor the requirements of general administration.[104]

To reform the peasant township, the conference advocated legalizing what it had already become in administrative practice: a territorial jurisdiction for all residents regardless of estate. In place of the elder, the conference proposed a new township supervisor [*volostel'*], elected to a six-year term by the county zemstvo assembly and confirmed by the governor's provincial board. Thus responsible to both zemstvo and provincial administration, this elected official was to be the primary representative of civil authority in local life. Through elections, the conference hoped to draw local residents with "practical experience and a good [university or secondary] education" into local administration, but given how small was the number of such individuals, it defined quite broadly the requirements for candidacy to this post and, contrary to zemstvo experience, did not stipulate landownership. The electoral sanction of the zemstvo assembly, it was hoped, was the best assurance of prestige and

102 Ibid., pp. 85–86.
103 Ibid., p. 101.
104 *Trudy o.k., Ob"iasnitel'nye zapiski*, (Volostnoe upravlenie), p. 4.

legitimacy for the new supervisor, who, unlike a government official, would not be "a stranger [*chuzhoi*] to the local population, but instead inspire it with confidence."[105]

Laws, rational institutions, stipulated administrative goals, and legitimate government authority—the conference believed that a generalized administrative structure could begin to stabilize rural civil society. A unified, decentralized provincial administration would ensure for the central government effective local supervisory power. A defined institutional relationship between local bureaucracy and zemstvo self-administration would bind the two together in an authoritative civil government. An educated, elected township supervisor of an all-estate territory would bring civil authority closer to the rural populace. Yet, in effect, the supervisor represented the last outpost at the frontier dividing civil society from the realm of the rural peasantry. In its project to establish all-estate organs of village public self-administration [*sel'skoe obshchestvo*], the conference proposed to colonize this culturally distinct peasant world. It intended to foster civil values by establishing civil institutions.

The conference was profoundly aware that the policy toward peasant administration since 1861 had been a double-edged fiasco. On the one hand, the principle of "estate segregation [*soslovnaia obosoblennost'*]," which in 1861 had been intended as a temporary measure applied only to seigneurial serfs, had been extended to all categories of peasants. Estate institutions, in turn, had been saddled with tasks of general state administration that were "totally beyond [their] capacity." On the other hand, by converting the peasantry's public institutions and officials into a subordinate administrative mechanism, the state had not only accentuated the gulf between peasant and civic cultures but also left itself without institutions capable of addressing the problem:

> Because the estate character [*soslovnost'*] of the peasants' administrative structure has been so extended, the peasants, 80% of the empire's population, are entirely segregated from other strata of society and in many ways constitute a distinct, vast state within the state. This segregation . . . could not but have produced a series of consequences that at present constitute unconquerable impediments both to the successful development of the peasants themselves and to the structuring of a local administration that can aid the government in sat-

[105] *Trudy o.k., Ob"iasnitel'nye zapiski* (Uezdnoe upravlenie), pp. 18–25, and *Trudy o.k., Polozhenie* (Uezdnoe upravlenie), pp. 12–15. The new official, an agent of the proposed county board as well as the zemstvo, was responsible for a long list of supervisory duties: circulation of county board directives; management of annual military conscription; temporary veto power over the decisions of peasant village institutions, officials, and judges; civil administrative tasks ranging from the issue of certificates (*svidetel'stva*) to statistical compilations; and, finally, acting as a police agent until such time as police or court investigators arrived at the scene of a crime.

isfying local public-state needs [*mestnye obshchestvenno-gosudarstvennye nuzhdy*].[106]

The impediments were most evident in village administration. Because at the time of emancipation the village community (*sel'skoe obshchestvo*) had been organized on the basis of seigneurial land allotments, there was at best a tenuous connection between the institution and actual patterns of rural residence. The village community might coincide with a single settlement, but it also might encompass several separate villages, or one large village might be divided among several distinct administrative units. Table 2.1 illustrates the problem: it compares the discrepancies between the number of "significant" rural settlements in 1885 and the corresponding number of seigneurial estates from which village institutions were formed in 1861. These data buttress the subjective conclusion drawn by the conference. In village institutions based on communal land allot-

TABLE 2.1

Rural Settlement in European Russia by Geographical Region

Geographical Region	No. of Provinces	Rural Settlements (1880–85)	Seigneurial Estates (1859–60)[a]
Lower Volga	5	5,292	6,014
Central Agricultural	8	9,457	28,743
Little Russian and Southwest	6	8,071	20,481
Lakes	4	3,265	7,941
Moscow Central Industrial	6	7,467	16,090
Far North and Urals	6	9,189	2,336
Lithuanian and White Russian	7	3,760	16,259
New Russia	4	2,903	5,803
Total	46	49,404	103,667

Source: Data for rural settlement are found in Ministerstvo vnutrennykh del, Tsentral'nyi statisticheskii komitet, *Volosti i vazhneishie seleniia Evropeiskoi Rossii: Po dannym obsledovaniia, proizvedennogo statisticheskim uchrezhdeniiam MVD, po porucheniiu statisticheskogo soveta*, editions 1–8 (St. Petersburg). Comparative figures for seigneurial estates are from A. Troinitskii, ed., *Tsentral'nyi statisticheskii komitet: Krepostnoe naselenie v Rossii po 10-i narodnoi perepisi* (St. Petersburg, 1861), p. 45.

[a] Seigneurial estates are only an approximate measure of total village communities (*sel'skoe obshchestvo*).

[106] *Trudy o.k., Ob"iasnitel'nye zapiski* (Sel'skoe obshchestvo), pp. 2–3.

ments, "public-administrative questions"—the election of officials, public welfare, famine relief, charity, proper selection of military recruits—were subordinated to the "private-economic" matters of land management that most immediately preoccupied the village community.[107]

The conference did not contemplate abolishing the existing village community, as it possessed neither the mandate nor the inclination to confront the politically sensitive and complex issue of the communal land allotments upon which the institution in fact rested. Rather, paying respects to the "state significance and political importance" of the commune, the conference circumvented the entire issue by declaring land relations to be a private matter subject to civil law. This provided a legal stratagem to distinguish the commune [zemel'noe obshchestvo] from the public interests of village residential life, from "the concept of the village community as the sum total (sovokupnost') of all village residents who constitute a single public-state entity."[108]

This legal and institutional demarcation of village public affairs was a significant innovation in the state regulation of rural life. So it would continue to be until, at the turn of the century, the central government would begin to confront the underlying economic dilemmas of communal land use. For the moment, however, the conference possessed a lever with which it might pry open a status quo of officialdom and estate institutions that it viewed as an impediment to the evolution of local civil society:

> In the course of 23 years . . . life in the villages has witnessed the most diverse developments; . . . if purely peasant villages still exist with the initial character foreseen . . . in the statute of 19 February [1861], many others of an entirely different type exist alongside it. . . . Villages have appeared in which a multitude of people have settled who are not of the peasant estate or even cultivators [sel'chany], but [are] primarily craftsmen and traders. The number of such individuals, who are pouring into the midst of the agricultural population, into its centers of public life [obshchestvennaia zhizn'], increases annually; at present such settlements are hardly an exceptional phenomenon.[109]

Existing laws and institutions distorted these processes of change. Under present law, all village residents who were not communal peasants were effectively "extraneous individuals [postoronnye litsa]," often having no right to participate in the village assembly and no obligation to pay its tax levies. The fact that village residents were developing informal methods to overcome these difficulties—private agreements for raising funds, constructing bridges, or hiring night watchmen—only reinforced

107 Ibid., pp. 3–4, 8–10.
108 Ibid., pp. 12–13.
109 Ibid., pp. 2–4.

the conviction that law lagged behind reality. Moreover, it was often the case that the village assembly, constituted from communal peasants who usually defined "public interests" in terms of "private questions of the communal economy," rendered "a [general] community of interests [*obshchnost' interesov*] in practice impossible." Senatorial investigations revealed that as a result, groups that could not obtain satisfaction from official village institutions—non-Orthodox religious denominations or sects, handicraft artels, ethnic communities, charity organizations, or economic and industrial enterprises—were creating their own "private assemblies" to attend these concerns.[110] "Public life [*obshchestvennaia zhizn'*] in the villages" was burgeoning, but lacked an institutional structure in which it could evolve properly. The village required

> a jurisdiction [*krug del*] that possesses general and equal importance [*obshchee i ravnoe znachenie*] for all members of the village community, regardless of the estate or faith to which they belong, the basis on which they utilize their land plots, the trade by which they seek the means of survival, or the union, brotherhood, or society they join.[111]

At no other juncture in its organizational plan was the conference's insistent imposition of legal and institutional order upon rural reality more evident—nor were the constraints imposed by this reality more apparent. Figuratively transposed to the mud of a village lane, the conference's members in exquisite detail constructed there the legal framework of a village public community. The new all-estate village institution—which would incorporate all communal, private arable, commercial, or industrial property in the area—was charged with supervising the public welfare and order, all tax collection, the execution of court orders, and military conscription. It was empowered to raise its own taxes and elect its own official to oversee these concerns. Yet these rights remained obligations, and to ensure their fulfillment the conference invested the township supervisor, and through him the county board, with broad supervisory power over village self-administration. The supervisor could veto or appeal the legality of any action taken by the village assembly or its elected official, and, despite warnings against the measure, the village elder was given the power to levy administrative fines and to arrest village residents. Members noted the utility of force at a time when "a respect for legality . . . is very weakly ingrained in our fatherland, especially at its low levels." Finally, neither rights nor obligations extended to private es-

[110] Ibid., pp. 6–12. See also *Trudy o.k.*, Kovalevskii, *Zapiska . . . krest'ianskikh uchrezhdenii*, pp. 73–76.

[111] *Trudy o.k.*, *Ob"iasnitel'nye zapiski* (Sel'skoe obshchestvo), pp. 13–14.

tate owners, who were allowed to decide for themselves whether to join the village and shoulder the burden of its tax assessments.[112]

Indeed, both here and elsewhere in its discussions the conference had been torn between the riveting image of a peasant whose low level of civil development reinforced perceptions of social instability and their own compelling desire to close the cultural distance separating this rural world from educated society. Hence, members were willing to compromise their opposition to peasant estate institutions in the case of the township court, citing "the peculiar [svoeobraznye] concepts of law in the peasant milieu, which are often based on entirely different principles than civil laws." They could only hope that the presence of the justice of the peace at the court's sessions could inculcate "truer concepts of law and justice."[113] The conference rejected proposals for a township zemstvo, fearing that a malleable peasant majority might support politically "unreliable people [sluchainye lichnosti] in such a small assembly." "This idea could become reality," the conference insisted, only in the future, when a more developed, rural "public life" existed in the villages, when "the economic and especially the intellectual level of the population" was raised, when "prosperous and enlightened [prosvechennye] people" lived "everywhere" in the township.[114] The conference knew that senatorial investigations had indicated peasant indifference, if not hostility, to zemstvo institutions. The "peasant estate," Kovalevskii wrote, regarded "its participation in the zemstvo as the fulfillment of an obligation placed upon it by the law." Shamshin added that the "peasant mass" thought the zemstvo to be, essentially, "a source of new tax assessments," nothing more.[115] Yet, members had expanded zemstvo supervision over peasant self-administration in order to eliminate the alienation in which such attitudes were rooted.

It would distort the significance of the conference's sweeping reform plan, however, to conclude a discussion of its work on this note. Specifically, the conference did attempt to revise the zemstvo electoral system,

[112] Only property of specified acreage (perhaps 25 desiatins, or 70 acres) or value was included in the village structure; property owners above this limit participated in village affairs at their discretion. In general, see Trudy o.k., Polozhenie (Sel'skoe obshchestvo), pp. 1–7; also Trudy o.k., Ob"iasnitel'nye zapiski (Sel'skoe obshchestvo), pp. 15–20, 25–31.

[113] Trudy o.k., Ob"iasnitel'nye zapiski (Volostnoe upravlenie), Prilozhenie, p. 7. See also Peter Czap, Jr., "Peasant Class-Courts and Peasant Customary Justice in Russia, 1861–1912," Journal of Social History 1, no. 2 (Winter 1967): 149–76.

[114] Trudy o.k., Ob"iasnitel'nye zapiski (Volostnoe upravlenie), pp. 9–10.

[115] Trudy o.k., Kovalevskii, Izvlechenie, p. 11; and Trudy o.k., Shamshin, Izvlechenie, p. 7. Shamshin observed that zemstvo delegates elected by the peasantry were often township elders or clerks, and that many served only one three-year term. Trudy o.k., I. I. Shamshin, Zapiska po voprosam otnosiashchimsia k zemskim uchrezhdeniiam (St. Petersburg, n. d.), pp. 10–14.

urging that it be altered to accommodate the changes in population, land values, and landownership that had occurred since emancipation. As this policy affected the peasantry, the conference wanted to increase its representation in the county assembly and allow qualifying smallholders to vote in the first electoral curia of private landowners.[116] This evolutionary dimension of the conference's thinking was even more pronounced in its principled defense of the township supervisor. To be sure, it had granted to a representative of the zemstvo broad legal discretion over peasant institutions. Yet his usefulness to future civil development rendered him a far more appropriate supervisory authority than the land captain (*zemskii nachal'nik*), an official exercising administrative and police-judicial authority over only peasant estate institutions. Although this idea, which would dominate reform discussions later in the decade, was already favored by some circles, the conference repudiated the proposal, terming it "a return to an outmoded police state." Russia had at least moved beyond "the first steps in the development of economic and civil life [*grazhdanskaia zhizn'*]," beyond the point at which such methods were applicable.[117]

In the final analysis, that which distinguished the thinking of the Kakhanov Commission was not its demand for institutional order but the purposes that order was to serve. Like the policy initiatives of Loris-Melikov, the Kakhanov Commission's projects presupposed that authority and law, when capricious and irrational, bred disrespect for the two pillars upon which a state order rested. In educated society such attitudes had produced political crisis. Among the masses they had assured cultural alienation and the stagnation of civil growth. Enlisting the cooperation of educated Russia, the reformers of the Kakhanov Commission thus proposed a movement to the people: the implantation of a legal system, a civic order in the countryside. This was admittedly only the edifice, but it could, they believed, foster in rural Russia the cultural values that both state officials and public opinion were deemed to uphold. The state and its officials would thus remain the guardians of rural Russia, but public officials from educated society would join them. The rural population, surrounded by an institutional structure intended to foster its acculturation, remained the object of legislative dreams. These dreams, however, were of future citizens.

The conference completed the initial draft of its local reform projects in the spring of 1883. Editorial work and final corrections were finished

---

[116] *Trudy o.k., Ob"iasnitel'nye zapiski*, (Uezdnoe upravlenie), pp. 28–36; and *Trudy o.k., Polozhenie* (Uezdnoe upravlenie), pp. 52–54. Druzhinin, *Russkaia derevnia*, p. 142, calculates that by 1880, peasants had purchased some 4.8 million desiatins (13 million acres) of privately owned land through approximately 110,000 bills of sale.

[117] *Trudy o.k., Ob"iasnitel'nye zapiski* (Volostnoe upravlenie), p. 10.

by the following November. Plenary sessions of the full commission, however, did not begin until October 1884. During this interim period, serious opposition to the reforms began to surface. This was particularly noticeable in a compendium of provincial governors' commentaries sponsored by Minister of Internal Affairs D. A. Tolstoi.[118] Appointed in May 1882 to replace Ignat'ev, Tolstoi had made no secret of his "great contempt" for the Kakhanov Commission. He allowed its work to proceed because he supposedly feared public accusations of inhibiting "a very significant matter." He also knew that the conference's proposals would later be resubmitted to the full commission, whose composition he was empowered to alter.[119] When the full commission finally convened, its membership indeed had been changed considerably since 1882; open hostility to the conference plan was the order of the day (see chapter 3). The commission debated local reform for some five months, and then, in March 1885, Tolstoi issued an abrupt order to terminate the proceedings. The materials of the Kakhanov Commission were relegated to the archives, not to appear again until a far greater crisis of autocracy than that of the early 1880s began to rack the state at the turn of the century.

A period of state reform that began in 1880 with Loris-Melikov's challenge to complete the work of the Great Reforms had ended in ignominious defeat. Yet its attempted redefinition of the character and goals of autocratic rule established precedents for the future—and raised significant consequences for the more immediate present.

Loris-Melikov and the Kakhanov Commission delineated compelling rationales for the reform of the autocratic order. Both acknowledged that the two decades since emancipation had witnessed the initial stages of an evolutionary process transforming Russia's estates and fostering their amalgamation as a civil society. The emergence of revolutionary ideologies, the growth of civic consciousness in educated society, the halting socioeconomic transformation of the peasant populace—all this change from below necessitated reform from above. Statesmen had the duty of adapting the political and social structures of the old regime to these developments. A government unable to accomplish that task threatened to undermine the authority of the autocrat it served.

The solution given in the early 1880s was legal autocracy. In many respects, the reform proposals of Loris-Melikov and the Kakhanov Commission were patterned after the German *Rechtsstaat*: a state order of laws and rational bureaucratic institutions that assured proper civil life

[118] *Trudy o.k., Svod mnenii Gg. Gubernatorov po predlozheniiam ob ustroistve mestnogo upravleniia* (St. Petersburg, n.d.).

[119] Polovtsev, *Dnevnik Polovtseva*, 1:148 (25 November 1883); and Feoktistov, *Vospominaniia*, pp. 248–49.

for all members of society. Yet the term "legal autocracy" more accurately conveyed the distance that still separated both government and society in Russia from the Rechtsstaat ideal of central European statecraft. A profound recognition of backwardness and change, of serfdom and modernity, of what Russia had been and what it ought to become, had informed the reform debates of the period. Rule by law and rational bureaucracy were ideals still contradicted by arbitrary power and tutelary officialdom. So, too, a civil society that valued a culture of law and individual rights was a nascent phenomenon in a country whose political traditions had been shaped by the superordination inherent in the estate structure through which the state regulated its subjects. Under such conditions of backwardness, Loris-Melikov and the Kakhanov Commission attempted to equip autocracy with a legal administrative order that would mediate and assure the further civil evolution of Russian society. Their unsuccessful efforts nevertheless established critical precedents and legislative materials to which later reformers would return.

Their failure, however, also complicated the dilemmas that subsequent reformers would have to confront. As the downfall of Loris-Melikov confirmed, legal autocracy was a contradiction in terms. The imposition of law and civil order on the personalized politics of autocracy raised implicit threats to the prerogatives of the tsar. Even before the death of Alexander II, Loris encountered profound difficulties in attempting to persuade the sovereign that the authority of *his* government depended upon rule of law and the public support from moderates that it engendered. Indeed, he had justified state reform and the legitimate aspirations of the public to participation in political affairs by attacking this government and emphasizing the need to expand the social base of autocracy in order to protect it against the more dangerous threats of revolutionary violence or constitutionalism. After the accession of Alexander III, the legitimacy of autocratic authority brooked no challenge, particularly from official servitors arguing that its viability rested upon law and public confidence. Of course, these aspirations, intensified and transformed by the experience of Alexander's reign, were to be articulated again in the later 1890s by both society and government.

The drive to implant legal autocracy in Russia also accentuated the superordinate role of the Russian state, which loomed as large in the 1880s as it had in earlier periods of "crisis" or social change. Both Loris and the Kakhanov Commission premised their reform programs on the preeminent significance of state power in Russian life. Indeed, the political and social instability perceived to be endemic in urban and particularly peasant Russia necessitated a rationalized administrative mechanism that would strengthen state power and increase its ability to influence society. To be sure, the reform proposals of this period had significantly redefined the purposes to which this power would be applied and the character of relations with the society it ruled, but no one had contemplated abandoning the state's role as mediator, through laws and institutions, of the conflicting interests present in civil life. When this effort to strengthen autocracy with the values of legality, civil order, and legitimate political authority failed, however, the premise, and perceived necessity, of superordinate power and authority remained. In the first decade of Alexander III's reign, the era of the counterreforms, new values arose in government and society for the legitimation of autocratic rule. They fundamentally contradicted those that had dominated the first crisis of autocracy.

CHAPTER III

Rural Counterreform in the 1880s:
The Reassertion of Unrestricted
Autocratic Authority

E. M. FEOKTISTOV, director of the Main Administration for Press Affairs, recalled in his memoirs that the appointment of D. A. Tolstoi to the Ministry of Internal Affairs in May 1882 had had a sobering impact on liberal and conservative circles of opinion alike. "Instead of the previously feverish ferment," Feoktistov wrote, "everything grew quiet under the influence of the idea that now, at last, a powerful authority [*sil'naia vlast'*] had appeared in our country."[1] K. P. Pobedonostsev, thinking as he read the proposals of Kakhanov's conference that he "was having some kind of awful nightmare," protested in a letter of September 1883 that the plan was "written as if purposefully not only to smash all authority in Russia, but [also] to divide it up into a myriad of little sand castles not bound together by anything."[2] Attacking the zemstvo liberal V. Iu. Skalon in March 1885, M. N. Katkov wrote in his influential conservative daily *Moskovskie vedomosti* that all efforts to expand the authority of self-administration were misguided. "Evil" had appeared in Russia because "the government had distanced itself too much from the most important functions of public and state life." "In our view," Katkov instructed, "anything that is labeled authority, anything that is obligatory, should belong to the government and only to the government."[3]

Arguments that contravened the principles recently upheld in both official and public opinion were to be heard in the provinces as well. The aged warrior of the reform era A. I. Koshelev, shortly before his death, raged against the changed attitudes that by 1883 had become apparent in the "zemstvo world" of Riazan province, where the views of "enlightened" nobles were increasingly shaped by the dictates of "narrow estate and even personal interest." It was, Koshelev wrote, "especially sickening

---

[1] Feoktistov, *Vospominaniia*, p. 226.

[2] K. P. Pobedonostsev, *K. P. Pobedonostsev i ego korrespondenty*, vol. 1, pt. 1, p. 317 (to D. A. Tolstoi, 11 September 1883); see also Meshcherskii, *Moi vospominaniia* (St. Petersburg, 1897), 3:184–86.

[3] M. N. Katkov, *Sobranie peredovykh statei Moskovskikh vedomostei 1885* (Moscow, 1889), p. 113 (1 March 1885); see also *Sobranie 1881*, pp. 175–76 (8 April 1881), 205 (26 April 1881), and 243 (19 May 1881).

that the younger members of the estate adhere more to this trend than to [the civil ideals of the 1860s]. . . . Is Russia really going backwards and are the young greater reactionaries than those who lived and worked in the time of serfdom?—Pitiful!"[4] From Simbirsk province in late 1884 came a tract entitled "The Contemporary Situation of Russia and the Estate Question," penned by a little-known county marshal of the nobility named A. D. Pazukhin. It condemned "the principle of equality or the so-called mingling of estates" that officials had embraced since the 1860s. Theirs were theoretical values, Pazukhin charged, ones that ignored a still viable societal order of estates. As recent history proved, misguided officials were creating cultural anomie and social crisis and allowing autocratic authority to be undermined:

> A significant transition [occurred] in our history from order to disarray, from respect for the law to the collapse of the force of authority, from enthusiasm to total apathy. . . . A love for practical affairs was replaced by the most insane doctrines, the sorriest ideas. . . . All public elements were in ferment; all classes of society were consumed by the passion for profit; the rule of phrases and lies had begun . . . ; the supreme authority, seeming to lose all moral bonds to the people, was also losing its stability; . . . in a word, the condition that Russia now finds herself in had begun.[5]

Powerful authority, authoritative power, obligation, the viability of estates, and moral decay: this was a very different vocabulary than that which had recently dominated public discourse. The commentators who expressed such sentiments differed on any number of issues afflicting Russia, but they all shared an antagonism to the principles of a legalistic and civic culture that was deemed to be a threat to the foundations of autocratic power and authority. From their perspective, the crisis of the early 1880s did not result simply from the external attacks of revolutionaries or liberal constitutionalists. It derived as well from the assault that reformist officials had mounted against the still viable political and social order of autocracy. Attempts to impose law and administrative rationality on government or to ground authority in the confidence of educated society denied the attributes and heritage of Russian autocracy, and the society and culture it had established.

Not coincidentally, these arguments grew more audible as the government stamped out revolutionary violence and adopted repressive police

---

[4] A. I. Koshelev, *Zapiski Aleksandra Ivanovicha Kosheleva (1812–1883)* (Berlin, 1884; reprinted by Oriental Research Partners, 1976), pp. 287–88.

[5] A. D. Pazukhin, "Sovremennoe sostoianie Rossii i soslovnyi vopros," *Russkii vestnik* 1 (January 1885): 8–13.

measures that dampened political dissidence in educated society.[6] The monarchy was secure enough now that the long-delayed coronation of Alexander III had finally occurred, in May 1882. Yet the issues that had provoked reform initiatives in the late 1870s and early 1880s remained in general unresolved. Indeed, because twenty years of purportedly liberal legislation had disintegrated into a void of cultural decline, civil disorganization, political instability, and regicide, the necessity of state activism was an uncontested fact. How to effect it was the issue that perplexed the government of Alexander III during the decade of the 1880s. The period that historians have labeled the era of counterreforms, and often interpreted as political reaction against the innovations of the great reforms, witnessed legislative activity in rural affairs as impressive as the work of that earlier period. To interpret the counterreforms as a reactionary phenomenon, a return to a political and social *status quo ante*, is to ignore the essential significance of these years in autocratic political history. This period—which witnessed both the assertion of autocratic political authority to unify society and the extension of state power to influence any aspect of civil life deemed essential to its interests—represented a conservative effort to mediate the political and social transformation of Russia.[7] The values and perspectives of an autocratic political culture shaped state policy toward rural society in the 1880s.

THE DEBATES OF THE KAKHANOV COMMISSION: CONFLICTING PERSPECTIVES OF STATE AND SOCIETY

Before Tolstoi closed the Kakhanov Commission in March 1885, it spent five months debating the reform project of the commission's conference.[8] The arguments advanced in these proceedings, which denigrated the reformist initiatives of 1880–83, were an important stage in the development of the counterreforms, one that provided the outlines for proposals

[6] Zaionchkovskii, *Rossiiskoe samoderzhavie*, pp. 155–64 details the statute of 14 August 1881 that allowed suspension of all legal procedure during the imposition of "reinforced safeguard" and "extraordinary safeguard" in territories of the empire. Under terms of this legislation, a committee of the MVD exiled some seven thousand individuals during 1881–85 who were accused of state crimes. In 1883 the government promulgated the statute that created the *Okhrana*, "On the Structure of a Secret Police in the Empire."

[7] On the counterreforms, see especially Zaionchkovskii, *Rossiiskoe samoderzhavie*; Yaney, *Urge To Mobilize*, chaps. 2–3; L. G. Zakharova, *Zemskaia kontrreforma 1890 g.* (Moscow, 1968); Pearson, "Ministerial Conflict and Local Self-Government Reform"; and Heide W. Whelan, *Alexander III and the State Council: Bureaucracy and Counter-Reform in Late Imperial Russia* (Rutgers University Press, 1982).

[8] These debates are summarized in published journals that attribute arguments to groups and occasionally individuals. *Trudy o.k., Zhurnaly osoboi kommissii dlia sostavleniia proektov mestnogo upravleniia* (hereinafter *Zhurnal*) (St. Petersburg, n.d.), nos. 1–19.

that would become law later in the decade. They also substantiated a renewed commitment to administrative power and estate institutions as the most suitable weapons with which to confront rural social change.

Within the full commission, the members of the conference encountered withering criticism from two different groups. First, the expanded commission included thirteen ministerial officials, most of them unsympathetic to the conference's plan. Notable among them were I. N. Durnovo, an assistant minister of internal affairs, and Prince M. S. Volkonskii, an assistant minister of education whose father had been a Decembrist. In addition, two senior officials, P. A. Shuvalov and K. Palen, had received special imperial appointments in order to "paralyze the harmful side" of the commission's proceedings.[9] Supporting the scepticism of this audience was the compendium of provincial governors' commentaries that the Ministry of Internal Affairs had published in 1883.[10]

Second, the commission also included fifteen provincial "experts"— marshals of the nobility, zemstvo delegates, and governors invited by Kakhanov and the minister of internal affairs. Five of these men—including I. A. Gorchakov and D. A. Naumov, the chairs of the St. Petersburg and Moscow provincial zemstvo boards, respectively—were moderate zemtsy. They supported the reforms but—as they witnessed the defeat of their own demands for greater zemstvo influence in rural society—did so reluctantly.[11] Overshadowing them, however, was a faction of conservative marshals of the nobility and provincial governors. The most outspoken of them was A. D. Pazukhin, the thirty-nine-year-old Alatyr' county marshal from Simbirsk province. Others included the provincial marshals Prince A. D. Obolenskii (Penza), G. V. Kondoidi (Tambov), and A. E. Zarin (Pskov); S. S. Bekhteev, a county marshal of Orel province; and governors A. V. Bogdanovich of Voronezh, S. N. Gudim-Lefkovich of Kovno, and A. K. Anastas'ev of Perm. Hostile and uncompromising, they repudiated the civic ideals that had informed the projects of the conference.[12]

[9] Polovtsev, *Dnevnik Polovtseva*, 1:256 (6 November 1884).

[10] *Trudy o.k., Svod mnenii Gg. gubernatorov.*

[11] See, for example, *Trudy o.k., Zhurnal*, no. 9, pp. 23–34 ("public theory" of self-administration); ibid., no. 9, pp. 27–49 (zemstvo jurisdiction); ibid., no. 5, pp. 3–8 (small zemstvo unit). See also minority gubernatorial opinion in *Trudy o. k., Svod mnenii*, pp. 14–15 (governors of Ekaterinoslav and Chernigov in support of all-estate *sel'skoe obshchestvo*), pp. 27–28 (governors of Kazan, Samara and Kharkov in support of township supervisor), and p. 28 (governors of Bessarabia, Vladimir, Ekaterinoslav, Poltava, Perm, Tula, and Kherson in support of the small zemstvo unit).

[12] Although the question is largely unexplored in the historical literature, there is sufficient evidence to suggest that the disorder of 1878–81 and the impact of Alexander II's assassination fostered a reassertion of conservative values in provincial society, particularly among younger zemstvo activists. See, for example, Veselovskii, *Istoriia zemstva*, 3:283–84

The more immediate objection to the conference's projects, however, came from that first group of ministerial police officials and governors who opposed strengthening the authority of zemstvo institutions and instead demanded greater power for provincial administration. According to their published commentaries, twenty of the thirty governors polled had taken this position.[13] Thirteen opposed election by the zemstvo of the county administrative board chairman.[14] Ten of the governors repudiated altogether "the incongruous" zemstvo presence on these collegial bodies because it promised to provoke "disagreements" that would "paralyze" the effectiveness of county administration. Only the governor of Vladimir was said to have raised the political implications of a measure whose "continued evolution . . . would inevitably lead to corresponding changes at higher administrative levels. . . ."[15]

Such suspicion of independent authority, and the authoritarian police mentality that it reflected, found niggling expression throughout the debates. A majority rejected zemstvo election of the county official in favor of the more reliable marshal of the nobility.[16] M. S. Volkonskii successfully led the opposition to expanding zemstvo involvement in the employment of primary school teachers. Objecting that the essence of the school was the "knowledge imparted in it, the teacher's way of thinking, discipline, etc.," he urged against transferring "into other hands . . . one of the most important institutions of state."[17] Because all such matters belonged to the higher authority of the governor and minister, the commission also rejected a "superfluous" proposal to allow the resolution of certain zemstvo petitions by the county administrative board.[18] It deemed a proposal to permit provincial and regional zemstvo congresses to be "premature," despite the support of the conference and fifteen governors; twelve other governors emphasized the potential political consequences of such action.[19]

The most graphic illustration of this police mentality was the commis-

---

and 289–91; S. Iu. Witte, *Samoderzhavie i zemstvo: Konfidentsial'naia zapiska Ministra finansov Stats-Sekretaria S. Iu. Vitte (1899)* (Stuttgart, 1901), pp. 120–24; Obolenskii, "Nabroski iz vospominanii D. D. Obolenskogo," p. 269; and Seymour Becker, *Nobility and Privilege,* chap. 3–5.

[13] *Trudy o. k., Svod mnenii,* pp. 77–79.

[14] Ibid., p. 84.

[15] Ibid., p. 81.

[16] *Trudy o.k., Zhurnal,* no. 9, pp. 9–14 and 92. Officials supported the motion because the marshal was deemed to be politically more reliable, noble conservatives supported it because the marshal represented the noble estate, and some zemstvo moderates hoped to salvage public influence in a local bureaucratic administration.

[17] *Trudy o.k., Zhurnal,* no. 9, p. 40. See also I. N. Durnovo, and the marshals A. E. Zarin and S. S. Bekhteev, ibid., pp. 32–45. Seventeen governors wanted to restrict zemstvo jurisdiction over education. *Trudy o. k., Svod mnenii,* p. 99.

[18] *Trudy o.k., Zhurnal,* no. 9, pp. 46–48.

[19] Ibid., p. 72, and *Trudy o.k., Svod mnenii,* pp. 131–33.

sion's refusal to dismantle the system of peasant estate administration. It rejected the all-estate village community and found no compelling reason to universalize an institution, which, critics insisted, was primarily concerned with the land affairs of the communal peasantry.[20] Only conference members and moderate zemstvo experts dissented from majorities that opposed any zemstvo role in peasant administration, be it a small zemstvo unit or an official elected by the county assembly; the government's exclusive supervisory powers in these jurisdictions were to be preserved.[21] Agreeing that the measure left the state without "any authority" over the villages and harmed "the interests of the treasury," ministerial officials and conservative provincial experts united to block the elimination of the peasant township.[22] Finally, having thus resurrected the estate administrative system, a majority of the commission voted to place a government-appointed township supervisor at the head of this structure and increase his influence over peasant affairs by granting discretionary "punitive power [karatel'naia vlast']" over all peasants resident in the territory.[23]

The fact that commission members who supported a general intensification of administrative power in the countryside also defended peasant estate institutions was not coincidental. Both proposals derived from a view of rural society that differed markedly from the evolutionary concerns that had preoccupied reformers. Indeed, the term "rural society" poorly conveyed their perception of an impoverished, mass peasant populace whose wholesale alienation from civic values constituted an immediate threat to the stability of the autocratic order. Not surprisingly, opponents had singled out the proposed all-estate village community, and its institutional separation from the land commune, to refute the goals of civil evolution embraced by the conference's plan.

It fell to the marshals of the nobility Pazukhin, Bekhteev, Zarin, and Obolenskii to argue that the emancipation statute had purportedly based all peasant administration on the "unique, indigenous, and national [svoeobraznyi, samobytnyi, natsional'nyi]" institution of the land commune.[24] Although less inclined to this kind of cultural argumentation, ministerial officials did agree that the conference's theoretical desire to separate peasant communal from public affairs threatened to compromise an essential "administrative entity, a political grouping that [was] dangerous to touch."[25] The land commune and its system of communal

[20] Trudy o.k., Zhurnal, no. 4, pp. 53–55.
[21] Ibid., no. 5, pp. 3–8, 15–34.
[22] Ibid., pp. 3, 53–56.
[23] Ibid., no. 5, pp. 44–46, and no. 16, pp. 4–5.
[24] Ibid., no. 4, p. 22.
[25] Ibid., p. 10.

responsibility (*krugovaia poruka*)—which assured revenues, redemption payments, population control, and economic subsistence sufficient to attenuate the rural instability afflicting industrial Europe—were of critical significance. Perceiving growing socio-economic instability in the countryside, a majority of the commission deemed a village institution "whose members [would] not be bound by the unity of landholding and cultural conditions [*bytovye usloviia*] . . . [to be] hardly useful from the state's point of view [*gosudarstvennaia tochka zreniia*]." At present, the statement continued, the peasants were anything but future citizens: "There will be little interest in [the problems of] a shared settlement [*obshchaia osedlost'*] because the majority of peasants are debtors and they must think primarily about paying taxes and [earning] their daily bread, not about cleaning the streets and other measures of a well-ordered public life."[26]

Similar preconceptions about peasant behavior had informed the thinking of the conference, but they had compelled its insistence that state institutions accommodate and foster rural civil evolution. Officials and opponents from the nobility alike, however, perceived that goal to be almost utopian, given the rural poverty and social instability that dominated the countryside. Indeed, among these commission members the conviction prevailed that the failure to buttress village and township estate organs with strong supervisory power had allowed the entire system to deteriorate, so that now the government was unable to defend the peasant population from the consequences of rural economic transformation—a situation boding ill for the future. Already, the majority opinion maintained, market sale of peasant allotment land had allowed "all sorts of plunderers" access to the economic decision making of village assemblies and "free rein to exploit the dark mass of the peasantry." "Noble landowners," whose enlightened influence had figured in the reform project, were themselves succumbing to market forces. Their family estates were falling "into the hands of upstarts [*raznochintsy*] of every sort" and "townsfolk [*meshchane*]" were taking up residence in the village. Indeed, in the view of Orel county marshal S. S. Bekhteev, all criticism of a segregated peasantry ignored the essential fact that the supervision of this vast, impoverished majority was the primary obligation of a government charged to defend what little civil order existed in the countryside.[27]

---

[26] Ibid., p. 26. The commission defeated the proposal by a vote of 17 to 13; 12 members of the majority became members of the commission after Tolstoi's appointment to the MVD. Ibid., p. 56. Only 2 of 30 governors supported the all-estate village. *Trudy o.k.*, *Svod mnenii*, pp. 14–15.

[27] *Trudy o.k.*, *Zhurnal*, no. 4, pp. 23–24. Most provincial governors agreed and worried that the village would fall under the influence of "*meshchane* and *raznochintsy*." By profession chiefly "tavern owners, innkeepers, renters of grain mills, and such types," they were

During the debates, it had been these perceptions of rural instability, and the administrative priorities that they dictated, that gave legitimacy to the principle of peasant estate segregation. The marshals of the nobility Pazukhin, Bekhteev, and Obolenskii had utilized the opportunity to advance their call for a "district supervisor [uchastkovyi], a concept that prefigured the land captain statute of 1889, which created a landowner from the hereditary nobility, appointed by the government and granted broad administrative and judicial authority over peasant estate administration.[28] Rejecting the zemstvo-elected township supervisor—a centerpiece of the conference's plans to establish an effective local government serving state, zemstvo, and rural society—the three provincial experts had explained that "the chief and most pressing reason for the disorder existing in the countryside" was the absence of a knowledgeable, authoritative local official to guard Russia's peasant masses. The three marshals stated bluntly that the primary goal of any reform "should be not zemstvo and government work but the supervision of that special administration that affects 80% of Russia's population."[29]

Commission members rejected the proposal by a vote of 21 to 10, but that majority coalesced for differing reasons.[30] Some protested the injection of nobiliary estate interests into the debate; most objected to the discretionary administrative and judicial power that was to be invested in the proposed official. That prospect was unpalatable not only to moderates, who feared the resulting "arbitrariness and corruption" inherent in such an institution, but also to ministerial officials, who looked askance at a situation where the central government never "could be certain of its [local] organs."[31] They were as adamant in opposing the dispersion of administrative power here as they had been when considering zemstvo self-administration. They did not, however, repudiate the marshals' underlying premise that state interests required a distinct administration of peasant affairs. The bureaucrats Durnovo, Fillipov, and Volkonskii, as well as all participating governors, joined provincial critics in preserving, by a vote of 19 to 15, the peasant township administration, an "order to which the population has accustomed itself and with which it has coexisted for more than twenty years."[32] The vote dealt a final blow to the

"morally deficient" people from whose ranks came the "so-called kulaks and *miroedy*." *Trudy o. k., Svod mnenii*, p. 8.

[28] *Trudy o.k., Zhurnal*, no. 5, pp. 3–12, 23–24.

[29] Ibid., pp. 11–12.

[30] Ibid., pp. 23, 27. The proposal was more favorably viewed by provincial governors, fourteen of whom advocated restoring the peace arbiters. *Trudy o.k., Svod mnenii*, p. 44.

[31] *Trudy o.k., Zhurnal*, no. 5, pp. 29–30.

[32] Ibid., p. 53. Seventeen of thirty provincial governors also took this position. *Trudy o.k., Svod mnenii*, pp. 22–26.

structure of the all-estate, civil administration that had been drafted by the conference.[33]

That body's original desire to create legitimate government authority through legality and civil order had become a minority view in the commission. Indeed, as several concluding debates demonstrated, the very appropriateness of law as an instrument of rural administration was coming into question. In the waning days of its existence, the commission had delegated former minister of Justice K. I. Palen, Senator I. I. Shamshin, and Marshals of the Nobility Pazukhin and Bekhteev to review once more the issue of granting discretionary administrative and judicial authority to the township supervisor. Their report explained that "punitive power [*karatel'naia vlast'*]" was necessary to assure "public safety . . . and private property interests" in rural areas. Local courts of law, which lacked the "speed, steadfastness, and proper strictness" necessary to adjudicate and punish crime, were unsuited to this critical task, they noted. Worse, courts acted to confuse the "majority of illiterate and semi-literate people," who often saw "a sharp disparity between their views of justice [*pravo*] and the laws [*zakony*] that guide a judge in rendering his decisions." With crime on the rise as peasants entered into "general civil life and economic relations with individuals of other estates," a popular perception was growing, "to the detriment of [peasant] public morality," that "petty crimes are not even prosecuted and the guilty too often go unpunished." Legality was encouraging civil disorder—a situation that only an authoritative official could reverse.[34]

Although the full commission closed before it could discuss this report, it did approve a related proposal granting the township supervisor discretionary authority to levy administrative fines and imprisonment on any member of a taxed estate. Only five members objected that "punitive power will not strengthen [the township official]; authority is strengthened not [by the granting of] extraordinary rights but by lawful actions [*pravomernaia deiatel'nost'*] and the respect that it thereby acquires." Appeals to law and civil authority, however, carried little weight among ministerial police officials and provincial experts, who believed that "the culture [*byt*] of the masses of the fatherland's population" necessitated an

---

[33] Only ten commission members supported the original plan to establish an elected, all-estate township official. *Trudy o.k., Zhurnal*, no. 5, p. 15. Conference members included Semenov, Mordvinov, Barykov, Andreevskii, and Vaganov; Kakhanov abstained from the vote. Five zemtsy joined this group: Naumov, Gorchakov, Chaplin, Karpov, and Konstantinovich.

[34] *Trudy o.k., Zhurnal*, no. 16, pp. 12–15. This passage is central to George Yaney's thesis that the creation of the position of land captain was a radical administrative reform that allowed the government to intervene directly in village life without the constraints of a law code often irrelevant in peasant culture. Yaney, *Urge To Mobilize*, pp. 68–96.

official "so influential that failure to fulfill his demands could not go unpunished." Only this would prevent "the denigration of the legitimacy of
authority [*avtoritet vlasti*], which is so necessary in the structure of local
administration."[35] The commission was not aiming to establish and foster
the values of civil culture in rural society. It was instead preparing to project superordinate power and authority through estate institutions into
the village itself.

THE PROVINCIAL NOBILITY AND ESTATE SOCIETY

In the Kakhanov Commission, ministerial officials and conservative noble
experts had agreed that reestablishing rural social order and increasing
supervisory authority over peasant life as a means to this end were interests of state. Yet provincial men had defined social order quite differently
than had their bureaucratic colleagues concerned about containing societal instability. Of primary importance to the nobiliary perspective was
the integrity of a rural society of estates. Power and authority were necessary to buttress the network of socioeconomic, political, and cultural
relationships that bound together nobility and peasantry as a still viable
social foundation of autocratic rule. And power was to be exercised not
by an impersonal officialdom, but by members of the hereditary noble
estate, whose ascriptive traditions of state service and family landowning
assured both the tsar and the lowest peasant legitimate authority in the
local areas. These values had motivated the proposal of a noble district
supervisor, and were apparent as well when marshals and governors
urged the Kakhanov Commission to restructure zemstvo elections according to estate criteria. The latter proposal provoked in the commission
an astounding debate.

The new electoral system was to exclude all non-noble rural landowners from the first electoral assembly in which they presently had the right
to participate. Most would join owners of urban property in the second
assembly, while peasant smallholders were to be sent to the third, peasant
curia.[36] Critics within the commission had expressed disbelief at these
proposals.[37] "What will be the bond among members of the proposed
estate electoral groups?" they had queried. The concept confused legal
and social status, mixing in one electoral grouping "descendants of cen-
turies-old noble families . . . and personal nobles" who had attained that

[35] *Trudy o.k.*, *Zhurnal*, no. 16, pp. 4–5.

[36] Ibid., no. 17, pp. 21–22.

[37] These were conference members Kakhanov, Semenov, Shamshin, Andreevskii, Mordvinov, Barykov, and Vaganov. The majority also included moderate zemstsy, as well as
some provincial experts and ministerial officials who usually did not support the positions
of conference members. *Trudy o.k.*, *Zhurnal*, no. 17, pp. 4, 23.

rank in state service. It also ignored differences of occupation. Some nobles were "landowners, others factory owners and industrialists." To be
sure, opponents maintained, the nobility (*dvorianstvo*) "possessed, by its
hereditary character and long-established organization and rights, all the
attributes of a legal estate," but Russia "in reality [knew] no other estates
in the way they were understood in the West: our law recognizes legal
standing [*sostoianiia*], life [recognizes] social classes [*obshchestvennye
klassy*]." Even the situation of peasants—who "as a class or legal category
of rural smallholders and ploughmen" were indeed bound together by
communal traditions that had been "cemented by the possession of allotment land"—was "still far from the concept of estate."[38]

Of course, the moderate officials and provincial zemtsy who advanced
this argument did not envision a democratized zemstvo. Little proposed
at the Kakhanov Commission's proceedings was intended to alter the significant role played in the assemblies by local landowners, most of whom
were still nobles. Yet these moderates feared that to permit the noble estate special privileges in public assemblies—and from the course of the
debate it would seem that the zemstvo here symbolized society as a
whole—would create "a broad arena for political, estate conflict." Critics
raised the specter of class struggle in order to argue that noble privilege
would lend "a political coloration" to the conflicting "economic interests" already obvious among landowners, urban groups ("the commercial legal order of the urban merchantry and the legal order of urban
townsmen"), and peasants: "relations among social classes will be exacerbated, and one must foresee that this will create a limitless source of
confusion and disorder [*smuta*], something that has occurred in almost
all Western states, but which [so far] Russia has fortunately avoided."[39]

Proponents of the new zemstvo electoral system had also acknowledged the potential for rural conflict, as that which their critics labeled
"civil development" inundated the social order of the autocracy. Yet the
marshals of the nobility Pazukhin, Obolenskii, Bekhteev, and Zarin, together with the provincial governors Bogdanovich and Kondoidi, deemed
this Western analytical construct inappropriate to any explanation of
changes taking place in rural estate society.[40] Provincial conservatives
knew well, they said, what had transpired in the countryside since emancipation. In twenty years' time, "an entirely new group of landowners,
primarily from the commercial class, with interests and motivations opposed to . . . [those of] the landowning estate" had appeared in local life.
Along with "the ever-multiplying class of peasant smallholders," such in-

[38] Ibid., pp. 26–28.
[39] Ibid., p. 28.
[40] Ibid., pp. 17, 4. Supporters also included P. A. Shuvalov, K. I. Palen, and three ministerial officials.

dividuals wanted nothing from the estates they purchased but "easy and quick enrichment." They were an "alien element [*prishlyi element*]," not tied to "property by those tight bonds of family traditions and rights of hereditary ownership that constitute the definitive characteristics of noble landholding." The state, having failed to restrain such change, was now witnessing the disruption of estate society, a form of social organization in which individuals "belonged to one social milieu, possessed a single culture, a single social status [*sotsial'noe polozhenie*], shared common motivations and moral criteria." This society had not resulted from law or institutional regulation: "the *natural* indication of this unity is an individual's membership in one or another estate."[41]

"Daily experience" convinced provincial conservatives "that estates have been assimilated very clearly and definitively into popular consciousness, that several of the estates are quite stably organized." It went without saying that these were the nobility and the peasantry. The objective of the legislator, then, was to legitimate this reality and extend "the same kind of representation to other groups of the population." Applied to the zemstvo—and again the discussion reached far beyond the parameters of local self-administration—such policy assured "the confidence of the government in zemstvo institutions." Autocracy could not "base itself . . . on organs that [were] subject to constant change and lack[ed] stability." Only an estate structure, which had coexisted with autocracy throughout Russia's history, provided a viable foundation for autocratic rule: "The government, and each one of us, well knows the distinctive attributes of these [estate] groups, and, knowing the component parts, can therefore judge correctly concerning the whole and regulate the mutual relations of the parts."[42]

Of course, provincial conservatives were manipulating the traditions of the estate system in order to legitimate the political preeminence they demanded for rural Russia in general and for its hereditary landowning nobility in particular. Indeed, insistence on the centrality of noble service to the state and the peasantry had not been so pronounced since the reform debates of the later 1850s. As had been the case then, so, too, was it now argued that the nobility protected an agrarian order threatened by both legal theorists and the inroads of commercial property and profit. Thus it was not narrow estate self-interest, as critics had charged, that motivated the allocation of eighty percent of all places in the assemblies to delegates elected by the noble and peasant estates. Rather than obfuscate, such proposals simply acknowledged the true character of social and political life in "Russia, [where] given the structure of its existence, the agrarian es-

[41] Ibid., p. 18. Emphasis added.
[42] Ibid., pp. 19–20.

tates should occupy the primary position in the zemstvo." This institution was "not a joint-stock company where every investor demands rights of participation equivalent to his contribution." It was "an organ of state administration in which the decisive role" belonged to knowledgeable hereditary nobles, whose traditions of service and landowning made them "concerned for the order of local life and most capable of assuming leadership [*rukovodstvo*] within it." In order to guarantee the reliability of this institution—or any others—the state would have to consider "all the moral conditions that define the significance of one or another estate." It was obliged "to penetrate to the fundamental aspects of our local life."[43]

The Kakhanov Commission did not resolve this issue before its work ended; some five years passed before an estate-based electoral system became law—in the zemstvo statute of 1890. But the debates that occurred in the commission were not simply the legislative prehistory of this important act. They were also symptomatic of broader movements within the provincial landowning nobility during the 1880s, a period when the economic and social standing of the first estate was under broad assault. Ascriptive noble status, and the larger estate society in which it was preeminent, were significant focuses of noble opinion, particularly at a time when issues of autocratic power and authority also increasingly dominated government and public debate. The symmetry was hardly coincidental: both drew on the same historical tradition to legitimate the institutions of an old regime confronted by social change.

In the Kakhanov Commission, provincial marshals and governors had provided impressionistic evidence in their descriptions of the economic and social difficulties encountered by noble landowners since emancipation. These problems were indeed imposing. By 1877 nobles had sold some twelve percent of the agricultural land they owned at the time of emancipation, a process of land loss subsequently exacerbated by the collapse of the international grain market during the 1880s.[44] The economic decline of the nobility and the gradual growth of Russia's urban and industrial sectors fostered new social elements that competed with the old agrarian elite. Less immediately apparent but equally threatening was the challenge that an expanding civil bureaucracy—it quadrupled in size between 1857 and 1903—posed to the political status of the nobility.[45] As the civil service expanded, so did the opportunity for ennoblement it of-

---

[43] Ibid., pp. 21–22.

[44] Korelin, *Dvorianstvo*, pp. 54–62; and T. M. Kitanina, *Khlebnaia torgovlia Rossii v 1875–1914 gg.* (Leningrad, 1978), pp. 35–36. Noble-owned arable land decreased from 87.1 million desiatins (235 million acres) in 1861 to 77 million desiatins (208 million acres) in 1877. During the long depression, total noble landowning was reduced a further 27%, down to 53.9 million desiatins (146 million acres) by 1895.

[45] Zaionchkovskii, *Pravitel'stvennyi apparat*, pp. 68–71.

fered to members of nonprivileged estates; some forty thousand individuals and their family members received noble status in this manner during the last quarter of the nineteenth century.[46] Moreover, the factors that had been transforming state service since midcentury—education, professionalization, and landlessness—rendered the ascriptive standards of noble service increasingly less important to success in a larger and more specialized administrative apparatus. Indeed, some evidence suggests that the new commercial element that was vilified in the commission debates was partially made up of career officials, who were using the salary and status they had earned in civil service to either purchase or obtain through marriage estate lands formerly owned by the hereditary nobility.[47]

Petitions from assemblies of the nobility during the 1880s reflected the growing concern that these developments were generating in the provinces. To the extent that nobiliary interests coincided with those of the state, the response from St. Petersburg was generally sympathetic. For example, numerous petitions in 1883–85 urged the government to establish state-guaranteed, low-interest land credit for noble landowners, a measure necessary not only to salvage bankrupt estates but also to provide investment capital for agricultural improvement. This request was partially satisfied by the creation of a Noble Land Bank in 1885.[48] Despite the budgetary constraints of the period, the crown was not stingy about extending to the landowning nobility other forms of financial aid as well.[49] Later in the decade some twenty provincial assemblies advocated the extreme measure of entailed hereditary estates in order to halt the economic decline of the nobility. A commission formed in 1892 to consider the measure never produced results.[50] Noble petitions also revealed a preoccupation with the social and political status of the first estate. As-

[46] Korelin, *Dvorianstvo*, p. 28.

[47] For a fuller discussion of these developments, see my article "The Land Captain Reform of 1889 and the Reassertion of Unrestricted Autocratic Authority," *Russian History/Histoire Russe* 15, no. 2–4 (1988): 300–308; also Zaionchkovskii, *Pravitel'stvennyi apparat*, pp. 131–70 and 200–218 passim.

[48] *Obzor deiatel'nosti Ministerstva Finansov v tsarstvovanii Imperatora Aleksandra III (1881–1894)* (St. Petersburg, 1902), pp. 28–31; Korelin, *Dvorianstvo*, pp. 255–57; Iu. B. Solov'ev, *Samoderzhavie i dvorianstvo v kontse XIX veka* (Leningrad, 1973), pp. 170–74; and Zaionchkovskii, *Rossiiskoe samoderzhavie*, pp. 141–42. The provincial noble assemblies of Orel, Smolensk, Voronezh, Kostroma, Bessarabia, Chernigov, Penza, Samara, Kaluga, Tambov, Saratov, and Kharkov all despatched such petitions.

[49] Korelin, *Dvorianstvo*, p. 267. The institution of obligatory redemption in 1881 compensated affected landowners with an additional twelve percent of their redemption claim, a cost of some 46 million rubles to the state treasury. After 1885, the Noble Land Bank purchased almost 26 million rubles worth of noble land mortgages from private banks, converting these obligations at a rate five percent lower than market value. The State Bank also extended short-term investment credits during 1883–84.

[50] Ibid., pp. 263–64.

semblies requested that the state restrict the process of hereditary enno-blement through civil service, ensure the exclusive right of children of the nobility to attend military cadet schools, guarantee nobiliary representa-tion in the zemstvo, and provide hereditary nobles with trials by their own courts of honor instead of by jury.[51]

In January 1885, however, two months before the centenary of Cathe-rine the Great's Charter to the Nobility, a protest more significant than a mere petition appeared in M. N. Katkov's *Russkii vestnik*. Pazukhin's "The Contemporary Condition of Russia and the Estate Question" framed the issue of nobiliary decline as a concern of fundamental political significance to the autocracy. A participant in the ongoing Kakhanov Commission when he wrote the essay, Pazukhin proclaimed to the read-ing public that which he had maintained in official debates:

> We see a Russia seemingly divided in two. There exists a historic Russia, resting on those foundations that have developed over a millennium and dedicated to ideals that the past has entrusted to her. . . . Together with her lives a different Russia, not knowing her history, not possessing any ideals, any respect for the past, any concerns for the future. . . . The entire structure of life that is coming into being suppresses historic Russia.[52]

In his critique of contemporary events, Pazukhin displayed the same penchant for selective historical memory that characterized so many of his contemporaries. For example, he could indict most of the great re-forms for having institutionalized values of legality and civil equality in-compatible with autocracy and its social structure of estates. At the same time, however, he could praise the greatest of these acts, the abolition of serfdom, because it had resulted from the long process of intellectual en-lightenment that since the eighteenth century had led both nobility and autocracy to recognize the evils of the institution. As a result, they had succeeded in abolishing serfdom while preserving the old order's "two most important estates . . . on their old historic foundations: the peas-antry, the primary element of state strength, and the nobility, the pre-server of state consciousness [*soznanie*] and political traditions."[53] What rendered Pazukhin's carping hostility to civil society fascinating and com-pelling was precisely this romantic evocation of the struggle that autoc-racy and its estates had endured throughout their history to build a stable political and social order.[54]

---

[51] Ibid., pp. 258–59. Also Solov'ev, *Samoderzhavie . . . XIX veka*, pp. 175–76, which notes that the restrictions on hereditary ennoblement would have excluded from such status all but seven of the 12,701 officials who attained it during the years 1875–84.

[52] Pazukhin, "Sovremennoe sostoianie," p. 6.

[53] Ibid., pp. 9–11.

[54] Ibid., pp. 41–58.

Reaching back to the consolidation of Muscovite rule, Pazukhin attributed this central moment of Russia's past to the unity that had existed between autocracy, which protected the land from external danger, and its estates, whose services fostered the power that brought order and general well-being to the populace. The nobility, "the service-landed estate," had provided the military force necessary "to gather [together] all the Russian land"; in return, it received land grants from the Muscovite princes. The "[enserfed] agricultural peasant estate" provided the income that allowed the nobility to serve, thereby guaranteeing itself domestic peace. "Townspeople [*posadskie liudi*]," secure in their places of residence, supplied revenue to the state. The clergy and boyars, "the oldest estates," retained their traditions even as they adapted to new conditions of life. All estates differed in the service they rendered, the obligations they bore, and the rights they received. Yet each received protection and justice from tsarist authority, and thus each sensed its inherent equality with the others before an autocrat that all willingly served: "Between tsarist authority and the estates . . . appeared total solidarity and mutual trust came into being. The estates saw the defense of their interests and the satisfaction of their needs only in autocracy, which, in turn, found in them support during all the difficult moments of [its] history." Autocracy guaranteed order—not mere institutional regularity but a just hierarchy in which tradition ascribed the place and dignity of each individual. "Each citizen of the Muscovite state," he continued, "stood absolutely in a particular rank, belonged to a certain estate that was obligated to render one or another state responsibility." This structure, he emphasized, had not been the product of "intellectual speculation" but was rather an organic reality that each Russian "drew from [his] experience of life."[55]

If medieval Muscovy helped Pazukhin explain a conception of order, then the Time of Troubles of the early seventeenth century, the second historical memory in his universe, gave meaning to the word "crisis."[56] It was then, he said, that Russia first learned what it "could expect from a non-estate principle." The parallels between that time and the 1880s were all too obvious. In the turbulent decade that preceded the founding of the Romanov dynasty, "homeless, wandering people, who had broken their

[55] Ibid., p. 42.

[56] The comparison was noted elsewhere to different effect. See, for example, "Ocherk nashei vnutrennoi politiki za 1881 g.," *Poriadok*, 31 December 1881, p. 1. Commenting on the tragedy of Alexander II's assassination, *Poriadok* cited other "tragic political crises" in Russian history and reminded readers that "in 1612 the people . . . had to restore state authority following the moral collapse into which the despotism of Ivan the Terrible and [his] *oprichnina* . . . had led it." See also the appearance of S. F. Platonov's master's dissertation on the Time of Troubles, "Drevno-russkie skazaniia i povesti o smutnom vremeni XVII v., kak istoricheskii istochnik," (Master's diss., St. Petersburg University, 1888).

ties with the land," rushed to destroy the state and its estate system. Peasants thought themselves landowners, merchants became government officials, bureaucrats courtiers, and middle gentry servitors aristocratic boyars: all were "antisocial elements" who lacked an "estate consciousness [*sklad poniatii*]." Pazukhin saw them as "the liberals of the early seventeenth century, who upheld the principles of personal freedom and personal accomplishment and set them against the principle of estates, who demanded political rights that had never existed in the Muscovite state, and always acted on the basis of mercenary and egoistic goals."[57] Against this egoism—a word that captured Pazukhin's abhorrence for the inroads of Western development—rose the "people of the land," that popular militia of provincial noble servitors and peasants that retained "a firm consciousness, did not want any changes, any kind of novelty, which placed on [its] banners a return to a strict estate organization under the protection of an autocratic tsar chosen with the counsel of all ranks of the Russian land." And, when the first Romanov was crowned in 1613, it had been the nobility, the first estate, that had led the land back to its autocrat. However fanciful this rendering of early seventeenth century history, the reunification of autocracy with its estates—portrayed here as a repayment of the debt owed by the estates to the Russian tsars—occupied the third, honored place in Pazukhin's ideological universe.[58]

What had followed was a natural, evolutionary process, that stabilized both the estate system and the nobility's primary position in it. Peter the Great, to whom Pazukhin paid tribute, had not disrupted tradition as the Slavophiles charged. His legislation had further consolidated the structure of estates, rendering them "united social unions, with defined rights and obligations and with exactly defined relationships of one to the others and [of all] to the Supreme Power."[59] As important, the Table of Ranks, "one of Peter's most important laws," opened the nobility to "a mass of low-born people who were relatively gifted, daring, and dedicated to the reformed order." Abetted by the subsequent policies of Catherine the Great, the nobility became a vitalizing force in state administration and local life, "the single educated, cultured estate in Russia," "the motive force of enlightenment and progress."[60]

Thus, when in conclusion Pazukhin returned to consider his own era, he used history to condemn a government that was now yielding the very foundations of autocratic authority to a civil society of wealth and individualism. He had few illusions about the "deep changes" that the two decades since emancipation had produced "in the habits and views of

[57] Pazukhin, "Sovremennoe sostoianie," pp. 43–44.
[58] Ibid., p. 45.
[59] Ibid., p. 48.
[60] Ibid., pp. 50–51.

society." To repair the damage and restore Russia to the heritage of its estate life would require immediate action by "the legislative power."[61] Both the land captain and zemstvo estate elections were essential first steps toward reasserting the nobility's preeminence in local service. Just as necessary were financial backing for its tottering landholding and even the ennoblement of very wealthy, non-noble landowners to supplement local corporative bodies thinned by economic decline. Yet all legislative measures were insufficient if they left untouched "the fiction of the political equality of the estates, of their identical political capacity." Only when autocracy guaranteed that the nobility again would become "a service estate and the highest estate of the land [*vyshee zemskoe soslovie*]," could social stability return to Russia.

Pazukhin insisted that his ideas contained not the slightest trace of "aristocratic exclusivity or caste [*soslovnaia zamknutnost'*]," concepts whose political implications he deemed alien to Russian history.[62] Yet, both his policy objectives and his values attached exclusive political significance to the nobility's role as mediator between tsar and people. Only firm "bonds between government and nobility and between nobility and the land," not legality or rational administration, assured autocracy's political and social stability. Only the nobility, not the intelligentsia or educated society, retained its bond to the rural populace and acted as "the support of the throne." Only the nobility, not the zemstvo or officialdom, could utilize authority so as to reestablish order among the peasants. Only the nobility could "bridle the elements of anti-estate Russia" (civil society), and thereby put a final halt to the onrush of "troubles, exploitation, and power-lusting demands" (socioeconomic and political transformation). Even new, rising landowners, if ensconced in corporative bodies of the nobility, would not alter but rather assimilate their traditions, thereby fortifying the estate "materially and morally" and raising "its political significance, which has become the essential requirement of Russia's contemporary condition."[63]

To be sure, Pazukhin's entreaties for state support of the nobility were still consonant with the subordination of the empire's first service estate to the autocratic government. Above all else, the establishment of firm authority in rural life was required to preserve a declining noble presence. Yet, in a fashion uncharacteristic of the servitor, Pazukhin demanded that the government "raise among the population the authority of [autocratic] power" and warned of the consequences if it failed to do so. This task required a legitimation of the historical "solidarity" between the state

[61] Ibid., p. 53.
[62] Ibid., pp. 56–57.
[63] Ibid.

and its estates, those "defined historical forces which are well-known to the government." The nobility, of course, was best known. The provincial life that it would administer and imbue with traditional values would guarantee the viability of autocracy, the unity of tsar and people. This educated, propertied, and loyal estate would again lead the people of the land, the traditional zemstvo, to the autocratic throne as it had in 1613. "Then unity will be achieved without excessive exertion," he concluded, "because it will be based on moral bonds whose solidarity has been experienced." Pazukhin's nobleman undoubtedly still served the tsar. At the same time, however, the transformations occurring in Russia were already eliciting from the hereditary nobility the first discernable outlines of an exclusive caste mentality.[64]

To the extent that Pazukhin was advocating autocratic dependency on the provincial nobility, he had little to offer a regime whose stated goal was the preeminence of its authority and power. Consistently, the recent debates of the Kakhanov Commission had revealed the government's refusal to dispense authority to any entity it did not control. K. P. Pobedonostsev, who gave his loyalty only to the integrity of autocratic power, said as much in a letter he wrote to Alexander III several months after the publication of Pazukhin's essay. History had accustomed the nobility "on the one hand to serve and on the other to command," Pobedonostsev acknowledged. A tradition of service made "the noble landowner always more trustworthy than the merchant landowner, and, among the people, more trusted because they know that the merchant primarily thinks of his own profit." Thus, particularly at a time of disorder, the government ought to encourage nobles "to live on their estates in the interior of Russia . . . [and not] gravitate to the capitals," as their presence was a stabilizing influence in rural life. To confuse service obligation with estate privilege, however, was an unacceptable error. No estate, Pobedonostsev insisted, excelled another in "the special quality of loyalty to tsar and fatherland," and none of them could claim immunity from "oppositionists." This included nobles, some of whom had been "traitors in Russia's times of trouble."[65] As long as the nobility did not challenge the autocracy's monopolization of political authority, Pobedonostsev was willing to rejuvenate and utilize its traditional service role. In service, noble landowners possessed an important role in the state organism; outside this body, they lost their significance.

Yet Pazukhin's imagery—a personalized, paternalistic rural community as emotionally evocative as the figure of the autocratic tsar—ought

[64] Leopold H. Haimson, "Conclusion: Observations on the Russian Countryside (1905–1914)," in Haimson, ed., *Politics of the Russian Countryside*, pp. 261–300.

[65] K. P. Pobedonostsev, *Pis'ma Pobedonostseva k Aleksandru III*, 2:115–16.

not be discounted in analyses of the 1880s. The imagery of tsar and rural estates stood as a ceremonial monument throughout Alexander III's reign. The new tsar's widely reported remarks at his May 1882 coronation ceremonies, made before delegations of peasant township elders and provincial marshals of the nobility, were taken to indicate the importance that his reign placed upon the personal relationship between the autocrat and his two rural estates. Telling the assembled peasant officials that he was glad to see them again (!), the tsar reminded his children to "follow the advice and leadership of your marshals of the nobility." To the latter, he expressed his belief in the "sincere sentiments of the noble estate" and his certainty that it would remain what it had been: "a support of everything that is good for the welfare of the throne and the fatherland."[66]

The same reassuring ideals informed the imperial rescript of April 1885 that marked the centenary of the Charter to the Nobility. Drafted by Pobedonostsev, the imperial rescript praised the historic unity of purpose that had allowed Russian autocrats to employ their hereditary servitors as protectors of popular well-being and morality. It expressed the tsar's personal will that the first estate retain the ascriptive traditions bequeathed to it by land and service, aiding him as it had his predecessors:

> And now, as in an older time, the good of the state demands that Russian noblemen preserve the first place, which history and the will of monarchs has granted them, in the ranks of the marshals, in state service, in matters of local administration and justice, in selfless care for the needs of the local population, in the propagation by their example and leadership of the rules of faith and honesty, of the true principles of popular education, good customs, and good work.[67]

In declining health at the end of a public career that had championed the autocratic state, even the conservative publicist M. N. Katkov found the vision of a stable estate society alluring. His political views had shifted often since his intellectual debut in the 1840s, but Katkov had never abandoned the conviction, engendered by German idealism, that the state was the instrument of national progress in the modern era. Nor did he entirely lose hope that the Russian nobility, despite the political pretensions of its liberals and aristocrats, might fulfill the same stabilizing role in rural society as had the landed gentry in England. In an editorial entitled "What Is That Which We Call an Estate?" Katkov marked the charter centenary by expressing his wish to see the new Noble Land Bank foster a unified "landholding nobility [*pomestnoe dvorianstvo*]" from an estate fractured by divisions of wealth and social status. That prospect,

---

[66] B. B. Glinskii, "Period tverdoi vlasti (istoricheskie ocherki): Vnutrennaia politika Rossii v epokhu vosymidesiatykh godov," *Istoricheskii vestnik* 127 (1912): 685–86.

[67] Pobedonostsev, *K. P. Pobedonostsev i ego korrespondenty*, vol. 1, pt. 1, p. 522.

"a political measure of great importance," was essential to ensure that the estate retained the place in local service granted it in the eighteenth century.[68]

Just as he urged the revitalization of the noble estate, so too Katkov believed in general that estates allowed the state to create unity and political stability in the disparate population of the empire. To the query posed by his title, Katkov answered that the estate was, "in its totality, an organism of a national people [gosudarstvennyi narod]." If one wanted "to conduct affairs with the Russian people," Katkov instructed, "turn to it in its estates." They were "not castes that incarcerate and divide the people," he explained, but "natural, historically evolved entities based upon different kinds of life and occupations." Through them, the state shaped the population, gradually establishing a "correct" organization for each and a milieu of "general civil freedom" in which all could evolve. That process, Katkov believed, was already underway; "education [was] equalizing and drawing together individuals of all estates." Yet, by grounding itself on the traditional estates, autocracy assured itself that modernity would strengthen the old order, just as "blood circulating through the body does not destroy but [rather] nourishes its organs."[69]

Katkov's paean to the estate, however, much more resembled the convictions of Nikolai Miliutin twenty years earlier than it did the claims of Pazukhin. Estates remained the proper and essential instruments through which the state influenced civil development. Yet, unlike the statesmen of the 1860's, Katkov and Pazukhin, both statists and critics from the nobility, now viewed the estate system, albeit from conflicting perspectives, as a legitimate alternative to the civil and legal theories of the reform era. To abandon the estate system, whether Pazukhin's organic rural community or Katkov's social organization, was thus to ignore a realistic alternative to Western capitalism and to reject a stable national life in which each individual held to and was enriched by a place in the social hierarchy of the autocratic order. During a reign that had raised the banner of untrammelled autocratic power and authority as the *sine qua non* of political life, the estate order provided a social reality in which to plant it.

LOCAL REFORM AND THE ZEMSKII NACHAL'NIK

When Pazukhin was appointed to direct the chancellery of the Ministry of Internal Affairs in late autumn 1885, theory began to influence legis-

[68] M. N. Katkov, "Chto zhe takoe soslovie?" in idem, *Sobranie* 1885, pp. 195–196 (22 April 1885). On Katkov's "unconditional" approval of Pazukhin's legislative recommendations for local reform, see Feoktistov, *Vospominaniia*, p. 251. On Katkov, see Feoktistov, *Vospominaniia*, and V. A. Tvardovskaia, "Ideolog samoderzhaviia v period 'krizis verkhov' na rubezhe 1870–1880-x godov," *Istoricheskie zapiski* 91 (1973): 217–67.

[69] Katkov, "Chto zhe," *Sobranie* 1885, p. 195.

lative practice. Several times that autumn Alexander III had vented his impatience about the fact that Tolstoi had not yet offered a local reform plan to replace that of the Kakhanov Commission.[70] Contemporaries agreed that Pazukhin's compelling essay on the estate question, which contained theses he had defended vigorously in the commission's debates, swayed Tolstoi.[71] An influential ministerial official of long standing, Tolstoi was also a hereditary noble of impoverished origins, who owned an estate in Riazan province. There he often sought refuge from the suffocating atmosphere of St. Petersburg to work in his large private library and pursue research on the era of Catherine the Great, the purported golden age of the Russian nobility.[72] Yet his subordinate's efforts to draft a proposal for the reform of local government dragged on through the following months with few concrete results. Pazukhin labored over proposals to alter the zemstvo statute and create a land captain (*zemskii nachal'nik*) but so completely isolated himself that even Tolstoi had little idea of what his assistant was writing. Feoktistov later remarked that Pazukhin's experience illustrated how often talented theoreticians proved to be "not entirely talented architects" of practical statutes.[73]

During September–November 1886 the work was transferred to an MVD committee that developed more detailed drafts. That body, chaired by Prince K. D. Gagarin, the assistant minister of internal affairs, included Pazukhin, A. E. Zarin, the Pskov provincial marshal, and G. V. Kondoidi, the governor of Tambov; all four men had participated in the Kakhanov Commission.[74] Finally, in December 1886, Tolstoi tendered his formal recommendations to Alexander III. It then became apparent that the ministerial official who wielded state power was retextualizing the original perspective of the provincial noble servitor.[75] Like Pazukhin, Tolstoi sketched a picture of wholesale social disarray in the countryside. He shared the marshal's fears that the legislation of the 1860s had led rural Russia toward a foreboding future blithely labeled by liberal officials "civil society." Yet Tolstoi regarded the repudiation of estates as a primary symptom of a more fundamental flaw whose origins lay in reform legislation that had weakened the influence of autocratic authority in

[70] Polovtsev, *Dnevnik Polovtseva*, 1:343–44 (21, 25 October 1885) and 356 (23 November 1885).

[71] Ibid., 2:59 (17 December 1887) and 189–90 (25 April 1889); Feoktistov, *Vospominaniia*, pp. 248–49; and Meshcherskii, *Moi vospominaniia*, 3:184–86 and 197.

[72] Feoktistov, *Vospominaniia*, pp. 163–89 and 230–31 passim. Whether Tolstoi's academic interests influenced his choice of Pazukhin is open to speculation.

[73] Ibid., pp. 273 and 249–50. Also Zakharova, *Zemskaia kontrreforma 1890 g.*, p. 91.

[74] Zaionchkovskii, *Rossiiskoe samoderzhavie*, p. 369.

[75] Quotations here are taken from Glinskii, "Period tverdoi vlasti," pp. 688–90; see also Zaionchkovskii, *Rossiiskoe samoderzhavie*, pp. 369–72 and Zakharova, *Zemskaia kontrreforma*, pp. 97–100.

Russian life. The path to popular order lay in its reassertion. All great reform legislation required reconsideration in this light.

Some of his contemporaries suggested that Tolstoi had repudiated the "liberal reform epoch of Alexander II's reign" and that visceral emotion had driven him to overturn its legislative heritage.[76] Feoktistov, who knew Tolstoi from the perspective of an MVD subordinate and shared this view, also maintained that the minister was the consummate police official, suspicious of any activity that occurred outside the supervision of the state.[77] Seemingly, both perspectives informed Tolstoi's rejection of reforms whose proponents had succumbed, he told the tsar, to "the alien ideals of Western European state theory and practice." Only "a lucid understanding of the fundamental, independent principles of Russian state life" could assure effective local reform: "the primary and truest condition for the success of the envisioned reform is to coordinate, strictly, all changes in local institutions with the fundamental principle of our state structure—autocratic imperial authority [samoderzhavnaia imperatorskaia vlast']."[78]

It is revealing that he employed both the personal and institutional personae of autocratic authority and insisted that "all parts of the state edifice [gosudarstvennoe zdanie] [were required to] be . . . directly linked to its chief foundation," because each administrative organ was a mere conduit manifesting the authority of the tsar before the population. History "bore witness," Tolstoi said, "that autocratic authority possesses a vital power, a creative spirit; only those institutions through which this authority can freely and correctly influence popular life are stable and organic, and, on the contrary, those that inhibit this influence disrupt the functioning of the state organism."[79]

Most organs of local administration and self-administration fell into the latter category; thus, as even a brief critique revealed, Tolstoi intended to restructure most of these institutions. An overly legalistic local administration weakened "the government's prestige [avtoritet] among the people" by depriving them of "an authority [vlast'] whose personal directives could redress the violations of law in matters arising from the needs of

[76] Polovtsev, Dnevnik Polovtseva, 2:190 (25 April 1889); Feoktistov, Vospominaniia, p. 218.

[77] Feoktistov, Vospominaniia, pp. 175–79 and 214–18. He related Tolstoi's comment that the most significant act of Peter the Great's reign had been the General Regulation of the Clergy. To Feoktistov's objection that this statute had caused servility and immorality in the Russian clergy, Tolstoi reportedly replied: "Any church hierarch conceals in his soul the dream of becoming pope; create a more independent position for the hierarchy and they will utilize all their powers to subordinate the state to the Church." Ibid., p. 218.

[78] Glinskii, "Period tverdoi vlasti," p. 688.

[79] Ibid.

their simple agrarian milieu."[80] Similarly, the "broad independence" that was being permitted to zemstvo organs rendered the government impotent to "prevent the abuse of power and redress transgressions" against individual interests, which, if Tolstoi were to be believed, they habitually committed. The "extraneous formalism" of jurisprudence and law that afflicted local courts left them ill-equipped, particularly given "the patriarchal customs of life" predominant among peasants, for the task "of quickly restoring order and, where possible, providing a rapid defense of the population's violated rights and interests." Demanding a significant expansion of state administrative power in rural life, Tolstoi concluded his report by reiterating that "all local institutions should be government institutions, linked with central government authority." The population's "confidence and trust" in local administration could be heightened "by bringing the best local people" to its service, a reference to a hereditary nobility that had figured far more centrally in Pazukhin's earlier writings. In general, he assured Alexander, the realization of his plan was guaranteed success because "all classes of the population are shaped by an unconditional loyalty to the historic foundations of state life."[81]

Many of Pazukhin's concerns had receded as Tolstoi's Ministry of Internal Affairs sought to impose a more systematic, hierarchical administration on the rural population. In one important respect, however, Tolstoi retained a fundamental concern of the nobiliary perspective: a preoccupation with the question of authority at a time of socioeconomic change and political uncertainty. Local administration had to be structured in such a manner that it manifested and reinforced autocratic authority in an agrarian social order whose peasantry purportedly accepted the tsar as legitimate. Thus, when Tolstoi submitted a formal draft of the land captain legislation to the State Council in February 1887, he also announced that the ministry had for the moment decided against a systemic reform of all rural administration and instead intended initially to promulgate only the land captain statute. Skewing the debate away from issues of law and civil government toward the imperative of authority, Tolstoi proclaimed that the MVD took its most pressing task to be the creation of "a special organ of administration that would subsume under [its] jurisdiction all the most important interests of the rural population and receive the necessary powers to guarantee order and tranquility" to rural life.[82]

[80] Ibid., p. 689.

[81] Ibid., pp. 689–90.

[82] "Po povodu proekta polozheniia o zemskikh nachal'nikakh, s"ezdakh sikh nachal'nikov i o gubernskikh po sel'skim delam prisutstviiakh," *Otchet po deloproizvodstvu Gosudarstvennogo Soveta za sessiiu 1889 g.* (St. Petersburg, 1889), p. 7. See in particular Yaney, *The Urge To Mobilize*, pp. 49–96.

In its details, the draft legislation established a territorial subdivision (*uchastok*) of the county that encompassed only peasant estate institutions—the village community and township—and those small urban settlements that, given "their cultural and economic conditions," resembled villages. The captain would be empowered to supervise and veto the actions of the landholding commune, the village assembly, village and township officials, and the township customary-law court. Moreover, he was assigned adjudicative authority over criminal misdemeanors and civil suits. The Ministry of Internal Affairs would appoint these officials from lists of local hereditary noble landowners compiled by governors in consultation with provincial marshals of the nobility. To be suitable, candidates would have to fulfill certain property, educational, and service requirements. The land captain would be subordinate to a new provincial board, the governor, the minister of internal affairs, and the Senate—the only institution capable of removing him from office.[83]

In a written presentation to the State Council's Joint Departments, Tolstoi substantiated this radical assertion of government authority in terms that indicated how forcefully his own dim perceptions of the agrarian social order were influencing policy. Previous attempts to create well-ordered peasant institutions, which he termed the state's primary "requirement in local administration," had suffered from an excessive reliance on "formalistic and distant" legal structures. Government supervision thus had "become illusory and peasant public institutions . . . in essence, [had been] left to themselves."[84] Worse, this abandonment had occurred at a time when rural economic change was fostering new, more exploitative social relations in the village. People obsessed with "their own material advantage"—speculators, merchants, peasant kulaks, lower-class townspeople—were, with growing regularity, influencing the decisions of village assemblies and township courts for personal gain, "while the interests of the peasant majority went undefended."[85] "Motivated only by personal goals," corruptible officials in these institutions at present could "not enjoy respect among peasants" because they "lacked the imprimatur of government legitimacy [*otpechatka pravitel'stvennogo avtoriteta*]."

[83] "Po povodu proekta polozheniia o zemskikh nachal'nikakh," pp. 6–9. Also Zaionchkovskii, *Rossiiskoe samoderzhavie*, pp. 374–77 and Mandel, "Paternalistic Authority."

[84] "Po povodu proekta polozheniia o zemskikh nachal'nikakh," p. 11. Tolstoi's minority position was joined by Pobedonostsev, Minister of Justice N. A. Manasein, Minister of Finance I. Ia. Vyshnegradskii, and State Council members Filosofov and Mansurov II.

[85] Ibid., p. 12. Legislation regulating the peasant economy included statutes limiting divisions of family households (*razdely*) in 1886, communal land repartitions (*peredely*) in 1893, and the market sale of allotment lands in 1893. On government policy toward peasant agriculture and its shifting perceptions of the land commune, see Macey, *Government and Peasant*, pp. 18–30, and I. V. Chernyshev, *Agrarno-krest'ianskaia politika Rossii za 150 let* (Petrograd, 1918), pp. 210–31.

That kind of "authority," Tolstoi believed, "never has enjoyed and probably never will enjoy significance in the eyes of the people."[86]

A dangerous situation now existed in the countryside: "the peasants have lost faith in their self-administration and expect its improvement solely from the government." If, at a time when "discipline and a feeling of legality were severely shaken," the population could still turn instinctively to the government, it did so only because "patriotism and love of the tsar" encouraged a willingness "to endure and await relief."[87] Autocratic authority, and the promise of moral justice and right that it represented, retained legitimacy; if the peasantry came to perceive that the government was indifferent to its concerns, however, the damage done could be incalculable. The overriding question of the moment thus became the creation of the land captain, an omnipotent authority acting directly in the tsar's name, whose leadership and influence could arrest the decay rotting out the country's social roots:

> It must not be forgotten that the peasantry constitutes no less than eighty percent of the empire's population, that it is a force . . . susceptible to any influence, often the most ill-intentioned, and that if, losing faith in the government, it began to correct the evil apart from and outside of government leadership, this could cause deep shocks to the entire state structure, the extent and consequences of which are hardly possible to predict.[88]

Throughout 1887 and 1888, Tolstoi's proposal provoked stormy protest among its opponents in the State Council, most of whom had served directly under Alexander II and were not prepared to forget either the reform era or the goals of civil evolution that it had posited.[89] Indeed, the land captain statute renewed the same debates that had divided the Kakhanov Commission and provoked a majority of the State Council into advocating an all-estate "district captain," a government-appointed local landowner supervising all civil, police, and public institutions in his territory. Justices of the peace were to retain juridical authority in the countryside.[90]

This counterproposal brought together the three policy issues that agitated opponents of the land captain statute. First, the proposed official

[86] Ibid. Also see Pobedonostsev, Pis'ma k Aleksandru III, 2:204 (31 December 1888), "Authority, in order to be real authority, must bear the seal of the state and derive its support outside of and above the environment of the local area."

[87] Ibid.

[88] Ibid., pp. 12–13.

[89] Polovtsev, Dnevnik Polovtseva, 2:5–139 passim.

[90] Ibid., 2:104–6 (13, 14 November 1888); Zaionchkovskii, Rossiiskoe samoderzhavie, pp. 389–90; Chernyshev, Agrarno-krest'ianskaia politika, pp. 233–38. Similar proposals were advanced in the Kakhanov Commission, Trudy o. k., Ob"iasnitelnye zapiski (Volostnoe upravlenie).

threatened the existence of rural justices of the peace, an institution that was a monument to the rational separation of powers embedded in the thinking of Russian officialdom and an instrument that defended the personal and property rights of civil society.[91] Although the MVD never formally advocated their elimination before Alexander III ordered them abolished in early 1889, opponents had from the outset been quick to criticize the admixture of juridical and executive powers in a single official.[92] Second, opponents protested the appointment of hereditary nobles to the post of land captain. Both sides of the debate acknowledged that the government lacked the financial resources and personnel necessary to place crown officials in the more than fifteen hundred territories that the new statute would create. Of necessity, the land captain would be appointed from the "best local people" in these areas. Moreover, although both sides agreed that landownership was a predictable measure of local influence and expertise, the majority of the State Council found the idea of requiring a noble pedigree to be anachronistic.[93] Kakhanov, for example, objected that the more meaningful requirements of education and property ownership "were being not only subordinated but [also] sacrificed" to the idea that hereditary noble status uniquely qualified an individual to supervise the peasantry. In fact, he countered, ascriptive status, if it still existed at all, did not guarantee "the broad intellectual viewpoint" necessary for this difficult administrative task.[94]

Third, opponents held that the land captain statute fundamentally misconstrued the character of rural society and hence the goals of state administration that it dictated. In the first formal critique organized by State Council opponents, eighteen members of the Joint Department of Laws

[91] Zaionchkovskii, *Rossiiskoe samoderzhavie*, pp. 378–88; and Polovtsev, *Dnevnik Polovtseva*, 2:157–60 (28, 30 January 1889).

[92] Protests concerning the land captain's encroachment on the justice of the peace occurred twice during the more than two years of debate: ministers' comments upon the initial MVD draft of 1886–87; and the State Council's response to Alexander III's unexpected decision in early 1889 to abolish the justice of the peace in rural areas, "Po povodu proekta polozheniia o zemskikh nachal'nikakh," pp. 39ff. Polovtsev maintains that the tsar always supported Tolstoi in his intention to implement this measure, Polovtsev, *Dnevnik Polovtseva*, 2:154–55 (28 January 1889).

[93] "Po povodu proekta polozheniia o zemskikh nachal'nikakh," pp. 41–42. The requirements demanded of nobles appointed to the post of land captain reflected the shortfall of qualified personnel. In descending order, they included: those who had one three-year term as county marshal of the nobility; noble landowners owning land qualifying them to vote in zemstvo elections; and noble landowners with university education or service in provincial administration with one-half the zemstvo property franchise. Given possible "shortfall," the final draft statute also allowed any hereditary noble living in the province to qualify for appointment. Moreover, as was routine in such debates, the Ministry of Finance forced a reduction in the proposed salary of the new official, ibid., pp. 133–34.

[94] Zaionchkovskii, *Rossiiskoe samoderzhavie*, p. 382.

did not dispute the need "to establish strong government authority in local areas.[95] Yet, they continued, because "the existing disorder" there affected "all strata of society," the state required "a universal administrative" structure to cope with it.[96] Advanced as heatedly here as it had been in the Kakhanov Commission, this defense of civil government went to the heart of the State Council's opposition. In December 1888 it appeared in the the State Council's formal majority opinion, which presented Alexander III with a clear choice between policies and defined the underlying perspectives that informed them.

The majority opinion contained two by now familiar premises. On the one hand, the idea of the land captain had been constructed on an illusory analysis of rural social structure. It was "possible and understandable only if the peasantry in Russia was a closed estate [*zamknutnoe soslovie*], living a totally segregated existence," but "in reality" these conditions no longer existed. The economic and social character of the village was diversifying "in a completely natural way," the majority insisted, and "village residents find themselves in the most variegated, everyday relationships and contacts with other strata of the population."[97] On the other hand, local disorder resulted from inevitable processes of social change—and not, as Tolstoi maintained, from the disintegration of authority. His untenable proposal—which the majority opinion implicitly attributed to fantasy—threatened, however, to become a self-fulfilling prophecy. The majority charged that the land captain could not create either effective administrative power or legitimate government authority because he was not equipped to regulate the increasingly diverse interests of rural civil society:

> The holy and great affair of the peasants' emancipation has been concluded successfully: they have been provided with land. What remains is to establish a strict hierarchy within local administration, a powerful and legalistic [*zako-nodeistvuiushchaia*] government authority in the local areas, and unity. . . . [T]here is no need at all to establish a special peasant organ, able to act successfully only within the narrow framework of estate interest. On the contrary, an authority is needed that will reconcile and unify the benefits and needs of all classes of the population. Only an institution that belongs to the general government structure of the state can accomplish this task properly.[98]

Even as these arguments were being heard in the State Council, however, Tolstoi was assured of the tsar's confidence and full support. In late

---

[95] "Po povodu proekta polozheniia o zemskikh nachal'nikakh," p. 15. These included Kakhanov, former Minister of Finance A. A. Abaza, D. M. Sol'skii, and E. A. Perets; all were allies of Loris-Melikov in 1880–81.

[96] Ibid., pp. 16–17.

[97] Ibid., p. 32.

[98] Ibid., pp. 34–35.

December Alexander told A. A. Polovtsev that he agreed with Tolstoi about "the impossibility of establishing an all-estate county captain." Apparently he had accepted Tolstoi's argument that the legal and administrative complexities of this idea would intolerably delay the implementation of the land-captain statute, without which, Alexander insisted, "peasant uprisings will without fail flare up in the coming summer."[99] The imperial state secretary lamented in his diary on New Year's Eve that "the sovereign had unconditionally agreed with Tolstoi about everything, had ordered him to dissent every time the Council disagreed with him, and had promised his total support."[100]

And so when Tolstoi rose in the State Council's general assembly, for the last time before his death, to rebut officials propounding the civil values of the reform era, he had little to fear in his attack on the one legislative act of the 1860s that had remained sacrosanct: the emancipation statute itself. Together with six other ministers, Tolstoi argued the minority position: the emancipators had been mistaken in thinking that the supervision of the peasantry was only a "provisional" measure. The task had not terminated with initial land settlements and the establishment of village institutional life, Tolstoi stated, but was, instead permanent, because

> as long as the peculiar conditions of peasant social structure continue to exist peasant administration cannot be left without the vigilant supervision of government organs charged with this [task] and granted the authority necessary to perform it. The supervision of the peasant matter, given its complexity and the importance of state interests tied to it, demands permanent care and indefatigable concern.[101]

These interests—social stability, economic prosperity, and political stasis—demanded "the permanent care and indefatigable concern" of tsar, government, and, ultimately, an uncontested, personal representative of this authority who would preside only over the peasantry. His opponents were wrong to look toward an all-estate government, Tolstoi declaimed. Supervision of the peasantry was "impossible for organs obliged to fulfill other administrative functions that have nothing in common with peasant administration." They were wrong to overemphasize the "significant changes" that had occurred in the countryside since 1861. Petty renters, rural townspeople, settlers, and others engaged in agriculture had appeared alongside "the indigenous peasantry," but these "rural residents differed in essentially no other way but name from the peasants."[102] Ultimately, they had been wrong to embrace the principles of legal order and civil society. Significant changes in Russian society did not require

[99] Polovtsev, *Dnevnik Polovtseva*, 2:132 (22 December 1888).
[100] Ibid., 2:138 (31 December 1888).
[101] "Po povodu proekta polozheniia o zemskikh nachal'nikakh," pp. 23–24.
[102] Ibid., p. 24.

abstract legality or rational institutions designed to accommodate them. Instead, they required an authority able to defend a traditional agrarian order against the processes that were undermining it.

To some modern observers, this may seem to be all idealizations and rhetoric to justify the extension of administrative hegemony into rural society. Certainly, a review of the land captain legislation promulgated in July 1889 indicates that administrative and police concerns dictated much of the final statute. The conclusion is inescapable that the Ministry of Internal Affairs utilized the peasant estate structure primarily as an administrative category through which it could control the amorphous rural mass population of the countryside. Supervision of peasant institutions and officials, and the right to fine or imprison any member of a nonprivileged estate subject to these jurisdictions, alone were sufficient to make the land captain the unchallenged master of his territory.[103] Through his legal control of the peasant township court, which heard most civil or criminal suits between peasants, he could intervene in the most mundane affairs of daily rural life. Revealingly, the first criminal violation subject to the land captain's adjudication was disobedience or insult of any imaginable government official.[104] Moreover, with the abolition of justices of the peace the land captain obtained adjudicatory jurisdiction over the growing number of disputes between peasants and private landowners: leases, day-labor contracts, damage and trespass on private or state property, wrecking of "complex" agricultural machinery, theft, and internal passport regulations. All these provisions, the State Council noted, would assure "the peaceful utilization of property."[105]

When Tolstoi in 1887 had first outlined the administrative functions of the land captain, he had emphasized such concerns. Yet the minister also cautioned the new official to exercise "care [*popechenie*] for the needs of the peasants, for their moral and economic success."[106] What remained of this guardianship role, and how did Tolstoi, who justified the land captain in part by referring to peasant expectations, imagine that a peasant would equate care with the imposition of ubiquitous, threatening authority?

If concerns for order are seen as demands for deference, the authorita-

[103] MVD, *Sbornik uzakonenii o krest'ianskikh i sudebnykh uchrezhdeniiakh, preobrazovannykh po zakonu 12-ogo iiulia 1889 goda* (St. Petersburg, 1894), articles 23–31, 61.

[104] "Ustav o nakazaniiakh, nalagaemykh Mirovymi Sudiami," articles 30 and 31, and "Vremennye pravila o Volostnom Sude v mestnostiakh, v kotorykh vvedeno Polozhenie o Zemskikh Uchastkovykh Nachal'nikakh," article 17 in *Sbornik uzakonenii o Krest'ianskikh i sudebnykh uchrezhdeniiakh*.

[105] "Po povodu proekta polozheniia o zemskikh nachal'nikakh," pp. 56–57 and 119; and *Sbornik uzakonenii*, "Ustav o nakazaniiakh," articles 51, 57–60, 63, 153–69, 172–74.

[106] "Po povodu proekta polozheniia o zemskikh nachal'nikakh," p. 14.

tive guardianship of the nobiliary land captain over a shaken yet still viable estate society appears with greater clarity. In its final deliberations, the State Council had mandated that the peasant township court, whose cases and decisions after the promulgation of the statute became subject to the supervision of the land captain, would sentence peasants to a public flogging of twenty lashes for certain stipulated crimes. Members cited the "humiliating character" of this punishment and warned that its too frequent application could exert a "corrupting influence on the population, inculcating a feeling of shame and humiliation." Yet crimes designated for such "serious" punishment were precisely those that reflected the social and economic transformation disrupting traditional forms of village behavior. Violations of decorum (*blagochinie*)—public brawling, disturbances of the peace, professional begging, public threats against life or property, any use of force without serious injury—all represented affronts to the established order. More immediately, neglect of elderly parents and public insulting of officials, family elders, or any individual whose position required proper respect all showed a flagrant disregard of social hierarchy. They manifested in microcosm the general disintegration of traditional peasant society that Tolstoi—and Pazukhin—had decried.[107]

Thus a forceful imposition of authority on village life was not intended merely to enforce administrative regulation. Powerful authority could mobilize and stabilize a social order. The land captain, omnipotent and ubiquitous, would root out the exploitative elements that afflicted peasant life. With his guiding example he would restore to the peasant majority, as if to essentially good but potentially unruly children, justice, morality, and tranquility. Finally, contrary to the present economic disarray of the village, the land captain would also foster prosperity. Protecting communal land against proletarian influences, guaranteeing the rights of private property whose income and produce fueled local life, and preserving the social hierarchy from the immoral influences of economic change, the land captain would bring "order" to local life. But his was a patriarchal order that would complement, in the locality, the autocratic order of estates so idealized throughout this decade.

In the land captain debates there appeared the allure of a political culture that, whether it was historically valid or not, assumed an aura of legitimacy because it coalesced with the conceptions of authority ascendant in the reign of Alexander III. Officials who confronted uncertainty in the present had found assurance in a history shaped by the authority and power of autocracy. Autocracy gathered the land, built the state, unified a society—and could reinvigorate a social structure displaying signs

[107] Ibid., p. 108. *Sbornik uzakonenii*, "Vremennye pravila o Volostnom Sude," article 17, and "Ustav o nakazaniiakh," articles 30–174 passim.

of stress. Tolstoi did more than justify institutional adjustments of the domestic administrative apparatus when he addressed the State Council. He also declared that personal authority was again the central factor in state life and that Russia, thus rearmed, would confront the contagion of Western social development in its own way, with principles organically developed by its own history.

The land captain statute was not the single accomplishment of the counterreform decade, nor did it represent the irreversible destruction of the great reforms. Yet its promulgation, and the defeat this inflicted on its opponents, dealt a serious blow to the hope, of Alexander II's last years, for gradual, evolutionary social change. Two very different views of Russian society and political authority had clashed in these debates. Neither the minority of the Kakhanov Commission nor the majority of the State Council had abandoned their commitment to the state's decisive, controlling influence on Russian life. Indeed, the necessity of this role was underscored by the sharply contrasting values of a cultured, educated society and a majority population that remained largely unassimilated to its values. Yet these reformers had taken account of an emerging, propertied civil society in Russia—a universalistic phenomenon rendering anachronistic not only the particularistic divisions of estates but also, increasingly, the paternalistic notions of government that rested upon them. Property and individualism were phenomena common to both educated and peasant culture, and they were slowly bridging the chasm between these two worlds. The state was obliged not only to recognize these currents as legitimate, but also to accommodate them within its own government apparatus. Hence a legal and rational institutional order was an indispensable instrument for the task of guiding an orderly transition to civil society and stabilizing the autocratic regime itself.

In the 1880s, however, powerful advocates of what we have called an autocratic political culture refuted and partially repudiated these arguments. It should be reiterated that this was not a reactionary phenomenon, a desire to return to the *status quo ante*. However divergent their viewpoints, public, nobiliary, and official proponents of these views all recognized the irreversible social transformation that was convulsing the country. This factor alone—it manifested itself in the village, in educated society and the intelligentsia, among provincial landowners—dictated the attempts to ensure that the state would be strong, and have the power necessary to control and manage socioeconomic change. The decade witnessed a significant expansion of administrative regulation and power, a trend that accelerated to an even faster pace in the 1890s. In rural society this process further rigidified the administrative segregation of the peasant populace, heightened the influence of officials who propounded the priority of police concerns in domestic policy, and intensified the suspicion of public autonomy that always had existed within Russian officialdom.

And yet it was not only state power that took precedence in the era of the counterreforms. The question of authority, its political character and function in society, had also become a critical focus of the decade. In this respect the reformers of the early 1880s had left their mark on subsequent debate. Although they had neither questioned their own *raison d'être* nor challenged the legitimacy of autocratic authority, they had argued that civil evolution dictated essential reforms of autocratic government, of the ways in which authority was exercised. The epithets subsequently hurled at this argument reflected not only an abhorrence for alien, Western European social and political development, but also an attempt to assert against it the historicity of autocratic authority and a society embodying the heritage, if not the reality, of the estates through which the Russian state had been consolidated.

This interpretation varied according to the constituency that expressed it. Within the provincial nobility appeared a renewed emphasis on the ascriptive traditions of noble service and its bonds of personal duty to the sovereign and the rural community, as well as on the preeminent importance of the noble estate to the political and social stability of the autocratic regime. Provincial petitions of the 1880s indicated that Pazukhin was not alone in willfully projecting the particularistic concerns of his estate as essential interests of state. The government was obliged to stabilize the society from which autocracy had arisen and in which its authority was unquestionably legitimate. Thus emerged the vociferous requests to resist the dissolution of estate society, arrest the disintegration of its traditional values and hierarchy, and reaffirm the local socioeconomic status of the landowning nobility.

Within the government, which was, to be sure, sympathetic to noble petitions, the essence of the question was not the reestablishment of estate society, but the reassertion of the unrestricted authority of the autocrat, a legitimating force that alone assured the prestige of state power and its stability in a traditional social order under assault from modernity. Hence, the land captain, although an institution intended to intensify administrative regulation of the peasant masses, was also a hereditary noble exercising unlimited authority in the village. The conclusion that power ultimately depended upon authority, which before the first crisis of autocracy had never been so plainly articulated, led the government to have its agents penetrate more deeply into the countryside than ever before. That it tried to assure its legitimacy, however, by relying on the personalized authority of officials to impose order and justice within the estate institutions of the peasantry only compounded the dilemmas that the state already confronted.

The economic and social transformation of the Russian countryside, of course, continued. Yet the counterreforms had strengthened the estate framework of rural life, arming it with a political legitimacy that now approached the level of dogma. As late as 1902, when substantial opinion in both government and public circles favored the abolition not only of estate administration but also of communal land tenure, the Ministry of Internal Affairs publicly defended the counterreform legislation as a viable expression "of Russian self-consciousness, grounded on the principles of Orthodoxy and on the unlimited loyalty of the Russian people to the unified Supreme authority of its sovereign." The land captain, this official text asserted, had instilled order in "the rural way of life." "The best people of the village have greeted this new government authority with signs of indisputable respect and complete trust." Village assemblies now acted "with careful consideration," not "under the influence of vodka," and spent their funds more correctly because they sensed "the presence of a close supervisory authority."[108]

Moreover, even in government circles, such official denigration of civil society quieted but did not silence its proponents. Indeed, the most notable failure of Tolstoi's local reform plan was his inability to revoke the independence of zemstvo self-administration, seen by moderate opinion as the very symbol of local civil society. To be sure, little official protest arose against the estate-based electoral system instituted by the 1890 zemstvo statute. Various observers acknowledged that this measure did not alter the existing domination of the assemblies by provincial nobility landowners—although it did effectively abolish peasant electoral rights by requiring governors to appoint peasant zemstvo delegates.[109] Yet the principle of self-administration remained intact because the State Council defended it as a legitimate expression of public service in the state:

> There were, especially at first, instances where the zemstvo did not accurately understand its purpose; . . . there were instances of careless, negligent, and even unscrupulous attitudes [shown] by elected zemstvo officials toward their obli-

[108] MVD, *Obshchii obzor deiatel'nosti Ministerstva Vnutrennykh Del za vremia tsarstvovaniia Imperatora Aleksandra III* (St. Petersburg, 1901), pp. 17–27. Also Mandel, "Patriarchal Authority," chap. 5.

[109] B. N. Chicherin, *Vospominaniia* (Moscow, 1929), p. 286; B. B. Veselovskii, "Detsentralizatsiia upravleniia i zadachi zemstva," in Veselovskii and Frenkel, *Iubileinyi Zemskii Sbornik*, pp. 44–46; and Thomas S. Fallows, "Forging the Zemstvo Movement: Liberalism and Radicalism on the Volga, 1890–1905" (Ph.D., diss., Harvard University, 1981), pp. 192–210.

gations. But, moving away from particulars, if one evaluates the general results of zemstvo activity over a quarter of a century, one will find beyond doubt that the summoning of local elected people to supervise local affairs significantly improved the conditions of provincial life and more fully satisfied the requirements of the local population.[110]

The survival of the zemstvo was nevertheless an exception to the growth of superordinate administration in the decade. Liberal spokesman and law professor Boris Chicherin wrote that the land captain statute best conveyed to him the essence of Alexander III's reign and the blows it had struck against the reform era's promises of legality and civil order. They had been replaced by arbitrariness and pursuit of power, he stated; "Russian youth were being corrupted by a habit of total arbitrariness in regard to those below them and slavish submissiveness to those above them. . . . The government mercilessly smashed our most treasured feelings, our best aspirations, supporting and agitating in society only servility and arbitrariness."[111]

Chicherin's remarks were quite appropriate. Power and authority now pervaded the bureaucratic lexicon. Quite naturally, these values only served to aggrandize the hegemonic impulses upon which so much of bureaucratic government rested. Bureaucrats who had entered service in the 1880s would ascend to positions of influence in the 1890s and the first years of the twentieth century. The experiences that had formed their perceptions were not those of the great reform era or of the varied attempts to pursue it characteristic of the 1870s and early 1880s. Rather, they had been schooled under Alexander III's autocracy and had learned the importance of authority and the exercise of force. The potential for conflict between such state men and a society entering an era of national politics was explosive. Perhaps the comments of a land captain, a petty official far from St. Petersburg to whom the state had delegated sweeping personal authority, expressed most eloquently the image that the state now conveyed—in this specific context to the peasantry, but in a more general one to all of Russian society:

> The view of the peasant as one . . . who is obliged to follow any kind of command, and the conviction of the peasant that he actually is obliged to execute these commands, creates abnormal relationships between the peasants and

---

[110] "Zemskie uchrezhdeniia," *Otchet po deloproizvodstvu Gosudarstvennogo Soveta za sessiiu 1890 g.* (St. Petersburg, 1890), pp. 122–23. On the development of this legislation, see N. N. Avinov, "Glavnye nachala v istorii zakonodatel'stva o zemskikh uchrezhdeniiakh," *Iubileinyi Zemskii Sbornik*, pp. 401–11; Zakharova, *Zemskaia kontrreforma*, chap. 6; and Zaionchkovskii, *Rossiiskoe samoderzhavie*, pp. 401–11.

[111] Chicherin, *Vospominaniia*, pp. 277–78.

their captains. . . . This is the chief reason why the peasant does not believe in the law; for him the law is the command of the captain. "You can do anything," the peasant tells you. . . . What is worse, the captain does not recognize that he acts criminally, but, on the contrary, is convinced that the law is bad, that it is his moral obligation to correct it.[112]

[112] A. I. Novikov, *Zapiski zemskogo nachal'niki* (St. Petersburg, 1899), pp. 26–27.

CHAPTER IV

Toward an Era of National Politics, 1894–1904

In 1899 S. Iu. Witte presented Tsar Nicholas II with a memorandum in which the minister of finance defended the accelerated industrial development that his ministry had overseen during that decade. Confronting mounting public criticism of his policies, Witte sought to assure the sovereign that his autocracy depended on the rapid development of a modern industrial society. In an age of European imperial expansion, the minister explained, Russia could not remain dependent on an underdeveloped agricultural economy and retain its status on the continent as a "politically independent, mighty power." A "national industry," Witte instructed, provided the autocracy with a necessary counterweight to "foreign industrial hegemony" and, perhaps more important for the future stability of the state, with "the enrichment of the entire nation [*natsiia*]." As long as Witte could ensure the Ministry of Finance's control of economic policy, the state would attempt to awaken the "more active and striving life" inherent in a modern industrial society. "Capital, knowledge, and entrepreneurship," the minister hyperbolized, "convert the illiterate peasant into a builder of railroads, a bold and leading industrial organizer, a multitalented financier."[1]

Russian industrialization was one of the great paradoxes of late imperial history. Nowhere else in Europe did the state play as central a role in the development of modern industry. Although this process can be traced back to earlier decades, it resulted in large measure from the fiscal, commercial, and investment policies of the later 1880s and 1890s. Emerging from the ideological framework of that period, state-sponsored industrialization was, as its primary architect Sergei Iul'evich Witte maintained at the turn of the century, a sweeping effort to bolster autocratic power with the economic and social structures of the contemporary industrial era. Yet any history of these years will reveal that the state, in its drive to accelerate the socioeconomic transformation of Russian society, encouraged processes that, seen in retrospect, fundamentally contradicted the foundations of autocratic rule. Rapid urbanization and professionaliza-

---

[1] "Vsepoddaneishii doklad ministra finansov S. Iu. Vitte Nikolaiu II o neobkhodimosti ustanovit' i zatem neprelozhno priderzhivat'sia opredelennoi programmy torgovo-promyshlennoi politiki imperii," in I. F. Ginden, "Ob osnovakh ekonomicheskoi politiki tsarskogo pravitel'stva v kontse XIX–nachale XX v.," *Materialy po istorii SSSR*, vol. 6 (Moscow, 1959), p. 182.

tion, the emergence of industrial labor and working-class movements, the commercialization and impoverishment of agriculture, the increasing bureaucratization of both government and society, and the coalescence of national political movements in opposition to autocratic government—by the turn of the century, state officials increasingly found themselves trapped within the social and political milieu of industrial modernity.[2]

They were also confronted with the necessity of political action, particularly as public dissidence and social conflict became pressing concerns in the decade before the first Russian Revolution in 1905. Efforts to address these problems brought to the fore the conflicting precedents that had arisen to explain the character of Russian social development and the role of the state in administering it. In retrospect, of course, we know that a political and social crisis was building within the autocratic system, one comparable only to that experienced in 1917. This was a perspective, however, that officials did not share until the revolutionary events of 1905 overwhelmed them. Indeed, their attempts to understand and respond to the prehistory of the 1905 Revolution created one crucial element of the revolutionary crisis: the discovery by officials that the political and social assumptions of their own past experience accorded little, if at all, with the reality of an era of national politics.

SERGEI WITTE AND THE MINISTRY OF FINANCE: VISIONS OF THE RECHTSSTAAT

Few other officials drank more deeply at the well of unrestricted autocratic authority than Sergei Iul'evich Witte, minister of finance (1892–1903), chairman of the Committee of Ministers (1903–05), and one of the most astute statesmen to serve the late imperial regime. Born a hereditary nobleman in 1849, Witte graduated from the mathematics faculty of Novorossiisk University in 1870 and for the next sixteen years worked in the railroad industry of the Ukraine, eventually becoming chief administrator on the privately owned Southwestern Railroad. There, in his own words, he acquired "more practical experience, practical gumption, and practical knowledge" than a career official could obtain "from books or Petersburg salons."[3] In 1886 he joined the civil service as director of the

---

[2] See Alexander Gerschenkron, "Problems and Patterns of Russian Economic Development," in Cherniavsky, *The Structure of Russian History*, pp. 282–308; Theodore S. Von Laue, *Sergei Witte and the Industrialization of Russia* (New York, 1969); L. E. Shepelev, *Tsarizm i burzhuaziia vo vtoroi polovine XIX veka* (Leningrad, 1981); F. Danilov, "Obshchaia politika pravitel'stva i gosudarstvennyi stroi k nachalu XX-ogo veka," in L. Martov et al., eds., *Obshchestvennoe dvizhenie v Rossii v nachale XX-ogo veka* (St. Petersburg, 1909), vol. 1, pp. 414–82; *Krizis samoderzhaviia v Rossii*, chap. 1.

[3] Witte, *Vospominaniia*, 1:385.

Ministry of Finance's Department of Railroad Affairs and chairman of its tariff committee. At the height of the great famine of 1891–92, he became minister of communications and won praise for organizing rail transport to assist the famine relief campaign. Seven months later, in August 1892, Witte succeeded his patron I. A. Vyshnegradskii as minister of finance. In a few short years, this talented outsider had reached the center of St. Petersburg's byzantine ministerial politics, where his unbridled ambition and brilliant tactical skills made him a most formidable combatant for the next fifteen years. One of his closest subordinates later recalled that "the appearance of Witte in St. Petersburg was an event, a historical phenomenon. Before everyone's eyes, with fantastic rapidity, appeared this powerful personality, who gradually conquered everyone and subordinated everyone, whether they were willing or not, to himself."[4]

The conservative publicist A. S. Suvorin remarked in early 1893 that within months of Witte's appointment, the new finance minister "was unrecognizable." Confidants reported that during his reports to Alexander III Witte assumed the visage of a man "who dreamt of things not of this world," an "authoritative manner, it was said, that the tsar liked."[5] The comment was revealing for an understanding of a man whose dedication to autocracy, its monopoly of both political authority and overwhelming state power, was uncompromising. V. I. Gurko, a most vitriolic and insightful critic of Witte, noted that the minister of finance did not seek power as a goal in itself. Rather, he perceived it as an instrument through which he could create that which he desired. In this sense, Gurko continued, the entire population became "the [raw] building material of state might," economic factors to be thrown into the struggle of building a modern industrial state.[6] Like a good political economist, Witte put the case in essentially the same terms when he wrote that Russian economic and political power depended on "three factors of production: natural resources, material and intellectual capital, and labor."[7] That the concen-

---

[4] Shepelev, *Tsarizm i burzhuaziia*, p. 196. On Witte's career and views, see especially the insightful comments supplied by B. V. Ananych, *Rossiia i mezhdunarodnyi kapital, 1897–1914: Ocherk istorii finansovykh otnoshenii* (Leningrad, 1970), pp. 19–28. Also B. V. Ananych and R. Sh. Ganelin, "P. A. Fadeev, S. Iu. Vitte i ideologicheskie iskaniia 'okhranitelei' v 1881–1883 gg.," Trudy AN SSSR, Institut Istorii SSSR, XII, *Issledovanie po sotsial'no-politicheskoi istorii Rossii* (Leningrad, 1971), pp. 299–326; V. I. Gurko, *Features and Figures of the Past: Government and Opinion in the Reign of Nicholas II* (New York, 1970), pp. 52–68; V. I. Gurko, "Chto est' i chego net v 'Vospominaniia grafa S. Iu. Vitte,' " *Russkaia letopis'*, no. 2 (1922) (reprinted Mouton, 1970); Von Laue, *Sergei Witte*, pp. 36–70; and M. N. de Enden, "The Roots of Witte's Thought," *Russian Review* 29, no. 1 (1970): 6–24.

[5] M. Krichevskii, ed., *Dnevnik A. S. Suvorina* (Moscow-Leningrad, 1923), p. 45.

[6] Gurko, "Chto est'," pp. 68–69 and 75–77.

[7] Witte, *Vospominaniia*, 1:410–11.

trated power of the autocracy allowed these breathtaking vistas explained, in large measure, Witte's unyielding loyalty to Alexander III, a paragon whose "powerful will and character" Witte sincerely admired.[8] Indeed, for Witte tsar and state were inextricably intertwined, the legitimate authority of autocracy assuring the sweeping state power necessary to impel Russian society into the competitive modern era that its Western European neighbors had already entered.

How broadly Witte construed the application of state power was first revealed in October 1893, when the Ministry of Finance presented the State Council with what Soviet historian L. E. Shepelev has termed "a radical turning point in the government's leadership of commercial-industrial development."[9] As the first comprehensive outline of the so-called "Witte system," the report detailed "the committed leadership [*rukovodstvo*]" required of the central government if it was to achieve the "rapid adaptation of a vast, still almost patriarchal Russian economy to the demands of a modern industrial and commercial culture." Interpreting state interests to extend not only to the large, but also to "the middling and small focuses of national labor . . . , to the entire organism of the Russian economy," the report supplied a compelling economic rationale for the superordinate power of autocratic government: "Only under conditions of the most immediate and strictly practical concern [*popechenie*] for the development of each distinct branch of our industry and commerce can the central administration develop general measures for the good of the national economy [*pol'za narodnogo khoziaistva*]."[10]

The report of October 1893 was a striking declaration of the universalistic perspective that guided the Ministry of Finance in its administration of the national economy. Yet it paid little attention to Russia's largest industrial branch, agriculture—a lapse that was not unintentional. Until the mid-1890s, ministerial policy toward agriculture was largely guided by the assumption that industrial development would foster the eventual commercialization of the rural economy by creating productive capacity, employment, and market demand. Although not ignored, agricultural prosperity was subordinated to the overriding, immediate concern of industrial growth. In large measure both private and peasant communal agriculture were sources of investment capital, which the treasury extracted through the grain trade and through the pervasive and indirect taxation of peasant consumption.[11]

[8] Ibid., 3:249–50 and in general, 331–70.

[9] Shepelev, *Tsarizm i burzhuaziia*, pp. 204–9 and generally pp. 217–47, which quote TsGIA, f. 1152, op. IX (1893), d.447, ll.2–46.

[10] Ibid., pp. 205–7.

[11] Von Laue, *Sergei Witte*, pp. 114–19, and Gerschenkron, "Problems and Patterns," pp. 43–46. On ministerial fiscal and tariff policies for the fostering of capital accumulation and

Witte's personal inexperience in agrarian affairs exacerbated this bias. When he became minister in 1892, his understanding of rural development was rudimentary, informed primarily by Slavophile conceptions of communal land tenure and the stability it engendered in the population.[12] Influenced partially by the admonitions of a predecessor, N. Kh. Bunge, by 1894 he had begun to reconsider these views and to advocate a general review of the peasant statute.[13] As his annual budget report of January 1895 demonstrated, however, Witte continued to believe that the needs of agriculture were of necessity secondary to the "general goals of the state power as regards the country's economic life." In the countryside, he declaimed, "God sets prices." Neither Russia's economy nor its industrial future could depend upon the weather and the success or failure of a single harvest.[14]

Such claims became difficult to sustain as provincial challenges to them grew in the second half of the decade. Tariff and investment policies perceived to favor industry continued to be a favorite target of nobiliary protest.[15] But a more compelling critique of rural economic conditions was being articulated in the zemstvos, where renewed public criticism of officialdom had been audible since the great famine of 1891–92—and had been greatly intensified by the flurry of petitions supporting representative institutions that Nicholas II had dismissed at the time of his coronation in 1894.[16] The Fifth All-Russian Congress of Agriculturalists in December 1895, for example, passed resolutions to expand zemstvo work in primary education and agronomy, as well as resolutions to create the all-estate small zemstvo unit that would facilitate such efforts. Like sev-

investment in manorial agriculture, see esp. Fallows, "Forging the Zemstvo Movement," pp. 444–49. Also Ministerstvo finansov, *Ministerstvo finansov, 1802–1902* (St. Petersburg, 1902), pt. 2, pp. 534–40.

[12] See Von Laue, *Sergei Witte*, pp. 34–35 and 50–64, and S. Witte, "Manufakturnoe krepostnichestvo," *Rus'*, no. 3 (1885): 18–19.

[13] On Bunge's views and the universalistic tradition in the Ministry of Finance, see George E. Snow, ed. and trans., *The Years 1881–1894 in Russia: A Memorandum Found in the Papers of N. Kh. Bunge*, Transactions, vol. 71, pt. 6 (Philadelphia, 1981). See also Macey, *Government and Peasant*, pp. 87–90; Mandel, "Patriarchal Authority," pp. 342–71; Gurko, *Features and Figures*, pp. 75–81; and Witte, *Vospominaniia*, 1:417–18.

[14] "Vsepoddaneishii doklad Ministra Finansov o gosudarstvennoi rospisi dokhodov i raskhodov na 1895 goda," *Vestnik finansov, promyshlennosti i torgovli*, 1 January 1895, pp. 5–6. One stark illustration of the bias was the following allocation of budgeted expenditures: Ministry of Finance, 144.3 million rubles; Ministry of Communications, 152.7 million rubles; construction of Trans-Siberian railroad, 49.8 million rubles; Ministry of Agriculture and State Properties, 31.4 million rubles.

[15] Solov'ev, *Samoderzhavie . . . XIX veka*, pp. 201–12; Korelin, *Dvorianstvo*, pp. 262–66; Becker, *Nobility and Privilege*, chap. 4; and esp. Fallows, "Forging the Zemstvo Movement," chap. 8.

[16] Veselovskii, *Istoriia zemstva*, 3:497–515.

eral other such gatherings in 1896, the congress urged regional meetings to coordinate concerns of mutual interest.[17] Most striking was a critique of state financial policy cosigned by twenty-six provincial marshals of the nobility in February of that year.[18] Gathered by Minister of Internal Affairs I. L. Goremykin, the marshals represented divergent political views.[19] On the right was the archconservative marshal of Ekaterinoslav province, A. P. Strukov, and on the "left" the liberal M. A. Stakhovich of Orel; all, however, dwelt on the dangers that Witte's financial policies posed to manorial agriculture and "the state significance of the noble estate." Articulating the same ascriptive values that had appeared a decade earlier, the marshals "openly declare[d] that without land there is no noble estate and without the noble estate the Russian land will become a different land."[20] Yet their criticism also asserted a community of economic interests within rural society extending beyond narrow estate concerns and led the marshals, drawing on their "long and extensive experience in provincial life," to the "unanimous conclusion that the economic well-being of rural Russia [*derevenskaia Rossiia*]" was not enjoying the benefits of the state's evident commercial-industrial development.[21]

Witte apparently took offense at this critique—particularly at the charge that his policies were detrimental to popular welfare. Several months later, the Ministry of Finance, under his signature, issued a detailed rebuttal that slandered the nobility for presuming to subordinate the general economic welfare to their own narrow self-interest. Plainly, provincial protest had not altered Witte's economic priorities. The content of the report did indicate, however, that the minister was reformulating his justification of state policy in light of rural public opinion. Industrialization, Witte began to insist, had become the means to achieve the goals of civil evolution intended by the great reforms. Taking the long view of the landed nobility's protests, Witte rhetorically acknowledged that emancipation had initiated a traumatic, "fundamental restructuring of the nobiliary landowning economy and a rupture of the age-old cus-

[17] Veselovskii, *Istoriia zemstva*, 3:379–80; Fallows, "Forging the Zemstvo Movement," pp. 459–78; and A. A. Stakhovich, "Obshchaia finansovaia politika i ee vliianie na sel'skokhoziastvennoi promyshlennosti," *Narodnoe khoziastvo* vol. 4, book 1 (January–February 1903), pp. 1–5.

[18] TsGIA, f.1284, op. 185 (1896), d. 37; also Solov'ev, *Samoderzhavie . . . XIX veka*, pp. 220–27.

[19] Suvorin, *Dnevnik A. S. Suvorina*, pp. 79 (20 January 1896) and 88 (14 April 1896).

[20] TsGIA, f. 1284, op. 185 (1896), d. 37, ll. 60–61. See also their arguments in favor of limiting hereditary ennoblement and against alteration of the land-captain statute, as the Ministry of Finance desired. Ibid., ll. 36–38 and 52.

[21] Ibid., l. 11. On the importance of the growing commercialization of noble agriculture, see Fallows, "Forging the Zemstvo Movement," chap. 2; Becker, *Nobility and Privilege*, chap. 1; and Manning, *Crisis of the Old Order*, chap. 1.

toms of an estate." Many noble landowners then (as now, was the implicit message) had been unable to survive it, but their disappearance, Witte maintained, was compensated for by results that had rendered Russia "unrecognizable politically, socially, and economically."[22] The transformation occurring within the landed nobility best illustrated these processes at work. Sobering statistics did portray the dimensions of noble land sales and indebtedness, but ample evidence also proved that some of these landowners were surviving and even prospering in difficult times.[23] During the years 1892–95, Witte noted, the nobility had invested some forty-three million rubles annually in new land purchases. In the southwestern, northwestern, and central agricultural regions, such purchases replaced 60 to 70 percent of the total land sold by nobles in these areas. Here, Witte retorted, was "a gratifying phenomenon" that indicated the transference of noble landownership "from weak, incapable hands into the hands of strong, knowledgeable, and enterprising owners, who are the most ardent representatives of the leading agricultural estate."[24]

The implication was clear. If state financial policy was aiding the economic reorganization of the landed nobility, then any claims to a unique, ascriptive status in the empire were at best anachronistic and at worst injurious to the future commonweal of rural society. Yet these conclusions ignored the charge—leveled both by the marshals' critique and, to a much greater extent, by zemstvo liberals—that the impoverishment of the peasantry, not simply the status of noble landholding, was at issue, and that this impoverishment gave the lie to ministerial claims to superordinate guardianship of rural welfare. Witte addressed this larger issue in his public budget report of January 1897, apparently prompted in part by the sympathetic hearing that Nicholas II gave to the marshals at a meeting with M. A. Stakhovich in late November.[25]

Here the finance minister readily admitted that the near-subsistence agriculture of the Russian peasantry created little cash income and thus precluded an immediate increase in its low standard of living. Yet, with four consecutive successful harvests since 1893 to support his point, he main-

[22] "Zamechanie ministra finansov S. Iu. Vitte na zapisku gubernskikh predvoditelei dvorianstva o nuzhdakh dvorianskogo zemlevladeniia," in I. F. Ginden and M. Ia. Gefter, "Trebovaniia dvorianstva i finansovo-ekonomicheskaia politika tsarskogo pravitel'stva v 1880–1890-kh godov," *Istoricheskii arkhiv* 4 (July–August 1957): 130–31.

[23] Ibid., pp. 133–36. Over 40% of noble land in European Russia was under some form of mortgage; this figure increased to 50% in some provinces of the central agricultural region and to 66% in the Volga provinces of Kazan and Saratov. Of the estates in these two regions whose mortgages were held by the State Noble Land Bank, only one-third and two-fifths of the loans, respectively, were considered risk-free.

[24] Ibid., p. 137. Witte makes this same distinction in his memoirs. Witte, *Vospominaniia*, 1:427.

[25] Suvorin, *Dnevnik A. S. Suvorina*, p. 136 (29 November, 2 December 1896).

tained that economic transformation was beginning to have a positive impact on some strata of the peasantry as well. Citing, as he would through 1902, increasing revenues from indirect taxation on consumption, Witte explained that "we are seeing . . . , as it was seen in all other countries, the transition from a purely agricultural period of economic life and a system of natural economy to an industrial period and a system of money economy." Some "distinct groups of the population [were] making their way to higher levels of prosperity," he said, a primary indication indeed that "national labor and entrepreneurship were diversifying."[26] As he had done in criticizing the marshals, Witte again asserted, against challenges to his policies, a more stable national economic future to which, despite the sacrifices involved, the state power had dedicated itself. It was, Witte wrote, "unreasonable to expect that the birth of a national industry, the creation of stable domestic markets for agriculture and labor, can be attained without violating some interests; the general law of organic development [*obshchii zakon organicheskogo razvitiia*]— the inevitability of sacrifices to attain great goals—must be applied to the state's economic growth."[27]

Notwithstanding this bold assertion of state hegemony over society— and the interests of the Finance Ministry over other institutional competitors—the next two years were ones in which Witte's industrial strategy confronted political and social challenges on several fronts. In April 1897 his attempt to override criticism from the nobility was blunted when Nicholas II approved the establishment of the Special Conference on the Needs of the Nobility. The new commission, designed to investigate the causes of decline, developed an agenda that included a reduction of import tariffs on agricultural machinery, the introduction of entail of hereditary estates, a prohibition on sales of noble lands to commoners, and other issues peculiar to the nobility alone.[28] From Witte's perspective, this irresponsible program that potentially threatened his own budgetary priorities was even less palatable given the significant involvement of the

---

[26] "Vsepoddaneishii doklad Ministra Finansov o gosudarstvennoi rospisi dokhodov i raskhodov," *Vestnik finansov, torgovli i promyshlennosti,* 5 January 1897, pp. 2–5. Also *Report of the Minister of Finance to H.I.M. the Emperor on the Budget of the Empire for 1899* (St. Petersburg, 1898), p. 20; and "Vsepoddaneishii doklad Ministra finansov o gosudarstvennoi rospisi dokhodov i raskhodov na 1902," *Narodnoe khoziastvo* 3, book 1 (January 1902): 173–75, where Witte, in the face of public charges of agrarian crisis, cited increasing per capita consumer consumption to demonstrate peasant prosperity.

[27] "Vsepoddaneishii doklad Ministra Finansov . . . na 1897," p. 6; also *Ministerstvo finansov, 1802–1902,* pt. 2, p. 533.

[28] Korelin, *Dvorianstvo,* pp. 275–76; and Solov'ev, *Samoderzhavie . . . XIX veka,* pp. 279–82, who attributes the program to A. S. Stishinskii. On the debates of the Special Conference, see Solov'ev, *Samoderzhavie . . . XIX veka,* pp. 276–360; and Becker, *Nobility and Privilege,* chaps. 4–5.

Ministry of Internal Affairs. The conference was chaired by the former minister I. N. Durnovo; the project was also supported by a former assistant minister under both Tolstoi and Durnovo, the talented imperial secretary V. K. Pleve.[29]

The special conference thus became another issue in a growing conflict between the empire's two most powerful domestic ministries. An episode at one of its earliest sessions in November captured both the intensity of the confrontation and the frustration that Witte was experiencing as his own views of state policy led him more and more deeply into the tangled web of rural interests. The conference was debating the cooptation of wealthy landowners into provincial corporations of the nobility when Witte, a member *ex officio*, objected that the entire system of nobiliary status "had outlived its time." Russia was beginning its own industrial transformation, Witte said, and ought to bear in mind the example of the West, where "the nobility was impoverished not because it had lost its privileges but because, compared to the industrial class, it had lost its significance." Unless measures were adopted to broaden the definition of hereditary nobility beyond state service and landowning, particularly in order to include commercial and industrial owners, he said, "no more than fifty years will pass before another wealthy class emerges [in Russia], similar to that which decided the fate of France, the bourgeoisie." It fell to Pleve to rebut these arguments, and he did so with vigor, arguing that one could not base all considerations on economic grounds or on uncontestable laws of science: "Russia has her own distinct history and unique structure. What is applicable to one state may be entirely untrue for another. The sooner we have the basis to hope that Russia will be spared the knout of capital and the bourgeoisie and the conflict of estates, the more peacefully will we take care of our business."[30]

Witte's forays into the realm of the special conference, as well as the nagging opposition that he encountered there from MVD officials, occurred while a much more significant challenge to the Finance Ministry was emerging in the countryside. The crop failure of 1897 was a stark reminder to the entire country of peasant impoverishment. In his public budget report of January 1898 Witte minimized the consequences of an "unsatisfactory" harvest that had been barely sufficient to feed the population; he remained confident that existing reserves would allow grain exports and revenue growth to continue.[31] The harvest of 1898, however, was even worse. Below average throughout the empire, the yields along the Kama and Volga River basins recalled the famine years of 1891–92

[29] Solov'ev, *Samoderzhavie . . . XIX veka*, pp. 245–51.

[30] *TsGIA*, f. 1283, op. 1 (1897), d. 229, ll. 2–4.

[31] *Report of the Minister of Finance to H.I.M. the Emperor on the Budget of the Empire for 1898* (St. Petersburg, 1897), pp. 6–8.

that had been most appalling in these same regions. With more concern, Witte stated in his December 1898 budget report that harvested tonnage in these areas had not even exceeded the amount of sown seed. High grain prices were threatening the population's subsistence and had forced the state treasury to allocate thirty-five million rubles to emergency famine relief.[32] This foreboding sign of the empire's fragile fiscal resources appeared as Russia felt the first spasms of a pan-European financial crisis, which by late 1898 had raised interest rates in the major stock markets of Western Europe and the United States, both of which were sources of revenue for the Russian government.[33]

In May 1898, amid these mounting economic difficulties, the tsar approved the recommendation of the Committee of Ministers that a general commission be convened to reconsider the entire institutional structure that governed the peasantry. A primary advocate of the measure was Witte, who now injected the principles of legality and civil order back into the debate over rural policy.[34] Still insisting that the expansion of industrial markets would eventually eliminate peasant poverty, he was coming to regard this problem—one that could starkly reflect the status of the general welfare—as a much greater and more immediate threat to his policies than noble protests about the decline of their manorial agriculture.[35] He thus moved to confront the peasant estate system and the Ministry of Internal Affairs that had enshrined it in law. Witte came to the fray armed not with the abstract theory that earlier proponents had utilized to substantiate these arguments, however, but with the compelling logic of national economic development—and with trepidation as to the dangers of failing to accommodate it.

A private letter of November 1898 urging Nicholas II to abandon the policy consensus of the counterreforms revealed the scope of Witte's assault. Attempting to counter the MVD and win control over the review

---

[32] Report of the Minister of Finance . . . for 1899, p. 15. The most alarming consequence of these harvest failures was a sharp jump in peasant crown tax arrears, which grew almost 25% from an already high 94 million rubles in 1896 to 116 million rubles two years later; in 1898, crown arrears equalled 115% of the total tax payment due from all village communities of European Russia. K. Iu. Kupalov, "Zemskie biudzhety i nedoimochnost' naseleniia," Narodnoe khoziastvo 4, book 6 (November–December 1903): 143–44. See also Witte, Vospominaniia, 1:430.

[33] Ananych, Rossiia i mezhdunarodnyi kapital, pp. 18–33; Report of the Minister of Finance . . . for 1899, p. 10; "Vsepoddaneishii doklad Ministra finansov o gosudarstvennoi rospisi dokhodov i raskhodov na 1901 god," Narodnoe khoziastvo 2, book 1 (January 1901): 175.

[34] Polovtsev, "Iz dnevnika A. A. Polovtseva (1895–1900)," KA, no. 46 (1931):118 (4 January 1899); generally see Macey, Government and Peasant, pp. 34–40.

[35] Report of the Minister of Finance . . . for 1899, pp. 16–22; see also "Vsepoddaneishii doklad . . . o neobkhodimosti opredelennoi programmy torgovo-promyshlennoi politiki," pp. 173–83.

that had been approved the previous spring, Witte raised the banner of economic initiative and charged that the absence of a rational civil order in the countryside explained why a universal phenomenon of contemporary civil life had had so little impact on the Russian peasantry:

> Each human being by his nature seeks something better. The development of the well-being of society and state is based upon this quality in the human being. But if this impulse is to develop in the individual, he must be placed in the proper environment. . . . A slave, recognizing that the improvement of his life and that of his dear ones is unattainable, turns to stone. . . . [It] is necessary to liberate him from the slavery of arbitrariness, to give him legality and enlighten him.[36]

In some detail, the finance minister portrayed the debilitating effects of the peasant estate system, targeting especially the land captain and suggesting, in one of his first attacks upon the peasant commune, the benefits to productivity of laws allowing the inheritance of allotment land.[37] Yet Witte had appealed to the sovereign, in an area outside his immediate ministerial jurisdiction, not simply to remove what he considered to be institutional impediments to economic progress—an effort whose success in any case appeared less likely when, in January 1899, Nicholas ordered that all discussions of reform be left to the MVD. Witte also spoke to win approval for principles of policy—merit, property, legal norms, general civil administration—that were assuming central importance in his views by 1898. Opposition to these ideas, he feared, reflected the more significant inability to undertake the serious economic and civil reforms required of a modern state order.

This intransigence was very much on his mind when he wrote the tsar: "Any matter depends on people, on the movement of their ideas and inspirations." Impugning the critique that the MVD had made to discredit and partially reverse one of the autocracy's great accomplishments, Witte tried to persuade Nicholas II that the great reforms had not created "the crisis of the 1880s." Rather, although "liberalism" in the press, the schools, "public administration," and government had led to the tragedy that initiated his father's reign, the very appearance of Alexander III had resolved that threat by returning Russia to the "true path of administration by autocratic authority." Witte's emphatic "now we must start moving" expressed his concern that the opportunity thus presented had subsequently been squandered.[38] The finance minister knew all too well the rising public criticism that was directed in the first instance at his own

---

[36] Witte, *Vospominaniia*, 1:430.
[37] Ibid., 1:430–34.
[38] Ibid., 1:430.

economic policies, but more generally against the system of state administration that they represented, and he feared that a conjuncture similar
to that of the early 1880s was appearing again at the turn of the century.
The disastrous harvest and famine had "everyone in an uproar," he complained. Gentry landowners were pressing the "question of a land crisis"
and insisting on "the valor of particular estates and even their support of
the throne." And, of course, "what a joy peasant disarray is for all the
declared and concealed enemies of autocracy. . . . Our journals, newspapers, and underground pamphlets, some with good and some with bad
intentions, relish this theme."[39] This quintessential man of the 1880s,
whose loyalty to autocracy was rivalled only by his commitment to state
power and the vision of industrial modernity that it afforded, was beginning to apprehend that both would be threatened if the bureaucratic state
failed to assert its leadership by addressing the dislocation and disaffection growing in society. As his ruminations on the peasant question suggested, Witte had reached the conclusion that the stability of autocratic
authority and power rested in the *Rechtsstaat*.[40]

These views received their most articulate expression in the winter of
1898–99, when Witte took issue with the Ministry of Internal Affairs
over—significantly—its proposed extension of zemstvo self-administration to the Western borderlands.[41] In a letter to Pobedonostsev, Witte
objected and suggested that this was an opportunity to show the merits
of effective bureaucratic administration. When properly organized, bureaucratic administration would work "better than the zemstvo" and, if
coupled with a reformed provincial administration, could show the country the government's capacity to resolve the "chaos" in provincial life. To
Pobedonostsev's refrain that all zemstvo institutions ought to be eliminated, Witte replied that the idea would simply enflame political passions.
"Generally," he said, "we do not need a struggle with the zemstvo but

[39] Ibid., 1:432–33. On the most noted instance of liberal zemstvo dissidence in late 1897
and early 1898, a series of conferences held by the Free Economic Society to discuss the
causes of repetitive crop failures, see Veselovskii, *Istoriia zemstva*, 3:507–8, and Von Laue,
Sergei Witte, pp. 168–69. On the more immediately threatening conservative nationalist
protest against foreign capital investment, see Von Laue, *Sergei Witte*, pp. 177–78; Ananych, *Rossiia i mezhdunarodnyi kapital*, pp. 20–24; Shepelev, *Tsarizm i burzhuaziia*, pp.
219–23; Witte, *Vospominaniia*, 1:411–12; and Polovtsev, "Iz dnevnika A. A. Polovtseva,"
pp. 119–20 (4 January and 13 February 1899). The latter describes the tsar being swayed
by the "beer-hall patriotism" of those arguing that "the real picture of the people's impoverished condition" was being concealed "by his ministers."

[40] On the expansion and specialization of the Ministry of Finance in the later nineteenth
century, see Zaionchkovskii, *Pravitel'stvennyi apparat*, pp. 70–71; also see Witte's description of his subordinates in the Ministry, *Vospominaniia*, 3:282–319.

[41] Ananych, Diakin, et al., *Krizis samoderzhaviia v Rossii*, pp. 96–113, and Veselovskii,
Istoriia zemstva, 3:511–15.

[rather] a firm program of action that would ultimately render it superfluous." He added:

> In my opinion, self-administration in the West defeated unitary authority chiefly because the government was unable to maintain the organization of its administration at the height of contemporary needs. Life moved ahead but the administration was not improved; in the end, everyone lost faith in it and sought salvation in self-administration. Something similar is happening here. [With the western zemstvo proposal] the MVD itself has declared that you can do nothing with bureaucracy [*biurokratiia*], with petty officials—you must give them up for lost and seek salvation in the zemstvo.[42]

Witte's economic policies and forays into rural politics already had indicated that he had not yet abandoned his belief in rational bureaucracy and law—as did his sponsorship of a most significant political essay, *Autocracy and the Zemstvo*. A comprehensive attempt to oppose the western zemstvo, the document also contained a debate of political principle—as Witte wrote, a broader "exchange of opinions concerning the political significance of [self-administered] institutions in the system of our state administration." His position from the outset was clear-cut. The zemstvo was not only "a poor means of administration" in a bureaucratic state but also a fount of popular sovereignty whose expansion would inevitably "lead to the authoritative participation [*vlastnoe uchastie*] of elected representatives of the population in legislation and supreme administration."[43]

The 1890s had witnessed sufficient conflict between central bureaucratic organs and zemstvo assemblies, Witte believed, to prove their mutual incompatibility. In 1895 his own ministry had issued new rules mandating greater zemstvo spending on rural road construction; zemstvo boards used various accounting ruses to continue funding more favored local needs, especially education. Similarly, despite two legislative acts and pressure from the Ministries of Internal Affairs and Finance, many zemstvos had not conducted property tax assessments as ordered by the government in 1893—notwithstanding "the broad and very comprehensive statistical work" for which some provinces were renowned. The most grating phenomenon was the unceasing growth of zemstvo expenditures and tax rates. Noting that the zemstvo's discretionary budget allocations had more than doubled in thirteen years, Witte termed such actions irresponsible when agricultural conditions had been "extremely unfavorable

---

[42] "Perepiska Vitte s Pobedonostsevym (1895–1905 gg.)," *KA*, no. 30 (1928): 105.

[43] Witte, *Samoderzhavie i zemstvo*, p. 4. Witte initially responded to Minister of Internal Affairs Goremykin in December 1898. Goremykin answered in February 1899, which prompted this memorandum. Ananych, Diakin, et al., *Krizis samoderzhaviia v Rossii*, pp. 106–11. See also Petr Struve's introduction to this volume, pp. v–xliv.

for landowners and peasants." He did not mention that such actions constituted a most unwelcome competition for scarce treasury revenues. Finally, the zemstvo bureaucracy was expanding: "vast chancelleries attached to zemstvo boards; specialists; statisticians; agronomists; teachers; doctors; etc." These "petty officials," who, he acknowledged, were often "fully moderate and deserving [of] total respect," had nevertheless acted "uncontrollably" and had heaped additional financial burdens upon the population.[44]

The zemstvo apparatus was an obstacle to rational state management of rural society; what alarmed Witte, however, was the fact that all attempts to incorporate it into the state hierarchy had only served to intensify opposition to bureaucratic interference among zemstvo activists. "The political tendency of the zemstvo," he wrote, "had not disappeared," but was instead reemerging even more powerfully than in the 1860s or 1880s. Citing the coronation petitions of 1894–95, Witte maintained that "as previously, the zemstvo senses the government's distrust of it" and warned that such attitudes encompassed both "leaders [*vozhaki*]" and "the vast majority of the most noble, moderate zemtsy." The "movement" evident now in the provinces was "more moderate in external form but in internal content much more significant than the strident movement of 1879–83."[45]

This was more than alarmist rhetoric. Almost half of the text was devoted to a historical examination of the zemstvo movement since the 1860s, as well as of the various legislative schemes that the government had considered as ways of regulating relations between itself and these self-administered organs. The document paid particular attention to the structural reorganization of county government advocated by the Kakhanov Commission and others in the 1880s.[46] Unlike those projects, however, Witte believed it possible to create rational *bureaucratic* administration in the provinces, which administration could then become the foundation of a "legalistic state [*pravovoe gosudarstvo*]." With a regularized administrative hierarchy and a "firm, defined framework of law," the government could, Witte wrote, "tranquilly regard manifestations of personal and public initiative, of freedoms of speech and thought, ensuring

---

[44] Ananych, Diakin, et al., *Krizis samoderzhaviia v Rossii*, pp. 146–65. See also *Ministerstvo finansov: Po voprosu o raskhode na narodnye uchilishche* (St. Petersburg, n.d.), in Witte, *Samoderzhavie i zemstvo*, pp. 1–3; "O predel'nosti zemskogo oblozheniia," in *Otchet po deloproizvodstvu Gosudarstvennogo Soveta za sessiiu 1899–1900 gg.* (St. Petersburg, 1900), pp. 680–86; Ministerstvo finansov, *Ministerstvo finansov, 1802–1902*, pt. 2, pp. 448–52; and Thomas Fallows, "The Zemstvo and the Bureaucracy," in Emmons and Vucinich, eds., *Zemstvo in Russia*, pp. 214–18.

[45] Witte, *Samoderzhavie i zemstvo*, pp. 165–69.

[46] Ibid., pp. 183–94.

only that no one, including the administration, exceeded the framework of this law and demanding from all unquestioning obedience to it."[47]

Although the Rechtsstaat had been an ideal of Russian statesmen throughout the nineteenth century, few had defended it as passionately as Witte. He refused to accept the emerging public perception that "bureaucracy [was] a too imperfect form of administration," that "it impeded public initiative [and] oppressed the people." In fact, Witte claimed, the bureaucracy represented all that was good in Russian society. As a product of the Table of Ranks, it was "to the highest degree a democratic institution, striving to form an aristocracy of labor and educated culture [*obrazovannost'*]." Bureaucratic officials were not divorced from educated society, but constituted "all its most cultured strata." They were "members of Russian society, by whose actions one can judge the average quality of society, the degree of development of public forces, public intelligence and the maturity of society. Every progressive movement in society is reflected in the bureaucracy; stagnation in the former [brings] reaction in the latter." Moreover, as products of educated society, bureaucrats shared its traditional commitment to bringing enlightenment and culture to the unassimilated peasant people. "One could not seriously think," Witte insisted, "that the administration represents among the people some kind of alien, hostile force that rains misfortunes down upon it." The bureaucracy was not "set off against either society or the people"; it was not an isolated caste. Rather, it was "one of the necessary conditions of national-state life [*obshchestvenno-gosudarstvennaia zhizn'*], serving together with others the general welfare [*obshchee blago*], the gradual social acculturation of the people."[48]

When *Autocracy and the Zemstvo* was published abroad in 1901, Petr Struve objected, in an editorial footnote, to what he considered the notorious bravado of this argument. "If the administration was not set off against society or the people," Struve asked, "then why did Mr. Witte build his entire essay on this opposition and why does he refuse to allow the participation of society in legislation and administration?"[49] Despite its polemical intent, the query was a fundamental one, as among all the constituent elements of Russian educated society the professional bureaucrat idealized by Witte was the one it found most alien. Oriented to the state's service and dependent on the authority of the autocracy, these administrators and supervisors worked in Russian society, but contrary to Witte's claims they were largely not of it—nor could they be while the autocratic regime reserved all legitimate political life to itself.

---

[47] Ibid., pp. 196–97. See also the discussion in Von Laue, *Sergei Witte*, pp. 160–62; and Weissman, *Reform in Tsarist Russia*, pp. 9–11.

[48] Witte, *Samoderzhavie i zemstvo*, pp. 204–5.

[49] Ibid.

Judging from the juxtaposition of the two alternatives posed in *Autocracy and the Zemstvo*, it would appear that Witte to a certain extent already understood this dilemma. If one believed, he noted in concluding, "that each state in its political development must come to a constitution," and that only broadly developed self-administration could "guarantee the good of the people," then the zemstvo ought to be allowed the necessary independence to achieve these goals. Witte did not personally share this point of view, but, as he said, "I understand it." At the turn of the century, however, he continued to advocate autocratic rule but knew that its stability required a comprehensive reform of bureaucratic administration to realize the ideals of the Rechtsstaat and eliminate the grounds from which constitutionalism was growing. Continuing this present drift would threaten disaster. Witte wrote in conclusion:

> Nothing so enflames the revolutionary spirit as the absence of institutional harmony and the contradiction between the laws or theoretical principles of administration and the latter's practice. . . . [Nothing] so suppresses the initiative of society, so undermines the prestige of authority as the frequent and broad application of repressive measures. These measures are dangerous and their continuation will either lead to an explosion or in fact render the population an "alienated crowd," "human dust"![50]

Few officials before the turn of the century perceived the political challenge to autocracy that was emerging from society as perceptively as Witte. It is true, however, that few possessed the perspective or the experience of the minister of finance. Witte was indeed a statesman of his time, convinced that a social order depended upon the structure of power and authority that organized it. These convictions were already implicit in the career of a railroad administrator who gave coherence to a regional transportation network, but they found their true medium in the autocratic state. His unquestionable allegiance to state power, and to the autocratic principle that assured it legitimacy, were to be explained in large measure by the opportunity that both commitments afforded this creative and megalomaniacal personality to influence the transformation of an entire national economy. Yet, over the course of the decade, Witte gradually came to recognize the paradox of his position, as the socioeconomic and civil changes that he encouraged began to strain against the structure of autocratic state power and authority that, in his view, had created them. Committed to the state that he deemed a precondition of Russian modernity, Witte recognized that the modernization of bureaucratic government thus had become essential in order to preserve its legitimacy and deflect the political opposition rising against the autocratic regime. Even

---

[50] Ibid., pp. 211–12.

before the turn of the century, Witte had arrived at a conclusion that he would propound, with growing frustration, for the next five years. The Rechtsstaat was not a theoretical ideal, but a political necessity.

THE LEGITIMACY OF THE AUTOCRATIC STATE, 1900–1904

At the turn of the century, the central government began to confront conditions that, by 1904–05, had coalesced into a national movement of political opposition to autocratic rule. Its consolidation within educated society, and the collective expressions of mass protest spawned in both urban and rural Russia, fundamentally altered the contours of old-regime society and politics. Yet this second crisis of autocracy, whose emergence in retrospect appears inevitable, in fact transpired as a stream of bewildering events and circumstances that continually redefined the perspectives and behavior of historical actors, testing established traditions even while demanding the articulation of new values to confront a novel universe. What was true for all groups of Russian society applied in particular to its highest state officials, against whom the rising tide of political opposition was directed. Their efforts to respond, to grapple simultaneously with the old and the new, proved to be a constituent element of the crisis that autocracy experienced.[51]

In the first two years of the new century, a flood of evidence inundated those who might previously have denied the depths of civil and political instability in Russia. Most pronounced were signs of severe economic dislocation. Since 1899–1900, industrial depression in both Europe and America had been spreading to Russia. The constriction of foreign investment funds, declining industrial production, and rising unemployment cut short the rapid economic expansion of the later 1890s and intensified public criticism of state financial policy.[52] In agriculture poor harvests continued to render peasant impoverishment a central issue of

[51] See esp. Martov et al., *Obshchestvennoe dvizhenie*, vols. 1–2. See also Manning, *Crisis of the Old Order*, chaps. 4–6; Haimson, "The Parties and the State," pp. 309–40; Teodor Shanin, *Russia 1905–07: Revolution As a Moment of Truth*, vol. 2 of idem, *The Roots of Otherness: Russia's Turn of Century* (Yale University Press, 1986); Ananych, Diakin et al., *Krizis samoderzhaviia v Rossii*, pt. 1, chaps. 2–6, pt. 2, chap. 1; and Walter Sablinsky, *The Road to Bloody Sunday: Father Gapon and the St. Petersburg Massacre of 1905* (Princeton University Press, 1976).

[52] On the Finance Ministry's reaction, see "Vsepoddaneishii doklad ministra finansov . . . na 1901 god," pp. 175–78; "Vsepoddaneishii doklad ministra finansov . . . na 1902 god," pp. 169–74; and "Soobshchenie ot Ministerstva finansov po povodu zatrudnenii v promyshlennosti," *Narodnoe khoziastvo* 2, book 10 (December 1901): 179–88. Also see A. A. Polovtsev, "Dnevnik A. A. Polovtseva (1901–1903)," *KA* 3 (1923): 87–99 passim (March–July 1901).

the day.[53] The crop failure of 1901, which by official estimates produced lower than average yields in forty-two provinces and regions, wrung from the Ministry of Finance a public acknowledgment that repeated shortfalls since 1897 had cost the national economy some one billion rubles in anticipated investment capital.[54] Writing to D. S. Sipiagin in July, Witte, for one, was "more than a little alarmed" that a growing economic crisis threatened his investment policies as well as his personal influence with the tsar.[55]

Mounting social disorder accentuated economic uncertainty. University student protests, which first erupted in the winter semester of 1899, resumed in early 1901 and culminated in the famous, or scandalous, political demonstration before Kazan Cathedral that marked the fortieth anniversary of emancipation. On May Day 1901 significant industrial strikes broke out in St. Petersburg for the first time since 1895–96, marking the emergence of a labor movement that would grow in scope and intensity over the next two years. Peasant disturbances, which had not occurred on a broad scale throughout the difficult 1890s, erupted suddenly in Kharkov and Poltava provinces during March–April 1902.[56] The Ministry of Internal Affairs explained that the rural disorders, admittedly arising in conditions of impoverishment, had been instigated by revolutionary propaganda.[57] This statement came less than a month after the socialist-revolutionary Balmashev assassinated minister D. S. Sipiagin. Viewing the murder as evidence of "the anarchistic-revolutionary spirit" loose in the land, the reactionary daily *Moskovskie vedomosti* claimed in May that the Kharkov-Poltava riots revealed "the savagery and barbarity" concealed in the depths of the peasant population.[58] A more skeptical *Novoe vremia*, acknowledging the influence of propaganda, obliquely

[53] M. S. Siminova, "Problema 'oskudeniia' tsentra i ee rol' v formirovanii agrarnoi politiki samoderzhaviia v 90-kh godakh–nachale XX v.," in Akademiia nauk SSSR, Institut istorii, *Problemy sotsial'no-ekonomicheskoi istorii Rossii* (Moscow, 1971), pp. 236–63 and A. D. Polenov, ed., *Issledovanie ekonomicheskogo polozheniia Tsentral'no-Chernozemnykh gubernii: Trudy osobogo soveshchaniia 1899–1901 g.* (Moscow, 1901).

[54] "Pravitel'stvennye rasporiazheniia," *Novoe vremia*, 20 August 1901, p. 4; "Ot zemskogo otdela MVD," *Narodnoe khoziastvo* 2, book 7 (September 1901): 171–77; and "Vsepoddaneishii doklad ministra finansov . . . na 1902 god," pp. 169–70.

[55] "Pis'ma S. Iu. Vitte k D. S. Sipiaginu (1900–1901)," *KA* 18 (1926): 45–46 (12 July 1901). One year later, Witte was forced to admit before the State Council that the taxpaying capacity of the peasant population had been exhausted. *Ministr finansov i Gosudarstvennyi Sovet o finansovom polozhenii Rossii: Zhurnal Obshchago Sobraniia Gosudarstvennogo Soveta 30 dek. 1902 g.* (Stuttgart, 1903).

[56] Ananych, Diakin, et al., *Krizis samoderzhaviia v Rossii*, pp. 121–22.

[57] *Novoe vremia*, 29 April 1902, p. 2. See also Gurko, *Features and Figures*, pp. 234–36, and Witte, *Vospominaniia*, 1:169.

[58] "Novoe prestuplenie," *Moskovskie vedomosti*, 2 April 1902, p. 1; and "Plody revoliutsionnoi idei," *Moskovskie vedomosti*, 30 April 1902, p. 1.

blamed the government for the disturbances when it noted that the peasantry was still "segregated from the life of the rest of society, completely separated from those processes of intellectual and civil evolution that create a cultured life."[59]

By the first half of 1902, then, economic and social instability was slowly acquiring political undertones in the eyes of both government and educated society. Indeed, organized political opposition to autocratic government was emerging at this time as a critical focus of contemporary life. This was true not only of Marxist Social-Democrats and the heirs of radical populism, the Socialist-Revolutionaries, both of which existed as underground parties by 1901–02 and both of which witnessed the consolidation of potential worker and peasant constituencies that gave credibility to their contrasting visions of national revolution. It also applied to liberal constitutionalists, who in May 1902 organized abroad the journal *Liberation* (*Osvobozhdenie*). Its founders, urban professionals and zemstvo liberals who in 1905 would eventually establish the Constitutional Democratic Party (shortened to the "Kadets"), sought to mobilize a broad national coalition of political opposition to autocratic rule. Their plans, in the first instance, targeted the zemstvo, where Russian liberalism had traditionally been rooted and where, in 1901–02, dissident sentiments were becoming much more noticeable.[60]

During the regular zemstvo session of autumn 1901, which met under the twin shocks of harvest failure and the recently published *Autocracy and the Zemstvo*, many provincial and district assemblies joined a campaign to advocate the creation of a small zemstvo unit—new zemstvo institutions in territories closer to the local populace than were the existing county and provincial organs. Raised the previous February by a congress of zemstvo agronomists in Moscow, the proposal had been crafted in political terms that contrasted the potential benefits of an all-estate zemstvo institution to the present backwardness assured by a segregated estate administration and the officialdom ruling it. Although stricken from agendas in at least seven provinces on account of the question's "general state significance," the proposal was nevertheless raised in twenty-one provinces, supported officially by eight provincial assemblies, and opposed only by two.[61] According to *Novoe vremia*, these discussions had

[59] "Pravitel'stvennoe soobshchenie o krest'ianskikh bezporiadkakh," *Novoe vremia*, 30 April 1902, p. 2.

[60] Terence Emmons, *The Formation of Political Parties and the First National Elections in Russia* (Harvard University Press, 1983), pp. 23–30, and idem, "The Beseda Circle, 1899–1905," *Slavic Review* 32, no. 3 (September 1973), pp. 476–79. See also K. F. Shatsillo, "Taktika i organizatsiia zemskogo liberalizma," *Istoricheskie zapiski* 101 (1978): 250–57.

[61] "Agronomicheskii s"ezd v Moskve," *Narodnoe khoziastvo* 3, book 5 (March 1901):

been unusually "interesting" because they dwelt less on "local welfare and needs" and more on "the interests of the zemstvo as a public organization."[62]

Compared to the radical and liberal political opposition that was coalescing in Russian society, this surge of zemstvo concern for local rural society at best represented muted involvement in national affairs. From the perspective of the government, however, the revitalization of rank-and-file zemstvo dissidence, at a time of socioeconomic instability, was a familiar yet unwelcome signal. Revealingly enough, the government roused itself to undertake the long-anticipated and -stalemated discussion of peasant reform in January 1902, months before the outbreak of rural unrest in the south and the founding of *Liberation*, but in the aftermath of the 1901 zemstvo season. The official most responsible for this shift in government policy was Witte.

Since August, the finance minister had been prodding the tsar to sponsor reform, emphasizing Witte's own opposition to communal land tenure.[63] In late January 1902 Witte partially achieved this objective when Nicholas II appointed him chair of a new Special Conference on the Needs of Agriculture. This interministerial body was charged to investigate agriculture and, after vigorous lobbying by Witte, was also granted the right to make recommendations concerning "general state" questions of law and administration. Yet, some eight days before this announcement, the tsar had also reactivated peasant reform discussions in the MVD, in effect sanctioning the efforts of Sipiagin to guarantee his ministry's jurisdictional control over any alteration of statute law.[64] That March, Witte related to A. A. Polovtsev his discontent at the prospect that the rival ministry would yet again frustrate serious efforts to "organize life and property" by defending its outmoded conceptions of peasant society:

> Isn't it necessary to start from the idea that they are people and ought to be legally recognized as such [*pravosposobnyi*], so that their labor, based on the

---

139–40; "Zemstvo o mel'kikh organakh samoupravleniia," *Narodnoe khoziastvo* 3, book 5 (May–June 1902): 125–43; and S. I. Shidlovskii, *Zemstvo*, pp. 69–74, vol. 23 of *Vysochaishe uchrezhdennoe Osoboe Soveshchanie o nuzhdakh sel'sko-khoziastvennoi promyshlennosti. Svod trudov mestnykh komitetov*. See also P. D. Dolgorukov and D. I. Shakhovskoi, eds., *Melkaia zemskaia edinitsa: Sbornik statei* (St. Petersburg, 1902).

[62] "Melkaia zemskaia edinitsa v zemskikh sobraniiakh," *Novoe vremia*, 18 December 1901, p. 3; see also the debate in "Dlia chego nuzhny melkie zemskie edinitsy," *Moskovskie vedomosti*, 24 October 1901, p. 1; and "Dlia chego nam nuzhna melkaia zemskaia edinitsa," *Novoe vremia*, 9 February 1902, pp. 2–3.

[63] Polovtsev, "Dnevnik A. A. Polovtseva (1901–1903)," pp. 103 (19 August 1901) and 105 (29 December 1901).

[64] Macey, *Government and Peasant*, pp. 43–70; "Dnevnik Polovtseva (1901–1903)," pp. 114–16 (26, 29 January 1902); Witte, *Vospominaniia*, 1:436–37; and *Novoe vremia*, 25 January 1902, p. 2, and 31 January 1902, p. 2.

firm right of property, could develop and be solidified as the individualism of each of them grew, or should the herd principle [*stadnoe nachalo*] and powerful tutelage [*opeka*] be preserved . . . ? [Sipiagin] has convinced the sovereign of the need to preserve the commune and the herd principle inviolate.[65]

Still confronting the intractability of an old institutional nemesis, and with the economy and his own personal prestige in decline, Witte began seeking political support, within moderate circles of provincial society, for policies he considered essential.[66] In early February the Special Conference resolved to convene provincial and county committees throughout European Russia and to utilize their local expertise in preparing rural reforms.[67] Eventually involving some twelve thousand officials, landowners, zemstvo delegates, and peasants in their work, the local committees represented a compromise between Witte, who had wanted to consult zemstvo assemblies directly, and Sipiagin, who feared such tactics might provoke political debate that would extend beyond local agricultural problems.[68] For the author of *Autocracy and the Zemstvo*, his sponsorship of the largest public debate of rural issues since emancipation was an abrupt reversal of earlier convictions. It reflected Witte's growing trepidation about the stalemate in state domestic policy—and his willingness to break the logjam by reaching outside the ministries to public opinion.

There were reasonable grounds to pursue such a strategy, as the first unofficial zemstvo congress of May 1902 indicated.[69] The gathering drew

[65] Polovtsev, "Dnevnik Polovtseva (1901–1903)," p. 126 (12 March 1902). Also Gurko, *Features and Figures*, p. 131.

[66] See especially the comments of MVD officials: Gurko, *Features and Figures*, pp. 205–6, and "Otryvki iz vospominaniia D. N. Liubimova, 1902–1904," *Istoricheskii arkhiv* 6 (1962): 77–81.

[67] "Vysochaishe uchrezhdennoe osoboe soveshchanie o nuzhdakh sel'sko-khoziastvennoi promyshlennosti: Zasedaniia 2, 9, 26 fev. 1902 g.," *Narodnoe khoziastvo* 3, book 5 (May–June 1902): 174–75. The Special Conference announced that consultation with zemstvo assemblies would be too time-consuming and would preclude testimony from local officials, the corporative nobility, and other experts. Provincial and county marshals of the nobility, along with all members of the provincial zemstvo executive board, were to be members of the provincial committees; the county marshal and zemstvo board were included in the county committee. For more information on the committees' agenda, which excluded discussion of peasant and zemstvo legislation as well as that of state tariff policy, see "Vysochaishe uchrezhdennoe osoboe soveshchanie: Zasedaniia 23, 24 marta 1902 g.," *Narodnoe khoziastvo* 3, book 6 (July–August 1902): 158–60 and Polovtsev, "Dnevnik A. A. Polovtseva (1901–1903)," pp. 126, 128 (14 and 21 March 1902). The committees were allowed to discuss any question "from whose resolution one might . . . expect an improvement of agricultural industry," a clause intended by Witte to encourage criticism of MVD peasant policy.

[68] Fallows, "Forging the Zemstvo Movement," pp. 670–76.

[69] Witte's personal contacts with national zemstvo leaders, limited to moderates such as Orel provincial marshal A. A. Stakhovich, D. N. Shipov, and V. D. Kuzmin-Karavaev, fostered the conviction that compromise on these grounds was possible. Witte, *Vospominaniia*, vol. 2, esp. pp. 55, 94, 133, 339, and 441.

more than sixty zemstvo activists from twenty-five provinces to formulate a program governing zemstvo participation in the local committees. Although convened because the government had refused to consult zemstvo assemblies directly, the congress proved disillusioning to zemstvo-constitutionalists, who had urged it to boycott the local committees altogether.[70] It was less so for Witte, who saw the congress repudiate the system of estate segregation upheld by the Ministry of Internal Affairs.[71] On the other hand, this denunciation of the rural status quo was directed not only against the MVD, but also, more generally, against the system of bureaucratic administration that reserved all power for local officialdom and sustained a legal system considered ruinous to the peasant majority. A resolution charging that state economic policy had ignored "the essential requirements of the local population" by restricting treasury expenditures on agriculture and overtaxing the peasantry heaped criticism upon Witte's Ministry of Finance as well. And when the congress insisted that only "broad freedom of public discussion" could fully illuminate the country's economic plight—a demand that stopped well short of constitutional aspirations—it did assert the benefits of zemstvo leadership against the decay caused by the bureaucratic state.[72]

Thus, in his efforts to cultivate moderate provincial opinion, Witte was treading a very thin line between public support for state reform and political opposition to statist hegemony. That line had become thinner even before the zemstvo congress, however, when his arch-rival, V. K. Pleve, was appointed in early April to replace the assassinated Sipiagin as minister of internal affairs. "Everybody was aware," the MVD official Gurko recalled, "that Pleve and Witte advocated different policies and that there was deep animosity between them." The "bureaucratic world," he noted, anticipated a "clash between these two powerful and clever men and the pleasure of watching the conflict."[73] The same certainly could not have been said of Witte, who deemed the appointment a personal affront and a potential disaster. Indeed, Witte almost immediately began to voice his alarm that this person, whom he later would call "an intelligent, cultured, and unscrupulous policeman," would only exacerbate the political dissidence arising against the state.[74] A week after Pleve's elevation, Witte was said to have told the tsar: "You are deceiving yourself if you think that all our present problems can be rooted out with strong police measures. . . . The government has strayed from the legal path and is giving the

[70] Veselovskii, *Istoriia zemstva*, 3:557–58; and *Russkie vedomosti*, 1 January 1903, pp. 6–7.

[71] Veselovskii, *Istoriia zemstva*, 3:560–61.

[72] Ibid.; and Fallows, "Forging the Zemstvo Movement," pp. 684–704.

[73] Gurko, *Features and Figures*, p. 100.

[74] Witte, *Vospominaniia*, 1:177, and, generally, 169–82.

population an example of illegality. Everywhere all we have is the arbitrariness of petty officials [*chinovniki*], [and] the population answers with violent actions."[75]

Witte's views were undergoing a metamorphosis. The more precarious his own position became, the more he doubted the capacity of the government to effect reform and the more he feared that the scenario he had sketched in *Autocracy and the Zemstvo* was coming to its fruition. Indeed, as Pleve's MVD badgered outspoken local committees during the summer and fall,[76] Witte's personal frustration and concern grew more and more pronounced. The issue came to a head in October 1902, when the two men attended a private dinner party in Yalta. An MVD subaltern, D. N. Liubimov, recorded a fascinating confrontation.

The conversation had turned to the local committees and Pleve's suspicion that some of them were fronts for dangerous political radicalism. But the administrative hectoring undertaken by the MVD, Witte insisted, was entirely inappropriate: "It is impossible to think that the movement now being observed in society was created by the agricultural committees." Repeating a view that he had held since the late 1890s, he told Pleve that "the drive to crown the edifice, the desire for freedoms, for self-administration, and for society's participation in legislation and administration" were of long duration and were rooted in the great reforms of the 1860s. Exasperated, he warned that it was dangerous to ignore these sentiments. The government "not only ought to meet the movement halfway, but ought, to the degree possible, stand at its head, coopting it [*ovladev im*]. . . . At present one must consider public opinion; the government must rely on the educated classes. Otherwise on whom can it rely?—on the peasant populace [*narod*]? But this is only a phrase . . . [of those who] do not want to reckon with life, with a situation in flux."[77]

Pleve replied that he well understood the "roots" of the zemstvo movement, but it was quite evident that he took his frame of reference from the early 1880s, when as director of the MVD's Department of Police he had overseen the campaign to restore order in the aftermath of Alexander II's death. The committees, he maintained, were arenas for "unrest," where "the so-called educated classes, public elements, intelligentsia" found another opportunity to propagate "all their theories and utopias." Ridiculing Witte's call that the government stand at the head of the movement, Pleve said: "At present the campaign of public elements against

[75] Polovtsev, "Dnevnik A. A. Polovtseva (1901–1903)," pp. 135–36 (12 April 1902); Also pp. 138–39 (18 April 1902), 158 (1 September 1902), and 164 (30 December 1902).

[76] Gurko, *Features and Figures*, pp. 234–42; "Otryvki iz vospominaniia D. N. Liubimova, 1902–1904," pp. 78–81; Veselovskii, *Istoriia zemstva*, 3:545–51 and 557–60; and *Russkie vedomosti*, 1 January 1903, p. 30.

[77] Liubimov, "Otryvki iz vospominanii," pp. 81–82.

bureaucracy is the slogan of a struggle that conceals another goal: the destruction of autocracy. *Here, in essence, is the entire concept of the present movement* [emphasis added]. How can a Minister of Internal Affairs of an autocratic sovereign not struggle with it?" Indeed, the alienation of public opinion concerned him little as long as permitting it to agitate disorder in the mass population loomed as a much more foreboding threat. "The prestige of tsarist authority is still strong in the people, and the sovereign has a loyal army," Pleve insisted, but the "so-called educated classes" were threatening to undermine these bastions with an "artificial, thoughtlessly made revolution." Pleve had not spent almost a quarter-century wielding ministerial power to think now that reform was unnecessary. He willingly acknowledged the need to undertake legislative initiatives, but only those that originated at the impartial behest of the state—not the self-interested demands of radicals and public factions. Only "the tsarist government possessed the experience, traditions, and customs to administer" a country as diverse as Russia, said Pleve. "All our most useful, most liberal reforms," he insisted, "were realized exclusively by government authority." Witte himself was "a clear example of what a talented and energetic Russian minister could do for his motherland without a constitution." Pleve was "convinced that only our historically evolved autocracy can shoulder the task of renewing Russia."[78]

In what Pleve had said, Witte concluded, was "much with which one could not but agree." Witte also remained committed to the state and autocratic authority, but, having taken the measure of the political challenge arising against bureaucracy, he now feared much more than he had in 1899 the threat posed to the regime's authority. Four years before he had anticipated this moment and had begun to advocate civil reform as a way of reasserting the authority of government. By 1902, with the time of accounting no longer pending but at hand, he proffered a political stratagem that few officials had dared to consider since the downfall of Loris-Melikov:

> I never recommended as a way out of the situation that the Minister of Internal Affairs stand at the head of a movement openly opposed to the government. I said that the government must coopt the movement, this is entirely different. . . . The majority of revolutions proceed from the fact that a government does not satisfy new requirements in time. The reminder from society about the arrival of this time is justified. Not to take account of this is impossible. But, above all, the government needs society's sympathy, which at this time it does not have. One cannot deny this. Indeed, on what could such sympathy focus— only repressive measures are undertaken. One must obtain this sympathy. Otherwise, on whom can the Minister of Internal Affairs rely under these condi-

[78] Ibid., pp. 82–83.

tions? Not really only on the officials of the Ministry or the Corps of Gendarmes?[79]

Witte's query was rhetorical, as he well knew that his own influence in government was waning and that, in the realm of domestic policy, that of the powerful minister of internal affairs was on the rise.[80] Yet he was quite correct to suggest that this experienced statesman, whose career was rooted in the reign of Alexander III, intended to manifest and defend the authority of the autocracy by manipulating the administrative system and police powers of the state.

Contrary to much received opinion, Pleve was not the reactionary chameleon that he is often portrayed to have been.[81] When he became minister in April 1902 even a liberal newspaper like *Russkie vedomosti* recognized him as "one of Russia's most eminent contemporary statesmen," whose reputation as "an experienced, educated jurist" and "a specialist in various branches of domestic administration" was widely recognized.[82] Well-educated indeed, Pleve had graduated from the juridical faculty of Moscow University in 1867, where he had supplemented his legal training with lectures on the natural sciences and with Solov'ev's course on Russian history. At the age of twenty-one he began his career as an investigator in the Moscow circuit court.[83] Promoted through the provincial judicial system, by 1881 he had become state prosecutor of the St. Petersburg appeals court, a post from which Loris-Melikov appointed him director of the newly formed Department of State Police. He remained in the Ministry of Internal Affairs for the next fourteen years as an assistant minister. First under Tolstoi, many of whose ideas became his "fundamental viewpoints," and then under I. N. Durnovo, who taught him "the art [*iskusstvo*] of administering people," Pleve oversaw much of the legislative work produced by the ministry. He was particularly active in rural reform, including the land captain statute and the law on inalienability of allotment land.[84] From 1894 until his appointment to the MVD, he was imperial state secretary of the State Council, where he controlled the

[79] Ibid., p. 83.

[80] See in particular David McDonald, "Autocracy, Bureaucracy, and Change in the Formation of Russian Foreign Policy (1895–1914)" (Ph.D. diss., Columbia University, 1988), chap. 2.

[81] The best treatments of Pleve are Weissman, *Reform in Tsarist Russia*, chaps. 2–3, and Edward H. Judge, *Plehve: Repression and Reform in Imperial Russia, 1902–1904* (Syracuse, 1983).

[82] *Russkie vedomosti*, 6 April 1902, p. 1; also *Novoe vremia*, 6 April 1902, p. 2, and *Moskovskie vedomosti*, 6 April 1902, pp. 1–2.

[83] D. N. Liubimov, *Pamiati V. K. Pleve* (St. Petersburg, 1904), pp. 5–8.

[84] Liubimov, *Pamiati*, pp. 15–16 and 21. Pleve paid tribute to Tolstoi and Durnovo in a speech upon his departure from the ministry in 1894.

appointment of talented young officials to the prestigious Imperial Chancellery and participated in almost all Council deliberations on "pressing political matters." In addition, from 1899 on he served as minister-state-secretary of Finland.[85]

A policeman, an undeviating adherent of autocratic authority, and a skilled administrator: it is perhaps more accurate to say that Pleve, having acquired his views during and after the first crisis of autocracy, was the living incarnation of its second one. The views of the police official who after 1902 undertook to suppress even moderate zemstvo political opposition, and thereby crippled his relations with most political groups in educated society, had already found expression in a report that he had written as director of the Department of State Police in 1882. In the aftermath of Alexander II's assassination, Pleve had been convinced that all public dissidence reflected the "distinct world of ideas and concepts" that constituted the revolutionary ethos of the intelligentsia. Communicated through the press and literature, its ideologies of communism, materialism, and atheism infected society and especially youth, so that the state confronted not an enemy of "flesh and blood," but one of ideals and spirit. In the short term, censorship and repression could manage the disease; to cure it completely, however, required the antidote of "a similar spiritual force," obtainable only through the "religious-moral reeducation" of the intelligentsia and strict "discipline in all areas of public life subject to the control of the state."[86]

For Pleve, who in 1899 had written of the need to accentuate "the spiritual side of autocracy" and "its service ... to the good of the people," that force was to be found in the legitimate political authority of autocracy.[87] Police power might guarantee the state public order, but political legitimacy derived only from the autocratic persona, which substantiated the state's claims to administer impartial justice and commonweal. As ardent an adherent of autocratic prerogative as his enemy Witte, Pleve after 1902 not only refused to compromise it, but also regarded autocratic authority as a weapon that could be employed in the struggle against revolution and disorder.

One prominent example of such efforts was the elaborate ceremonial staged when Nicholas II attended military maneuvers near Kursk in late August 1902. Accompanied by Pleve and several other ministers, the tsar attended a round of crowded public appearances and receptions where he displayed his solicitude for the concerns of the local population. The trappings of corporate and estate life were on full display at a formal

[85] Zaionchkovskii, *Rossiiskoe samoderzhavie*, pp. 190–201 and 385–95; Liubimov, *Pamiati*, pp. 13–21; and *Russkie vedomosti*, 6 April 1902, p. 1.

[86] Liubimov, *Pamiati*, pp. 11–12.

[87] Ibid., p. 28.

welcoming ceremony of 29 August. At the Kursk railroad terminal, the sovereign greeted the assembled deputations of local officials, the clerical hierarchy, the nobility, the zemstvos and towns, peasant township elders, members of the provincial merchantry, townsmen and craft guilds, decorated army veterans, even a delegation from the Kursk Jewish population.[88] In a meeting with the Kursk nobility, Nicholas expressed his heartfelt thanks for "true, unselfish service to the throne," praised the nobility's "leadership of peasant administration" since the creation of the land captains, and promised reforms of both nobiliary and peasant agriculture. In sharp contrast to this, however, the tsar's encounters with the Kursk zemstvo were at best correct.[89] Addressing a deputation led by the liberal provincial executive board chair N. V. Raevskii, the sovereign allowed that the zemstvo was summoned by law to supervise local "economic needs" and promised his "sincere goodwill" as long as these concerns remained the sole focus of its work.[90]

Particular emphasis was placed on encounters with the peasantry.[91] A deputation of eighty-seven township elders greeted Nicholas with bread and salt upon his arrival in Kursk, while a separate delegation of peasant artisanal workers, whose mastery of religious iconography was anything but an industrial occupation, also paid homage to the sovereign.[92] His most publicized encounter with "the people" occurred at an audience attended by peasant village and township officials gathered from provinces bordering the area of the previous spring's rural disorders. With the minister of internal affairs at his elbow, the tsar threatened retribution for any recurrence of the unrest and recalled the memory of his father to impress upon the assemblage that the local nobility represented his authority. He added assurances of his own continuing personal attention to

[88] *Moskovskie vedomosti*, 31 August 1902, p. 2.

[89] *Moskovskie vedomosti*, 4 September 1902, p. 2, listed guests attending an imperial banquet on 2 September: the tsar, his suite, ministers and provincial officials, military officers, clergy, governors from the region, provincial and county marshals of nobility, town officials of Kursk, and even the Kursk county sheriff (*ispravnik*). No representative of the zemstvo attended in an official capacity.

[90] *Moskovskie vedomosti*, 31 August 1902, p. 2; "Slovo russkogo imperatora o russkom dvorianstve i zemstve," *Moskovskie vedomosti*, 1 September 1902, pp. 1–2; "O pomestnom elemente v Rossii," *Novoe vremia*, 4 September 1902, p. 2, and 6 September 1902, p. 3. See also *Russkie vedomosti*, 8 September 1902, p. 2, which editorialized that day about the importance of the local committees of the Special Conference and the need to heed "public opinion" and assure the "cooperation of society" when developing rural legislation.

[91] See Gurko, *Features and Figures*, pp. 228–29. Also Solov'ev, *Samoderzhavie i dvorianstvo v 1902–1907 gg.* (Leningrad, 1981), pp. 74–76, who argues that Pleve sought to utilize court religious ritual (Nicholas II's pilgrimage to the tomb of St. Serafim in May 1903) as a means to tap "the religiosity of the people and its feeling of loyalty to the motherland."

[92] *Moskovskie vedomosti*, 31 August 1902, p. 2.

the peasantry's well-being and ordered the officials to take his words back to their villages:

> I remind you of the words spoken [by Alexander III] . . . "Obey your marshals of the nobility and do not believe false rumors. Remember that you become prosperous not by seizing someone else's property but by honest toil, by thrift and a life lived according to the Lord's commandments." Pass on to your fellow villagers everything, exactly as I have told it to you, and also tell them that I will not give up my concern for their true needs.[93]

It was a paradox of the early twentieth-century autocratic state that a man such as Pleve, who so rigidly upheld the traditions of police power and superordinate authority, could at the same time regard himself, and be regarded by others, as an individual whose administrative talents and experience guaranteed reform. Yet in a December 1902 speech commemorating the centenary of the Ministry of Internal Affairs, Pleve first raised such public expectations by announcing that general economic development and "changes in public life" necessitated "improving the means of administration."[94] Seven weeks later these allusions to reform became more concrete when the government issued the Sovereign Manifesto of 26 February 1903. A state proclamation that for the first time recognized "the troubles" but did so solely by emphasizing the government's concern to create "a stable structure of local life," the manifesto emphasized three issues of longstanding concern to both government and society. It promised to continue its review of the peasant statute in order to assure both "the inviolability of the communal structure" and the right of individuals to leave it. The manifesto also declared the government's intentions to reorganize provincial and county administration. "Local people," supervised by "strong and rational" authority, were to receive a more prominent role in resolving "the needs of rural life." And, responding to the demands for a small zemstvo unit, the Manifesto of 26 February offered to bring "public administration" closer to the local populace by establishing, "where possible," parish guardianship councils (*prikhodskoe popechitel'stvo*) attached to local Orthodox churches.[95]

Even under the strict censorship of that time, the liberal daily *Russkie*

---

[93] *Moskovskie vedomosti*, 3 September 1902, p. 2; also "Gosudareva zabota o krest'ianstve," *Moskovskie vedomosti*, 4 September 1902, p. 1, and "Rech' Gosudaria k starshinam i sel'skim starostam," *Novoe vremia*, 3 September 1902, p. 2. See also Gurko, *Features and Figures*, pp. 228–29.

[94] "Prazdnovanie stoletiia ministerstv," *Novoe vremia*, 30 December 1902, pp. 2–3; also "Biurokratiia i tvorcheskaia sila strany," *Sanktpeterburgskie vedomosti*, 1 January 1903, p. 1; "Preobrazovaniia vo vnutrennem upravlenii," *Moskovskie vedomosti*, 3 January 1903, pp. 1–2; and *Russkie vedomosti*, 1 January 1903, p. 2.

[95] *Novoe vremia*, 27 February 1903, p. 1; also Gurko, *Features and Figures*, pp. 217–21.

vedomosti was unable to conceal its perplexity at this "act of great state significance." The manifesto left the development of general reform proposals to the central ministries and thus, the editorial stated, ignored "the knowledge and experience possessed by society and [its] representatives [*predstaviteli*]." In short, it did not address the legitimate national political aspirations of educated society that were causing the unrest.[96] Pleve, of course, had never intended to address these concerns, given the revolutionary threat he believed these sentiments posed to autocracy. Moreover, he considered such political concessions irrelevant to the resolution of economic and social dysfunction, the causes of which resided in the irrationality of the autocracy's administrative system.

In a letter he wrote to A. A. Kireev in August Pleve remarked that the reasons for the present unrest were "more complex than the domination in our administration of the bureaucratic over the public structure." Citing the "civil development [*grazhdanskoe razvitie*] of the last half-century," Pleve maintained that the state's inability to adapt its institutions to the "growth of public consciousness [*obshchestvennoe soznanie*]" and to rapid "social evolution [*sotsial'naia evolutsiia*]" had inevitably exacerbated socioeconomic dislocation. As a result, "a certain part of educated society" had lost faith in bureaucracy and had begun "to see a panacea for all social evils" in the idea of "political freedom." If, however, the government moved to institutionalize "the gradually and organically established norms of civil community [*grazhdanskoe obshchezhitie*]" that strengthened social order, dissidence would disappear as all "the best people, . . . summoned to [public] affairs by the obligation of being both subjects and citizens," rallied behind the authority of "our historic autocracy." Pleve remained convinced that autocratic authority and a perfected bureaucratic machine, whose lumbering apparatus he had helped to construct in the 1880s, was Russia's salvation: "Society will only follow an authority [*avtoritet*] that rests on strength, knowledge, and labor. The art of administration [*iskusstvo upravleniia*] consists in the ability to obtain this authority."[97] Poignant and insightful, Kireev's reply recognized the antecedents of Pleve's argument and the futility of applying failed formulas to resolve the autocracy's present crisis:

There is nobody for you to rely upon, you are alone. . . . Your predecessors developed the same enlightened-bureaucratic (more truly absolutist) idea with the same courage (Katkov, D. Tolstoi) . . . and they also did not rely on anybody, even went against the current. . . . *But that was long ago*! What was possible *then* is (I think) impossible now. The authority of the government was

[96] *Russkie vedomosti*, 28 February 1903, p. 1.
[97] "Pis'mo V. K. Pleve k A. A. Kireevu (31 avgust 1903)," *KA* 18 (1926): 201–3.

incomparably stronger, and the strength of the opposition was much weaker, more stupid, less capable.[98]

Indeed, because Pleve resurrected the administrative solutions of the 1880s to treat the much different social and political dilemmas of the early twentieth century, his reforms were fraught with contradictions. In peasant affairs, he was a man torn between two sets of dogma and consequently lacked "a stable, definite ideology concerning this basic question of public life." So spoke V. I. Gurko, who supervised much of the MVD's work on this problem. On the one hand, Pleve was attracted to Gurko's contention that only economic competition, individualism, and proprietorial agriculture could serve as a long-term solution to the agrarian problem.[99] And by late 1903 the MVD's Editing Commissions, under Gurko's de facto leadership, had in fact compiled a multivolume program of peasant land and administrative reform. Although the work defended the principles of estate segregation and communal inviolability, Gurko had drafted it in such a way as to make inescapable the conclusion that these archaic legal structures were impeding the needed economic transition from unproductive peasant communal agriculture to more advanced forms of land use and technology.[100] On the other hand, Gurko ventured, the compromised nature of MVD plans derived from Pleve's refusal to eliminate a legal structure that he had helped to construct in the 1880s and that, twenty years later, he still considered to be a guarantee against social disorder. Gurko noted that the Kharkov-Poltava disorders of 1902 had reinforced Pleve's conviction that the mass peasant population remained susceptible to revolutionary agitation. Pleve, Gurko opined, thought that no peasant "possessed the germs of moral and cultural progress" and "as a social factor all peasants—rich and poor, landowners and members of communes—were alike." To dismantle the institutional and economic barriers of the estate system at a time of unrest was impossible.[101]

[98] Solov'ev, *Samoderzhavie . . . v 1902–1907 gg.*, p. 83.

[99] Gurko, *Features and Figures*, pp. 171–72.

[100] MVD, *Trudy redaktsionnoi komissii po peresmotru zakonopolozheniia o krest'ianakh*: vol. 1 (*Svod vyrabotannykh komissiei zakonoproektov*); vol. 2 (*Proekt polozheniia o krest'ianskom obshchestvennom upravlenii s ob"iasneniiami*); and vol. 5 (*Proekt polozheniia o nadel'nykh zemliakh s ob"iasneniiami*). (St. Petersburg, 1903). This interpretation follows Macey, *Government and Peasant*, chap. 3.

[101] Gurko, *Features and Figures*, pp. 171–72. Also Polovtsev, "Dnevnik A. A. Polovtseva (1901–1903)," p. 144 (1 May 1902), which quotes Pleve's comments one month after the unrest: "Collectivism and its manifestation—communal tenure—are rubbish, leading only to disarray. . . . [But] I cannot allow the sudden extension of general civil rights in their entirety to the peasants; the transference to such a structure should be gradual and should initially be accompanied uninterruptedly [by bureaucratic supervision]. I also consider necessary the preservation of a certain portion of the allotments in the peasants' inalienable

Pleve's attitude toward the zemstvo, and moderate public opinion generally, was equally contradictory. He recognized the central place that the zemstvo occupied in the provincial administrative structure—both its legal obligations to the local economy and the sensibilities of the noble landowners who filled its ranks. Possessing established contacts with conservative elements of the landowning nobility that dated back to the counterreforms, Pleve continued an MVD policy of appointing prominent local nobles and zemtsy to provincial administrative posts. In 1902–03 he held consultations with zemtsy and marshals of the nobility concerning new veterinary, fire-insurance, food-supply, and road-construction zemstvo statutes.[102] Finally, the minister initiated work on several MVD reforms affecting local self-administration: a lowered property franchise for zemstvo elections; a provincial council to advise the governor that included public representatives; and a Council on Local Economy within the MVD, approved in early 1904 but never implemented, to institutionalize consultation between appointed zemtsy and officials concerning issues of local import.[103]

Yet, as attempts to incorporate the zemstvo into state administration, they failed to address—indeed, rather exacerbated—the increasingly pronounced political opposition prevailing in these institutions. As early as the summer of 1902, Pleve told D. N. Shipov that he recognized the need to bridge "the gulf that [divided] . . . the government and the public." He said that "well-informed men who [were] well acquainted with local conditions and needs"—in the parlance of the 1880s, enlightened experts—could consider local issues under terms set by the government. This was "all that the government now need[ed]."[104] Pleve paid little attention to issues that were galvanizing even moderate zemstvo opinion.[105] He re-

---

possession (Bauerland) and I do not allow for the possibility that all the land might become latifundia and the peasant population exclusively hired workers."

[102] Veselovskii, *Istoriia zemstva*, 3:575–77 and 587. Among prominent local activists promoted by Pleve were: Grodno governor P. A. Stolypin (provincial marshal), the Tambov vice-governor Prince S. D. Urusov (county marshal), St. Petersburg governor A. D. Zinov'ev (provincial marshal), and the director of the MVD's Main Administration for Affairs of Local Economy S. N. Gerbel (provincial zemstvo executive board chair).

[103] On initiation of statistical work in preparation for zemstvo electoral reform, "Tsirkuliarnoe otnoshenie GUMKh, MVD" (10 December 1902), in TsGIA f. 1288, op. 2, ed. khr. 7, chast' 2, ll. 9–10. On provincial reform, "Usilenie gubernatorskoi vlasti: Proekt von-Pleve," *Vsemirnyi vestnik* 6 (June 1907): especially pp. 37–43. On the Council of Local Economy, *Narodnoe khoziastvo* 4, book 6 (November–December 1903): 169–76. In general, see Weissman, *Reform in Tsarist Russia*, pp. 40–92, and Gurko, *Features and Figures*, pp. 201–49.

[104] D. N. Shipov, *Vospominaniia i dumy o perezhitom* (Moscow, 1918), pp. 174–78.

[105] "Zapiska predstavitelei zemskikh uchrezhdeniiakh v komissiiu o tsentre," *Narodnoe khoziastvo* 4, book 6 (November–December 1903): pp. 201–20. Eighteen zemstvo delegates, five of whom were members of the Union of Zemstvo Constitutionalists and two

fused to lower the institutional barriers of peasant estate administration, did not consider the expansion of peasant participation in zemstvo assemblies, and moved to replace the small-zemstvo concept with voluntary organizations built around the local parishes of the Orthodox Church.[106]

Moreover, in refusing to countenance political or constitutional opposition in society, he applied the same administrative repression to zemstvo assemblies that he had directed earlier against the local committees of the Special Conference. In early January 1904 an imperial order suspended the authority of the Tver provincial and Novotorzhsk county executive boards, both bastions of zemstvo liberalism. Shortly thereafter, the MVD refused to confirm the re-election of D. N. Shipov to the chair of the Moscow provincial executive board, and in June it published a revision of the Moscow zemstvo system, which concluded that its work had fallen under the control of salaried zemstvo employees, the so-called third element, which the MVD regarded as a cancerous source of political radicalism.[107]

Revealingly enough, the one aspect of Pleve's domestic policy that did not display these contradictory tendencies was his consistent strengthening of the state's administrative and police powers. His program of provincial administrative reform, detailed after the Manifesto of February 1903, projected a significant expansion of gubernatorial authority over all branches of provincial administration and self-administration so as to decentralize administrative power to the provinces. Although never implemented during the Pleve years, the plan envisioned a governor able to control information to and from the central ministries, to exercise greater discretion in dismissing politically disloyal officials, to order zemstvo funding of legally mandated obligations, and to review the agendas of zemstvo and municipal assembly debates.[108] In 1903–04 the MVD also moved to strengthen its police apparatus; it created a state-funded mounted rural police force (*strazhniki*) and increased the complement of

---

others of the Beseda Circle, resolved that the primary cause of peasant and hence rural impoverishment was "the peasant legal order." The law regarded peasants as "a special type of people, distinct from people of other estates. . . . A separate legislative code, the uncertainty of property rights, the total irresponsibility of contractual relationships, the multiplicity of appointed and elected supervisors who frequently do not supervise within limits set by the law—all this creates a situation that acts on the world view [*mirosozertsanie*] of the people in a completely demoralizing way, degrades a sense of individualism, represses initiative and independence." Ibid., p. 207.

[106] MVD reform discussions of the zemstvo electoral system only began after December 1904, TsGIA, f. 1288, op. 2, ed. khr. 15, chast' 3, ll. 74–79. On Pleve's opposition to the small zemstvo unit, see Gurko, *Features and Figures*, pp. 330–31.

[107] *Russkie vedomosti*, 1 January 1905, pp. 30–31, and "Vsepoddaneishii raport tovarishcha ministra vnutrennykh del, senatora, tainogo sovetnika Zinov'eva," *Novoe vremia*, 30 June 1904, pp. 3–4; 1 July 1904, p. 4; and 3 July 1904, p. 4.

[108] "Usilenie gubernatorskoi vlasti," pp. 1–49.

police officials in towns, rural districts, and on some railroads. Finally, in 1904 the ministry issued instructions that attempted to regulate the activities of the land captains and increase their subordination to directions from the center.[109]

On 12 July 1904, some six months after the outbreak of the Russo-Japanese War, Pleve was assassinated—his body horribly shattered by a terrorist's bomb. His efforts to stabilize the autocratic state had been decimated by military defeat in the Far East and growing political instability at home. In his obituary, *Novoe vremia* lamented that too many in Russian society had come to think of Pleve as "a reactionary." They had been enraged by his use of police power, the paper wrote, but had failed to realize that the minister "had not sought salvation in constitutional tendencies, but in the capable, enlightened direction and operation of the existing state mechanism."[110] Yet even Witte, whose views in the 1890s had much in common with those his arch-rival articulated after 1900, had come to understand that legal regulation, rational administration, and police methods were by themselves no longer capable of upholding the political legitimacy of the autocratic state. Some concessions to the political aspirations building in civil society were required. Witte had feared several months before the assassination even more than he had in 1902 that Pleve was "deliberately stirring things up" and "creating a concealed psychological process . . . in the population, one that can bring many afflictions." "God help us!" Witte wrote General A. N. Kuropatkin.[111]

Pleve, however, had remained more loyal than Witte to the heritage of Alexander III's reign. He believed that the state, if it possessed a competent administrative system and defended legitimate autocracy with all the means at its disposal, remained the sole, essential arbiter in a country whose populace was only beginning to experience the "norms of civil community." Drawing on his experience of the 1880s, Pleve insisted that autocratic authority exercised by a rational administrative power continued to be the key to future social and political stability. It had instead opened the antechamber to revolution.

THE FIRST CRISIS OF AUTOCRACY REVISITED, SUMMER 1904–WINTER 1905

Pleve's death only thickened the atmosphere of political instability that surrounded the government in the summer of 1904. Even Witte, hardly grief-stricken by the passing of his nemesis, remarked in a letter of mid-

[109] *Russkie vedomosti*, 1 January 1904, pp. 6–7.
[110] "Pamiati V. K. Pleve," *Novoe vremia*, 20 July 1904, p. 2.
[111] "Perepiska S. Iu. Witte i A. N. Kuropatkin v 1904–1905 gg.," *KA* 19 (1926): 68 (19 April 1904); also 70 (spring 1904).

August how "horrible" it was that "one heard only a sigh of relief and condemnation of [Pleve's] memory" when public opinion marked the assassination. After six months of military defeat and domestic repression, this reaction conveyed not only the dissipation of the nationalist fervor that had marked the first months of the war, but also the re-emergence of political opposition in educated society as well. This turn of events, emboldening constitutionalists in the national zemstvo movement and the Union of Liberation, led Witte in late August to the conclusion that, "especially in view of the war, a sharp alteration of the entire regime [was] necessary in order to correct the situation."[112]

The announcement on 25 August of the appointment of Pleve's successor seemed to indicate that such a change was underway. Adjutant-General Prince P. D. Sviatopolk-Mirskii effected an abrupt change in the tone, if not the substance, of the regime's domestic policy. A career military officer, Mirskii had served as Kharkov provincial marshal of the nobility briefly in the mid-1890s, as governor of Penza and then Ekaterinoslav provinces (1895–1900), and as assistant minister of internal affairs under Sipiagin. Finally, as governor-general of the Baltic provinces (1902–04), he had enjoyed general esteem for his cooperation with the public.[113] In statements to the press and to officials of his new ministry, Mirskii made known his sympathies for self-administration, moderate public opinion, and the "mutual confidence" between government and society necessary to effect reform.[114] He was more explicit at a private audience with Nicholas II in late August, insisting that the state had to seek an accommodation with public moderates by abandoning Pleve's repressive tactics, fostering "the expansion of self-administration," and summoning elected representatives to St. Petersburg for discussions of legislative reform.[115] In presiding over a sudden, springlike liberalization, the new minister of internal affairs—as one newspaper later commented—achieved "a popularity enjoyed by no other Russian high official since the time of Count Loris-Melikov."[116]

The comparison with Loris-Melikov was instructive not only for the

[112] Ibid., 72 (19 August 1904).

[113] *Novoe vremia*, 28 August 1904, p. 2, 12 September 1904, p. 3; *Russkie vedomosti*, 16 September 1904, p. 1. See also, Aleksei Achkasov, ed., *"Poveialo vesnoiu": Rechi g. ministra vnutrennykh del kniazia P. D. Sviatopolk-Mirskogo i tolk o nikh pressy* (Moscow, 1905).

[114] "Iz besedy frantsuzskogo zhurnalista s kn. P. D. Sviatopolk-Mirskim," *Novoe vremia*, 1 September 1904, pp. 3–4; "Rech' ministra vnutrennykh del" and "Soobshchenie Rossiiskogo Telegrafnogo Agenstva," *Novoe vremia*, 17 September 1904, pp. 2–4; and *Russkie vedomosti*, 18 September 1904, p. 1.

[115] "Dnevnik Kn. E. A. Sviatopolk-Mirskoi za 1904–1905 gg.," *Istoricheskie zapiski* 77 (1965): 242 (25 August 1904).

[116] *Russkie vedomosti*, 20 January 1905, p. 1.

response that official liberalism elicited from public opinion, but, more important, for the incongruity growing between the government's reform proposals and the demands of the political opposition. Throughout the autumn Mirskii devoted himself to the development of a program whose key provision was the incorporation of elected public representatives into the State Council. Simultaneously, and with the minister's tacit endorsement, preparations were underway to convene the pivotal November 1904 zemstvo congress, at which a majority of the country's zemstvo leadership for the first time demanded the creation of an elected national assembly with legislative, not merely consultative powers.[117] Yet, at a time when even the censored liberal press was calling for "the replacement of the existing bureaucratic order with a legal order guaranteeing the people freedom and a voice in the resolution of state questions," Mirskii was engaged in a torturous effort to convince a suspicious tsar that measures vetoed a quarter-century previously might satisfy the emerging national political movement against the autocratic government.[118]

His exertions produced the ukase of 12 December 1904, a new reform manifesto that was stillborn, lacking the promise of popular representation that Mirskii had deemed essential to its success.[119] Although the primary responsibility for this decision rested with Nicholas II, the one adviser most responsible for undermining Mirskii was none other than Witte, who had made little secret of his adamant opposition to an idea that he found "incompatible with autocracy."[120] At a special conference of 8 December chaired by the tsar, Witte insisted that including public representatives in the State Council was a meaningless gesture. If concessions were to be made, it was better, he said, "to go over to a constitution."[121] The other option was immediate state reform under the aegis of

[117] In general, see Sviatopolk-Mirskaia, "Dnevnik Sviatopolk-Mirskoi," pp. 241–67 (August–December 1904); S. E. Kryzhanovskii, *Vospominaniia* (Berlin, 1938), pp. 15–27; Gurko, *Features and Figures*, pp. 292–323; Solov'ev, *Samoderzhavie . . . v 1902–1907*, pp. 117–140.

[118] *Russkie vedomosti*, 13 November 1904, p. 1; also 17 November 1904, p. 1; 18 November 1904, p. 2; 24 November 1904, pp. 1–2. Also see the discussion of more circumscribed representative plans first discussed during the 1870s in "Eshche o proekte Kn. Vasil'chikova," *Novoe vremia*, 24 November 1904, p. 3, and K. Golovin, "Po povodu zapiski kniazia A. I. Vasil'chikova," *Novoe vremia*, 29 November 1904, pp. 2–3.

[119] Compare the reactions of "Vysochaishii ukaz," *Novoe vremia*, 14 December 1904, p. 3 ("the general spirit and character of this ukase corresponds exactly to the idea of liberalism in the most moderate meaning of this word"), and *Russkie vedomosti*, 17 December 1904, p. 2 ("An important step toward the renewal of our state and public structure has been taken. . . . [It] is necessary to summon elected representatives of the people").

[120] Sviatopolk-Mirskaia, "Dnevnik Sviatopolk-Mirskoi," pp. 260–61 (3 December 1904) and 265 (12, 13 December 1904). Also Shipov, *Vospominaniia i dumy*, pp. 286–90; Kryzhanovskii, *Vospominaniia*, p. 26; and Gurko, *Features and Figures*, p. 304.

[121] Sviatopolk-Mirskaia, "Dnevnik Sviatopolk-Mirskoi," p. 262 (8 December 1904); also p. 266 (14 December 1904).

a unified central government. When Nicholas vetoed Mirskii and charged the Committee of Ministers, chaired since mid-1903 by the former finance minister, with the implementation of the ukase, Witte achieved a goal, as he himself remarked, toward which he "had striven ten years ago."[122] Essential to the realization of his aspirations was the de facto unification of ministerial government in the Committee of Ministers. This institution provided a lever, and, if skillfully utilized, an opportunity, to force other ministries toward legislative reform.[123] Now, having prevented the convocation of representatives, Witte was in a position to implement his vision of the Rechtsstaat. State reform directed toward civil order and astute concessions to public opinion would, he believed, defuse the political opposition.

The ukase of 12 December provided three avenues toward these goals. First, it promised the rule of law, "the most important support of the throne in an autocratic state." Under this rubric were included the judicial prosecution of administrative abuses of power, a review of the extralegal administrative statutes, rights for religious and national minorities, a reform of press censorship, and the right of judicial redress for all, particularly peasants. Second, the ukase announced pending reforms of zemstvo and urban self-administration—expanding its authority in local affairs, broadening popular participation in these institutions, and creating a small zemstvo unit. Finally, the program of 12 December favored the rural reform proposals of Witte's Special Conference. In contrast to the estate-oriented manifesto of 26 February 1903, the ukase stipulated that peasant law and institutions were to be unified with "the general legislation of the empire." The eventual goal of this work was to return to peasants the status originally granted them in 1861: "free rural residents invested with full rights."[124]

With the implementation of the ukase invested in the Committee of Ministers, and with that of peasant legislative reform invested in his Special Conference, Witte had assumed de facto responsibility for two critical areas of domestic legislative concern.[125] Outside the chancelleries of St. Petersburg, however, the political opposition in educated society,

[122] "Perepiska Vitte i Kuropatkina," p. 75 (19 January 1905). Also Witte, *Vospominaniia*, 1:290–91, and Gurko, *Features and Figures*, pp. 311–12.

[123] See McDonald, "Autocracy, Bureaucracy, and Change in the Formation of Russian Foreign Policy," chap. 2.

[124] *Novoe vremia*, 14 December 1904, p. 3. Also Komitet ministrov, Kantseliariia. *Zhurnaly Komiteta Ministrov po ispolneniiu Ukaza 12 dekabria 1904 g.* (St. Petersburg, 1905), pp. 4–6.

[125] See *Zhurnaly komiteta ministrov* and Witte, *Vospominaniia*, 1:290–306. See also the committee's decision in late December to create two special commissions on zemstvo and municipal reform, which were to include elected representatives from both institutions; the commissions never met. TsGIA f. 1288, op. 2 (1905), ed. khr. 15, chast' 3, l. 74.

which he was attempting to defuse with promises of local reform, was rapidly becoming a constitutional movement. In part, Witte's belief that he could resist changes in the central institutions of government resulted from the peculiar configuration of events in November–December 1904, particularly the absence of large-scale popular upheaval and a pending mobilization of army reservists that caused the postponement of many zemstvo assembly meetings until January.[126] In large measure, however, Witte acted from his own longstanding conviction that bureaucratic leadership, the effective and programmatic utilization of state power, would solidify the authority of the autocratic state. Applying a credo that he had internalized as minister of finance to the unfamiliar realm of national political conflict, Witte believed that he could divert the challenge to autocracy without compromising its authority or undermining the state.

Pobedonostsev, who wrote Witte in late December to protest such reformist chimeras, believed that this moment had passed long ago. "We do not have the strength to reestablish authority, it lies powerless," the distraught old man lamented. "But if we are powerless, we nevertheless should preserve the very idea and the very principle of authority . . . in the sense of the element which binds any order together." In his rejoinder, Witte parted company with a man whose views of autocracy he had often found compelling. Autocratic authority, Witte replied, was meaningless without the government leadership necessary to preserve it. The "reasons for our present situation," Witte wrote, were clear: "the horrible war and the absence of a strong, definite authority that knows what it wants." Pobedonostsev was right to be horrified by "an insane crowd" that seemed to be carrying him "into an abyss," but, Witte retorted, it was "insufficient to state that an insane crowd is on the move." One had to determine "why it has gone insane and why it is on the move and also how to halt it." At present, Witte acknowledged, "the embittered and oppressed" populations of city and countryside were indeed threatened by the constitutional and socialist invective of opposition intellectuals. Yet to argue, as Pobedonostsev seemed to imply, that the government could "shut everyone up, intern them in prison, exile them, coerce their conscience and spirit" was to pursue the same strategy that officials had used for many years to "stifle indiscriminately everything that although not dangerous to Russia was inconvenient and undesirable for them." This "large, insane crowd, which is screaming at us 'Out!' " presently wielded such powerful influence because the government had become an

---

[126] *Russkie vedomosti*, 1 January 1905, p. 37. Roberta Thompson Manning, "Zemstvo and Revolution," in Haimson, *Politics of Rural Russia*, pp. 37–42 shows that by January 1905 only five provincial zemstvo assemblies had passed resolutions supporting the November zemstvo congress.

entity that appeared to think only "how not to do anything, how to reduce every idea, every requirement to nothingness."[127]

Central to Witte's calculations were the rural reform discussions of his Special Conference and the legislation they would produce to address the needs of the majority rural populace. On 8 December, its membership—some thirty ministerial officials, State Council members and senators—convened to deliberate over Witte's *Note on the Peasant Matter*, his recently published statement of the conference's legislative agenda.[128] As a broad reversal of both economic and administrative policy toward the peasantry, Witte's *Note* was a significant moment in the long-term evolution of agrarian reform. It envisioned the voluntary right of individual peasants to leave the commune with land and begin the "transition to individual household proprietorship [*podvornoe vladenie*]," as well as the implementation of measures to facilitate this process.[129] Yet the *Note* was also a document of immediate political significance. It not only held out the promise of government leadership on this critical issue of domestic policy, but also offered legal proposals that addressed concerns shared by moderates in the zemstvo movement.

Witte proposed to eliminate the estate segregation of the peasantry and to expand zemstvo participation in a reformed, all-estate rural administration to a greater degree than earlier government projects—most notably those of the Kakhanov Commission—had ever contemplated. All-estate village institutions were to become small zemstvo units. Concerns arising from common residence in the village—"medicine, schools, roads, fire insurance, social welfare, agronomic aid, and, in general, public life"—were to be subject to "the supervision of elected organizations, which do not have an estate character, [and] are joined with existing zemstvo institutions." The program also hinted that these might assume certain local administrative powers as well, mentioning, for example, the employment of local police, tax collectors, and draft board inspectors. Second, Witte advocated the elimination of peasant township courts and customary law; imperial civil and criminal codes, adjudicated by zemstvo-elected justices of the peace, were to be the governing norms of peasant life. Finally, these reforms would abolish the judicial responsibilities

[127] "Perepiska Vitte s Pobedonostevym," pp. 106–8 (25 December 1904).

[128] S. Iu. Witte, *Predsedatel' vysochaishe uchrezhdennogo Osobogo Soveshchaniia o nuzhdakh sel'sko-khoziastvennoi promyshlennosti: Zapiska po krest'ianskomu delu* (St. Petersburg, 1905). These debates were recorded in *Vysochaishe uchrezhdennoe Osoboe Soveshchanie o nuzhdakh sel'sko-khoziastvennoi promyshlennosti: Protokoly po krest'ianskomu delu* (St. Petersburg, 1905) (hereafter *Protokoly*).

[129] *Zapiska po krest'ianskomu delu*, pp. 156–61. On the origins of this document and the emerging bureaucratic consensus concerning the agrarian reform that lay behind it, see Macey, *Government and Peasant*, chap. 4.

of the land captain and allow him to become a local administrative official for the entire population.[130]

Taking the measure of contemporary politics, even *Novoe vremia* editorialized that Witte's effort seemed "somewhat belated," but it acknowledged that his reform proposals were "a significant turn of events," given "the archaic servile [*krepostnicheskie*] tendencies that for some inexplicable reason" still existed among a minority of MVD officials.[131] Commenting on the day the Special Conference opened its debates, *Russkie vedomosti* was much less sanguine, although it believed that Witte's plans reflected "a political axiom" of educated society. Full legal rights for the peasantry, its emancipation from administrative tutelage, and its access to independent courts were all well and good. Yet, the newspaper queried, given the existing "conditions of Russian state life," what guaranteed that this new trend in government thinking would not again be reversed by "contradictory tendencies incompatible with the most elementary demands of civil order, justice, and freedom?"[132]

As the movement for national representation grew in educated society, it was becoming less necessary to read between the lines for the answer to this question. Witte's response, judging from the debates that occurred in the Special Conference, however, was that *he* guaranteed reform—and a reformed autocratic state, a Rechtsstaat, would ensure civil order and rights. Addressing the Special Conference on 11 December, Witte conspicuously identified a program that he had advocated since the late 1890s with the strivings of the nation. "Russia wants the quickest return to those ideas that inspired the reform of 1861," he said. "I would consider it a great step forward if we restored all those principles that were proclaimed in 1861 and subsequently subjected to undesirable changes." It went without saying that the realization of these goals, which Witte believed to be essential interests of state, would generate public confidence in the government.

He acknowledged, of course, that "the essence" of local reform entailed replacing the structure of bureaucratic tutelage that segregated the peasantry within its own institutional and legal system. Witte knew as well in late 1904 as he had in the 1890s, that "the population's local interests could be satisfied with some kind of purely administrative-bureaucratic organization—not, of course, in the sense that the country lately understands the word 'bureaucracy' but in the best meaning of this word." Yet the exigencies of practical politics demanded some compromise of hallowed, personal principle. Witte, in fact, was not prepared to

[130] *Zapiska po krest'ianskomu delu*, pp. 147–55.
[131] *Novoe vremia*, 5 December 1904, p. 3.
[132] *Russkie vedomosti*, 8 December 1904, p. 1.

concede very much. "Purely economic needs," he stated, could "be given over to the management of society itself, with control invested in the [government]." The "all-estate zemstvo" was charged to supervise such matters in the county—whether it did so "well or poorly was a completely different question," he remarked. "Simple historical logic" therefore dictated that the existing zemstvo system be granted smaller assemblies to aid in its work.[133] At the first meeting after the publication of the ukase of 12 December, Witte hastened to add sovereign imprimatur to the logic of history and insisted that imperial will had "predecided" the creation of a small zemstvo unit.[134]

Witte's program did not, however, go unchallenged in the Special Conference. Only four individuals opposed eliminating estate administration outright. All were conservative nobles or officials associated with the MVD: A. S. Stishinskii, a very senior assistant minister whom Sviatopolk-Mirskii had discharged and sent to the State Council; N. A. Khvostov, ober-procurator of the Senate's Second (peasant) Department and an Orel provincial landowner active in rightist circles; Prince A. G. Shcherbatov, a stalwart rightist of the Moscow provincial nobility; and Count S. D. Sheremetev, a wealthy court aristocrat and former marshal of the nobility of Moscow province.[135] Stishinskii and Khvostov registered their objections in a minority opinion to the conference's proceedings. They allowed certain minor alterations in peasant administration, but preserved the essential features of estate segregation intact.[136]

In debate, both men repeated the refrain, familiar since the 1880s, that a communal peasantry ensured social stability in an era when agrarian capitalism created impoverishment and grounds for economic conflict. With rising urban unrest and military defeat sowing the seeds of social disorder in the countryside, arguments in favor of an estate system that was deemed to preserve public order assumed even greater urgency than before. Labeling himself a "nationalist" who opposed the "abolition of the commune" or the "destruction of the peasant family way of life," Khvostov attacked "cosmopolitans," a slur in the first instance directed against Witte, for thinking that Russia "need not fear a proletariat be-

[133] *Protokoly*, 11 December 1904, pp. 17–18; also p. 30.

[134] Ibid., 15 December 1904, p. 2.

[135] Ibid., 12 January 1905, pp. 20, 22. All four opposed the all-estate village and defended the preservation of the peasant commune. Sheremetev was absent when the others voted against reform of the land captain.

[136] Ibid., p. 29, gives the minority opinion: (1) preservation of the existing village community with allowances for members of other taxed estates to participate in the assembly when it discussed village public needs; (2) preservation of the peasant township, with similar provisions for other taxed estates; (3) assumption of township administration expenses by the state treasury to relieve peasants of inequitable obligations; (4) permission for county zemstvo assemblies to place agents in the township; and (5) no changes in the structure of local police.

cause a proletariat also exists in Western Europe."[137] As a more astute analyst of the agrarian problem, Stishinskii accepted in theory the desirability of peasant proprietorship but refused to contemplate abandoning the "strong public union" supplied by the "great commune" and the estate structure that protected it. Without them, Stishinskii warned, "each peasant will be left to his own devices and will probably not survive the struggle with capitalist interests and pretensions—a struggle that constitutes the essence of economic life at the present time."[138] In a countryside rife with socio-economic conflict, the disorder threatened by the dismantling of estate institutions was only rivaled by the chaos that would ensue if they were replaced by zemstvo institutions. The very idea of accommodating the "antithetical interests . . . of the large noble landowner and the peasant," Stishinskii said, was "absolutely unthinkable: these individuals will stand in irreconcilable enmity [vrazhda] to each other."[139]

Other MVD officials, unwilling to indulge the extremist views of Stishinskii, were equally reluctant to accept Witte's assurances that the path to civil stability and political order ran through either all-estate institutions or expanded self-administration. Insisting that legal equality was possible in a system of estates, the former minister I. L. Goremykin clung to the argument that "the entire population of Russia is divided into estates, which possess their own specific institutions and thus administration." He saw no contradiction in preserving the MVD administrative network and guaranteeing peasants "proper utilization" of those rights that had been granted to them as an estate in 1861.[140] Dedicated to sweeping agrarian reforms, V. I. Gurko did not share the views of a Goremykin or Stishinskii, but neither did he accept Witte's views of self-administration. He supported an all-estate rural administration, if it excluded large landed estates from the jurisdiction, but only in order to create fiscal and administrative territories under bureaucratic supervision. A small zemstvo unit, "either now or within a significantly long period of time," was out of the question. Pleve "was right," Gurko stated in Witte's presence, "when he maintained that the small zemstvo unit is not achievable in our country." The shortfall of prosperous landowners, the looming majorities of impoverished peasants, and the conflict endemic to their relations meant, in bureaucratic parlance, that Russia "lacked the material for creating that kind of organization in our local areas."[141]

[137] Ibid., 11 December 1904, pp. 1–2.

[138] Ibid., 8 December 1904, p. 29.

[139] Ibid., p. 28.

[140] Ibid., 15 December 1904, p. 29. See also ibid., 5 February 1906, pp. 1–9, where Goremykin quoted at length from Witte's arguments in 1893 favoring MVD legislation on the inalienability of allotment lands.

[141] Ibid., 11 December 1904, pp. 3–7. Only Senator G. A. Evreinov took a similar position in these debates, ibid., p. 22.

Most participants in the Special Conference, however, supported the elimination of estate segregation and favored expanded public self-administration in the village and township. Yet even among this group, which included officials presently or soon to be affiliated with the MVD, there was considerable uncertainty concerning the scope of these reforms and the wisdom of exposing landowning interests to volatile peasant majorities. A. I. Lykoshin, assistant ober-procurator of the Senate's Civil Affairs Department, favored the zemstvo-elected township supervisor scheme proposed by the Kakhanov Commission a quarter-century previously, but, again, only if wealthy property-owners were excluded from its jurisdiction.[142] St. Petersburg governor A. D. Zinov'ev, a former provincial marshal of nobility (1897–1903) and a zemstvo delegate since 1893, accepted the Witte program in principle, but cautioned that the creation of new zemstvo institutions should be at the discretion of individual county assemblies.[143] Assistant minister of internal affairs N. N. Kutler had only recently been appointed to his post from the Ministry of Finance, where this former tax inspector had distinguished himself as an expert on agrarian reform. Repudiating a peasant estate administration that represented nothing more than "the powerful discretion of the land captain," Kutler was even willing to allow an all-estate village and a "zemstvo township assembly" authority to control local police officials. Yet although "far from the idea that the interests of landowners uncompromisingly contradict those of the peasants," he urged protection for the propertied minority by granting large landowners automatic membership in the township assembly and allowing the government to set township tax rates.[144]

Indeed, with unease over rural unrest lurking in the background, few officials issued an unqualified endorsement of Witte's plans, and only two participants thought that the potential antagonism of peasants was overstated. One was D. I. Pikhno, a professor of political economy at Kiev's St. Vladimir University and editor of the conservative daily *Kievlianin*. Viewing the village as "a general place of residence just like the city," Pikhno—perhaps for that reason—saw no reason "why antagonism [between landowners and peasants] would inevitably arise" there.[145] The other was Witte, who insisted, as did the zemstvo liberals whose support he was seeking, that expanded self-administration and the moderate leadership they would attract could exert a stabilizing influence on a country-

---

[142] Ibid., 11 December 1904, pp. 13–15.
[143] Ibid., 15 December 1904, p. 18.
[144] Ibid., pp. 20–25.
[145] Ibid., 8 December 1904, pp. 29–32.

side threatened by radical agitation.[146] "I am an advocate," Witte lectured on 15 December, "of the unification of [cultured and uncultured] elements. . . . I maintain that our peasantry is situated in such a way that only petty officials and revolutionaries have access to it. I think that enmity between the cultured element and the uncultured will be an exception."[147]

Whether Witte argued from conviction or from ignorance of rural conditions (the latter seems the more likely possibility), his perception of rural civil instability had been endemic to official thinking since the first crisis of autocracy. So, too, was the response to these conditions now contemplated by the Special Conference. All its members, with the exception of Stishinskii and Khvostov, approved a general resolution to establish a "small zemstvo organization"—although the proposal was broad enough to allow opponents like Gurko to join the majority.[148] A majority constituted largely from senior officials ratified this centerpiece of the Witte program and resolved to dismantle estate institutions, repudiate administrative tutelage, and expand zemstvo influence in rural public life. Combined with the economic reforms of communal land use under consideration in both the Special Conference and the Ministry of Internal Affairs, these proposals reflected a conviction that state power could create civil order through general laws, rational institutions, and effective self-administration. Under the conditions existing outside chancellery walls in late 1904, political disorder and the threat of social instability, to be sure, had influenced this decision, supplying a compelling rationale for pursuing a reformist strategy discredited since the 1880s. The strategy itself, however, derived from established state precedents and was designed to serve the fundamental interests of the state.

A. P. Nikol'skii, director of the Ministry of Finance's State Savings Bank, succinctly articulated the prevailing conviction that the times required the state to direct its efforts toward the long-neglected task of strengthening legal and civil order in the countryside. "Obviously," he said, the peasant could not believe in the rule of law when the daily experience of "people at their discretion adjust[ing] the law to every particular event" had convinced him of its irrelevance. This explained why, he added, the peasant was "unusually gullible before every foolish and unbelievable rumor . . . for example about taking the land away from noble landowners." Without a "concept of justice and legality," peasants lacked

---

[146] See, in particular, N. N. L'vov and A. A. Stakhovich, eds., *Nuzhdy derevni po rabotam komitetov o nuzhdakh sel'sko-khoziastvennoi promyshlennosti: Sbornik statei* (St. Petersburg, 1904), 2 vols. Also Fallows, "Forging the Zemstvo Movement," pp. 693–719.

[147] *Protokoly*, 15 December 1904, p. 12.

[148] Ibid., 13 January 1905, p. 27. The final resolution allowed members to support a small zemstvo, an all-estate village, or both.

"a basis for sober criticism of such rumors, which ill-willed people [were] using to agitate unrest." Yet Nikol'skii was also expressing the underlying unease, noticeable throughout the conference's deliberations, that the times perhaps no longer accommodated the ideals of reformist statesmen:

> To allow a separate legal consciousness [*pravosoznanie*] to grow strong among one hundred million peasants, who constitute the foundation of the Russian state, would be to prepare a pitiful fate for our entire civilization [*tsivilizatsiia*], because a thin stratum of the population that lives by the principles of [the Code of Laws] will not survive a separate peasant legal consciousness . . . different from the one by which we define our civil existence [*grazhdanskii byt*] and legal order and, moreover, our entire sense of citizenship [*grazhdanstvennost'*].[149]

On 30 March 1905, Nicholas II unexpectedly ordered the work of the Special Conference terminated and its materials transferred to a new commission, one directed by I. L. Goremykin.[150] "The king is dead, long live the king," sarcastically exclaimed *Russkie vedomosti* to mark its complete indifference to an event that was already a footnote in the overwhelming historical chronicle of 1905.[151] For as military defeat, political opposition, and popular unrest swept the country, the actions of the state became ever more superfluous to the national political life that educated society, and—in their own way—the awakening urban and rural populations of Russia, were not only orchestrating but in a very real way creating for the first time.

These months were overwhelming, an unending stream of events, each compounding, redefining, and exacerbating the conditions that preceded it: the shooting of Petersburg workers on the Bloody Sunday of 9 January; the humiliating news of Port Arthur's surrender to the Japanese two days later; the unprecedented industrial strikes and university disorders that racked urban Russia in January; the growing number of zemstvo assemblies joining the liberation movement and calling for a national representative institution with legislative powers; the stunning yet circumspect Bulygin rescript of 18 February, in which Nicholas II ordered his minister of internal affairs to define the composition and consultative role of an elected popular assembly; and the first reports in early March of

---

[149] Ibid., 29 December 1904, pp. 47–48.

[150] M. S. Simonova, "Politika tsarizma v krest'ianskom voprose nakanune revoliutsii 1905–1907 gg.," *Istoricheskie zapiski* 75 (1965): 241. Witte blamed D. F. Trepov and I. L. Goremykin for convincing the tsar that the Special Conference program was "threatening to the state structure," Witte, *Vospominaniia*, 1:440–43. Gurko, *Features and Figures*, pp. 335–37, simply states that the tsar had again lost faith in his talented but replaceable minister.

[151] *Russkie vedomosti*, 3 April 1905, p. 1.

peasant unrest.[152] The challenge to autocratic authority and the specter of popular upheaval began to have a paralyzing effect on government as officials found themselves isolated and unable to control the unprecedented events unfolding around them.

Gurko described the Ministry of Internal Affairs in winter 1905 as a place where "there was no trace of legislative work in any department." Even "the most pressing demands of national existence had been relegated to a secondary position by current events, which were becoming more revolutionary" by the day. All concerns, he complained, focused on the "need for popular participation in the government," a preoccupation that Gurko repudiated. This quintessential statist official, alarmed as " 'the liberation movement' began affecting all classes of society," could only "view these events as a man firmly persuaded that Russia and her people were not adult enough for self-government, and that her intellectual classes represented not a constructive but a destructive force."[153]

Witte as well was withdrawing to the refuge of the superordinate state. In mid-January 1905, he wrote to A. N. Kuropatkin of a domestic situation so severe that any exit from it depended not on people, but on "Providence." Military defeat had "produced an utter stench in public self-consciousness." "Anarchists, revolutionaries, constitutionalists" were trumpeting their propaganda and all Russia was beginning "to scream: 'what has the government done to us.' " After Bloody Sunday and Port Arthur, even moderates in "the zemstvos and the nobility are against the autocratic sovereign"—which is an accurate statement if one substitutes "bureaucratic government" for "autocratic sovereign." Indeed, amidst this growing political chaos, the only touchstone remaining to the stalwart autocratic statesman was the peasant populace (*narod*), a dubious political base indeed: "And the narod, the narod so far wants one thing, to have the land taken from private owners and granted to it; everything else in their head is confused. But, of course, instinctively they are for the tsar. But let the domestic struggle continue and then nothing will be certain."[154]

V. I. Kovalevskii, one of Witte's most capable assistant ministers during the 1890s, gave a more insightful analysis of events when he wrote to Nicholas II in April—but he reached the same conclusion: the state was

---

[152] The confusion of these months is recoverable only through the national press. This reproduces *Russkie vedomosti*, January–March 1905 passim. See also Ananych, Diakin et al., *Krizis samoderzhaviia v Rossii*, pp. 189–214.

[153] Gurko, *Features and Figures*, pp. 359–61.

[154] "Perepiska Vitte i Kuropatkina," pp. 73–76 (15 January 1906). See also his "Proekt manifesta o sobytiiakh 9 ianvaria" in "Iz arkhiva S. Iu. Vitte," *KA* 11–12 (1925): 26–38. Similar sentiments are expressed in A. S. Ermolov, "Zapiski A. S. Ermolova," *KA* 8 (1925): 51–67.

isolated and irrelevant. Urging only weeks after the Bulygin rescript the creation of a representative assembly with legislative authority, Kovalevskii told the tsar that he confronted a "national revolutionary movement [obshchenarodnoe revoliutsionnoe dvizhenie]." Kovalevskii had resigned his post in 1902 to work in private industry, a position from which he now regarded a government that had shown itself to be "totally powerless to cope with the justified strivings of the country ... for fundamental improvements of its life within the existing regime." "Confidence in and respect for authority" was collapsing, "authority is tossed from wave to wave by the pressure of daily chance. It concedes, retreats, then consciously closes its eyes to phenomena of public life that it has condemned, because it is now powerless to stop them. ... [This] is clear evidence of disintegration and a precursor of terrible events."[155]

That this political crisis had arisen was due, in the final analysis, to the tortuous defense of autocratic prerogative mounted by Nicholas II and conservative elements in both government and society since 1894. This resistance would be overcome, and then only partially, by the revolutionary general strike of October 1905. Yet the intensity of the crisis derived as much from the failure of the statesmen who had wielded authority and the limitations that their own superordinate perspective had imposed on legitimate efforts to accommodate within the autocratic state the civil and political transformations occurring in Russian society.

Witte was the primary but not the sole example of such an official. As minister of finance, he had energetically sought to aggrandize the power of the state, fostering national economic development and the propertied civil society arising from it in order to transform the social foundations on which the autocratic regime rested. His efforts to hasten Russia's economic development had forced him to grapple with the inevitable civil and political consequences of his actions, and, by the late 1890s, he had become an advocate of the Rechtsstaat. Autocratic authority in the modern era could not depend solely on power or the dynasty, but required legal order and a rational bureaucratic state to administer it. Only thus could the regime create the civil stability and public confidence that alone assured the legitimacy of its rule. Yet the explicit assumption in Witte's thinking—and there is really no other term to describe this fundamental precept of his career—was that only the bureaucratic state possessed the talent and vision necessary to arbitrate the issues of national life. In December 1904, when Witte effectively achieved his cherished goal of directing a unified program of state reforms, he acted in the belief that such

---

[155] "Ob"iasnitel'naia zapiska V. I. Kovalevskogo ot 7 aprelia 1905 g., predstavlennaia N. Romanovu," in "Iz arkhiva S. Iu. Witte," KA 11–12 (1925): 109–14.

an assertion of government authority could coopt public support and prevent constitutional change.

Pleve, for all the hostility between Witte and him, possessed a similar understanding of the task confronting the state. He too recognized that profound processes of social and civil change were at work in Russian society; he too envisioned the establishment of legal norms and orderly institutional structures to preserve autocracy as it confronted the challenge of modernity. Yet, having learned "the art of administration" during the 1880s in the Ministry of Internal Affairs, Pleve understood state reform to mean the rationalization of institutions that either, in the case (*delo*) of the peasantry, left the subordination of the Russian population to bureaucratic rule intact, or, in the case of the zemstvo, intensified it. Moreover, he remained a servitor, undeviating in his conviction that only the authority of the autocrat assured the legitimacy of the state. Any movement for public independence, or any attempt to obtain the confidence of educated society, was thus a challenge not simply to the state, but also to the very existence of the authority that sustained it.

As national political life in late 1904 began to outstrip the boundaries of previous bureaucratic experience, the autocracy was left with very little with which to defend itself. The "springtime" of Sviatopolk-Mirskii and the ukase of 12 December 1904, although attempts to address the crisis brewing in Russia, were rooted in the precedents and experience of the 1880s. Mirskii's expressions of "confidence" in society, Witte's attempts to establish rule of law and civil order, Stishinskii's adherence to the peasant estate structure, and Gurko's conviction that Russia had not reached the maturity required for political freedom: these were maxims and precepts that were increasingly irrelevant to contemporary life. By early 1905, as the political legitimacy of bureaucratic government was shaken by military defeat and challenged in the name of civil society, officials found themselves isolated in a state that they could defend only with police suppression or with reliance on autocratic authority and the peculiar peasant culture in which it purportedly could exist.

CHAPTER V

From the October Manifesto to the First Duma: The Witte Ministry and the Revolution of 1905

WITTE recalled returning from the United States in September 1905 to find Russia in a state of "total unrest." He wrote in his memoirs that the "government had lost the power to act, everyone either did nothing or went their separate ways, and the prestige of the existing regime and its sovereign head was trampled." "All classes of the population"—he listed in detail educated society, youth, zemstvo and municipal assembly delegates, the commercial-industrial class, urban professionals and the university professoriate, workers, national minorities, peasants, government employees, the army—"had been engulfed by the troubles and the common slogan was a heartfelt cry, 'Life cannot continue like this any longer,'—in other words, it is necessary to be done with the existing regime." Everyone, he concluded, "was united in a [common] hate for the current regime and only when [the October Manifesto] decided what would replace that which was hated was the unity . . . destroyed."[1]

Witte's memoirs displayed an unusual clarity when he described the events of autumn 1905, perhaps because these events possessed singular historical import in the late imperial era. Even as its educated classes had witnessed the ascendancy of nationalism in Europe and its masses had experienced the transformations of industrial growth, the disparate elements of the Russian population had always found "freedom" to be an ill-defined, unachievable, yet intoxicating dream. By late 1905, as Witte had noted, an unprecedented awakening of mass politics had provided, quite suddenly, the opportunity for all classes of the population to believe that this goal was within reach. The objectives on which all shades of public opinion had agreed in the winter of 1904–05—fundamental civil liberties and political representation for the Russian people—by autumn were becoming the means to more sweeping programs of constitutional change: constituent rights for the Russian nation; the creation of a democratic, federal republic; and, on the far left, republican government as a prelude to radical socialism. Moreover, even as the life of the political nation took shape, the lower depths of the social order, where "freedom"

[1] Witte, *Vospominaniia*, 1:453–55.

possessed a less articulate but equally powerful significance, began to re-verberate with the tremors of an even more far-reaching upheaval.

For an autocratic government whose authority had been crumbling, the autumn of 1905 revealed an abyss, and the state order stood at its very edge.[2] Indeed, as Witte had testified, the autocratic regime confronted a choice that it had long attempted to avoid. It could grant political rights to the "nation" and concede the prerogatives of unrestricted tsarist authority, or it could endanger the survival of state power itself. To a states-man of Witte's caliber, which way to decide was a foregone conclusion. The transition to a new political order that was begun by the Manifesto of 17 October 1905, however halting and ill-defined, was as fundamental and irreversible for officials as it was for all other groups of Russian society. Yet, as was true for the parties and classes, the leap across the abyss led the government as well into an uncharted world, where precedent and learned experience were redefined even as they were applied. How the government was to construct a reformed state order, how it was to go about reestablishing political authority, and how it was to govern in this new era of national political life were issues wholly unresolved in October 1905. Ironically, the culmination of Witte's career as a statesman, his brief tenure at the head of a unified cabinet pledged to fundamental re-forms of the old order, revealed the depths of the political crisis confront-ing the new.

CONFRONTING REVOLUTION: THE WITTE MINISTRY, THE OCTOBER MANIFESTO, AND THE REFORMED BUREAUCRATIC STATE

Bolstered by his successful peace negotiations with Japan, Witte returned from the United States bearing the title of count, which the tsar had be-stowed on his suspect yet seemingly indispensable adviser. He also carried the aura of the one man capable of confronting the revolution now threat-ening the state. In his inimitable fashion, Witte did nothing to discourage these hopes. Plunging back into the world of official high politics, Count Witte again began to advocate, as he had in early 1905, the unification of ministerial government under a reformed Council of Ministers, an idea

[2] In general see, Witte, *Vospominaniia*, 2:1–44; Gilbert S. Doctorow, "The Government Reform Program of 17 October 1905," *Russian Review* 34, no. 2 (1975): 123–36; Verner, *Crisis of Russian Autocracy*, chap. 7; Howard D. Mehlinger and John M. Thompson, *Count Witte and the Tsarist Government in the 1905 Revolution* (Indiana University Press, 1972), pp. 29–47; Geoffrey A. Hosking, *The Russian Constitutional Experiment: Govern-ment and Duma, 1907–1914* (Cambridge University Press, 1973), pp. 1–13; Fedor Dan, "Obshchaia politika pravitel'stva i izmeneniia v gosudarstvennoi organizatsii v period 1905–1907 gg.," in *Obshchestevnnoe dvizhenie*, vol. 4, pt. 1, pp. 334–64; and E. D. Cher-menskii, *Burzhuaziia i tsarizm v revoliutsii 1905–1907 gg.*, 2d ed. (Moscow, 1970).

under consideration in a conference chaired by D. M. Sol'skii.[3] Recommended during the summer by Minister of Internal Affairs Bulygin and his ghostwriting subordinate S. E. Kryzhanovskii, this long-sought reorganization was considered to be essential if the autocratic state was to assure the Duma, and through it society and the press, of "the firmness and stability of government policy."[4] For Witte, however, the issue went further. A united cabinet would also provide its chairman with the legal basis to become prime minister and impose, on both the administrative apparatus and a vacillating sovereign, the bureaucratic leadership that he deemed essential to the reestablishment of government authority.[5]

Such was the background from which Witte presented a historic report to Nicholas II on 9 October 1905.[6] In it he analyzed the grave political crisis confronting the state, outlined how he intended to combat it, and effectively demanded imperial support for his program were he to assume direction of the government. With a general strike paralyzing St. Petersburg and unrest intensifying throughout the country, Witte did not deny that popular revolution was "something possible in the future," but he insisted, as he had since 1902, that the essence of the present moment lay in the wholesale alienation of educated society from government authority, in the "ideological revolution [*ideinaia revoliutsiia*]" that already existed. Citing prominent demands for universal male franchise, female suffrage, nationalization of the land, and national autonomy, which only "the most extreme elements of society" had advocated in late 1904, Witte sought to convince the tsar that "extremist ideas alone" were now dominating public opinion. Increasingly, it appeared to be "inconsequential whether a given idea was practicable," and, he warned, this "most dangerous indication of an approaching explosion" proved beyond doubt that moderate support for the government was wasting away "by the day." The more protracted the collapse of government authority, the greater the threat to the very existence of the state. In this situation, fundamental reforms were indispensable.[7]

True to the precedents that had informed his thinking since the late 1890s, Witte raised the issue of the autocracy's first crisis in the 1880s to attack those of the tsar's advisers who were still attempting to sway him toward a policy of repression and military dictatorship. "Police repres-

[3] Polovtsev, "Dnevnik A. A. Polovtseva (15 September 1905–10 August 1906; 5 March–2 May 1908)," *KA* 4 (1923): 63–74.

[4] MVD, *Materialy po uchrezhdeniiu Gosudarstvennoi Dumy* (St. Petersburg, 1905), p. 6. Also Kryzhanovskii, *Vospominaniia*, pp. 50–52.

[5] McDonald, "Autocracy Bureaucracy, and Change in Russian Foreign Policy," chaps. 2–3.

[6] "Zapiska Vitte ot 9 oktiabria," in "Iz arkhiva S. Iu. Witte," *KA* 11–12 (1925): 51–61.

[7] Ibid., pp. 53–54.

sion," then as now, was "powerless to halt an ideological movement" in educated society. Even less, he argued, could the political authority of autocracy rest on monarchist illusions about "the passive peasant masses," who were, quite simply, "always inert" and not "a reliable basis [for] statecraft [*aktivnye meropriiatiia*]." To be sure, Witte said, the government still could—and, as subsequent months revealed, would—try to manipulate the sentiments of the rural populace, where "loyalty to the idea of the tsar undoubtedly exists." Yet the unrestrained growth of radicalism, inevitable as long as the government ignored more moderate political demands in society, was threatening to create conditions in which the "populace [*narod*], in an unrestrained flood and in the name of the tsar, can bring down everything upon which not only the monarchy but the state itself stands."[8] It was all the more imperative to realize, Witte continued, that contrary to the 1880s, when autocratic government had not encountered "theoretical repudiation," educated Russians were now displaying "malice toward the government": "they do not respect it, they do not believe it." Society was convinced only of "its own significance and its own powers—its capacity to deprive the government of support and force it to capitulate." Particularly amidst a potential social crisis, the idea of capitulation could not be an acceptable strategy for a statesman who had always believed, as he repeated here, that "the government not fictitiously but actually ought to lead [*rukovodit'*] the country." Thus, the task at hand was to reestablish, in deed and in the eyes of society itself, the capacity of the bureaucratic state to guide Russia's transition into the new era of national life opening before it:

> Leadership primarily requires a clearly stated goal. An ideological [*ideinaia*] goal, supreme, recognized by all. Society has offered this goal, its importance is great and completely indestructible, for there is truth in this goal. The government should therefore adopt it. The slogan of "freedom" should be the slogan of government activity. There is no other option to save the state.[9]

Judging from the specific measures he recommended in the report, Witte was entertaining a broad interpretation of this slogan. His three primary objectives, eventually promised by the tsar in the Manifesto of 17 October, were legal guarantees of the freedoms of person, conscience, speech, and assembly; legislative authority for the State Duma; and an expansion of the restrictive electoral franchise that had been announced in August. Yet he also hinted at other, even more substantial concessions to public opinion. All either had been demanded at the September zemstvo congress or would soon be debated at the landmark November

[8] Ibid., p. 54.
[9] Ibid., p. 56.

congress: universal male suffrage; labor legislation; the controlled sale to peasants of rented manorial land, a "form of expropriation" necessary to satisfy rural "land hunger"; and limited administrative autonomy for the populations of Poland, Georgia, and the Caucasus. Moreover, he was considering alloting ministerial portfolios to "individuals enjoying public confidence" to foster the image of a government "dedicated to the pending reforms." Whatever the outcome of this effort, the government intended to exert "indirect leadership" on the new Duma by presenting its representatives with a coherent legislative agenda for their consideration when they convened. He added that this task required "extreme sensitivity to the attitude of the majority."[10]

Witte characterized his report as "a program of government activity that could successfully . . . take the liberation movement in hand and thereby save the fatherland."[11] Only subsequent months were to prove how accurately he had gauged the political crisis of late 1905 and, in particular, whether the basic assumptions of a reformist tradition of the later nineteenth century could accord with the national politics of the early twentieth. There was no denying, however, that the sovereign's approval of the October Manifesto and the simultaneous announcement of Witte's appointment as chairman of the Council of Ministers represented a turning point for the old regime. The concession of legislative power to elected representatives of society signified, however heatedly adherents of autocracy attempted to dispute the fact, a principled restriction of tsarist authority. A grant of legitimacy to the political interests of the nation— to be sure, defined with the same vagueness that characterized the nascent national politics suffusing the Russian empire—established a new precedent with which the Witte ministry and those that succeeded it would have to contend. Yet the transitional moment of October 1905 was also fraught with paradoxes, for the concession of civil and political rights was made with the conviction that a bureaucratic government, displaying its commitment to fundamental reforms of the state structure, would retain political leadership over the "nation" and remain, as before, the decisive arbitrative power in Russian life.

This amalgam of old and new was especially reflected in the programmatic statement of the Witte ministry that appeared, together with the Manifesto, in the press on 18 October. Its recognition that "Russia had outgrown the form of its existing structure" did not invalidate but only revised the character and role of the state power. Thus the new chairman of the Council of Ministers promised "a legal order based on civil free-

---

[10] Ibid., pp. 56–60. On the zemstvo congresses, see Veselovskii, *Istoriia zemstva*, 3:636–41, and Manning, *Crisis of the Old Order*, pp. 83–88, 106–11, 131–37.

[11] Ibid., p. 59.

dom," not a constitution. Civil liberties were guaranteed, as long as they did not violate the "tranquility and peace of the state." Rural economic reform was forthcoming, but it would not violate "the property and civil rights that [were] recognized in all cultured countries." The government intended to uphold the "prestige" of the Duma and honor its "decisions, to the extent that [they] . . . did not diverge fundamentally" from the existing state order. It allowed the possibility of broadening the Duma's authority, but would not heed the "sharply expressed demands of certain circles" for constituent powers. The Witte ministry stood ready to establish the Rechtsstaat and the gradual civil evolution that it guaranteed, but, the premier cautioned, the "foundations of a legal order are realized to the degree that the population becomes accustomed to them—[and acquires] civil experience [*grazhdanskii navyk*]." Any immediate achievement of that task in "a country with a multiethnic population of 135 million people and a vast administration, both of which were immersed in different values" was impossible, rendering all the more necessary the guiding presence of a unified, reformist government that could promulgate "the primary stimuli of civil freedom." The first minister remained convinced that public moderates possessed "the political tact" to accept this program; it is "unthinkable," he proclaimed, "that Russian society desires anarchy, which threatens, in addition to all the horrors of social conflict [*bor'ba*], the dismemberment of the state."[12]

Few other officials were as sure as Witte that the October Manifesto would produce this result, but then their personal reputations were not tied so directly to its success. They acknowledged more readily that this unprecedented political transformation of the state order had in fact created wholesale uncertainty about the future character of autocratic government. A. D. Obolenskii, a Witte confidant who shared his superior's conviction that October was a culminating moment in a tradition that reached back to "the reforms and renewal of Russian life begun in the reign of Alexander II," nevertheless remembered the "sorrowful, painful, oppressive" atmosphere in which the decision to grant the manifesto had been taken.[13] Gurko, whose own career after 1905 revealed an unusual willingness to engage in rightist politics, believed that most officials, suddenly confronted with "the end of an epoch in Russian history many centuries long," had fallen into a state of "total demoralization."[14] Receiving the news in Manchuria a long week after publication of the manifesto, A. N. Kuropatkin acknowledged that "constitutional rule [*pravlenie*] had been introduced" and "autocratic authority restricted." What was to fol-

---

[12] *Russkie vedomosti*, 18 October 1905, p. 1.
[13] "Dnevnik kn. A. D. Obolenskogo," in "Iz arkhiva S. Iu. Vitte," *KA*, 11–12 (1925): 70.
[14] Gurko, *Features and Figures*, pp. 393–99.

low, however, he could not predict; he feared that with "wave upon wave, reaching ever higher," the revolutionary movement might "sweep away the very foundations of the Russian order."[15] His bureaucratic superior, Minister of War A. F. Rediger, maintained that the "constitution" granted by the October Manifesto had altered everything and defined nothing: "old laws were no longer considered to be in effect and new ones had not yet been developed, and, as a result, total lawlessness and unbelievable chaos reigned over the entire country."[16] S. E. Kryzhanovskii most graphically portrayed the burden that October had placed upon the shoulders of high officials:

> We saw a complete paralysis of authority, which guaranteed the citizen neither justice nor freedom, nothing. We lived in a cloud, wandered about without sustenance. We were in an extremely new but totally unbearable situation. . . . The general impression was confused: something will happen and Russia will move along a new path; will it be national development or some other kind of [foreign] development, into whose hands was the future construction of state life to be given?[17]

Kryzhanovskii's query went to the heart of the matter, for even as the Witte government was unfurling the banner of reform, the increasingly evident contours of social conflict, or popular revolution, were challenging the political preconceptions upon which the October Manifesto had been premised. When the St. Petersburg general strike eased enough to allow *Novoe vremia* to publish news of the reforms on 22 October, the newspaper warned that "the events of the bitter state crisis now being experienced by Russia move with stunning swiftness. . . . The ubiquitous disquiet in the population is a volcano capable at any minute of spewing forth from its quaking depths disasters both terrible and unexpected."[18] No rhetoric, however, could adequately describe the stream of events that flooded the winter of 1905–06: the month-long existence of the St. Petersburg Soviet of Workers' Deputies; industrial work stoppages and strikes by postal, telegraph, and railroad workers that paralyzed the country in November and December; the early December armed uprising in Moscow; rising unrest in the Manchurian army causing fears for the state's military power; and disorders in the national borderlands.

Amidst these events came the most stunning outburst of all: peasant rebellion. In November–December 1905, a countryside already smolder-

[15] "Iz dnevnika A. N. Kuropatkina," *KA* 7 (1924): 55 (23 October 1905).

[16] "Zapiski A. F. Rediger o 1905 g.," *KA* 45 (1931): 90.

[17] P. E. Shchegolev ed., *Padenie tsarskogo rezhima: Stenograficheskie otchety doprosov i pokazanii, dannykh v 1917 g. v chrezvychainoi sledstvennoi Kommissii Vremennogo pravitel'stva.* (Moscow-Leningrad, 1924–27), vol. 5. pp. 395–96.

[18] *Novoe vremia*, 22 October 1905, pp. 13–14.

ing with unrest burst into open rebellion.[19] Over the course of sixty days, peasants concentrated in the provinces of the Volga River valley and central agricultural region looted and destroyed the agricultural infrastructure of some two thousand private estates. Inflicted largely on the provincial landowning nobility, property damage exceeded thirty million rubles by January.[20] The peasant "movement," which is now known to have been a pivotal moment for noble landowners who began to repudiate liberal causes as they witnessed the social consequences of political opposition, confirmed for officials as well the depths of the revolutionary crisis they now confronted.[21] Mass peasant unrest directed against private property was an assault on the social order and so it was treated, often with brutality. By December, six weeks after the October Manifesto, twenty-eight provinces were under martial law and an additional twenty-three were being ruled by some form of extralegal statute.[22]

What rendered the scope and depth of popular disorder even more threatening, however, was the failure of the October Manifesto to still political opposition in "educated society." That "educated society" might moderate its demands—a goal defined by the experience of public life as it had existed in Russia before the revolution—was based on a set of assumptions that proved to be incapable of accounting for the unfamiliar national politics emerging in the wake of the manifesto. National and local political organizations were mushrooming across Russia. Group interests became more articulate, conflict among them more endemic, power and the opportunity to exercise it a desired commodity to which the bureaucratic government lacked any overriding claim.[23] This disconcerting, cacophonous reality bore little resemblance to the political standards that had governed public debate before 1905. Looming above the

[19] "Krest'ianskie bezporiadki," *Novoe vremia*, 18 November 1905, pp. 3–4; "Bezporiadki v Saratovskoi gubernii," *Russkie vedomosti*, 6 November 1905, p. 3, and 22 November 1905, p. 1.

[20] "Sostavlennaia MVD spravka ob ubytakh, prichenennykh agrarnymi bezporiadkami v 20 guberniiakh Evropeiskoi Rossii," TsGAOR f. 434, op. 1, d. 228/9, ll. 11–14, and Manning, *Crisis of the Old Order*, pp. 169–75.

[21] "Agrarnoe dvizhenie v 1905 g. po otchetam Dubasova i Pantaleeva," in "Iz arkhiva S. Iu. Vitte," *KA* 11–12 (1925): pp. 182–92; "Doklady S. Iu. Vitte Nikolaiu II," in ibid., pp. 146–55; "Ezhenedel'naia zapiska po departamentu politsii za period vremeni s 8 . . . po 29 dek. 1905 g.," in ibid., pp. 159–81; and "Vsepoddaneishii doklad predsedatelia soveta ministrov gr. S. Iu. Vitte po agrarnomu voprosu (10 ianvaria 1906 g.)," in B. B. Veselovskii, ed., *Agrarnyi vopros v sovete ministrov (1906 g.)* (Moscow-Leningrad, 1924), pp. 71–75.

[22] Dan, "Obshchaia politika pravitel'stva," pp. 365–67; "Tsirkuliar upravliaiushchago MVD po departamentu obshchikh del ot 23 dek. 1905 g.," *Novoe vremia*, 16 February 1906, p. 3; Verner, *Crisis of Autocracy*, chap. 8.

[23] See, in particular, Martov et al., *Obshchestvennoe dvizhenie*, vol. 3 ("Partii—ikh sostav, razvitie i proiavlenie v massovom dvizhenii, na vyborakh i v Dume"). Also, Mehlinger and Thompson, *Count Witte and the Tsarist Government*, pp. 251–65.

fray was the preeminent demand of the Constitutional Democrats (the Kadets) and parties on their left for a constituent assembly; yawning below was the abyss of social upheaval. Thus it was not surprising that S. E. Kryzhanovskii would view Witte as a man in whose "head was chaos, a bunch of impulses, a desire to satisfy all."[24] Kryzhanovskii, and others who repeated this opinion, however, did not have to grapple with the fluid and unpredictable political universe of post-October events.

The Witte ministry did, and the experience was a sobering one. Indeed, only one day after the proclamation of the manifesto, Witte appealed "as a Russian man, as a citizen" to representatives of the Petersburg press to moderate their reporting of events. Expressions of no confidence and demands for a general amnesty, a position advocated by the Union of Unions to which some of the editors belonged, greeted this attempt to engage the political tact of society.[25] His hopes of forming a coalition cabinet from representatives of the moderate, minority wing of the zemstvo movement, which was already foundering on the reluctance of future Octobrists to join a ministry that excluded representatives of the majority Kadets, were dashed by the November zemstvo congress and its resolution that approved constituent powers for a Duma elected by the four-tail suffrage.[26] A piqued Witte in late November issued a press statement warning unnamed "public groups" to mind "the consequences toward which their refusal . . . to cooperate with state authority might lead the fatherland at a time decisive for the fate of Russia."[27] By January, he had begun to lament, publicly, how public opinion was still expecting "political and social rebirth from . . . loud phrases" and was flippantly ignoring "rational and patient labor, obedience to the law, respect for a feeling of duty."[28] In late December he expressed his disillusionment much more explicitly, during a private meeting with a delegation of the St. Petersburg branch of the Octobrist Party central committee. To their charges that

[24] Kryzhanovskii, *Vospominaniia*, p. 68. See also Gurko, *Features and Figures*, pp. 442–44; V. N. Kokovtsov, *Out of My Past* (Stanford University Press, 1935), pp. 59–70; Paul Miliukov, *Political Memoirs, 1905–1917* (University of Michigan Press, 1967), pp. 58–59.

[25] "Interv'iu S. Iu. Vitte s predstaviteliami pechati," in "Iz arkhiva S. Iu. Vitte," *KA* 11–12 (1925): 102–4. Also Witte, *Vospominaniia*, 2:47–52. Witte was quoted as saying at this meeting: "Help me, give me several weeks. All inconveniences, all disorders in the world and revolution always proceed from misunderstandings. . . . It is difficult for the population to achieve the universal right of election without railroads and without social organization. We will only come to this gradually." "Interv'iu," p. 104.

[26] V. I. Startsev, *Russkaia burzhuaziia i samoderzhavie v 1905–1917 gg. (Bor'ba vokrug "otvetstvennoga ministerstva" i "pravitel'stva doveriia")* (Leningrad, 1977), pp. 8–52; Shipov, *Vospominaniia i dumy*, pp. 334–39 and 350–80; "Iz vospominanii A. I. Guchkova," *Poslednye novosti*, 9 August 1936, p. 2; P. N. Miliukov, *Tri popytki* (Paris, 1921), pp. 45–55; and Miliukov, *Political Memoirs*, pp. 59–69.

[27] *Russkie vedomosti*, 2 December 1905, p. 1, and 24 November 1905, p. 1.

[28] *Novoe vremia*, 15 January 1905, p. 2.

government repression was undermining society's trust in the government and repeating the mistakes of past "bureaucratic regimes," Witte replied—according to those who attended—that "there had been a time when he had worried about confidence, when he had sought confidence, but it had not been shown to him then, and now he does not worry about this, now he has one goal—to save Russia—'and I will save it; I know how this will be done.' "[29]

At a time of revolutionary and political upheaval, this was a gargantuan task, and Witte must be given his due for the legislative acts of December 1905–April 1906 that shaped the reformed state order. The revised electoral law of December 1905, the State Duma and State Council statutes of 20 February 1906, and the new Fundamental Laws of 26 April together made possible the election of Russia's first legislative assembly, an achievement without which, Witte knew, the reestablishment of state authority was impossible. Yet although these reforms accommodated the existence of new representative institutions, they were also a deliberate attempt to preserve and reinforce the prerogatives of the state power in law *before* the convocation of the Duma, which Kadets and those to their left would view as a constituent body.

The December electoral law, for example, attempted to accommodate public demands for universal male franchise without dismantling the system of indirect curial elections established by the Bulygin Duma statute of August 1905.[30] In particular, despite arguments against this, the new statute retained separate peasant elections designed to assure the influence of large numbers of peasant voters at the provincial electoral assemblies. It was assumed that the peasants would support prominent local landowners or, an even more desirable outcome, peasants like themselves, producing a loyal Duma majority whose conservatism and pliable character was an assumption that went largely unquestioned.[31] Similarly, the

[29] TsGAOR, f. 115, op. 1, d. 45, ll. 34–35.

[30] "Soobrazheniia Ministra Vnutrennykh Del po nekotorym voprosam, voznikaiushchim pri osushchestvlenii Vysochaishikh predukazanii, vozveshchennykh v reskripte 18 Fevralia 1905 goda," in MVD, *Materialy po uchrezhdeniiu Gosudarstvennoi Dumy*, pp. 92–97, and *Petergofskoe soveshchanie o proekte gosudarstvennoi dumy pod lichnym ego Imperatorskogo Velichestva predsedatel'stvom—sekretnye protokoly* (Berlin, n.d. [192?]). The broadened franchise requirements of the December 1905 electoral law affected rural smallholders in the landowner's curia, professional and middle classes in the cities, and, if least significantly, industrial workers. See Mehlinger and Thompson, *Count Witte and the Tsarist Government*, pp. 112–24 and 241–45, and Leopold H. Haimson, "Introduction: The Russian Landed Nobility and the System of the Third of June," in Haimson, *Politics of Rural Russia*, pp. 9–15.

[31] Kryzhanovskii, *Vospominaniia*, pp. 40–45 and 69–70. The peasant electoral structure established in August had stipulated a four-stage voting process: representatives from each *sel'skoe obshchestvo* to the *volost'* electoral assembly; two delegates from each *volost'* to a peasant county electoral assembly; peasant delegates to the provincial electoral assembly;

Duma and State Council statutes of February 1906, which granted significant legislative, budgetary, and interpellative powers to both bodies, sought at the same time to preserve the executive power of the state.[32] The sovereign and his cabinet retained control over most foreign and military affairs, any initiation of changes in the empire's Fundamental Laws, and the right to disband the Duma and schedule new elections. Through a provision eventually included in the Fundamental Laws under Article 87, the government was able to promulgate emergency legislation when the Duma was not in session. Witte remarked in debate that this "critically important" measure served as "a cane [kept] in the corner" at a time when the representative experiment was just beginning.[33] Finally, the transformation of the State Council into an upper legislative chamber was, according to Witte, "necessary to guarantee a conservative state structure" against the potential inroads of radical parties. Indeed, half of the upper chamber's members were to be appointees of the tsar. The others were elected: a smaller number from large cities, commercial-industrial organizations, and the universities; the greater part from provincial zemstvo assemblies, landowners of nonzemstvo provinces, and, through indirect elections, the provincial assemblies of the nobility.[34]

The Fundamental Laws of 26 April 1906 codified these institutional changes and in essence constructed around them a wall of legality that could be altered only at the emperor's behest—and with the legislative sanction of both chambers. Thus, the Fundamental Laws ensured, or so it seemed, the prerogatives of the bureaucratic government to implement the social and economic reforms that Witte had advocated since the turn of the century. This was particularly true of rural reform, which, under the impact of peasant disorders, was a central preoccupation of the Coun-

---

election of one peasant Duma deputy by peasant delegates before the general provincial election. Counterproposals advocated by a joint Octobrist-Kadet committee and supported by Kryzhanovskii were premised on general elections in the region (*volost'*, *okrug*), where educated landowners could influence peasant voting more directly than would be possible at provincial electoral assemblies where peasants would be much less familiar with non-peasant electors. These plans were rejected because the government doubted its capacity to prevent radical agitation in numerous small electoral assemblies. Kryzhanovskii, *Vospominaniia*, pp. 40–45, and Shchegolev, ed., *Padenie tsarskogo rezhima*, 5:380–81; Shipov, *Vospominaniia i dumy*, pp. 351–52.

[32] "Soobrazheniia," in MVD, *Materialy po uchrezhdeniiu Gosudarstvennoi Dumy*, pp. 31–71.

[33] "Tsarskosel'skoe soveshchanie: Protokoly sekretnogo soveshchaniia v fevralia 1906 g. pod predsedatel'stvom byvshego imperatora po vyrobotke Uchrezhdenii gosudarstvennoi Dumy i gosudarstvennogo Soveta," *Byloe* 5–6 (27–28) (November–December 1917): 296.

[34] "Svod osnovnykh gosudarstvennykh zakonov," *Svod zakonov Rossiiskoi Imperii*, 1906: vol. 1, pt. 1; "Uchrezhdenie Gosudarstvennogo soveta," *Svod zakonov Rossiiskoi imperii*, 1906: vol. 1, pt. 2, no. 2; "Uchrezhedenie Gosudarstvennoi Dumy," *Svod zakonov Rossiiskoi imperii*, 1906: vol. 1, pt. 2, no. 3.

cil of Ministers during the pre-Duma months. Here, perhaps even more than at the level of national politics, the Witte ministry exhibited the constraints imposed by the statist tradition on its efforts to restructure the political and social order of the old regime.

RURAL REFORM AND THE IMPACT OF PEASANT REBELLION

In the three months following the October Manifesto, discussions of rural reform took place in the heightened atmosphere generated by peasant rebellion. It was during this period that the Witte ministry gave serious consideration to a limited but compulsory sale of private estate lands to the peasants. To be sure, proposals to expand peasant landholding, the best known of which was authored by N. N. Kutler, director of the Main Administration of Land Reorganization and Agriculture (Glavnoe upravlenie zemleustroistva i zemlediia [GUZiZ]), were construed as one aspect of a more complex land reform intended to convert peasant communal land use to more advanced and intensive forms of agriculture.[35] Yet because rural disorder was perceived to result from a general "land hunger" that had left the rural populace vulnerable to its own conceptions of injustice, the idea of forced alienation of land seemed to some in government to be a means of dampening rural protest and retaining peasant loyalties. As late as early January Witte was still urging this view upon the tsar, arguing that long-term economic reform did not "relieve the government of its obligation to moderate public life immediately." Peasant declarations, he said, were consistently expressing the "firm if idiosyncratic [svoeobraznyi] viewpoint . . . that they possess rights to lands that they rent, having paid their value many times over."[36] One advantage of distributing these lands in a controlled way, plainly, was to prevent their seizure in an uncontrollable one.[37]

The most immediate result of these discussions, however, was to promote reaction against them in both government and society. Gurko, who authored an anonymous note in November that labeled compulsory alienation "an act of insanity," argued that no amount of land could satisfy a mass rural populace suffering the impoverishment caused by an unproductive, extensive communal agriculture. To expect that whetting

[35] On the Kutler project, see "Proekt zakona o merakh k rasshireniiu i ulushcheniiu krest'ianskogo zemlevladeniia i ob"iasnitel'naia zapiska . . . ," in Veselovskii, *Agrarnyi vopros*, pp. 27–63; "Agrarnyi vopros proekt eks-ministra zemlevladeniia," *Rus'*, 8 February 1906, p. 3; and N. Kutler, "O zemel'nom voprose," *Rus'*, 14 February 1906, p. 4, and 16 February 1906, p. 1. In general, see Macey, *Government and Peasant*, chap. 5 and Yaney, *Urge To Mobilize*, pp. 240–50.

[36] "Vsepoddaneishii doklad grafa Vitte po agrarnomu voprosu (10 ianvaria 1906)," in Veselovskii, *Agrarnyi vopros*, pp. 77–78.

[37] See, in particular, Witte's comments in *Vospominaniia*, 2:156–63 and 287.

appetites with offers of more land could "calm the rural population and even create from it a powerful bulwark" against urban radicalism was unthinkable. Even to mention the plan publicly, Gurko insisted, would instigate a peasant assault on the private estate economy that could become a national economic disaster and undermine those "cultured" provincial noble landowners whom the state utilized in "administration, the courts, and local self-administration."[38] Gurko's was not an isolated voice. His perception that the commune was a source of impoverishment and social antagonism was gaining broad acceptance under the impact of peasant rebellion—and the government's rumored willingness to compromise property rights in order to dampen it. This was especially true within the provincial nobility, where a general conservative reaction against the revolution was being fed by a growing abhorrence for the commune and the threat it posed to private property.[39]

By January these protests and demands to preserve inviolate the rights of property had reached Nicholas II and swayed him against compulsory alienation altogether.[40] Coupled with expressions of the sovereign's disapproval, the same pressure influenced the Council of Ministers, which, Witte reported on 10 January, had decided not to go forward with the Kutler plan, but rather to reserve it, and all other such projects, for further consideration. At the same time, the council resolved to begin legislative discussion of comprehensive land reform, a decision that refocused the government's attention on the juridical abolition of communal tenure and the reorganization of communal agriculture that was favored by officials such as Gurko.[41] The development of statutes, a tortured process

[38] "Zapiska o nedopustimosti dopolnitel'nogo nadeleniia krest'ian," in Veselovskii, *Agrarnyi vopros*, p. 67 and generally pp. 63–82.

[39] Macey, *Peasant and Government*, pp. 133–46 and 183–94; Manning, *Crisis of the Old Order*, pp. 218–26; "Zaiavlenie tambovskikh dvorian V. M. Andreevskogo i N. L. Markova v Tambovskoe dvorianskoe deputatskoe sobranie," in Veselovskii, *Agrarnyi vopros*, pp. 95–98; "S"ezd gubernskikh i uezdnykh Predvoditelei Dvorianstva, 7–11 ianvaria 1906 g.," TsGAOR, f. 483, op. 1, d. 1, ll. 4–8, contains the resolution of this meeting to the effect that all agrarian reform ought to be based on the inviolability of private property and ought to facilitate "the free transition from communal tenure to household [*podvor*] and farmstead [*khutor*] tenure, with the right to freely sell" allotment lands.

[40] *Rus'*, 21 Jan 1906, p. 5, contains the following comments of Nicholas to a delegation of Kursk peasants: "You, brothers, should know of course that any right of property is inviolable; that which belongs to the estate owner belongs to him and that which belongs to the peasant belongs to him. . . . It cannot be otherwise, and there can be no argument about this. I desire that you tell this to your fellow villagers. . . . The State Duma is being summoned and together with Me it will discuss how best to resolve [your needs]. All of you can rely on Me, I will help you, but, I repeat, always remember that the right of property is sacred and ought to be inviolable."

[41] "Vsepoddaneishii doklad grafa Witte po agranomu voprosu," pp. 77–80; *Novoe vremia*, 15 January 1906, p. 5, and 13 February 1906, pp. 3–4.

that occurred primarily under Gurko and GUZiZ director A. I. Krivo-shein, occurred over the next four months. By mid-April the land-reform legislation that later bore the name of P. A. Stolypin was essentially complete. The government stood poised to subordinate the village economy to state power and law, to utilize its political instruments in as sweeping a manner as had occurred during industrialization and emancipation.[42]

Agrarian rebellion, and the perceptions of rural social instability that it spawned, influenced policy toward local administrative reform as much as they had shaped the government's stance on the land question. Here as well, the Witte ministry responded to perceived crisis by attempting to enhance the influence of state power in rural life—thus ignoring those concerns for expanded popular participation in civil government that had figured so prominently in official deliberations before 1905. Indicatively, the major impetus for administrative reform came from the Ministry of Internal Affairs, where by early December Acting Minister P. N. Durnovo had formed a commission to draft legislation.[43] Chaired by Assistant Minister S. D. Urusov, the Urusov Commission drew together the directors of the ministry's four major departments: Gurko (Land Section); S. N. Gerbel (Main Administration for Affairs of Local Economy [Glavnoe upravienie po delam mestnogo khoziaistva—GUMKh]); A. A. Lopukhin (Department of Police); and D. N. Liubimov (Chancellery). Reviewing the materials of the Kakhanov Commission, the Special Conference, and the provincial administrative reforms developed under Pleve, the commission spent the month of December devising a reorganization of rural government.[44] Over that period, the MVD's statist and police traditions were decisive in the formulation of reform proposals.

In the first instance, however, the discussions of the Urusov Commission showed the marked influence that revolution had exerted on these concerns. Returning full circle to positions advocated by the Kakhanov Commission, the membership repudiated peasant estate administration in favor of territorial civil government embracing all estates. Given the formal legitimacy granted civil liberties by the October Manifesto, this repudiation of the principle of estate segregation engendered no debate whatsoever. A general reference in the commission's journal to the rationales of the Special Conference, where the dangers of the peasantry's legal isolation had been underlined repeatedly, conveyed the scorn officials felt for the administrative structures that had contributed to rural disorder.[45]

[42] Macey, *Peasant and Government*, p. 213, and chap. 6. Also Yaney, *Urge To Mobilize*, chap. 6.
[43] TsGIA, f. 1288, op. 2, ed. khr. 38, l. 1 (Durnovo to Witte, n.d.).
[44] "Zhurnaly komissii po razrabotke proekta preobrazovaniia mestnogo upravleniia," (hereinafter "Zhurnaly komissii") TsGIA, f. 1288, op. 1 (1906), d. 3, l. 2.
[45] Ibid., ll. 2–3.

The presence of Gurko and his assistant I. M. Strakhovskii, whose critiques of peasant estate administration had appeared in the liberal legal journal *Pravo*, supplied additional impetus to the decision to abolish the estate character of the village community, township, and land captain.[46]

Resolving to create civil government, the commission almost as unanimously recommended its unification under a county supervisor (*uezdnyi nachal'nik*): "the highest representative of administrative authority and the primary director of administration in the county."[47] Although the antecedents of this proposal could also be traced to the Kakhanov Commission, the new structure of county government had more recently been considered during Pleve's tenure, when minister Durnovo and three other commission members had participated in the work. Indeed, only N. L. Psheradskii of the GUMKh, who at the time was reviewing future reforms of self-administration, urged the Urusov Commission to allow zemstvo election of this official, a route that had been envisioned in the early 1880s. It was testimony not only to the times but also to the increased professionalization within bureaucratic ranks that the reliance on zemstvo personnel was rejected out of hand, as was the use of the county marshal of the nobility, whom "the law [did] not equip with actual authority."[48] The county supervisor was to be a crown official, appointed by and subordinated to the provincial governor. His responsibilities would extend to all police business, prosecution of official malfeasance, auditing (*reviziia*) of state and zemstvo institutions, and review of administrative appeals from lower echelons of the county apparatus.[49] With the notable exception of police affairs, this work would be conducted through a county council (*uezdnoe prisutstvie*), whose bureaucratic membership would include two zemstvo representatives.[50] The commission left little doubt that the changed political environment now existing in the empire not only allowed, but, more important, demanded a strengthening of government power through a rationalized, more effective administrative apparatus that would possess "the broadest prerogatives [*polnomochiia*]" in local society:

> One must not forget that with the reform of our entire structure on the basis of the Manifesto of 17 October, the exercise of administrative power unavoidably

[46] I. M. Strakhovskii, "Obosoblennost' i ravnopravnost' krest'ian," *Pravo* 1903, pp. 2109–22, 2149–61, and 2197–2211.

[47] "Zhurnaly Komissii," l. 30.

[48] Ibid., ll. 27–28.

[49] Ibid., ll. 30–31. The supervisor was to be appointed at the fifth rank of the Table of Ranks at an annual salary of four thousand rubles.

[50] Ibid., l. 31. The county supervisor would chair a council constituted from his administrative assistant, the Ministry of Justice's senior procurator, the Ministry of Finance's tax inspector, the chair of the county zemstvo board, and an elected representative of its assembly.

assumes an entirely different character. If formerly it was necessary to observe a certain degree of caution in limiting the authority of administrative officials in order to constrain [their] arbitrariness, under the new conditions—freedom of the press, interpellations in the State Duma, etc.—it is desirable on the contrary to grant to administrative power the greatest prerogatives possible, because there is little doubt that, given the changing circumstances in which power is exercised, its representative will employ it with the necessary caution.[51]

The near-unanimity displayed in these decisions to reform the institutions and powers of government administration, however, concealed deep differences as to the goals that both confronted in the new, "post-October" era of political freedom and social conflict. Nominally, the issue that provoked contentious disagreement was the small zemstvo unit that had been promised in the ukase of 12 December 1904. In principle, however, debate centered on the extension of self-administration to all-estate village and township territories—and, consequently, on the degree to which officials were willing to expand popular participation in local civil affairs as a strategy to restore order and authority in the countryside. This question, which in large measure had been only theoretical when the Kakhanov Commission had considered it in the 1880s, assumed irrefutable political importance in the winter of 1905–06.[52]

Four commission members—Urusov, Lopukhin, Liubimov, and I. Ia. Gurliand—were prepared to accept significant changes. They advocated all-estate village self-administration and new zemstvo institutions in the territory (uchastok) currently administered by the land captain. The latter could levy its own taxes, write budgets, hire employees, and elect an executive board. The land captain, having lost his raison d'être with the abolition of estate institutions, would be eliminated altogether and "certain" of his administrative functions (tax collection, the annual military draft, and some local police responsibilities) would be transferred to the zemstvo executive board. These elected officials would thus become the primary executive agents of the county supervisor. In essence, this proposal aimed to expand and deepen the authority of zemstvo institutions in local administration. The law would allow provincial zemstvos to shut down county assemblies and divert their resources and personnel to the new institutions.[53]

This drive to incorporate the local populace into official structures of public self-administration was even more apparent in the majority's recommendations concerning the electoral franchise, which determined who

---

[51] Ibid., l. 28.

[52] These were the most time-consuming and heatedly debated issues of the commission's work. Ibid., ll. 4–9, 13–22.

[53] Ibid., ll. 15, 19, 22, 29–31, and *Novoe vremia*, 21 December 1905, p. 4.

participated in these institutions. Under existing law, voting rights belonged only to local residents owning rural or urban property that was subject to zemstvo taxation. All members of the commission were willing to broaden this rubric somewhat to include long-term rented property and any commercial license.[54] Going much further, A. A. Lopukhin and I. Ia. Gurliand argued for a franchise based solely on residence because it alone would allow salaried professionals to participate in the institution. Aware of the hostility and suspicion with which the MVD regarded the zemstvo "third element," Lopukhin and Gurliand preferred legitimate public endeavor to an exclusionary strategy that had provided grounds for political radicalism "and thereby convert[ed] useful forces into harmful ones."[55] Although he refused to jettison the principle of property ownership, Chairman Urusov did join his two colleagues in advocating both a franchise based upon payment of zemstvo tax and the so-called Prussian or "class system of elections," which distributed all taxpayers among three electoral assemblies organized according to assessed wealth.[56] Supporting as it did a regressive system that allocated to the wealthy minority the same number of zemstvo delegates as the other two assemblies, this proposal did not portend the democratization of zemstvo institutions. Yet, as Urusov explained in a special opinion, it was a significant alteration of a system that had been dominated since 1864 by provincial noble landowners. "The franchise," Urusov said, was "a personal right, not the representation of a particular property value." He aimed to assure the conservative influence of wealth and property, yet guarantee "a just and equal representation of diverse class interests [*klassovye interesy*]."[57]

This entire scheme provoked heated opposition from GUMKh director S. N. Gerbel, and especially from V. I. Gurko, whose opposition to the small zemstvo unit had not cooled since the meetings of the Special Conference in 1904. In the first instance, although both accepted the small zemstvo as a fait accompli, neither envisioned anything more than an executive appendage of the county assembly, which would define the tax rates and budget of the new institution. More important, both of these

[54] Ibid., l. 6. This measure did not include most peasants renting private land, who usually leased for one planting season. Nevertheless, however erratically, zemstvo property taxation encompassed a large part of the rural male population and most forms of economic activity: privately owned agricultural land; forests; peasant allotment land; all residences in towns or rural areas; commercial and industrial buildings; licenses for commerce and trade, extending from large industrial enterprises to rural shops selling or producing consumer goods, Veselovskii, *Istoriia zemstva*, 1:33–125.

[55] "Zhurnaly Komissii," l. 7.

[56] Ibid., l. 8. The proposal arose at a time when the Ministry of Finance was considering the introduction of a progressive income tax, "Memoriia soveta ministrov, 7 marta 1906," TsGIA, f. 1276, op. 2, d. 4, l. 59.

[57] "Zhurnaly Kommissii," l. 8.

prominent MVD officials were reluctant to expand the authority and scope of an institution whose presence implicitly challenged statist regulation of the countryside. Objecting to any administrative empowerment of zemstvo officials, they insisted that all executive functions remain the responsibility of a bureaucratic hierarchy working through all-estate township officials (*starshina*), and, in Gurko's formulation, through reformed land captains as well.[58]

Rather than principled opposition to self-administration per se, however, it was the perceived political and social consequences of allowing broader popular participation in civil government that reinforced the statist convictions of these officials. Indeed, D. N. Liubimov, who supported the small zemstvo in theory, joined Gerbel and Gurko in attacking the proposed electoral reforms intended to give it significance in popular life. All three rejected the tax franchise and reforms of the electoral structure, preferring only minor adjustments of the existing system to accommodate smaller private estate owners.[59] All also singled out the support expressed by Gurliand and Lopukhin for a residency franchise to protest an apparent willingness to ignore the influence that political radicals wielded within the local population.[60] If allowed unrestricted access, salaried professionals, "in current parlance labeled the 'third element,' " would use the small zemstvo unit for only one reason: "political agitation [*politikanstvo*] . . . and in the majority of cases for propaganda of socialist ideas [*propaganda soltsialisticheskikh idei*]."[61]

Liubimov, it should be noted, opposed only the liberalization of franchise requirements; unlike Gurko and Gerbel he supported powers of administration and taxation for the new zemstvo. Apparently retaining views widespread in his ministry before 1905, he believed that communal peasants, if protected from radical influence and made to see a role for themselves in zemstvo self-administration, could be a conservative force in the institution. Such was also the view of his superior P. N. Durnovo,

[58] Ibid., ll. 15, 19, 30–31. In their version, budgetary and taxing power belonged only to the county zemstvo assembly. Both Gurko and Gerbel favored retention of the township territory as an administrative and fiscal jurisdiction. The *starshina*, elected by the entire local populace, was subject to state supervision only. Gurko in addition advocated a reformed land captain (*uchastkovyi komissar*), as the immediate supervisor of several townships.

[59] Ibid., ll. 8, 30. They recommended: a 50% reduction of the existing property franchise; separate electoral assemblies for communal peasants and full-census landowners; and preliminary elections for private smallholders.

[60] Gerbel's GUMKh had already been considering a long list of administrative measures to eliminate zemstvo political radicalism, TsGIA, f. 1288, op. 2, 1905, ed. khr. 37, ll. 41–42, which included gubernatorial supervision of zemstvo elections, assembly proceedings, requests for extraordinary sessions, violations of state laws or interests, elected and salaried officials, executive boards, and instances requiring state expenditure of zemstvo funds.

[61] "Zhurnaly Kommissii," l. 7.

who in a letter of January noted that peasants, placed in the proper environment, would "become interested in zemstvo economy and administration." Their "well-known drive to curtail wasteful expenditures and their dislike for the salaried element, which lately has been gaining strength in the zemstvo," would exert a "most beneficial" influence upon public affairs.[62] Gurko and Gerbel shared no such illusions about peasant majorities. To allow their domination in village and small zemstvo assemblies, the two maintained, was to predetermine "extreme taxation of more prosperous individuals, their liability for taxes that are not of equal interest for all." Peasants in the existing estate township might be left to tax themselves, but in an all-estate zemstvo their uninhibited access to the income of noble private property would only exacerbate rural socioeconomic instability:

> It is inadmissable to forget that our country lacks a middle agricultural class [*srednyi zemel'nyi klass*]. Here there exist either the grey, impoverished millions of peasant farmers or a few relatively prosperous noble landowners. Between the property status of the one and [that of] the other lies a huge abyss [*tselaia propast'*]. . . . The heterogeneity of the population's class composition [*klassovyi sostav*] will result in peasants living at the expense of noble landowners [pomeshchiki] and pomeshchiki being crushed by unbearable taxes.[63]

Of course, in other forums Gurko had expressed a more nuanced view of agrarian society and knew well that patterns of rural property-holding were more diversified than he and his colleague depicted here. Indeed, these processes were sufficiently advanced to have rendered Gurko the most committed advocate in the MVD of civil and economic reform: land reform intended to accelerate rural socioeconomic transformation; institutional reform to dismantle the peasant estate structure; and administrative reform to establish effective bureaucratic authority in the local areas. Yet, particularly at a time of political and social disorder, state reform

---

[62] TsGIA, f. 1288, op. 2, ed. khr. 38, chast' 4, ll. 1–3 (P. N. Durnovo to S. Iu. Witte, 26 January 1906). See also "Organizatsiia obshchestvennykh sil," *Novoe vremia*, 16 January 1906, p. 2. Durnovo's letter was prompted by his disapproval of a proposal, forwarded to him by Witte, to expand peasant membership in the zemstvo assemblies and allow them to initiate discussions of the land question. The idea was premised on the assumption that if peasant zemstvo deputies witnessed land reform discussions beginning in a forum they controlled, they would become "avid supporters and defenders of order and, given their influence, [would] restrain their fellow villagers," "O neobkhodimosti nemedlennogo preobrazovaniia sostava zemskikh uezdnykh sobranii—Proekt Kailenskogo, zemlevladelets Sudzhanskogo uezda," TsGIA, f. 1288, op. 2 (1905), ed. khr. 7, chast' 2, ll. 152–55.

[63] "Zhurnaly Komissii," l. 9. They offered three possible solutions: invest all budgetary authority in the county zemstvo; allot large landowners votes in the small zemstvo assembly commensurate with the value of their property holdings; mandate itemized taxation for each projected expenditure (*predmetnye sbory*). Ibid., ll. 9, 15, 30.

that entailed an expansion of rural self-administration or a reorganization of rural public life was rejected because it threatened the pillars of state power and private estate agriculture, which at present upheld the old order. To undermine either of them was tantamount to abandoning the long-term opportunity for reform that Gurko wanted to pursue. Social antagonism in the countryside dictated civil and economic reform but militated against all but the most superficial expansion of popular participation in rural public affairs, in rural political life.

The Urusov Commission completed its deliberations on 2 January 1906. Some three weeks later the Council of Ministers included local rural reform in a resolution ordering all ministries to prepare legislative initiatives for consideration by the State Duma. Such work, it remarked, was necessary "to direct the activity of the State Duma immediately along a defined, business-like course." Empasizing in this regard that the "peasant question" in both economic and legal aspects was of primary significance, the Council instructed the MVD to prepare a local reform based on the elimination of estate segregation, a principle that suffused the "legislative code in almost all branches of national [*narodnyi*] life." The creation of the Duma—and, implicitly, the projected reforms of the agricultural economy—had rendered it illegitimate:

> Peasants form a class of petty proprietors [*klass mel'kikh sobstvennikov*]. To preserve and maintain their estate segregation is unacceptable when . . . peasants have been summoned to assist the Monarch in the great affair of general state construction. Under these conditions it would be plainly inconsistent to refuse peasants the right to free utilization of their property [and] to preserve for them a separate court, which does not rely on laws, or the guardianship [*opeka*] of the land captain.

Property, legality, and rational administration: these were the principles of the Rechtsstaat that had informed the resolutions of Witte's Special Conference and the ukase of 12 December 1904, and the council duly noted these precedents. On the issues that divided the MVD, however, the cabinet simply allowed that different options were available for defining local administration and self-administration, thus leaving the matter in the hands of the ministry.[64]

Novoe vremia reported in mid-February that Minister of Internal Affairs Durnovo had taken local reform discussions under his direct supervision, and that the ministry was not inclined to create a small zemstvo unit, but instead planned only to reorganize the village and township into all-estate institutions.[65] That Durnovo had sided with Gurko's version of

---

[64] "Memoriia Soveta ministrov, 24 January 1906," TsGIA, f. 1276, op. 2, d. 4, ll. 13–16.
[65] *Novoe vremia*, 18 February 1906, p. 4; also 1 February 1906, p. 4, which reports that

local reform became evident over the next two months. In March Gurko replaced Urusov as assistant minister; in early April he represented the MVD on the Nikol'skii Commission, which finalized the rural reform program that the government intended to present to the Duma. On the eve of its convocation he was preparing to chair a commission to write new statutes for local administration.[66] The clearest indication of his influence, however, was the legislative program of the Witte ministry, formally presented by its chairman on 23 April, nine days after he had in fact resigned from office.[67]

The "Witte program," which was primarily devoted to the ministry's proposed economic and legal reforms of rural society, did represent, as its preamble stated, the triumph of a reformist tradition that had long sought "to realize the chief principle of the statute of 19 February 1861— the acculturation of the peasants to general civil life [*priobshchenie krest'ian k obshchegrazhdanskoi zhizni*]."[68] Peasant estate administration and courts were to be abolished in favor of all-estate institutions and justices of the peace elected by the zemstvo.[69] A rationalized county bureaucracy, based on a reformed land captain supervising village and township institutions, was to be established. Restrictions on the right to leave the land commune were to be eliminated, and the mechanisms to

zemstvo reform had not yet been developed and was unlikely to be ready until after the convocation of the Duma.

[66] TsGIA, f. 1291, op. 122, d. 46, ch. 4, ll. 1–2 (Durnovo to M. G. Akimov, 12 April 1906) contains the notification that a commission chaired by assistant minister Gurko would begin meeting on 24 April "for examination of a project of rural administration."

[67] "Vsepoddaneishii doklad Grafa Witte, 23 aprelia 1906 g." and "Programma voprosov, vnosimykh na razsmotrenie Gos. Dumy," TsGIA, f. 1276, op. 2, d. 4, l. 205–23. The program contained proposals from the MVD (peasant reform); GUZiZ (land reorganization); Ministry of Justice (local courts; civil and criminal liability for official malfeasance); and the Ministry of Trade and Industry (legislation affecting the commercial-industrial and working classes [particularly illness and accident insurance, housing, child and female labor law, working day, hiring practices and wages, factory inspectorate, industrial arbitration boards]).

[68] Ibid., l. 208. "Proekt osnovnykh polozhenii dlia izmenenii zakonodatel'stva o krest'ianakh," ll. 209–15, outlined the ministry's proposals concerning peasant property rights, administration, courts, land reorganization, and expansion of landholding through the Peasant Bank.

[69] Ibid., ll. 210–12. The principles of the proposed rural justice of the peace were: equality of all estates before the law; judicial independence; proximity to the population; simplified procedure; utilization of imperial criminal and civil law codes. The proposed justice would possess adjudicatory authority over all civil suits seeking damages of less than one thousand rubles and criminal misdemeanors. The justice would be elected by the county zemstvo and confirmed in office by the First Department of the Senate. He was to be a full-census property owner with exceptions made for academic accomplishment: graduates of university juridical faculties; or graduates of universities and gymnasiia, providing they passed a bar examination administered by the *okrug* court.

effect the reorganization of communal agriculture were to be put in place. These were institutional and legal structures through which the state could oversee and foster the transformation of rural society. Yet at the same time the program ignored jurisdictional relations between bureaucratic and zemstvo institutions as well as electoral reform, and left the creation of small zemstvos to the discretion of county assemblies—an increasingly unlikely prospect in the strife-torn spring of 1906.[70]

From the perspective of the previous half-century, the Witte ministry had proposed significant alterations of autocratic government. That a unified ministerial cabinet was presenting a national assembly with a legislative program to consider in itself conveyed the depths of Witte's achievement. Only twelve months previously both institutions had been unacceptable infringements on tsarist prerogative. Even more fundamental was the effort to create, through state law and the long-term socioeconomic transformation of the Russian peasant, a civil order no longer threatened by the social conflict of 1906. From the perspective of contemporary events, however, what was equally striking about the Witte program was its disregard of local politics, of the issues of rural self-administration that had preoccupied the chairman before 1905 as he sought to avoid the national politics over which he now presided. Most immediately, this gap was attributable to policy-making in the MVD. Rural social conflict had reinforced the perceived necessity for state power to police agrarian society; an expansion of self-administration, and even more acutely a realignment of its constituencies, threatened to undermine the political and social foundations on which the state rested.

There was, however, a second factor that explained the abandonment of what before 1905 had been a key element of Witte's political strategy. Reforms of self-administration had then been viewed as both an instrument of civil acculturation and a concession to educated political opposition that was limited to local concerns. In the aftermath of the October Manifesto, social disorder and the creation of the State Duma had rendered such objectives not only potentially dangerous but also irrelevant. Instead, the ministry turned its attention to the long-term goal of agrarian reform and the immediate task of constructing the legal and civil order that would reestablish the legitimacy of government authority in the still novel world of national politics. Believing that it confronted a crisis of political opinion in educated society alone, the ministry ignored local politics because it anticipated that a mass peasantry, as had been the case in

---

[70] Ibid., ll. 210–12. County assemblies could petition to create these new institutions, define their jurisdiction in the zemstvo economy, determine the extent of their authority and budgetary powers, and decide the form of their electoral system. Tax rates would be fixed in law as some percentage of county revenues.

other European states, could still be manipulated to support the government.

That view had played a role in the flirtation with forced alienation of private property in the early winter. It had informed the outlines of the December electoral law and continued to influence the thinking of many throughout the months preceding the convocation of the Duma. Witte himself, noting in a January interview with the London *Daily Telegraph* the government's successful suppression of peasant disorders, also applauded the common sense of those villagers who were realizing the truth about revolutionary propaganda directed against "God and Tsar": two images, he said, that represented "religion, morality, patriotism, and duty," the very "essence of the spiritual life of the peasantry." Even a statesman contemplating the transformation of the land commune, it would appear, could find reassuring the hope that peasants were beginning to recognize that "lack of faith and rebellion against the tsar stand beyond the pale of [even] the most extreme and irrational crimes."[71]

Nor was it coincidental that the Witte ministry lavished attention on reforms of the rural economic and legal order as it prepared a legislative program in March and April. These plans were an official and appropriate version of land and freedom, the hallowed peasant demand that had echoed throughout the countryside that winter. When on 5 March 1906 the Council of Ministers first set in motion the final formulation of the agrarian reform program, it noted that "considerations of a political character" were motivating the decision:

> Whatever the first Duma's composition—and it is possible and even likely that it will be significantly [composed of] peasant[s]—the question of the structure of peasant life [krest'ianskoe ustroistvo], which affects the interests of all rural residents, will hold the attention of the Duma to a significant degree. . . . [With a government program before it], there will be fewer grounds for fearing the fruitless waste of the Duma's power on conflicts with representatives of government authority, given the path toward creative, serious work that will open before it.[72]

Indeed, in late March the ministry moved to obtain State Council sanction of land-reform legislation before the convocation of the Duma, thereby, as both Witte and A. P. Nikol'skii explained, diverting peasant deputies from the alluring but unacceptable plans for forced alienation likely to be put forward by the Kadets and other radical elements. Although supporting the legislation in principle, a majority of the Council

[71] *Novoe vremia*, 15 January 1906, p. 2.

[72] "Memoriia Soveta ministrov, 5 March 1906," TsGIA, f. 1276, op. 2, d. 4, l. 53. See also "Memoriia, 24 January 1906," ibid., l. 12, and "Memoriia Soveta ministrov 17 and 24 February 1906," in Veselovskii, *Agrarnyi vopros*, pp. 126–27.

rejected the measure because an act of such significance could not be approved without the sanction of the Duma and its probable complement of peasant deputies.[73]

Gurko, who had no illusions that the government could manipulate peasant sentiments, supplied telling testimony about his colleagues' convictions by recalling a meeting of the Council of Ministers in early March, when Duma elections were already underway. Reports of preliminary voting in rural townships and counties had indicated that many peasant delegates would attend the provincial assemblies to elect Duma deputies, Gurko remembered. "Everyone present was pleased." The ministers happily discussed their pending legislative program: "now it will be easier; now we shall pass this measure through this Duma." It occurred "to no one," he wrote, "that the fact of being a peasant did not constitute a guarantee of political loyalty."[74] Grand Duke Konstantin Aleksandrovich, writing in his diary on 7 March, confirmed Gurko's retrospective commentary. Newspapers reported that the early balloting was producing many "individuals of extreme-leftist tendencies," but, he added, "the overwhelming majority will be from the peasants"—a turn of events that was "extremely desirable."[75]

Most revealing of this willful belief that the peasant population remained susceptible to tsarist and thus ministerial authority, was the editorial line that the daily newspaper *Russkoe gosudarstvo*, the mouthpiece of the Witte ministry, took in analyzing the Duma elections.[76] On 23 March, two days after the Kadet party scored its first major victory in the city of St. Petersburg, the paper suggested that exultation about a Kadet majority dominating the new assembly might be premature. Noting that some forty percent of the delegates to provincial electoral assemblies remained to be selected, it found even greater significance in the fact that "the overwhelming majority" of delegates already chosen were peasants who did not adhere to any party. Whether communal villagers, small proprietors, or priests, the "peasants," it was becoming apparent, preferred "independence and complete freedom in politics [*v dele politiki*]." Such individuals, who did not belong to "the intelligentsia" and knew little of

---

[73] "Zasedanie Gosudarstvennogo Soveta," *Novoe vremia*, 20 March 1906, p. 1; "Vopros o formakh krest'ianskogo zemlevladeniia," *Russkoe gosudarstvo*, 21 March 1906, pp. 1–2; and Polovtsev, "Dnevnik A. A. Polovtsev," pp. 96–97 (18 March 1906). The project under consideration was developed in the MVD by Gurko, "Proekt osnovnykh polozhenii zakona o svobodnom vykhode krest'ian iz obshchiny i rasprostranenii operatsii Krest'ianskogo banka na ukreplenye v chastnuiu sobstvennost' nadel'nye zemli, namechennyi pravitel'stvom dlia izdaniia do sozyva Gos. Dumy (19 fevralia 1906)," S. M. Sidel'nikov, *Agrarnaia reforma Stolypina* (Moscow, 1973), pp. 58–61.

[74] Gurko, *Features and Figures*, p. 454.

[75] "Iz dnevnika Konstantina Romanova," *KA*, 45 (1931): 114 (7 March 1906).

[76] Witte, *Vospominaniia*, 2:252–53.

towns where opposition political parties drew most of their support, were likely to vote for "people who were honorable, dedicated to the Motherland, loyal to its Sovereign, and above all not falsifiers" like the Kadets.[77]

When the first provincial elections took place on 26 March 1906 and results indicated a significant number of "leftist" [i.e., Kadet] deputies, *Russkoe gosudarstvo* registered its unease, as "nobody from personal experience suspected that the mass of the Russian populace was in any way imbued with radical political ideas."[78] Yet, as the paper noted on 4 April, there was a distinct difference between the radicalism shown by "the majority of peasant representatives," whose desire for land could only be understood "from the perspective of socioeconomic issues," and "the purely political viewpoint" of those party organizations that sought to create a constituent assembly or a democratic republic. Most peasants "held to the idea of tsarist authority too fervently" to accept such proposals. Admittedly, political extremism was going to tell "very strongly" on the "chances for moderation in the Duma," but it was for this very reason that a defined government program on the land question was essential to allow "the consolidation of representatives of the people who seriously desire to see to their affairs" when the Duma convened.[79]

Like most of the national press in early April, *Russkoe gosudarstvo* was coming to the conclusion that "the peasant masses in all likelihood [would] be strongly represented" in the coming Duma.[80] Conducting detailed statistical analyses of the some 190 deputies already elected in order to divine their probable political orientation, the paper began to emphasize that "the majority of deputies [were] semi-literate," a fact that not only conveyed the preponderant influence of peasants but also raised questions whether they "would follow the intelligentsia or stand aloof in the Duma." The high percentage of deputies unaffiliated with a party suggested that peasants were assuming a passive but centrist position, identifying neither with extreme rightist circles nor left-wing radicalism and thus still amenable to government influence:

> The peasantry does not possess a detailed political platform, it is unable to orient itself properly within the complex system of contemporary political goals, it needs authoritative and enlightened leadership. Clearly and con-

[77] "Kto budet v Gosudarstvennoi Dume?" *Russkoe gosudarstvo*, 25 March 1906, p. 4. See also "Znachenie stolichnykh vyborov," *Novoe vremia*, 22 March 1906, p. 3.

[78] "Vybory i Kadety," *Russkoe gosudarstvo*, 31 March 1906, p. 3; also "Luchshie liudi," p. 4. The Kadets began to claim victory for "progressive elements" after this date, citing especially the votes of peasants, *Russkie vedomosti*, 28 March 1906, p. 1.

[79] "Krainye levye i Gosudarstvennaia Duma," *Russkoe gosudarstvo*, 4 April 1906, pp. 2–3.

[80] "Krest'ianskoe predstavitel'stvo," *Russkoe gosudarstvo*, 5 April 1906, p. 3.

sciously it can only say that it cannot live without God and Tsar and that the land is the foundation of its material welfare and spiritual development.

Thus it was all the more essential to fulfill "the political ideals and desires of this class," particularly at a time when radicals, competing for the same base, believed that the opportunity still existed to achieve "the reeducation of the people in the spirit of revolutionary doctrines."[81]

Indeed, only three days later *Russkoe gosudarstvo* reported that peasant deputies arriving in St. Petersburg were holding private meetings to discuss "the formation of a Duma peasant party"—a process eventually leading to the creation of the *Trudovik* fraction, which stood to the left of the Kadets in the first assembly. The paper applauded the actions of "these energetic and active people" because they were creating "a Duma center." While "Kadet and Union [of Unions] orators and publicists" fruitlessly debated theory, "peasants were acting—and doing so quite energetically."[82] On the eve of the second round of provincial elections, whose results would largely decide the Duma's actual composition, one editorialist went so far as to argue that the Duma would be divided between "two strata: the intelligentsia and the people [*narod*]." Looking to the most traditional foundation of government authority and hoping for the defeat of its most traditional opponent, this author emphasized that peasants had exhibited "energy and firmness" in electing their own to the Duma. "They did not trust the intelligentsia," he said, primarily because their own "self-consciousness as a defined and distinct social group" was developing "at a rapid pace." Preserving "their [historic] ideals" in the face of democratic and republican doctrine, peasant deputies were assuredly going to insist on "fruitful and expeditious work" in the Duma and would deprive intelligentsia radicals of a base from which to pursue their ideals.[83]

After the second round of provincial elections on 14 April, however, a Kadet victory could no longer be denied. Nor, as press interviews with arriving peasant deputies revealed a staunch insistence on obtaining land, was speculation about a moderate peasant bloc realistic.[84] *Russkoe gosudarstvo* signaled its disillusionment on 18 April, but a note of self-justifying incredulity still persisted in its protestations. Perhaps the majority

---

[81] "Tsifrovye resultaty vyborov," *Russkoe gosudarstvo*, 5 April 1906, p. 2. See also a similar analysis, which, however, emphasized the peasantry's interest in the Kadet land program, in *Russkie vedomosti*, 7 April 1906, p. 1.

[82] "Krest'ianskie deputaty," *Russkoe gosudarstvo*, 8 April 1906, p. 3.

[83] "Budushchaia Gosudarstvennaia Duma po tsifrovym dannym," *Russkoe Gosudarstvo*, 13 April 1906, p. 3.

[84] "Rossiia nakanune rokovykh sobytii," *Novoe vremia*, 20 April 1906, p. 3, compared events to the opening of the French Estates-General in May 1789. See also "Krest'ianskie deputaty v Peterburge," *Novoe vremia*, 21 April 1906, p. 3.

of deputies were "the most honorable people deserving the full respect and confidence of the country," the paper noted, but from its perspective the first attempt at elections had not "given a true result." Only one generation previously, in the 1870s and 1880s, peasants had resisted populist radicalism. Had the German social democrat Bebel or the French socialist Jaures gone into the "backwater of the provinces" at that time, they too would have been handed over to the local police. "Hence," the paper concluded,

> theoretically such unexpected phenomena as the election [of radical deputies] from the peasants are totally incomprehensible; such individuals cannot be voices of the Russian popular spirit and representatives of this ultraconservative milieu. . . . The people . . . could not have been remade in such a short interval to the extent that they would elect and entrust their fate to personalities of this kind. . . . Clearly, all this was the artificial work of the leaders of the electoral campaign.[85]

What in theory had seemed incomprehensible was emerging as the preeminent fact of Russian political life. Only the subsequent months of the First Duma's tenure would prove that the "ultraconservative peasantry" had been neither duped by radical agitators nor remade, but simply revealed as a groundless illusion. When the First Duma was convened with solemnity at the Winter Palace on 27 April, I. L. Goremykin might have been able to rejoice, as he was reported to have done, at the highly successful idea of opening the Duma "amidst all the splendor of court pomp." What "a great impression" all of this made "on the members of the Duma, particularly the peasants," said Goremykin, recounting how one of the deputies, a "*muzhik* [peasant], for the first time in his life entering the Winter Palace, gasped, crossed himself, and exclaimed: 'And they want to encroach upon this kind of majesty [*velichie*]!' Isn't it true," Goremykin added, "that this is characteristic [of them]!"[86] The new chairman of the Council of Ministers, who had replaced a disillusioned Witte on 23 April, would himself quickly discover, as had his predecessor, that even this pillar of government authority had collapsed.

In his memoirs Witte blames everyone but himself for the failure of his reform program to reestablish the legitimacy of autocratic government in Russian society. "All those who were truly enlightened [and] not embittered, and [who] still believed in the political honesty of the higher-ups,

---

[85] "Chto bylo, chto est' i chto budet," *Russkoe gosudarstvo*, 18 April 1906, pp. 1–2. This issue, appearing four days after Witte tendered his resignation from office, was the last to convey the official tone that previously had characterized the newspaper's editorial writing. On 16 May, the paper was renamed *Vechernye pribavleniia k Pravitel'stvennomu Vestniku*.
[86] L.D Liubimov, *Na chuzhbine* (Moscow, 1963), p. 47.

understood," he wrote, "that *society had been given everything* [emphasis added] for which . . . it had sacrificed so many noble lives, beginning with the Decembrists." The litany that followed, however, revealed how few of the truly enlightened had rallied to the premier's support. The "embittered, the unbalanced, those who had lost faith in autocracy" had battled the "regime" and the "autocrat."[87] The "cultured classes of the population" had failed to repudiate radicalism, proving that educated society as a whole lacked the "political and state experience" demanded by the times.[88] By turning against his agrarian reform plans and damaging his credibility with the sovereign, provincial noble landowners had proven that they had been "boudoir liberals" concerned more for their "bulging pockets" than for peasant welfare. Not even the tsar, whom Witte blamed for the debacle of the First Duma elections, escaped indictment. By withdrawing his support for compulsory land sales, Witte charged, Nicholas had left his government holding an electoral law designed to convene "a primarily peasant Duma," while depriving it of the legislative symbol that might have convinced the peasants that they still "could seek supreme justice from the autocrat."[89]

Perhaps Witte should be excused the deep antagonism he showed to those he perceived as having undermined his ministry. His appointment to chair the Council of Ministers and the promulgation of the October Manifesto had not only been the crowning achievements in the distinguished career of this great statesman. They had represented as well a fundamental transition in the history of the autocratic state. Particularly when considered in the context of the previous half-century, unification of ministerial government, limitation of autocratic authority, and popular election of a representative legislative assembly had effected far-reaching changes in Russian political life. Although these initiatives had not created, nor, indeed, been intended to create, a constitutional order, this ought not detract from the skill with which Witte attempted to secure the administrative system, legal guarantees, and, contrary to his inclinations in the 1890s, representative institutions of the Rechtsstaat. Having struggled before 1905 to avert the imposition of limitations on autocratic authority and bureaucratic government, Witte had understood better than most the necessity of these measures as a barrier against a revolution that might undermine state power altogether. They became, as he had intended, precedents for a new political order; future attempts to overturn them would raise not only the specter of prereform tutelage, but also that

[87] Witte, *Vospominaniia*, 2:43.
[88] Ibid., pp. 266–67.
[89] Ibid., p. 287.

of the revolutionary upheaval that in October 1905 had necessitated such fundamental acts of state.

Witte's retrospective bitterness, however, also reemphasized the limitations that long service to the autocratic state had placed on his political vision. His actions in 1905–06 had been informed by a conviction that state power and government authority were instruments as essential in an era of revolution as they had been during the industrialization of the 1890s. Political stability, and the realignment of state life necessary to achieve it, had thus been means to greater goals. Together they were to have solidified state authority and to have guaranteed it the opportunity to create, at long last, the civil order foreseen at the time of the Great Reforms. Yet Witte *expected* educated society to heed his views of the national interest. Judging from his memoirs, the chagrined premier never fully realized how fundamentally the panoply of political parties and interest groups replacing "educated society" had altered the political topography on which these false expectations had rested. As an unfamiliar national politics contradicted this heritage of enlightened bureaucratic leadership, so too grew Witte's Bonapartism: a term that can be understood not as Lenin applied it to post-1905 Russia, but as European commentators interpreted Louis-Napoleon's or Bismarck's reliance on the peasant vote. In order to preserve superordinate state power Witte was willing to manipulate the purportedly conservative political sympathies of the peasantry, a policy whose risks only became fully apparent as the former minister went into retirement.

In the final analysis, what was most striking about the Witte ministry was that it had not fully encountered, and thus had not comprehended, the true scope of the political crisis confronting autocracy. Only the elections of March–April 1906 and the experience of the First Duma that they produced provided convincing proof that the state confronted a systemic collapse of all political authority. An assembly whose largest bloc was constituted from the Kadet party, whose character had largely been determined by the votes of peasant Russia, and whose primary political demand was the compulsory alienation of private lands signaled the absence of a foundation on which the authority of the bureaucratic government could rest. The First Duma also marked the beginning of a period in which an isolated state would attempt a process of political reconstruction to mobilize the political authority that it now lacked. "There appeared," Witte brooded in his memoirs, "the gallant orator from the school of Russian provincial zemstvo assemblies, oiled from head to foot in Russian liberalism, who achieved the state coup d'état of 3 June [1907]," P. A. Stolypin.[90]

---

[90] Ibid., p. 288.

CHAPTER VI

"Reform at a Time of Revolution": Government and Politics under the Stolypin Ministry, July 1906–June 1907

RATHER THAN alleviate the political crisis of 1905–06, the First Duma deepened it. A. A. Polovtsev, an appointed member of the reformed State Council but still a diligent diarist, noted on 5 July 1906 that council business had kept him from recording events for almost three weeks. "Besides," he added in despair, "events, truly horrifying ones occur daily one atop another," so that he found it difficult to write. The newspapers reported nothing but "plundering, armed robberies, and murders." The Duma, pretending "to play the role of a national convention," was dispatching "agents in all directions to organize an armed uprising" and demanding a cabinet responsible to the assembly. The government exhibited indecisiveness; the army was so disorganized that even the Preobrazhenskii Guards had staged an uprising; a law-abiding individual could not walk the streets of the capital for fear of attacks by the unemployed and hooligans. "Threatening clouds are building on every horizon," Polovtsev cried.[1]

Even allowing for the exaggeration that underlay comments such as these, their sense of crisis and political isolation accurately conveyed the autocracy's plight in the spring and early summer of 1906. Social unrest, much less intense, to be sure, than that of late 1905, still roiled cities, factories, and villages. In the provinces, the single most propitious development—the abandonment of the liberation movement by the majority of the landowning nobility—had produced little moderation in national politics. The agrarian disorders of 1905–06 and the increasing radicalization of the Kadet Party after the October Manifesto had produced an abrupt rightward shift, particularly in provincial zemstvo assemblies, prompting many to oust Kadet-dominated executive boards, challenge their budgets, and sack the suspect third element they employed.[2] All the more shocking, then, had been the propensity of peasants to blackball

[1] Polovtsev, "Dnevnik A. A. Polovtseva," p. 116 (5 July 1906).

[2] Veselovskii, *Istoriia zemstva*, 4:21–79; Manning, "Zemstvo and Revolution," pp. 30–66; and "O povorotakh v nastroenii zemskikh sobranii," TsGIA, f. 1288, op. 2, 1906, d. 76, ll. 1–253.

conservative landowners during the First Duma elections.[3] In the center, the government confronted what it regarded as a radical national assembly, dominated by the Kadet Party but elected in large measure by peasants seeking an unconscionable resolution of their demand for land. And the Duma seemed only to exacerbate this desire through its published debates concerning the compulsory sale of private estate property. Convinced that compromise with the First Duma was impossible, and resolved to dismiss it, the Goremykin cabinet nevertheless wavered before the unknown consequences of this act. Some ministers supported the scheduling of new elections, Goremykin contemplated a revision of the December 1905 electoral law, and the rightist ministers Stishinskii and Shirinskii-Shikhmatov advocated abolishing the legislature altogether.[4]

Into this environment stepped P. A. Stolypin, unquestionably the last great statesman of the imperial era.[5] While some view him as a constitutionalist—a claim difficult to sustain—most studies of Stolypin tend to treat his tenure (1906–11) as contiguous with the accumulated experience of bureaucratic rule in the late nineteenth century. They emphasize in some form the slogan of "order and reform" frequently attached to his policies. The term itself often implies that Stolypin cured the paralysis afflicting autocratic government in 1905–06. Forceful repression and provincial government by fiat hastened the ebb of the revolutionary tide. Stolypin placated conservative elements of educated society with the veneer of Duma representation, judiciously gerrymandered by the dissolution of two Dumas and the so-called coup d'état of 3 June 1907—by which he prorogued the second Duma and decreed a new, more restric-

[3] See, in particular, the statistical analysis in Manning, *Crisis of the Old Order*, p. 207, which compares the preponderance of Kadets (52.5%) among the 101 provincial zemstvo landowners elected to the first Duma and the Octobrist and right deputies that the provincial zemstvo assemblies and corporative organizations of the hereditary nobility elected to the State Council: of 34 zemstvo deputies, 41% were Octobrists-centrists and 35% were rightists; of the 18 noble deputies, 39% were Octobrist-centrists and 56% were rightists.

[4] Startsev, *Russkaia burzhuaziia*, p. 68; Polovtsev, "Dnevnik A. A. Polovtseva," p. 114 (4 June 1906); Gurko, *Features and Figures*, pp. 472, 483; Alexander Izvolsky, *The Memoirs of Alexander Izvolsky* (Academic International Press, 1974), p. 178; and Kokovtsov, *Out of My Past*, p. 155.

[5] On the Stolypin era, see Diakin, *Samoderzhavie, burzhuaziia i dvorianstvo v 1907–1911 gg.* (Leningrad, 1978) and Manning, *Crisis of the Old Order*, chaps. 12–15. See also A. Ia. Avrekh, *Tsarizm i tret'eiiunskaia sistema* (Moscow, 1966), and "Tret'eiiunskaia monarkhiia i obrazovanie tret'eiiunskogo pomeshch'e-burzhuaznogo bloka," *Vestnik Moskovskogo Universiteta, Istoriko-filologicheskaia seriia* 1 (1956): 3–70; A. Izgoev, *P. A. Stolypin: Ocherk zhizni i deiatel'nosti* (Moscow, 1912); Mary Schaeffer Conroy, *Peter Arkad'evich Stolypin: Practical Politics in Late Tsarist Russia* (Westview Press, 1976); Hosking, *The Russian Constitutional Experiment*; Weissman, *Reform in Tsarist Russia*, chaps. 5–7; and A. Levin, "Peter Arkadeevich Stolypin: A Political Appraisal," *Journal of Modern History* 4 (1965): 445–63.

tive, electoral law—and thus retained a monopoly of power for a weakened but essentially uncompromising autocracy. Order, in turn, allowed him the breathing space necessary to reform the social and economic foundations of the old regime.[6]

To a certain extent, of course, this perspective is quite accurate. A paragon of the old order, Stolypin opposed revolution and suppressed it, not only in order to effect reform but in principle to preserve the autocratic regime from an era of mass politics that he understood but abhorred. Yet it was precisely this acute understanding that rendered the very idea of simply reconstituting autocratic state power irrelevant to the thinking of a statesman whose views of government were shaped not by the ministerial chancellery of the late nineteenth century, but by provincial life and the experience of provincial revolution in 1904–06. Order and reform indeed constituted the essence of Stolypin's policy, but his was an attempt to shape a new national politics: to reconstruct the societal base of the autocratic government (*pravitel'stvo*) and foster a new consciousness of national politics (*gosudarstvennost'*).

P. A. Stolypin: A Governor of Russia

Other officials had acquired their experience of autocratic administration outside the ministries of St.Petersburg. Few had immersed themselves in the life of provincial Russia as fully as Petr Arkad'evich Stolypin.[7] Born in 1862 to an old hereditary noble family, he was the son of a general of artillery. His father, who also enjoyed a passing reputation as sculptor and essayist, managed to squander the family's estate holdings after emancipation. Coming of age during the crisis years of 1878–81, Stolypin enrolled at St. Petersburg University, where, rather than read the law, he entered the physics-mathematics faculty and studied agronomy. Intent on a career in state service, Stolypin requested and received an appointment to the Ministry of Internal Affairs while still at university. With two years already registered on the Table of Ranks, he graduated in 1885 and joined the Ministry of State Properties' Department of Land and Agriculture. Already married to a daughter of the influential Neidgardt clan, the

---

[6] Weissman, *Reform*, pp. 124–30; Diakin, *Samoderzhavie*, pp. 19–37; Miliukov, *Political Memoirs*, pp. 216–28; Shipov, *Vospominaniia i dumy*, pp. 480–84; and Guchkov, "Iz vospominanii," *Poslednye novosti*, 26 Aug. 1936, p. 2.

[7] The following discussion is drawn from "Formuliarnyi spisok," TsGIA, f. 1162, op. 6, d. 511, ll. 60–75; M. P. Bok, *Vospominaniia o moem otse P. A. Stolypina* (New York, 1953); Izgoev, *P. A. Stolypin*, pp. 7–10; Manning, *Crisis of the Old Order*, pp. 21–28; A. Stolypin, *P. A. Stolypin, 1862–1911* (Paris, 1927); and V. V. Shul'gin, *Vospominaniia byvshego chlena Gosudarstvennoi Dumy* (Novosti, 1979). The whereabouts of Stolypin's personal papers is a mystery. His archive, TsGIA, f. 1162, only contains scattered materials concerning his personality and politics.

young official made good use of family ties to obtain court rank in 1888. A year later, he accepted appointment as marshal of the nobility of Kovno county in the Lithuanian borderlands, where he owned a hereditary estate of some 800 desiatins (approximately 2,200 acres), and left St. Petersburg for the provinces. There he would spend the next eighteen years of his life.

The decade he spent in Kovno, most biographers agree, was a formative experience. Russians of the day attested, sometimes less than benignly, that Kovno was a "cosmopolitan" place. Near both Kovno and Vilnius, major cities in the Jewish Pale of Settlement, Kovno county contained an ethnically mixed population of Lithuanians, Jews, Polish Catholics, Germans, and a minority Russian Orthodox community. Close by the border with German Poland, life for a Russian nobleman here undoubtedly led to heightened nationalistic sentiments; by all accounts, however, the county marshal mixed well in society and performed the ceremonial duties required from the corporative officer of the local nobility. Moreover, unlike many appointed marshals he took an active interest in rural administrative affairs. In his service record Stolypin noted that he had actually presided for a decade on the county council of arbiters of the peace. Through this administrative appeal board he came to know the details of land disputes, criminal or civil misdemeanors, and the daily events of peasant life that often crossed ministerial desks in St. Petersburg as statistical compilations or summary reports.

As important, he spent his time in Kovno acquiring the perspective of a landowner actively engaged in the management and improvement of his estate's agriculture. Together with his own educational background, the setting of Kovno was itself conducive to the effort. Over half the county's land was owned by nobles, and peasant allotments were held in hereditary tenure. The local agricultural economy, devoted to grain export and some flax production, was thus fairly diversified and capitalistic.[8] Apparently successful at his work, Stolypin, when he died in 1911, still owned two estates that he had inherited, the one in Kovno and a second in Penza. He had purchased a third of some 800 desiatins (approximately 2,200 acres) in Nizhnii Novgorod province and with his wife possessed large Neidgardt family holdings in Kazan.

By 1899 a prosperous noble landowner and a local official with some expertise in rural affairs, Stolypin had acquired the credentials that marked out a promising candidate for promotion in provincial administration.[9] That year, he received an imperial appointment as Kovno pro-

[8] "Kovenskii uezd," *BE,* 11:128.
[9] Richard G. Robbins, Jr., *The Tsar's Viceroys: Russian Provincial Governors in the Last Years of the Empire* (Cornell University Press, 1987), chap. 2.

vincial marshal of the nobility. In May 1902 Pleve designated him governor of neighboring Grodno province, making Stolypin one beneficiary of the minister's policy of promoting prominent provincial nobles to administrative posts. After a year, he was transferred to the governorship of Saratov province, a major agricultural region in the Volga River valley that was a hotbed of political activism—radical, liberal, and conservative. Indeed, in a biography that largely dwelt on the personal, Stolypin's daughter remembered how the family had been struck by the altogether different tenor of public life in Saratov as compared to the Western region, a fact she attributed to the existence of zemstvo self-administration in the province.[10] Stolypin remained in this turbulent provincial center until the spring of 1906, and it was here that he lived through the 1905 Revolution.

Two aspects of Stolypin's Saratov experience in 1904–06 deserve particular attention: his analysis of the revolutionary crisis, and his use of gubernatorial authority to combat it. The first he detailed in the annual summary of Saratov provincial affairs that he submitted to the tsar in January 1905.[11] Here Stolypin emphasized that the state confronted two dire threats to civil order. Peasant unrest was rising, but, he hinted, to attribute it solely to revolutionary propaganda trivialized the scope of the problem. Social instability in the villages was chronic; poverty, the unproductive system of communal agriculture that intensified it, and the growing desperation of peasants forced to pay exorbitant land rents inevitably created "enmity" toward estate owners and "animosity to the existing order." Dangerous because they were intractable in the short-term, these structural problems thus provided "enemies of the state [with the opportunity] ... to create sedition"—a prognosis that became reality in the counties of Saratov during and after the summer.[12] There was, moreover, small consolation in the fact that, "excepting the [question] of land," most peasants appeared indifferent to the second issue that concerned the governor: "the public movement [obshchestvennoe dvizhenie]" sweeping all "other classes of the population." Indeed, because fertile economic grounds for radical agitation existed, the volatility of Saratov "political life"—an unusually candid expression in an imperial report—threatened

[10] Bok, Vospominaniia, p. 118.

[11] "Vsepoddaneishii otchet saratovskogo gubernatora P. Stolypina za 1904 g.," in "K istorii agrarnoi reformy Stolypina," KA 17 (1926): 83–87.

[12] Ibid., pp. 83–85. Stolypin advocated the consolidation of peasant smallholdings as the only path to assure "peaceful labor in the village based on mutual agreement of landowner and peasant." He foresaw both free exit from the commune and state-supported land reorganization as the "single counterweight to the communal principle." See also "Donesenie gubernatora Saratovskoi gubernii," in N. Karpov, Krest'ianskoe dvizhenie v revoliutsii 1905 goda v dokumentakh (Leningrad, 1926), p. 162. On the Saratov agricultural economy, see Fallows, "Forging the Zemstvo Movement," pp. 39–150.

to ignite the very sedition against which the governor warned. And, as Stolypin knew, provincial politics was already escaping his control:

Zemstvo [and] public men and all individuals of the free professions stand in the forefront of the movement; they have attracted in their wake the worker element and student youth. . . . All of this, *given the absence until now of a political life [politicheskaia zhizn']* *in the country,* seems so new that . . . it cannot but summon displays of extreme intemperance by public groups and . . . attempts by radical circles to direct the entire movement onto a revolutionary path. Moreover, in view of the distrust toward the government that legal groups in Saratov province have articulated, the public atmosphere has become antigovernmental, [it is] of a negative, denunciatory character.[13]

In short, government authority was being challenged in all strata of Saratov society, and his administration was becoming more and more powerless to influence events that threatened to become revolutionary.

His attempts to exercise gubernatorial authority under these conditions were thus all the more instructive. In the first instance, he relied on force and administrative power, the oldest weapons in a governor's arsenal. Saratov peasants particularly felt their firepower in 1905–06. Stolypin's widespread employment of police and troops, applied especially to all forms of collective action, was energetic enough to attract frequent notice in the liberal national press, as well as an expression of personal gratitude from Nicholas II.[14] He also harassed zemstvo third element employees, especially doctors and primary school teachers, whose presence in rural areas, combined with the often democratic, sometimes socialist politics of the Saratov third element, rendered their professional activities suspect.[15] This assault on the "influential, even powerful" third element reflected as well a general apprehension before zemstvo liberalism. Stolypin made full use of the veto and administrative rulings in an attempt to bridle political opposition in the Saratov zemstvo, which, it should be noted, was one of the most influential sources of liberal and conservative provincial activism in the country.[16]

---

[13] "Vsepoddaneishii otchet saratovskogo gubernatora," pp. 86–87. Emphasis added.

[14] TsGIA, f. 1162, op. 6, d. 511, l. 60. Stolypin included the following telegram from Nicholas II in his service record: "To Saratov Governor Stolypin. Informed through the Minister of Internal Affairs of the exemplary action shown by you in despatching troops on your own personal initiative to suppress disorders within the borders of Novouzensk county, Samara province, and long esteeming your loyal service, I declare to you my sincere gratitude. Nicholas." See also reporting of Saratov politics in *Russkie vedomosti*, 22 July 1905, p. 4; 19 August 1905, p. 3; 25 August 1905, p. 4; 12 September 1905, p. 5; 4 November 1905, p. 3; and 28 January 1906, p. 4.

[15] "Donesenie 26 aprelia 1905," Karpov, *Krest'ianskoe dvizhenie*, pp. 144–45, and "Donesenie 11 ianvaria 1906," ibid., pp. 161–62.

[16] Fallows, "Forging the Zemstvo Movement," pp. 754–76. Also *Russkie vedomosti*, 20 July 1905, p. 4; 7 October 1905, p. 5; 18 October 1905, p. 4.

In view of his own immersion in provincial public life and politics, however, Stolypin was well aware that the days when a governor relied exclusively on instruments of repression had passed. These were means to establish order, not consolidate authority. Indeed, in his January 1905 report, he recognized that the urban, intellectual, and professional elements whom he classified under the heading third element were declaring their "pretensions to a leading role" in provincial life for good reason. They possessed "boldness, industriousness, energy, and knowledge," which, he realized, had allowed many professionals to become "politicos [*politikany*], the necessary concomitant of a country's political life." This explained "why many public activists of other classes [were] constantly looking to the third element." It was a mistake, Stolypin said, "to ignore and fail to consider this party [*partiia*]." The government could not "rely on it because it [was] hostile," but "to act against it at present exclusively with force" would only exacerbate public alienation and "strengthen" the hand of extremists. "Local administrative authority" must, he urged, stand firm, approving "that which is useful in the actions of the third element" and placing "an unconditional 'veto' where its progressive [*progressivnaia*] activity begins to become revolutionary." Moreover, he wrote, "this party, as a negative example, might be useful, if others, who stand amongst the people [*imet' pochvu v narode*], could contain it." The mobilization of political support for the government was necessary in order for it to reassert its authority: "In the future, one must await and support the birth of a party of the land that has roots in the people, which, opposed to theoreticians, might render the third element harmless."[17]

Stolypin's remarks referred most directly to the consolidation of a potential political base among provincial noble landowners like himself, particularly among those engaged in zemstvo work. Only a year later, however, did these prospects begin to appear realistic. In January 1906 he was able to report a "sharp reaction" occurring in the Saratov provincial zemstvo against its former liberal majority.[18] Although this was a political sea change extending far beyond the actions of a single individual, Stolypin had done his best in the heated atmosphere of 1904–05 to encourage the growing conservatism of Saratov noble landowners. The governor maintained personal ties with moderate and conservative circles in the provincial zemstvo.[19] His defense of order and property fostered a

[17] "Vsepoddaneishii otchet saratovskogo gubernatora," pp. 86–87.

[18] "O povorotakh v nastroenii zemskikh sobranii," TsGIA, f. 1288, op. 2, 1906, d. 76, l. 249. Also *Russkie vedomosti*, 11 February 1906, p. 4.

[19] Bok, *Vospominaniia*, pp. 125–28, 142–51; Kryzhanovskii, *Vospominaniia*, p. 214; Manning, *Crisis of the Old Order*, pp. 266–69. His cordial personal relations with the Saratov moderate N. N. L'vov probably helped to explain why Stolypin's name arose as a candidate for minister of internal affairs during Witte's early negotiations with Octobrists for a coalition cabinet. Witte, *Vospominaniia*, 2:85 and Izgoev, *P. A. Stolypin*, pp. 23–25.

growing reputation as a strong and competent governor.[20] Moreover, it was striking that amidst press reports of prohibited public assemblages came the news in late September 1905 that Stolypin had endorsed "an unofficial noble conference" summoned by provincial marshal M. F. Melnikov and N. A. Pavlov to discuss the founding of an "All-Russian Union of Noble-Landowners."[21]

Yet Stolypin construed the mobilization of political support more broadly than reliance on landowners of the provincial nobility alone. Even as he deployed troops and proclaimed marshal law to combat intense unrest in the wake of the October Manifesto, a joint proclamation by Governor Stolypin, the elected mayor of Saratov, and the chairman of the provincial zemstvo executive board urged all "citizens" to resume work and to await the Duma's approval of the "fundamental rights of civil freedom" promised by the tsar.[22] Reports in early January revealed that thirty thousand leaflets had been distributed throughout the province urging the "rural populace" to remain calm and show "confidence" in "reforms undertaken for the renewal of Russia."[23] Finally, replying at the same time to an MVD request to analyze the relationship of rural unrest and peasant land hunger, Stolypin rejected the implied assumption that government authority could rest on an impoverished peasantry. An expansion of peasant landholding, he warned, at best promised "a breathing space" and not the elimination of the economic conjuncture that had rendered the peasantry ripe for radical agitation. Advocating communal land reform, he believed that the "creation of a class of petty proprietors, this fundamental cell of a state," could alone transform peasants into "opponents of destructive theories" and "cultured activists [kul'turnye deiateli]."[24] Only the fact that he so forcefully contested the apparent program of his superiors in St. Petersburg rivaled this willingness to consider the economic *and* political reconstruction of rural society. Durnovo, in a summary read by the tsar, emphasized that Stolypin's advice stood out from the litany of complaints against radical agitation and requests for

[20] Bok, *Vospominaniia*, pp. 142, 151; Shul'gin, *Vospominaniia*, p. 53.

[21] *Russkie vedomosti*, 22 September 1905, p. 4. See also Geoffrey Hosking and Roberta Manning, "What Was the United Nobility?" in Haimson, *Politics of Rural Russia*, pp. 147–50.

[22] *Russkie vedomosti*, 7 November 1906, p. 4; *Novoe vremia*, 20 December 1905, p. 3.

[23] *Russkie vedomosti*, 19 January 1906, p. 5. Press reports in 1905 also indicate that Stolypin, besides applying force in the villages, instructed local officials and land captains to explain the actual legal content of government manifestos, in an apparent effort to counteract propaganda and peasant self-interpretation. *Russkie vedomosti*, 16 July 1905, p. 4; 22 July 1905, p. 3; 28 January 1906, p. 4.

[24] "Donesenie gubernatora Saratovskoi gubernii, 11 ianvaria 1906," in Karpov, *Krest'ianskoe dvizhenie*, pp. 161–62.

increased repression that characterized most other gubernatorial reports.[25]

On the eve of the convocation of the First Duma, Stolypin was appointed minister of internal affairs in the Goremykin cabinet. Reputed to be a young, capable administrator with knowledge of provincial society, he was otherwise a virtual unknown in St. Petersburg circles.[26] Within three months, however, the new minister had won the trust of Nicholas II, who came to believe that in Stolypin he had found a man capable of supervising the government and restoring order. It was this relationship of personal confidence more than any other factor that led the sovereign to hand over to Stolypin the chairmanship of the Council of Ministers on 9 July, the day that he dissolved the first Duma.[27] Retaining control over the MVD and its domestic administration, the provincial landowner and administrator assumed the power to govern all Russia, which he would relinquish only at his death in 1911.

If the Saratov governor needed additional proof, his first months in St. Petersburg must have provided abundant evidence as to how difficult that task would be. Among the political parties there was little confidence displayed toward the government. Twice during the summer Stolypin failed to entice into the Council of Ministers the representatives of the Kadets and of the more moderate Octobrist and Peaceful Renewal parties.[28] At the same time, he came under increasing pressure from the far right for even toying with tactics that smacked of constitutionalism. The Permanent Council of the United Nobility registered a sharp protest in July, even as it initiated a campaign for a new electoral law to restore to the nobility its "former predominant position" in national life.[29] The premier refused to countenance such measures, but did recognize the inadequacies of the existing statute, which, he told Nicholas II, had been based on the false "impression of peasants as a loyal support of the existing political structure."[30] Generally, amidst repetitive reports of peasant disorders, as-

[25] "Doklad MVD Durnovo o prichinakh krest'ianskikh besporiadkov po doneseniiam gubernatorov," in Karpov, *Krest'ianskoe dvizhenie*, pp. 94–97.

[26] *Novoe vremia*, 22 April 1906, pp. 2–3; *Russkie vedomosti*, 26 April 1906, p. 1; Polovtsev, "Dnevnik A. A. Polovtseva," pp. 104–5 (25 April 1906); Witte, *Vospominaniia*, 2:278; Izwolsky, *Memoirs*, p. 199; and Gurko, *Features and Figures*, pp. 460–61.

[27] Verner, *Crisis of Autocracy*, chap. 10; McDonald, "Autocracy, Bureaucracy, and Change in the Making of Russian Foreign Policy," chaps. 3–4.

[28] Startsev, *Russkaia burzhuaziia*, pp. 89–123; Miliukov, *Tri popytki*, pp. 59–78; A. I. Guchkov, "Iz vospominanii," *Poslednye novosti*, 16 August 1936, p. 2; Izwolsky, *Memoirs*, pp. 206–10; Shipov, *Vospominaniia*, pp. 484–92.

[29] "Protokol, 20 July 1906," TsGAOR, f. 434, op. 1, d. 75, l. 16, and "Protokol, 22 July 1906," ibid., d. 10/38, l. 2.

[30] Chermenskii, *Burzhuaziia i tsarizm*, p. 338, quoting TsGAOR, f. 601, op. 1, d. 912, ll. 13–22.

sassinations, industrial strikes, and street crime, only the provincial zemstvo elections of early 1906 had indicated that a propitious rightward moderation was occurring in national politics.[31] Thus Stolypin confronted a situation in which the reforms of 1905–06, concessions granted by the autocracy to restore government authority, had further undermined it. Order, as has so often been noted, was essential for the implementation of reform; Stolypin immediately undertook the task by turning first to the provincial administrative apparatus of which he had so recently been a part.

In one of his first circulars as minister of internal affairs, dated 9 May 1906, Stolypin detailed for all governors the principles that were to guide their actions "at a time of crisis." With Duma debates on the land question threatening to inflame peasant unrest, he instructed subordinates to understand that the state order was under assault by "people"—implicitly all leftist parties beginning with the Kadets—who agitated "sedition" and wanted to force "a government [that] desires broad reforms . . . to adopt party views and diverge from strict principles of state." Because the recent "fundamental reforms of popular life" had created rampant civil instability, governors now bore the weightiest responsibility for impressing on society that the government remained "firm, resolute in the fulfillment of its duty, and unwavering, . . . the single pillar on which the preservation of order, property, and life rested." To uphold these principles was the first, essential step toward the reconstitution of government authority among those strata of the population still willing to accept it, and the only means of reestablishing the social stability necessary to create a reformed state order. Only if "the healthy part of the population [found] support and defense in the authorities," Stolypin wrote, could "the country pass without convulsion through this epoch of reconstruction [*pereustroistvo*], whose necessity has been proclaimed from the throne."[32]

Stolypin was neither a constitutional monarchist nor an enemy of the 1905–06 reforms who sought to render them meaningless. As had other officials of the period, he assumed that sovereign decree and state law were irreversible; the speculation that he strove to eviscerate the post-October order is an oversimplification. Yet politically and, it might be said, psychologically Stolypin never contemplated abandoning the state's arbitration of national life. As the work of both Soviet and Western social historians has indicated, he understood legitimate politics within the narrow framework that his own "class" biases, not surprisingly, dictated. Only those social groups and political parties that acknowledged a struc-

---

[31] For example, "V smutnoe vremia" and "Sveaborgskii bunt," *Novoe vremia*, 22 July 1906, p. 3, and "Obshchestvennaia reaktsiia," *Novoe vremia*, 30 July 1906, p. 2.

[32] "Tsirkuliar' ministra Vnutrennykh Del Stolypina ot 9 maia 1906 g.," TsGAOR, f. 102, Osobyi otdel, op. 1905, ed. khr. 975, t. 3, ll. 290–91.

ture of public life existing within the reformed autocratic order were deemed to be legitimate. Only they, to use the term often employed at the time by government and conservative circles, possessed a consciousness of *gosudarstvennost'*, an untranslatable parallel formation from the phrase "public self-consciousness [*obshchestvennost'*]" that subsumed it and conveyed the idea that without the autocratic state the nation lacked meaning. A national state, rather than a nation-state was, to be sure, a prescription for political reaction, one directed against the diverse popular aspirations of 1905 for freedom and sovereignty. The campaign of repression that began in the late summer of 1906 with the intention— as the tsar had commanded—of "root[ing] out sedition and restor[ing] order," aimed to limit radical liberalism and suppress altogether the democratic and socialist politics that had swept urban Russia and inflamed the peasantry. Military field courts-martial, provincial government by fiat, exile, imprisonment: these were the days of the noose, the "Stolypin necktie." The popular epithet was hung on a man whose ministry marked for many the end of the 1905 Revolution.[33]

The scope and depth of this crackdown was evident in a secret directive that Stolypin circulated to all MVD provincial officials in September 1906.[34] Read from a somewhat different perspective, the document also revealed the dearth of societal allies on whom the government could rely and thus its own assiduous search to find allies, to create political support for governmental authority. In the countryside the brunt of the government's attack was directed against political agitation in the village. The arrest of "outside agitators [*prishlye agitatory*]," especially ringleaders from "the peasant milieu," who if unpunished would acquire "prestige in the eyes of the populace," was "the primary task" of local police. Provincial administrators were told to appear personally in unruly areas in order to display "the unyielding firmness of government authority." Force was the crudest instrument against peasant land protests, but the ministry also urged provincial officials to utilize more positive forms of influence with the local populace. They were told to defuse economic grievances by hastening the conclusion of any land purchase by a peasant household, and were expected as well to exert quiet but firm pressure on estate owners whose "extreme demands" were creating resentment in village communities. Local zemstvo assemblies and landowners, it was noted, could offer useful assistance in instructing peasants about the economic conse-

[33] "Perepiska N. A. Romanova i P. A. Stolypina," *KA* 5 (1924): 103–4. In general see Dan, "Obshchaia politika pravitel'stva," pp. 58–85, and Diakin, *Samoderzhavie*, pp. 26–30.

[34] "Tsirkuliar' predsedatelia Soveta ministrov P. A. Stolypina ot 15 sentiabria 1906 g. general-gubernatoram, gubernatoram i gradonachal'nikam," in "Mobilizatsiia reaktsii v 1906 g.," *KA* 32 (1929): 158–82.

quences of a ruined private estate agriculture. The clergy could be utilized in a similar manner. Should all these measures fail and disorders still erupt, the authorities were to move against them immediately with troops, "halt the movement," and arrest "leaders and agitators."[35]

Stolypin recognized that outside the village the constraints of law and, more important, the demands of ministerial policy "severely restricted" the government's ability to supervise political activity. All local administrative action against "agitation in the intelligentsia strata of society," he insisted, was thus subordinate to the center's "understanding . . . of [differing] political tendencies." These were clearly stated. All political parties pursuing "republican" goals—"the social-democrats, the socialist revolutionaries, the [Jewish] Bund, and other such circles"—were illegal and subject to criminal prosecution. Other organizations required legal registration to be considered parties, and administrative sanction would not be extended to any entity—the Kadets went unmentioned—surreptitiously pursuing "socialist" or "democratic" objectives. On the far right, where "patriotic and monarchical societies" might render "an essential service to local crown organs," the government sought "unconditionally loyal support" from such groups, not advocacy of "civil violence, terrorist undertakings, etc."—precisely the kind of proto-fascist activity emerging under the label of "the Black Hundreds."[36]

With regard to other autonomous forums for public initiative, the government's missives were more sweeping. Professional unions, especially those within the Union of Unions—"engineers, lawyers, teachers, and other circles"—were politically suspect and, unless registered under government auspices, illegal. Unregistered unions among the mass population—"workers, artisans, petty service workers, . . . individuals in state and public service, and so-called peasant unions"—were to be rooted out and their leadership arrested. Students in primary and middle schools who belonged to illegal student organizations were liable to administrative trial by officials of the Ministry of Education. Although the corporative rights of the universities prevented such interference in their internal affairs, any student arrested off campus was subject to immediate prosecution. Editors, publishers, and authors utilizing press organs to agitate illegal acts against the government were liable to administrative action under the censorship laws.[37]

Stolypin wrote in conclusion that he recognized the "complexity" of the work he was demanding from subordinates, but unremitting efforts were required at this "historic moment, when new forms of [the state's]

[35] Ibid., pp. 163–68.
[36] Ibid., pp. 169–71, 180.
[37] Ibid., pp. 172–81.

political structure [*politicheskoe ustroistvo*] [were] coming into existence." And he made it clear to local officials that the Council of Ministers and its chairman were the decisive arbiters of this reformed system—not political parties, not conflicting ministerial interests, and certainly not provincial administrators themselves:

> The government stands firmly on the ground of an *unshakable desire* to promulgate the reforms proclaimed by the monarch, but at the same time *its greatest duty is to preserve law and society from criminal attack by whatever means are necessary*. All local authorities without exception must recognize that the [cabinet] *government, not subordinate administrative organs*, guides high policy. . . . Interdepartmental disagreements do not have a place [at a time when] central institutions have been unified; this idea should be accepted once and for all by all local representatives of authority, with the recognition that the conflict that had become routine in the service class [*sluzhilyi klass*] is *a cruel evil for all interests of the country*.[38]

The results of the Second Duma elections in January 1907 would tell how successful Stolypin's efforts to establish order had been; already in late summer 1906 the outlines of a circumscribed national politics were becoming evident. Entry into the circle required acknowledgment that the ultimate arbiter of the reformed political order remained the autocrat, and that the instrument through which his authority was exercised was a bureaucratic government crowned by the Council of Ministers. Only within this narrowly delimited framework, which, it should be emphasized, contained the State Duma and State Council, could national political life occur. Liberal, democratic, and socialist politics, or the more messianic visions of popular sovereignty emanating from the peasant village, were excluded because they challenged constituted authority and the values it propounded. Thus, to consolidate government authority and its capacity to promulgate reforms, Stolypin was forced to begin removing from legitimate politics much of the "nation" that had created it. What remained was a narrow base indeed: moderate and rightist parties; propertied classes, especially the provincial landowning nobility; and an officialdom that Stolypin willed to become a professional service class. But it was within this Russia, as S. E. Kryzhanovskii later recalled, that Stolypin intended to govern:

> Governors were obliged to become friends with society [*sblizhenie s obshchestvom*]. Stolypin . . . instructed the governors to retreat from their former pomp, estrangement, isolation [*razroznennost'*], quarrels, . . . to get closer to the circles that possessed influence, and to incline them favorably toward the government. These kinds of instructions were given frequently . . . and the gov-

[38] Ibid., pp. 181–82.

ernors changed their attitude to the zemstvos and to strata of society that possessed influence.[39]

To another, more critical assistant minister, Stolypin's behavior was alien if not altogether incomprehensible. V. I. Gurko noted that Stolypin "brought with him to St. Petersburg his provincial way of doing things. . . . He was much more a politician than an administrator." The comment was an apt portrayal of the new era of autocratic government that began under the Stolypin ministry. Gurko, an accomplished bureaucrat, carped at Stolypin's lack of "talent . . . for selecting assistants" or his unfamiliarity with "the needs of the people and those organic reforms which were necessary for the normal development of the country."[40] In light of Stolypin's provincial experience and articulate views on rural policy, this seems a spurious charge, but also a telling indication of the values separating the Petersburg administrator from the provincial "politician."

Gurko used power to regulate and shape the population, to impel it to become what he wanted it to be. This statist impulse was present, to be sure, in Stolypin as well, despite Gurko's protestations, but he channeled it in an entirely different direction than officials of the last two decades had done. To a much greater extent than even the astute Witte, Stolypin—because he had learned the lesson in the provinces—understood that the revolution of 1905 signaled the near disintegration of state authority throughout Russian society, in both its educated and mass strata. Thus the task at hand was not simply the reconsolidation of state power in order to effect "organic reforms" and assuage "the needs of the people." More important was the reconstitution of a reformed autocratic order that possessed legitimacy in strata of society stable enough to uphold it. Gurko would reach this conclusion only on the eve of the First World War. Stolypin, to judge from Gurko's criticisms, had already perceived it:

> [Stolypin] understood well enough the significance of public opinion, just as he also realized that the stability of the state and internal order depended on the attitude of the people toward the government. . . . [H]e was less concerned with the reforms themselves and their actual results than with the degree to which they would be approved by the people and would thus strengthen the position of the government.[41]

Kryzhanovskii, like Gurko a skilled MVD official, seconded the opinion that his chief "was not a creator in the realm of ideas." All of the

---

[39] Shchegolev, ed., *Padenie tsarskogo rezhima*, 5:402–3. See as well his description of government expenditures to support conservative political organizations, press organs, and anti-leftist pamphleteering campaigns. Kryzhanovskii claimed these expenditures averaged some three million rubles annually. Ibid., pp. 403–12, and *Vospominaniia*, pp. 98–105.

[40] Gurko, *Features and Figures*, pp. 461–63.

[41] Ibid.

legislative reforms that Stolypin undertook existed in some form within the ministries before he came to power. However, he "breathed life into them."[42] Indeed, Kryzhanovskii argued, administrative expertise was not the standard by which to evaluate Stolypin. "Petr Arkad'evich Stolypin was a new phenomenon in our state life." Seeking "support not only in the strength of authority [*sila vlasti*] but in the opinion of the country," Stolypin cut a figure quite different from "the usual type of minister—the bureaucrat [*biurokrat*], floating with the tide in pursuit of his own personal gain."[43] His contribution to the old regime was "above all in the area of state psychology [*gosudarstvennaia psikhologiia*]—the creation of an atmosphere favorable to the government and its initiatives."[44]

Kryzhanovskii exaggerated somewhat. Other statesman had sought public support in response to perceived crisis: Valuev in the 1860s; Loris-Melikov in the 1880s; Witte before 1906. Yet none of them had been forced to confront, or in Witte's case able to understand, a crisis in which the state, its hegemony over Russian life shattered, had become only *one* of the actors vying to control the civil and political order. Unlike the political parties, and even more unlike the less organized social groups, the Stolypin ministry possessed a preponderance of force, and began utilizing it freely to define as legitimate only that national politics in which government authority was recognized and its values of law, public order, and property propounded. There could be few illusions, however, that authority could rest on such hastily constructed, unstable foundations.

Stolypin recognized this reality. A public statement of his ministry's program, issued on 24 August, left no doubt that the government intended to preserve "the very idea of *gosudarstvennost'* " and, as it announced the creation of military field courts-martial, to "oppose force with force." Yet the ministry also insisted that such measures were "only a means, and not the goal" of government policy. It was, the report stated, "the greatest mistake to see [repression] as the single objective of state authority, [thus] forgetting the profound reasons" that had created the revolution and the necessity of effecting reforms to correct them. The "government" could not heed those "public circles" on the right who demanded a halt to "all reforms" and wanted "the might of the state to be directed exclusively against the struggle with treason." Nor would it follow leftist parties who believed, incorrectly, that revolution would recede once officials stood aside and allowed the promulgation of their "liberationist" ideals. The "path of the government" lay between these two extremes. Suppressing "revolutionary phenomena," it intended to pursue

[42] Kryzhanovskii, *Vospominaniia*, pp. 215–16.
[43] Ibid., p. 209.
[44] Ibid., p. 220.

"the path of construction in order to create a stable order based on legality and a rationally understood, true freedom." The ministry's report contained a long list of legislative measures, headed by communal land reform and the elimination of "archaic [estate] restrictions" placed upon the peasantry, both of which it intended to promulgate via Article 87. In addition to these, the next Duma would consider other important proposals, including reform of local administration that aimed to "accommodate [*postavit' v neposredstvennuiu sviaz'*]" government administration with "reformed organs of self-administration, including a small zemstvo unit."[45]

As Kryzhanovskii later noted, Stolypin believed land reform to be a primary way of "strengthen[ing] civil consciousness [*grazhdanstvennost'*]" in the countryside.[46] This program, although crucial, constituted only one component of a far-reaching civil and political transformation. The task of reform that confronted the former provincial governor at a time of revolution demanded the reconstruction of the social foundations on which political authority in the old regime rested.

THE STOLYPIN LOCAL REFORMS

In autumn 1906 the Stolypin ministry used Article 87 of the Fundamental Laws to promulgate rural economic and legal reforms. Separate imperial decrees of 9 and 15 November initiated the attempted conversion of peasant communal agriculture to proprietorial ownership and land use.[47] A month previously, on 5 October, an ukase proclaiming "equality of rights" among members of taxed and untaxed estates eliminated some of the most blatant discriminatory laws leveled on the peasant estate.[48] Most immediately, it restored direct peasant voting in the pending zemstvo elections of 1907 by rescinding the gubernatorial appointment of peasant delegates. It also allowed peasant smallholders to vote in the appropriate landowner's curia.[49] As the MVD noted in its presentation to the Council

---

[45] "Pravitel'stvennoe soobshchenie," *Novoe vremia*, 25 August 1906, p. 1. The report was part of a process that Stolypin had initiated on 7 August, when he requested all ministers to report to the Council of Ministers concerning those reforms under preparation in their departments. He specifically inquired whether these measures could await the Duma's convocation or required promulgation via Article 87. These projects were compiled, discussed in the Council on 12 January 1907, and received the tsar's approval as the government's legislative program on 15 February 1907, TsGIA, f. 1276, op. 2, d. 4, ll. 226–537.

[46] Shchegolev, ed., *Padenie tsarskogo rezhima*, 5:391–92.

[47] Macey, *Government and Peasant*, chaps. 9–10, and Yaney, *Urge To Mobilize*, chaps. 6–7.

[48] *Novoe vremia*, 15 September 1906, p. 4.

[49] "Ob uravnenii lits byvshikh podatnykh soslovii v pravakh po sostoianiiu s otstal'nymi sosloviiami imperii," TsGIA, f. 1291, op. 122, d. 46, ll. 1–2, 13–15, 45–48, and 76–80.

of Ministers, the legislation abrogated "the segregation of the peasant estate from other classes of the population" and "assure[d] the equality of all citizens before the law." The elimination of estate distinctions in peasant administration, the report noted, was under consideration in the ministry and would be the subject of separate legislation.[50]

This work, it will be recalled, had been taking place in the MVD before Stolypin assumed office, primarily under the aegis of Gurko and his Land Section. Aiming to rationalize and strengthen local administrative power, the MVD had resisted significant changes in the structure of self-administration, changes deemed threatening to the county zemstvo and the provincial noble landowners who dominated it. Within a month of Stolypin's appointment as head of the ministry, however, press reports first indicated that the MVD's GUMKh, which had been studying reform of local self-administration since early 1905, opposed the Gurko strategy.[51] Officials in this department—Kryzhanovskii had worked there until the summer of 1905, and Stolypin appointed N. L. Psheradskii, one of the more liberal voices in the Urusov Commission, to be its assistant director in August 1906[52]—argued that the elimination of estate institutions did not necessitate abolishing those organs of self-administration that in theory at least already existed in the village and township. Opponents focused particularly on Gurko's opposition to the small zemstvo assembly and urged the conversion of the existing peasant township administration to an organ of all-estate self-administration with some administrative powers.[53]

As the ministerial program of 25 August 1906 had indicated, Stolypin was drawing on the work of both the Land Section and GUMKh to develop a comprehensive reform of all provincial government. Sometime during that month, the minister convened a private conference of MVD officials to develop the outlines of this work. *Novoe vremia*, which was usually reliable, quoted one anonymous participant who explained that the conference was examining the relations between state administration

---

Other provisions of the ukaz included: entry into the civil service or higher educational institutions without loss of rights to allotment lands; relaxed residence and passport regulations based on place of work or permanent residence to accommodate mobility into the cities.

[50] Ibid., l. 76.

[51] GUMKh presented a summary of zemstvo reform discussions to the Council of Ministers in November 1905 and recommended that the department be included in any consideration of local reform, TsGIA, f. 1288, op. 2 (1905), ed. khr. 15, ch. 3, ll. 74–79.

[52] "Po peresmotru zemskogo i gorodskogo polozhenii," TsGIA, f. 1288, op. 2, ed. khr. 38, ll. 1–9, and *Novoe vremia*, 18 August 1906, p. 4. Psheradskii became GUMKh director in November. Ibid., 21 November 1906, p. 4.

[53] "Proekt reformy krest'ianskogo upravleniia," *Novoe vremia*, 9 May 1906, p. 3 and 10 May 1906, p. 3; also 21 May 1906, p. 4.

and self-administration in all territorial jurisdictions of the province. The source also noted that such clarification was undertaken with an eye to avoiding the fate suffered by the Kakhanov Commission, the last such attempt at local reform and apparently a precedent for the present effort.[54] Discussions continued into the fall; on 2 October Gurko circulated a preliminary plan of local reform to all concerned MVD officials. This internal memorandum set out two conflicting "opinions": both advocated the creation of a county vice-governor, but differed over whether to create all-estate township and village organs of self-administration. Gurko continued to insist that establishing any new township institution was a decision best left to the discretion (fakul'tativno) of the county zemstvo; it was sufficient, he said, to incorporate all heads of households, regardless of estate, into the existing village community—a measure that excluded most other forms of private property from its jurisdiction and thus from liability for its taxes.[55] Stolypin called his advisers to a series of private meetings the following week, at which time the decision to override Gurko's objections was taken.[56] By early November, the ministry's Land Section had drafted a local reform plan that aimed both at strengthening government administration and at expanding popular involvement in organs of self-administration. Stolypin presented this project to the Council of Ministers in mid-December.[57]

Although Stolypin sponsored reform of provincial government, much of the responsibility for its conceptual coherence belonged to S. E. Kryzhanovskii, the assistant minister whose legislative skills had been utilized frequently during the previous decade and an adviser whom one MVD subordinate called "the second Stolypin."[58] In his retrospective but valuable memoirs, Kryzhanovskii explained that local reform had been designed to address the political crisis of 1905, which had resulted, he be-

[54] "K voprosu o reforme mestnogo upravleniia," Novoe vremia, 26 August 1906, p. 3.

[55] "Obshchii proekt ustroistva uezdnogo upravleniia (2 October 1906)," TsGIA, f. 1291, op. 122 (1906), d. 79, ll. 1–5.

[56] Novoe vremia, 6 October 1906, p. 2, and 10 October 1906, p. 3. Gurko was forced to relinquish his posts in mid-November, when he was implicated in a food-relief scandal involving the grain merchant Lidval'; he was convicted of administrative corruption by the Criminal Cassation Department of the Senate in October 1907. Novoe vremia, 14 November 1906, p. 3; 19 November 1906, p. 4; and 26 October 1907, p. 3. See also Gurko, Features and Figures, pp. 507–10.

[57] "Glavnye nachala ustroistva mestnogo upravleniia (2 November 1906)," TsGIA, f. 1291, op. 122 (1906), d. 84, ll. 1, 20–34, and "Ob ustanovlenii glavnykh nachal ustroistva mestnogo upravleniia (11 December 1906)," f. 1291, op. 50 (1906), d. 33, ll. 136–54.

[58] S. N. Paleolog, Okolo vlasti (St. Petersburg, 1912), pp. 157–58. Kryzhanovskii authored: the MVD rebuttal to Witte's Autocracy and the Zemstvo; Pleve's legislation creating the Council on Local Economy in 1904; the reform program of Sviatopolk-Mirskii; the Bulygin Duma statute; the December 1905 electoral law; the February 1906 reform of the State Council; the electoral law of 3 June 1907. Kryzhanovskii, Vospominannia, pp. 7–8.

lieved, from the distortions that the centralized state had created in local public life since the mid-nineteenth century. Without a civil administration to satisfy their growing desire for autonomous initiative (*deiatel'-nost'*), Kryzhanovskii maintained, "the quickly multiplying local intelligentsia classes" had sought to escape "the tutelage" of the state, "even if at the price of destroying its structure"; by 1905, the two had become locked in an uncompromising, centralized struggle for power. To defuse it required the "decentralization of both administration and legislation," by which Kryzhanovskii meant not simply the decentralization of bureaucratic affairs to more effective echelons of the state apparatus, but also the creation of a provincial civil administration that would engage broader strata of society in the business of government and thus reconstruct the societal foundations of state authority.[59]

It was Kryzhanovskii, writing "for the minister" on 2 December, who first detailed the three major components of local reform legislation.[60] "Rationalization of administration," "incorporation of self-administration," and "expansion of popular participation" might have served him well as organizing headings. The program's first goal was the transformation of peasant estate institutions—village and township self-administration and the land captain—into rationalized territorial structures of provincial civil administration.[61] Second, the MVD sought to restructure all county and provincial "organs of [state] administration and supervision," a category in which Kryzhanovskii included organs of local self-administration. Here, the program aimed to create "a strong, regularized and responsible political authority [*rukovodiashchaia vlast'*]" by strengthening gubernatorial power, unifying provincial administration,

[59] Kryzhanovskii, *Vospominaniia*, pp. 121–25. Kryzhanovskii in 1908 proposed a radical reform of tsarist administration, based on the creation of eleven regional territories (*oblast'*) in the empire, each with its own government administration and zemstvo assembly. The latter would possess broad legislative rights on all matters that did not possess "general state significance." Ibid., pp. 131–32. This idea was never formally discussed in the Council of Ministers, although it is reported that Stolypin was still toying with it at the time of his death. Zenkovsky, *Pravda o Stolypine* (New York, 1956), chap. 3.

[60] "Programma deiatel'nosti Ministerstva vnutrennykh del (2 December 1906)," TsGIA, f. 1276, op. 2, d. 4, ll. 379–403.

[61] Ibid., ll. 380–81. On the reformed land captain, see "Proekt polozheniia o pravitel'-stvennykh uchastkovykh kommisarakh," TsGIA, f. 1284, op. 185 (1907), d. 5a, ch. 1, ll. 72–82, and "Polozhenie o pravitel'stvennykh uchastkovykh kommisarakh," ibid., ll. 100–103. This official was required to be twenty-five years of age and to possess a middle or university education, or sufficient service experience. He was not required to be a hereditary noble. He could hold no other state office, but could be a zemstvo or municipal assembly delegate. His duties included: confirmation in office of village and township officials; administrative review of these institutions and appeals against them by private individuals; supervision of the land reform; tax collection; the military draft; and execution of county government directives. Unlike the land captain, he would not possess judicial authority.

and placing crown vice-governors in the counties. At the same time, it looked to limit administrative interference in self-administration, expand "the jurisdiction and activities of zemstvo and municipal institutions," and incorporate state and zemstvo organs within a single institutional system where, "mutually reinforcing each other," they might work to develop local public life.[62] Finally, Kryzhanovskii relied on the ukase of December 1904 to justify the objectives of broader popular participation in self-administration and the creation of a small zemstvo unit, adding that his ministry also regarded zemstvo electoral reform as a measure of special significance.[63]

Already evident in Kryzhanovskii's memorandum, and even more pronounced in the statutes and explanatory notes that the ministry drafted over the next two months, was a strong commitment to the leveling of estate distinctions in local administration, wherever they existed. To possess authority, provincial administration required a rationalized territorial apparatus that encompassed all civil relations in rural society. Thus, presenting the reform program to the Council of Ministers in mid-December, Stolypin referred to the "broad masses of the populace [involved] in political life" and to "the principle of civil equality [*printsip grazhdanskogo ravenstva*]" established by the October Manifesto to demonstrate that no basis existed any longer for the preservation of the archaic principles of peasant "estate segregation" or "paternalistic [*popechitel'noe*] administration." Nor, he continued, could there be any question that the province as a whole required an administrative "system in which the varied interests of the local population would find complete, uniform reflection and direction, devoid of estate distinctions."[64] In a similar manner, the premier could repudiate the "obsolescence" of estate elections in the zemstvo. The "estate structure," which, he told the Council of Ministers, never possessed "strong, historical roots in . . . Russian public life [*obshchestvennost'*]," had been "undermined" by the "natural course of economic and social development." To preserve "an electoral system that divide[d] people bound by the most intimate unity of general economic and professional interests" would weaken an institution of central importance to local government.[65]

Most telling in this regard was Stolypin's refusal to mandate that the

[62] Ibid., ll. 382–83.

[63] Ibid., l. 384.

[64] "Ob ustanovlenii glavnykh nachal ustroistva mestnogo upravleniia (11 December 1906)," TsGIA, f. 1291, op. 50 (1906), d. 33, l. 136. See also "Proekt polozheniia o posel'kovom upravlenii, 20 February 1907," TsGIA, f. 1284, op. 185 (1907), d. 5a, ch. 1, ll. 54–55, and "Zhurnal . . . soveshchaniia dlia rassmotreniia dolzhnostei uezdnogo upravleniia," ibid., l. 123.

[65] "Ob ustanovlenii," TsGIA, f. 1291, op. 50 (1906), d. 33, ll. 143–44.

marshal of the nobility, by virtue of his office, assume the post of county vice-governor. Subordinated to the provincial governor, the vice-governor was envisioned as the link between a strengthened provincial government and all county bureaucratic and zemstvo institutions.[66] To be sure, the proposed official, whom the MVD labeled a "powerful," "unifying" bureaucratic representative, would supervise relations between the central government and local society in a manner patterned after the role traditionally ascribed to the local nobility as mediator between autocracy and peasantry. Stolypin, certainly aware of such arguments when he addressed the Council of Ministers, saw nothing to indicate that the marshal of the nobility, despite the preeminence in county administration traditionally accorded this elected officer, possessed the proper education or career experience required for an important administrative position.[67] His ascriptive status was irrelevant.

It should be emphasized, however, that neither Stolypin nor the MVD was bowing to liberal public sentiment in opposing estate distinctions. Administrative logic worked against these archaic obstacles to a more powerful and influential local government. Thus, in the case of the vice-governor, the MVD flatly rejected its transfer into the hands of any public entity, be it nobiliary corporation or organ of zemstvo self-administration, as Kadets and even some Octobrists at this time were arguing. "No central authority, whatever the existing form of its state administration," the ministry argued, could "do without its own representatives and agents in local areas."[68] This was particularly true at a time when efforts were underway to convert the governor into an "an organ of the Supreme Government [*Vyshii Pravitel'stvo*]," as stated in a legislative proposal drafted by the MVD in January 1907. Although it would remain a prerogative of the tsar, the gubernatorial appointment that would occur through the recommendation of the Council of Ministers was designed to

---

[66] "Proekt zakliuchenii ob izmenenii i dopolnenii deistvuiushchikh uzakonenii ob uezdnykh ustanovleniiakh, 20 February 1907," TsGIA, f. 1284, op. 185 (1907), d. 5a, ch. 1, ll. 28–33. Originally, the vice-governor was to possess powers of administrative review over any ministerial official in the county. After jurisdictional objections from the Council of Ministers, the right of review was restricted to MVD civil and police officials only; the vice-governor would be able to make inquiries of other local officials. "Osobyi zhurnal Soveta ministrov" (19, 22 December 1906 and 3, 6 January 1907), ibid., l. 10.

[67] "Ob ustanovlenii glavnykh nachal," TsGIA, f. 1291, op. 50 (1906), d. 33, l. 141. Individuals eligible for appointment to the post were those with service experience as: provincial vice-governors; marshals of the nobility; permanent members of provincial peasant boards; chairmen of the county appeals board of land captains; high-level provincial administrative staff; chairmen of provincial or county zemstvo executive boards; other suitable provincial or county officials. Ibid., l. 28. The marshal of the nobility had been included in this list at the insistence of the Council of Ministers in order to avoid "expressions of distrust toward the noble estate." "Osobyi zhurnal," ibid., ll. 11–12.

[68] "Ob izmenenii i dopolnenii," TsGIA, f. 1284, op. 185 (1907), d. 5a, ch. 1, ll. 18–20.

assure the cabinet that it would have reliable executive agents for its do-mestic policy.[69] Subordinate vice-governors, in turn, would bring this same unity of purpose to the county. Hence, rationalized civil administra-tion provided the conduit for a more powerful administrative presence in the countryside; the Stolypin government was poised to achieve an objec-tive sought by ministerial officials since the great reforms.

Yet, unlike the statist tendencies that had been so pronounced in MVD thinking under Pleve, for example, Stolypin's local reforms predicated greater state power on its capacity to buttress political authority in public life and thus sought an equally significant realignment of self-administra-tion at all levels of the provincial apparatus. Indeed, in its explanatory memorandum to the Council of Ministers of February 1907, the MVD emphasized that the political sea change of 1905 had opened up an op-portunity to incorporate both state and zemstvo organs as interdependent components of a single government. Historically, N. L. Psheradskii rec-ognized, the state had denied the zemstvo any "authority" and had viewed it as a "public institution" that was "isolated from government organs." As he delicately put the case, the resulting "antagonism" had contributed to "the well-known contradiction between the principle of [popular representation] and the bureaucratic structure [*biurokratiche-skii stroi*] of the state"—a conflict rendered moot with the creation of the State Duma.[70] Now, Psheradskii argued, three legislative tasks were es-sential [in order] to assure the "expedient and effective activity of [local] state institutions": the "regularization [*uporiadochenie*]" of state-zemstvo relations, increased authority for self-administration, and elec-toral reform that eliminated estate distinctions and allowed "broader strata of the population" to participate in local public life.[71]

In the first instance, revealingly, regularization meant preventing the reemergence of the political opposition that had swept these institutions before 1905. Thus legislation was proposed that under stipulated proce-dures would allow the central government to assume extraordinary pow-ers over affairs of individual zemstvos, including expenditure of funds and appointment of officials to manage the institution for a three-year period.[72] Consistently justified in terms of government oversight, such "broad powers"—as the Council of Ministers resolved when approving them in December 1907—were also political cudgels whose use, although sure to be an "extremely rare" phenomenon, could "prevent the disrup-

---

[69] "Ob ustanovlenii glavnykh nachal ustroistva gubernskikh uchrezhdenii (7 January 1907)," TsGIA, f. 1276, op. 3, d. 18, ll. 8–20.

[70] "Ob ustanovlenii glavnykh osnovanii preobrazovanii zemskikh i gorodskikh uchrezh-denii," TsGIA, f. 1276, op. 3, d. 22, ll. 4–10.

[71] Ibid., l. 2.

[72] Ibid., ll. 12–14. These measures applied to municipal institutions as well.

tion of order in these institutions and keep them on the path of conformity to the law."[73] At a time when zemstvo assemblies had shifted their political sympathies to the right, however, extraordinary measures were unlikely to be used in any but the most extreme circumstances. In general, the ministry's proposals sought greater cooperation between local state and zemstvo organs, an atmosphere considered essential to effective government in the provinces. Both governors and county vice-governors, for example, would also be accorded the right to attend sessions of the zemstvo assembly. This unprecedented official presence, the ministry said, was not intended to inhibit "freedom of discussion and decision." In place of the formalistic correspondence through which relations had previously been conducted, "mutual and public discussion" might assure a level of "understanding and confidence" that could "gradually abolish the fundamental alienation and enmity that had existed . . . to the detriment of harmonious and correct administration."[74] A provincial governor or county vice-governor rising in the primary forum of local rural politics to cajole zemstvo opinion reflected political strategies far different than the veto and petition of the pre-1905 era.

The ministry also projected a number of measures to institutionalize and expand the authority of existing zemstvo institutions. Of primary importance were statutes (ustavy) to define their jurisdiction in law and eliminate the "capricious character" of government supervision.[75] Increased zemstvo participation in primary education, economic development, telephone and telegraph communications, famine relief, and public health, as well as the right to issue rulings that bore the force of law, were deemed the best ways of assuring the development of the rural public infrastructure.[76] A system of state treasury aid, which had been created in 1903, was to be expanded in order to facilitate the zemstvo's role in campaigns for universal primary education and agricultural reform. The three-percent annual ceiling on the growth of zemstvo taxation, which had been established at the same time, would be removed. The MVD proposed a zemstvo-town state bank to provide investment capital at below-market rates. It hoped to revive the moribund Council on Local Economy and use it as a forum where elected zemstvo and municipal representatives could meet officials to discuss legislative issues of mutual interest. Similar plans were afoot for the technical specialists of the ministry's GUMKh, whose expertise would be made available to local

[73] "Osobyi zhurnal Soveta ministrov (7, 18 December 1907)," TsGIA, f. 1276, op. 3, d. 22, ll. 151–54.

[74] "Ob izmenenii i dopolnenii," TsGIA, f. 1284, op. 185 (1907), d. 5a, ch. 1, l. 22.

[75] "Ob ustanovlenii glavnykh osnovanii preobrazovanii zemskikh i gorodskikh uchrezhdenii," TsGIA, f. 1276, op. 3, d. 22,, ll. 7–8.

[76] Ibid., ll. 14–43, outline statutes in all areas of zemstvo responsibilities.

institutions. Finally, the MVD supported public participation in the county and provincial advisory councils, the bodies that were intended to facilitate the unity of administrative activity in both these venues.[77]

These proposals were intended in the first instance to elicit political support from the provincial nobility, who presently controlled the zemstvo assemblies. Yet, particularly in the aftermath of rural disorders and electoral defeats, it was also quite evident that zemstvo landowners were a minority of a much larger populace that, given its systematic exclusion from local public affairs, was isolated from government authority, indifferent to its concerns, and susceptible to political radicalism. The MVD's proposed extension of limited self-administration to the township and the village and its reforms of the zemstvo electoral system were fundamental attempts to restructure zemstvo politics and expand, to a much greater extent than contemplated before, the popular constituencies over which government authority held sway.

Village and township public self-administration thus assumed particular importance in the local reform program. In the case of the village, which would not be subordinate to the institutional hierarchy of the zemstvo, the government intended to create all-estate "self-administering unions in fact and not just on paper." Only in declared emergencies were their officials to be subject to the authority of the police. Elected assemblies with the power of taxation were to be established immediately in populous, townlike settlements. The MVD's draft statute also established a mechanism by which county officials could extend this structure to smaller agricultural villages as their social composition diversified—a measure that took account of land reform.[78] Any resident who paid at least two rubles annual property tax, a figure including most heads of peasant households, could vote in village assembly elections.[79] In no case, however, were landed estates and commercial-industrial enterprises lying outside village boundaries to be incorporated under an institution likely

[77] Ibid., ll. 9–12.

[78] "Proekt . . . i polozhenie o posel'kovom upravlenii," TsGIA, f. 1284, op. 185 (1907), d. 5a, ch. 1, ll. 49–92. The village project was mandated in any rural settlement that did not contain a land commune, assuming this to be the criterion designating a commercial, industrial, or suburban area. Second, it applied to any village in which at least ten percent of the registered populace were not members of a land commune. Any "exclusively" communal village would receive the institution upon exceeding this mark; until that time, affairs of public self-administration were to be invested in the *zemel'noe obshchestvo*. Originally, the MVD had proposed the application of all-estate self-administration to all rural settlements. The Council of Ministers objected that the measure was too "complex" and recommended these variations instead, which, it believed, accounted for the "accelerating development of local life." Ibid., ll. 7–8.

[79] Ibid., ll. 84–86. All residents in villages of less than 150 people participated in the assembly. Representative assemblies of between thirty and sixty individuals were to be elected in larger villages.

to overtax these properties.[80] Although its powers of tax assessment were subject to other restrictions as well, the village assembly was authorized to raise revenues and fund municipal services.[81] All these proposals were consistent with the cautious protection of propertied interests that informed much of the local reform program. Yet they also reflected a general drive to encompass broader strata of rural society within institutions of village public life (*mestnoe blagoustroistvo*), where they could in turn be subject to the authority of the government and the influence of its values.

The same thinking motivated the MVD's proposed "township administration."[82] Quite deliberately, the ministry labeled the township an organ of administration because it intended the elder (*starshina*) to remain an agent of local crown and zemstvo officials, obliged to execute the orders of both branches of the county government.[83] Yet he was to be elected by an all-estate township assembly, which the ministry, with characteristic caution, granted the legal identity of "a self-administering union managing affairs of local public welfare": jurisdiction over primary school construction, medical stations, famine relief, credit, and technical aid for agriculture; the right to petition; the prerogative to bring charges of malfeasance against the elder; and the election of some delegates to the county zemstvo.[84] The powers to tax, write budgets, and contract loans, although restricted, would belong to the new institution.[85]

The township assemblies would vary in size between thirty and fifty members, depending on local population. They were to be elected from two curiae: one for peasants holding communal allotments, and a second

[80] Ibid., l. 58. Any landed estate owner or commercial-industrial entrepreneur in the vicinity could join the village corporation if he or she desired.

[81] Ibid., ll. 84, 87. The village could tax the household property at discretion; all other property was taxed according to county zemstvo assessments, with an upper limit set in law. The village assembly's jurisdiction at a minimum included: salaried police officials; fire laws; public works; schools and medical stations; poor houses and orphanages; rights of petition; and the right to contract loans. Additionally, either via petition or the decision of the county vice-governor, larger settlements could issue obligatory rulings on matters involving public health, public works, primary education, aid to agriculture, etc.

[82] "Proekty i polozhenie . . . volostnogo upravleniia," TsGIA, f. 1284, op. 185 (1907), d. 5a, ll. 49–82 and 93–100.

[83] Ibid., ll. 97–100. These were described under categories relating to: general administration; zemstvo executive board; township institutions; public order and safety; crimes committed against property, agriculture, and contracts; military draft; tax collection; public health; famine relief; insurance; public construction; passports.

[84] Ibid., ll. 69–70 and 94–97.

[85] Ibid., l. 97. Township taxes were collected according to assessments of the county zemstvo and limited to a maximum percentage of its annual revenues. The township assembly thus could not change property assessments and depended upon the spending policies of the county zemstvo for its own funding. Within this framework, however, it could establish its own budgetary priorities.

for all private proprietors who paid two rubles in annual zemstvo property tax. Here, too, the MVD inserted measures to favor propertied interests.[86] In particular, the stipulation of a minimum tax payment excluded the majority of individuals (wage workers, salaried professionals, renters) who did not own property. According to MVD estimates in 1908, only some 548,000 smallholders were enfranchised under these terms, which represented a small 26 percent of the two million owners of rural and urban private property assessed by county executive boards.[87] It was within this narrow but elastic framework—communal peasants and the small but growing stratum of rural smallholders they promised to generate—that the ministry believed it was exposing "the broadest strata of the population" to "the spirit of initiative [*samodeiatel'nost'*]" that the new institution was intended to engender.[88]

Zemstvo electoral reform was both a logical and a necessary complement to these plans. When Stolypin first presented the local reforms to the Council of Ministers in December, he said that "local self-administration [was] a vital foundation and the best school of experience for public initiative in the political arena."[89] It was a characteristic yet perhaps wistful comment for the provincial politician to make, for—as he knew without reminding his colleagues—the existing structure of zemstvo representation precluded its use as a means of political acculturation. The imperial decree of 5 October 1906 had corrected the most glaring shortcoming of the 1890 zemstvo statute—female disenfranchisement gave different meaning to the paternalism of the old regime—when it reinstated direct peasant election of zemstvo delegates and allowed peasant smallholders to vote in the second electoral curia. Still, communal peasants were alloted by law some 31 percent of all seats in the county assemblies at a time when their allotments accounted for 60 percent of the landed prop-

[86] The MVD draft of February 1907 allowed groups of property owners to declare themselves to be a subcuria and elect delegates to the volost' assembly commensurate with the aggregate tax payments represented by their holdings; a minimum of three electors was required to elect one delegate, six for two, etc. The measure was seen as a means of protecting any property interest within the township territory. Ibid., ll. 72–75.

[87] MVD, Zemskii otdel, *Povolostnoe raspredelenie zemel'nykh i prochikh nedvizhimykh vladenii v 34 zemskikh guberniiakh* (St. Petersburg, 1908), p. 293.

[88] "Proekty i polozhenie . . . volostnogo upravleniia," ll. 71–72. The original MVD program of November 1906 had not established any minimum for participation in township elections beyond payment of some zemstvo property tax. TsGIA, f. 1291, op. 122 (1906), d. 84, ll. 22–24 and 29–30. The Council of Ministers inserted the two-ruble provision, largely to prevent "the owner of the most insignificant chunk of land" insinuating himself into the township assembly. TsGIA, f. 1284, op. 185 (1907), d. 5a, ch. 1, ll. 12. Nevertheless, Psheradskii, the project's author, believed that the township franchise was still low enough to account for "the massive exit from the commune" in heavily populated agrarian regions like Kursk, where two and one-half desiatins (seven acres) "was already a large amount of property." TsGIA, f. 1288, op. 1 (1908), d. 25, l. 120.

[89] "Ob ustanovlenii glavnykh nachal," TsGIA, f. 1291, op. 50 (1906), d. 33, l. 144.

erty and over half the total assessed value of all rural and urban property taxed by the zemstvo.[90] That the peasants regarded the zemstvo as another source of burdensome taxation, a charge scandalously popularized by Anton Chekhov in his short story *Peasants*, was confirmed in 1906 and 1907 when they curtailed these payments in many rural areas.[91]

Moreover, as the following compilation of GUMKh statistics indicated, the county zemstvo was accessible to only a thin stratum of private property owners; the institution primarily remained a preserve of hereditary noble landowners. All 129,000 property owners eligible to vote in 1906–07 constituted just six percent of the two million taxpayers (see table 6.1). Even this figure, however, was deceiving. Urban representation in the zemstvo, lower than the figures noted above for a second curia that included all non-nobiliary rural property owners, was so discriminatory that towns consistently petitioned after 1900 for representation commensurate with their tax payments or separation from the zemstvo altogether.[92] Moreover, almost three-quarters of enfranchised property owners voted indirectly through the preliminary assemblies, where they elected an artificially low 2,800 representatives to participate in zemstvo elections. Had the same proportional representation been applied to these voters as was used for full-census hereditary noble landowners, their total assessed property value in 1906–07 would have required that twenty-six thousand representatives be sent to the curial elections.[93] The low rates of participation in both the first and second preliminary assemblies reflected the reality of zemstvo representation for such voters. They also attested to the most salient fact of zemstvo life: control by the landowning nobility. More than half of all county assembly seats were reserved for less than 15 percent of all enfranchised voters and less than 1 percent of all zemstvo taxpayers. In the traumatic years of 1906–07, two-thirds of these noble landowners did not even vote.

The Stolypin local reforms did not aim to democratize an unrepresentative institution, as Kadets who supported a four-tail suffrage urged in early 1907.[94] Nor did they encompass proposals as sweeping as the "Prussian" electoral structure or the elimination of franchise restrictions that the Urusov Commission had advocated in early 1905. In all, the

---

[90] *PSZ* 1890, no. 6297 (12 June 1890), p. 501, and *Povolostnoe raspredelenie*, p. 293.

[91] TsGIA, f. 1276, op. 3, d. 18, l. 73, cites MVD and Ministry of Finance emergency allocations of some eight million rubles to 180 zemstvos in order to cover budget deficits. Some zemstvo petitions for aid referred specifically to the shortfall of peasant taxation. TsGIA, f. 1288, op. 2, 1905, d. 38, ch. 4, ll. 16, 24–25, 56, 62, 71–79, 92–95, and 100.

[92] TsGIA, f. 1288, op. 2 (1905), d. 15, ch. 3, prilozhenie, ll. 10–275.

[93] "Litsa, imevshie pravo . . . v zemskikh izbiratel'nykh s"ezdakh," TsGIA, f. 1288, op. 2 (1906), d. 113, ll. 2–3.

[94] See, for example, *Samoupravlenie*, 13 January 1907, pp. 1–7, and 17 February 1907, pp. 1–3; also "Ministerskii zakonoproekt o zemskikh vyborakh," *Russkie vedomosti*, 30 May 1907, pp. 1–2.

TABLE 6.1

Enfranchised Property Owners and Rates of Voting Participation in the County Zemstvo Elections of 1906–1907, 34 provinces

Voter Category	% Allocation of Assembly Seats, 1890 Statute	No. of Enfranchised Voters (% of All I and II Curiae Voters)	No. of Enfranchised Voters Participating in Elections
I curia of full-census hereditary landowners[a]	55	18,838 (14.6)	6,412 (34)
I preliminary assembly of noble smallholders[b]	—	13,341 (10.3)	2,391 (18)
II curia of full-census rural and urban property owners[c]	14	15,218 (11.8)	3,222 (21)
II preliminary assembly of smallholders[d]	—	81,664 (63.3)	9,240 (11)
Total	69	129,061 (100)	21,265 (16.5)

Source: "Litsa, imevshie pravo uchastiia i deistvitel'no uchastvovavshie v zemskikh izbiratel'nykh sobraniiakh pri vyborakh na tekushchee trekhletie, 1906–1909: Pogubernskie itogi [Those persons having the right to participate, and actually participating, in the zemstvo electoral assemblies during elections for the three-year term, 1906—1909: Summary totals by province]." TsGIA, f. 1288, op. 2 (1906), d. 113, 11. 8–11; "Litsa, imevshie pravo uchastiia i deistvitel'no uchastvovavshie v zemskikh izbiratel'nykh s"ezdakh pri vyborakh na tekushchee trekhletie 1906–1911: Pogubernskie itogi [Those persons having the right to participate, and actually participating in the preliminary zemstvo electoral meetings for the three-year term, 1906–1909: Summary totals by province]." Ibid, 11. 2–3; and PSZ 1890, no. 6927 [12 June 1890], p. 501.

[a] Hereditary noble landowners owning landed property of a minimum area of 150–475 desiatins (400–1300 acres).

[b] Personal nobles and other noble landowners owning less than the full census but at least one-tenth this amount.

[c] All full census, non-noble landowners; all urban property and rural or urban commercial-industrial enterprises with an assessed value of at least fifteen thousand rubles.

[d] Same groups owning less than full census but at least one-tenth this amount.

MVD's proposed electoral reform promised immediately to enfranchise 765,000 (37 percent) of the two million zemstvo taxpayers registered in 1908. This figure represented a sixfold increase over the 129,000 individuals eligible to vote in 1906 and loomed over the 10,000 full-census property owners who actually participated in those elections.[95] Hardly a radical restructuring, the specifics of the electoral reform nevertheless

[95] MVD, Zemskii otdel, Povolostnoe raspredelenie, p. 293.

demonstrated that the ministry planned to facilitate the gradual expansion of the constituencies engaged in zemstvo work.

The county electoral system that Stolypin presented to the Council of Ministers in December 1906 eliminated the estate divisions of the 1890 statute, but retained a curial system of elections that was intended, he said, to assure the representation of "landowning, commercial-industrial, and agricultural classes" in the zemstvo and account "for the cultural distinction between the interests of large and small proprietorship."[96] These proposals provided additional confirmation that property, economic success, and the social stability they imparted to rural society—not the preservation of status ascribed by birth to particular groups of the population—were primary concerns motivating government policy. Yet they also revealed the strong bias toward wealth and land that shaped the ministry's views of zemstvo reform. MVD statistics suggested that its proposals would effect only slight readjustments in the existing distribution of delegates among the three electoral curiae (see table 6.1). Thus, a first curia of full census landowners filled 44 percent of all assembly seats. The second curia, constituted from owners of urban property and rural commercial-industrial enterprises, contributed 20 percent; preliminary elections from the towns in this category reduced the influence of less wealthy urban strata. A third curia of all rural smallholders and communal peasants, elected through the township assembly, supplied the remaining 36 percent.[97]

To the extent that noble landowners were the holders of landed wealth, the Stolypin projects aimed to preserve their influence in self-administration. In subsequent debate, Kryzhanovskii referred to provincial nobles as "enlightened and experienced individuals" who historically had comprised "the basic cell of the assemblies"; their absence, he said, "could hardly aid zemstvo business."[98] N. L. Psheradskii, the principal author of these proposals, similarly acknowledged that without legislative restraints "to preserve a significant presence in the zemstvo for the landowning class, as the most cultured element," the "very character of zemstvo activity" would change.[99] Indeed, the MVD included extraordinary measures to protect the interests of wealthy property owners, especially provincial nobles, in electoral contests. Very wealthy landowners or commercial-industrial entrepreneurs, Stolypin suggested, ought to be included automatically in the county assembly in order to guarantee "the

[96] "Ob ustanovlenii glavnykh nachal ustroistva mestnogo upravleniia," TsGIA, f. 1291, op. 50 (1906), d. 33, l. 144.

[97] Ibid., ll. 143–46; "Spravka," TsGIA, f. 1276, op. 2, d. 63, l. 39; and "Chislo uezdnykh zemskikh glasnykh po polozheniiu 1864 i 1890 gg. i zakonoproektam MVD i Soveta po delam mestnogo khoziastva," TsGIA, f. 1288, op. 2 (1907), d. 15, ll. 1–26.

[98] TsGIA, f. 1288, op. 1 (1908), d. 28, l. 21.

[99] Ibid., d. 25, l. 120.

minority [that] influence in local zemstvo life" that accorded with "their economic weight" in rural society.[100] The Council of Ministers objected, fearing that a provision grossly favoring "large land or commercial-industrial capital" might breed resentment within the majority population. It opted instead for a less offensive strategy for achieving the same result.[101] The Council also ordered one-fourth of each assembly's seats to be reserved for delegates elected from the landowner's curia. Designed to assure that "the landowning element would not be placed in the background in the future zemstvo," this provision provoked Nicholas II's only comment on any document of the local reform program, an exclamation of agreement.[102] As a result of this proviso, the MVD felt obliged to guarantee delegates elected from the township one-third of all assembly seats and the second curia a token two places, giving further expression to the rural bias that informed the entire project.[103] The ministry thus predetermined the distribution of more than half of the county assembly delegates.

Within this structure, however, the MVD did envision significant long-term changes in the social composition of the zemstvo. The ministry was well aware, in the first instance, that provincial landowners from the hereditary nobility were increasingly unable to fill the places designated for them under the terms of the 1890 statute. Indeed, its statistics suggested that the ongoing realignment of rural property relations, and in particular the break-up of large landed estates, made it unlikely that under the existing statute they could assure even one-fourth of the delegates in many counties.[104] Thus, the ministry sought means to broaden the ranks of

[100] "Ob ustanovlenii glavnykh nachal," TsGIA, f. 1291, op. 50 (1906), d. 33, l. 146. Specifically, these individuals (*polnotsensoviki*) were those owning ten times the zemstvo franchise. The measure was intended to serve the landed nobility, but was primarily of symbolic importance. The MVD apparently based this proposal on the existing composition of the provincial zemstvo assemblies, which were dominated by hereditary noble landowners. In the 34 zemstvo provinces in 1906, they comprised 81% of all provincial zemstvo delegates. Only 173 of these delegates (9%) owned ten times the current land census; an additional 68 county and provincial marshals (3.5%) also reached this level. "Lichnyi sostav gubernskikh zemskikh sobranii tekushchago trekhletiia (1906–09, 1907–10): Raspredelenie glasnykh po sosloviiam i razmeru prinadlezhashchikh im imushchestv," TsGIA, f. 1288, op. 2 (1906), d. 113, ll. 35–38.

[101] "Osobyi zhurnal Soveta ministrov," TsGIA, f. 1284, op. 185 (1907), d. 5a, ch. 1, l. 15. The council substituted "proportional elections" by which electors in any of the three curiae could declare themselves blocs and elect a number of delegates to the assembly proportional to the total amount of property represented in their bloc.

[102] Ibid., l. 19.

[103] "Ob ustanovlenii glavnykh osnovanii," TsGIA, f. 1276, op. 3, d. 22, l. 55. It was planned, however, to exempt large urban centers of more than 100,000 people from inclusion in the zemstvo system. Ibid., ll. 64–66.

[104] Ibid., l. 55. Of 283 zemstvo counties (77% of total), only 14 possessed sufficient num-

landowners participating in zemstvo work. Eliminating the estate distinctions of the 1890 statute was a first step in this direction, as it extended suffrage to any landowner who possessed the requisite property franchise. A proposed reduction of this requirement by fifty percent would add immediately some twenty-three thousand individuals to the first curia—doubling the number of those enfranchised to vote there at present.[105] Finally, at the urging of the Council of Ministers, the MVD took steps to shift the franchise to a "uniform standard" of zemstvo property tax payments. Less static than the existing system of assessed property values and owned acreage, the tax franchise provided a neutral barometer of voting rights that, given the anticipated increase of zemstvo taxation and the parcelization of rural landholding, promised a growing number of new voters for the first curia.[106] With allowances for adjustments if it proved too high, the tax franchise was targeted at twenty-five rubles, the approximate equivalent of 50 to 100 desiatins (135 to 270 acres) of land. This figure, three times less than existing limits, defined a "prosperous [zazhitochnyi] landowner who conducts a more complex agriculture, which signifies a somewhat higher level of [intellectual] development."[107]

The MVD reforms attempted to increase access to zemstvo assemblies for other rural smallholders as well. Here, as N. L. Psheradskii noted, the government confronted two contradictory pressures. On the one hand, it sought to assure that first curia landowners, individuals "with a certain level of culture, wealth, and social stability," retained their ability to influence zemstvo proceedings. On the other, it wanted to "provide the propertied class [imushchii klass] an adequate number of places" in the county assemblies, by which Psheradskii meant the much larger population of rural property owners currently absenting themselves from preliminary elections or altogether excluded from the process.[108] The proposed system of township elections struck a compromise between these conflicting concerns. As only those delegates who were communal peasants or rural smallholders elected the township assembly's zemstvo representatives, the ministry was in effect separating wealthier landed and

bers of noble landowners to provide one-half the assembly delegates under the existing property franchise. Only 80 could supply one-fourth the delegates.

[105] MVD, Zemskii otdel, *Povolostnoe raspredelenie*, p. 293.

[106] Originally, the MVD had based its franchise proposals on assessed land values. "Ob ustanovlenii glavnykh nachal," TsGIA, f. 1291, op. 122 (1906), d. 84, ll. 29–30. The Council of Ministers ordered the utilization of the tax franchise. "Osobyi zhurnal Soveta Ministrov," TsGIA, f. 1284, op. 185, d. 5a, ll. 18–19, and "Ob ustanovlenii glavnykh osnovanii," TsGIA, f. 1276, op. 3, d. 22, ll. 51–52.

[107] TsGIA, f. 1276, op. 3, d. 22, l. 53. See also, for example, the comments of assistant minister A. I. Lykoshin, who applied the term landowning "minority" to peasant proprietors purchasing land through the Peasant Land Bank. TsGIA, f. 1288, op. 1, d. 25, l. 28.

[108] "Ob ustanovlenii glavnykh osnovanii," TsGIA, f. 1276, op. 3, d. 22, l. 53.

commercial-industrial property owners from the otherwise overwhelming domination of the majority populace. This was a critical stratagem, because the aggregate tax payments contributed from each category of property represented in the county assembly determined the distribution of zemstvo delegates among the three electoral curiae. Unless they were somehow artificially reduced, peasant allotment lands and the substantial tax revenues they generated would necessitate that a majority of any zemstvo's delegates would come from the township. Psheradskii later noted that direct elections from the townships "would increase the quantity of peasant deputies to the point that the county zemstvo assembly would lose all capacity to work effectively [*rabotosposobnost'*]."[109]

Yet township elections, which occurred in a viable organ of public self-administration, were also viewed as a viable means to coopt into zemstvo work those activists among smallholders who were at present indifferent to preliminary county zemstvo elections, proprietors previously excluded from the zemstvo system by its high franchise requirements, and heads of communal households. Although by law guaranteed only a third of the county zemstvo seats, the number of delegates elected from the township could be significantly higher than that figure, especially in areas where first- and second-curia property owners lacked the number of individuals necessary to fill their designated places in the assembly—a prospect that the agrarian reform not only envisioned but also encouraged.[110] Township delegates engaged in local public life had a place in the reformed zemstvo alongside other propertied elements of rural society. At a time of revolutionary unrest, the participation of these "cultured" strata—in the village, the township, the county, and all of provincial life—was essential to the long-term viability of the reformed old regime.

Indeed, it was this attempt to heighten the public role of new propertied elements in the countryside that distinguished the Stolypin program from previous efforts to effect local reform. Stolypin confronted a vastly different society, and a far graver political crisis, than had the Kakhanov Commission or the statesmen of the 1850s, and consequently his plans went far beyond that which his predecessors had considered possible. In conjunction with the transformation of peasant agriculture and property relations, the local reforms aimed at modernizing autocratic government and politics from above by creating a civil order in which a far greater range of strata of the population would be subject to the mobilizing influence and authority of the bureaucratic government. Yet there was still a great disparity between ministerial theory and the actual conditions of Russian political and social life in winter 1906–07. Russia in large mea-

[109] TsGIA, f. 1288, op. 1 (1908), d. 25, l. 2.
[110] "Ob ustanovlenii glavnykh osnovanii," TsGIA, f. 1276, op. 3, d. 22, l. 80.

sure lacked what Stolypin wanted to achieve. State authority was not legitimate in provincial life. Zemstvo self-administration did not engage the local population in fruitful public endeavor. Civic initiative was not a characteristic feature of the township and village populace; a stable propertied society did not yet provide a solid foundation for a reformed old regime. The test of Stolypin's political acumen, and that of the autocracy he served, lay in the ability of both, combined, to promulgate this vision of the national future.

Gosudarstvennost' and the Coup d'État of 3 June 1907

On 5 February 1907, the day before the beginning of provincial elections to the Second State Duma, advertisements for party meetings and publications filled the front page of *Novoe vremia*. More than one reader must have noticed, amidst this cacophonous display, the bold-faced announcement of a new drama by the playwright N. Iu. Zhukovskii, entitled *Chaos*.[111] This seemed an apt description of domestic politics in winter 1907, as Russia went to the polls for the second time in less than a year to select a national assembly.

Stolypin had wagered much of his personal prestige on the outcome of this ballot. Although the ministry chose to retain the December 1905 electoral statute, in late autumn 1906 it had reinterpreted some of the law's provisions. These Senate interpellations were intended to bolster the representation of conservative, propertied elements by inhibiting the voting rights of peasants, industrial workers, and those of the urban lower-middle classes.[112] The government's campaign of repression had also aimed at influencing electoral results. A mid-January circular from the premier, addressed to all "representatives of government authority in the provinces," reiterated that free elections did not mean allowing "political parties" to "demean the actions and intentions of the government" with "revolutionary agitation" and "untrue rumors." Yet, it continued, the sovereign intended the State Duma to be "a foundation of the legislative structure of the Empire," and his government therefore anticipated "fruitful, creative" cooperation with the assembly. All but explicitly naming the Kadets, Stolypin also warned that mutual endeavor had its limits; only activity within the framework delineated by the Fundamental Laws

---

[111] *Novoe vremia*, 5 February 1907, p. 1.

[112] Dan, "Obshchaia politika pravitel'stva," pp. 80–83, and Kryzhanovskii, *Vospominaniia*, pp. 96–97. These changes included: the exclusion of peasant smallholders from the landowner's curia; the redefinition of urban residence requirements to restrict Kadet support in the cities; the exclusion of industrial workers from all other electoral curiae but their own. They also attempted to bolster the representation of more wealthy, propertied elements in city and countryside.

could "preserve Monarchical confidence." Denying rumors that the government intended to dissolve the Duma and return to "the old order," Stolypin emphasized his commitment to "immediate legislation": altering the zemstvo electoral structure, expanding self-administration, unifying county and provincial government, and securing approval of the government's land-reform program. This "enormous work of reconstruction . . . [was] a historic obligation of the State Duma, the State Council, and the government."[113]

Although a far from conservative body, the assembly that was elected in early February did differ from the First Duma. Because the Social-Democrats and Socialist-Revolutionaries had abandoned their boycott of the electoral campaign, 102 socialist deputies (19 percent) occupied the far left benches of the chamber. Together with an additional 104 peasant Trudoviki, the "left" accounted for over 40 percent of the Duma membership, a total that eventually became a primary cause of its downfall. Still uncertain in February, however, was the balance of forces among this bloc, the now much smaller Kadet center (36 percent), and an amorphous right wing (14 percent) that stretched from Octobrists to a handful of extreme monarchists.[114] Differing political perspectives yielded conflicting appraisals of the Second Duma's prospects.

Stunned by the party's electoral defeat, the Kadet press charged that the government had only its own repressive policies to blame for the leftist strength of the Second Duma. *Russkie vedomosti* announced that the Kadet Party would seek a centrist coalition with moderates on both left and right who valued the foundations of a constitutional Russia, an early signal of the Kadet effort to "save the Duma" from the radicalism of the left and the obscurantism of the government.[115] On the extreme right, *Moskovskie vedomosti* saw no difference between a Kadet First Duma and the mélange of leftists filling the Second. It ridiculed the Stolypin ministry for thinking that a "revolutionary electoral law" might have achieved anything different. The "sole correct" strategy now available to the government was to abolish the Duma altogether. Failing this, the paper urged the assembly's dispersal at the first opportunity, and the convocation of an assembly of the land (*zemskii sobor*) to write a new electoral law for a consultative chamber stripped of its legislative authority. Any other scenario, from the issuance of a new electoral law to concessions by the government, threatened [to bring on] "revolutionary

[113] "K vyboram v Gosudarstvennuiu Dumu," *Novoe vremia*, 18 January 1907, p. 1.

[114] Manning, *Crisis of the Old Order*, pp. 294–95, and Alfred Levin, *The Second Duma* (Yale University Press, 1966), pp. 66–69.

[115] *Russkie vedomosti*, 8 February 1907, p. 2; 10 February 1907, p. 2; and 15 February 1907, p. 2.

chaos."[116] The more moderate conservative daily *Novoe vremia*, however, saw less cause for alarm in the Duma's makeup. Indeed, it welcomed the appearance of a distinct left wing likely to push the Kadets toward the right and toward support of the government. Although the paper would soon discover that it had greatly exaggerated the case, it could argue in early February that "the country had moved to the right. . . . We are undoubtedly moving out of a phase of political romanticism and entering a phase of real politics." Although this "turnabout," an accomplishment of the Stolypin ministry, had only begun, it indicated that Russia's "multitudinous population" was recognizing how "powerless it was without gosudarstvennost'."[117]

Stolypin initially took a similar position regarding the Duma. The possible moderation of the Kadets, a substantial minority of Octobrists and moderate rightists, and the presence of a genuine and threatening democratic left all rendered conceivable a centrist Duma coalition willing to support the government and its programs. In the first weeks after the Duma's convocation on 20 February, the premier assured the tsar that "the attitude of [this] Duma differs greatly from last year's."[118] Nicholas, using Stolypin's language during an audience in late February with the new Duma president, the Kadet F. A. Golovin, spoke of the many legislative projects that required the assembly's attention and inquired about the possibilities of a Duma "center capable of work [*rabotosposobnyi*]."[119] Stolypin's maiden speech to the Duma on 6 March, in which he outlined the ministry's legislative agenda and emphasized the local reforms, reiterated that the premier remained committed to cooperation between government and Duma in order to promulgate the "state structure's new foundations." The "government," Stolypin said, was "prepared in this regard to apply the greatest efforts: its labor, good will, and accumulated experience are at the disposal of the State Duma." The Duma, he was certain, would be "a collaborator [*sotrudnik*]" in the ministry's quest "to preserve the historical bequest of Russia and reestablish order and tranquility in her."[120] The ministry's semi-official press organ, *Rossiia*, consistently returned to this theme throughout the month of March.[121]

---

[116] "Pravitel'stvo pred kadetskoi pobedoi," *Moskovskie vedomosti*, 9 February 1907, p. 1. Beginning with its issue of 24 March, the paper appeared daily under a banner headline that read "The Duma Ought To Be Dissolved."

[117] "Vidy na budushchee v G. Dume," *Novoe vremia*, 10 February 1907, p. 4.

[118] "Perepiska N. A. Romanova i P. A. Stolypina," pp. 108–9 (20 February, 6 March 1907).

[119] "Zapiski F. A. Golovin," *KA* 19 (1926): 118.

[120] *Stenograficheskii otchet Gosudarstvennoi Dumy* (hereafter *SOGD*), II Duma session 2, meeting 5, 6 March 1907, p. 120.

[121] See, for example, "Zametki ekonomista," *Rossiia*, 18 March 1907, p. 2, and "Angliiskaia pechat' i Duma," *Rossiia*, 23 March 1907, pp. 1–2.

Accommodating a center-right coalition that included the suspect Kadets, Stolypin was pursuing what for him was a familiar strategy. The premier sought political stability for the state and allies for the government wherever he could find them. Yet as Roberta Thompson Manning has shown, Stolypin's personal determination to find a base of public support in the Duma was also reinforced by the implacable opposition that his reform initiatives were encountering on the far right of autocratic politics. Since mid-1906, a constellation of influential former officials and provincial noble landowners, positioned in the right bloc of the State Council and the organs of the United Nobility, had been registering loud protests, with the premier and at the imperial court, against ministerial policy. Having previously refused entreaties to alter the electoral law, in early 1907 Stolypin further exacerbated rightist antagonism by announcing that he sought cooperation with the Duma and intended to present it with a legislative program that included basic alterations of rural administration and self-administration. Indeed, as Manning has shown, the proposed reconstruction of rural institutions, and the far-reaching changes of the rural status quo that it portended, was exploited by rightist circles to create widespread opposition to the Second Duma within provincial zemstvo assemblies.[122]

Even before the February elections, Stolypin was well aware of opposition to the local reforms "in higher spheres." In the days following approval of the program by the Council of Ministers on 6 January, a document condemning the proposals and urging that they be withheld from the second Duma made its way to Stolypin. He noted in his own hand the authorship of Count K. I. Palen, the venerable former minister of justice,

---

[122] Manning, *Crisis of the Old Order*, chaps. 12–13. The treatment accorded these events here differs with Manning in terms of chronology and interpretation. It is not clear to this author that *provincial zemstvo* protest against the local reforms was as central a factor in the crisis leading to the 3 June coup as Manning suggests. She stands on firm ground in portraying the government's awareness that far-right circles of the capital and the more radical elements of the United Nobility envisioned not only a revision of the electoral law but also a possible diminution or elimination of the Duma's legislative powers (see especially ibid., pp. 306–10). Equally convincing is her contention that the provincial campaign against the local reforms was a broad protest against allowing a radical Duma to consider fundamental reforms of rural life (see especially p. 317). Finally, she is right to suggest a confluence of conservative national and local politics. Yet my reading of the sources does not support the contention that in the spring of 1907 the MVD or the Council of Ministers (two organs that followed zemstvo politics closely) equated rightist opposition to the legislative Duma and provincial protest against the local reforms as a single campaign to prevent the elimination of "the last vestiges of gentry political influence in a country dominated by a largely landless bureaucracy and a relatively democratic Duma" (pp. 304–5), particularly since both the local reforms and the Duma itself still bore the sanction of the sovereign autocrat that nobles and officials both served. These dynamics were a product, not a cause of the coup of June 3.

and identified the sponsors as "a group on the extreme right of the State Council." It is most likely that this was an attempt to influence the tsar's pending decision on the recommendations of the Council of Ministers that the reform program be approved.[123] Certainly a damning critique, it termed Stolypin's initiatives even more incomprehensible than "a fundamental disruption of an army during a military campaign." The ministry was contemplating "a fundamental disruption of the entire administrative mechanism in the heat of a revolution that is also a war, but one with an internal enemy that is much more dangerous than any foreign foe."[124]

Three features of the Stolypin program came under intense attack. The position of vice-governor—a "petty official [*chinovnik*]" who as an outsider lacked "the authority enjoyed by the majority of county marshals"—promised neither improvement of local administration nor aid to the rural populace. Useless to the state, this reform served only to register a "mark of distrust" against the landowning nobility and to "increase the number of those dissatisfied with the Government." Ministerial plans for township and zemstvo electoral reform, both containing excessive franchise reductions, were considered to be even more myopic. They portended assemblies in which "cultured and prosperous" noble landowners were "lost" amidst communal peasants, "a mass of small proprietors from the agricultural, commercial, and industrial classes," and "leaders" from the third element. Such statutes, proposed at a time of agrarian strife, guaranteed that the townships would become "permanent sources of homegrown revolution," and zemstvo assemblies the organs of an "intelligentsia . . . antagonistic to the existing state and social order."[125] The most severe criticism of the projects, however, was reserved for their willingness to tamper with the preeminence of local landowning nobilities at a time when these had finally abandoned "political opposition to the Government" and come to "stand . . . in defense of state authority, property, and order." The zemtsy "had turned to the right" and were "displaying a firm intention . . . of assisting the Government by every means in its struggle with the revolutionary movement." The reforms threatened to "undermine" these developments by altering the zemstvo's "composition [in a manner] extremely advantageous for leftist tendencies." With nobiliary influence eliminated, the zemstvos "would again be sucked into the whirlpool of political agitation" and used to advance goals "plainly destructive to the entire state order."

[123] "Zapiski gr. Palena (n.d.)," TsGIA, f. 1284, op. 185 (1907), d. 5a, ch. 3, ll. 151–58, and "Zamechaniia po zapiske gruppy krainei pravoi Gosudarstvennogo Soveta (n.d.)," ibid., l. 150. Both documents were found in the premier's personal files after his assassination in September 1911. Ibid., d. 5a, ch. 1, l. 309.

[124] "Zapiski," l. 152.

[125] Ibid., ll. 154–55.

The critique concluded by demanding that the government withhold its reforms of local administration and the zemstvo electoral system from the upcoming Duma. In the likely event that this advice went unheeded, it urged Stolypin at least to allow all provincial zemstvo and noble assemblies to examine the statutes before initiating the legislative process. Their conclusions might balance out the even more radical alternatives to the government's proposals likely to surface in a leftist Duma still obsessed with the four-tail suffrage. Stressing how dangerous it was to rely on a chamber that knew nothing "about the requirements of contemporary zemstvo Russia," rightists insisted that consultation with provincial assemblies might establish a useful "precedent" for discussing other legislative measures, thereby allowing "the government to discover support in the zemstvos for the struggle with the radical excesses of the Duma."[126]

With its emphasis on revolutionary disorder, the rightist critique of the local reforms echoed earlier opposition from statist officials within the MVD, one that had already been discounted as exaggerated and shortsighted. The strategy of turning to the zemstvos violated the premier's intentions to elicit stable relations with the Duma. Both positions contradicted the interests of the state as Stolypin defined them, and neither of them was a persuasive reason to abandon reform. In a handwritten personal memorandum he replied:

> Reform at a time of revolution is necessary because the shortcomings of the domestic order [uklad] in large measure spawned the revolution. Solely engaging in struggle with the revolution at best eliminates the consequences and not the cause: one sore is healed, but the infected blood creates a new ulceration. Moreover, this path of reform has been solemnly proclaimed, the State Duma has been created, and it is impossible to turn back. That would be a dreadful mistake—where a government has repressed revolution (Prussia, Austria), it succeeded not exclusively by physical force, but, by relying on strength, by bravely standing in the forefront of reform. To reduce all the creativity of the government to police measures is to admit that the ruling authority [praviashchaia vlast'] is powerless.[127]

This argument, or one like it, assured the support of Nicholas II, who gave his formal approval to the local reform program on 11 February.[128]

---

[126] Ibid., ll. 157–58.

[127] "Zamechaniia," ibid., l. 150. The only specific policy disagreement treated in this note was the replacement of the marshal of the nobility, which Stolypin justified with reference to his own service in the provinces. Ibid.

[128] TsGIA, f. 1284, op. 185 (1907), d. 5a, ch. 1, l. 1. The drafts of village, township, uchastok (district), and county reforms were distributed within the MVD for final editing on the following day. TsGIA, f. 1291, op. 122 (1907), d. 17, l. 9. The reform of the county zemstvo electoral system, to which the tsar also gave his approval, was part of a separate

Yet, as the Second Duma convened later that same month, both State Council rightists and the Permanent Council of the United Nobility continued to press the issue. The Permanent Council wrote to the premier on 17 February to urge preliminary consideration of the projects by provincial noble and zemstvo assemblies, but Stolypin replied that "general political circumstances" required him to follow established legislative procedure.[129] A week later two State Council members, former MVD Assistant Minister A. S. Stishinskii and the provincial noble landowner A. A. Naryshkin, visited Stolypin to reiterate that the local reforms would expose the village to the "politically disloyal third element" and undermine the "entire significance of the noble estate in the countryside." Stolypin, according to the report that the two gave to the Permanent Council, responded that the "estate principle had lost all importance," whereas the "non-estate principle [bezsoslovnost']" and "the small zemstvo unit" were concepts that he intended to implement. As to their fears of the third element, Stolypin, who undoubtedly thought that he had taken sufficient precautions in this regard, replied that peasants knew "perfectly well who in fact can lead local [public] life."[130] Discussing this outcome at meetings of the 27th and 29th, members of the Permanent Council were somewhat despondent and unsure how to proceed, given their repeated failures to sway the premier. Indeed, some, including the chairman A. A. Bobrinskii, urged delaying the organization's third congress, which was scheduled at the end of March to discuss the local reforms, for fear that a publicized assault by the United Nobility might weaken right deputies in the Duma and hasten the passage of the legislation. Naryshkin and A. I. Mosolov successfully contended that the congress was an imperative means to mobilize provincial assemblies of the nobility against the reforms.[131]

A more substantial and, for Stolypin, consequential source of provincial opposition was emerging from the zemstvos. From January through early March, small groups of activists met privately in Moscow and St. Petersburg; they were also considering how to divert the local reforms from the Duma and looked to the convocation of a zemstvo congress as

statute incorporating all aspects of zemstvo reform. The Council of Ministers reviewed it on 17 February and ordered an interministerial commission to review the contentious jurisdictional issues affecting the relations of each ministry to the zemstvo; this body did not debate electoral reform TsGIA, f. 1276, op. 3, d. 22, ll. 82–86. The Council of Ministers only handed down final approval of zemstvo reform in December 1907, so that it was never brought before the Second Duma. "Osobyi zhurnal Soveta ministrov (7 and 18 December 1907)," ibid., ll. 149–72.

[129] TsGAOR, f. 434, op. 1, d. 75, l. 53, and d. 76, l. 76. The text and Stolypin's reply is TsGIA, f. 899, op. 1, d. 94, l. 2.

[130] TsGAOR, f. 434, op. 1. d. 76, ll. 90–91.

[131] Ibid., ll. 91 and 95–97.

a fulcrum of this campaign.[132] The Saratov provincial zemstvo and two of its stalwart conservatives, A. A. Uvarov and D. A. Olsuf'ev, a moderate member of the United Nobility's Permanent Council, were key players in this game. On 6 March the Stolypin ministry formally introduced the local reforms into the State Duma.[133] Six days later an extraordinary meeting of the Saratov assembly petitioned the minister of internal affairs to allow the zemstvos to examine the projects before their approval by the Duma and State Council. A telegram to the former governor left little doubt that Stolypin was contaminating himself with his association with the Duma. It charged that the government's reforms had been "prepared by the old bureaucratic path, without the aid of vital public forces, without the participation of zemstvo activists who have an intimate knowledge of local welfare and needs. To replace the broad experience of local zemtsy," the petition concluded, "with [that] knowledge of life [possessed] by members of the State Duma . . . [was], especially given the composition of [its] members, absolutely inadmissable."[134] At the same time, the Saratov assembly resolved to notify all other provincial executive boards that their zemstvos should despatch similar petitions to the government. Finally, it asked the Moscow board to obtain official permission from the government for a zemstvo congress in that city to review the reform projects.[135]

Indirectly replying to the Saratov petition, on 15 March the MVD informed provincial governors that zemstvo assemblies were free to discuss statutes relating to self-administration, but remained conspicuously silent about the campaign for prior examination.[136] Yet the ministry had sup-

---

[132] *Stenograficheskie otchety 1-ogo Vserossiiskogo S"ezda Zemskikh Deiatelei v Moskve: Zasedaniia 10–15 iiunia 1907 g.* (Moscow, 1907), pp. 1–2.

[133] All the local reform statutes, excepting zemstvo self-administration, were given to the Duma on 7 March: village; township; district kommisar; county administration; and the land reform and peasant civil rights legislation promulgated via article 87. *SOGD*, II Duma, session 2, meeting 6 (7 March 1907) p. 180. Provincial reform was introduced on 12 March. Ibid., pp. 341–42.

[134] TsGIA, f. 1288, op. 2 (1907), ed. khr. 37, ll. 1–2, Saratov provincial executive board to Minister of Internal Affairs (14 March 1907). Whether Uvarov and Olsuf'ev were acting in tandem with the United Nobility is unclear. Attendance records for the Permanent Council's twenty-nine meetings between 26 May 1906 and 14 February 1907 show that Olsuf'ev stopped regularly participating after the dissolution of the First Duma, and subsequently was present only at two meetings in November 1906. TsGAOR, f. 434, op. 1, d. 75.

[135] *Zhurnaly Chrezvychainnogo Saratovskogo Gubernskogo Zemskogo Sobraniia 12 Marta 1907 g.* (Saratov, 1907), pp. 6–7. This action served to inform other provincial zemstvos of the movement growing against consideration of the reforms by the Second Duma. See, for example, *Zhurnal chrezvychainnogo Vologodskogo Gubernskogo Zemskogo Sobraniia, 29 maia 1907* (Vologda, 1907), pp. 5–9; TsGIA, f. 1288, op. 2 (1907), d. 38, ll. 11–12 (Ekaterinoslav governor to GUMKh, 26 May 1907); and Gr. D. A. Olsuf'ev, *Ob uchastii zemstv v obsuzhdenii zemskoi reformy* (Saratov, 1907).

[136] TsGIA, f. 1288, op. 2 (1907), ed. khr. 37, l. 4, GUMKh to governors of zemstvo prov-

plied a legal opening that both the United Nobility and the organizers of the zemstvo congress moved quickly to fill. When the third congress of the United Nobility began in St. Petersburg on 27 March, it appointed Olsuf'ev chair of a commission with delegates from all attending provincial affiliates that was charged to devise a strategy against the reforms. On the 30th the commission recommended that the congress formally support prior examination by provincial noble and zemstvo assemblies, and instructed the Permanent Council to distribute copies of the statutes to these bodies should they not be forthcoming from the MVD. Recognizing that Duma approval was not foreseeable "in the near future," it also advised the creation of a committee to develop a detailed critique that could be sent to provincial assemblies of the nobility and serve as the basis for their petitions.[137]

The next day a private "conference" of ninety-two delegates from twenty-seven provincial zemstvo assemblies, many of whom were attending the congress, also endorsed the idea of prior examination and issued the formal call for a zemstvo congress in Moscow to articulate a united position on these issues. The congress's provisional council, elected by the conference, met with Stolypin in early April, at which time he sanctioned the Moscow meeting and released copies of the ministry's reform statutes.[138] In mid-April the council dispatched these materials to the provincial zemstvo boards. An accompanying letter detailed the strategy pursued by the congress organizers. All provincial assemblies were requested to hold extraordinary sessions in April and May to "acquaint" their members with the local reforms and elect delegates to the upcoming congress. The executive boards would also designate special commissions to review the projects in detail, and would distribute the statutes to county assemblies for consideration at their regular autumn meetings. Together with the conclusions of the zemstvo congress, all these materials would then allow provincial assemblies to present their opinions to the government at the end of the year.[139]

---

inces (15 March 1907); ibid., l. 8, Zemskii otdel to governors of zemstvo provinces (29 March 1907). This permission did not extend to reforms of county and provincial administration, "Spravka po GUMKh (n.d.)," ibid., ll. 6–7; and ibid., l. 10, GUMKh to governors of zemstvo provinces (17 May 1907).

[137] *Rech'*, 31 March 1907, p. 2; "Postanovleniia kommissii po voprosu o peredache zakonoproektov o mestnoi reforme na razsmotrenie mestnykh uchrezhdenii," TsGAOR, f. 434, op. 1, d. 12/55, ll. 47–48; and *Trudy tret'ego s"ezda upolnomochennykh dvorianskikh obshchestv 32 gubernii s 27 marta po 2 aprelia 1907 g.* (St. Petersburg, 1907), pp. 337–38.

[138] "Protokol postoiannogo soveta (12 April 1907)," TsGAOR, f. 434, op. 1, d. 77/307, l. 3; and TsGIA, f. 1291, op. 122 (1907), ed. khr. 17, l. 27 (P. Geiden to N. L. Psheradskii, 11 April 1907). An announcement of the congress appeared in *Rossiia*, 17 April 1907, p. 3.

[139] TsGIA, f. 1288, op. 2 (1907), ed. khr. 38, ll. 11–12 (Ekaterinoslav governor to GUMKh).

The provincial zemstvos of Saratov, Kursk, and Simbirsk—all rightist assemblies with strong ties to the United Nobility—actually issued reports in the spring that were critical of the local reforms. Kursk, a bastion of political reaction, adopted the extreme position of defending the 1890 statute and its estate structure, while Saratov and Simbirsk, although acknowledging the need for electoral reform, expressed strong reservations about township self-administration.[140] All other provincial assemblies followed the lead of the zemstvo congress's provisional council. They met in extraordinary sessions, primarily during the last days of May, to elect delegates to the June zemstvo congress and appoint investigative commissions.[141] In addition, some sixteen of the thirty-four zemstvos approved petitions requesting prior investigation of the projects.[142] At Stolypin's order, however, the MVD pocketed these resolutions: they were "left unanswered."[143]

This mobilization of zemstvo opinion confronted the Stolypin ministry with two different challenges. On the one hand, the premier had encountered signs of serious provincial opposition to the substance of his rural reform program. Although only a handful of assemblies had issued any critique of the legislation, it was still evident that the hostility his program had encountered from rightists in the State Council and United Nobility could be found in the provinces as well, and not merely in the antechambers of the capital. The character and extent of this opposition, however, was entirely unclear. Indeed, the authoritative *Rossiia*, responding on 10 May to Kadet attacks on the reactionary character of the upcoming June zemstvo congress, expressed little fear about an assemblage "that, given its political orientation, . . . lacks revolutionary aims and will not allow

---

[140] "Doklad komissii po izmeneniiu zemskogo izbiratel'nogo zakona," *Zhurnal Zasedaniia Ekstrennogo Kurskogo Gubernskogo Zemskogo Sobraniia 15 maia 1907 g.* (Kursk, 1907), pp. 165–224; *Zhurnaly i doklady Simbirskogo Gubernskogo Zemskogo Sobraniia Chrezvychainnoi Sessii 28 aprelia i 5 iiunia 1907 g.* (Simbirsk, 1907); and *Doklad i Protokoly Zasedanii Kommissii po reforme zemskogo polozheniia* (Saratov, 1907), pp. 1–57.

[141] The list of delegates and the date of their election is *Stenograficheskie otchety 1-ogo s"ezda*, pp. 105–12.

[142] "Po khodataistvam zemstv o peredache na predvaritel'nye obsuzhdeniia zemskikh sobranii zakonoproektov kasaiushchiesia reform zemskikh uchrezhdenii," TsGIA, f. 1288, op. 2 (1907), d. 38, ll. 1–81. These were (together with the date of the vote): Saratov (14 March); Novgorod (17 April); Bessarabia (20 April); Simbirsk (30 April); Kherson (20 May); Iaroslavl' (23 May); Orel (25 May); Ekaterinoslav (26 May); Tula (26 May); Perm (28 May); Vologda (29 May); Moscow (1 June); Pskov (17 June); and Tambov (15 December). Also St. Petersburg and Tver, *Zhurnaly zasedanii Sankt-Peterburgskogo Gubernskogo Zemskogo Sobraniia Chrezvychainykh Sessii 10–16 maia i 20 iiunia 1907 g.* (St. Petersburg, 1907), pp. 11–13, and *Zhurnaly Tverskogo Ocherednogo Gubernskogo Zemskogo Sobraniia sessii 1907 goda (8–19 dek.) i chrezvychainnogo sobraniia 16–17 maia 1907 g.* (Tver, 1908), p. 1474.

[143] Ibid., d. 38, l. 4.

itself any unlawful decisions or actions."[144] The more compelling challenge confronting the government was a campaign of protest that was in fact not focused on legislation, about which the assemblies generally lacked detailed information, but on the prospect of the government allowing the second Duma to resolve issues essential to the future of the zemstvo and the landowning nobility that presently controlled it. Both in the provincial assemblies that petitioned against the Duma and in those that did not, debate swirled around the unrepresentative character of a national assembly whose membership stood far to the left of zemstvo opinion and, as had been the case in the First Duma, excluded all but a smattering of provincial zemtsy.[145] The government's association with this body was creating a new crisis of authority within one of the primary constituencies to which Stolypin looked for support.[146]

Thus, the consolidation of conservative opinion in the zemstvos, which two years earlier had been bastions of liberalism, was a threatening phenomenon only as long as the ministry chose to seek an accommodation with the Second Duma, which by April it was less and less inclined to do. The same factors that agitated provincial opposition to the Duma exerted no less of an impact on the government, particularly as the issue that had doomed the first assembly again reared its head in the second: the land question.[147] By late March and early April instances of local peasant disorders and the speeches of left-wing deputies demanding compulsory alienation of property were raising the specter of rural unrest. Writing to Stolypin on 31 March, Nicholas II expressed his outrage at "the extreme speeches on the agrarian question being distributed all over Russia," which, he feared, posed "a serious danger to peace in the village." Stoly-

[144] *Rossiia*, 10 May 1907, p. 1. See also the paper's treatment of the second congress of the Octobrist Party, particularly its supportive stance toward the government local reform program. *Rossiia*, 8 May 1907, p. 4; 10 May 1907, p. 3, 12 May 1907, p. 3.

[145] See, for example, a review of debates in the Moscow provincial zemstvo on 1 June 1907. TsGIA, f. 1288, op. 2 (1907), d. 38, ll. 7–8; *Nizhegorodskoe Gubernskoe Zemskoe Sobraniia XLII Ocherednoi sessii 25 noiabria–14 dekabria 1906 g. i chrezvychainnoi sessii 7 maia 1907 g.* (Nizhnii Novgorod, 1907), pp. 364–65; and *Doklady Kharkovskoi Gubernskoi Zemskoi Upravy Gubernskomu Zemskomu Sobraniiu chrezvychainnoi sessii 4-ogo maia 1907 g.* (Kharkov, 1907), pp. 1–3.

[146] The results of a survey of zemstvo political sympathies, which GUMKh conducted in the last days of May, emphasized the far more conservative orientation of the provincial assemblies, while also indicating that the extreme right did not dominate provincial opinion. "So svedeniiam o prinadlezhnosti k politicheskim partiiam rukovodiashchego bol'shinstva glasnykh v zemskikh sobraniia," TsGIA, f. 1288, op. 2 (1907), d. 2. The characterization of thirty-two provincial zemstvo assemblies was: right (28%); moderate right (28%); moderate (31%); moderate left (3%); and left, i.e., Kadet, (9%). The latter were the zemstvos of Viatka, Kostroma, and Ufa provinces.

[147] Manning, *Crisis of the Old Order*, pp. 310–12; Hosking, *Russian Constitutional Experiment*, chap. 1; and Ananych, Diakin, et al., *Krizis samoderzhaviia v Rossii*, pp. 320–23.

pin replied on 9 April that he had arranged an audience between the tsar and Duma President Golovin so that the sovereign could warn him against "revolutionizing the people from the Duma tribune," but he also agreed that the assembly seemed increasingly to display "a general incapacity to work."[148] When in early May a Duma commission rejected the government's land-reform legislation in favor of a bill incorporating compulsory sale of property, the minister went before the assembly to hint that his patience had been exhausted. Acknowledging "the irrefutable desire, demand, aim of broad circles in society to place state work on correct, legal foundations and move toward . . . the improvement of the country's life," Stolypin charged that many Duma deputies wanted simply "to strengthen unrest in the country, to sow the seeds of agitation in the population, with the goal of raising distrust toward the government in order to undermine its significance." Stolypin thundered: "the state will not allow this line to be crossed. . . . [O]therwise it ceases to be a state."[149]

That so much of Russia, among both its political parties and its mass population, still stood on the wrong side of this line embodied the dilemma confronted by a government that insisted on its right to draw the limits of acceptable national politics. "Several weeks of cooperation with the Second Duma convinced the government," Kryzhanovskii recalled, "that one could not live with" this assembly. Stolypin soon decided to dissolve it and issue a new electoral law. Certain that Kryzhanovskii's pet project of elections via the zemstvo assemblies constricted the Duma's representative character to an unacceptable degree, Stolypin ordered his assistant to craft a statute that "would assure the more prosperous, and consequently more cultured, strata [of the population] access to the Duma." At the same time, he persuaded the tsar to oppose the missives of State Comptroller P. Kh. Shvanebakh and other rightist officials in the State Council to suspend the Duma for an unlimited period of time and rule, in effect, by dictatorship—an idea no more persuasive in mid-1907 than it had been in late 1905.[150] Yet by altering a law that itself had been far from democratic, the Stolypin government established by fiat the narrow limits of the political nation, limits that it had been unable to secure by other means for over a year. Reducing peasant participation in the

---

[148] "Perepiska N. A. Romanova i P. A. Stolypina," pp. 109–10 (31 March 1907), and Shchegolev, ed., *Padenie tsarskogo rezhima*, 5:372–73.

[149] *Rossiia*, 11 May 1907, pp. 1–2.

[150] Kryzhanovskii, *Vospominaniia*, pp. 107–16; and Ananych, Diakin, et al., *Krizis samoderzhaviia v Rossii*, pp. 320–24. Kryzhanovskii maintained that a Duma electoral law based on the county zemstvo and the township could guarantee representation of propertied and conservative elements. Ibid., pp. 36, 90.

electoral system, the government ensured that its land demands would not preoccupy the third Duma. Realigning the voting equation in the cities in favor of large urban property, it undermined the Kadet party's primary political constituency. And by allocating the single largest bloc of Duma electors to large and middling provincial landowners, the Stolypin ministry staked its hopes for political stability on the moderate conservatism of the provincial nobility and the long-term evolution of rural civil society.[151]

The issuance of the new electoral law by sovereign manifesto, the so-called coup d'état of 3 June 1907, was an act that contravened the Duma's right to approve any alteration of the Fundamental Laws of the Empire. To Kryzhanovskii, however, the formalities of law in this case had rightfully given way to the political interests of the state. Both the first and second Dumas, he wrote, had revealed that "the fire of social hatred lurking in the depths of Russia, in its semi-educated strata . . . threaten to incinerate the very structure of gosudarstvennost'." Leftist parties had fueled it, the Kadets had proved unable to contain it, and the "voice of moderate elements was lost" in the conflagration. Stolypin seized on the only option open to him; he attempted "to close the air-vent" feeding the flames in the hope that "the fire would subside and allow time to adopt measures aimed at putting it out and strengthening the government apparatus." "To tear the State Duma from the hands of the revolutionaries, join it with [Russia's] historic institutions, propel it into a system of state administration—this," Kryzhanovskii argued, "was the goal that stood before the Supreme Authority and the government." Those who insisted that the third of June marked "a dangerous blow to popular legal consciousness" had failed to understand that the experience of the first two Dumas had supplied convincing evidence that such consciousness barely existed in the masses. "This consciousness still had to be created and inculcated in them," Kryzhanovskii concluded, and the task "demands long years of peaceful, creative labor."[152] Whether the third of June system created by the coup d'état would provide this necessary interval was, however, an issue that in the summer of 1907 still remained entirely unresolved.

To be sure, little Western parliamentary theory informed this act that imposed state hegemony on national political life. Reserving all executive power to itself and the autocrat, the government remained the arbiter of

[151] Dan, "Obshchaia politika pravitel'stva," p. 145, and Haimson, "Introduction," in idem, ed., *Politics of Rural Russia*, pp. 1–29.

[152] Kryzhanovskii, *Vospominaniia*, pp. 116–17; see also Shchegolev, ed., *Padenie tsarskogo rezhima*, 5:423–30.

state life, able to define the acceptable limits of Russian social and political development. It was revealing that on the eve of the coup Stolypin's newspaper *Rossiia*, in attacking both socialists and liberals for seeking to overthrow the state order (the former through a revolutionary republic and the latter through the peaceful means of "parliamentarism") quoted approvingly from a Reichstag speech of Otto von Bismarck that condemned German liberalism:

> You are striving for a parliamentary regime, you desire that the imperial government submit to your majority; in other words, you want the primacy of a party. Already, however, this is not a monarchy, but a republic . . . I cannot cross this line, and I will try to protect my emperor from a situation in which he would be forced to execute the will of the majority. In this sense, your majority is not authoritative for me. I was hostile to many of the parliamentary parties but worked with them when I saw that they agreed with what I considered necessary in the interests of the state and the emperor.[153]

Indeed—*Rossiia* maintained the next day—only Duma parties that rejected all "revolutionary groupings" and evidenced "a sincere desire to preserve Russian gosudarstvennost' " could assure themselves a place in the body politic.[154] Under the third of June system, the nation could not exist without the state, the national interest could not be expressed without the pronounced influence of the government, and political legitimacy was available to parties and ministers alike only within a framework of law acceptable to the autocratic sovereign.

Yet, if the third of June system thus represented Stolypin's "victory" over the revolution of 1905, that triumph was only partially complete, if a triumph at all. Indeed, to view the events of 1906–07 as a reactionary conquest, or to expect a more democratic perspective from a statesman of monarchical Russia than the era itself was capable of producing, says in fact very little. That Stolypin chose to tie the fate of the old regime to urban wealth and especially to rural noble landowning, which *Rossiia* in June termed "the country's cultured film [*kulturnaia plenka*]," was no more surprising than his repression of a peasantry whose own rational demand for land confirmed widespread public perception that peasants were at present politically incapable.[155] As *Rossiia* wrote on 6 June, the first two Dumas had almost produced "the final destruction of even that small culture that the country with such difficulty had accumulated." The electoral law of 3 June promised a modicum of political stability that

---

[153] "Revoliutsionnaia panacea," *Rossiia*, 24 May 1907, p. 2.
[154] *Rossiia*, 25 May 1907, p. 1.
[155] *Rossiia*, 13 June 1907, p. 1.

"would protect the more stable and cultured public elements to some degree from the attacks of groundless demagoguery."[156] Indeed, in this sense, the coup d'état and the system it produced succeeded not so much in conquering revolution as in institutionalizing an extremely fragile and contradictory national politics.[157]

Despite sentiments to reverse the concessions of the October Manifesto, the formerly unrestricted authority of the tsar remained limited, on the one hand, by the legislative powers of the State Duma and, on the other, by a unified ministerial government over which Stolypin presided. That the Duma was neither constituent assembly nor genuine parliament did not remove its significance as a symbol of the post-October political order, a forum for national political debate, and a potential base of support for a reformist cabinet. Moreover, the superordinate traditions of bureaucratic rule, although plainly not destroyed, had been constrained, in part by the Fundamental Laws but in larger measure by the fait accompli of political parties, press, and public opinion that Stolypin, more than most public figures, was skilled at manipulating as the situation demanded. Yet, the former provincial governor recognized that the very fragility of the third of June system, the narrow social base from which the government could lay claim to legitimate rule, dictated not only the preservation of the state reforms of 1905–06, but also the gradual civil and political transformation needed to stabilize a reformed autocratic order. The third of June created a temporary respite from political conflict. It was now, as Stolypin's *Rossiia* insisted on 1 July, "necessary to work." Socialists, the paper complained, understood this slogan to mean striving for social upheaval, for the Kadets it meant securing party dominance in the next Duma, and for rightist groups it meant condemning "almost all authority for its creation of revolution." Stolypin, to judge from these editorial comments, believed his government would, in the Third Duma, prove to be capable of circumnavigating such political shoals:

> When we say it is necessary to work, we understand this to mean selfless labor, guided, on the one hand, by the disinfection of the air from the miasma established by the so-called "liberation movement," and, on the other, by the . . . gradual improvement of the real conditions of the real life of real people. . . . History knows examples of new peoples building entirely new orders in new

[156] *Rossiia*, 6 June 1907, p. 2.

[157] Lenin's brief analytical examinations of post-1907 domestic politics are quite revealing in this regard. See especially, V. I. Lenin, "O sotsial'noi strukture vlasti (4 March 1911)," *Polnoe sobranie sochinenii* (Moscow, 1961), vol. 20, pp. 187–88; "O znachenii krizisa (16 April 1911)," ibid., pp. 223–27; and "Ob otsenke tekushchego momenta (1 November 1908)," ibid., 17:271–84.

places. But Russia is not a new place and the Russian people are not a new people; we can only build a new order by means of . . . gradual and organic evolution. . . . Otherwise, we will be hopelessly doomed to the endless cycle of contradictions that characterize our times.[158]

Having repudiated the ideals that sparked the liberation movement and the revolution of 1905, Stolypin knew that reform was essential if the old regime as a whole was to survive the endless cycle of contradictions that had brought autocracy near collapse.

[158] "Nado rabotat'," *Rossiia*, 1 July 1907, p. 1.

CHAPTER VII

Provincial Politics and Local Reform: Conflicting Visions of the Nation, 1907–1909

WHEN STOLYPIN first addressed the "lofty assemblage" of the Third State Duma on 19 November 1907, he looked out upon the conservative body that the third of June electoral law had been intended to produce. Some two-thirds of the new deputies belonged to moderate-right and rightist parties, beginning with the single largest fraction, the Octobrists, which controlled 32 percent of the Duma votes, and ending with the extreme right, which occupied 11 percent of the seats. In the Second Duma, these same parties had clung to 74 places (14 percent). Zemstvo landowners, limited to 53 votes (10 percent) in early 1907, saw their ranks swell to 141 deputies (32 percent). Members of the nobility, who accounted for one-third of all deputies in the First Duma, now supplied one-half. In 1906, almost half of these nobles had been liberal professionals; in the Third Duma, more than 80 percent were provincial landowners.[1] This was a Duma of "stable" and "cultured" public elements.

Although proclaiming his commitment to the same legislative agenda that had been presented to the Second Duma earlier in the year, Stolypin told the assembled deputies that "the conditions under which we now must work and achieve these goals have not remained unchanged."[2] As "thunderous applause" greeted his condemnation of "the destructive movement [*razrushitel'noe*; not "liberation"—*osvobozhditel'noe*] created by extreme leftist parties," it was clear that the premier was addressing a Duma whose political sentiments had shifted sharply to the right. Nine months earlier he had spoken to the Second Duma of the government's duty to guard against "the abuse of newly granted freedoms"; now, he promised to oppose with force "antisocial criminal elements that debauch the younger generation." Then he had pledged the government to legislative reform "guided by the sovereign manifesto of 17 October 1905." Before the third assembly, he guaranteed "a stable, legal structure corresponding to Russian national consciousness" and the government's commitment to the "representative structure" granted by the sovereign.[3]

---

[1] Manning, *Crisis of the Old Order*, pp. 295, 327, and 500.

[2] TsGIA, f. 1276, op. 2, d. 4, ll. 640–736 is the government program.

[3] *SOGD*, Duma 2, session 2, meeting 5 (6 March 1907), pp. 322 and 324, and *SOGD*, Duma 3, session 1, meeting 7 (16 November 1907) p. 307.

"Applause from the center and from the right," the stenogramme of the proceedings noted, greeted this muted reference to the October Manifesto, but the words that followed it evoked an ovation from the right of the Duma chamber. They were references that deputies of the Second Duma had never heard from the head of "his majesty's government":

> The phenomenon of Tsarist Authority during all time has shown the people clearly that historic Autocratic Authority (thunderous applause and exclamations of bravo from the right) . . . historic Autocratic Authority and the free Will of the Monarch are the most treasured achievements of Russian state consciousness [*russkaia gosudarstvennost'*], because only this Authority and this Will, creating existing institutions and preserving them, are summoned, in moments of shock and danger for the state, to save Russia and direct her onto the path of order and historic justice.[4]

Offering talk of legality and representation to the Duma's Octobrist center, Stolypin also showered the right with grandiloquent references to autocracy that said nothing of the October Manifesto. The appeal to two different audiences spoke volumes about the accelerating rightward shift of Russian provincial politics in the six months that had passed since the coup d'état of June 1907. Indeed, as the dust settled from an act that had eliminated the threat of Duma radicalism and purportedly initiated a new era in Russian public life, Stolypin began to realize that his fate rested less in the realm of high politics and more in rural areas, where he had hoped to construct the core of a reformed autocratic order. The course of provincial politics from 1907 to 1909 was to reveal that the landowning nobility, bearing the cultural heritage of a service estate, embraced a very different vision of the nation and its future than that which Stolypin had summoned rural landowners to the Third Duma to confirm.

BENEATH THE STATE DUMA: PROVINCIAL POLITICS AND THE LOCAL
    REFORMS

The self-styled All-Russian Zemstvo Congress convened on 10 June 1907 in Russia's second capital, Moscow. From 32 provincial assemblies 124 representatives gathered to discuss the topic of the hour: the zemstvo electoral reform so recently saved from the second Duma. Reflecting the repudiation that liberalism had endured in the zemstvo milieu, only 10 Kadets (8 percent) attended the congress. They were joined by 4 center-left progressives, 2 of whom, the provincial marshal M. A. Stakhovich and the zemstvo executive board chairman S. N. Maslov, hailed from the

---

[4] *SOGD*, Duma 3, p. 312.

same province, Orel. That which remained of the liberal bloc that had dominated the 1904–05 zemstvo congresses was dwarfed by a conservative majority: 44 Octobrists (35 percent), 33 moderate-rightists (27 percent), and 33 rightists (27 percent). The congress elected right Octobrist M. V. Rodzianko its chairman and selected three assistant chairmen: Octobrist party leader A. I. Guchkov; D. A. Olsuf'ev, now an elected member of the State Council from Saratov; and the rightist Poltava provincial marshal S. E. Brazol. Like Olsuf'ev, Brazol was an active member of the United Nobility.[5]

Before the congress convened, its provisional council had drafted an analysis of the Stolypin zemstvo electoral reform that, although to the right of the government's proposals, did not express uncompromising opposition. Despite "all the difficulties . . . of present political conditions," the council agreed that a zemstvo electoral reform eliminating estate distinctions was necessary, and believed that the benefits of "revitalizing" zemstvo work with "new forces" outweighed the risks of change. It supported as well the government's proposals to base the zemstvo franchise on tax payments and halve this requirement. Nevertheless, even these theses, which reflected moderate-right sentiments within the Octobrist Party, took aim at two critical components of the MVD plan. Although that project already guaranteed one-fourth of the county zemstvo's seats to the landowner's curia, the council believed the figure to be too low. More important, the council recommended against conducting elections from the township assembly, insisting instead that communal peasants and petty proprietors vote separately in different curiae. Intended to divide and restrict their combined electoral weight, the measure benefited the first curia of landowners.[6]

Although its recommendations displayed some apprehension of broader popular participation in the zemstvo, the provisional council seemed to offer the government grounds for compromise. All the more shocking, then, was the raucous protest that exploded when the zemstvo congress opened. From the outset, when the provisional council proposed that the congress endorse the necessity of zemstvo reform, heated opposition arose from the congress's right wing and members of the United Nobility. The Smolensk Kadet Przhevalskii set the tone when he charged that rightists denying the necessity of reform were "blind men" unable to acknowledge that Russia's new constitutional order could not prevent revolution unless it allowed "the broad participation of citizens in self-

[5] *Rossiia*, 15 June 1907; and *Stenograficheskie otchety*, p. 6.

[6] "Voprosnye punkty i otvety Vremennogo Soveta," in *Zhurnaly i postanovleniia vserossiiskogo s"ezda zemskikh deiatelei v Moskve s 10 po 15 iiunia 1907 g.* (Moscow, 1907), pp. 113–16.

administration."[7] Picking up the gauntlet, N. E. Markov II of Kursk, soon to be an extreme right deputy in the Duma, replied that if he and his colleagues had gone blind, then the Kadets suffered from a more serious disease: "hallucinations, that is, they see what isn't there." Representing a provincial zemstvo already on record in defense of the 1890 estate franchise, Markov railed against all proponents of "democratization" who ignored the recent experience of the first two Dumas—implicitly numbering among them a premier apparently determined to alter the existing statute: "Can you, putting your hand on your heart, say that our peasantry in its current state is actually capable of running zemstvo business? . . . I am talking about what exists now, I am not hallucinating, I cannot speak about what will be, I am speaking about what exists now."[8]

Other speakers echoed this enraged, even visceral reaction to the ministerial reforms. Conveying the shock registered by agrarian rebellion and the repudiation suffered when peasants voted against them in the first two electoral campaigns, the speakers' comments evidenced a heightened sense of isolation, threatened status, and a refusal to think about the future given the reality of the present. Prince Kasatkin-Rostovskii, the provincial marshal of Kursk, charged that in its haste to promulgate a liberal zemstvo electoral reform the government was forgetting "that mess" it had created with the second Duma.[9] Those supporters of "democratizing" the zemstvo who thought reform could "give the country tranquility," N. A. Melnikov of Kazan objected, were committing "a state crime" if they dared allow "into the very heart of Russia" the same radical elements that had ruled the Second Duma. "In normal times," said Penza delegate A. L. Tsitovich, peasants would "gladly entrust the direction of the zemstvo ship to representatives of large landowning," but these were extraordinary days. Peasants seemed to "have lost all sense of the principles of a civil order [grazhdanskii pravoporiadok]":

> The desire to seize that which does not belong to them, to resolve the economic question with fire and force, incited in the peasants a distrust and hate for people who for more than forty years had led zemstvo business and managed it for the welfare of the peasants. As the pitiful experience of the first and second Dumas proved, a feverish vapor forced our essentially loyal peasants to entrust the defense of their interests to enemies of all order and legality, to enemies of state consciousness [gosudarstvennost'], and it would be even more pitiful if . . . we placed the zemstvo on this same dangerous and slippery path.[10]

[7] Stenograficheskie otchety, p. 14.
[8] Ibid., p. 17.
[9] Ibid., p. 29.
[10] Ibid., pp. 34–35.

The congress must reject and rework the current government bill, S. A. Tsurikov of Orel said: "Its consequences will be completely the opposite of those expected—instead of life we will get death."[11]

Not all congress delegates adopted this intransigent stance. Like the Octobrists A. A. Uvarov of Saratov and V. M. Petrovo-Solovovo of Tambov, they accepted the government's electoral reform as a basis for further negotiations, but indicated that the instability evident in both the cities and the countryside dictated limits that, particularly with township elections, the Stolypin proposals were exceeding.[12] Only a minority of the delegates fully shared Stolypin's views; most notable in this regard was A. D. Golitsyn, the Kharkov left-Octobrist soon to win election to the Third Duma. Expanding popular participation in local public affairs, Golitsyn objected, could not be confused with democratization and elimination of noble influence. From "an acculturative [vospitatel'nyi] point of view," the measure was imperative because the time had come to transform a majority presently "incapable of state life" into "conscious citizens." Irresponsible rightist opponents were "blinded by the glow of fires" if they thought that the "social enmity [sotsial'naia rozn']" revealed by recent events did not necessitate "the unification of those classes that possess general property interests."[13]

That Golitsyn's position was a minority view, however, indicated the depth of the prevailing opposition. Indeed, as this debate concluded, M. D. Ershov, a member of the provisional council that already had recommended restrictions of the MVD statute, noted: "If someone came in at the end of the meeting and was not here in the beginning, he would think that we were discussing a colossal reform, something new, whereas we are talking about changing several parts of the electoral law."[14] Many delegates clearly did not agree with this, however. Voting on general resolutions, the congress unanimously supported the principle of zemstvo electoral reform, but split in half when asked to approve submission of the government project, as amended by the provisional council, to the Duma. By a vote of 50 to 48, the congress narrowly defeated a resolution of Markov II that the bill be rewritten and, in essence, scrapped. When the wording of this motion was softened to a reworking of the government bill, the measure passed 60 to 37, even though it did not mention the Duma at all. The final compromise, which soothed moderates alarmed at a blatant affront to the legislative order, gained near unanimous approval, but still offered small consolation to the Stolypin minis-

[11] Ibid., p. 42.
[12] Ibid., pp. 18–20 and 49–50.
[13] Ibid., pp. 36–37.
[14] Ibid., p. 51.

try. The congress was willing to support a reform bill in the Duma only after all county and provincial assemblies had reworked the government project *and* yet another zemstvo congress had reexamined it in line with these conclusions.[15] Because many assemblies were already preparing to debate the local reforms in the autumn and winter, the congress's action presaged a process extending well into 1908.

If the June zemstvo congress was not an unmitigated disaster, it had raised serious objections to the projects. To be sure, all but four participants endorsed the ministry's projected lowering of the land census, but two-thirds of the delegates rejected the proposed tax franchise.[16] Moreover, the congress also voted down the MVD's electoral system and specifically repudiated use of the township assembly as a third curia.[17] On the last day of the congress, apparently after many of the most hostile rightist critics had departed, it did approve, by a vote of 43 to 27, the advisability of creating this small zemstvo unit, but it advocated delaying the debate of this controversial measure until a second congress scheduled for later in the summer.[18] In sum, the congress had taken a number of decisions that constrained the flexibility that the government had built into its statutes. Opposing the tax franchise and elections from the township, urging that a higher percentage of assembly seats be reserved for landowners, establishing a zemstvo electoral system with five voting curiae: the congress exhibited much more of a conservative tilt toward nobiliary landed property than did the already biased ministerial projects. Combined with a scandalous rightist resolution demanding the restoration of order before the promulgation of reform, the results of the congress did not bode well for the government.[19]

That conclusion, at least, seemed to be the judgment of press commentary following the June proceedings. On the far right, *Moskovskie vedomosti*, each day printing under its masthead the headline "Now It Is Necessary Above All To End Sedition," rejoiced that the congress had exhibited "a fully correct understanding" of current events by demanding the suppression of revolution, as if no talk of reform had occurred at all.[20]

---

[15] Ibid., pp. 53–55, and *Novoe vremia*, 12 June 1907, p. 3, and 13 June 1907, p. 2.

[16] *Stenograficheskie otchety*, pp. 90–115, and *Novoe vremia*, 14 June 1907, p. 3.

[17] *Novoe vremia*, 15 June 1907, p. 3, and *Rossiia*, 14 June 1907, p. 4, and 15 June 1907, p. 3. The congress supported five curiae, a system that reduced the influence of rural smallholders and urban property. These curiae would contain, respectively: (1) full census rural landowners, including agricultural processing factories; (2) rural landowners below the full census; (3) communal peasants and peasant cooperatives with land purchased through the Peasant Land Bank; (4) full census urban and commercial-industrial property owners; (5) urban and commercial-industrial property owners below the full census.

[18] *Rossiia*, 16 June 1907, p. 3, and *Novoe vremia*, 16 June 1907, p. 3.

[19] *Stenograficheskie otchety*, pp. 57–64.

[20] "Vremia-li dlia korennykh reform?" *Moskovskie vedomosti*, 15 June, 1907, p. 1.

More accurate in its appraisal, the Kadet Party organ *Rech'* remarked that "noble landowners had not exhibited the slightest inclination toward liberal reforms" and wondered whether the government would again "find itself at odds with a popular assembly" if the third Duma was to be filled with deputies resembling those who had attended the congress.[21] Usually more moderate than its St. Petersburg counterpart, *Russkie vedomosti* deemed criticism of the ministerial projects, which already tended "to defend certain class interests," to be both "biased and unjust." Shocked by this "exhibition of truly noble views," the paper nevertheless was less disposed than *Rech'* to think that the third Duma could be quite so unnerving; not all delegates, it emphasized, had been "adherents of old, archaic structures."[22] As was to be expected, *Novoe vremia* leaped to defend the congress from such liberal criticism, but even this conservative daily expressed concern that rightists might lack the impartiality necessary to stand "above estate and revolutionary tendencies." Were some perhaps "too frightened by . . . revolution" and concerned with "estate interests more than they should be?" the paper queried. How many provincial nobles were prone "to forget that life goes forward?"[23]

In its editorials of 13 and 14 June, *Rossiia* expressed more official displeasure with the congress's right. This faction was exploiting the word "democratization" to establish an illusory connection between "political groups different in spirit, general attitude, composition, and tactics." Plainly, the paper's unofficial senior editor, Stolypin, resented the accusation. The tendency of the "left" to equate zemstvo reform and the elimination of local nobiliary influence, *Rossiia* noted, was not at all evident in the government's attempts "to broaden the circle of individuals who could be attracted to the management of local economy." Why, then, did unidentified critics act as if the premier intended to eliminate "the most cultured part of the population" from participation in these affairs?[24] Of course, Stolypin intended nothing of the kind, but he did desire provincial noble landowners to assume in a reformed zemstvo the leading role that, as they maintained, belonged to them. "It is time," *Rossiia* wrote the next day, "to recall that long, complicated, difficult work lies ahead . . . [in order to achieve] the thorough renewal [*obnovlenie*] of Russia as a united and undivided state." Albeit in veiled terms, the paper was chastising the large number of congress delegates who refused to recognize the national political responsibilities now before them: "Narrow party views [*partiinost'*] should give way to a broad state viewpoint. He who does not accept this . . . will remain powerless and isolated. The demand is to live

---

21 "Po povodu zemskogo s"ezda," *Rech'*, 15 June 1907, p. 2.
22 *Russkie vedomosti*, 15 June 1907, p. 1.
23 "Rabota vserossiiskogo s"ezda zemskikh deiatelei," *Novoe vremia*, 15 June 1907, p. 2.
24 *Rossiia*, 13 June 1907, p. 1.

and to develop energetically within the state organism [*gosudarstvennyi organizm*]."[25]

That the congress had not demonstrated this capacity firmly enough, however, probably explained why, shortly after it closed, Stolypin met with its chairman, M. V. Rodzianko, in an effort to restrain rightist protest and devise some compromise that might soothe the anxieties of congress moderates. Rumors circulated in the capital that the MVD was reexamining the local reforms in this light.[26]

Conditions worsened during the summer and early fall. In August a second zemstvo congress considered MVD plans for township self-administration in more detail. Boycotted by the moderate and Kadet minority of the first congress, the second was dominated by rightist delegates and rejected the township project out of hand. It recommended instead that all decisions concerning these institutions be left to the discretion of county zemstvo assemblies, an idea initially advocated by some MVD opponents in 1906.[27] By early autumn a substantial body of information, all of it to some degree critical, was growing with respect to the reforms. Either through delegates attending the congresses or communication among provincial boards, much of it was reaching provincial and even county assemblies, which were scheduled to review the projects at the end of the year.[28] Finally, between July and October at least eight provincial

[25] *Rossiia*, 14 June 1907, p. 1.

[26] " 'Zemtsy' i pravitel'stvo," *Rus'*, 26 August 1907, p. 3; also Manning, *Crisis of the Old Order*, pp. 333–34. The government in fact did adjust its zemstvo electoral reform proposals somewhat, in particular abandoning the tax franchise and raising the number of guaranteed first curia seats to one-third of the assembly. "O poriadke izbranii uezdnykh i gubernskikh zemskikh glasnykh (n.d.)" and "Ob izbranii uezdnykh i gubernskikh zemskikh glasnykh (n.d.)," TsGIA, f. 1288, op. 1, 1908, d. 18, ll. 43–66.

[27] *Kratkie zhurnaly obshchezemskogo s"ezda v Moskve s 25–28 avg. 1907 g.* (Poltava, 1907). Also "Obshchezemskii s"ezd," *Novoe vremia*, 26–30 August 1907, passim, and "Zachem opiat' sobiraetsia obshchezemskii s"ezd," *Russkie vedomosti*, 23 August 1907, p. 2.

[28] For example, *Zhurnaly zasedanii Bessarabskogo gubernskogo zemskogo sobraniia XXXIX ocherednoi sessii v 1907 g.* (Kishinev, 1908), pp. 286–92; "Doklad no. 86-i: Kommissiia po reforme zemskikh uchrezhdenii," *Zhurnaly chrezvychainnogo Orlovskogo gubernskogo zemskogo sobraniia zasedaniia 1-ogo iiulia 1908 g.* (Orel, 1908), pp. 1–28; *Zhurnal . . . ocherednogo Penzenskogo gubernskogo zemskogo sobraniia 9–22 dek. 1907 g.* (Penza, 1908), pp. 707–9; *Zhurnaly zasedanii Chernigovskogo gubernskogo zemskogo sobraniia 43 ocherednoi sessii 1907 goda (26 noiabria–11 dekabria 1907)* (Chernigov, 1908), pp. 1–8; *Khersonskoe Gubernskoe Zemskoe Sobranie: Sessiia Piat'desiat Pervaia 12–20 dek. 1907 g.* (Kherson, 1908), pp. 102–8; *Poltavskoe gubernskoe zemskoe sobranie XLIII ocherednogo sozyva. Doklady . . . 1907* (Poltava, 1907), pp. 314–17; *Zhurnaly Sankt-Peterburgskogo gubernskogo zemskogo sobraniia sorok vtoroi ocherednoi sessii 12–19 dekabria 1907 i 10–18 ianvaria 1908 g.* (St. Petersburg, 1908), pp. 113–17; *Doklady Vladimirskoi gubernskoi zemskoi upravy ocherednomu gubernskomu zemskomu sobraniiu 1907* (Vladimir, 1907), pp. 157–61; *Postanovleniia 43 ocherednoi sessii 15–23 dek. 1907*

noble assemblies either planned to consider or passed resolutions condemning the local reform program.[29]

Once again the hand of the United Nobility's Permanent Council was seen stoking opposition sentiment. Since May it had been circulating among provincial marshals and organization members two detailed critiques of the local reform plan—the work of committees delegated by the Third Congress of March 1907.[30] One considered the reforms of village and township administration, as well as the land captain; the other studied changes of county government and the planned displacement of the county marshal of the nobility.[31] What was most immediately striking about these documents was their authors. They were former MVD officials and noble landowners whose careers dated back to the counterreforms.[32] The well-travelled A. S. Stishinskii, who had helped lead the State Council protest of early 1907, had authored the final draft of the land captain legislation in 1889. B. V. Shturmer worked in a variety of ministerial posts from 1872 to 1892. A. P. Strukov, a wealthy landed magnate and Ekaterinoslav provincial marshal during the years 1886–1902, served in the MVD under Pleve, as had Stishinskii and Shturmer. The noble landowners Kasatkin-Rostovskii of Kursk, Brazol of Poltava, and S. S. Bekhteev of Orel all served in local zemstvo or noble institutions during the 1880s as well.[33] Of particular interest in this regard was Bekhteev, who as a county marshal had joined A. D. Pazukhin in the Kakhanov Commission to help refute that earlier version of the local reform program.

The presence of statist officials and noble landowners on the same commission produced a critique of the local reforms that combined two differing strands of conservative opinion. In their first report, these conservatives from the Alexandrine era emphasized the danger that eliminating peasant estate administration posed to public order and to the landown-

g. i 3–13 ianvaria 1908 g. Kazanskogo Gubernskogo Zemskogo Sobrania (Kazan, 1908), pp. 297–320.

[29] These were the provincial noble assemblies of: Moscow, Orel, Samara, Ekaterinoslav—Postoiannyi sovet Ob"edinennykh Dvorianskikh Obshchestv: 6-i material po voprosu o mestnoi reforme (St. Petersburg, 1908), pp. 3–5; Tula—TsGAOR, f. 483, op. 1, d. 10/38, l. 176; Kazan and Tambov—ibid., d. 13/57, l. 119; and Kharkov—TsGIA, f. 1283, op. 1 (1906), d. 34, ll. 98–99.

[30] "Protokol, 26 March 1907," TsGAOR, f. 434, op. 1, d. 76, ll. 119–22 and d. 12/55, ll. 47–48.

[31] Postoiannyi sovet ob"edinnenykh dvorianskikh obshchestv, 1-i material po voprosu o mestnoi reforme—Reforma posel'kovogo upravleniia (St. Petersburg, 1908) and idem 2-i material po voprosu o mestnoi reforme: Reforma uezdnogo upravleniia (St. Petersburg, 1908). Both documents are dated from pp. 21 and 7 of the two texts, respectively.

[32] TsGAOR, f. 434, op. 1, d. 77/307, l. 4.

[33] TsGIA, f. 1283, op. 1, d. 26, ll. 4–16 (Strukov); ibid., op. 1 (1901), d. 32, ll. 99–109 (Kasatkin-Rostovskii); and ibid., d. 43, ll. 22–36 (Brazol).

ing nobility whose prosperity depended on it. Converting the peasant village into an all-estate organ of public self-administration, the report charged, would serve no other purpose than to threaten "more prosperous individuals, i.e. noble landowners . . . and owners of [rural] factories," with ruinous overtaxation by "a mass of peasants and representatives of smallholdings."[34] Still more dire consequences loomed for "the cultured element" if the ministry's township reform became law. It was "impossible to assume the possibility of amicable, mutual work" in assemblies where, given "the increasingly strident land question, the peasantry will undoubtedly be hostile to large and middling landowning." Seeing few distinctions in "a united opposition of [communal] peasant delegates and smallholders," the report thus repeated the charge made consistently since the 1880s that abolishing the peasant township would exacerbate social conflict. At the very least, proprietorial "kulaks" and "*miroedy*"—those who live off the commune—would exploit scarce township revenues to their own advantage. Much worse would be the consequences of third- element radicalism, sure to appear in the township assembly given "the false franchise" of the government statute. Not surprisingly, the commission also demanded that the land captain retain special "supervision" over communal peasants—"given their existing standard of living."[35]

In its second report, a slashing attack on the county vice-governor, the commission raised what was becoming the symbolic center of the local reform debate: the MVD's plan to replace the county marshal of the nobility. Having emphasized primarily statist concerns in its critique of peasant administrative reform, the authors here evoked the most ingrained strains of the nobiliary service tradition in portraying the dangers confronting the autocratic political order should the marshals be eliminated from county government. Like A. D. Pazukhin some two decades earlier, they emphasized the capacity of elected marshals to mediate between the autocratic state and the local populace.[36] Yet under conditions of political and social conflict that Pazukhin would have found unimaginable a quarter century previously, this argument held loyalty to be the most unique of the attributes that a tradition of state and local service had inculcated in representatives of the hereditary nobility. Was the removal of the marshal, the report queried, wise at a time "when all the attention, power, and labor of the government and the cultured part of

---

[34] Postoiannyi sovet ob"edinnenykh dvorianskikh obshchestv, *1-i material*, pp. 3–7. The members of the committee authoring this commentary were Strukov, Stishinskii, B. V. Shturmer, Ia. A. Ushakov, and P.N. Semenov.

[35] Ibid., pp. 15–19.

[36] Postoiannyi sovet ob"edinnenykh dvorianskikh obshchestv, *2-i material*. The members of this committee were Bekhteev, Stishinskii, Olsuf'ev, and Brazol.

society are devoted to accommodating a new state structure . . . to the old habits and views of a people [*narod*] far from prepared for it?" Was it justifiable "when the same attention and same labor ought to be devoted to the unceasing struggle with antistate forces and the support of wavering state principles?"[37]

The answers to these rhetorical questions came, as had those of Pazukhin, wrapped in romantic imagery; what was singularly remarkable about the report's argument, however, was the frame of historical reference that it utilized. Unlike Pazukhin's preoccupation with the Time of Troubles, and the unity of tsar and land that they evoked, this note referred to the notoriously arbitrary reign of Ivan the Terrible, when Muscovy was divided between the royal court holdings of the *oprichnina* and "the land [*zemshchina*]." As if offering the present monarch a distinct choice, the report emphasized that local administration had then rested "in the hands of the two estates of the land—the nobility [*dvorianstvo*] and the peasantry [*krest'ianstvo*]—who under the name *zemshchina* together constituted the power of the Russian land [and] whose elected representatives divided authority [*delili vlast'*] with tsarist protégés [*stavlenniki*]."[38] The distinction between a harmonious rural community and the repugnant absolutism of Ivan, the report implied, was relevant to contemporary events, as the *zemshchina*, having survived centuries of "the bureaucratic knout," in a sense still existed as a foundation of autocratic rule. Through the leadership of provincial nobles, the rural community could stand solidly against "principles threatening the state idea" and prevent them from penetrating "Russian life and popular consciousness." By threatening to displace the marshal, Stolypin was not only renewing bureaucratic oppression but also leading the government, and the autocrat, toward a disaster more terrible than that which Ivan had inflicted on Muscovy:

> Forgetting historical continuity, forgetting that the strength of central authority rests on alliance [*sliianie*] with the public element, continuing to seek examples and instructions not in the history of its native country but in the ready forms of the West, the government is now attempting to inflict the final blow on the *zemshchina*, the foundation of local administration.[39]

To level this charge was not only to deny the validity of the MVD's proposed vice-governor, but to demean the very legitimacy of Stolypin's efforts to enhance the political authority of the government. Authority had to remain strong, but it could do so only if based on the autocrat and

[37] Ibid., pp. 4–5.
[38] Ibid., p. 7.
[39] Ibid., p. 8.

the nobility that retained its loyalty to him. Removing the marshals was equivalent to entrusting unruly rural areas and the political authority of autocracy resting on them to officials like Stolypin, bent on paying "homage to a passing political fantasy" about eliminating estate distinctions and oblivious to the dangers confronting Russia:

> How can one not see that [by] eliminating the single . . . support of Russian state-consciousness in the village—. . . the only independent conservator of legality, order, and true freedom—the government is itself undermining the foundation of a strong edifice, and when this happens no artificial reforms, no matter how rationally or finely crafted they might be, will save the country from the principles [threatening] to destroy it.[40]

The United Nobility's theses on the local reforms thus challenged the Stolypin ministry on two fronts. They questioned whether his domestic reforms would foster economic prosperity and public order or would in fact risk dangerous civil instability. They also contested the legitimacy of government political authority by charging that ministerial policy was undermining the traditional estate foundations of autocratic rule. Circulating through the provincial conduits of the United Nobility, these arguments undoubtedly influenced the rising chorus of right-wing rhetoric audible throughout the summer and fall. In particular they permeated a long, detailed refutation of the local reforms, which the prestigious provincial assembly of the Moscow nobility issued on 8 October.[41]

The Moscow nobility traditionally was influential, as some of the country's wealthiest landowners, who possessed access to the imperial court, maintained their residence in Russia's second capital. Endorsing a report written by A. D. Samarin and other conservatives active in the United Nobility, its pronouncements in the case of the local reform program were unequivocal.[42] In the words of the commission report, the local re-

---

[40] Ibid., p. 13. The report acknowledged a primary tenet of the government program: namely, that the process of land loss was reducing the numbers of local noble landowners and making the election of marshals in some areas difficult. The committee answered that marshals could be reimbursed by the government for their expenses, thus maintaining the honorific principle of duty without salary. Nobles from anywhere in the province could fill the post in counties lacking suitable candidates. Ibid., pp. 15–18.

[41] "Doklady komissii izbrannoi Moskovskim Dvorianskim Deputatskim Sobraniem po rassmotreniiu zakonoproektov o reforme mestnogo upravleniia," *Trudy chetvertogo s"ezda upolnomochennykh dvorianskikh obshchestv 32 gubernii s 9 po 16 marta 1908 g.* (St. Petersburg, 1909), pp. 381–481. The Moscow provincial marshal of the nobility, P. A. Bazilevskii, requested copies of the United Nobility's commentary on 26 July 1907. TsGAOR, f. 434, op. 1, d. 13/57, l. 17. The Moscow report subsequently became a primary source for provincial opposition to the projects. See copies in TsGIA, f. 899 (A. A. Bobrinskii), op. 1, d. 94, ll. 8–62; f. 1288 (GUMKh), op. 1 (1908), d. 26; f. 1284 (Departament obshchikh del—DOD) op. 185, d. 72, ll. 18–61.

[42] *Russkie vedomosti,* 9 October 1907, pp. 3–4. See the history of this report in "Doklad

form program represented "a fundamental rupture of . . . local administration," which the state reforms of 1905–06—a "political structure that
was far from fully delineated"—in no way necessitated.[43] The report especially attempted to debunk the link between 1905 and the local reforms, which indeed was a fundamental component of the government's
argument. It charged that the Stolypin ministry, which "was at one stroke
reconstructing totally anew" an institutional structure that had existed
for "many decades," was inadvertently aiding rather than diverting the
forces of revolution. Drawing on examples from English and French history, the report pointed to the former as a country whose local institutions evolved over time and thus slowly adapted "to changing political,
social, and economic conditions." It was Russia's misfortune that her
government was "more inclined to follow the example of France . . . during the revolutionary period."[44] Challenging Stolypin's commitment to
accommodating state institutions to the post-October political order, the
Moscow nobility maintained that "existing institutions" could be retained "under the new state structure" without any "inconveniences . . .
either for the government or the population."[45]

The day after the resolutions of the Moscow assembly were announced, *Russkie vedomosti* reacted by remarking that if rural life was as
"dangerous" as critics maintained, the "natural inclination" ought to be
to change it. Yet, the "the leading estate" seemed to be saying that "the
present is bad and thus we must preserve it." To heed this opinion, the
paper concluded, was to assure that those "conditions creating the nightmare" of noble opponents would persist for a long period of time.[46] Such,
it would seem, was also Stolypin's conclusion. One week after the Moscow resolution, in a move that coincided with provincial elections to the
Third Duma, he acted to preempt the mounting protest against the reforms. The premier announced in circulars to provincial governors that
the government was temporarily withholding the local reforms from the
third Duma, and was submitting them instead to the MVD's Council on
Local Economy, whose permanent bureaucratic membership would be

---

chrezvychainomu Moskovskomu Dvorianskomu Sobraniiu 8-ogo oktiabria 1907 g.,"
TsGIA, f. 899, op. 1, d. 94, ll. 1–7. It was initially conceived by P. A. Bazilevskii in April
1907, after the third congress of the United Nobility. The Moscow nobility, thinking that
the reforms would not receive Duma approval in the immediate future, commissioned the
report on 7 April. Members of the committee included: Bazilevskii; A. D. Samarin, the
report's primary author and a conservative activist since 1900; his brother F. D. Samarin;
Count Pavel Sheremetev, a wealthy and influential court confidant; D. A. Olsuf'ev; and
Poltava Provincial marshal Prince N. G. Shcherbatov. Ibid., l. 4.

[43] "Doklady komissii izbrannoi Moskovskim . . . Sobraniem," p. 396.

[44] Ibid., pp. 382–83.

[45] Ibid., p. 394.

[46] *Russkie vedomosti*, 10 October 1907, p. 2.

supplemented by elected representatives from provincial zemstvos and municipal assemblies. Acknowledging that the statutes had been developed "exclusively by central institutions" and would thus perhaps be "in insufficient accord with contemporary social and economic conditions," the government was in effect yielding to demands for provincial examination of the local reforms. Yet the ministry had decided to undertake this process in St. Petersburg, hoping to save time and avoid the "often conflicting results" of local debates—a decision, *Moskovskie vedomosti* noted when it broke the news, that overturned the decision of the June 1907 zemstvo congress.[47] Indeed, because most provincial assemblies were preparing to debate the reforms at their upcoming regular meetings in December and January, this decision to convene the council appeared to be an attempt to divert the local reform debate from the provinces to the center, where it could be more easily contained and defused.

Plainly, agitation against his reforms from the provincial right had forced Stolypin to a decision that six months previously he had refused to make. Moreover, summoning the council at least implicitly impugned the legislative authority of the Duma at the very time when the government was witnessing the election of the conservative assembly it had sought in launching the June 1907 coup d'état.[48] Stolypin was taking a calculated risk, that he could define a compromise satisfying provincial opinion yet preserve the core of the local reforms intact. He allowed all thirty-four provincial zemstvo assemblies and twelve city Dumas to elect delegates to the proceedings.[49] Although the MVD altered its projects in some instances, most notably by abandoning the zemstvo tax franchise, the program that the premier presented to the Council on Local Economy when it assembled in March 1908 largely resembled that of early 1907. Addressing the first session of the council, Stolypin told the provincial men that they constituted "a pre-Duma" whose activities "could invigorate and add vital force to the ministry's proposals" before their consideration by the State Duma. He believed that this forum, a meeting place for bureaucrats and local "individuals who represent the most varied interests," would allow "an explanation of misunderstandings."[50] He was to be sorely mistaken.

[47] *Moskovskie vedomosti*, 20 October 1907, p. 4, and TsGIA, f. 1288, op. 2 (1907), d. 38, l. 65 (Tambov governor to Tambov zemstvo executive board, 19 October 1907), and *Doklady Khersonskoi Gubernskoi Zemskoi Upravy* (Kherson, 1907), pp. 175–76.

[48] *Russkie vedomosti*, 21 October 1907, p. 2; 24 October 1907, p. 1; and "Deklaratsiia G. Stolypina," *Rus'*, 17 November 1907, p. 2.

[49] "Spisok lichnogo sostava SDMKh vesennei sessii 1908 g.," TsGIA, f. 1288, op. 1 (1908), d. 11, ll. 1–3.

[50] *Russkie vedomosti*, 13 March 1908, pp. 2–3.

THE COUNCIL ON LOCAL ECONOMY: GOVERNING THE NATION OR
PRESERVING THE LAND?

Responding to the third Duma's failure in November 1907 to include the
term "unrestricted autocratic authority" in its formal address to the
throne, the provincial assembly of the Moscow nobility created a public
scandal when it greeted the tsar in early February 1908:

> Great Sovereign! In days of tragic events, which have more than once befallen
> the Russian land, the ancient service estate, together with all the Russian peo-
> ple, has expressed throughout the ages, in both word and deed, their faith in
> the fundamental strength of autocratic tsarist authority in all its totality and
> indivisibility. That faith has not yet been shaken in the Moscow nobility. . . .
> Now as of old there is no political authority in Rus' equal to tsarist authority.
> . . . Ancient tsarist authority is higher in the consciousness of the people than
> transient, artificial laws. The tsarist word gives life to the dead letter of the
> law.[51]

Ignoring the State Council, the State Duma, and law itself, the Moscow
nobility had fired a salvo against the reformed state order and the ministry that was attempting to govern within it. A. A. Stolypin, the premier's
brother and a regular contributor to *Novoe vremia*, complained that the
assembly was confusing "loyalty to the Supreme Authority" and opposition to "reformist activity in the state, which undeniably was sanctioned
by the same" autocrat.[52] The journalist was correct in pointing out the
contradiction; increasing pressure was being brought to bear on both the
minister who sponsored and the sovereign who sanctioned reform.

The Moscow address prefigured the difficulties awaiting the local reforms in March. Four days before the Council on Local Economy convened, the fourth congress of the United Nobility met in St. Petersburg.
Adopting the Samarin report of the Moscow provincial nobility as its official position, the congress rejected the all-estate village, the self-administering township assembly, the county vice-governor, and the divestiture
of the land captain's juridical authority over the peasant estate. Indeed, it
discounted Stolypin's conciliatory gesture of summoning the Council on
Local Economy and charged that this forum, termed "a foreign form of
centralization and an evasion of the traditions . . . of our national history," could not replace local consultation.[53] Finally, the organization's
Permanent Council ordered a summation of the congress's conclusions,

---

[51] *Rossiia*, 2 February 1908, p. 4; *Russkie vedomosti*, 2 February 1908, p. 1; *Rus'*, 2
February 1908, p. 2. See also Diakin, *Samoderzhavie*, pp. 98–100.

[52] *Novoe vremia*, 3 Feb. 1908, p. 3.

[53] *Svod postanovlenii I-X s"ezdov upolnomochennykh ob"edinennykh dvorianskikh obshchestv 1906–1914 gg.* (Petrograd, 1915), pp. 48–52.

to which Stolypin's former colleague and opponent V. I. Gurko contributed, and presented it to Nicholas in early April.[54] At this audience A. A. Bobrinskii spoke of the "immediate necessity, for the good of the state, to preserve the importance of the county marshals." Hearing as well a refutation of the zemstvo electoral reform, the tsar promised "to pay the most serious attention to the questions raised by the deputation."[55]

The Council on Local Economy convened on 13 March to consider village, township, and zemstvo electoral reform. Although far from a rubber stamp, its membership seemed to promise confirmation of the ministerial projects. Most of the 35 elected representatives of provincial zemstvo assemblies were prestigious and influential members of their local societies. Among their number were counted 1 State Council member, 3 Duma deputies, 4 provincial and 5 county marshals of the nobility, and 13 provincial and 2 county zemstvo board chairmen.[56] To be sure, 9 of the 34 zemstvo provinces were represented by delegates who had also attended the United Nobility's congress (Bessarabia, Ekaterinoslav, Kazan, Kaluga, Kursk [2 delegates], Pskov, Samara, Saratov, and Tula).[57] Seven other rightist delegates to the council did not belong to the organization (Vologda, Viatka, Novgorod, Penza, Riazan, Tver, and Iaroslavl). The zemstvo complement thus was divided equally between these 17 rightists and 18 other, more moderate representatives: 1 Kadet (Ufa); 2 Progressives (Orel and Chernigov); 12 Octobrists (Vladimir, Voronezh, Moscow, Olonets, Poltava, Pskov [second delegate], St. Petersburg, Simbirsk, Tauride, Tambov, Kharkov, and Kherson), and 3 moderate rights (Kostroma, Nizhnii Novgorod, and Smolensk).[58] Together with delegates from twelve municipal assemblies, who generally took moderate positions in these debates, and the contingent of 23 MVD, Ministry of Finance, and GUZiZ officials led by Stolypin and Kryzhanovskii, the premier possessed the bloc of votes necessary for obtaining a formal

[54] "Protokol, 24 March 1908," TsGAOR, f. 434, op. 1, d. 78/307, l. 16, and "Kratkii obzor trudov chetvertogo s"ezda upolnomochennykh dvorianskikh obshchestv 32-x gubernii," TsGIA, f. 899, op. 1, d. 84, ll. 1–4. The two authors of this document were A. A. Bobrinskii and V. I. Gurko.

[55] TsGAOR, f. 434, op. 1, d. 78/307, l. 24.

[56] TsGIA, f. 1288, op. 1 (1908), d. 11, ll. 1–3, and "formuliarnye spiski" in ibid., f. 1283, op. 1; f. 1162, op. 6, 7; and f. 1282, op. 2. Four delegates were provincial officials serving in the zemstvo departments of provincial administration; three others were attached to GUZiZ or the MVD, and one was a land captain.

[57] "Spisok upolnomochennykh 32-x ob"edinennykh Dvorianskikh Obshchestv," TsGAOR, f. 434, op. 1, d. 15/61, ll. 104 ff.

[58] TsGIA, f. 1288, op. 1 (1908), d. 11, ll. 1–3. Political orientation from "Spisok"; Veselovskii, Istoriia zemstva, 4:36, 58; TsGAOR, f. 115, op. 1, d. 45, ll. 20–24; and in several cases on the bases of positions taken in the debates. The position of the Perm delegate P. V. Ivanov, an "engineer-mechanic," is unknown.

imprimatur for his reforms. Yet what was really at issue in the upcoming session was defusing the objections of provincial activists and, if moderates among them could be persuaded, a compromise with a majority of the zemstvo representatives. In the course of droning legislative debate, it would become eminently clear that hereditary noble landowners were unwilling to assume the role in rural civil society that Stolypin had presumed they would play in constructing a national state.[59]

Throughout the assembly's examination of the village and township proposals, majorities of the zemstvo representatives utilized a harsh economic arithmetic against the MVD's desire to grant the rural populace limited fiscal and administrative powers. Most approved the principle of all-estate village self-administration. In actual fact, however, both rightists and some more moderate provincial Octobrists voted to compromise principles whenever they thought their own minority status to be threatened by village assemblies with peasant and smallholder majorities.[60] On the question of the village's fiscal powers, a rightist minority bloc of 14 to 15 zemstvo representatives wanted to strip all budget-making authority from the village assembly.[61] Failing that, they agreed with Samara provincial marshal A. N. Naumov that no private landowner should be forced into the village's taxing jurisdiction. What a man had built "on his own risk and responsibility," Naumov said, could not be subject to a village assembly "where the given individual has extremely limited representation."[62] While Octobrists found this formulation too egotistical, they did agree with the essential concern. How, I. I. Sterligov asked, could the statute avoid turning the new village institution into "a parasite that lives at the expense of the nearest factory or rich landowner?"[63] From the Bessarabia rightist M. V. Purishkevich to the Kharkov left Octobrist A. D.

---

[59] The materials of the council are in TsGIA, f. 1288, op. 1. A methodological note on the documents. The council divided itself into working commissions to study each statute and draft a formal report. Generally, only several officials would attend these sessions, so that commission majorities were comprised from elected delegates. Commission proceedings, however, were preserved only in the form of summaries. References to the commissions in the following discussion are made only if the document allowed a conclusion about voting blocs on particular issues. Each commission report was submitted to the council's general assembly for debate and vote. Unless the issue was critical, officials again did not attend in large numbers. The records of the assembly's proceedings, kept haphazardly as journals and stenogrammes, generally do not identify individual voters but only majorities and minorities. When reference is made to the assembly, the conclusions are based upon a best estimate of alliances as understood from the commissions' and assembly's debates.

[60] "Zhurnaly kommissii po posel'kovom upravlenii," TsGIA, f. 1288, op. 1, d. 13 and "Obshchee prisutstvie: Stenogrammy o posel'kovom upravlenii," d. 14.

[61] Ibid., d. 13, l. 128, and d. 14, ll. 68–70.

[62] Ibid., d. 14, l. 53.

[63] Ibid., d. 14, l. 52.

Golitsyn, the answer was the same: transfer effective regulation of village tax rates to the county zemstvo.[64]

Moreover, the same fear of isolation within the village framework led the assembly to place a limit on the total taxes any one wealthy property owner might pay the village. "I am thinking about a landowner's estate with a huge house, a park, and a large fruit orchard," said the Pskov Octobrist N. S. Brianshaninov.[65] Despite the protests of an Octobrist minority, a majority for these same reasons supported Kaluga rightist S. A. Popov's proposal that large taxpayers need not stand for election in order to participate in village assembly deliberations.[66] Finally, the council's village commission recommended that the elected village elder should bear some duties as a subordinate of the police. Its chairman, the Octobrist Sterligov, recalled "those days [of 1905–06] that we and everyone remember," and the commission report insisted that "the absence of such authority, threatening anarchy in the village, is felt especially in agrarian settlements, amidst the typical 'gray' of our village." This was "a fundamental departure from the project's basic idea" of making the elder "a leader of village public welfare and well-being," retorted MVD representative I. M. Strakhovskii. Only urban representatives supported the government's view when the assembly voted to reimpose police obligations on an institution of rural self-administration.[67]

Trepidation for the security and well-being of individual landowners assumed a collective character when the assembly considered the proposed township and its limited role in managing zemstvo affairs.[68] Although its proposals in this regard were themselves hedged, the government had presented council delegates with a facsimile of the small zemstvo unit that provincial activists had demanded throughout the late nineteenth century. Council representatives thus had to declare whether the country's majority population ought to assume a greater role in

[64] Ibid., d. 14, ll. 52–55.

[65] Ibid., d. 14, l. 65. In general the assembly's debates of taxation occupied more time than any other issue of the village project, consuming two of the four sessions devoted to the subject. Ibid., d. 14, ll. 52–71.

[66] Ibid., d. 14, ll. 75–76.

[67] Ibid., d. 14, ll. 42–44, and d. 13, l. 101. The government presented statistics to illustrate its contention that administrative obligations diverted funds that the villages would be better off spending on public needs. In 1905 village communities in all fifty European provinces budgeted 44.8 million rubles of expenditures. Of these monies, 23% supported the costs of administration. The three largest categories of peasant spending on public welfare were primary education (9.5%), fire prevention (5%), and agriculture (25%). "Raspredelenie volostnykh i sel'skikh sborov v 1905 godu, TsGIA, f. 1288, op. 1 (1908), d. 18, ll. 67–68.

[68] "Doklady i zhurnaly kommissii po volostnomu upravleniiu," TsGIA, f. 1288, op. 1 (1908), d. 18; "Obshchee prisutstvie: Stenogrammy o volostnoi reforme," ibid., d. 25; and "Postanovleniia," ibid., d. 17.

zemstvo self-administration. Here the responses of rightists and moderates differed sharply.

Filing a special opinion, representatives of the far-right Kursk and Tula provincial assemblies were alone in repudiating not only a small zemstvo, but the very idea of an all-estate township. Maintaining that the "estate-corporative structure of county life" remained viable, these representatives summarized positions taken earlier by their assemblies.[69] Noble landowners, the Kursk zemstvo had argued, maintained their hereditary ties to the land and to a peasant estate unprepared for independent civil life. Fulfilling their service obligations unselfishly in the zemstvo since 1890, they "had concerned themselves solely with the interests of the population's lower classes, had pursued almost no other goal but the welfare of the peasants." The anarchy of 1905–06, which had been particularly intense in both Kursk and Tula, had not derived from internal causes, and thus had nothing to do with the actions of the local nobility, but rather was agitated by revolutionary elements: zemstvo liberals, radical "antistate groups and parties" and the third element's "petty service intelligentsia." Now, when order was returning to the country, the MVD thought to "reinvigorate public independence" with the proposed township. This, the Kursk assembly charged, was the ruse of a radical bureaucracy that intended to replace "the two estates of nobles and peasants [that] in places still exist, . . . to create . . . something new, which exists in the abstract, to depersonalize vital estate groups and give access to elements that do not belong there, [to do this] no matter how insignificant they are or how dubious their role in zemstvo activity will be."[70]

Few other zemstvo representatives defended the integrity of the traditional estate structure; indeed, only the representatives of five other provinces (four with ties to the United Nobility) wanted to delay and effectively squelch the creation of township self-administration.[71] Agreeing that the proposed institution was necessary, the remaining provincial delegates, an overwhelming majority, rejected the rightist contention that uncertain revolutionary times heightened the danger of reform. "Let us wait," Poltava county board chairman D. N. Miloradovich, an Octobrist, sarcastically stated, "for the house to become a total ruin, for it to collapse." "In the majority of cases," said Pskov senator N. S. Brianchaninov, the peasants viewed the county zemstvo as "a bureaucratic institu-

---

[69] "Osoboe mnenie M. Ia. Govorukho-Otrokha, Grafa V. F. Dorrera i Kniazia A. P. Urusova," ibid., d. 17, ll. 4–6.

[70] *Zhurnal zasedaniia ekstrennogo Kurskogo sobraniia*, pp. 10–11. Also *Zhurnaly chrezvychainogo Tul'skogo gubernskogo zemskogo sobraniia 26 maia 1907 g.* (Tula, 1907), pp. 5–8.

[71] TsGIA, f. 1288, op. 1 (1908), d. 25, ll. 13 (S. A. Popov, Kaluga), 14 (A. N. Naumov, Samara), 14 (M. V. Purishkevich, Bessarabia), and 16 (S. P. Mezhakov-Kaiutov, Vologda).

tion, often far away from the population's life and needs." Kharkov left-Octobrist A. D. Golitsyn, an "ardent supporter" of immediate reform, castigated those who referred to disorders as a rationale for opposing "any reform." Few disagreed in principle with the Moscow provincial zemstvo board chairman, Octobrist N. F. Rikhter, that the county zemstvo needed to "come closer to the local population," to create an institution whose absence "in a constant and daily way paralyzes our zemstvo activity."[72]

Yet supporting principle did not mean creating a township assembly that might compete with or challenge the county zemstvo's dominant position in rural public affairs. The MVD's draft statute already contained measures that constrained the powers of the township assembly to a large degree: a specified list of zemstvo functions; tax assessment tied to a percentage of the county assembly's rates; a cap on township taxation set by the county executive council. All these measures aimed at protecting against overtaxation, preventing the parcelization of county zemstvo operations, and preserving a strong supervisory role for county officials and zemtsy. Nevertheless, I. M. Strakhovskii insisted, the law had to establish a degree of independence for the new assembly if it was to generate popular interest and participation.[73] Precisely a recognition that the government intended to implement this general legislative principle, and an underlying suspicion that its project did not protect the county zemstvo, led a majority of the council to resolve, as had the June 1907 zemstvo congress, that the actual structure and powers of the township be left to the discretion of each county assembly.[74]

From the remarks of zemstvo representatives, it was evident that once this decision reverted to the local areas, the MVD's hopes might very well be dashed. Kherson Octobrist S. T. Varun-Sekret argued that for the populace of the township, "zemstvo business will be *terra incognita*." To establish anything more than an executive official or board under the county's "leadership" could result in "giving these organs autonomy and thus killing zemstvo business, not moving it forward."[75] S. I. Zubchaninov, the rightist provincial board chairman from Pskov who initially moved the resolution, expressed the council majority's attitude to a population that the MVD viewed as a source of future civil evolution: "I maintain that at the present level of our population's development and the degree to which it is accustomed to this business, there is absolutely no possibility of form-

---

[72] Ibid., d. 25, ll. 13–15.
[73] Ibid., d. 18, l. 119.
[74] Ibid., d. 17, l. 14.
[75] Ibid., d. 25, l. 20.

ing township zemstvos in all of mother Russia . . . this will be ruinous [*pagubno*] for the business."[76]

Only seven zemstvo representatives protested this decision. They argued that the Council was creating "purely bureaucratic [*na-chal'stvennye*] relationships between county and township zemstvos" by allowing the imposition of arbitrary local norms on the population. Such tactics would only "impede" zemstvo work in the township.[77] To the extent that the dream of a small zemstvo unit still existed in 1908, it remained alive among this minority. Chernigov Progressist provincial board chairman N. P. Savitskii, a self-proclaimed adherent of Prince Vasilchikov's writings on "the public theory" of zemstvo self-administration, objected to a decision that merely transferred tutelage from bureaucratic to zemstvo administration.[78] P. F. Korapachinskii of Ufa, the sole Kadet provincial board chairman remaining in the empire, decried "the chasm that exists between the administrators and the administered" in zemstvo affairs.[79]

Other Progressists and also Octobrists were to be found in this minority, most notably S. N. Maslov and V. V. Meller-Zakomel'skii, the provincial board chairmen of Orel and St. Petersburg provinces, respectively. The Progressist Maslov in fact directed most of his criticism not against noble rightists but against the MVD. By limiting the township's jurisdiction and powers of taxation, he said, the government was eviscerating "vital zemstvo business . . . in the name of the dead letter of the law."[80] Yet Maslov, standing to the left of the Octobrist coalition, was thus arguing a position that the government deemed precipitous, but could accept—while zemstvo colleagues further to the right found it unconscionable. Indeed, during the work of the Orel provincial commission that had studied the zemstvo reform proposals, Maslov and a slim majority had barely sustained a defense of the small zemstvo unit with their use of arguments widespread in 1902–04. The creation of the new institution, this majority had stated, was not premature but rather imperative in the wake of revolution. "Thanks to the darkness of the mass population, the most unfounded charges circulate against any public institution and official, and serve as one of the chief reasons for all disorders." Zemtvo men had

---

[76] Ibid., d. 25, l. 46.

[77] Ibid., d. 17, ll. 17–18. These were the Octobrists Meller-Zakomel'skii (St. Petersburg), Rikhter (Moscow), Petrov (Vladimir), Kolchanov (Tauride), the Progressists Maslov (Orel) and Savitskii (Chernigov), and the rightist Beketov (Kazan).

[78] *Zhurnaly zasedanii Chernigovskogo gubernskogo zemskogo sobraniia 43 ocherednoi sessii 1907 goda* (Chernigov, 1908), pp. 5–8.

[79] "Doklady i zhurnaly kommissii po volostnomu upravleniiu," TsGIA, f. 1288, op. 1 (1908), d. 18, l. 212.

[80] Ibid., d. 18, l. 132.

to recognize their isolation, take steps to facilitate the "acculturation [*vospitanie*]" of this population, and encourage greater "communication [*obshchenie*] among people in the sphere of public interests."[81] For Maslov, the township was an arena, a meeting ground where the populace would come to know its county zemstvo benefactors.

Yet even Maslov could not escape the superordinate perspective toward the majority population that informed much of the provincial opposition to independent township self-administration. Nor did he neglect the necessity of county zemstvo administrative supervision that it dictated. Indeed, Maslov, like most other provincial delegates, conceived the county zemstvo's role in the township from the same perspective of paternalistic tutelage that he condemned in the practice of state administration. There was no need to impose legal regulation upon the jurisdiction of the township assembly, he said, given "the very close bond" existing between it and the county assembly. The law need only assure that "the authority [*vlast'*] of the higher [county] entity will have the right to exercise discretion in disputes."[82] Maslov attacked legal limitations on the total amount of taxes a township assembly could assess annually on its population, and thought the threat of overtaxation better managed if the county zemstvo wrote the township budget—an idea the MVD official Strakhovskii thought "odious for organs of self-administration."[83] Perhaps with more sympathy and certainly with more ambivalence than his rightist colleagues, Maslov still regarded "his" population, less than two years removed from 1906, as a mass to be administered—by the county zemstvo.

Indeed, as compared to the ministerial officials who authored the village and township statutes, most provincial delegates exhibited little inclination to cross the divide separating the administrators from the administered. Much of this intransigence derived from perceptions of economic self-interest. A preoccupation with fiscal powers concealed an insistence on protecting the propertied minority from the dictates of a peasant and smallholding majority. Listening to the assembly's debates of the zemstvo electoral system, however, it became increasingly clear that defense of what might be misconstrued as purely class interests was inseparable from fundamental concerns for the hereditary nobility's heritage and identity as a service estate.[84] Confronting an electoral network prem-

[81] "Doklad 86-i," *Zhurnal chrezvychainnogo Orlovskogo gubernskogo zemskogo sobraniia zasedaniia 1-ogo iiulia 1908 g.*, pp. 6–9.

[82] "Doklady i zhurnaly kommissii po volostnomu upravleniiu," TsGIA, f. 1288, op. 1 (1908), d. 18, l. 212.

[83] Ibid., d. 25, ll. 2, 8, and d. 18, l. 119.

[84] "Stenograficheskii otchet so"edinennogo zasedaniia kommisii po zemskomu tsenzu,"

ised upon the common economic and social interests of wealth and property, most zemstvo representatives were unable to act as the landowning class that the MVD had assumed the provincial nobility to have been when it structured the reform program. Although provincial delegates recognized that the majority population threatened their minority economic and social status, this realization did not create a willingness to seek alliances with other propertied elements, whether existing or envisioned. Rather, it expressed itself in a defensive reaction against social change and an insistent reiteration of the hereditary nobility's preeminent cultural position in local society. Zemstvo delegates repeatedly emphasized that preserving the tradition of service to the land—their leadership in the zemstvo—was the state's primary obligation and the county's sole hope for future development.

These views were evident, first of all, when the council debated the MVD's proposal to allow zemstvo elections from the township assembly. In the council's zemstvo commission, whose majority was comprised of Octobrists and moderate rights, delegates repeatedly protested that the township populace, too numerous and unreliable, would overwhelm the ability of noble landowners to influence county zemstvo affairs. The zemstvo commission, with only the left Octobrist A. D. Golitsyn and Kadet P. F. Korapachinskii dissenting, voted against this proposal altogether.[85] It was reinserted into the statute only after the government conceded that each provincial zemstvo assembly could set the franchise that determined the extent of popular participation in these elections.[86] Without this measure, Kazan rightist S. A. Beketov argued, the county assembly would witness a flood of individuals indifferent or hostile to those like himself—landowners who "were interested in zemstvo business [and] possessed economic experience and a close bond with the local area."[87]

Ministerial officials and moderate zemtsy alike warned that restrictive measures against the township were foolhardy. They would only exclude proprietors, especially the new peasant smallholder, while leaving to an unreliable communal peasantry the same sizable representation it presently possessed in the zemstvo.[88] Yet provincial critics of the proposal were not so much concerned with culling reliable property owners from the township populace as they were determined to exclude suspect social and political elements from the electoral process. Allowing that small-

---

ibid., d. 9, ll. 1–13; "Zhurnaly kommisii po zemskoi izbiratel'noi reformy," ibid., d. 28, ll. 1–164; and "Obshchee prisutstvie o zemskoi izbiratel'noi reforme," ibid., d. 25, ll. 88–243.

[85] Ibid., d. 28, ll. 5–6 and 133–45.

[86] Ibid., d. 25, ll. 115–27.

[87] Ibid., d. 25, l. 115.

[88] Ibid., d. 25, ll. 127 (A. D. Golitsyn, left Octobrist), 117 (P. F. Korapachinskii, Ufa Kadet), 120 (N. L. Psheradskii), 27 (A. I. Lykoshin); and ibid., d. 18, l. 118 (Ia. Ia. Litvinov).

holders were a desirable element in principle, the right Duma deputies M. V. Purishkevich of Bessarabia and A. P. Urusov of Tula foresaw that wage workers and political agitators would slip into the zemstvo system. The government plan allowed access to "that fellow whose bond with the local area is minuscule, who does not possess this bond, who is alien [*chuzhoi*] to the region."[89] There was in fact considerable minority sentiment that the communal peasantry was a stable base for zemstvo elections as long as their delegates were selected in a separate curia, where voters would not "fall prey to outside influence" as had happened in the Duma elections of 1906 and 1907.[90]

Most provincial representatives, including some rightists, acknowledged that social and political change in rural society rendered zemstvo electoral reform imperative. S. I. Zubchaninov, the rightist Pskov provincial board chairman, knew that the county zemstvo could not survive unchanged, given both "the gradual decline in the number of zemtsy and the necessity of filling the gulf that as the experience of 1905–06 revealed, divides the population from the zemstvo."[91] When the council's general assembly voted on the zemstvo electoral reform, majorities—which included government officials—accepted the major premises of the MVD's plan: the elimination of estate distinctions; a halving of the landowner's franchise—which the ministry had already agreed would be based upon landholding, not tax payments; a somewhat smaller cut for non-landed property owners; separate representation for municipal dumas; and, over objections, elections from the township assembly.[92]

Yet these votes apparently required significant concessions from the government. As the final act of the council's spring 1908 session large majorities added several "corrections" to the assembly's conclusions. Thirty-eight representatives voted to restrict urban representation in the zemstvo to a maximum one-sixth of all county assembly seats and refused to allow an exception even in industrial provinces. Twenty-eight then supported placing a cap on township representation so that at most only one-third of the zemstvo might be elected from the new institution. They thus refused to allow that township delegates in agrarian counties might fill seats originally allocated to landowners, but left unoccupied because too few remained in the area. Effectively, therefore, the council voted the landowner's curia fifty percent of all assembly seats, five percent less than it presently held.[93]

[89] Ibid., d. 25, l. 117.
[90] Ibid., d. 28, ll. 154, 133–45, and 5–6.
[91] Ibid., d. 28, l. 23.
[92] Ibid., d. 25, ll. 88–107.
[93] Ibid., d. 25, ll. 235–40. *Russkie vedomosti*, 20 April 1908, p. 2, noted this decision as

These inflexible barriers made a mockery of the MVD's electoral scheme. How, government bureaucrats frequently asked, did the assembly think that large landowners could supply so many zemstvo delegates through the first curia, when their numbers in the countryside were dwindling?[94] Was it not time, asked Orel Octobrist mayor N. N. Rostovtsev, to recognize that "the cultured element" of gentry landowners was selling its land and that "the cultured element of the towns" should have a much greater say in zemstvo affairs?[95] Could the delegates not understand, queried Kharkov left-Octobrist A. D. Golitsyn, that they were isolating themselves in the landowners' electoral assembly, that "the interests of large zemstvo taxpayers fully coincide, regardless of whether they are landowners, industrialists, factory owners, or commercial traders?"[96] "Undoubtedly," Kharkov mayor A. P. Pogorel'ko agreed, the question of the hour was the "contradiction between wealth and poverty, between the haves and the have-nots." To fix such obvious privilege for one group in the electoral system would raise "irritation" and "censure" among the majority population.[97]

> One cannot in fact conceal from oneself what is happening everywhere, one must account for life's changing conditions, one cannot leave the zemstvo in its present situation or else we will arrive at the point where the zemstvo will be by itself and life, society by themselves. There will be no relationship between them and we will be faced with the danger of the collapse of the local administration.[98]

Significantly, these critics were officials and municipal mayors. Among the zemtsy, A. D. Golitsyn stood as one of a few stark exceptions to a majority that did not speak their language of wealth, property, and class.[99] Yet, contrary to Pogorel'ko's indictment, provincial delegates had attempted to account for life's changing conditions. Their response, however—an insistence that an ascriptive rural universe of land and service still possessed validity—contradicted the civil world of wealth and prop-

---

evidence that "large noble landowners" wanted to be "the undisputed lords of the situation" and preferred no delegates at all to individuals elected from the township assemblies.

[94] Ibid., d. 25, l. 26. Also d. 28, l. 164 (N. L. Psheradskii); and d. 18, l. 118 (Ia. Ia. Litvinov).

[95] Ibid., d. 25, l. 230 (N. N. Rostovtsev). Also l. 226 (N. M. Perepel'kin), l. 227 (A. K. Pogorel'ko), l. 228 (A. M. Memorskii), l. 229 (A. O. Nemirovskii), l. 229 (P. F. Korapachinskii). The first four delegates represented towns; Nemirovskii was an MVD official; and Korapachinskii was a Kadet.

[96] Ibid., d. 28, l. 27.

[97] Ibid., d. 9, l. 2.

[98] Ibid., d. 9, l. 8.

[99] The views of N. P. Savitskii, the Progressist provincial board chairman of the Chernigov zemstvo, approximated those of Golitsyn, ibid., d. 9, ll. 8–9.

erty posited by the MVD's projects. The council had allowed that the township population fill one-third of the zemstvo assembly only after it had assured zemstvo control over the franchise defining smallholder participation in the elections, a measure that gave predominance to communal peasants. Because the numbers of noble landowners were declining, delegates were willing to broaden access to the landowner's curia. Yet Octobrist N. S. Brianchaninov believed that "leadership in the zemstvo will remain with nobles, in whose hands reside . . . a love for the matter and an ability to sacrifice their interests."[100] To ensure this fact, provincial zemstvo assemblies would decide the actual size of the decreased land franchise.[101] Even when considering their own electoral curia, provincial delegates exhibited an unwillingness to ally themselves with other property owners, to transcend the enveloping parameters of their own cultural milieu. Indeed, the council's zemstvo commission, concerned that the representation of noble landowners ought not to result in the exclusion of other categories of property from the county assemblies, had engaged in a tortured process to accommodate "cultural characteristics [*bytovye priznaki*] and levels of propertied wealth [*imushchestvennaia sostoiatel'nost'*]" throughout the electoral system. Securing one curia for the existing cadre of zemstvo landowners necessitated dividing the rest of the voting population among four, five, and even six different groups to assure that all forms of property—rural and urban, wealthy and smallholding, private and communal—might be represented in a structure still shaped by "the distinctions of cultural conditions," in the words of P. P. Golitsyn of Novgorod.[102]

One issue more than any other revealed how the nobility's heritage as a service estate delegated a unique role in contemporary rural society to zemstvo landowners. The overwhelming majority of provincial representatives reacted with scorn when the idea of a zemstvo tax franchise, already abandoned by the MVD, was raised again by A. D. Golitsyn in the name of the Kharkov assembly. Golitsyn insisted that the concept be reconsidered as a more rational and reliable means of assuring the representation of wealth and property. Yet the measure reduced the importance of hereditary landholdings, which were not simply a source of income but also a symbol of the nobility's place and preeminence in the rural community—a fact that peasants had understood when during 1905–06 they had attempted in some areas to destroy them. The family estate of a noble was conceptually its own universe; the suggestion that zemstvo representation ought to be determined by an arithmetic calculation of tax assessments was greeted as if it were a revolutionary act.

"This is not reform, but a complete rupture," A. E. Kubarovskii of

[100] Ibid., d. 25, l. 115.
[101] Ibid., d. 25, ll. 92, 96, and 99.
[102] Ibid., d. 28, ll. 142–44.

Smolensk said.[103] Octobrist I. I. Sterligov looked to an "ideal" democratic franchise arising in "100 years or so," but warned against changing a system that had served well for four decades: "We ought not uproot our foundations, we ought not place our zemstvo in unstable circumstances."[104] Since 1864 the size of a man's landholdings, Tula rightist A. P. Urusov proclaimed, had produced "that complement" of public men who "were known to the zemstvo assemblies." Change was "dangerous" because the "arbitrary" tax franchise supplied little guarantee that these same landowners would remain zemstvo delegates.[105] "We live in cultural conditions," declaimed S. I. Zubchaninov, the owner of 1,000 desiatins (2,700 acres) of hereditary land in the county where he had served for seven years as marshal of the nobility. "We are distinguished not only by the amount of our property; we are primarily distinguished from each other and united with each other by those cultural conditions that from time immemorial have unified us in established estates, in established corporations." Perhaps these legal distinctions were becoming less relevant, but the land remained, anchoring rural society, guaranteeing that "the large landowner and the small always will *feel* [emphasis added] the unifying foundation that historically bound them together." With those others of the outside world—the world of money, individualism, and economic status that the local reforms addressed—no unifying bond could exist.

> They say: those who pay much should be united in one group and those who are poor, let them go below. In principle both the tax and land franchises encompass cultural groups of the population, but we part ways when we begin to define [them]. They give preference to money, to capital. They say capital is the alpha and the omega. The golden calf has enveloped us in its embrace and we ought to submit to it here, there, and everywhere, even in the zemstvo assembly.[106]

Ultimately, most provincial zemstvo representatives could only understand their present circumstances, and Russia's future with which they were joined, within the traditional framework of their heritage as an estate and the parameters of their own particularistic world. Confronted from below by a volatile rural populace, the delegates in large measure could not accept the government's premise that stable economic and social relations in civil society were the best protection of property and order. Indeed, they repudiated this argument, insisting that the historical organicity of the rural community rendered it a still viable social foundation for the zemstvo and the state. However illusory this unique world,

[103] Ibid., d. 9, l. 3.
[104] Ibid., d. 9, l. 6.
[105] Ibid.
[106] Ibid., d. 9, l. 14.

they defended it heatedly. Only here did their own cultural heritage, traditions of service, and preeminent position in the state possess importance. Without this ascriptive universe, their past history was rendered meaningless by a world of property, wealth, and modernity.

Civil society, viewed in the ministerial chancellery as the basis of all social and political order, became in the eyes of many zemstvo delegates a universe of disorder, a war of all against all. It gave rise to the peasant smallholders, merchants, and all the "outsiders [*prishlye*]" who purchased rural property purely for "mercantile" concerns.[107] It was the city, the disdained commercial-industrial class, the intelligentsia, and an industrial world that had spread revolution to the countryside. It was changing the face of rural Russia. Surrounded by this civil universe, the delegates had been asked by Stolypin to accept the unthinkable: that capital was the "alpha and the omega." Revealingly, they withdrew to their land, insisting that owning land and living on it secured for them a unique heritage, solidified a common experience, bequeathed to them a mutually shared perspective and set of values. Only among "individuals united by certain identical cultural conditions," claimed Samara provincial marshal A. N. Naumov, could he say, "Yes, I elect this person because I know him."[108]

Most critical for the plans of the government, this denial of civil society, whose accommodation Stolypin deemed essential to the political stability of the nation, possessed a powerful rationale. Council delegates knew that economic development and agrarian unrest had weakened the provincial nobility's position in the countryside. Yet when they voted to solidify their dominance of the zemstvo, these nobles claimed to act not from a desire to protect economic self-interest or social privilege, but to preserve the nobility's tradition of selfless local service. The zemstvo would no longer be an estate institution; all elements of the population would be represented in it.[109] But the landowner's curia, largely retaining its noble complexion, would have to possess a majority, moderate N. S. Brianchaninov said, "because it includes representatives of the entire county territory who will be capable of pursuing state goals and defending the interests of the entire county, unrestricted by the interests of the township or petty property."[110]

Similarly, rightist S. I. Zubchaninov depicted the landowner's curia as a focal point between the state and the rural community. Only a landowners' majority of one-half the assembly could guarantee the zemstvo's "capacity to fulfill state obligations." Like prerevolutionary autocracy, the old zemstvo, controlled by noble landowners but constituting a "vital,

[107] Ibid., d. 9, l. 10 (S. A. Popov, Kaluga rightist).
[108] Ibid., d. 9, l. 3.
[109] Ibid., d. 28, l. 5.
[110] Ibid., d. 28, l. 232.

whole organism," had worked "for the general welfare [*obshchee blago*] and general interests." Performing state service in his home county, the noble landowner still remained loyal to the cultural heritage of his estate (*soslovie*). He transcended personal concerns and translated the desires of the center into concrete action. He alone, however, had inherited this unique distinction. To allow the domination of the assembly by township and urban delegations thus threatened to destroy not only the zemstvo's traditional character but also its ability to assure the commonweal. Zubchaninov resolutely contrasted Stolypin's zemstvo to his own:

> The single hope that our zemstvo will remain ideal, that people will be in it who actually are capable of work and not simply people defending parochial interests, is that the predominant element in the zemstvo assembly be the first electoral curia. It will be the cement binding the separate, disunited parts of the whole into one.[111]

After these deliberations of zemstvo electoral reform, the spring 1908 session of the Council on Local Economy ended. Two conclusions were apparent to Stolypin, both of them evident in his actions over the following six months. On the one hand, as a "pre-Duma" the spring session had achieved its objectives. Officially, the body approved each of the reforms presented for its consideration. Village, township, and zemstvo electoral reform were passed out of the council. The final votes on these matters were generally not contested. In October the government presented a township reform bill to the third Duma and in December submitted village reform legislation as well. As promised, the government dispatched the printed records and opinions of the council along with its own proposals.

On the other hand, Stolypin had not reached an accommodation with representatives of the provincial zemstvos. Significantly, the township legislation submitted in the fall contained not a word about that assembly's place in county zemstvo elections.[112] For that matter, the entire issue of zemstvo electoral reform reverted to the MVD, where the legislation was being reworked.[113] Finally, provincial opposition in the spring had forced Stolypin to make concessions for the upcoming November session of the council, when it was scheduled to discuss the reforms of county and provincial administration. In early November the premier invited ten provincial marshals of the nobility to attend these deliberations.[114] His renewed

---

[111] Ibid., d. 28, l. 231.

[112] TsGIA, f. 1291, op. 50 (1906), d. 33, ll. 1–53, and *Obzor deiatel'nosti gosudarstvennoi dumy, tret'ego sozyva, 1907–1912 gg., chast' 2-aia, zakonodatelnaia deiatel'nost'* (St. Petersburg, 1912), pp. 67–71.

[113] TsGIA, f. 1288, op. 2 (1909), ll. 15–16.

[114] TsGAOR, f. 483, op. 1, d. 7, ll. 37–38 (Smolensk provincial marshal V. M. Urusov to the Permanent Council, 8 November 1908).

attempt to conciliate rightist opinion failed, however, as eight of these marshals arrived in St. Petersburg and consulted the United Nobility's Permanent Council, looking "to act in common" against the projected replacement of the county marshal.[115]

When debate resumed again in November, the government had already made one minor concession in its county legislation, allowing that an acting county marshal might be appointed vice-governor.[116] Moreover, in commission discussions, the MVD agreed without objection to equalize the number of public and bureaucratic representatives sitting on the county advisory council.[117] Yet on the primary point of contention Stolypin was unyielding, and he refused to countenance an elected public official at the head of county government—"estate or nonestate, it makes no difference," said I. M. Strakhovskii.[118]

Stolypin, in a rare appearance during general assembly debate, tried to explain to his critics that he did not intend "to construct all local administration on bureaucratic foundations [biurokraticheskie nachala], destroying the entire structure of local life by which Russia [had] lived to the present time." Restating the premises that had guided the local reform program, he asserted that "the public element" was participating in "state activity" in a variety of ways. Primarily, of course, the public was involved in "political activity that occurred in" the Duma and State Council. It also worked in "local self-administration" and joined in "administrative activity" as well—the county council, school boards, land reorganization committees, and so forth. Yet, at a time when the government planned to broaden the competence of local self-administration, it required "a firmly established and energetically active administrative authority" of its own in rural society. Thus the choice that the council confronted was quite clear. The premier desired "a strong local authority and the attraction to this authority of local public elements . . . [within] a local administration led by this central unifying authority," that is, strong local authority able to rally broad public support for the government. His no-

[115] TsGAOR, f. 434, op. 1, d. 78/307, ll. 28 and 30. Only Kharkov marshal N. A. Rebinder and Kiev marshal Prince P. A. Kurakin did not attend. The other marshals were: A. D. Samarin (Moscow); V. A. Drashusov (Riazan); Gr. V. F. Dorrer (Kursk); V. N. Polivanov (Simbirsk); S. S. Tolstoi (Kazan); Prince V. M. Urusov (Smolensk); Prince N. P. Urusov (Ekaterinoslav); and Prince N. B. Shcherbatov (Poltava). TsGIA, f. 1288, op. 1 (1908), d. 29, ll. 77–78.

[116] TsGIA, f. 1288, op. 1, d. 3, l. 2.

[117] "Zhurnaly kommissii po proektu polozheniia ob uezdnom upravlenii," TsGIA, f. 1284, op. 185 (1907), d. 5a, ch. 1, ll. 211, 217.

[118] Ibid., l. 217. An important component of the government's argument against the marshal was a statistical survey of his administrative activity during the period 1 January 1905–1 August 1908. The survey revealed that the 318 elected county marshals attended administrative councils—which by law they were charged to chair—only 46 percent of the time that these organs convened. Ibid., l. 153.

biliary opponents, however, were refusing to recognize the new realities of political life in Russia and were, he warned, threatening the very reform plans that were intended to address such change:

> If representatives of the public in the Council cannot accept this viewpoint, if they obstruct its promulgation in local life, raising instead another view based on established traditions and considerations that a rupture of the existing county structure is undesirable, then of course serious complications [will] arise for the reform of county administration on new foundations.[119]

When he spoke on 2 December 1908, the premier already knew that his plan had encountered these complications—and this viewpoint. A week before the speech, the council's commission on county administration had rejected the county vice-governor plan. It demanded that the marshal remain the county's chief administrative officer.[120] In its report to the council, the commission contradicted Stolypin's political thinking, opposing to it the same historic rural culture and the same nobiliary leadership that had influenced the debates of the previous autumn. Eliminating the county marshal, the report stated, "ought not to be seen merely as an affront to the interests of the noble estate, but primarily as the diminution of the land [*nachalo zemskogo*], of public independence." Although elected only by the corporative nobility, the marshal nevertheless was "one chosen by the public [*obshchestvennyi izbrannik*]," who stood above the population but enjoyed its trust. As a member of an estate that traditionally had dedicated itself "to serve Tsar and Fatherland," the marshal was best suited to be a loyal executor of government orders in the local areas. Thus, "without any real need," the ministry was removing "the unifying link between the administrative mechanism and the local population." Opposing the land to the nation, contrasting nobiliary leadership with bureaucratic authority, the commission resolved that the proposal of a county vice-governor was inopportune. It "could hardly be considered cautious to undermine that element of the county structure that exerts a conciliatory and mollifying influence on all aspects of local life."[121]

[119] "Zhurnaly Obshchego Prisutstviia SDMKh," ibid., l. 221.

[120] Ibid., l. 198. The vote was 13 to 9. In the majority were: Prince P. P. Golitsyn (Novgorod zemstvo State Council representative, right); Prince N. B. Shcherbatov (Poltava provincial marshal, right); A. N. Naumov (Samara provincial marshal, right); A. G. Rat'kov-Rozhnov (Iaroslavl', moderate-right); E. K. Brodskii (Ekaterinoslav county marshal, right); S. T. Varun-Sekret (Kherson county marshal, Octobrist); Prince A. I. Kurakin (Kiev provincial marshal, [unknown]); S. A. Popov (Kaluga county marshal, right); A. I. Mukhlynin (Tver, [unknown]); M. Ia. Govorukho-Otrok (Kursk provincial zemstvo board chair, right); S. A. Panchulidze (Saratov right); and Prince V. M. Urusov (Smolensk provincial marshal, right). Ibid., ll. 196–97.

[121] Ibid., ll. 209. The nine dissenting members of the commission included four provincial

The resolution of this issue took place on 2 December, immediately after Stolypin had addressed the assembly. In the premier's presence and with most government members attending, the council accepted the MVD's plan by a vote of 39 to 30. In fact, however, the tally concealed a debacle.[122] Twenty-nine of the 39 affirmative votes had come from governors, officials, and municipal mayors. Representatives of 29 zemstvo provinces were present. Only 10 of these delegates supported the government, but because in four instances a second delegate from the same province voted against, in fact only 6 zemstvo provinces could be counted in Stolypin's column.[123] The representatives of 19 zemstvo provinces voted nay; moreover, 7 of the 10 provincial marshals invited to the proceedings were also numbered in the opposition. If the final vote is tabulated in this manner, zemstvo or noble representatives from only 6 provinces unanimously supported the MVD and 24 provinces were opposed. Of these, 16 were located in the country's black-earth belt, the heartland of the landowning nobility and the monarchy.[124]

Agitation around this issue continued even as the council was concluding its deliberations on 9 December 1908. Twenty-five delegates, led by A. D. Samarin, filed a petition requesting that final approval of the county reform be delayed, for even Stolypin had said that the vote was evenly split. Kryzhanovskii denied this request, arguing that all votes of the council were legally binding. The minority could, if it so desired, develop a counterproject for the ministry's consideration before the bill was introduced to the Duma.[125] Subsequently, the matter became a primary topic for the United Nobility's fifth congress, which was held in February 1909.[126] Like the zemstvo electoral law, however, the county reform remained within the MVD for further review.[127]

Even the MVD's proposed reforms of the land captain and provincial administration encountered difficulties in the council. Although delegates

---

governors, four urban delegates, and one zemstvo representative, the Moscow Octobrist N. F. Rikhter.

[122] Ibid., l. 221.

[123] These were Tver, Vologda, Tauride, Viatka, Kostroma, and Tambov. Ibid., ll. 215 and 221.

[124] These were Kiev, Kherson, Ekaterinoslav, Poltava, Chernigov, Kharkov, Kursk, Voronezh, Orel, Tula, Kaluga, Riazan, Kazan, Simbirsk, Saratov, and Samara. Ibid., ll. 215 and 221. See also A. N. Naumov, *Iz utselevshikh vospominanii, 1868–1917* (New York, 1954), 2:135–39.

[125] "Zhurnal obshchego prisutstviia, 9 December 1908," ibid., ll. 235–36.

[126] "Doklad K. F. Golovnina V-omu S"ezdu upolnomochennykh ob"edinennykh dvorianskikh obshchestv, 'Predpolozhennye administrativnye reformy,' " TsGAOR, f. 434, op. 1, d. 23/84, ll. 1–4. See also the petitions of the Nizhnii Novgorod and Kursk provincial noble assemblies in support of the marshals (December 1908–January 1909), TsGIA, f. 1283, op. 1 (1907), d. 55, ll. 92–93, and d. 92, ll. 9–11.

[127] TsGIA, f. 1284, op. 185 (1907), d. 5a, ll. 78–79 and 115–19.

were willing to support the reformulation of the land captain's administrative functions, they overwhelmingly opposed the proposal that he be
selected by the Ministry of Internal Affairs. Instead they insisted that the
position remain a gubernatorial appointment after consultation with the
county marshal and zemstvo board chairman, thereby leaving the post a
patronage sinecure for local landowners.[128] When the council debated
provincial reform, rightist delegates exploited statutory language describing the governor as the provincial representative of the central government, and not the personal agent of the sovereign, to charge that the project demeaned the autocrat. They forced a rewording of the law to this
effect.[129]

Although the council completed its examination of the provincial statute only during spring 1909, serious objections arose against both of its
other essential features as well. Most delegates, whether rightist or moderate, protested that the expanded supervisory authority of the governor
over both administrative institutions and local self-administration required more precise legal definition.[130] Second, a number of council members, including some appointed governors, opposed the attempted unification of provincial administrative affairs under the aegis of the
governor's council. Although a minority opinion, one primary argument
advanced against this effort to render civil government more effective was
that it eliminated the provincial board charged with administrative oversight of the peasantry. This function, it was argued, would "undoubtedly
for a long time" remain a concern of provincial government because "the
abolished peasant estate [had] not in fact lost its intrinsic character as an
estate of rural residents."[131]

Thus, by late 1908, well before the naval staff crisis of March–April
1909, the dimensions of the government's defeat in the Council on Local
Economy were evident—and stunning. Indeed, the intractable situation
into which the Stolypin government was falling was only confirmed by
this more renowned "ministerial crisis," which arose over a minor appro-
priation passed by the Duma in mid-1908 to fund a reorganization of the
navy's general staff. Charging that the Duma, with the ministry's conniv-
ance, had infringed on the autocrat's prerogatives in military affairs, State
Council rightists seized on a pretext that finally forced Nicholas II to articulate publicly his own sentiments about the third of June political sys-

[128] "Doklad kommissii ob uchastkovykh nachal'nikov," and "Zhurnaly obshchego prisutstviia," TsGIA, f. 1288, op. 1 (1908), d. 12, ll. 35–41 and 73–75.

[129] *Russkie vedomosti*, 6 December 1908, p. 4.

[130] "Doklad kommissii po proektu preobrazovaniia uchrezhdenii gubernskogo upravleniia," TsGIA, f. 1288, op. 1, d. 23, ll. 1–3.

[131] "Doklad kommissii po proektu . . . gubernskogo upravleniia," TsGIA, f. 1288, op. 1
(1908), d. 30, ll. 70–73, and "Osoboe mnenie," d. 23, ll. 38–39.

tem and the premier who had created it. The emperor's eventual veto of the legislation in April—despite Stolypin's support for Duma Octobrists and deployment of his cabinet ministers to force the bill through the State Council in March—filled the national press with debates about the reformist capacities of the ministry and swirling rumors of Stolypin's imminent resignation. In fact, the premier did indeed threaten to retire if the tsar refused to support him, but Nicholas, ignoring his own decision to side with the right, demanded the continuing service of his subordinate.[132]

In the aftermath of these events Stolypin turned back to consider the previous fiasco he had endured at the Council on Local Economy. In July, I. Ia. Gurliand delivered two notes, requested by the premier, analyzing the political implications of the council's proceedings.[133] The first examined the debate that had arisen over the marshal of the nobility.[134] Gurliand cited several factors that had sparked opposition among council delegates. First, he noted, some "leftists" in the council and society at large had taken advantage of the issue to protest what they regarded as a bureaucratic attack on "the public realm [obshchestvennost']." They objected to the strengthening of state authority, and desired to "leave [to] the government" a perfunctory role in local life.[135] This appraisal was less than comforting, of course, as it reflected the increasingly strained relations of the ministry to moderate Progressists and left-center Octobrists. Indeed, at the party's third congress in October 1909, the latter spoke out in favor of local reform legislation approximating the original intent of the 1906–07 government proposals. That these supporters of reform were growing hostile to the government undoubtedly made the primary conclusion of Gurliand's analysis even less comforting.[136] The chief source of the government's defeat had been the rightist sentiments of the provincial nobility and the provincial nobility's inability to accept reforms critical to the long-term political stability of the national state.

Extreme rightists, he said, were enraged by a government intent on undermining the noble estate, as if to say to the "Russian *dvorianstvo*: You are not necessary to us anymore, you have played out your role." These rightists believed that Stolypin aimed either at establishing a bureaucratic

---

[132] Diakin, *Samoderzhavie*, chap. 6; Ananych, Diakin, et al., *Krizis samoderzhaviia v Rossii*, pp. 467–72; and *Russkie vedomosti* and *Novoe vremia*, 21 March–1 May 1909, passim.

[133] TsGIA, f. 1284, op. 185 (1907), d. 5a, ch. 3, l. 96 (Gurliand to Stolypin, 20 July 1909).

[134] "Uezdnaia reforma," ibid., ll. 111–21.

[135] Ibid., ll. 116–18; also *Russkie vedomosti*, 28 November 1908, p. 2; 30 November 1908, p. 1; 4 December 1908, p. 1; 7 December 1908, p. 1.

[136] TsGAOR, f. 115, op. 1, d. 47, ll. 90–94. A. D. Golitsyn urged a zemstvo reform based upon a tax franchise and the Prussian system of curial elections. Iu. N. Glebov supported township reform that fully implemented the idea of a small zemstvo unit. A. I. Ursul advocated all-estate village administration along the lines of the MVD statute given to the Second Duma.

dictatorship or, worse, at converting the country to "a constitutional-parliamentary style [of government]." Either way the premier became the sponsor of a drive to remove a loyal nobility from its position of influence. More moderate opponents spoke about a potential loss of both local patronage and access to provincial administrative office if the marshal was displaced. Even they, however, feared that the removal of the marshal signaled the beginning of a time when "noble-landowners will be distinguished from other landed property owners only by the amount of their possessions. To the extent that it still exists, this will cause the final end of the nobles' way of life [dvorianskii byt]."[137] Perhaps in public, Gurliand noted, the provincial delegates had devoted their attention to legislative detail and occasional outcries against "bureaucratic tendencies," but only these more substantive concerns for their estate had consumed long periods of "unusually agitated private discussions." And always, all opponents returned to "their basic point of view":

> The introduction of the county vice-governor is the end of the nobility as a foundation of Russian public strength in local areas, and this at a moment when the government should be extremely careful or at least understand that either it relies on a conservative nobility loyal to the monarchical principle or it will again run hopelessly aground, will give itself up to fate; then it will have to retreat before the noisy onslaught of radical elements and the silent disdain of the Russian dvorianstvo.[138]

Gurliand drew no other conclusions from these events. Yet, for the government to rely on the nobility meant abandoning not only the local reforms but also, in large measure, the attempt that these reforms represented to render government authority effective and legitimate in an era of national politics that many noble landowners apparently refused to accept. Gurliand's second report, however, which answered a question presumably put to him by Stolypin, expressed a clear recognition that nobiliary opposition of this magnitude dictated precisely such consequences. Gurliand was asked to analyze the history of local government in nineteenth-century Prussia, and in particular to determine how "the introduction of a constitutional form of rule" had influenced its development there. He replied that Prussia had replaced its system of estate administration in 1850, but that these "half-hearted," artificial legal constructs were in large measure a "compromise" dictated by the 1848 Revolution, had been revoked in 1853, and then were not put into practice again until 1872. To be sure, Gurliand noted, Prussia "abruptly turned back to a preconstitutional local order" in 1853, but in doing so had

---

[137] "Uezdnaia reforma," ll. 111–12.
[138] Ibid., ll. 112–13.

acted properly, as the government had "risked destroying that which had evolved historically" without providing "any stable basis for the . . . development of local life." As Prussian national politics evolved in the 1850s and 1860s, local administration had thus "survived both liberal and conservative stances in the government and the legislature, and remained essentially unchanged for another twenty years." Gradually, however, "a constitutional structure, having been strengthened and developed, became an inalienable possession of national consciousness," and, two decades later, a "real foundation for the further, more fundamental reform of the local order" had finally come into being.[139]

There was no record of the premier's reaction to this argument. Yet by the summer of 1909 the impetus behind local reform had been dissipated to the point that even if the reforms of village and township estate administration were to pass the Duma in a form acceptable to the government, they awaited an uncertain future in the State Council. The premier's domestic policy had been hamstrung by rightist opposition in the center and the provinces. His own personal authority, both with the sovereign and with the provincial landowning nobility that he once had regarded as his favored constituency, had grown alarmingly weak. And the "constitutional structure" of the third of June, an alliance with property and wealth needed to stabilize a reformed autocratic order, was proving itself to be anything but an inalienable possession of national consciousness. If Stolypin believed that the regime possessed twenty years to eradicate such weaknesses, he was soon to be disabused of this illusion as well.

One of the many paradoxes that characterized the last decades of autocratic rule was revealed in the two years following the coup d'état of June 1907. For the better part of a half-century, successive generations of reformist statesmen had seen their plans for the transformation of rural society scuttled by the contention—which they themselves shared—that the mass population of the country was unprepared for civil and political rights. Although—as the 1907 electoral law illustrated amply enough— the Stolypin government remained influenced by these preconceptions, it nevertheless understood that the consequences of failing to address this most inbred legacy of serfdom were far more risky than the uncertainty associated with gradual social and political reform. Moreover, the government possessed in Stolypin a statesman convinced that he could achieve this transformation without abandoning the prerogatives of an autocratic state essential to the control and mediation of this process—

[139] "Skoro-li posle vvedenie v Prussii konstitutsionnogo obraza pravleniia byla zadumana reforma organov mestnogo samoupravleniia, kakimi etapami ona shla i kogda okonchatel'no osushchestvlena?" TsGIA, f. 1284, op. 185 (1907), d. 5a, ch. 3, ll. 107–8.

that he could construct a national state, an edifice of gosudarstvennost' allowing the autocracy to survive the early twentieth century. Yet Stolypin only discovered in 1908 that he confronted, in the ranks of the provincial landowning nobility, a stratum of society as unprepared in its own way for civil life and national politics as many perceived the mass populace to be. As Gurliand's analysis had indicated, the government was wondering how long it would need to await the evolution of a national consciousness within the most legitimate constituency of the third of June system.

Indeed, Stolypin was realizing that the *coup d'etat* had created conditions that, rather than allowing the government to wield authority and effect reforms, had rendered it increasingly unable to act. Having depoliticized all but the cultured minority of the "nation," Stolypin by 1909 confronted a situation in which most of the political constituencies supporting reform—the Kadets, Progressists, and left Octobrists—were those whom Gurliand had labelled "leftists," primarily because their programs excluded or greatly reduced the prerogatives of the autocratic government within national life. Yet that constituency deemed most prepared to construct an edifice of gosudarstvennost', the provincial landowning nobility, was either unwilling to undertake these reforms or actively repudiated the government that attempted to implement them.

Criticism of the local reforms revealed a nobility driven by the fear that Stolypin's attempts to reform the state order would undermine the ascriptive culture that lent the nobility its status, identity, and place and provided the autocracy with its firmest guarantee of social order. In this sense, despite the coup d'état and Stolypin's thorough suppression of revolution, Stolypin's ministry was as much a "leftist" and illegitimate entity as all other parties, public groups, and social classes whose struggle for political ascendancy violated the principles upon which autocratic history rested. The third of June system, with which Stolypin had intended to govern the nation, was in fact turning out to be an empty shell.

CHAPTER VIII

Isolation and Defeat: Bureaucratic Reform on the Eve of the War

THE POLITICAL chronicle of the Stolypin ministry after 1908–09, and of the reform initiatives it had attempted to implement, was a story of isolation and defeat. Dependent on a sovereign increasingly apathetic about his goals and values, Stolypin continued to endure criticism from the Russian right. With the western zemstvo crisis of March–April 1911, however, he was forced into a political confrontation with these opponents. This conflict cost him both the confidence of Nicholas II and the base of public support from which his government had derived its political legitimacy. The premier's assassination the following September thus functioned only to provide a tragic but convenient marker to date the demise of the third of June system and the collapse of the opportunity for state reform of the autocratic order it was intended to facilitate.

"System," however, was something of a misnomer as applied to the governing structure that, forged by the coup d'état of 3 June 1907, had institutionalized in an ad hoc manner the contradictions left unresolved by the 1905 revolution. Nominally following Lenin, Soviet historians have emphasized the inherent instability of an autocratic state too weak after 1905 to reestablish the *status quo ante* but nevertheless powerful enough to reassert its primacy through the coup. This act allowed the Stolypin ministry to "maneuver [*lavirovat'*]" in the representative forum of the Duma, and through it in society at large, between parties of the liberal left and conservative right, or the class interests of bourgeoisie and nobility whose views they purportedly reflected. Neither the government nor the parties could challenge the existence of the other, because each recognized the broader threat posed to it by the persistence of a "general revolutionary situation" and thus feared that political instability might re-ignite the social revolution of 1905–06. However, even scholars holding to this "bonapartist" model, as V. S. Diakin was first to recognize, believe that its most debilitating—and, by 1911, fatal—dysfunction was the clash between a bureaucratic government that deemed the third of June system to be a vehicle for reform and a nobility that viewed reform as an assault on its own class interests. By obstructing even minimal state reconstruction, the nobility undermined the ministry's ability to appeal to the "left" and thus alienated the bourgeois elements of Octobrism and Kadet liberalism, driving them into an unstable oppositional coalition against the government.[1]

Freed from its overly rigid ideological constraints, this analysis suggests some guidelines for how one might understand the fate of the third of June system and the crisis of autocracy that its demise signaled. The system, to be sure, was inherently unstable, in the first instance because it had only papered over the incompatibility of autocracy and representative institutions. The laws that had secured broad prerogatives for the tsar had left intact his personal right to rule, a powerful symbol of superordinate authority that resonated deeply within autocratic political culture and increasingly reinforced similar conceptions of authority among officials and the landowning nobility. Remnants of this tradition were reflected as well in a ministerial policy that *assumed* the primacy of government views and the legitimacy of its political authority in national life, even when such primacy and legitimacy could be retained only at the cost of excluding most of the nation that the third of June system was intended to govern. Undertaken to effect order and reform, Stolypin's coup only further exacerbated the instability of civil society, deepening the gulf between its heights and depths (*verkhi i nizy*); at the same time, it left undefined, for all constituent parties and social groups, the nature of a constitutional or representative political culture that encompassed only a minority of the population.

The third of June system was in this sense as fragile as the society and nation it governed: all were caught within the same still incomplete process of transformation that rendered the prewar landscape of imperial Russia a confusing amalgam of conflicting belief systems and social orders. It was a mark of Stolypin's historical importance that he had been able to maneuver for six years within this system in the hope of effecting civil and political reform without undermining the autocratic order he had pledged to serve. Yet by 1909 the effort had already strained the capacities of the third of June system; when put to the test again in 1911, it disintegrated. With the passing of the last great reformer of imperial Russia, the final three years before the Great War would see the recrudescence of an autocratic political culture whose underlying values concealed debilitating consequences for the survival of the old regime.

THE WESTERN ZEMSTVO CRISIS: TWILIGHT OF THE STOLYPIN MINISTRY

By early 1911 Stolypin had recognized that his personal prestige and the political authority of his government had significantly declined, but he

---

[1] See especially, Diakin, *Samoderzhavie*, pp. 3–25, and the biased criticism of his argument in A. Ia. Avrekh, *Tsarizm i IV Duma, 1912–1914 gg.* (Moscow, 1981), pp. 10–17.

had not yet lost either the ability or the will to exercise power. In an interview given anonymously to *Novoe vremia* that January, the premier acknowledged the growing public criticism of the Third Duma "for its ineffectiveness" and of the Octobrist "majority party" for its inability to provide the assembly with the "necessary weight and strength" that had been expected earlier, in 1907. Noting as well the "arguments and discord" now characteristic of relations between the Duma and the State Council, Stolypin could blame Duma "leftists" only partially for the situation, and he admitted the complicity of the right. "Extremist wings of the Duma" had obstructed legislation, he said, and "opposition" in the State Council, although not "overwhelming [*strashno*]," had been quite apparent. Nevertheless, he countered, important legislation—especially land reform and the Finnish fundamental laws—had been implemented. Although the local reforms were stalled for both procedural and political reasons, he still expected their eventual passage. And, assiduously cultivating nationalist support, he predicted an early passage for the western zemstvo legislation, insisting that it was "impossible to deprive an entire region of self-administration." "The machine is screeching at the moment," Stolypin admitted, but he remained confident enough of his own personal influence to speculate about the electoral tactics necessary to produce a Fourth Duma nationalist coalition more favorably disposed toward government policy.[2]

Whatever solid ground there had been under his feet in the first months of 1911, however, crumbled in March with the beginning of the western zemstvo crisis. Since coming to power in 1906, Stolypin had contemplated the extension of zemstvo institutions to the six southwestern provinces of Belorussia and the right-bank Ukraine, but he had pursued the idea only seriously after 1909.[3] In part, a characteristic desire to expand self-administration motivated the legislation; indeed, in 1910 his government had supported Duma amendments broadening the franchise for electoral participation in these new institutions.[4] Yet "the central question of the legislative project," as Stolypin told the State Council on 4 March, was a zemstvo electoral structure allowing representation by property and nationality.[5] This attempt to create a viable zemstvo infrastructure while limiting the influence of the Polish landholding gentry

[2] "O vnutrennoi politiki," *Novoe vremia*, 13 January 1911. Stolypin is acknowledged as the source of the interview in "Iz poslednei besedy s P. A. Stolypina," ibid., 10 September 1911, p. 4.

[3] The proposal first became a topic for public discussion at the Council on Local Economy during its fall 1909 session. TsGIA, f. 1288, op. 1 (1908), d. 29.

[4] Hosking, *Russian Constitutional Experiment*, pp. 116–34, and Diakin, *Samoderzhavie*, pp. 200–201 and 213–18.

[5] *Russkie vedomosti*, 5 March 1911, p. 2.

dominant in the region was key to the emerging alliance between Stolypin and the Nationalists, a Russian, agrarian coalition based primarily in southwestern Russia and whose growing influence already figured in the government's Duma strategy.[6] A proposal expanding zemstvo self-administration and possibly solidifying Stolypin's tenure, however, offered an inviting target for the premier's many enemies. The State Council's rejection on 4 March of the so-called national curiae initiated a "ministerial" or "parliamentary" crisis that riveted the attention of public opinion throughout that spring's political season in the capital. At stake was Stolypin's political survival.

The story of this crisis has been told in much greater detail elsewhere.[7] Several of its characteristics, however, deserve mention here because they illuminate the political conjuncture that by 1911 afflicted reformist elements of the autocratic government. With some twenty-eight rightist officials and center-right provincial zemtsy providing the decisive votes on 4 March, the primary—and publicly most evident—feature of the conflict was the willfulness of State Council rightists in their attempts to undermine Stolypin and his legislative program.[8] A second and more critical component of the crisis was its impact on the personal relations of Stolypin and Nicholas II. Allowing State Council opponents "to vote [according to] their conscience" on the curial question, the tsar had abandoned his premier—an act, one newspaper noted, that "rocked the entire bureaucratic world [biurokraticheskii mir]."[9] Indeed, this sign of imperial apathy (if not outright disfavor) led Stolypin to request a meeting with Nicholas on 5 March so that he could resign. A written summary of the confrontation, dictated by Stolypin on his return from the meeting, portrayed more than just a stormy clash between a suspicious sovereign and a statesman aware that his influence at court was waning. From Stolypin's perspective, the autocrat neither sympathized with nor understood the task of governing a reformed political order.[10]

[6] Robert Edelman, *Gentry Politics on the Eve of the Russian Revolution: The Nationalist Party, 1907–1917* (Rutgers University Press, 1980), pp. 116–30.

[7] Hosking, *Russian Constitutional Experiment*, pp. 134–49; Diakin, *Samoderzhavie*, pp. 212–41; Edelman, *Gentry Politics*, pp. 116–26.

[8] "Okolo dumy," *Russkie vedomosti*, 6 March 1911, p. 4, and 9 March 1911, p. 4; "Ministerskii krizis," *Russkie vedomosti*, 9 March 1911, p. 2; and "Dnevnik A. A. Bobrinskogo," *KA* 1(26) (1928): 133–50. Generally, see Alexandra Shecket Korros, "The Landed Nobility, the State Council, and P. A. Stolypin (1907–1911)," in Haimson, *Politics of Rural Russia*, pp. 135–38; and Diakin, *Samoderzhavie*, pp. 213–17.

[9] "Ministerskii krizis," *Russkie vedomosti*, 8 March 1911; also 6 March 1911, p. 4; "Dnevnik Bobrinskogo," pp. 144–45 (5–7 March 1911); and Shul'gin, *Vospominaniia*, pp. 108–14.

[10] *Novoe vremia*, 9 March 1911, p. 2, and "Izlozhenie razgovora P. A. Stolypina s Niko-

To Nicholas's face, Stolypin labeled V. P. Trepov and other State Council rightists, who had attempted to persuade the tsar that his premier had manufactured artificial expressions of public support for the western zemstvo proposal, as "secretive, obtuse, and lying reactionaries [*reaktsionery*]." Expressing his chagrin at the fact that Nicholas appeared to believe the rumors they had spread, Stolypin explained, in the language of the servitor, that such "intrigue" merely aimed "at dividing us, as one might divide an overseer and a landlord." In his written summary, however, Stolypin used the language of the statesman—he vented his frustration at an emperor who, like those rightists "leading us to our death, . . . apparently himself believes . . . [that] it is not necessary to govern [*zakonodatel'stvovat'*] but only to administer [*upravliat'*]." Stolypin well understood how the persistent slander of legislative institutions had reduced his own political capital and stoked the tsar's suspicion of the political values linked with the premier's name since 1906–07. These tactics, he now realized, had succeeded in attenuating relations between tsar and first minister: "I felt that the sovereign believed I was attempting to push him into the background [*zaslonit'*], as if to stand between him and the country." Having concluded from all of this that "there was no more support [for his work]," Stolypin had enough personal honor to insist that Nicholas replace him.[11] Maneuvers behind the scenes between the two men continued for a week, until 12 March, when Stolypin acceded to the emperor's demand that he remain at his post, but he did so only after winning what the press called "compensation." The cost to Nicholas was unprecedented and undoubtedly remembered by the emperor. The tsar forced leaves of absence upon the two leaders of the State Council right group, V. P. Trepov and P. N. Durnovo, and signed an imperial order proroguing both legislative chambers for three days, during which time the Duma's version of the western zemstvo bill was promulgated via Article 87.

The cost of these acts to Stolypin, however, was even higher, for not only did he exacerbate Nicholas's antagonism, he also alienated most of his remaining support among the political parties. By late April this loss of support was apparent in the fact that both the State Duma and State

---

laem II po povodu slukhov o predstoiashchei otstavke Stolypina," TsGIA, f. 1662, op. 1, d. 325, ll. 1–2.

[11] Ibid. See also Guchkov, "Iz vospominanii," *Poslednye novosti*, 5640, 2 September 1936, and S. I. Shidlovskii, *Vospominaniia* (Moscow, 1924), p. 198. V. N. Kokovtsov relates the following comments of empress Alexandra Fedorovna some four weeks after Stolypin's death: "Listening to you, I see that you are always comparing yourself to Stolypin. . . . Remain true to yourself, don't seek support among political parties; they are so insignificant in our country. Rely on the confidence of the sovereign—God will help you. I am certain that Stolypin died to give you his place and this is for the good of Russia." Count V. N. Kokovtsov, *Iz moego proshlogo* (Mouton reprint, 1969), vol. 2, p. 8.

Council had voted to censure Stolypin's use of Article 87, which they considered to be a blatant misuse of the Fundamental Laws. In the State Council, only 53 of 152 deputies sided with the premier's handling of the western zemstvo legislation.[12] In the State Duma, a vote of 202 to 82 registered an even more resounding defeat. Opposed only by the favored Nationalists, a majority—which included the defecting Octobrists— found Stolypin's rationales "unsatisfactory" and his actions "illegal [*nezakonomernyi*]."[13]

In the final analysis, this third feature of the western zemstvo crisis was its most significant. Forced to extreme measures by the right, Stolypin squandered the slim base of public support on which he had wagered so much of his government's political legitimacy. Those in the opposition, most notably the Kadets, found little surprise in "this constant readiness to overstep lawful boundaries," as *Russkie vedomosti* commented on 13 March.[14] On the far right, the western zemstvo crisis only cemented hostility to all that Stolypin represented. In early 1912, shortly after the premier's death, the Duma's rightist fraction premised much of its platform for the approaching Fourth Duma elections on opposition to Stolypin's prominent ministers, to most of his reform plans, and, by advocating even further restrictions, even to the third of June electoral law.[15] Most devastating, however, was the final blow that the western zemstvo crisis struck against Octobrism. Octobrism's ostensible commitment to the ideals of the October Manifesto had already weakened a party whose provincial noble constituency was attaching less and less significance to those ideals. By late 1909 the Octobrists, with some 128 Duma deputies, maintained party organizations in only thirteen percent of zemstvo counties in European Russia.[16] Yet Octobrism's influence on the right center of Russian politics ultimately had rested on the party's ability to hold this sizable bloc of deputies together and place them at the service of a reformist cabinet. Under the plainly anticonstitutionalist blows of prorogation and Article 87, both supports disintegrated.

The western zemstvo crisis exacerbated the internal contradictions of the party and was a crucial step toward the eventual split in 1913 between oppositional Left Octobrists and the rump Zemstvo-Octobrist fraction.[17] Its more immediate consequence, however, was to destroy what remained

---

[12] *Russkie vedomosti*, 3 April 1911, pp. 1, 4.

[13] *Russkie vedomosti*, 29 April 1911, pp. 1–2.

[14] *Russkie vedomosti*, 13 March 1911, p. 1.

[15] G. Iurskii, *Pravye v Tretei Gosudarstvennoi Dume* (Khar'kov, 1912), pp. 9–16.

[16] "Alfavitnyi spisok gubernskikh i uezdnykh gorodov, s ukazaniem otdelov soiuza 17 okt.," TsGAOR, f. 115, op. 1, d. 47, ll. 46–73.

[17] Shidlovskii, *Vospominaniia*, pp. 202–7; Hosking, *Russian Constitutional Experiment*, pp. 182–88; and Avrekh, *Tsarizm i IV duma*, pp. 20–29.

of Octobrist allegiance to Stolypin. On 12 March the party's Duma deputies formally distanced themselves from the government, resolving to oppose any bill that was implemented through "the illegal act" of Article 87. Left Octobrists threatened to join a proposed mass resignation of Kadet and left deputies in order to deprive the Duma of a quorum, thereby instigating the calling of new elections.[18] A measure far too radical for most Octobrists, it was taken up, symbolically, only by A. I. Guchkov, who resigned his position as president of the Duma on 14 March in order to protect himself and the party from the flood of public criticism inundating Stolypin.[19] "In several days," Guchkov told assistant minister of war A. A. Polivanov with a certain incredulity, "Stolypin has managed to insult all the parties and lose everyone's confidence."[20]

There was an added significance to this general collapse of support for the Stolypin ministry. The public had always suspected that Stolypin's dedication to reform was mere window dressing for the unaltered tutelage and administrative hegemony of the bureaucratic state, and, as the political legitimacy of the government disintegrated, this belief became more and more widespread. With a note of self-vindication, *Russkie vedomosti* argued that Stolypin's actions during the western zemstvo crisis reflected an "organic incapacity to understand the spirit of a legal state [*pravovoe gosudarstvo*]," a sure sign that "the old bureaucratic regime [*staryi biurokraticheskoi rezhim*]" persisted.[21] The left Octobrist S. I. Shidlovskii, despite respect for the premier's perspicacious attempt to effect "the fundamental alteration . . . of the antiquated nobiliary estate structure," observed in his memoirs that "the Petersburg bureaucratic atmosphere [*peterburgskaia biurokraticheskaia atmosfera*]" by 1911 had rendered Stolypin "more majestic and less accessible."[22] M. O. Menshikov, the anti-Semitic nationalist columnist of *Novoe vremia*, emphasized that the premier was reminding "all Russia . . . of the arbitrariness of the old, bureaucratic regime," which had never acknowledged that the state was "an *organized* structure, [that] its organization excludes everything that is sudden and not established by law."[23] Even on the far right, A. A. Bobrinskii echoed this hostility when he impugned the bureaucratic "milieu" that had imparted to Stolypin a tyrannical willfulness (*samodur-*

[18] "Protokol, 12 March 1911," TsGAOR, f. 115, op. 1, d. 19, l. 25 and *Russkie vedomosti*, 13 March 1911, pp. 3–4.

[19] *Russkie vedomosti*, 22 March 1911, p. 4; also Guchkov, "Iz vospominanii," *Poslednye novosti*, 26 August 1936, p. 2.

[20] A. A. Polivanov, *Iz dnevnikov i vospominanii po dolzhnosti voennogo ministra i ego pomoshchnika 1907–1916 g.*, edited by A. M. Zaionchkovskii (Moscow, 1924), p. 104 (23 March 1911).

[21] *Russkie vedomosti*, 22 March 1911, p. 1. See generally Miliukov, *Political Memoirs*, pp. 216–28.

[22] Shidlovskii, *Vospominaniia*, p. 190.

[23] *Novoe vremia*, 16 March 1911, p. 4, and 12 March 1911, p. 4.

stvo), which, Bobrinskii insisted, Stolypin had contracted from contact with "these Gerbels, Kryzhanovskiis, all these stooges who have made Petr Arkad'evich extremely sick."[24]

Stolypin made few excuses for his behavior; indeed, in speeches before the State Council and the State Duma, he justified his actions by asserting the right of the government to further any political reform that clearly served the country's interests. Ironically, however, these attempts to prove that government authority remained relevant and legitimate in national life only exacerbated the public suspicion that the bureaucratic state preferred power to the delimitations of legal order and representative institutions. Speaking before the State Council, Stolypin shielded the use of Article 87 behind "the right of the crown [*pravo korony*]" to act in extraordinary circumstances: flimsy rationales indeed, given the widely rumored concessions forced from an unforgiving Nicholas II.[25] His central theme was that the bureaucratic government, confronted by intransigent State Council rightists opposed to reform, had been forced to promulgate "from above" measures that served the interests of state and society. He used the metaphor of an emergency tracheotomy to explain government intervention in a suffocating legislative process.[26] Before the State Duma, where he castigated State Council rightists and emphasized the common interests that ought to ally government and Duma against them, Stolypin maintained that there were certain

> extraordinary moments when the government itself must struggle for its political ideals [*politicheskie idealy*]. . . . The government must decide whether it is worthwhile to continue spinning its wheels correctly and mechanically, preparing projects that will never see the light of day, or whether the government, which is the spokesman and executor of the directives of the Sovereign will, has the right and the obligation to act according to a defined, clear policy.[27]

This defense reveals a final commentary on the paradox of Stolypin's ministry. Throughout his tenure Stolypin had exhibited a lucid understanding of the political ideals that the 1905 Revolution had imposed on the Russian state. The legitimacy of its authority required reform of the empire's socioeconomic and administrative structures that would be

---

[24] "Dnevnik Bobrinskogo," p. 146 (14 March 1911).

[25] V. V. Logachev, *Sbornik rechei Petra Arkad'evicha Stolypina proiznesennykh v zasedaniiakh Gosudarstvennogo Soveta i Gosudarstvennoi Dumy (1906–1911)* (St. Petersburg, 1911), p. 124.

[26] Ibid., pp. 127–28.

[27] *Russkie vedomosti*, 28 April 1911, p. 3. One source notes that Stolypin as late as May 1911 was still considering proposing sweeping plans for state reform, which included reorganization of the ministerial structure and passage of zemstvo reform. See Zenkovskii, *Pravda o Stolypine*, chaps. 2–5.

sweeping enough to adapt autocracy to the representative political culture grudgingly conceded in 1905. From the outset, that task had proven difficult; only through repression and violation of the Fundamental Laws could Stolypin carve out for himself ill-defined but legal boundaries of a national politics within which the government would possess both legitimacy and the public support necessary to pursue its initiatives. Yet the social and political reforms that strengthened these slim foundations contradicted established patterns of autocratic authority and political culture; these remained deeply embedded in officialdom, in the provincial nobility, and in the mind of a sovereign whose inability to understand that "it was necessary to govern and not only to administer" had so unnerved his premier.[28] Reform deprived Stolypin of constituencies whose interests this scion of a hereditary noble family was attempting to serve. By mid-1911, as many of his critics had charged, he had indeed been left few other options but to rely upon an old—and, for the premier, familiar—weapon that above any other most alienated moderate and liberal supporters of Russian constitutionalism: the state's own superordinate power and obligation to define the national interest. Yet to a very large extent he had been forced to this position because old-regime society was proving incapable of adapting to the evolution of a reformed political order.

BUREAUCRATIC REFORM IN RETROSPECT: LOCAL REFORM ON THE EVE OF THE WAR, 1911–1914

During the three years between Stolypin's assassination in September 1911 and the beginning of World War I, the capacity of the central government to influence national politics disintegrated.[29] To no small degree, this situation resulted from the dissipation of the reformist ethos that Stolypin had sponsored and the further coalescence of the traditional values he had hoped to restrain. Without the moderation and perspective of reformers, the Russian state by 1914 existed in a vacuum of its own making, as even its power became increasingly irrelevant to the nation's life. Adherents of unrestricted autocratic authority, superordinate bureaucratic power, and the ascriptive cultural traditions of the hereditary nobility could and did posit an alternative to the values of law, rational government, and civic political culture. Moreover, because advocates of an autocratic political culture possessed institutional power—in the imperial court, the ministries, the State Council, the State Duma, and the unre-

---

[28] Verner, *Crisis of Autocracy*, epilogue.

[29] Ananych, Diakin, et al., *Krizis samoderzhaviia v Rossii*, pp. 500–543; Thomas Riha, "Constitutional Developments in Russia," in Stavrou, *Russia under the Last Tsar* (University of Minnesota, 1971), pp. 108–12; S. S. Oldenburg, *Last Tsar*, 3:138–39.

formed organs of provincial government still dominated by the landown-ing nobility—they supplied the drumbeat to which the old order marched off to war and its own demise.[30]

After 1911, proponents of unrestricted autocracy increasingly spoke in tones pre-dating the October Manifesto, mincing few words in their ex-pression of hostility before the State Duma and the political culture it represented. Indeed, rightists campaigning for the Fourth Duma in 1912 emphasized the incompatibility of "Tsarist Autocracy" and a "constitu-tional system"; they also broadly hinted that only a consultative Duma could serve as "an assistant of the Autocratic Sovereign, Who retains the entire totality of supreme authority, which by its very nature is indivisi-ble."[31] The tsar's long-standing personal disdain was expressed in the February 1913 manifesto marking the tricentenary of the Romanov dy-nasty. Praising the estates of the realm and the institutions that had con-tributed to autocracy's glorious history, the manifesto failed even to men-tion the Duma.[32] By the autumn Nicholas was indulging the urging of his minister of internal affairs N. A. Maklakov to consider a new state coup d'état that would render the Duma a consultative body.[33] Autocratic pre-rogative also clashed with the by now tattered ideal of unified bureau-cratic government, which both Witte and Stolypin had considered essen-tial to the maintenance of the integrity and sway of government authority within society. The growing willingness of Nicholas to undertake per-sonal relations with individual ministers rather than with the cabinet as a whole weakened the effectiveness of bureaucratic policy and thereby ex-acerbated its inability to influence national politics.[34]

Accompanying the reemergence of autocratic apologetics was a recru-descence of superordinate attitudes and practice in bureaucratic admin-istration, to a degree that had not been seen since before the 1905 Revo-lution. As the need to accommodate public opinion and political parties waned, the central government did indeed become indifferent to the civil reforms that had been hallmarks of the Stolypin period. Compared to the significant legislation that the Ministry of Internal Affairs had offered to the Second and Third Dumas, the program that Stolypin's former assis-tant minister A. A. Makarov prepared for the Fourth Duma was paltry:

---

[30] Haimson, "Conclusion," in idem, ed., *Politics of Rural Russia.*

[31] Iurskii, *Pravye v Tretei Gosudarstvennoi Dume*, p. 70.

[32] *Russkie vedomosti*, 21 February 1913, p. 2.

[33] Ananych, Diakin, et al., *Krizis samoderzhavie v Rossii*, pp. 518–27. Ibid., p. 526, notes that the signed but undated ukaz dissolving the Duma is in TsGIA, f. 1276, op. 20, d. 68, l. 51. See also E. D. Chermenskii, *IV gosudarstvennaia duma i sverzhenie tsarizma v Rossii* (Moscow, 1976), pp. 38–46.

[34] V. N. Kokovtsov, *Iz moego proshlago*, 2:311–40; Gurko, *Features and Figures*, pp. 516–18; Avrekh, *Tsarizm i IV Duma*, pp. 255–84; and McDonald, "Autocracy," chap. 5.

restrictive revisions of press and assembly laws; territorial realignment in Tomsk province; limitations on Asian and Finnish immigration into the empire; and prohibitions against Polish rural landowning in the western region.[35] Even the Kadet daily *Russkie vedomosti* admitted in April 1914 that despite his superficial "oratory," Stolypin "outlined before the second and third dumas an entire program of legislative work" and strove "to enlist [the Duma's] support" in order to assure its implementation. In comparison, the editorial continued, the inaugural address of the venerable chair of the Council of Ministers, I. L. Goremykin, to the new Duma "in no way differed from those speeches with which newly appointed [bureaucratic] bosses [*nachal'niki*] address [their] subordinates."[36]

Perhaps the best illustration of these tendencies, however, was supplied by the fate of local reform after 1911. Significantly, of all the initiatives undertaken during the Stolypin years, only police reform continued to engage the attention of the central government. When first developed in 1905–06, these proposals had aimed at professionalizing the empire's local police apparatus and at delegating many of its administrative responsibilities to local state and zemstvo bureaucracies. By 1913–14, under the guidance of Maklakov, these goals had yielded to concerns for strengthening the police power of provincial administration.[37] In March *Novoe vremia* complained that what Maklakov called "decentralization" many others labeled "the unconcealed reinforcement of the authority of the governors," and it compared these efforts unfavorably to Stolypin's plan for "decentralization . . . with the aid of a preliminary reform of the entire structure of local administration."[38]

With the exception of police realignments, most other local reforms were indeed stalemated. As late as the summer of 1911, S. E. Kryzhanovskii had prepared revised statutes for the reorganization of county administration and the district land captains.[39] Neither project received further attention until January 1913, when the recently appointed Maklakov ordered his subordinates to halt consideration of land captain reform. Generally opposed to "all this that is new," Maklakov stated in a letter to an assistant minister, Ia. Ia. Litvinov, that removing the often criticized judicial responsibilities of this official simply to accommodate

---

[35] *Novoe vremia*, 14 November 1912, pp. 2–3.

[36] *Russkie vedomosti*, 24 April 1914, pp. 1–2. Generally see Chermenskii, *IV gosudarstvennaia duma*, esp. pp. 38–67; and Avrekh, *Tsarizm i IV Duma*, esp. chap. 1.

[37] Neil Weissman, "Regular Police in Tsarist Russia," *Russian Review* 44, no. 1 (January 1985): 45–68. Also see reports concerning "Soveshchanie gubernatorov," *Novoe vremia*, 9–12, 14, 15 February 1913.

[38] *Novoe vremia*, 5 March 1913, p. 4.

[39] TsGIA, f. 1284, op. 185 (1907), d. 5a, ch. 2, ll. 38–39 (letter of S. E. Kryzhanovskii to A. A. Makarov, 8 August 1911); and "Proekt polozheniia ob uezdnom reforme" and "Ob"iasnitel'naia zapiska," ibid., ll. 40–79.

the "non-estate principle [*bezsoslovnost'*]" was unnecessary.[40] Only in June 1914 did Maklakov appoint a special conference of officials within his personal chancellery to review the question of county administration. Ironically, it was the son of V. K. Pleve, Assistant Minister N. V. Pleve, who supervised work on this issue that occurred briefly in the first autumn of the war years. In a manner reminiscent of his father before 1905, Pleve directed the discussions toward the "specifically administrative [*sobstvenno administrativnyi*]" requirements of establishing a crown-appointed "vice-governor" and a bureaucratic structure that would approximate the proposals made on the eve of emancipation. More from procedural acknowledgment of what had transpired than from an active interest in their promulgation, the conference at its initial meeting merely noted that the reform manifestos of 1903–06 had dictated far broader concerns than these: peasant and nobiliary estate distinctions in rural government, expansion of the zemstvo franchise, and extension of self-administration to the township and village.[41]

By early 1914 these civil and political initiatives of the Stolypin years were moribund as well. The project to create an all-estate village self-administration, which had never been considered by the Third Duma, in May 1913 was still buried in the MVD archives, a victim of bureaucratic indifference.[42] Despite the sounds of paper-shuffling in MVD chancelleries, earlier plans to expand the institutional authority of self-administration had largely been forgotten.[43] Indeed, in spring 1914 the MVD rejected a Progressist proposal to revive the legality (*zakonnost'*) clause of the 1864 zemstvo statute because, as it wrote in an advisory note to the Council of Ministers, possessing only "formalistic supervision" meant abandoning the overriding obligation of "a government responsible before the country and the Monarch for the success of general administration."[44]

Still more striking was the government's virtual abandonment of earlier efforts to reform the zemstvo electoral system. In February 1912, Kokovtsov's Council of Ministers termed "inadvisable" an Octobrist proposal

---

[40] TsGIA, f. 1284, op. 185 (1907), d. 5a, ch. 2, l. 128 (Ia. Ia. Litvinov to A. D. Arbuzov, 19 January 1913).

[41] "Zhurnal osobogo soveshchaniia po rassmotreniiu uezdnoi reformy pri MVD," TsGIA, f. 1282, op. 2, d. 29, ll. 46–48.

[42] TsGIA, f. 1284, op. 185 (1907), d. 5a, ll. 186–217.

[43] "Obshche-zemskaia reforma," TsGIA, f. 1288, op. 2 (1909), d. 12, ll. 15–16, and "Svedeniia o zakonodatel'nykh rabotakh po GUMKh," ibid., l. 69.

[44] TsGIA, f. 1288, op. 2 (1909), d. 12, l. 18. Generally on renewed government antagonism toward zemstvo independence, see V. S. Diakin, "Zemstvo i samoderzhavie v tret'eiiun'skoi monarkhii," in *Voprosy istorii Rossii XIX–nachala XX veka* (Leningrad, 1983), pp. 127–41.

containing the MVD tax franchise of 1907.[45] More than two years later, in May 1914, Zemstvo-Octobrists complained in the press that both Goremykin and Maklakov were indifferent to zemstvo electoral reform: at least this is the way they explained the refusal to release MVD statistical material to a Duma committee.[46] Speaking before his party's central committee in May 1913, A. D. Golitsyn vented his exasperation at government intransigence. When "the consciousness [*samosoznanie*] of the village grows unbelievably," Golitsyn remarked, the failure to open "an escape valve . . . in productive [zemstvo] work in the provinces" threatened to render the zemstvo altogether superfluous to rural society. And he was quite pessimistic about the possibility that the mood currently prevailing in the capital might prevent such a disaster. "That which we are now experiencing," Golitsyn queried, "is it not a return to the old [regime] [*k staromu*]?"[47]

Some of Golitsyn's pessimism was fed by his justifiable fears about the township zemstvo bill, which he, like Stolypin, considered to be a critical institutional instrument of acculturation and a centerpiece of any effort to restructure rural government. This bill was the only part of the 1907 local reform program still under active consideration, and it had received Duma approval in May 1911 only after that body had expanded the township's role in zemstvo self-administration. Less than enthusiastic government support for the measure continued into 1912, but N. A. Maklakov's hostility was public knowledge, and he withdrew ministerial support in 1913.[48] Yet bureaucratic indifference, as Golitsyn knew by the spring, was only one factor explaining the difficulties that the township legislation was encountering.

The bill had become the obsession of bureaucratic and noble opponents in the United Nobility and the State Council; indeed, it became the object of a striking alliance aimed at defeating the reform in the upper chamber. Nobiliary opposition to township reform had been a major focus of the Eighth Congress of the United Nobility in March 1912, which conveyed to V. N. Kokovtsov a formal resolution that the Duma bill was "wholly unacceptable."[49] Moreover, through their discussions of the project, congress delegates provided important information and support

[45] TsGIA, f. 1288, op. 2, d. 61 (1908), ll. 10–13, 22.

[46] *Novoe vremia*, 23 May 1914, p. 2, and *Russkie vedomosti*, 22 May 1914, p. 2.

[47] A. D. Golitsyn, *Blizhaishie zadachi zemskoi reforme: Doklad chleny 3-ei Gosudarstvennoi Dumy kniazia A. D. Golitsyna v zasedanie Tsentral'nogo Komiteta Soiuza 17-ogo Oktiabria 5 maia 1913 g.* (Moscow, 1913), pp. 14 and 4. See similar comments in "Iz besedy s zemtsami," *Russkie vedomosti*, 7 March 1913, p. 2, and 12 March 1913, p. 2.

[48] Stenograficheskii otchet Gosudourstvennogo Sovet (hereinafter *SOGS*), 1913–14, p. 2156, and *Russkie vedomosti*, 15 May 1914, p. 3.

[49] "Postanovleniia s"ezda," TsGAOR, f. 434, op. 1, d. 35/195, ll. 19 and l. 40 (A. A. Naryshkin to V. N. Kokovtsov).

to State Council rightists who, the Orel magnate and council member A. A. Naryshkin promised, "unanimously" opposed it.[50] Unanimity was an exaggeration, but hostility was not.

Having ignored the measure throughout the 1911–12 legislative session, a committee of the State Council finally began considering the Duma bill in February 1913. Committee rightists labeled it "not only harmful but directly fatal for Russia" if passed, and led by the former MVD ministers P. N. Durnovo and A. S. Stishinskii, along with Naryshkin, they almost succeeded in convincing the committee to refuse even to study the reform.[51] One month later, the Ninth Congress of the United Nobility again returned to the fray, dispatching to N. A. Maklakov a report with a detailed repudiation of legislation that would "cut to the very quick [*vsia tol'shcha*] of popular life [and] threaten new shocks to the life of the peasantry."[52] Considering the bill for another year, the committee largely rewrote it, adding a number of measures to protect rural propertied wealth.[53] Nevertheless, when the committee finally completed its work in April 1914, only pressure from the State Council presidium yielded the favorable vote of 14 to 13 and prevented the public scandal of a council committee rejecting its own project outright after a three-year delay.[54] Finally, in May, after four days of heated debate, the council's general assembly rejected the project, by a vote of 76 to 72, without a first reading.[55] The majority included most members of the council's right group and majorities of its right-center and zemstvo groupings.[56] Hence, some six weeks before the outbreak of World War I and some eight years after Stolypin had first advanced a similar proposal, the State Council repudiated the last vestige of rural civil reform.

In a stinging editorial that castigated the State Council's decision, *Novoe vremia* blamed the defeat on "the very ideology [*ideologiia*] of the council's majority, which clings convulsively to the debris of the past in order to keep the country from every reform that might distance it from the prerevolutionary system [*dorevoliutsionnyi stroi*]."[57] Correctly em-

[50] *Trudy sed'mogo s"ezda Upolnomochennykh Dvorianskikh Obshchestv 37 gubernii s 5 marta po 11 marta 1912 g.* (St. Petersburg, 1912), p. 274; see generally pp. 240–302.

[51] "Burnoe zasedanie volostnoi kommissii G. Soveta," *Novoe vremia*, 8 February 1913, p. 1.

[52] "Doklad soveta ... po proektu polozheniia o volostnom zemskom upravlenii," TsGAOR, f. 434, op. 1, d. 35/195, ll. 66, and ll. 112–14 (A. A. Naryshkin to N. A. Maklakov).

[53] *SOGS*, 1914, 2147–62.

[54] *Russkie vedomosti*, 20 April 1914, p. 4, and 22 April 1914, p. 3; also *Novoe vremia*, 22 April 1914, p. 3.

[55] *SOGS*, 1913–14, pp. 2147–2212, 2213–84, 2289–2352, 2354–94.

[56] "V kommissiakh i gruppakh G. Soveta," *Novoe vremia*, 16 May 1914, p. 2.

[57] "Otkaz ot zakonodatel'stva," *Novoe vremia*, 21 May 1914, pp. 4–5.

phasizing what it called ideology, the newspaper nevertheless simplified when it portrayed rightist opposition as myopic and reactionary—although one has to admit that such terms have their place in an analysis of rightist politics. The May debates of the State Council, as well as those that occurred earlier within the United Nobility, revealed a confluence of prescriptive, traditional political values that allowed for an alliance of proponents of both statist and nobiliary superordinate power against this final legacy of bureaucratic reformism. From differing perspectives, officials and nobles were able to agree, perhaps even more vociferously in the early twentieth century than some had done as younger men in the 1880s, that politics and society in rural Russia rested on the system of estates.

It was more than an ironical twist that two leading State Council opponents of township reform were the former bureaucrats Stishinskii and Durnovo. Both were hereditary nobles without family land. Both received juridical degrees and began their professional bureaucratic careers in the uncertain 1870s, Stishinskii as a young clerk in the elite State Chancellery and Durnovo, after twelve years of naval service, as a Ministry of Justice district court prosecutor. Both rose to positions of prominence in the MVD in the 1880s and 1890s.[58] Finally, both mounted adamant opposition to township reform from the statist perspective imparted by careers that spanned the 1880s and the 1905 Revolution. The existing rural administrative structure, primarily one of local MVD police officialdom imposed on a distinct system of peasant estate institutions, was an instrument to maintain political and social order. To alter it might exacerbate the threat disorder posed to the old regime.

Good bureaucrats, both Stishinskii and Durnovo devoted considerable attention in their presentations before the State Council to the complexities of the statute and its potential for excessive taxation.[59] Informing such institutional commentaries, however, was a vision of an agrarian mass population conveying the same haunting images of rural particularism, social instability, and political uncertainty that had shaped the views of statist police officials since the counterreform era. In the main, Durnovo and Stishinskii maintained in a memorandum circulated to members of the State Council, local areas remained populated by "communal peasants completely unprepared for broad participation in local self-administration given their poverty, their low intellectual level, and their political immaturity."[60] While both acknowledged that rural social transformation was taking place, they viewed it, as in the past, as a destabilizing

---

[58] "Formuliarnyi spisok," TsGIA, f. 1162, op. 6, d. 510, ll. 141ff., and d. 190, ll. 82–109.

[59] SOGS, 1913–14, pp. 2201–6 and 2300–2302.

[60] On the State Council commission, see Russkie vedomosti, 15 May 1914, p. 4, and SOGS, 1914, pp. 2147–62; on the United Nobility, see TsGAOR, f. 434, op. 1, d. 35/195, l. 66.

influence that required a defense of bureaucratic power and what remained of the local landholding elites, the only unifying centers in an uncertain agrarian environment.

Proponents of the township bill consistently refuted this perspective, emphasizing the higher quality of military draftees, the continuing success of land reform, and the remarkable growth of consumer and producer cooperative organizations as evidence of the rural population's socioeconomic and cultural development.[61] Yet particularly from Durnovo's perspective, the promise that land reform or civil development might ameliorate the underlying social antagonism in rural society was groundless, as enmity between elites and masses, he believed, was characteristic of all modern societies. "The peasant dreams [only] of obtaining a gratuitous share of somebody else's land; the workman, of getting hold of the entire capital and profits of the manufacturer," Durnovo wrote in a February memorandum to the tsar, one that perceptively warned of approaching pan-European war and "social revolution in its most extreme form" should Russia be defeated.[62] He remained under the influence of this way of thinking in May, probably assisted in no small measure by the labor strikes raging in the streets of St. Petersburg at that time. He warned the State Council that township zemstvo self-administration and self-taxation were "unthinkable" when "all thoughts of the have-nots [*neimushchie*] are directed toward taking away the land of the haves [*imushchie*]."[63] Such change could not be arrested or reversed, but police bureaucracy and peasant estate administration could defend social and political order in the provinces from its consequences. As such, both served the interests of state.

A former prosecutor and policeman, Durnovo thus did not evoke historico-cultural imagery to defend instruments that allowed the state to isolate the rural population from political radicalism. His specter was more immediate. To heed "the consistent and uninterrupted propaganda . . . from liberal books, liberal journals, and liberal circles" in favor of the all-estate zemstvo township, Durnovo maintained, would mean creating institutions where radicals could breed political and social conflict perhaps more threatening than that of 1905:

Activists like these . . . feel a need to have the people politically acculturate [*politicheskoe vospitanie*] in a certain direction, to eradicate in the people the old ways [*zavety*] and introduce them to [the activists' own ideology of] nega-

---

[61] See, for example, the speeches of Count F. A. Uvarov and A. D. Zinov'ev in *SOGS*, 1913–14, pp. 2166–72 and 2266–73.

[62] This memorandum, first published in *Krasnaia nov*, 6 (November–December, 1922), has been reprinted in a number of English translations.

[63] *SOGS*, 1913–14, p. 2300.

tion and criticism. . . . [Already] the people are beginning to resemble the stereotype of the conscious worker. . . . When agitation inevitably penetrates the new township assembly, it will find relatively prepared ground there. The new law will transfer the entire affair of local administration and [zemstvo] economy into the hands of the peasants—the same peasants who only eight years ago plundered and burned out landowners and who still harbor a lust for land at the expense of noble landowners.[64]

Durnovo discounted the proposed law as the work of "our heirs," concluding that "the very archaic conditions and relations of our life do not allow [us] to alter them radically." Social and political order in a rural society that was still particularistic and still organized, if only administratively, into estate groupings dictated stasis.

Many of the 58 State Council members elected from the provincial zemstvos and the hereditary nobility lent their support to this statist repudiation of the township. Judicious estimates of the positions taken by 41 of these individuals revealed that at least 28 of them (70 percent) voted against the reform.[65] Zemstvo representatives in this sample split almost evenly, 12 for and 13 against, but at least 15 of the total 18 State Council members elected from the hereditary nobility joined in opposing the bill. Most of this latter group had some institutional affiliation with the United Nobility. Yet unlike bureaucratic rightists, spokesmen from the nobility acted not simply from a desire to prevent rural disorder, but more from profound sociocultural apprehensions about a reform that, by "mixing the estates," was deemed to risk the privileges, influence, and identity of the nobility. Moreover, to an unprecedented degree, those nobles who advanced such arguments did so with hardly a mention of the nobility's traditions of public leadership and state service. They displayed a stunning preoccupation with their own economic affairs and an inability to represent the broader interests of a rural society in which they found their socioeconomic status threatened. Adamantly insisting that the state shape its policy to serve the nobility, that it repudiate a reform deemed to threaten the superordinate power that they derived from their manorial agriculture and institutions of rural government, these influential elected representatives of the provincial nobility displayed a castelike mentality reminiscent of the last decades of serfdom.

[64] Ibid.

[65] The identity of members was determined from the service records of State Council members found in TsGIA, f. 1162, op. 6. Determination of voting (which in some cases was not possible) was based on the following rubric: statement of position in the press (*Russkie vedomosti*, 20, 22 April 1914, or *SOGS*, 1913–14, pp. 2131–2403); party affiliation found in Veselovskii, *Istoriia zemstva*, 4:36; membership in the United Nobility in 1908–09 (TsGAOR,, f. 434, op. 1, d. 15/61, ll. 104ff.) or 1914 (TsGAOR, f. 434, op. 1, d. 7, l. 498); previous position taken in the Council on Local Economy.

As had occurred in earlier rounds of such debates, nobiliary opponents of the township excoriated the threat that excessive taxation posed to noble landholding and agriculture. Yet given the wealth of those protesting, the preoccupation seemed exaggerated, almost excessive. A. P. Strukov, a Ukrainian magnate who owned over 65,000 desiatins (175,000 acres) of land and sat in the upper chamber as a representative of the hereditary nobility, worried that township levies added to already extensive zemstvo taxation might cripple "agriculture"—a remarkable claim for someone whose extensive involvement in the sugar-beet industry placed him among the wealthiest landowners in Russia.[66] Similarly, Stolypin's brother-in-law A. B. Neidgardt, a moderate conservative who represented the Nizhnii Novgorod zemstvo and controlled hereditary and purchased family holdings in the province exceeding 4000 desiatins (11,000 acres) drew on his provincial expertise to demonstrate that a working manorial economy, whose income supported a landowning family and twenty agricultural laborers, already paid land taxes only ten times less than those levied on communal allotments. Alarmed by the threatened increase of this burden, he never mentioned either the injustice or the long duration of this very real imbalance between noble and peasant holdings.[67]

For these and other speakers, implicit in the issue of township taxation was the same disquieting image that had afflicted their bureaucratic colleagues: isolated noble landowners confronting unruly, peasant-dominated assemblies. Unlike officials, who primarily feared the insidious political agitation through which outsiders radicalized peasants, many noble members were as obsessed, if not more so, with the palpable antagonism that they perceived in the peasants in and around their estates. The Nationalist I. E. Rakovich, a former ally of Stolypin who had been appointed to the post of Podol'ia provincial marshal of the nobility by him in 1910 and who in 1914 had been elected to the State Council by the province's new zemstvo, was a prosperous provincial proprietor who had expanded his holdings by purchasing an 800-desiatin (2,200-acre) estate in the county where he had been marshal of the nobility since 1897. Rakovich insisted that further rural economic development should precede the creation of a township zemstvo, apparently preferring to await a more diversified smallholding class than to contend with the proprietorial peasantry that already inhabited the western region. Quoting "the great historian of the French revolution" Taine, he warned against the social and political disorder that excessive tampering with local institutions

---

[66] SOGS, 1913–14, pp. 2264–66.
[67] Ibid., pp. 2238–47, and "Formuliarnyi spisok," TsGIA, f. 1162, op. 6, d. 355, ll. 159ff.

might engender within "this huge ocean and sphinx that is the people."[68] D. D. Levshin of Tula province—a council representative elected from the nobility, a member of the United Nobility, and coowner with his wife of 300 hereditary desiatins (800 acres) in the county where he had served in noble offices for three decades—was less delicate than Rakovich. He knew that peasant majorities in township assemblies would further isolate the "home nests" of those noble proprietors left in the countryside after the 1905 Revolution.[69]

V. I. Karpov, who represented the nobility from Ekaterinoslav province, and who like Levshin was a United Nobleman, brought before the State Council a related argument that had dominated the more evangelical atmosphere of the organization's eighth congress in March 1912. Perceived peasant hostility had driven Karpov to withdraw from the very ideal of rural nobiliary leadership, a principle fundamental to the nobility's service identity since the late nineteenth century. He called it an "idyll" whose supporters deluded themselves with "the touching picture of enlightened leaders [from the local nobility] standing behind the masses of new [peasant] township administrators who listen humbly and [let themselves be] enlightened without objection." In fact, Karpov retorted, the measure threatened to place the entire administration of the empire "in the hands of the least cultured and most inert mass of the population."[70] At the 1912 congress, when Prince A. A. Kropotkin of Saratov defended the ideal of noblesse oblige "to lead the people [rukovodit' narod]," he provoked an outraged response.[71] This was an "idyll," said V. N. Oznobishin of Saratov. The "bringing together [sblizhenie]" of nobles and peasants was as unrealizable as "equal rights for Jews" in Russian society, jabbed rightist publicist K. F. Golovnin of Tver.[72] D. N. Khovanko of Kharkov stated with remarkable candor that nobles could not be "mixed into the general mass [obshchaia massa]" because that act would "destroy our distinct independent position, which alone gives us influence in the local areas." He emphasized the very essence of the nobility's superordinate relationship with the local population:

> I possess influence not because I possess a voice among the peasantry, but because my own position, which is to be found outside the peasantry [vne krest'ianstva], places me above it and gives me the opportunity to give it that advice and those orders that, once we are not talking about taking away my

[68] SOGS, 1913–14, p. 2224; and "Formuliarnyi spisok," TsGIA, f. 1162, op. 6, d. 781, ll. 8–13.
[69] SOGS, 1913–14, pp. 2302–8, and "Formuliarnyi spisok," TsGIA, f. 1162, op. 6, d. 735, ll. 27–35.
[70] SOGS, 1913–14, pp. 2308, 2311–13.
[71] Trudy VIII s"ezda, pp. 258–59.
[72] Ibid., pp. 263–67.

land, it will accept because it senses in me a power that is useful to it and beyond it. . . . What peasant will listen to someone lower than he?[73]

Critics within the State Council pilloried this increasingly rigid isolationist mentality, which relied so exclusively on the particularism of the power and status of the nobility. To relinquish the nobility's obligation of rural public service and leadership, they insisted, was to withdraw from all ability to exert influence in rural society: an act of political irresponsibility that placed the autocratic order at risk. Indeed, so stark was this abandonment of the nobility's service traditions that criticism of it came not from State Council liberals, but from elected zemstvo representatives with well-established conservative pedigrees. Most remarkable in this regard was the representative of the Saratov zemstvo, Count D. A. Olsuf'ev. A wealthy landowner and a conservative activist even before the 1905 Revolution, Olsuf'ev, it will be recalled, had helped in 1907 to mobilize provincial opposition to Stolypin's zemstvo program. Some seven years later, he was "a convinced adherent" of township reform. What in earlier days had seemed to be an excessively liberal, even radical measure sponsored by unreliable government bureaucrats by 1914 had become a necessary act of statesmanship. The extremism of rightist politics had rendered Olsuf'ev a moderate.

Distinguishing the "right wing of zemstvo Russia" from that of the State Council, Olsuf'ev repudiated the latter's "blind conservatism" and pointed out its two primary defects. Council rightists, he knew, were ignoring the socioeconomic transformation of the rural society in which they lived. "A strong patriarchal structure" no longer existed there; "age and authority, youth and obedience [were] no longer synonymous" in a village that had "become diverse [*pestroe*]—communal peasants, smallholders, commercial traders, and [in the cooperative movement] even its own third element." Second, in refusing to seek "the conditions of amicable, neighborly work" that the township might create, they forgot that "the political interests" of the nobility required that it regain "its lost influence in the village" and prevent its displacement by "other leaders of the peasant mass." Olsuf'ev reminded his listeners of the years before 1905–06. Then, too, "many noble conservatives [*konservatory-dvoriane*] had wanted to ignore the existing zemstvo" and had become active in local affairs only after destructive agrarian unrest. Virulent opposition to the township bill, he feared, indicated that influential noble leaders of the provincial nobility were once again lapsing into a particularistic preoccupation with their own affairs and abandoning their broader responsibilities to national politics. "Again," Olsuf'ev declaimed, "we propose to the dvorianstvo that it withdraw from public affairs, that it go off to its

[73] Ibid., p. 263.

own nests and give itself over to its former political idleness." Echoing the words of his former Saratov opponent, P. A. Stolypin, Olsuf'ev warned that the State Council's "refusal to govern" would bring "the machine [of state] to a complete standstill."[74]

Several other prominent zemtsy agreed with these sentiments—although their minority status among the more extremist representatives of the hereditary nobility should be reiterated. Most vociferous was F. A. Uvarov of the Moscow zemstvo, who contributed a detailed portrayal of cooperatives and ad hoc zemstvo institutions, which in many instances the population itself was establishing to service rural society.[75] He feared that the State Council was letting slip "a final opportunity . . . to fill in the chasm that more and more broadly divides peasants and [nobles] in the provinces."[76] A second articulate—and, given his history, shocking—advocate of the measure was V. I. Gurko, who in 1914 was a representative of the Tver zemstvo who had qualified for election using the 800-desiatin (2,200-acre) hereditary estate that he owned in this former provincial bastion of Russian liberalism.[77] In 1906–07 this powerful assistant minister of internal affairs had been more concerned with the long-term stabilization of proprietorial landholding than with civil or political reforms, and in 1908 he had aided the United Nobility in its campaign against them. By 1914, however, Gurko had reappraised his analysis and arrived at several disturbing conclusions.

Gurko saw the State Council's repudiation of the "liberal" township bill to be yet another instance of the political polarization growing within both government and society, which, he feared, was stalemating moderate reform and necessary socioeconomic progress. Singling out his former bureaucratic colleagues, Gurko knew that some "conservatives fear any initiative that comes from liberal circles; they see in each such proposition . . . almost a desire to establish or propagandize social revolution [sotsi-al'naia revoliutsiia]."[78] If he was chastened by such extremism, he was positively perplexed by opponents in the nobility who failed to recognize that the provincial nobility's leadership in local society now hung in the balance. Above all else this realization pushed him to approve a reform that, if it required "a political label," he termed "profoundly conservative." Peasants and local nobiliary elites, Gurko declaimed, were indeed increasingly "separate [razroznennye]" and "antagonistic parts of the rural population." A burgeoning rural cooperative movement was indeed

[74] SOGS, 1913–14, pp. 2290–97.

[75] SOGS, 1913–14, pp. 2165–72.

[76] Ibid., pp. 2387 and 2381–87. See also the comments of D. M. Kalachov of the Iaroslavl' zemstvo, pp. 2213–17.

[77] "Formuliarnyi spisok," TsGIA, f. 1162, op. 6, d. 681.

[78] SOGS, 1913–14, p. 2197.

usurping many functions of the zemstvo and hence the public work that noble zemstvo men could perform. And third-element professionals would indeed find greater opportunity in new township institutions for "concrete, vital" employment that would distract them from "the world of abstractions [and] the world of utopias" that had supposedly radicalized them. Yet these premises were being repudiated, and Gurko expressed his deep concern that council rightists were abandoning to others—third-element employees, cooperative organizations, political radicals, and the peasantry itself—the obligations of the provincial nobility in the countryside:

> The time is coming, and it is not far off, when you will complain bitterly about [delaying this measure], but by then it will be too late. They will not let you into the township . . . because although you will be there, your influence will not. . . . I implore you, gentlemen, you are on a false path, you are deceiving yourselves. This is your last cup of salvation, and you are flippantly refusing it.[79]

In the final analysis, however, such criticisms of rightist myopia and the increasingly castelike mentality within the nobility made little impression. Indeed, prominent rightists vociferously denied them. Count A. A. Bobrinskii, an appointee of the tsar to the State Council and a former chair of the United Nobility, took umbrage at charges that the Russian nobility was indulging in the same kind of reactionary impulses as the French nobility before 1789. Unlike that "closed aristocratic caste based on feudal principles," the hereditary nobility, Bobrinskii proclaimed in ritualistic fashion, remained "a service estate, whose doors are always open to those from other estates." It acted not as an isolated group but as "a gigantic force imbibing and reflecting the mind-set [umozrenie], the beliefs, and the consciousness of the Russian people."[80]

Propounding rhetoric that flew in the face of much evidence adduced at these debates came easily to the aged A. A. Naryshkin as well. An elected representative of the nobility and vice-chair of the United Nobility, Naryshkin simply termed reform "unnecessary." A central figure in similar disputes since the 1880s, Naryshkin was well aware, as were all rightists, that agrarian transformation threatened the role of the hereditary nobility within the state. Yet, Naryshkin's reaction to the threat was to suggest that existing police-estate township administration would preserve order and the influence of the nobility in the provinces. He therefore demanded that the state avoid any administrative change that might undermine the nobility's privileges, justifying his stand with a portrayal of

[79] Ibid., pp. 2199–2200.
[80] Ibid., pp. 2233–2235.

superordinate nobiliary authority more commensurate with the pre-reform year 1839, when he was born, than the early twentieth century, which he had lived to see:

> Whoever says that the peasantry is at present too weak economically, and insufficiently developed intellectually, to act well in public institutions expresses the opinion of the peasantry itself, which wants to be administered and administered well. Concerning those nobles who remain in local areas, [holding] firmly to their roots and not selling their estates, their situation is not easy, and I think that it is not worthwhile to summon them to [the new institution]—they act without it and act for the good of the entire local population, never denying it cooperation, they help it in all its needs, both material and moral. I suggest that peace has established itself little by little in the village milieu, and, I repeat, you cannot guarantee this peace and good morals with regulations.[81]

Were Bobrinskii and Naryshkin mouthing antiquated rhetoric to disguise a calculated defense of the nobility's socioeconomic privilege? To be sure, references to the service traditions of the hereditary nobility or the cultural peculiarities of agrarian Russia were heard less frequently in these debates than previously. More often than not they were articulated by proponents of reform as reminders of once honored obligations in rural society and the dangers that their neglect posed to state stability. Opponents expressed a much greater concern with perceived threats to the nobility's economic and social dominance in the countryside, but it would be a mistake to regard the comments of a Bobrinskii or Naryshkin as remnants of a mentality quickly receding before an awakening Russian Junkerdom defending its class interests.[82] The sentiments with which noble rightists had repudiated the all-estate township zemstvo reflected those of a service estate disintegrating into a closed caste mentality, a nobility whose prominent representatives identified particularistic concerns for their own local economic and social status as the principle interests of the autocracy.

In May 1914 M. O. Menshikov, writing a perceptive summary of these events for *Novoe vremia*, commented that two "noble viewpoints" had clashed when the State Council defeated township reform. Obvious alienation between nobility and peasantry, at times resembling the "hostile relations of Europeans to the population of uncivilized [colonial] countries," had motivated the "relatively liberal" view advocated by Olsuf'ev and Gurko. They recognized the danger in a situation that would undermine the nobility's traditional "leading role" in local life; without the one, "the people was deprived of [its] cultured element, and without the

---

[81] Ibid., pp. 2324.
[82] Becker, *Nobility and Privilege*, chap. 8.

people, the nobility was deprived of its raison d'être as the highest estate [*vyshee soslovie*]." Moreover, Menshikov remarked, proponents of the bill also realized that refusal to establish the township would leave nobiliary elites almost powerless in a rural society whose own development was producing new educated strata now filling cooperatives and zemstvo third-element staffs—"all these popular teachers, agronomists, veterinarians, statisticians, insurance agents, store clerks, accountants, secretaries, mechanics, and so on [who] constitute a new educated estate, who are a part of the people and are closer to the people than the nobles are."[83]

Yet these arguments, Menshikov knew, had been ignored by noble opponents from the nobility in both the State Council and the United Nobility who found "the fundamental idea" of township reform "odious [*protivna*]." "The mixing of nobles with peasants and townsmen [*meshchane*], the de facto equality of estates" was, for many nobles, "psychologically unbearable."

> Interspersed within the grey peasant world [*mir*], little nooks of pomeshchik culture, these oases of civilization, will be sacrificed to the village masses who will in the end consume them. . . . Old nobles sense this, and this is the primary but usually unstated argument that led a congress of the united nobility of 33 provinces and the State Council to oppose the all-estate township and the small zemstvo unit.

A conservative commentator himself, Menshikov did not deny the "cultural consciousness and political instinct" evident among "the reactionary part of the nobility." Indeed, cultural and political traditions grounded its perceptions, but here was "the tragedy of their situation: they felt themselves to be *dvoriane . . .* and *organically could not* [emphasis in original] recognize themselves simply as citizens of Russia." Moreover, Menshikov concluded, this crippling disability was also a tragedy for the country, as "estate antagonism" between nobility and peasantry was not a fiction but a reality resulting from an inescapable, historic inequality between them. Even to attempt rationalizing it with the argument that "such antagonism should not exist" because service offered ennoblement to all, including the peasant, was "senseless." Perhaps, Menshikov chided, "the peasantry would accept a closed caste [*zamknutnaia kasta*] more readily than an open one," for at least the former possessed "a justification of its unique nature and accompanying attributes."

With such evidence before him, Menshikov doubted that the nobility possessed the perspicacity or will to outgrow its isolated position in Russian society. Another social structure and a new elite were necessary to effect this transformation and even Menshikov, archnationalist and ad-

---

[83] "Soslovnyi razdor," *Novoe vremia*, 24 May 1914, p. 4.

herent of autocracy, had difficulties articulating precisely where this brave new world might be. Menshikov called for "fundamental estate reform" to eliminate all its distinctions from imperial law and thereby "prepare an environment [*sreda*] distinguished by attributes beyond *soslovnost'* [*priznaki vne soslovnosti*]." "But," Menshikov concluded, "to rise above narrow estate [*uzkososlovnye*] interests to a state and civil perspective [*na vysotu gosudarstvennuiu i grazhdanskuiu*] requires an entirely different enthusiasm of spirit, which in our day is strange even to discuss."[84]

[84] Ibid.

Conclusion

ON THE EVE of the war, the Russian autocracy possessed an institutional system far more extensive and effective than that with which "enlightened officials" of the mid-nineteenth century had confronted serfdom. The administrative apparatus and supervisory bureaucracy of the state, together with the institutions of self-administration, justice, and political representation that it had created, allowed the central government to retain its dominant position in society and, after 1905, in national politics as well. And yet, as the empire mobilized for a conflict that would prove its undoing, the autocracy of Nicholas II did not govern as much as it ruled, ever more dependent on police power and the superordinate persona of the reigning sovereign to secure its place in a body politic becoming quite rapidly modern. Autocratic state power, which had played such a critical—if at times ill-defined—role in fostering Russian modernization, lacked authority, and thus legitimacy and relevance in national life.

From the time of the emancipation until the first turbulent years of the twentieth century, officials of the central government had foreseen and attempted to forestall this isolation. A central concern of this work has been to understand the conscious effort ministerial reformers made to accommodate the institutions and practice of the autocratic old regime to what they perceived to be a more progressive and pan-European era of civil and political equality. With remarkable persistence officials had striven to restructure the state in response to this transformation, an effort they deemed essential if the state was to guide an old order, which serfdom had shaped, toward the new social and political structures that industrial modernity required. Attempts to construct the Rechtsstaat—to rationalize institutions, imbue their personnel with a legal ethos, and create the civil stability necessary for individual initiative—thus became a primary objective, however distant its success might have seemed, for several generations of state reformers beginning with the officials of the Editing Commissions. Certainly by the time of Loris-Melikov, and then strikingly with Witte and Stolypin, these same officials began to appreciate the political consequences of socioeconomic change and, rather than trying to suppress them, acknowledged that the long-term authority of the state order they served dictated the utilization of state power to mobilize political support for themselves and for the government they intended to lead. Indeed, in this regard, Stolypin, although his efforts were the most concerted, stood at the end of a succession of reformist officials who had sought reform since the emancipation in order to ground the legitimacy of autocratic authority in its capacity to govern civil society and, following the 1905 Revolution, influence national politics in support of a reformed autocratic order as well. This work has attempted to suggest that, by the eve of the war, the failure of Stolypin's efforts reflected the broader failure that bureaucratic reformism had experienced in Russian national life. What had happened?

In the first instance failure was due to the tutelary and superordinate imperatives that historically had shaped Russian bureaucratic government, a heritage of problems deriving from serfdom, which officials who sought to guide and transform society exacerbated as often as they alleviated. Whether it was Nikolai Miliutin intent upon investing police power in the self-administering institutions of the newly emancipated peasantry; Loris-Melikov prosecuting revolutionary extremism; Witte combating public initiative as he attempted to coopt it; or Stolypin flouting the law in an attempt to achieve his "political ideals"—no official, however truly odious they found such methods to be, hesitated to rely on supralegal measures if they considered them necessary to achieve the higher interests of state as defined in their programmatic goals. Moreover, the most progressive tsarist officials remained in the final analysis conservators of order—*poriadok*—which had been and remained the most fundamental interest of the autocratic state. The connotation of this ubiquitous word, as the history of late imperial reform makes evident, became quite complex: the socioeconomic, fiscal, and public-moral concerns of the early nineteenth century acquired distinctively civil, proprietorial, and political contexts within a half-century. Yet, however diverse its meanings, the preservation of order was one primary raison d'être of autocratic administration, because in this objective lay the foundation of the institutional power and authority that would, in the minds of these reformers, ultimately guarantee stability to a society in which a mass population testified to the fundamental social and cultural instability of its society and culture.

That peasants were unprepared for life in civil society—an assumption that had dominated the debates of the Editing Commissions in the late 1850s—resounded with numbing regularity down through the entire late imperial era. Even officials who hoped that facilitating the evolutionary development of Russian society would allow a reformed autocracy to survive the demands of the twentieth century cautiously trod the line that divided civil progress—which state power, law, and institutions could control and supervise—from the unacculturated world of peasant "land and liberty" that potentially threatened to explode the civic culture whose isolation these reformers felt so acutely. To that extent, reformist initiatives, far-reaching as they were, hesitated to go too far toward the mass politics that were beginning to dominate Europe in the early twentieth century. The paradox of Stolypin—a statesman dedicated to the social and political reconstruction of autocratic Russia, who undertook a coup d'état to effect such change—testified most poignantly to the self-imposed constraints of the reformist perspective.

Yet to leave the analysis of late imperial reform at this level trivializes the larger sociocultural dilemmas that societal transformation raised for those officials attempting to encourage it. In recent years, historians have increasingly questioned the degree to which Russian "modernization" succeeded in leveling an ascriptive order of particularistic estates and in creating a universalistic civil society of classes. The question is nuanced and still unresolved—as the variety of analyses advanced to answer it indicates. Viewing the problem primarily in cultural terms, Gregory Freeze sees the estate order gaining strength and resilience at the end of the old regime. Seymour Becker, regarding the capitalistic agriculture and professional activity that increasingly preoccupied noble landowners with the same fascination it generated in Witte, believes estates were archaic legal constructs that bore increasingly less normative power in Russia's emerging class society. Alfred Rieber, speaking of the commercial-industrial bourgeoisie that never resolved the contradictions inherent in its heritage as a merchant estate and its more modern activity as an autonomous entrepreneurial class, or Leopold Haimson, when he discusses the "Januslike character" of a landowning nobility immersed in its traditions as a service estate, come closer to the mark in capturing the complex, confused, transitional character of social processes that partially, but never fully, articulated the new structures of life that were replacing the old.[1] Both in terms of the institutions through which they administered and the societal reality that shaped their *mentalité*, ministerial reformers themselves were caught in this milieu. That fact must balance critical judgments of their timidity with admiration for the conviction with which they sought to establish the legal and institutional constructs that would hasten the emergence of a modern civil society: the social and political foundation, they believed, of a reformed autocratic order.

Whether or not their analysis was correct—an issue that awaits further historical investigation, this work has attempted to demonstrate that bureaucratic efforts to define and fortify a civic political culture evoked debilitating opposition within the autocracy's elites. Indeed, given the unresolved, transitional nature of Russian social transformation, defenders of an autocratic political culture possessed abundant evidence to prove that such attempts would be an intolerable affront to systems of superor-

---

[1] Freeze, "The Soslovie Paradigm"; Becker, *Nobility and Privilege*; Rieber, *Merchants and Entrepreneurs*; and Haimson, "Conclusion," in *Politics of Rural Russia*.

dinate power and ascriptive status that, if perhaps no longer in the cities, still bore normative power in a rural society on whose stability the autocratic state depended. Particularly after the "first and second crises of autocracy" in 1881 and 1905, such opposition—found at court, in the ministerial apparatus, in the legislative chambers after their creation, and within the ranks of the provincial nobility—undermined the advocacy of law, civil reform, and political legitimacy that had been advanced by reformers.

Two very different sources fed this opposition. Advocates of ministerial police power, whose influence within the Ministry of Internal Affairs became pronounced during the decade of the counterreforms, regarded the agrarian social transformation that reformers were attempting to channel toward future civil stability as an immediate threat to public order, property, and the preservation of autocratic authority. Adding fears of economic impoverishment and political radicalization to the more traditional suspicion with which elites had regarded the subordinate masses even before emancipation, these officials heatedly defended, in debates of local reform, the system of peasant estate administration and segregation that the legislation of the counterreforms had done so much to rigidify. In the broader context of autocratic politics, they believed that bureaucratic hegemony and the autocracy's monopolization of power and authority were the sole instruments capable of preserving the old regime from the rural social conflict and political disorder rampant in a particularistic agrarian world. Like good policemen, they were the thin front line separating order from chaos, culture from dissipation, and autocratic authority from the political radicalism assaulting it.

Adherents of nobiliary power—one thinks first of Pazukhin as a symbolic totem of such opinion—were strange bedfellows for police officials, given the suspicious resentment that had so often characterized the relations between provincial nobility and ministerial bureaucracy in the last decades of imperial rule. Yet particularly once the rural uprisings and Duma elections of 1906 had worked their traumatic influence on the *mentalité* of the first estate of the realm, police order was the only means by which the status of the nobility in the countryside could be protected from the otherwise overwhelming forces of political and social change beating against it. Thus, police power and the bulwarks of peasant estate administration that it patrolled served a far greater goal. By protecting manorial property and nobiliary preeminence in local public life against the threats of radicalism and renewed popular upheaval, they allowed provincial nobles, on the one hand, to defend what remained of the bonds of community that had historically united nobility and peasantry and, thus on the other, to see themselves as being uniquely qualified to mediate between the demands of the center and the needs of the local populace.

State institutions thereby could preserve—and were required to do so—the service to the autocracy that history and contemporary life ascribed to members of the hereditary noble estate. Despite so much evidence that rural development was rendering the estate society that had justified such attitudes anachronistic, by 1914 prominent spokesmen of the provincial nobility found the hegemonic missives of a Stishinskii or a Durnovo far more comforting than they had found the risky speculation of a Stolypin. Rather than "reform at a time of revolution," state interests demanded nobiliary preeminence in the provinces, even if the growing caste mentality of this nobility threatened to make rural society a timebomb ticking at the very heart of the autocratic order.

To be sure, such opposition was only one aspect of Russia's prewar history. Some might argue that its obstruction and ultimate defeat of a circumscribed bureaucratic reformism was a relatively inconsequential spasm within an ever more isolated right wing of the Russian political spectrum. Yet it would seem that the conflict that arose here, and the inability of state reformers to defuse it, did indeed contribute to the polarization of Russian politics and the elimination of the public support necessary for moderate, centrist reform. Moreover, the social crisis that dominated urban Russia by the eve of the war found a resonance, however faint, in the countryside. There, despite the significant impact of land reform, growing agricultural productivity, and rural development in general, influential elements of both bureaucratic and nobiliary elites saw in the very fact of socioeconomic transformation a fundamental challenge to the social and political structures of the old regime—a challenge that, despite Stolypin's efforts, old Russia proved to be incapable of meeting.

A. O. Menshikov had plaintively observed in May 1914 that Russia required statesmen and citizens to assure future progress. Stolypin, its greatest statesman, however, was dead, his reform plans left to the hands of inquiring historians. Another reformer, V. I. Gurko, stood forlornly in the State Council as a representative of the Tver zemstvo, warning his former ministerial colleagues that their political myopia was endangering the very state order that they claimed to protect. The first rank of Russia's citizens was filled by members of the noble estate (*dvorianstvo*) who, despite the calls of some like Olsuf'ev that they resume the role of public leadership that had been a hallmark of the nobleman's identity, were ensnared in a particularistic preoccupation with their own affairs. On the eve of the war, ancien régime Russia was served by bureaucratic administrators and a nobility exposed to the mentality of caste. Both wielded "legitimate" power because both subordinated themselves to the superordinate authority of the autocratic tsar, an authority increasingly superfluous to the country over which it reigned. Herein lay one fundamental, ultimately fatal failing of the political order of the old regime.

Glossary

Article 87 — A provision of the Fundamental Laws of the Empire as they were issued in 1906. Article 87 provided that during periods when the State Duma and State Council were in recess, the emperor could decree legislation to have the force of law until such time as both chambers approved, amended, or rejected it. Stolypin used this provision legally in 1906 to promulgate reform legislation, used it illegally in June 1907 to issue a new electoral law, and then illegally again in 1911 to issue the western zemstvo legislation. Article 87 was broadly viewed as a legal formality through which the government could circumvent the legislature.

curia or *curiae* (pl.) — Electoral assemblies. These institutions provided the indirect systems of electing deputies to both the zemstvo and the State Duma. Electoral assemblies were defined on the basis of wealth, landed property, and, to some degree, membership in *sosloviia*.

desiatina — A measure of land equal to 2.7 acres.

dvorianstvo — The service estate of the nobility, often called the "first estate of the realm." The privileges, rights, and duty of service that marked the status of each Russian noble (*dvorianin*) and all nobles (*dvoriane*) together were defined both by law and historical tradition.

four-tailed suffrage — The term used in 1904–06 to convey the most liberal definition of the system necessary to elect deputies to the State Duma. Balloting was to be (1) secret, (2) direct (as opposed to the multitiered indirect system eventually utilized), (3) universal (despite pronounced movements in favor of female suffrage, more often than not applied only to adult males, but without the distinctions of ethnicity eventually adopted), and (4) equal (one person–one vote, as opposed to those considerations of legal status and wealth eventually used to define the franchise).

gosudarstvennost' — State self-consciousness. A term found repeatedly in the public statements of the Stolypin ministry and press organs supportive of its policies. It was a deliberate play on the word *obshchestvennost'*, or public self-consciousness, which was fixed firmly in the lexicon of Russian liberalism and conveyed the meaning of public autonomy. When opposed to *obshchestvennost'*, *gosudarstvennost'* conveyed the idea that without the autocratic state there could not be a nation. Here, the term is usually understood to mean national state, rather than nation-state.

Kadets, Kadet Party — An acronym (K-D) for Constitutional-Democratic Party, which formed in October 1905. The party drew political support from the cities—especially from their professional classes—and from liberal elements in the provincial landowning nobility that had been active in the zemstvo before the 1905 Revolution. Deemed the primary proponent of liberalism in Russian politics, the Kadet Party at times espoused a legislative agenda, whose contents, especially in the halcyon days of the First Duma, ranged far from the traditional positions of liberalism to embrace a constituent assembly and the forced sale of private property to resolve the land question.

krest'ianstvo, krest'iane, krest'ianin — The peasantry, peasants, peasant. In the nineteenth and twentieth centuries, the terms could be understood to mean a service estate or a class. In either case, they concealed a confusing diversity of economic, social, and cultural distinctions.

meshchanstvo, meshchane, meshchanin — The estate of the lower urban classes or townspeople, townspeople, townsman. These terms, particularly when used by members of the higher nobility, the intelligentsia, or some officials, could have a perjorative connotation.

miroedy — Individual peasants who, by economic exploitation of their fellow villagers, lived at the expense of the *mir*, or commune. In the discourse of officialdom, the word had a very perjorative connotation for those who viewed uncontrolled rural economic transformation with trepidation.

narod — "The people," often equivalent to the German *Volk*. The word had a variety of connotations depending on the perspective of the individual: a premodern and monarchist "rural populace"; the "rural masses"; or the people, understood as a precondition of national existence.

October Manifesto — The Sovereign Manifesto of 17 October 1905, the symbolic turning point of the first Russian Revolution of 1905–07. Its chief provision was the promised grant of legislative powers to the State Duma and thus the formal termination of the tsar's unrestricted political authority. The extent to which this promise was, or could be, fulfilled became an issue that subsequently dominated imperial Russian politics and, later, the writing of Russian history.

Octobrism — Used here to convey the political perspective of the Union of 17 October (1905), or the Octobrists. This moderate conservative political organization, which drew its support primarily from the ranks of the provincial landowning nobility, formed in 1905–06 on a platform of accepting the October Manifesto as a basis to begin the political and social reform of the old regime. During the period of the Third Duma (1907–12), the Octobrists controlled the single largest bloc of votes in the legislative assembly. Stolypin invested much of his political capital in an ultimately unsuccessful attempt to make the party a centrist foundation on which to build a cooperative relationship between government and Duma parties.

oprichnina — The royal bailiwick created in 1565 by Ivan the Terrible, subsequently a symbol of arbitrary absolutism in Russian history. During the conflict over the Stolypin program of local reforms, rightist provincial nobles adopted the term as an analogy with which to condemn the purported bureaucratic absolutism of the premier.

pomeshchik — Translated here as noble landowner or noble landowner-pomeshchik. The term, which was in use both before and after the abolition of serfdom, conveyed the involvement of the Russian nobility in manorial agriculture and, more broadly, life and service in the countryside.

Progressists, or *Progressisty* — A small but prominent political party whose fraction wielded an important swing vote in the Fourth Duma, 1912–17. The party was regarded as a left-of-center voice, articulating the views of industrial and business interests. Its political assertiveness derived less from big business as a whole and was more a product of the so-called big bourgeoisie of Moscow, its chief press organ, *Utro Rossii*, and especially the most prominent spokesman for both, the textile magnate A. I. Konovalov.

raznochintsy — Literally, people of varied rank, or plebians. This term of public discourse was used from the mid-nineteenth century on to characterize those individuals in Russian society who were not easily classified in one or another service estate. For conservative officials and conservative public opinion, the word possessed the connotation of political radicalism as well.

Rechtsstaat — The legal state, a political structure for wielding power and authority controlled by law and the respect for law that it inculcated in those who administered the state. Never a reality of Russian life, government by law and not by human will was one ideal of later imperial Russian officialdom.

sanovnik — An advisor of the tsar, whose influence derived less from rank and more from the personal relationship and trust that existed between sovereign and servitor.

sel'skoe obshchestvo — Village community, an institution of peasant self-administration and the smallest rural territorial jurisdiction that served to administer the peasantry. Often, the village community did not correspond to actual patterns of village settlement; one village community could encompass several neighboring villages or several village communities could divide one larger village. Throughout the post-emancipation era, the village community remained an estate institution that by law administered only peasants.

Socialist-Revolutionaries (S-Rs) — The underground political party, formed in 1901–02, that had inherited and in part reshaped the ideals of nineteenth-century radical populism. Given its roots in both radical terrorism and rural political organization, the Socialist-Revolutionaries were generally regarded by the government to be a subversive and illegitimate political organization.

soslovie, sosloviia (pl.), *soslovnost'* — Translated here as service estate or estate of the realm to distinguish it from *sostoianie* (see below). All native-born Russians, and some non-Russian imperial subjects, belonged to an estate either from birth or on the basis of status earned through some form of state service. The chief estates were the nobility (*dvorianstvo*), the clergy (*dukhovenstvo*), the merchantry (*kupechestvo*), the townspeople (*meshchanstvo*), and the peasantry (*krest'ianstvo*). The product of prolonged historical processes though which the autocratic state had sought to assure itself personnel and funds, Russian law in the late imperial era continued to define social status in terms of obligations of service, which each estate bore, and rights and privileges, which each thereby enjoyed. As opposed to *sostoianie*, the term *soslovie* possessed much more pronounced cultural and social connotations, as witnessed by the word *soslovnost'*, which conveyed the ethos created by belonging to a *soslovie*.

sostoianie or *sostoianiia* (pl.) — Legal status or standing. Russian law accorded legal standing to all subjects of the empire according to whether they were native-born ethnic Russians, non-Russian ethnic minorities, foreign-born nationals, or members of one or another of the estates (*sosloviia*) of the realm. In public discourse during the late imperial era, the terms *sostoianie* and *soslovie* were at times used interchangeably. The former, however, possessed a more legalistic and institutionalized connotation.

starshina — The elder, usually the elected officer of peasant volost' self-administration. This peasant—who, judging from official government investigations, was often semi-literate—was the primary executive officer through whom acted a wide array of higher organs—police, bureaucratic, zemstvo, and judicial.

State Council — A legislative advisory council of state first created in 1801. Its members, primarily ministers and retired senior officials, were appointed by the crown. In 1906 the State Council was converted into a second, upper legislative chamber to serve as a guarantee against the expected political radicalism of the State Duma. Approximately one-half of its membership was elected from various corporative bodies: the universities, commercial-industrial organizations, provincial zemstvo assemblies, and the hereditary nobility.

State Duma — The lower of the two legislative chambers that existed in the empire after 1906. It was created by the Soveriegn Manifesto of 19 February 1905, the Sovereign Manifesto of 17 October 1905, and subsequent legislation. Although its rights and representative character were constrained in a number of ways, it was an elected body that possessed legislative authority. No legislation could become law without its approval. Four Dumas existed in the period 1906–17.

Third of June system — A term first used in Soviet historiography to describe the political system that existed in Russia after the promulgation of the electoral law of 3 June 1907. The primary characteristics and viability of this system have been and continue to be a subject of debate for historians in both the USSR and the West.

Trudoviki — A Duma political grouping or fraction during the period of the First and Second Dumas. The *Trudoviki* were a loosely knit group of peasant deputies who stood to the left of the Kadets in the legislative assembly. Their insistent demand for a radical resolution of the land question, including broad expropriation of private property, was a critical element in the crisis atmosphere that permeated the central government in 1906–07.

uchastok — Translated here as district; a rural territorial jurisdiction intermediate between the township and the country. Each land captain after 1889 supervised an *uchastok* that was amalgamated from several townships.

uezd — Translated here as county. These territorial jurisdictions were the primary units of Russian rural administration outside the provincial capital.

volost' — Translated here as rural township, a territorial jurisdiction intermediate between the village community and the county. By the terms of the emancipation legislation of 1861, the *volost'* was also an institution of peasant public self-administration. Over subsequent decades, however, it became a territorial jurisdiction whose chief elected officer, the *volost' starshina*, was utilized extensively as an executive agent of both state administration and zemstvo self-administration. Throughout the post-emancipation era, the *volost'* remained an estate institution that by law administered only peasants.

zemstvo — Elected institution of rural self-administration first established in 1864 and somewhat altered in 1890. Zemstvo institutions existed in both provinces and counties of Great Russia proper and were extended into other areas, most notably parts of the Western borderlands, by 1914. They were charged to administer the "zemstvo economy" or public infrastructure of these local areas and to raise tax revenues and employ salaried professionals for that purpose. The zemstvo's contributions to the development of health care, primary education, statistical work, agronomic aid, etc. have been studied often. The governing body of these organs was an assembly of delegates, elected to three-year terms, who met annually to discuss zemstvo business and review the work of the zemstvo executive board, which managed the zemstvo's business throughout the year and whose chair was elected by the assembly. The asembly itself, said to represent all local "propertied interests," was elected through a complex system that gave a preponderant voice to landowners from the provincial nobility.

zemtsy — This term applied to those individuals who were active in zemstvo affairs, either as assembly delegates or zemstvo board chairmen. They were often, but not always, landowners of the hereditary nobility; their politics were often liberal, but could be conservative as well.

Bibliography

I. ARCHIVAL SOURCES

A. *Tsentral'nyi Gosudarstvennyi Istoricheskii Arkhiv SSSR (TsGIA)*

f. 899   (A. A. Bobrinskii)
f. 1162 (State Council)
f. 1276 (Council of Ministers)
f. 1282 (Chancellory of the Minister, MVD)
f. 1283 (Chancellory on Affairs of the Nobililty, MVD)
f. 1284 (Department of General Affairs, MVD)
f. 1288 (Main Administration on Affairs of Local Economy, MVD)
f. 1291 (Land Section, MVD)
f. 1662 (P. A. Stolypin)

B. *Tsentral'nyi Gosudarstvennyi Arkhiv Oktiabr'skoi Revoliutsii (TsGAOR)*

f. 115 (Union of 17 October)
f. 434 (Permanent Council of the United Nobility)
f. 483 (United Nobility)

II. PUBLISHED IMPERIAL GOVERNMENT DOCUMENTS

Doklad i zhurnaly vysochaishe uchrezhdennoi komissii dlia issledovaniia ny-neishego polozheniia sel'skogo khoziastva i sel'skoi proizvoditel'nosti v Rossii. St. Petersburg, 1873.
Garmiza, V. V. "Predlozheniia i proekty P. A. Valueva po voprosam vnutrennoi politiki (1862–1866)." *Istoricheskii arkhiv* 1 (1958): 138–52.
Gosudarstvennaia Duma. *Obzor deiatel'nosti gosudarstvennoi dumy, tret'ego sozyva, chast' vtoraia, zakonodatel'naia deiatel'nost'.* St. Petersburg, 1912.
———. *Stenograficheskie otchety Gosudarstvennoi Dumy pervogo sozyva.* St. Petersburg, 1906.
———. *Stenograficheskie otchety Gosudarstvennoi Dumy vtorogo sozyva.* St. Petersburg, 1907.
———. *Stenograficheskie otchety Gosudarstvennoi Dumy tret'ego sozyva.* St. Petersburg, 1912.
———. *Ukazatel' k stenograficheskim otchetam Gosudarstvennoi Dumy tret'ego sozyva.* St. Petersburg, 1908.
Komitetov ministrov, Kantseliariia. *Zhurnaly Komiteta Ministrov po ispolneniiu Ukaza 12 dekabria 1904 g.* St. Petersburg, 1905.
"Konstitutsiia grafa Loris-Melikova: Materialy dlia ee istorii." *Byloe* 4–5 (32–33) (April–May 1918): 125–93.
"Konstitutsionnye proekty nachala 80-x gg. XIX v. (Pervaia i vtoraia redaktsii proekta aristokraticheskoi konstitutsii gr. P. P. Shuvalova i proekt takogo zhe roda konstitutsii A. A. Bobrinskogo)." *KA*, no. 31 (1928): 118–43.
Materialy po zemskomu obshchestvennomu ustroistvu. 2 vols. St. Petersburg, 1885–86.

Materialy redaktsionnoi komissii. Pervoe i vtoroe izdanie materialov (MRK). St. Petersburg, 1859–1860.

Ministerstvo Vnutrennykh Del (MVD—Ministry of Internal Affairs). *Materialy po uchrezhdeniiu Gosudarstvennoi Dumy.* St. Petersburg, 1905.

————. *Trudy redaktsionnoi kommissii po peresmotru zakonopolozhenii o krest'ianakh.* 6 vols. St. Petersburg, 1903–04.

————. Zemskii Otdel. *Materialy po volostnoi reforme: Povolostnoe raspredelenie zemel'nykh i prochikh nedvizhimykh vladenii v 34 zemskikh guberniiakh.* St. Petersburg, 1909.

————. *Sbornik uzakonenii o krest'ianskikh i sudebnykh uchrezhdeniiakh, preobrazovannykh po zakonu 12-ogo iiunia 1889 goda.* St. Petersburg, 1890.

"O predel'nosti zemskogo oblozheniia." *Otchet po deloproizvodstvu Gosudarstvennogo Soveta za sessiiu 1899–1900 gg.* St. Petersburg, 1900.

Polnoe sobranie zakonov rossiiskoi imperii. Seria tretiaia. 33 vols. St. Petersburg, 1885–1916.

Polenov, A. A., ed. *Izsledovanie ekonomicheskogo polozheniia tsentral'no-chernozemnykh gubernii: Trudy osobogo soveshchaniia 1899–1901 gg.* Moscow, 1901.

"Po proektu polozheniia o zemskikh nachal'nikakh, s'ezdakh sikh nachal'nikov i o gubernskikh po sel'skim delam prisutstviiakh," *Otchet po deloproizvodstvu Gosudarstvennogo Soveta za sessiiu 1889 g.* St. Petersburg, 1889.

Semenov, N. P. *Osvobozhdenie krest'ian v tsarstvovanii imperatora Aleksandra II: Khronika deiatel'nosti komisii po krest'ianskomu delu.* St. Petersburg, 1889–93. 3 vols. in 4.

"Senatorskie revizii 1880 goda." *Russkii arkhiv* 11 (1912): 417–29.

Skrebitskii, A. I., ed. *Krest'ianskoe delo v tsarstvovanii Imperatora Aleksandra II: Materialy dlia osvobozhdeniia krest'ian.* Bonn, 1862–68. 4 vols. in 5.

Sovet ministrov. *Osobye zhurnaly.* St. Petersburg, 1906–17.

Stenograficheskii otchet: Gosudarstvennyi Sovet. St. Petersburg, 1907, 1914.

Svod zakonov Rossiiskoi imperii poveleniem gosudaria imperatora Nikolaia Pavlovicha Sostavlennyi. St. Petersburg, 1832 and 1906.

Svod zakonov Rossiiskoi imperii izdannyi 1857 goda. St. Petersburg, 1857.

Trudy komissiia o gubernskikh i uezdnykh uchrezhdeniiakh. St. Petersburg, 1860–63.

Trudy osoboi komissii dlia sostavleniia proektov mestnogo upravleniia (Trudy o. k.). Works entitled:

  Izvlechenie iz vsepoddaneishago otcheta Chlena Gosudarstvennogo Soveta i Senatora Kovalevskogo po reviziiu gubernii Kazanskoi, Ufimskoi i Orenburgskoi. St. Petersburg, n.d.,

  Izvlechenie iz vespoddaneishago otcheta Senatora Samshina. St. Petersburg, n.d.

  Materialy po preobrazovaniiu mestnogo upravleniia (dostavlenye gubernatorami, zemstvom i prisutstviiami po krest'ianskim delam). 3 vols. St. Petersburg, 1884.

  Ob''iasnitel'nye zapiski k proektu polozhenii ob ustroistve mestnogo upravleniia, sostavlennym Soveshchaniem, vydelennym iz sostava Vysochaishe uchrezhdennoi Osoboi Komissii. St. Petersburg, n.d.

Ocherk predpolozhenii bol'shinstva chlenov Soveshchaniia Osoboi komissii po sostavleniiu proektov mestnogo upravleniia. St. Petersburg, n.d.

Polozhenie ob ustroistve mestnogo upravleniia. St. Petersburg, n.d.

Shamshin, I. I. *Zapiska po voprosam osobogo nastavleniia revizuiushchim senatoram, otnosiashchimsia k zemskim uchrezhdeniiam.* St. Petersburg, n.d.

Svod mnenii Gg. Gubernatorov po predlozheniiam ob ustroistve mestnogo upravleniia. St. Petersburg, n.d.

Zapiska Chlena Gosudarstvennogo Soveta Senatora Kovalevskogo, zakliuchaiushchaia materialy, kasaiushchiesia polozheniia i deiatel'nosti krest'ianskikh uchrezhdenii po dannym, obnaruzhennym pri revizii gubernii Kazanskoi i Ufimskoi. St. Petersburg, n.d.

Zhurnaly osoboi kommissii dlia sostavleniia proektov mestnogo upravleniia. St. Petersburg, n.d.

"Tsarskosel'skoe soveshchanie: Protokoly sekretnogo soveshchaniia pod predsedatel'stvom byvshago imperatora po voprosu o rasshirenii izbiratel'nogo prava." *Byloe* 3 (25) (September 1917): 217–65.

"Tsarskosel'skie soveshchaniia: Protokoly sekretnogo soveshchaniia v aprele 1906 goda pod predsedatel'stvom byvshago imperatora po peresmotru osnovnykh zakonov." *Byloe* 4 (26) (October 1917): 183–245.

"Tsarskosel'skie soveshchaniia: Protokoly sekretnogo soveshchaniia v fevrale 1906 goda pod predsedatel'stvom byvshago imperatora po vyrabotke Uchrezhdenii Gosudarstvennoi Dumy i Gosudarstvennogo Soveta." *Byloe* 5–6 (27–28) (November–December 1917): 289–318.

"Usilenie gubernatorskoi vlasti: Proekt fon Pleve." *Vsemirnyi vestnik* 6 (June 1907): 1–49.

"Vsepoddaneishii doklad gr. P. A. Valueva i dokumenty k Verkhovnoi Rasporiaditel'noi Kommissii 1880 g. kasatel'nye." *Russkii arkhiv* 11–12 (1915): 216–48.

Vysochaishe uchrezdennoe. Osoboe soveshchanie o nuzhdakh selskokhoziastvennoi promyshlennosti. Works entitled:

Protokoly po krest'ianskomu delu: Zasedaniia s 8 dekabria 1904 goda–30 marta 1905 goda. St. Petersburg, 1905.

Svod trudov mestnykh komitetov. Otdelenie 1-i. A. A. Rittikh, *Krest'ianskii pravoporiadok.* St. Petersburg, 1904.

———. Otdelenie 2-i. A. A. Rittikh, *Krest'ianskoe zemlepolzovanie.* St. Petersburg, 1903.

———. Otdelenie 23-i. S. I. Shidlovskii, *Zemstvo.* St. Petersburg, 1904.

"Zemskie uchrezhdeniia," Otchet po deloproizvodstvu Gosudanstvennogo Soveta za sessiiu 1890 g. St. Petersburg, 1890.

III. Newspapers, Journals, Encyclopedias

American Historical Review
Bol'shaia entsiklopedia
Byloe
Canadian-American Slavic Studies
Canadian Slavic Studies

Canadian Slavonic Papers
Entsiklopedicheskii slovar'
Istoriia SSSR
Istoricheskie zapiski
Istoricheskii arkhiv
Istoricheskii vestnik
Jahrbücher für Geschichte Osteuropas
Journal of Social History
Katorga i ssylka
Krasnyi arkhiv
Moskovskie vedomosti
Narodnoe khoziastvo
Novoe vremia
Otechestvennye zapiski
Poriadok
Poslednye novosti
Pravitel'stvennyi vestnik
Pravo
Rech'
Rossiia
Rus'
Russian History/Histoire Russe
Russian Review
Russkaia letopis'
Russkaia starina
Russkie vedomosti
Russkii arkhiv
Russkii vestnik
Russkoe gosudarstvo
Samoupravlenie
Sanktpeterburgskie vedomosti
Slavic Review
Slavonic and East European Review
Vestnik evropy
Vestnik finansov, promyshlennosti i torgovli
Vsemirnyi vestnik
Voprosy istorii KPSS

IV. Published Materials of Provincial Zemstvo Assemblies Relating to the Local Reform Debate, 1907–1909

Bessarabian Provincial Zemstvo. [*Bessarabskoe gubernskoe zemstvo*]. *Doklady Bessarabskoi gubernskoi zemskoi upravy gubernskomu zemskomu sobraniiu XXXIX ocherednoi sessii v 1907 g.* Kishinev, 1908.
Chernigov Provincial Zemstvo [*Chernigovskoe gubernskoe zemstvo*]. *Zhurnaly zasedanii Chernigovskogo Gubernskogo Zemskogo Sobraniia chrezvychainoi sessii 1907 g.* Chernigov, 1907.

———. *Zhurnaly zasedanii Chernigovskogo Gubernskogo Zemskogo Sobraniia 43 ocherednoi sessii 1907 goda*. Chernigov, 1908.

Ekaterinoslav Provincial Zemstvo [*Ekaterinoslavskoe gubernskoe zemstvo*]. *Postanovleniia Ekaterinoslavskogo gubernskogo Zemskogo sobraniia 26–27 maia 1907 g*. Ekaterinoslav, 1907.

Iaroslav Provincial Zemstvo [*Iaroslavskoe gubernskoe zemstvo*]. *Zhurnal Ekstrennogo Iaroslavskogo Zemskogo Sobraniia 22 maia 1907 goda*. Iaroslavl', 1907.

Kazan Provincial Zemstvo [*Kazanskoe gubernskoe zemstvo*]. *Postanovleniia 65 Chrezvychainnogo Kazanskogo Zemskogo Sobraniia 2–5 maia 1907 g*. Kazan, 1907.

———. *Postanovleniia 43 ocherednoi sessii 15–23 dekabria 1907 g. i 3–13 ianvaria 1908 g*. Kazan, 1907.

Khar'kov Provincial Zemstvo [*Khar'kovskoe gubernskoe zemstvo*]. *Doklady Khar'kovskoi Gubernskoi Zemskoi Upravy Gubernskomu Zemskomu Sobraniiu Chrezvychainnoi Sessii 4-go Maia 1907 g*. Khar'kov, 1907.

———. *Zhurnaly Khar'kovskogo Gubernskogo Zemskogo Sobraniia Chrezvychainnoi Sessii 4–5 maia 1907 g*. Khar'kov, 1907.

———. *Zhurnaly Khar'kovskogo Gubernskogo Zemskogo Sobraniia Ocherednoi Sessii 1907 goda*. Khar'kov, 1908.

Kherson Provincial Zemstvo [*Khersonskoe gubernskoe zemstvo*]. *Khersonskoe Gubernskoe Zemskoe Sobranie Sessiia Piat'desiat' Pervaia*. Kherson, 1908.

———. *Doklady Khersonskoi Gubernskoi Zemskoi Upravy Gubernskomu Zemskomu Sobraniiu Ocherednoi Sessii 1907 g*. Kherson, 1907.

———. *Khersonskoe Gubernskoe Zemskoe Sobranie Chrezvychainnoi Sessii 20–21 Aprelia 1908 g*. Kherson, 1908.

———. *Khersonskoe Gubernskoe Zemskoe Sobranie XLIII Ocherednoi sessii 1908 g*. Kherson, 1909.

Kostroma Provincial Zemstvo [*Kostromskoe gubernskoe zemstvo*]. *Postanovleniia Kostromskogo Chrezvychainnogo Zemskogo Sobraniia 20 i 21 maia 1907 g*. Kostroma, 1908.

Kursk Provincial Zemstvo [*Kurskoe zemskoe sobranie*]. *Zhurnaly zasedanii Ekstrennogo Kurskogo Zemskogo Sobraniia 15 maia 1907 g*. Kursk, 1907.

———. *Zhurnaly zasedanii XLIII Ocherednogo Kurskogo Gubernskogo Zemskogo Sobraniia 1908 g*. Kursk, 1908.

Moscow Provincial Zemstvo [*Moskovskoe gubernskoe zemstvo*]. *Zhurnaly Chrezvychainnykh zasedanii Moskovskogo Gubernskogo Zemskogo Sobraniia sostoiavshchikhsia v 1907 godu*. Moscow, 1908.

Nizhnii Novgorod Provincial Zemstvo [*Nizhegorodskoe gubernskoe zemstvo*]. *Nizhegorodskoe Gubernskoe Zemskoe Sobranie XLII Ocherednoi sessii 25 noiabria–14 dekabria 1906 g. i Chrezvychainnoi sessii 7 maia 1907 g*. Nizhnii-Novgorod, 1907.

Novgorod Provincial Zemstvo [*Novgorodskoe gubernskoe zemstvo*]. *Stenograficheskii Otchet XLIII Ocherednogo Novgorodskogo Gubernskogo Zemskogo Sobraniia s 1 po 12 Dekabria 1907 g*. Novgorod, 1908.

Novgarod Provincial Zemstvo. *Sbornik Postanovlenii Zemskikh Sobranii Novgorodskoi Gubernii za 1907 g.* Novgorod, 1908.

Olonets Provincial Zemstvo [*Olonetskoe gubernskoe zemstvo*]. *Zhurnaly Olonetskogo Gubernskogo Zemskogo Sobraniia XL-i Ocherednoi Sessii s 28 noiabria po 17 dekabria 1906 g. i chrezvychainnykh 4–5 fevralia i 14–15 maia 1907 g.* Petrozavodsk, 1907.

Orel Provincial Zemstvo [*Orlovskoe gubernskoe zemstvo*]. *Zhurnaly izbrannoi chrezvychainnym gubernskim zemskim sobraniem 25 maia 1907 goda kommisii po reforme mestnogo upravleniia.* Orel, 1908.

———. *Zhurnaly Chrezvychainnogo Orlovskogo Gubernskogo Zemskogo Sobraniia byvshogo 24 i 25 maia 1907 g.* Orel, 1907.

———. *Zhurnaly Chrezvychainnogo Orlovskogo Gubernskogo Zemskogo Sobraniia zasedaniia i-ogo iiulia 1908 g.* Orel, 1908.

Penza Provincial Zemstvo [*Penzenskoe gubernskoe zemstvo*]. *Zhurnaly Chrezvychainnogo Zasedaniia 28–30 Maia i 29 Avgusta 1907 g. i ocherednoi sessii 9–22 dekabria 1907 g.* Penza, 1908.

Poltava Provincial Zemstvo [*Poltavskoe gubernskoe zemstvo*]. *Poltavskoe gubernskoe zemskoe sobranie XLIII ocherednogo sozyva, Gubernskie Zemskie Upravnye Doklady 1907 goda.* Poltava, 1907.

———. *Poltavskoe Gubernskoe Zemskoe Sobranie XLIII ocherednogo sozyva s 10 po 19 Dekabria 1907 g.* Poltava, 1908.

Pskov Provincial Zemstvo [*Pskovskoe gubernskoe zemstvo*]. *Doklady Pskovskoi Gubernskoi Zemskoi Upravy i Postanovleniia Chrezvychainnogo 17–19 iiunia 1907 g. i XLIII Ocherednogo 15–22 Dekabria 1907 Gubernskogo Zemskogo Sobraniia.* Pskov, 1908.

Riazan Provincial Zemstvo [*Riazanskoe gubernskoe zemstvo*]. *XXXIX Chrezvychainnoe Riazanskoe Gubernskoe Zemskoe Sobranie 21 maia 1907 g.* Riazan, 1907.

Samara Provincial Zemstvo [*Samarskoe gubernskoe zemstvo*]. *Postanovleniia Samarskogo Gubernskogo Zemskogo Sobrannie XXXIII ocherednoi sessii.* Samara, 1908.

Saratov Provincial Zemstvo [*Saratovskoe gubernskoe zemstvo*]. *Doklad 2-i kommissii po voprosam o zemskom izbiratel'nom tsenze i zhelatel'nykh izmeneniiakh deistvuiushchago Zemskogo Polozheniia Saratovskomu XXXVIII Ocherednomu Gubernskomu Zemskomu Sobraniiu.* Saratov, 1904.

———. *Zhurnaly Chrezvychainnogo Saratovskogo Zemskogo Sobraniia 12 Marta 1907 g.* Saratov, 1907.

———. *Doklad i Protokoly Zasedanii kommissii po reforme zemskogo polozheniia.* Saratov, 1907.

St. Petersburg Provincial Zemstvo [*Sanktpeterburgskoe gubernskoe zemstvo*]. *Zhurnaly zasedanii St.P-ogo Gubernskogo Zemskogo Sobraniia Chrezvychainnykh Sessii 10–16 maia i 20 iiunia 1907 g.* St. Petersburg, 1907.

———. *Zhurnaly zasedanii St.P-ogo Gubernskogo Zemskogo Sobraniia sorok vtoroi ocherednoi sessii 12–19 dekabria 1907 g. i 10–18 ianvaria 1908 g. i chrezvychainnoi sessii 3 fevralia 1908 g.* St. Petersburg, 1908.

Simbirsk Provincial Zemstvo [*Simbirskoe gubernskoe zemstvo*]. *Zhurnaly i do-*

klady Simbirskogo Zemskogo Sobraniia Chrezvychainnoi Sessii 28 aprelia i 5 maia 1907 g. Simbirsk, 1907.

———. *Zhurnaly Simbirskogo Gubernskogo Zemskogo Sobraniia Ocherednoi sessii 1907 goda.* Simbirsk, 1908.

———. *Stenograficheskii otchet Zasedanii Simbirskogo Gubernskogo Zemskogo Sobraniia ocherednoi sessii 1907 goda s 3–20 ianvaria 1908 g.* Simbirsk, 1908.

Smolensk Provincial Zemstvo [*Smolenskoe gubernskoe zemstvo*]. *Zhurnal Chrezvychainnogo Smolenskogo Gubernskogo Zemskogo Sobraniia zasedaniia 30 maia 1907 goda.* Smolensk, 1907.

———. *Zhurnal XLIII Ocherednogo Smolenskogo Gubernskogo Zemskogo Sobraniia zasedanii s 5 po 20 ianvaria 1908 g.* Smolensk, 1908.

Tauride Provincial Zemstvo [*Tavricheskoe gubernskoe zemstvo*]. *Zhurnal Zasedaniia Tavricheskogo Gubernskogo Zemskogo Sobraniia Chrezvychainnoi Sessii 24-ogo Marta 1907 goda.* Simferopol', 1907.

Tambov Provincial Zemstvo [*Tambovskoe gubernskoe zemstvo*]. *Zhurnal Gubernskogo Zemskogo Sobraniia chrezvychainnoi sessii 2 maia 1907 g.* Tambov, 1907.

———. *Zhurnal ocherednogo Tambovskogo gubernskogo zemskogo sobraniia sessii 1907 goda.* Tambov, 1908.

Tver Provincial Zemstvo [*Tverskoe zemskoe sobranie*]. *Zhurnal Tverskogo Ocherednogo Gubernskogo Zemskogo Sobraniia sessii 1907 goda i chrezvychainnogo sobraniia 16–17 maia 1907 goda.* Tver, 1908.

Tula Provincial Zemstvo [*Tulskoe gubernskoe zemstvo*]. *Zhurnal Chrezvychainnogo Tulskogo Gubernskogo Zemskogo Sobraniia 26 maia 1907 g.* Tula, 1907.

———. *Zhurnaly Tulskogo Gubernskogo Zemskogo Sobraniia chrezvychainnoi sessii 18 ianvaria 1908 g.* Tula, 1908.

———. *Zhurnal Tulskogo Gubernskogo Zemskogo Sobraniia: Sorok tret'ei ocherednoi sessii.* Tula, 1908.

———. *Zhurnal Chrezvychainnogo Tulskogo Gubernskogo Zemskogo Sobraniia 3 Marta 1908 g.* Tula, 1908.

Ufa Provincial Zemstvo [*Ufimskoe gubernskoe zemstvo*]. *Zhurnaly Zasedanii Ufimskogo Gubernskogo Zemskogo Sobraniia XXXII ocherednoi i XXXIX chrezvychainnoi sessii 1906 i 1907 godov.* Ufa, 1907.

Vladimir Provincial Zemstvo [*Vladimirskoe gubernskoe zemstvo*]. *Zhurnal Ocherednogo Vladimirskogo Gubernskogo Zemskogo Sobraniia 1907 g.* Vladimir, 1908.

———. *Doklady Vladimirskoi Gubernskoi Zemskoi Upravy ocherednomu gubernskomu zemskomu sobraniiu 1907 g.* Vladimir, 1907.

Vologda Provincial Zemstvo [*Vologodskoe gubernskoe zemstvo*]. *Zhurnal Chrezvychainnogo Vologodskogo Gubernskogo Zemskogo Sobraniia 29 Maia 1907 goda.* Vologda, 1907.

Voronezh Provincial Zemstvo [*Voronezhskoe gubernskoe zemstvo*]. *Zhurnaly Voronezhskogo Gubernskogo Zemskogo Sobraniia Ocherednoi sessii 11–20 dekabria 1906 g. i Chrezvychainnoi 2–5 maia 1907 g.* Voronezh, 1907.

Voronezk Provincial Zemstvo. *Zhurnaly Voronezhskogo Gubernskogo Zemskogo Sobraniia Ocherednoi sessii 1907 g.: 15–20 dekabria 1907; 9–16 ianvaria 1908 g.* Voronezh, 1908.

V. Dissertations

Fallows, Thomas S. "Forging the Zemstvo Movement: Liberalism and Radicalism on the Volga, 1890–1905." Harvard University, 1981.
Hirschbiel, Henry H. III. "The District Captains of the Ministry of State Properties in the Reign of Nicholas I: A Case Study of Russian Provincial Officialdom, 1838–1856." New York University, 1978.
MacDonald, David M. "Autocracy, Bureaucracy, and Change in the Formation of Russian Foreign Policy (1895–1914)." Columbia University, 1988.
Mandel, James I. "Paternalistic Authority in the Russian Countryside, 1856–1906." Columbia University, 1978.
Pearson, Thomas. "Ministerial Conflict and Local Self-Government Reform, 1877–1890." University of North Carolina, 1976.

VI. Other Sources

Abramov, Ia. V. *Shto sdelalo zemstvo i shto ono delaet: Obzor deiatel'nosti russkogo zemstva.* St. Petersburg, 1889.
Achkasov, Aleksei, ed. *"Poveialo vesnoiu": Rechi g. ministra vnutrennykh del kniazia P. D. Sviatopolk-Mirskogo i tolki o nikh pressy.* Moscow, 1905.
Adianov, S. *Ministerstvo vnutrennykh del: Istoricheskii ocherk.* 3 vols. St. Petersburg, 1902.
"Agrarnoe dvizhenie v 1905 g. po otchetam Dubasova i Panteleeva." *KA* 11–12 (1925).
Alekseev, S. A. *Samoderzhavie i liberaly v revoliutsii 1905–1907 gg.* Leningrad, 1925.
Alekseev, V. P. "Sekretnye komitety pri Nikolae I." In A. K. Dzhivelegov et al., eds. *Velikaia reforma*, vol. 1. Moscow, 1911.
Alston, Patrick L. *Education and the State in Tsarist Russia.* Stanford University Press, 1969.
Ananych, B. V. "R. A. Fadeev, S. Iu. Vitte i ideologichiskie iskazaniia 'okhranitelei' v 1881–1882." In *Issledovaniia po sotsial'no-politicheskoi istorii Rossii*, pp. 299–326. Trudy Akademii nauk SSSR, Institut Istorii, Leningradskoe otdelenie, 1971.
———. *Rossiia i mezhdunarodnyi kapital, 1897–1914: Ocherk istorii finansovykh otnoshenii.* Leningrad, 1970.
Ananych, B. V., V. S. Diakin, et al., eds. *Krizis samoderzhaviia v Rossii, 1895–1917.* Leningrad, 1984.
Ananych, B. V., and R. Sh. Ganelin. "I. A. Vyshnegradskii i S. Iu. Vitte—korrespondent 'Moskovskikh Vedomostei.' " In *Problemy obshchestvennoi mysli i ekonomicheskoi politiki Rossii XIX–XX vekov*, pp. 12–34. Leningrad, 1972.
Akademia nauk SSSR. Institut istorii (Leningrad). *Otmena krepostnogo prava: Doklady ministrov vnutrennykh del o provedenii krest'ianskoi reformy, 1861–1862.* Moscow-Leningrad, 1950.

———. *Vnutrenniaia politika tsarizma (seredina XVI–nachalo XXv)*. Leningrad, 1967.

Andreevskii, I. E. *Politseiskoe pravo*. 2 vols. St. Petersburg, 1871.

Anfimov, A. M. *Krest'ianskoe khoziaistvo Evropeiskoi Rossii, 1881–1904*. Moscow, 1980.

———. *Krupnoe pomeshchich'e khoziastvo evropeiskoi Rossii (konets XIX–nachalo XX veka)*. Moscow, 1969.

Astyrrev, N. *V volostnykh pisariakh: ocherki krest'ianskogo samoupraleniia*. Moscow, 1896.

Avinov, N. N. "Glavnye nachala v istorii zakonodatel'stva o zemskikh uchrezhedniakh." In *Iubileinyi zemskii sbornik, 1864–1904*. St. Petersburg, 1914.

———. *Graf M. A. Korf i zemskaia reforma 1864 goda*. Moscow, 1904.

Avrekh, A. Ia. "O nekotorykh voprosakh revoliutsionnoi situatsii." *Voprosy istorii KPSS* 5 (1966): 30–44.

———. "Russkii absoliutizm i ego rol' v utverzhdenii kapitalizma v Rossii." *Istoriia SSSR*, no. 2 (1968).

———. *Stolypin i tret'iaia duma*. Moscow, 1968.

———. "Tret'eiiunskaia monarkhiia i obrazovanie tret'eiiunskogo pomeshchich'e-burzhuaznogo bloka." *Vestnik Moskovskogo Universiteta (istoriko-fililogicheskaia seriia)*, no. 1 (1956): 3–70.

———. *Tzarizm i IV duma, 1912–1914 gg*. Moscow, 1981.

———. *Tzarizm i tret'eiiunskaia sistema*. Moscow, 1966.

———. "Utrachennoe ravnovesie." *Istoriia SSSR* 4 (1971): 60–76.

———. "Vopros o zapadnom zemstve i bankrovtstvo Stolypina." *Istoricheskie zapiski* 70 (1961): 61–112.

Barykov, F. L. et al. (eds.). *Sbornik materialov dlia izucheniia sel'skoi pozemel'noi obshchiny: Izdanie imperatorskogo Vol'no-Ekonomicheskogo i Russkogo Geograficheskogo Obshchestva*. St. Petersburg, 1880.

Becker, Seymour. *Nobility and Privilege in Late Imperial Russia*. Northern Illinois University Press, 1985.

Berlin, Isaiah. "A Remarkable Decade," in idem, *Russian Thinkers*. Penguin, 1979.

Bermanskii, K. L. "Konstitutsionnye proekty tsarstvovaniia Aleksandra II." *Vestnik prava*, no. 9 (1905).

Bervi-Flerovskii, V. V. *Zapiski revoliutsionera-mechtatelia*. Moscow-Leningrad, 1929.

Bezobrazov, V. P. "Iz dnevnika senatora." *Byloe* 9 (1907): 1–32.

Bilimovich, A. D. *Krest'ianskii pravoporiadok po trudam mestnykh komitetov o nuzhdakh selsokhoziastvennoi promyshlennosti*. Kiev, 1904.

Blum, Jerome. *Lord and Peasant in Russia From the Ninth to the Nineteenth Century*. Princeton University Press, 1961.

"Dnevnik A. A. Bobrinskogo (20 sentiabria 1910–2 aprelia 1911)." *KA*, no. 26 (1928): 127–50.

Bogdanovich, A. V. *Tri poslednikh samoderzhtsa. Dnevnik A. V. Bogdanovicha*. Moscow-Leningrad, 1924.

Bogoliubov, V. A. "Udelnye krest'iane," in A. K. Dzhivelegov et al., eds. *Velikaia reforma*, vol. 2.

Bok, M. P. *Vospominaniia o moem otse P. A. Stolypine*. New York, 1953.

Borodin, A. P. "Usilenie pozitsii ob"edinennogo dvorianstva v Gosudarstvennom sovete v 1907–1914 godakh." *Voprosy istorii*, no. 2 (1977): 56–67.

Brusnikin, E. M. "Krest'ianskii vopros v Rossii v period politicheskoi reaktsii." *Voprosy istorii*, no. 2 (1970): 34–48.

Byrnes, R. F. *Pobedonostsev: His Life and Thought*. Indiana University Press, 1968.

Charykov, Nikolai V. *Glimpses of High Politics, Through War and Peace, 1855–1929: The Autobiography of N. V. Tcharykov, Serf-Owner, Ambassador, Exile*. London, 1931.

Chermenskii, E. D. *Burzhuaziia i tsarizm v pervoi russkoi revoliutsii*. 2d ed. Moscow, 1970.

———. *IV Gosudarstvennaia duma i sverzhenie tsarizma v Rossii*. Moscow, 1976.

———. "Tsarizm i tret'eiiunskaia duma." *Voprosy istorii*, no. 1 (1973): 30–48.

Cherniavsky, Michael. "Ivan the Terrible as Renaissance Prince." *Slavic Review* 27 (1968), pp. 195–211.

———. "Khan or Basileus: An Aspect of Russian Medieval Political Theory." In *The Structure of Russian History: Interpretive Essays*. Random House, 1970.

Chernukha, V. G. *Krest'ianskii vopros v pravitel'stvennoi politike Rossii*. Leningrad, 1972.

———. *Vnutrenniaia politika tsarizma s serediny 50-kh do nachala 80-kh gg. XIX v.* Leningrad, 1978.

Chernyshev, I. V. *Agrarno-krest'ianskaia politika Rossii za 150 let*. Petrograd-Moscow, 1918.

Chicherin, B. N. *Vospominaniia*. Moscow, 1929–34.

"Chleny Gosudarstvennogo soveta s 1801 goda." *Entsiklopedicheskii slovar'*. A. and I. Granat. Vol. 23, pp. 642–735.

Chmielewski, E. "Stolypin and the Ministerial Crises of 1909." *California Slavic Studies* 4 (1967): 1–39.

———. "Stolypin's Last Crisis." *California Slavic Studies* 3 (1964): 95–126.

Conroy, Mary Schaeffer. *Peter Arkadevich Stolypin: Practical Politics in Late Tsarist Russia*. Westview, 1976.

———. "Stolypin's Attitude toward Local Self-Government." *Slavonic and East European Review* 46 (1968): 446–462.

Czap, Jr., Peter. "Peasant-Class Courts and Peasant Customary Justice in Russia, 1861–1912." *Journal of Social History* 1, no. 2 (Winter 1967): 149–78.

Dan, Fedor. "Obshchaia politika pravitel'stva i izmeneniia v gosudarstvennoi organizatsii v period 1905–1907 gg." Martov et. al. *Obshchestvennoe dvizhenie v Rossii* vol. 4, pt. 1. St. Petersburg, 1911.

Davidovich, A. M. *Samoderzhavie v epokhe imperializma*. Moscow, 1975.

de Enden, M. N. "The Roots of Witte's Thought." *The Russian Review* 29 (January 1970): 6–24.

Demidova, N. F. "Biurokratizatsiia gosudarstvennogo apparata absoliutizma v XVII–XVIII vv." In *Absoliutizm v Rossii*, pp. 206–42. Moscow, 1969.

Diakin, V. S. *Samoderzhavie, burzhuaziia i dvorianstvo v 1907–1911 gg.* Leningrad, 1978.

———. "Stolypin i dvorianstvo (proval mestnoi reformy)." In *Problemy krest'ianskogo zemlevladeniia i vnutrennoi politiki Rossii, dooktiabr'skoi periody*, pp. 238–82. Akademiia nauk SSSR, Leningrad, 1972.

———. "Zemstvo i samoderzhavie v tret'eiiunskoi monarkhii." *Voprosy istorii Rossii XIX–nachale XX veka.* Leningrad, 1983.

Doctorow, G. S. "The Fundamental State Laws of 23 April 1906." *Russian Review* 35, no. 1 (January 1976): 33–52.

———. "The Government Program of 17 October 1905." *Russian Review* 34, no. 2 (April 1975): 123–36.

Dolgorukov, Prince P. D., and Prince D. I. Shakhovskoi. *Melkaia zemskaia edinitsa: Sbornik statei.* St. Petersburg, 1903.

Dolgorukov, Prince P. D. and Count S. L. Tolstoi. *Krest'ianskii stroi: Sbornik statei.* St. Petersburg, 1905.

Drozdov, I. G. *Sud'by dvorianskogo zemlevladeniia v Rossii i tendentsii k ego mobilizatsii.* Petrograd, 1917.

Druzhinin, N. M. *Gosudarstvennye krest'iane i reforma P. D. Kiseleva.* 2 vols. Moscow, 1946.

———. *Russkaia derevnia na perelome, 1861–1880 gg.* Moscow, 1978.

Dubrovskii, S. M. *Stolypinskaia zemel'naia reform.* Moscow, 1963.

Dzhanashiev, G. A. *Iz epokhi velikikh reform: Istoricheskie spravki.* Moscow, 1893.

Dzhivelegov, A. K., et. al., eds. *Velikaia reforma: Russkoe obshchestvo i krest'ianskii vopros v proshlom i nastoiashchem.* 6 vols. Moscow, 1911.

Edelman, Robert. *Gentry Politics on the Eve of the Russian Revolution: The Nationalist Party, 1907–1917.* Rutgers University Press, 1980.

Egorov, A. E. *Stranitsy iz proshlego.* 2 vols. Odessa, 1913.

Emmons, Terence. "The Beseda Circle, 1899–1905." *Slavic Review* 32, no. 3 (September 1973).

———. *The Formation of Political Parties and the First National Elections in Russia.* Harvard University Press, 1983.

———. *The Russian Landed Gentry and the Peasant Emancipation of 1861.* Cambridge University Press, 1968.

Emmons, Terence, and Wayne S. Vucinich, eds. *The Zemstvo in Russia: An Experiment in Local Self-Government.* Cambridge University Press, 1982.

Eroshkin, N. P. *Istoriia gosudarstvennykh uchrezdenii dorevoliutsionnoi Rossii.* Moscow, 1968.

Ershov, M. D. *Doklad po proektu polozhenii o volostnom i posel'kovom upravleniiakh sostavlennyi po porucheniiu soveta obshchezemskogo s"ezda 1907 g. glasnym kaluzhskogo gubernskogo zemstva.* Moscow, 1907.

———. *Zemskaia reforma v sviazi s gosudarstvennym izbiratel'nym zakonom.* St. Petersburg, 1907.

Fallows, Thomas. "The Zemstvo and the Bureaucracy." In Terence Emmons and

Wayne Vucinich, eds. *The Zemstvo in Russia*. Cambridge University Press, 1982.

Feoktistov, E. M. *Vospominaniia E. M. Feoktistova: Za kulisami politiki i literatury, 1848–1896*. Leningrad, 1929; reprinted by Oriental Research Partners, 1975.

Field, Daniel. *The End of Serfdom: Nobility and Bureaucracy in Russia, 1855–1861*. Harvard University Press, 1976.

———. *Rebels in the Name of the Tsar*. Houghton Mifflin, 1976.

Fischer, George. *Russian Liberalism from Gentry to Intelligentsia*. Harvard University Press, 1958.

Flynn, James T. "The Universities, the Gentry, and the Russian Imperial Services, 1815–1825." *Canadian Slavic Studies* 2, no. 4 (Winter 1968): 486–503.

Freeze, Gregory L. "The Soslovie (Estate) Paradigm and Russian Social History." *American Historical Review* 91, no. 1 (February 1986): 11–36.

Galai, Shmuel. *The Liberation Movement in Russia, 1900–1905*. Cambridge University Press, 1973.

Garmiza, V. V. *Podgotovka zemskoi reformy 1864 goda*. Moscow, 1957.

Gerschenkron, Alexander. "Problems and Patterns of Russian Economic Development." In *The Structure of Russian History. Interpretive Essays*, edited by Michael Cherniavsky. Random House, 1970.

Gessen, Vladimir. "Sel'skoe obshchestvo i volost' v trudakh Kakhanovskoi kommissii." *Russkoe Bogatstvo* 8 (1903): 125–44; 9 (1903): 33–35.

Girchenko, V. P. *Iz vospominanii o grafe V. F. Dorrer*. Kursk, 1912.

Gleason, Abbott. *Young Russia: The Genesis of Russian Radicalism in the 1860s*. Viking, 1980.

Glinski, B. B. "Epokha mira i uspokoeniia (istoricheskie ocherki)." *Istoricheskii vestnik*. 123 (St. Petersburg, 1911): 262–88.

———. "Graf Sergei Iul'evich Vitte (Materialy dlia biografii)." *Istoricheskii vestnik* 141, no. 3 (August 1915): 520–55; 141, no. 4 (September 1915): 893–97.

———. "Period tverdoi vlasti (istoricheskie ocherki). Vnutrenniaia politika Rossii v epokhu vos'midesiatykh godov." *Istoricheskii vestnik*, 127 (St. Petersburg, 1912): 667–90; 128, pp. 219ff.

Golitsyn, A. D. *Blizhaishie zadachi zemskoi reformy: Doklad chleny 3-ei Gosudarstvennoi Dumy kniazia A. D. Golitsyna v zasedanii Tsentral'nogo Komiteta Soiuza 17-ogo Oktiabria 5 maia 1913 g*. Moscow, 1913.

Golovachev, A. A. *Desiat' let reform, 1861–1871*. St. Petersburg, 1872.

Golovin, F. A. "Zapiski F. A. Golovina: P. A. Stolypin." *KA*, no. 19 (1926): 128–49.

Golovnin, K. F. *Moi vospominaniia*. 2 vols. St. Petersburg, 1908–10.

Gosudarstvennyi dvorianskii zemel'nyi bank, 1885–1910. St. Petersburg, 1910.

Gosudarstvennyi sovet. *Obzor deiatel'nosti Gosudarstvennogo Soveta v tsarstvovanii imperatora Aleksandra III 1881–1894 gg*. St. Petersburg, 1902.

Gradovskii, A. D. *Istoriia mestnogo upravleniia v Rossii*. St. Petersburg, 1899.

———. *Itogi (1862–1907)*. Kiev, 1907.

Gurko, V. I. "Chto est' i chego net v 'Vospominaniia grafa S. Iu. Vitte.' " *Russkaia letopis'*, no. 2 (1922).

————. *Features and Figures of the Past: Government and Opinion in the Reign of Nicholas II*. Stanford University Press, 1939.

Haimson, Leopold H. "The Parties and the State: The Evolution of Political Attitudes." In *The Structure of Russian History*, edited by Michael Cherniavsky, pp. 309–40. Random House, 1970.

————. "The Problem of Social Identities in Early Twentieth Century Russia." *Slavic Review* 47, no. 1 (Spring 1988): 1–29.

————. "The Problem of Social Stability in Urban Russia." In *The Structure of Russian History*, edited by Michael Cherniavsky, pp. 340–80. Random House, 1970.

————, ed. *The Politics of Rural Russia, 1905–1914*. Indiana University Press, 1979.

Hosking, Geoffrey A. *The Russian Constitutional Experiment: Government and Duma, 1907–1914*. Cambridge University Press, 1973.

Ianson, Iu. E. *Opyt' statisticheskogo issledovaniia o krest'ianskikh nadelakh i platezhakh*. St. Petersburg, 1881.

Ignatovich, I. I. "Krest'ianskie volneniia," in A. K. Dzhivelegov, *Velikaia Reforma*, vol. 3.

————. *Pomeshchich'ie krest'iane nakanune osvobozhdeniia*. St. Petersburg, 1902.

Islavin, M. V. *Obzor trudov vysochaishe utverzhdennoi pod predsedatel'stvom stats-sekretaria Kakhanova Osoboi komisii*. St. Petersburg, 1908.

"Izpoved grafa Loris-Melikova." *Katorga i ssylka* 2 (1925): 118–25.

Iswolsky, Alexander. *The Memoirs of Alexander Iswolsky*. Edited and translated by Charles Louis Seeger. Academic International Press, 1974.

Iurskii, G. *Pravye v tret'ei gosudarstvennoi dume*. Khar'kov, 1912.

Izgoev, A. *P. A. Stolypin: Ocherk zhizni i deiatel'nosti*. Moscow, 1912.

Jones, Robert E. *The Emancipation of the Russian Nobility, 1762–1785*. Princeton University Press, 1973.

Judge, Edward H. *Plehve: Repression and Reform in Imperial Russia, 1902–1904*. Syracuse University Press, 1983.

"K diskussii ob absoliutizme v Rossii." *Istoriia SSSR* 4 (1972): 65–89.

Kabuzan, M. *Izmeneniia v razmeshchenii naseleniia Rossii v XVIII–pervoi polovine XIX v.: Po materialam revizii*. Moscow, 1971.

Kahan, Arcadius. "Government Policies and the Industrialization of Russia." *Journal of Economic History* (December 1967): 460–77.

Karpov, N. *Krest'ianskoe dvizhenie v revoliutsii 1905 goda v dokumentakh*. Leningrad, 1926.

Karyshev, N. A. *Zemskie khodataistva: 1865–1885 gg*. Moscow, 1900.

Kataev, I. M. *Doreformennaia biurokratiia po zapiskam, memuaram i literature*. St. Petersburg, 1911.

Kataev, M. M. *Mestnye krestianskie uchrezhdeniia, 1861, 1874 i 1889 (Istoricheskii ocherk ikh obrazovaniia i norm deiatelnosti)*. 3 vols. St. Petersburg, 1911–12.

Katkov, M. A. *Rol' uezdnykh predvoditelei dvorianstva v gosudarstvennom upravlenii Rossii: K voprosu o reforme uezdnogo upravleniia*. Moscow, 1914.

Katkov, M. N. *Sobranie peredovykh statei Moskovskikh vedomostei, 1863–1887 gg.* 25 vols. Moscow, 1897–98.

Kheifets, M. I. *Vtoraia revoliutsionnaia situatsiia v Rossii (konets 70-kh–nachalo 80-kh godov XIX veka).* Moscow, 1963.

Kitanina, T. M. *Khlebnaia torgovlia Rossii v 1875–1914 gg.* Leningrad, 1978.

Kizevetter, A. A. *Mestnoe samoupravlenie v Rossii IX–XIX st.: Istoricheskii ocherk.* Moscow, 1910.

———. "Vnutrenniaia politika." *Istoriia Rossii v XIX veke.* vol. 1, pt. 5. St. Petersburg, 1907.

Kliuchevskii, V. O. *Istoriia soslovii v Rossii.* St. Petersburg, 1886.

Klochkov, M. V. *Ocherki pravitel'stvennoi deiatel'nosti vremeni Pavla I: Zapiski istoriko-filologicheskogo fakul'teta Imperatorskogo Petrogradskogo Universiteta.* Petrograd, 1916.

Koenker, Diane. *Moscow Workers and the 1917 Revolution.* Princeton University Press, 1981.

Kokovtsov, V. N. *Out of My Past.* Stanford University Press, 1935.

Kolchin, Peter. *Unfree Labor: American Slavery and Russian Serfdom.* Harvard University Press, 1987.

Komitetov Ministrov, Kantseliaria. *Istorichiskii obzor deiatelnosti Komiteta ministrov: K stolettiiu Komiteta ministrov (1802–1902).* 5 vols. in 8. St. Petersburg, 1902–03.

Koni, A. F. *Sobranie sochinenii.* 8 vols. Moscow, 1966–69.

Korelin, A. P. *Dvorianstvo v poreformennoi Rossii, 1861–1904 gg.* Moscow, 1979.

———. "Rossiiskoe dvorianstvo i ego soslovnaia organizatsiia (1861–1904 gg.)." *Istoriia SSSR,* no. 5 (1971).

Korf, S. A. *Administrativnaia iustitsiia v Rossii.* vol. 1. St. Petersburg, 1910.

———. *Dvorianstvo i ego soslovnoe upravlenie za stoletiia 1762–1855 godov.* St. Petersburg, 1906.

Kornilov, A. A. *Iz istorii voprosa ob izbiratel'nom prave v zemstve.* St. Petersburg, 1906.

———. *Krest'ianskaia reforma.* St. Petersburg, 1905.

———. *Obshchestvennoe dvizhenie pri Aleksandre II.* Moscow, 1909.

Koroleva, N. G. *Pervaia rossiiskaia revoliutsiia i tsarizm. Sovet ministrov Rossii v 1905–1907 gg.* Moscow, 1892.

Koropachinskii, P. D. *Reform mestnogo samoupravleniia po rabotam Soveta po delam mestnogo khoziastva.* Ufa, 1909.

———. *Reforma mestnogo upravleniia i drugie zakonoproekty po rabotam vtoroi i tret'ei sessii Soveta po delam mestnogo khoziastva.* Ufa, 1910.

Koshelev, A. I. *Golos iz zemstva.* Moscow, 1869.

———. *Zapiski Aleksandra Ivanovicha Kosheleva (1812–1883).* Berlin, 1884.

Koval'chenko, I. D. *Russkoe krepostnoe krest'ianstvo v pervoi polovine XIX veka.* Moscow, 1967.

Kratkie zhurnaly obshchezemskogo s"ezda v Moskve v 25–28 avgust 1907 g. Poltava, 1907.

Krichevskii, M., ed. *Dnevnik A. S. Suvorina.* Moscow-Leningrad, 1923.

Kryzhanovskii, S. E. *Vospominaniia*. Berlin, 1938.

Kuropatkin, A. N. "Iz dnevnika A. N. Kuropatkina." *KA*, no. 7 (1924).

Lazarevskii, N. I. *Lektsii po russkomu gosudarstvennomu pravu*, vol. 2: *Administrativnoe pravo*. St. Petersburg, 1910.

LeDonne, John P. *Ruling Russia: Politics and Administration in the Age of Absolutism, 1762–1796*. Princeton University Press, 1984.

Lenin, V. I. *Polnoe sobranie sochinenii*. Moscow, 1961.

Leroy-Beaulieu, Anatole. *The Empire of the Tsars and the Russians*. 3 vols. Putnam's, 1893.

Levin, Alfred. *The Second Duma*. Yale University Press, 1940.

——. *The Third Duma, Election and Profile*. Archon Books, 1973.

——. "Peter Akadeevich Stolypin: A Political Appraisal." *Journal of Modern History* 37, no. 4 (December 1965): 445–63.

Lewin, Moshe. *The Making of the Soviet System: Essays in the Social History of Interwar Russia*. Pantheon, 1985.

Lincoln, W. Bruce. "The Genesis of an 'Enlightened' Bureaucracy in Russia." *Jahrbücher für Geschichte Osteuropas* 20, no. 3 (September 1972).

——. *Nikolai Miliutin: An Enlightened Russian Bureaucrat*. Oriental Research Partners, 1977.

——. *Nicholas I: Emperor and Autocrat of All the Russias*. Indiana University Press, 1978.

Liubimov, D. N. *Pamiati V. K. Pleve*. St. Petersburg, 1904.

Liubimov, L. D. *Na chuzhbine: Vospominaniia*. Moscow, 1963.

Liubimov, S. V. *Predvoditeli dvorianstva vsekh namestnichestv, gubernii i oblastei Rossiiskoi imperii, 1777–1910*. St. Petersburg, 1911.

Logachev, V. V. *Sbornik rechei Stolypina, proiznesennyk v zasedaniiakh gosudarstvennoi dumy i gosudarstvennogo sovet (1906–1911)*. St. Petersburg, 1911.

L'vov, N. N., and A. A. Stakhovich. *Nuzhdy derevnei po rabotam komitetov o nuzhdakh sel'sko-khoziastvennoi promyshlennosti: Sbornik statei*. St. Petersburg, 1904.

Macey, David A. J. *Government and Peasant in Russia, 1861–1906: The Prehistory of the Stolypin Reforms*. Northern Illinois University Press, 1987.

Maevskii, V. I. *Borets za blago Rossii: (K stoletiiu so dnia rozhdeniia)*. Madrid, 1962.

Maklakov, V. A. *Vlast' i obshchestvennost' na zakate staroi Rossii*. Paris, 1930.

Malia, Martin. *Alexander Herzen and the Birth of Russian Socialism*. Harvard University Press, 1961.

Manning, Roberta Thompson. *The Crisis of the Old Order in Russia: Gentry and Government*. Princeton University Press, 1982.

——. "The Zemstvo and Politics," in Terence Emmons and Wayne S. Vucinich, eds., *The Zemstvo in Russia*. Cambridge University Press, 1982.

Martov, L., et al., eds. *Obshchestvennoe dvizhenie v Rossii v nachale XX-go veka*. 4 vols. St. Petersburg, 1911.

Mehlinger, Howard D., and John M. Thompson. *Count Witte and the Tsarist Government in the 1905 Revolution*. Indiana University Press, 1972.

Meshcherskii, V. P. *Moi vospominaniia*. St. Petersburg, 1897–1912.

Mikhailov, Stefan. *Iz nabliudenii volostnogo pisaria.* St. Petersburg, 1883.

Miliukov, Paul N. *Gosudarstvennoe khoziastvo v pervoi chetverti XVIII stoletiia i reforma Petra Velikogo.* 2d ed. St. Petersburg, 1905.

———. *Political Memoirs, 1905–1917.* Edited by Arthur P. Mendell. University of Michigan Press, 1967.

———. *Tri popytki.* Paris, 1921.

Miliutin, D. A. *Dnevnik D. A. Miliutina.* Edited by P. A. Zaionchkovskii. 4 vols. Moscow, 1947–50.

Minarik, L. P. "Kharakteristika krupneishikh zemlevladel'tsev Rossii kontsa XIX–nachala XX v." In *Ezhegodnik po argrarnoi istorii Vostochnoi Evropy.* Minsk, 1964.

Ministerstvo finansov. *Ministerstvo finansov, 1802–1902.* St. Petersburg, 1902.

———. *Obzor dieiatel'nosti Ministerstva finansov v tsarstvovanii Imperatora Aleksandra III (1881–1894).* St. Petersburg, 1902.

Ministerstvo vnutrennykh del (MVD). *Ministerstvo vnutrennykh del: Istoricheskii ocherk.* 2 vols. St. Petersburg, 1901.

———. *Obshchii obzor deiatel'nosti Ministerstva Vnutrennykh Del za vremia tsarstvovaniia Imperatora Aleksandra III.* St. Petersburg, 1901.

Mixter, Timothy. "Of Grandfather-Beaters and Fat-Heeled Pacifists: Perceptions of Agricultural Labor and Hiring-Market Disturbances, 1872–1905." *Russian History* 7, pts. 1–2 (1980): 152–68.

"Nabroski iz vospominanii D. D. Obolenskogo." *Russkii arkhiv* no. 3 (1894): 256–69.

Natsionalisty v 3-ei Gosudarstvennoi Dume. St. Petersburg, 1912.

Naumov, A. N. *Iz utselevshikh vospominanii, 1868–1950.* New York, 1954.

"Dnevnik Borisa Nikol'skogo (27 fevralia 1905–3 iiulia 1907)." *KA* 6, no. 63 (1934): 55–97.

Nechkina, M. V., ed. *Golosa iz Rossii: Sborniki A. I. Gertsena i N. P. Ogareva.* Moscow, 1974.

Novikov, A. I. *Zapiski zemskogo nachal'nika.* St. Petersburg, 1899.

Obzor upravleniia gosudarstvennymi imushchestvami s 19 fevralia 1855 goda po 19 fevralia 1880 g. St. Petersburg, 1880.

Oldenburg, S. S. *Last Tsar. Nicholas II: His Reign and His Russia.* 4 vols. Translated by Leonid I. Mihalip and Patrick J. Rollins; edited by Patrick J. Rollins. Academic International Press, 1977.

Ol'sufev, Count D. A. *Ob uchastii zemstvo v obsuzhdenii zemskoi reformy.* Saratov, 1907.

Orlovsky, Daniel T. *The Limits of Reform: The Ministry of Internal Affairs in Imperial Russia, 1802–1881.* Harvard University Press, 1981.

"Otryvki iz vospominanii D. N. Liubimova, 1902–1904 gg." *Istoricheskii arkhiv* no. 6 (1962).

Paleolog, S. N. *Okolo vlasti.* St. Petersburg, 1912.

Pazukhin, A. D. "Sovremmenoe sostoianie Rossii i soslovnyi vopros." *Russkii vestnik* 1 (January 1885): 1–58.

Pereira, N.G.O. "Alexander II and the Decision to Emancipate the Russian Serfs, 1855–1861." *Canadian Slavonic Papers* 12, no. 1 (March 1980): 99–115.

"Perepiska N. A. Romanova i P. A. Stolypina." *KA*, no. 26 (1924): 102–8; 30 (1928): 80–88.

Perets, E. A. *Dnevnik 1880–1883 gg.* Edited by A. A. Sergeev. Moscow-Leningrad, 1927.

Perrie, Maureen. *The Agrarian Policy of the Russian Socialist-Revolutionary Party from its Origins through the Revolution of 1905–1907.* Cambridge University Press, 1976.

Pinchuk, Ben-Cion. *The Octobrists in the Third Duma, 1907–1912.* University of Washington Press, 1974.

Pintner, W. "The Russian Higher Civil Service on the Eve of the Great Reforms." *Journal of Social History* (Spring 1975): 55–68.

Pintner, W., and Don Karl Rowney, eds. *Russian Officialdom: The Bureaucratization of Russian Society from the Seventeenth to the Twentieth Century.* University of North Carolina Press, 1980.

Pipes, Richard. *Russia Under the Old Regime.* Charles Scribner's Sons, 1974.

———, ed. and trans. *Karamzin's Memoir on Ancient and Modern Russia.* Atheneum, 1966.

Pirumova, N. M. *Zemskoe liberal'noe dvizhenie: Sotsial'nye korni i evoliutsiia do nachala XX veka.* Moscow, 1977.

Pobedonostsev, K. P. *K. P. Pobedonostsev i ego korrespondenty.* 2 vols. Moscow, 1923.

———. *Pis'ma Pobedonostseva k Aleksandru III.* Moscow, 1925–26.

———. *Reflections of a Russian Statesman.* University of Michigan Press, 1965.

Polivanov, A. A. *Iz dnevnikov i vospominanii po dolzhnosti voennogo ministra i ego pomoshchnika 1907–1916 g.* Edited by A. M. Zaionchkovskii. Moscow, 1924.

Polovtsev, A. A. "Dnevnik A. A. Polovtseva (17 February 1901–10 January 1903)." *KA*, no. 3 (1923): 75–172.

———. "Dnevnik A. A. Polovtseva (15 September 1905–10 August 1906; 5 March–2 May 1908)." *KA*, no. 4 (1923): 63–128.

———. *Dnevnik gosudarstvennogo sekretaria A. A. Polovtseva.* Edited by P. A. Zaionchkovskii. 2 vols. Moscow, 1966.

———. "Iz dnevnika A. A. Polovtseva (1877–1878)." *KA*, no. 33 (1929): 170–203.

———. "Iz dnevnika A. A. Polovtseva (27 October–29 December 1884)." *KA*, no. 67 (1934): 168–86.

———. "Iz dnevkika A. A. Polotseva (1895–1900)." *KA*, no. 46 (1931): 110–32.

Postoiannyi sovet ob"edinennykh dvorianskikh obshchestv. *Material po voprosu o mestnoi reforme: Postanovleniia chrezvychainykh i ocherednykh gubernskikh dvorianskikh sobranii po voprosu o mestnoi reforme.* St. Petersburg, 1908.

———. *1-i material po voprosu o mestnoi reforme. Reforma posel'kogo upravleniia.* St. Petersburg, 1908.

———. *2-i material po voprosu o mestnoi reforme. Reforma uezdnogo upravleniia.* St. Petersburg, 1908.

Praviashchaia Rossiia: Polnyi sbornik svedienii o pravakh i ob"iazannostiakh ad-

ministrativnykh uchrezhdenii i dolzhnostnykh lits Rossiiskoi Imperii, ot Go-sudarstvennogo Soveta do sel'skogo starosty. 3 vols. in 1. St. Petersburg, 1904.

Presniakov, A. E. *Emperor Nicholas I of Russia. The Apogee of Autocracy, 1825–1855.* Edited and translated by Judith C. Zacek. Academic International Press, 1974.

———. *Moskovskoe tsarstvo.* Petrograd, 1918.

Raeff, Marc. *Michael Speransky: Statesman of Imperial Russia (1772–1839).* Mouton, 1957.

———. *Origins of the Russian Intelligentsia: The Eighteenth-Century Nobility.* Harcourt, Brace and World, 1966.

———. "The Russian Autocracy and its Officials." *Harvard Slavic Studies,* 4 (1957): 77–91.

———. *Understanding Imperial Russia: State and Society in the Old Regime.* Columbia University Press, 1984.

———. "The Well-Ordered Police State and the Development of Modernity in Seventeenth and Eighteenth-Century Europe: An Attempt at a Comparative Approach." *American Historical Review* 80, no. 5 (December 1975): 1221–43.

———. *The Well-Ordered Police State: Social and Institutional Change Through Law in the Germanies and Russia, 1600–1800.* Yale University Press, 1986.

Ransel, David L. *The Politics of Catherinian Russia: The Panin Party.* Yale University Press, 1975.

Rashin, A. G. *Naselenie Rossii za 100 let, 1811–1913 gg.* Moscow, 1956.

Rediger, A. F. "Zapiski A. F. Rediger o 1905 g." *KA,* no. 45 (1931).

Riasanovsky, Nicholas. *Nicholas I and Official Nationality in Russia, 1825–1855.* University of California Press, 1969.

Rieber, Alfred J. *Merchants and Entrepreneurs in Imperial Russia.* University of North Carolina Press, 1982.

———. *The Politics of Autocracy.* Mouton, 1966.

Robbins, Jr., Richard G. *Famine in Russia, 1891–1892.* Columbia University Press, 1975.

———. *The Tsar's Viceroys: Russian Provincial Governors in the Last Years of the Empire.* Cornell University Press, 1987.

Robinson, G. T. *Rural Russia under the Old Regime.* Los Angeles, 1969.

Rogger, H. "The Formation of the Russian Right, 1900–1906." *California Slavic Studies* 3 (1964): 66–94.

Romanovich-Slavatinskii, A. V. *Dvorianstvo v Rossii ot nachala XVIII veka do otmeny krepostnogo prava.* St. Petersburg, 1870.

Rowney, D. K. "Higher Civil Servants in the Russian Ministry of Internal Affairs: Some Demographic and Career Statistics, 1905–1916." *Slavic Review* 31, no. 1 (March 1972): 101–10.

Rubinshtein, N. L. *Russkaia istoriografiia.* Moscow, 1941.

Ryndziunskii, P. G. *Utverzhdenie kapitalizma v Rossii, 1850–1880 gg.* Moscow, 1978.

Sablinsky, Walter. *The Road to Bloody Sunday: Father Gapon and the St. Petersburg Massacre of 1905.* Princeton University Press, 1976.

Samarin, Iu. *Revoliutsionnyi konservatizm.* Berlin, 1875.

Semenov-Tian-Shanskii, P. P. *Epokha osvobozhdeniia krest'ian v Rossii (1857–1861)*. Petrograd, 1915.

Semevskii, V. I. *Krest'ianskii vopros v Rossii v XVIII i pervoi polovine XIX veka.* 2 vols. St. Petersburg, 1888.

Seredonin, S. M. *Istoricheskii obzor deiatel'nosti komiteta ministrov.* St. Petersburg, 1902.

Shanin, Teodor. *Russia 1905–07: Revolution As A Moment of Truth*, vol. 2 of idem, *The Roots of Otherness: Russia's Turn of the Century.* Yale University Press, 1986.

―――. "Socio-Economic Mobility and the Rural History of Russia, 1905–1930." *Soviet Studies* (1971): 222–35.

Shatsillo, K. F. "Taktika i organizatsiia zemskogo liberalizma nakanune pervoi russkoi revolutsii." *Istoricheskie zapiski* 101 (Moscow, 1978).

Shchegolev, P. E., ed. *Padenie tsarskogo rezhima: Stenograficheskie otchety doprosov i pokazanii, dannykh v 1917 g. v Chrezvychainoi sledstvennoi kommissii Vremennogo pravitel'stva.* 7 vols. Moscow-Leningrad, 1924–27.

Shepelev, L. E. *Tzarizm i burzhuaziia vo vtoroi polovine XIX veka: Problemy torgovo-promyshlennoi politiki.* Leningrad, 1981.

Sheremetev, Count Pavel. *Zametki, 1900-1905.* Moscow, 1905.

Shidlovskii, S. I. *Vospominaniia.* Moscow, 1924.

Shipov, D. N. *Vospominaniia i dumy o perezhitom.* Moscow, 1905.

Shul'gin, V. *Vospominaniia byvshego chlena gosudarstvennoi dumy.* Novosti, 1979.

Sidel'nikov, S. M. *Agrarnaia politika samoderzhaviia v period imperializma.* Moscow, 1980.

―――. *Agrarnaia reforma Stolypina (Uchebnoe posobie).* Moscow, 1973.

Simonova, M. S. "Agrarnaia politika samoderzhaviia v 1905 g." *Istoricheskie zapiski* 81 (1968): 199–215.

―――. "Bor'ba techenii v pravitelstvennom lagere po voprosam agrarnoi politiki v kontse XIX v." *Istoriia SSSR* 1 (1963): 65–82.

―――. "Krizis agrarnoi politiki samoderzhaviia nakanune pervoi russkoi revoliutsii." In *Ezhegodnik po agrarnoi istorii Vostochnoi Evropy, 1962 god*, Moscow, 1964, pp. 475–88.

―――. "Otmena krugovoi poruki." *Istoricheskie zapiski* 83 (1969): 159–95.

―――. "Politika tsarizma v krestianskom voprose nakanune revoliutsii 1905–1907 gg." *Istoricheskie zapiski* 75 (1965): 212–42.

―――. "Problema 'oskudeniia' Tsentra i ee rol' v formirovanii agrarnoi politiki samoderzhaviia v 90-kh godakh XIX–nachale XX v." In *Problemy sotsial'no-ekonomicheskoi istorii Rossii.* Moscow, 1971.

Skal'kovskii, K. A. *Nashi gosudarstvennye i obshchestvennye deiateli.* St. Petersburg, 1890.

Skalon, V. Iu. *Po zemskim voprosam.* St. Petersburg, 1905.

―――. *Zemskie vzgliady na reformu mestnogo upravleniia: Obzor zemskikh otzyvov i proektov.* Moscow, 1884.

Skrebitskii, A. I., ed. (see government documents).

Smirnov, V. "Zemskaia reforma 1864 goda i ee posleduiushchiia izmeneniia." *Russkaia Starina* 167, no. 8 (1916): 209–45.

Snow, George E., ed. and trans. *The Years 1881–1894 in Russia: A Memorandum Found in the Papers of N. Kh. Bunge. Transactions of The American Philosophical Society*, vol. 71, pt. 6. Philadelphia, 1981.

Solov'ev, Iu. B. *Samoderzhavie i dvorianstvo v kontse XIX veka*. Leningrad, 1973.

———. *Samoderzhavie i dvorianstvo v 1902–1907 gg*. Leningrad, 1981.

Starr, S. Frederick. *Decentralization and Self-Government in Russia, 1830–1870*. Princeton University Press, 1972.

Startsev, V. I. *Russkaia burzhuaziia i samoderzhavie v 1905–1917 gg. (Bor'ba vokrug "otvetstvennogo ministerstva" i "pravitel'stva doveriia")*. Leningrad, 1977.

Statistika pozemel'noi sobstvennosti i naselennykh mest Evropeiskoi Rossii. St. Petersburg, 1880–85.

Stavrou, T. G., ed. *Russia Under the Last Tsar*. University of Minnesota Press, 1969.

Stenograficheskie otchety 1-go Vserossiskogo S'ezda zemskikh deiatelei v Moskve: Zasedaniia 1–15 iiunia 1907 g. Moscow, 1907.

Stenograficheskie otchety 2-go Vserossiskogo S'ezda zemskikh deiatelei v Moskve: Zasedaniia 25–28 avgusta 1907 g. Moscow, 1908.

Sternheimer, Stephen. "Administering Development and Developing Administration: Organizational Conflict in Tsarist Bureaucracy, 1906–1914." *Canadian-American Slavic Studies* 9, no. 3 (Fall 1975): 277–301.

Stolypin, A. P. *P. A. Stolypin, 1862–1911*. Paris, 1927.

Strakhovskii, I. M. *Krest'ianskie prava i uchrezhdeniia*. St. Petersburg, 1904.

———. "Krest'ianskii vopros v zakonodatel'stve i v zakonosoveshchatelnykh kommissiiakh posle 1861 g." In *Krestianskii stroi: Sbornik statei*, I. Edited by P. D. Dolgorukov and S. Tolstoi. St. Petersburg, 1905.

———. "Obosoblennost' i ravopravnost' krest'ian." *Pravo* (1903): 2109–22, 2149–61, and 2197–2211.

Sviatopolk-Mirskaia, E. A. "Dnevnik Kn. E. A. Sviatopolk-Mirskoi za 1904–1905 gg.," *Istoricheskie zapiski* 77 (1965).

Svod postanovlenii I-X s"ezdov upolnomochennykh ob"edinennykh dvorianskikh obshchestv, 1906–1914 gg. Petrograd, 1915.

Terner, Fedor Gustavovich. *Vospominaniia zhizni F. G. Ternera*. St. Petersburg, 1910.

"Iz dnevnika L. Tikhomirova." *KA* no. 61 (1933): 82–128; no. 72 (1935): 120–59; no. 37 (1935): 170–90; no. 74 (1936): 162–91; no. 75 (1936): 171–84.

Tolmachev, I. S. *Krest'ianskii vopros po vzgliadam zemstva i mestnykh liudei*. Moscow, 1903.

Torke, Hans J. "Continuity and Change in the Relations between Bureaucracy and Society in Russia, 1613–1861." *Canadian Slavic Studies* 5, no. 4 (Winter 1971): 457–76.

Treadgold, D. W. "Was Stolypin in Favor of Kulaks?" *American Slavic and East European Review* 17, no. 1 (February 1965): 1–14.

Troinitskii, A. *Krepostnoe naselenie v Rossii, po 10-i narodnoi perepisi.* St. Petersburg, 1861.

Troitskii, S. M. *Russkii absoliutizm i dvorianstvo v XVIII v. (Formirovanie biurokratii).* Moscow, 1974.

Trudy chetvertogo s"ezda upolnomochennykh dvorianskikh obshchestv 32 gubernii s 9 marta po 16 marta 1908 g. St. Petersburg, 1909.

Trudy pervogo s"ezda upolnomochennykh dvorianskikh obshchestv 29 gubernii 21–28 maia 1906 g. St. Petersburg, 1906.

Trudy tret'ego s"ezda upolnomochennykh dvorianskikh obshchestv 32 gubernii s 27 marta po 2 aprelia 1907 g. St. Petersburg, 1907.

Trudy vos'mogo s"ezda Upolnomochennykh Dvorianskikh Obshchestv 37 gubernii s 5 marta po 11 marta 1912 g. St. Petersburg, 1912.

Trudy vtorogo s"ezda upolnomochennykh dvorianskikh obshchestv 31 gubernii (14–18 noiabr' 1906 g.). St. Petersburg, 1906.

Tvardovskaia, V. A. "Ideolog samoderzhaviia v period krizisa verkhov na rubezhe 70–80-x godov XIX v." *Istoricheskie zapiski* 91 (1973): 217–66.

Uvarov, A. A. *Doklad Graf A. A. Uvarova (o reforme zemskogo polozheniia).* N.p., 1907.

Valuev, Count P. A. *Dnevnik, 1877–1884.* Petrograd, 1919.

———. *Dnevnik P. A. Valueva, ministra vnutrennykh del.* Edited by P. A. Zaionchkovskii. 2 vols. Moscow, 1961.

———. "Dnevnik." *Russkaia starina* 72 (1891).

Vasil'chikov, A. I. *O samoupravlenii.* St. Petersburg, 1869.

Venturi, Franco. *Roots of Revolution: A History of the Populist and Socialist Movements in Nineteenth Century Russia.* Grosset & Dunlap, 1960.

Verner, Andrew M. *The Crisis of Russian Autocracy: Nicholas II and the 1905 Revolution.* Princeton University Press, 1990.

Veselovskii, B. B. *Istoriia zemstva za sorok let.* 4 vols. St. Petersburg, 1911.

———. *K voprosu o klassovykh interesakh v zemstve,* 1st ed. St. Petersburg, 1905.

———. ed. *Agrarnyi vopros v sovete ministrov, 1906 g.* Moscow-Leningrad, 1924.

Veselovskii, B. B., and Z. G. Frenkel, eds. *Iubileinyi Zemskii Sbornik.* St. Petersburg, 1914.

Volkov, N. T. *Nakaz zemskim nachal'nikam po administrativnym delam.* Moscow, 1907.

Von Laue, Theodore H. "A Secret Memorandum of Sergei Witte on the Industrialization of Russia." *Journal of Modern History* 16, no. 1 (March 1954): 60–74.

———. *Sergei Witte and the Industrialization of Russia.* Atheneum, 1969.

———. *Why Lenin? Why Stalin? A Reappraisal of the Russian Revolution, 1900–1930.* Lippincott, 1964.

[Vtoroi] *II-i material po voprosu o mestnoi reforme: Reforma uezdnogo upravleniia.* St. Petersburg, 1908.

Walker, Mack. *German Home Towns: Community, State, and General Estate, 1648–1871.* Cornell University Press, 1971.

Weissman, Neil B. *Reform in Tsarist Russia: The State Bureaucracy and Local Government, 1900–1914*. Rutgers University Press, 1981.

Whelan, Heidi W. *Alexander III and the State Council: Bureaucracy and Counterreform in Late Imperial Russia*. Rutgers University Press, 1982.

Witte, S. Iu. "Iz arkhiva S. Iu. Vitte." *KA*, nos. 11–12 (1925).

———. *Konspekt lektsii o narodnom i gosudarstvennom khoziastve, chitannykh ego imperatorskomu vysochestvu velikomu kniazu Mikhailu Aleksandrovichu v 1900–1902 gg.* St. Petersburg, 1912.

———. "Manufakturnoe krepostnichestvo." *Rus'* 3 (1885): 18–19.

———. *Ministr finansov Vitte i Gosudarstvennyi Sovet o finansovom polozhenii Rossii; zhurnal obshchago sobraniia Gosudarstvennogo Soveta*. Stuttgart, 1903.

———. "Perepiska S. Iu. Vitte i A. N. Kuropatkin v 1904–1905 gg." *KA*, no. 19 (1926).

———. "Perepiska Vitte s Pobedonostsevym (1895–1905 gg.)." *KA*, no. 30 (1928): 89–116.

———. "Pis'ma S. Iu. Vitte K D. S. Sipiaginu (1900–1901)." *KA*, no. 18 (1926).

———. *Po povodu neprelozhnosti zakonov gosudarstvennoi zhizni*. St Petersburg, 1914.

———. *Predsedatel' vysochaishe uchrezhdennogo Osobogo Soveshchaniia o nuzhdakh sel'sko-khoziastvennoi promyshlennosti: Zapiska po krest'ianskomu delu*. St. Petersburg, 1905.

———. *Report of the Minister of Finance to H.I.M. the Emperor on the Budget of the Empire for 1898*. St. Petersburg, 1897.

———. *Report of the Minister of Finance to H.I.M. the Emperor on the Budget of the Empire for 1899*. St. Petersburg, 1898.

———. *Samoderzhavie i zemstvo: Konfidentsial'naia zapiska Ministra finansov Stats-Sekrataria S. Iu. Vitte (1899)*. Stuttgart, 1901.

———. *Vospominaniia*. 3 vols. Moscow-Leningrad, 1923.

———. "Vsepoddaneishii doklad Ministra finansov o gosudarstvennoi rospisi dokhodov i raskhodov na 1895 goda." *Vestnik finansov, promyshlennosti i torgovli*, 1 January 1895.

———. "Vsepoddaneishii doklad Ministra finansov o gosudarstvennoi rospisi dokhodov i raskhodov na 1897 goda." *Vestnik finansov, promyshlennosti i torgovli*, 5 January 1897.

———. "Vsepoddaneishii doklad Ministra finansov o gosudarstvennoi rospisi dokhodov i raskhodov na 1901 god." *Narodnoe khoziastvo* 2, book 1 (January 1901).

———. "Vsepoddaneishii doklad Ministra finansov o gosudarstvennoi rospisi dokhodov i raskhodov na 1902." *Narodnoe khoziastvo* 3, book 1 (January 1902).

———. "Vsepoddaneishii doklad ministra finansov o polozhenii nashei promyshlennosti, fev. 1900 g." *Istorik-marksist*, no. 2–3 (1935).

———. "Vsepoddaneishii doklad ministra finansov S. Iu. Vitte Nikolaiu II o neobkhodimosti ustanovat' i zatem neprelozhno priderzhivat'sia opredelennoi programmy torgovo-promyshlennoi politiki imperii." In I. F. Ginden, "Ob osnovakh ekonomicheskoi politiki tsarskogo pravitel'stva v kontse XIX-nachale XX v.," *Materialy po istorii SSSR*, vol. 6. Moscow, 1959.

———. "Zamechanie ministra finansov S. Iu. Vitte, na zapisku gubernskikh predvoditelei dvorianstva o nuzhdakh dvorianskogo zemlevladeniia," Ginden, I. F., and M. Ia. Gefter, eds. "Trebovaniia dvorianstva i finansovo-ekonomicheskaia politika tsarskogo pravitel'stva v 1880–1890-kh godakh." *Istoricheskii arkhiv* 4 (July–August 1957): 122–55.

———. "Zapiska Vitte ot 9 oktiabria." In "Iz arkhiva S. Iu. Vitte," *KA*, nos. 11–12 (1925): 51–61.

Wortman, Richard S. *The Development of a Russian Legal Consciousness.* University of Chicago Press, 1976.

V pervye dni ministerstva Gr. M. T. Loris-Melikova: Zapiska o politicheskom sostoianii Rossii vesnoiiu 1880 goda. Berlin, 1881.

Yaney, George L. "Bureaucracy and Freedom: N. M. Korkunov's Theory of the State." *American Historical Review* 71, no. 2 (January 1966): 468–86.

———. *The Systematization of Russian Government: Social Evolution in the Domestic Administration of Imperial Russia, 1711–1905.* University of Illinois Press, 1973.

———. *The Urge To Mobilize: Agrarian Reform in Russia, 1861–1930.* University of Illinois Press, 1982.

Zablotskii-Desiatovskii, A. P. *Graf P. D. Kiselev i ego vremia.* St. Petersburg, 1882. 4 vols.

Zaionchkovskii, P. A. *Krisis samoderzhaviia na rubezhe 1870–1880 kh- godov.* Moscow, 1964.

———. *Otmena krepostnogo prava.* Moscow, 1968.

———. *Pravitel'stvennyi apparat samoderzhavnoi Rossii v XIX v.* Moscow, 1978.

———. *Provedenie v zhizn' krest'ianskoi reformy 1861 g.* Moscow, 1958.

———. *Rossiiskoe samoderzhavie v kontse XIX stoletiia.* Moscow, 1970.

Zakharova, L. G. "Perepiska ministra vnutrennykh del P. A. Valueva i gosudarstvennogo sekretaria S. N. Urusova v 1866 godu." *Istoriia SSSR* 2 (1973): 115–28.

———. *Samoderzhavie i otmena krepostnogo prava v Rossii.* Moscow, 1984.

———. *Zemskaia kontrreforma, 1890 g.* Moscow, 1968.

"Zapiska predstavitelei zemskikh uchrezhdenii v komissii o tsentre." *Narodnoe khoziastvo*, no. 6 (1903).

"Zapiski A. S. Ermolova." *KA*, no. 8 (1925): 49–69.

Zelnik, Reginald E. *Labor and Society in Tsarist Russia: The Factory Workers of St. Petersburg, 1855–1870.* Stanford University Press, 1971.

Zenkovsky, A. V. *Pravda o Stolypine.* New York, 1956.

Zhurnaly postanovleniia Vserossiiskogo S"ezda Zemskikh Deiatelei v Moskve 10 po 15 iiunia 1907 g. Moscow, 1907.

Zyrianov, P. N. "Sotsial'naia struktura mestnogo upravleniia kapitalisticheskoi Rossii (1861–1914)." *Istoricheskie zapiski* 107 (Moscow, 1982).

———. "Tret'ia duma i vopros o reforme mestnogo suda i volost'nogo upravlenia." *Istoriia SSSR*, no. 6 (November–December 1969): 45–67.

Index

Abaza, A. A., 60, 110n
address of the five, 35–36
Adlerberg, Count V. F., 19
Alexander II, 10, 17–18, 24, 38; anti-constitutionalism of, 58; assassination of, 60; his role in emancipation, 43–44
Alexander III, 60, 102, 104, 111, 122, 129, 143, 146, 151; coronation of, 85; and imperial manifesto of 29 April 1881, 61
Anastas'ev, A. K., 86
Andreevskii, I. E., 68
arbiters of the peace, 31–33
Article 87, 176, 210, 284, 286, 311
ascription, xv, 95
authority
—autocratic authority, ix, xii, xv, 45, 61, 105, 144, 170, 244, 256, 281, 288–89, 309; and bureaucratic administration, 147, 151, 155, 164–65, 308; and estate society, 84, 99, 254; legitimacy of, 47, 115–16, 129–32, 141–42; and rule of law, 59, 81, 133–34
—government authority, xii, 40, 54, 107, 142, 168, 170–71, 281, 287–88; collapse of, 164–65, 168, 194, 208; and political mobilization, 194, 201–2, 204, 207, 209–10, 226, 241–42, 279; and reliance on peasantry, 165, 169, 175, 177, 187–92; and tutelage, xiii, 37, 51, 68, 91
—nobiliary authority, 16, 37, 42, 302
—personalized authority, xv, 113, 116–18
Autocracy and the Zemstvo, 130–34, 137, 139, 141
autocratic political culture, xvi, 85, 113–14, 281, 288, 307

Barykov, F. L., 68
Bazilevskii, P. A., 255n
Becker, S., 307
Beketov, S. A., 265
Bekhteev, S. S., 86, 88–91, 93, 251
Bezobrazov, M. A., 38n
Bismarck, Otto van, 240
Black Hundreds, 206
Bloody Sunday, 162

Bobrinskii, A. A., 233, 258, 286, 301
Bogdanovich, A. V., 86
"bonapartism," xiv, 280
Brazol, S. E., 245, 251
Brianshaninov, N. S., 260, 262, 268, 270
Bulgakov, P. A., 34
Bulygin Rescript, 162
Bunge, N. Kh., 123
bureaucracy, x–xvi; expansion of, 95–97; as a modern bureaucratic state, xii–xiii, 133, 147; police officials in, xiv, 44, 87–92, 144, 251, 294, 308; social identity of, x–xi, 306–7; Weberian analysis of, xiv. *See also* authority; power; *Rechtsstaat*

caste. *See* hereditary service nobility
Charter to the Nobility, 5; centenary of, 97, 102
Cherkasskii, Prince V. A., 26, 34
Chernyshevskii, N. G., 22
Chicherin, B. N., 17, 117
Chuprov, A. I., 51
civic political culture, xv, 50, 84, 129, 171, 307
civil society, x, xii, 270, 307; pre-reform views of, 12–13
coalition cabinet, 174, 203
Committee of Ministers, 154
communal land tenure: and compulsory sale of private property, 170, 177–78, 196; in Editing Commissions, 27–28, 33–34; in Kakhanov Commission, 76, 88–89; before 1905, 129, 138–39, 148; under Witte and Stolypin, 178–79, 210
Constitutional-Democrats. *See* Kadets
"Contemporary Situation of Russia and the Estate Question," 84, 97. *See also* Pazukhin, A. D.
Council of Ministers, 167, 207, 216
Council on Local Economy, 149, 217; composition of, 258; decision to utilize, 255–56; and Gurliand reports, 276–78; and invited provincial marshals of the nobility, 271–72; and Stolypin, 256, 272

Studies of the Harriman Institute

Soviet National Income in 1937 by Abram Bergson, Columbia University Press, 1953.

Through the Glass of Soviet Literature: Views of Russian Society, Ernest Simmons, Jr., ed., Columbia University Press, 1953.

Polish Postwar Economy by Thad Paul Alton, Columbia University Press, 1954.

Management of the Industrial Firm in the USSR: A Study in Soviet Economic Planning by David Granick, Columbia University Press, 1954.

Soviet Politics in China, 1917–1924 by Allen S. Whiting, Columbia University Press, 1954; paperback, Stanford University Press, 1968.

Literary Politics in the Soviet Ukraine, 1917–1934 by George S. N. Luckyj, Columbia University Press, 1956.

The Emergence of Russian Panslavism, 1856–1870 by Michael Boro Petrovich, Columbia University Press, 1956.

Lenin on Trade Unions and Revolution, 1893–1917 by Thomas Taylor Hammond, Columbia University Press, 1956.

The Last Years of the Georgian Monarchy, 1658–1832 by David Marshall Lang, Columbia University Press, 1957.

The Japanese Thrust into Siberia, 1918 by James William Morley, Columbia University Press, 1957.

Bolshevism in Turkestan, 1917–1927 by Alexander G. Park, Columbia University Press, 1957.

Soviet Marxism: A Critical Analysis by Herbert Marcuse, Columbia University Press, 1958; paperback, Columbia University Press, 1985.

Soviet Policy and the Chinese Communists, 1931–1946 by Charles B. McLane, Columbia University Press, 1958.

The Agrarian Foes of Bolshevism: Promise and Defeat of the Russian Socialist Revolutionaries, February to October, 1917 by Oliver H. Radkey, Columbia University Press, 1958.

Pattern for Soviet Youth: A Study of the Congresses of the Komsomol, 1918–1954 by Ralph Talcott Fisher, Jr., Columbia University Press, 1959.

The Emergence of Modern Lithuania by Alfred Erich Senn, Columbia University Press, 1959.

The Soviet Design for a World State by Elliot R. Goodman, Columbia University Press, 1960.

Settling Disputes in Soviet Society: The Formative Years of Legal Institutions by John N. Hazard, Columbia University Press, 1960.

Soviet Marxism and Natural Science, 1917–1932 by David Joravsky, Columbia University Press, 1961.

Russian Classics in Soviet Jackets by Maurice Friedberg, Columbia University Press, 1962.

Stalin and the French Communist Party, 1941–1947 by Alfred J. Rieber, Columbia University Press, 1962.

Sergei Witte and the Industrialization of Russia by Theodore K. Von Laue, Columbia University Press, 1962.

Ukrainian Nationalism by John H. Armstrong, Columbia University Press, 1963.

The Sickle under the Hammer: The Russian Socialist Revolutionaries in the Early Months of Soviet Rule by Oliver H. Radkey, Columbia University Press, 1963.

Comintern and World Revolution, 1928–1943: The Shaping of Doctrine by Kermit E. McKenzie, Columbia University Press, 1964.

Weimar Germany and Soviet Russia, 1926–1933: A Study in Diplomatic Instability by Harvey L. Dyck, Columbia University Press, 1966.

Financing Soviet Schools by Harold J. Noah, Teachers College Press, 1966.

Russia, Bolshevism, and the Versailles Peace by John M. Thompson, Princeton University Press, 1966.

The Russian Anarchists by Paul Avrich, Princeton University Press, 1967.

The Soviet Academy of Sciences and the Communist Party, 1927–1932 by Loren R. Graham, Princeton University Press, 1967.

Red Virgin Soil: Soviet Literature in the 1920's by Robert A. Maguire, Princeton University Press, 1968; paperback, Cornell University Press, 1987.

Communist Party Membership in the U.S.S.R., 1917–1967 by T. H. Rigby, Princeton University Press, 1968.

Soviet Ethics and Morality by Richard T. DeGeorge, University of Michigan Press, 1969; paperback, Ann Arbor Paperbacks, 1969.

Vladimir Akimov on the Dilemmas of Russian Marxism, 1895–1903 by Jonathan Frankel, Cambridge University Press, 1969.

Soviet Perspectives on International Relations, 1956–1967 by William Zimmerman, Princeton University Press, 1969.

Kronstadt, 1921 by Paul Avrich, Princeton University Press, 1970.

Class Struggle in the Pale: The Formative Years of the Jewish Workers' Movement in Tsarist Russia by Ezra Mendelsohn, Cambridge University Press, 1970.

The Proletarian Episode in Russian Literature by Edward J. Brown, Columbia University Press, 1971.

Labor and Society in Tsarist Russia: The Factory Workers of St. Petersburg, 1855–1870 by Reginald E. Zelnik, Stanford University Press, 1971.

Archives and Manuscript Repositories in the USSR: Moscow and Leningrad by Patricia K. Grimsted, Princeton University Press, 1972.

The Baku Commune, 1917–1918 by Ronald G. Suny, Princeton University Press, 1972.

Mayakovsky: A Poet in the Revolution by Edward J. Brown, Princeton University Press, 1973.

Oblomov and his Creator: The Life and Art of Ivan Goncharov by Milton Ehre, Princeton University Press, 1973.

German Politics Under Soviet Occupation by Henry Krisch, Columbia University Press, 1974.

Soviet Politics and Society in the 1970's, Henry W. Morton and Rudolph L. Tokes, eds., Free Press, 1974.

Liberals in the Russian Revolution by William G. Rosenberg, Princeton University Press, 1974.

Famine in Russia, 1891–1892 by Richard G. Robbins, Jr., Columbia University Press, 1975.

In Stalin's Time: Middleclass Values in Soviet Fiction by Vera Dunham, Cambridge University Press, 1976.

The Road to Bloody Sunday by Walter Sablinsky, Princeton University Press, 1976; paperback, Princeton University Press, 1986.

The Familiar Letter as a Literary Genre in the Age of Pushkin by William Mills Todd III, Princeton University Press, 1976.

Russian Realist Art. The State and Society: The Peredvizhniki and Their Tradition by Elizabeth Valkenier, Ardis Publishers, 1977.

The Soviet Agrarian Debate by Susan Solomon, Westview Press, 1978.

Cultural Revolution in Russia, 1928–1931, Sheila Fitzpatrick, ed., Indiana University Press, 1978; paperback, Midland Books, 1984.

Soviet Criminologists and Criminal Policy: Specialists in Policy-Making by Peter Solomon, Columbia University Press, 1978.

Technology and Society under Lenin and Stalin: Origins of the Soviet Technical Intelligentsia by Kendall E. Bailes, Princeton University Press, 1978.

The Politics of Rural Russia, 1905–1914, Leopold H. Haimson, ed., Indiana University Press, 1979.

Political Participation in the USSR by Theodore H. Friedgut, Princeton University Press, 1979; paperback, Princeton University Press, 1982.

Education and Social Mobility in the Soviet Union, 1921–1934 by Sheila Fitzpatrick, Cambridge University Press, 1979.

The Soviet Marriage Market: Mate Selection in Russian and the USSR by Wesley Andrew Fisher, Praeger Publishers, 1980.

Prophecy and Politics: Socialism, Nationalism, and the Russian Jews, 1862–1917 by Jonathan Frankel, Cambridge University Press, 1981.

Dostoevsky and The Idiot: *Author, Narrator, and Reader* by Robin Feuer Miller, Harvard University Press, 1981.

Moscow Workers and the 1917 Revolution by Diane Koenker, Princeton University Press, 1981; paperback, Princeton University Press, 1986.

Archives and Manuscript Repositories in the USSR: Estonia, Latvia, Lithuania, and Belorussia by Patricia K. Grimsted, Princeton University Press, 1981.

Zionism in Poland: The Formative Years, 1915–1926 by Ezra Mendelsohn, Yale University Press, 1982.

Soviet Risk-Taking and Crisis Behavior by Hannes Adomeit, George Allen and Unwin Publishers, 1982.

Russia at the Crossroads: The 26th Congress of the CPSU, Seweryn Bialer and Thane Gustafson, eds., George Allen and Unwin Publishers, 1982.

The Crisis of the Old Order in Russia: Gentry and Government by Roberta Thompson Manning, Princeton University Press, 1983; paperback, Princeton University Press, 1986.

Sergei Aksakov and Russian Pastoral by Andrew A. Durkin, Rutgers University Press, 1983.

Politics and Technology in the Soviet Union by Bruce Parrott, MIT Press, 1983.

The Soviet Union and the Third World: An Economic Bind by Elizabeth Kridl Valkenier, Praeger Publishers, 1983.

Russian Metaphysical Romanticism: The Poetry of Tiutchev and Boratynskii by Sarah Pratt, Stanford University Press, 1984.

Ruling Russia: Politics and Administration in the Age of Absolutism, 1762–1796 by John P. LeDonne, Princeton University Press, 1984.

Insidious Intent: A Structural Analysis of Fedor Sologub's Petty Demon by Diana Greene, Slavica Publishers, 1986.

Leo Tolstoy: Resident and Stranger by Richard Gustafson, Princeton University Press, 1986.

Workers, Society, and the State: Labor and Life in Moscow, 1918–1929 by William Chase, University of Illinois Press, 1987.

Andrey Bely: Spirit of Symbolism, John Malmstad, ed., Cornell University Press, 1987.

Government and Peasant in Russia, 1861–1906: The Prehistory of the Stolypin Reforms by David A. J. Macey, Northern Illinois University Press, 1987.

The Making of Three Russian Revolutionaries: Voices from the Menshevik Past, edited by Leopold H. Haimson in collaboration with Ziva Galili y García and Richard Wortman, Cambridge University Press, 1988.

Revolution and Culture: The Bogdanov-Lenin Controversy by Zenovia A. Sochor, Cornell University Press, 1988.

A Handbook of Russian Verbs by Frank Miller, Ardis Publishers, 1989.

1905 in St. Petersburg: Labor, Society, and Revolution by Gerald D. Surh, Stanford University Press, 1989.

Iuzovka and Revolution. Volume 1, *Life and Work in Russia's Donbass, 1869–1924* by Theodore H. Friedgut, Princeton University Press, 1989.

Alien Tongues: Bilingual Russian Writers of the "First" Emigration by Elizabeth Klosty Beaujour, Cornell University Press, 1989.

The Menshevik Leaders in the Russian Revolution: Social Realities and Political Strategies by Ziva Galili, Princeton University Press, 1989.

The Crisis of Russian Autocracy: Nicholas II and the 1905 Revolution by Andrew M. Verner, Princeton University Press, 1990.